Contents

"A Personal View from the Top of the Stairs"

How I loved and admired that father of mine. Back in the 1920s and '30s he and his Air Corps friends, all WWI veterans — Andrews, Spaatz, McNarney, Kenney, Knerr, Eubank, George — men of steel in planes of wood — would gather at one another's homes on a Saturday night at Langley Field. Their merriment drifted to the top of the stairs, where this little boy sat entranced by songs of "Mademoiselle from Armentières" and the sad fate of people called Kiwis, whoever they were. "Tooey" Spaatz strummed the guitar and my Dad played the piano, both with a degree of uncertainty, but with great gusto. They sang and talked — talked of flying in the early days, of today, and of their hopes and dreams for the future.

As I matured and my perceptions deepened, I began to understand the meaning of those dreams. The memories of WWI underlay their determination to change things. No more would there be the horrors of the trenches, of stalemate, of attack and counterattack with thousands of casualties and no discernible gain. They would carry the war to the enemy, attack his industrial base and his lines of communication. They would destroy his transportation system, and they would erode his will to fight — all from the air, and with aircraft not yet built.

When publicly revealed, those ambitions garnered the thinkers scorn and downright resentment. My Dad and his Air Corps contemporaries were looked upon as lightweight "flyboys," whose limited capabilities were of no consequence in the grand scheme of land and sea warfare. Airmen could not occupy territory, nor rule the sea–lanes. Therefore what good were they, except to provide eyes for the real forces, and to try to deny those same eyes to the enemy. As for bombing, it was laughingly admitted that the Air Corps could probably penetrate enemy territory, but not much farther than good artillery, and certainly not as accurately nor as devastatingly. The Navy brass hadn't been impressed when Billy Mitchell sank the *Ostfriesland*. They claimed the test had been set up. There was no opposition, the target was anchored close to shore, and the release altitude unrealistically low. In a practical sense, the Navy was right. But it had proved possible to sink a dreadnought with explosives from the air, and that lesson was not entirely lost on the admirals.

And so it went throughout the decade of the 1920s and into the mid-'30s. Aviation and aviators were viewed with awed amusement, particularly by those who occupied the hallowed seats of government. On reviewing the Air Corps segment of the Army's annual budget request, President Coolidge is said to have asked why the service didn't buy just one airplane and let the aviators take turns flying it. At one point those same visionaries had even attempted to enforce a caveat that the Air Corps should not acquire any airplane having a flight range in excess of one day's march by the infantry. Failing in that, the combined efforts of the armchair generals and the battleship admirals managed for a while to restrict the airmen to operating no more than 100 miles from the coasts of the United States. General Billy Mitchell was court-martialed for his outspoken belief in the future of air power and for his criticism of those who would deny that potential. The trial outraged his followers and encouraged them to greater effort. Progress was painstakingly slow. Technology could not yet provide the airframes and engines to match the dream.

All that time the threat to world peace became ever more evident. Germany reacted to the harsh terms of the Treaty of Versailles, let Hitler take power, began rearming and, with scarcely any opposition from her former enemies, marched troops into the Rhineland. The die was cast.

When Hitler struck Poland, perhaps no nation was more shocked than America. Our Army and Navy were seen to be living in the past. Horse cavalry? Coast artillery? Battleships with great towers so that the lookout could see farther than the admiral on the bridge? A handful of aircraft carriers as a concession to the Navy's flyboys? In the Air Corps, our pilots still flew in open cockpits. But there was encouragement, however little and however late. By 1937 we had B-17s, all thirteen of them. They flew faster and higher than our so-called pursuit planes, and that suggested another problem. As a result we were blessed with the P-40, which was the best we could do at the time.

While Britain gallantly went it alone, America had time to build. Yet we were not fully ready when Japan struck Pearl Harbor. It took another two years to reach the point where America's air power could be said to have a meaningful impact on the campaigns being waged over Europe and Asia, and in the Pacific. Then vast fleets of bombers, escorted by hundreds of long-range fighters, struck the enemy heartlands. Men dropped from the sky into battle. Remote forces were supplied by trains of cargo aircraft. The giant stirred and the old dreams became reality. Eventually Germany crumbled and it was admitted that Allied air power had done much to bring about the defeat. In the Pacific a combined onslaught by sea, land, and air moved us inexorably towards the Japanese homeland. Then came Hiroshima and Nagasaki, and the world could never be the same.

Nuclear capability suddenly dominated all military thinking. The Air Force created Strategic Air Command and thought of itself as all-powerful. New doctrinal battles raged in Congress and the halls of the Pentagon. The Oval Office became directly involved. President Eisenhower theorized that a large, strategic nuclear force could provide for the common defense of the nation and its allies. Such a defensive deterrent plan was thought to be cost-effective, permitting the downsizing of the Army and Navy, and those Air Force commands other than SAC. A few dissenting voices, wise as they were, went unheeded. In short order, the main thrust of the Air Force was nuclear. It was proclaimed by none other than the Chief of Army Air Force Plans that the atomic bomb made conventional warfare and tactical air power "as old-fashioned as the Maginot Line."

We thought we had gained a lasting global peace, but the world divided to West and East. By 1949, the Soviets had the atomic bomb and the game was on in earnest. Each side strove to outdo the other in the arena of nuclear bragging rights:

"We have more missiles than you."

"No, you don't."

"We can make ours intercontinental."

"So can we."

"But ours are more accurate."

"Maybe, but we have ten warheads on each missile — try to top that."

"Yeah — well, we have nuclear armed submarines and you can't find them. And we have nuclear armed aircraft surrounding you.

So there!"

On it went, to the point where the whole game was to outshout the other fellow, make him fear your capability, recognize your readiness, and respect your determination. At the same time, each side had to make sure the other knew it was not intending to use the destructive forces being flaunted. "Peace is our Profession" was the SAC motto. Admittedly, all of this worked, far better than the well-intended efforts of the anti-nuke soapbox orators. Unbridled nuclear warfare did not, has not, and will not occur. If one nuclear missile had ever been launched in anger, the whole system would have failed in its single role, which was *NEVER TO BE USED.*

Meanwhile, in spite of lessons learned (and quickly forgotten) in Korea, planning for an effective conventional air power capability in the USAF languished. The emphasis was unashamedly nuclear. The bulk of the annual Air Force budget was dedicated to the provision and deployment of nuclear-capable men and machines. The world lived in the shadow of international suicide under apocalyptic labels devised by angry men on the thrones of power — massive retaliation, assured second strike, preemptive strike, graduated response — spine-tingling, knee-jerking terms affecting every facet of civilization and every human life.

Tactical Air Command, dominated and commanded by bomber adherents, embraced the nuclear strike role to survive. The F-100 was not as capable in its intended air combat role as was the F-86H it replaced. It even proved to be a mediocre performer in the ground support role. The next in line, the F-105, was designed as a nuclear strike fighter, complete with bomb bay. Pressed into a conventional role by circumstance, it was to prove invaluable over North Vietnam. There it was joined by the F-4, a Navy fleet interceptor hurriedly purchased by the USAF because no Air Force aircraft matched its capability. A ghost from the 1930s, that grand old lady, the C-47 "Gooney Bird," was resurrected to join the fighting in South Vietnam, as was another Naval aircraft, the huge propeller-driven A-1. That these diverse aircraft were so successfully employed in Southeast Asia is more to the credit of the air and ground crews than to the vision of the planners in the Pentagon.

Vietnam, ghastly as it was, can be credited with forcing a reevaluation of the role and mission of air power. Nuclear-armed B-52s were given a piece of the conventional action, and carpet bombing jungle-clad mountains became the rage. Practicing a policy of limited response, America's leaders denied our forces decisive action. Instead of cutting off the head of the snake, the Air Force was relegated to chopping away at the tail, which only grew longer and longer as time passed. Our departure from Vietnam was not a military defeat, but one of political policy.

Over the past fifty years and more what we have learned, sometimes slowly, often reluctantly, is that the greater and more massive the nuclear threat and counterthreat, the less likely its use, and the more likely the advent of conventional wars and confrontations. Nuclear power, rather than deterring all conflict, serves only to deter itself. No missile has ever been fired, and no nuclear bomb has been dropped, thanks to the dedication and personal sacrifice of men and women in uniform on both sides of the East-West divide. Though we must maintain a nuclear posture for the foreseeable future, the proven likelihood of conflict is that of iron bombs and bullets, and, in the 1990s, for the first time since 1945, America became truly ready to face that challenge. Just ask Saddam.

Let the faces and actions of the people in this book tell the story in full. Think of the security guard walking his lonely vigil in the sub-zero cold of Minot AFB, of the maintenance, supply, and armament people working to keep the force instantly ready, of the cooks and clerks and administrative troops who make it all work. Put youself in the cockpit of a B-52 or a KC-135 that flew the Arctic Circle on Looking Glass alert, facing a grim, direct threat; there because world tension had reached a point of near explosion and the words flying between Washington and Moscow needed the force of reality. Think of the men and women who, even today, spend half of each year deployed somewhere far away. Consider their families who wait, knowing their loved ones are there to make America's presence felt, to preserve the peace, but ready to fight if need be. Remember the fighter pilots who have flown hundreds of hours in combat in the battles we could not call wars. Recall with agony those who languished in the dank cells of Hanoi for endless years. These men and women, in their own way, served their country with steadfast loyalty, with uncomplaining devotion, and with pride. We owe them an immeasurable debt of gratitude.

Robin Olds
Steamboat Springs, Colorado
May 1997

PREFACE

A single volume on the history of the United States Air Force and its origins cannot begin to cover such a vast subject with any hope of being comprehensive, or even adequate. It is a powerful story, full of courage and daring under the physical challenges of operating military aircraft in war and peace, and of flair and determination in the face of the sometimes shortsighted views which bedevil the defense policies not only of the United States, but of all democratic nations. The history of American military aviation, from the acquisition of the first Wright Flyer as Signal Corps Aeroplane No. 1 in 1909 to the building of an air force for the 21st century, is an epic tale of air power and its continuous — often explosive — development. It has involved political struggle at the highest level, interservice rivalry at its most bitter, and continuous debate about the nature of air power and how it should be used. Advances have been made which have hugely expanded the frontiers of science and technology, and a bewildering variety of equipment has been produced with capabilities bordering on the magical. The wildest flights of imagination undertaken by prophets like H.G. Wells have been overtaken by the reality of events in the 20th century. Above the trenches at St. Mihiel and the oilfields of Ploesti, from Burma's mountainous "hump" to the beaches of Normandy, over burning German and Japanese cities and the Yalu River, in Southeast Asia and the Middle East, American air power has been a force which has shaped world events. There is every reason to suppose that it will continue to do so in the future. It would be difficult to do these matters justice with a whole library of books, let alone one.

All that having been said, it would not have been reasonable to let the 50th anniversary of the world's most powerful air force pass without attempting to review its background and achievements, however imperfect the end result might prove to be. In preparing just such a work, we looked for the "golden threads" which weave unbroken through the complex tapestry of Air Force history, prominent among them the threads of innovation, technical competence, and courage. In many ways, it is

remarkable that the grand design of this historical pattern was created by people who might think of themselves as ordinary Americans. It is they who have, for the most part, been behind the extraordinary accomplishments of the USAF and its predecessors. There have always been singular individuals who have drawn special attention and will be remembered by name, but they are the exceptions, and it can be argued that they serve only to dramatize the performance of the Air Force as a whole. It is no exaggeration to describe the Air Force which fought so hard and well in WWII, for example, as a citizens' force, formed in large part from youngsters who had been farmers or bank clerks or motor mechanics before the war. (Great names emerged, some of them already established as exceptional career airmen, but it might be noted that most WWII Medals of Honor were awarded to men who appeared at the time to be no more than average Americans doing their best to serve their country in its hour of need.) Demobilization sent most of them home in 1945, leaving those who remained in uniform to seek a new, postwar identity. Soon after becoming an independent service in 1947, the USAF moved to widen its peacetime personnel field by adopting policies which denied discrimination on the grounds of race, creed, or gender. Today's Air Force, with its superlative equipment, almost limitless capabilities, and global responsibilities, is organized and operated by a truly representative cross-section of the American people.

The epic scale of the history and the limitations of available space being what they are, it was necessary for us to be extremely selective, often painfully so, in choosing what to include in this book, and it is certain that many people will feel disappointed that much valuable and interesting material has had to be left out. Perhaps inevitably, the exploits of the personnel and machines at the Air Force's "sharp end," the operational units, have been given the lion's share. However, it should never be forgotten that operators cannot operate without their supporting cast of technicians, armorers, logisticians, administrators, medics, air traffic controllers, meteorologists, ca-

terers, and all the other specialists who combine to make the Air Force an effective military organization. Even when they are not directly mentioned, their efforts are recorded between the lines.

Anyone wishing to put flesh on the bones of the Air Force story told in the pages of this book could do no better than visit the United States Air Force Museum at Wright-Patterson AFB, near Dayton, Ohio. It would be hard to find a more appropriate place for the Museum than Dayton, home of the brothers who brought the first chapter of aviation history to a successful conclusion — Wilbur and Orville Wright. Since their remarkable achievements, the area which now has Wright-Patterson AFB at its center has remained at the forefront of Air Force research and development, expanding aeronautical frontiers and introducing successive generations of military aircraft to operational service. The USAF Museum is therefore appropriately sited, and is a treasure house of air power history, unsurpassed anywhere in the world for the size and quality of its aviation collection.

The Museum is also the repository for a significant piece of America's national fabric; the United States could not be the world's strongest nation without air power, and the artifacts which record the building of that power are at Dayton. Consequently, it seemed only right that the illustrations for a USAF 50th anniversary book should be drawn, as far as possible, from the resources of the USAF Museum. Most of the historical photographs came from the Museum's archives, and dramatic new color shots were taken of the major items on display in its extensive galleries. Since not everything could be included, the subjects for this new collection were chosen with an eye to following the line of the "golden threads," paying particular attention to the points of view of those who put on Air Force cloth and brought the machines to life. As the pages turn and the Air Force story unfolds, the evolution of those machines from the simple creations of wood, wire, and cloth of the early years into the sleeker shapes of exotic metals and composites of today is steadily revealed by

ACKNOWLEDGMENTS

the camera. Indeed, the eye of the lens often seems to take us further, seeing aircraft more as sculpture that flies than as mere technical achievement.

To complete the work of illustration, selected works of art from some of the world's leading aviation artists have been added, and, to give the reader who has not been to Dayton some idea of the USAF Museum and its atmosphere, each chapter (save the last, which looks to the future) is preceded by a few impressions of what a visitor would have seen in 1996 when walking through the galleries and reliving the drama of Air Force history.

If there is a message behind the story told in this book, and revealed by the illustrations which bring it to life, it is that the Air Force is an organization in which remarkable achievement has been and is the daily fare of typical Americans. The finished work is intended as a 50th anniversary tribute to those men and women whose combined efforts since the days of the Wright brothers have contributed to an inspiring tale of air power, and to the building of the modern United States Air Force — an air force for the 21st Century.

Ron Dick, Woodbridge, Virginia
Dan Patterson, Dayton, Ohio
October 1996

It was a surprise and a considerable honor for a retired Royal Air Force officer to be invited to put together a book in celebration of the United States Air Force's 50th anniversary. It was with some trepidation that I began reviewing the monumental achievements of an air force other than my own, but the nature of the task and the encouragement I received while completing it made the experience a memorable and enjoyable one. If the finished work does not do justice to its subject, the fault is mine alone. Inadequacies or inaccuracies cannot be ascribed to any of the many friends and advisers who offered advice and assistance during the book's preparation.

At the head of the list for my particular thanks comes my colleague, Dan Patterson, an aviation photographer of rare talent. His keen eye for the shapes and colors of aviation technology has given this book life. Turn the pages and you will see a collection of photographs which is not only unique, but often startling in its impact. His enthusiasm for his work is both inspired and infectious. I am equally grateful to Dr. Richard Hallion, the Air Force Historian, a gentleman and a scholar who was brave enough to think that I might be qualified to write the book in the first place. His staff in the Air Force History Support Office matched their title and were suitably supportive throughout.

Without the blessing of Dick Uppstrom, then Director of the United States Air Force Museum near Dayton, the job could never have been done; his staff was invariably helpful. During our exhaustive (and often exhausting!) searches through the archives, we were guided by Wes Henry and the encyclopedic mind of Dave Menard (MSgt, USAF, Retd), whose retentive memory for the details of USAF history is a valuable archive in itself. Elsewhere in the Museum we were offered cheerful assistance wherever we turned.

As we approached the later chapters of the book and began to deal with the Air Force of the present and future, the material at the USAF Museum became understandably sparse. The photographs of the current Air Force inventory came from Combat Camera in the Pentagon, where I

AF Museum staff who helped make the photographs in this book possible. From left, Robert Patterson, Ted Chapman, Dave Lazzerine, Randy Canady, Dick Daugherty, Paul Lee, Frank Mcvay, Tom Bachman, Robert Adair, Ray Patrusch, Kari Clark, Dave Robb, Dick Tobias, Don Scott, Charlie Weyrick, Roger Deere, Krista Strider, Steve West, Myrl Morris, Ted Beegle, Bob Spaulding.

Members of the Museum staff, family, and friends who helped make this book possible. Back row from left, Bob Bobbitt, Dave Menard, Diana Bachert. Middle row from left, Wes Henry, Bill Patterson, Paul Perkins, Tom Patterson. Front row from left, Brigitta Patterson, Joe Patterson, Nate Patterson, Teresa Jones.

was introduced to the wonders of digital photographic storage. John McDowell of *Airman* magazine and Colonel "Smoky" Greene were kind enough to add some more conventional images. Colonel Greene, together with several current Air Force operators, also offered helpful comments on the book's concluding chapter.

The International Association of Eagles in Montgomery, Alabama, has long supported aviation history projects, and has consistently encouraged this venture. The Association's annual "Gathering of Eagles," held at the USAF's Air University, enabled me to meet many of the famous aviators whose names appear in the following pages, and whose exploits add color to the narrative. Through the Association, too, the Curtiss-Wright Corporation, present-day successors of the men who started it all, made a generous contribution towards the costs of production.

Closer to home, I am deeply indebted to Don Babb for his meticulous proofreading of the text, and to Mike Harbison, a computer wizard who several times saved me (and the manuscript) from the potentially disastrous consequences of my own ineptness in handling computers. Finally, I am grateful to my family for their patience and fortitude during the months when the book was for me the center of the Universe. To my wife, Paul, in particular, my heartfelt thanks for her tolerance of my obsession with aviation and, especially, of its latest manifestation. I hope she thinks the result is worth all the turbulence which accompanied its extended gestation and difficult birth.

Ron Dick

The years that have gone into this work have had an impact not only on myself, but also on a circle of family and friends who pitched in to help me accomplish the daunting task of shooting all the photographs. Literally thousands of images have been edited down to the selections seen on these pages. I need to thank those who helped make this possible.

Ron Dick, my friend and colleague. We have developed a very comfortable working partnership and our mutual commitment to nothing but the best is very satisfying. The friendship of Ron and his wife Paul helped to keep me going through some difficult times.

My children Nate, Brigitta, and Joe. All have helped with lights and equipment, climbing through airplanes to put lights in just the right place, and have endured the long hours of editing and designing after the photos were done. My parents, Bill and Jane Patterson, have offered endless support and advice. As I have told them many times, without their efforts...I wouldn't be here. Dad and my brother Tom helped me shoot several of the more complex photographs, and they did the portrait of Ron and me.

Cheryl Terrill, for an understanding friendship.

Many others, especially Paul Perkins, my lifelong friend. Kurt Wiedner, Tim Thompson, Mike Fessler, Tom Whalen, Kelly Miller, Ron Kaplan. All of whom learned about lights, hydraulic lifts, extension cords that weren't quite long enough, and ladders that just didn't quite reach. I owe them my thanks.

The USAF Museum staff was generally helpful, but a few names must represent them all. Diana Bachert, Museum Public Affairs. Her efforts made everything possible. Bob Bobbitt, also from Public Affairs. Wes Henry and Dave Menard from the museum's research department offered every encouragement and answered some very obscure questions. The Museum's volunteers were constantly involved, with Bob Spaulding serving as the cog to keep the wheels turning. Dick Tobias gave every possible assistance.

Ross and Elinor Howell of Howell Press, who continue to believe in what I do and how I do it. Ross's commitment to quality publishing is greatly appreciated.

Dan Patterson

Chapter 1

Hopes and Dreams

"I said to my brother Orville that man would not fly for fifty years."

(Wilbur Wright, 1901)

"We'll go through the air; for sure the air is free."
(*The Metamorphoses*, Ovid)

"I suppose we shall soon travel by air vessels; make air instead of sea voyages; and at length find our way to the moon, in spite of the want of atmosphere."
(Lord Byron, 1822)

"Aerial navigation will form a most prominent feature in the progress of civilization."
(George Cayley, 1809)

"I have not the smallest molecule of faith in aerial navigation other than ballooning, or expectation of good results from any of the trials we hear of."
(Lord Kelvin, 1896)

Octave Chanute (1832-1910), the first significant aviation historian and a crucial link between the aeronautical communities of Europe and America. His 1894 book, **Progress in Flying Machines**, *summarized the facts and fantasies of mankind's eternal fascination with flying, drawing together the threads of a story which had been in the making for thousands of years. Among other things, the book helped to motivate the Wright brothers as they began their aeronautical experiments. Perhaps just as important, Chanute remained a constant source of encouragement to the Wright brothers as they worked towards their ultimate success.*

In telling the story of any nation's air power, it is sensible to begin by digging back through time to discover something about the foundations on which that power is built. The history of man's contemplation of flight and of efforts made by people the world over to emulate the birds is mankind's common heritage. The United States Air Force Museum's first gallery offers a brief reminder of the thousands of years of human fantasies and aspirations which preceded manned flight. The displays lead the visitor from the winged figures of early religions through fable

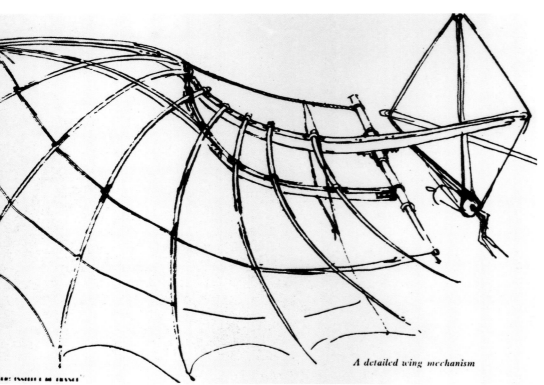

A detailed wing mechanism

Leonardo da Vinci studied the anatomy of birds and sketched designs for man-sized wings to be made of wood and fabric. Flapping was to be accomplished by means of a continuous cable running round a hand-turned winch. Surprisingly, he does not seem to have realized that human muscles could never have provided the power necessary for flight.

and legend to the stumbling experiments of men who dared to reach for the sky. There is also an introduction to those who found success by choosing the lighter-than-air flight of balloons and airships, and to those who tried but failed to achieve controlled flight with various heavier-than-air contraptions. The gradual progress represented by these failures and near successes sets the scene for the final triumph of the Wright brothers, and begins the process of gathering together the many

threads which were later combined to weave the fabric of American air power.

1903 was a vintage year for widening the horizons of the American people. The Ford Motor Company was incorporated to produce Henry Ford's Model A, the Harley-Davidson motorcycle was introduced, and, in a fifty-two day epic, a Packard was driven from San Francisco to New York to complete the first successful transcontinental journey by car. Hardly noticed at the time, but more significant than any of these, was the fact that two brothers from Dayton, Ohio, accom-

plished something human beings had dreamed of doing for thousands of years. On December 17, 1903, when the thoughts of most Americans were turned towards the coming Christmas celebrations, Wilbur and Orville Wright braved the icy winds of the Kill Devil Hills near Kitty Hawk, on North Carolina's Outer Banks, to experience powered, controlled flight for the first time. As Orville himself later described their accomplishment, it

was "the first in the history of the world in which a machine carrying a man had raised itself by its own power into the air in full flight, had sailed forward without reduction of speed, and had finally landed at a point as high as that from which it had started."

The achievement of the Wright brothers passed almost unremarked in 1903, even though they had taken the first small step along an aerial highway which would, in the course of the twentieth century, lead to a change in the way of life of every society on Earth. Those who did hear of the event generally reacted to the news with skepticism. People refused to believe the claims of the Wrights in the absence of the evidence of their own eyes. It demanded too great a leap of the imagination to accept that human flight was possible. Indeed, there may actually have been a subconscious rejection of the feat at first. The idea of flight had a mystic quality to it which was necessarily diminished if mere mortals could lift themselves into the third dimension.

Flights of Fancy

There is ample evidence that a reverence for the heavens and a recognition of the powers flight could bestow appeared at a very early stage in human development. Eyes seemed naturally drawn upward to search the skies for deities. Gods, angels, and other immortals were often imagined as having wings. In the evolution of religions everywhere, wings were used to enhance the supernatural qualities of such divine figures as the Egyptian Isis, the Hindu Garuda, and the Greek Hermes and Eros, who became the Roman Mercury and Cupid. Christian artists have almost invariably depicted angels with the wings thought necessary to carry them between Heaven and Earth.

Legends in which some form of flight is imagined for mere humans have come to us from well before recorded history. The earliest written account is from the *Chinese Annals of the Bamboo Books* from at least four thousand years ago when the Emperor Shun is said to have flown by putting on "the work clothes of a bird." Many years later, another Chinese, Ki-kung-shi, seems to have commanded an airborne chariot. A King of Persia apparently flew in a jeweled throne fitted with several spears. Four tethered eagles were induced to provide the necessary motive power by impaled hunks of meat just out of their reach on spearpoints. As if the genuine achievements of Alexander the Great were not legendary enough, he was said to have viewed the heavens towed by four similarly encouraged griffins, while the inhabitants of Arabia relied on even more exotic magic carpets.

The best known Western legend of manned flight, recorded by the Roman poet Ovid, tells how Daedalus and his son Icarus escaped captivity on the island of Crete. The fatal dive of Icarus after the sun melted the wax in his wings was emulated at intervals in later centuries by scores of less legendary but still hopeful aviators who jumped off cliffs and towers supported by little more than faith and a few feathers. Feathers were thought to possess the quality of "lightness" which, when enough were attached to the body, would enable a person to float in the air. The aspiring aeronauts usually floated in air like bricks in water and most fell to their deaths or were sadly mutilated.

As time went by, more scientific approaches were taken to the problem of flight, and manned flight in particular. Kites were in use by the Chinese and Japanese for centuries before they were even thought of in the West, and many of them were quite capable of carrying a man. In Europe, the first man to approach flying scientifically was Leonardo da Vinci. In the late fifteenth and early sixteenth centuries, this remarkable Renaissance man thought deeply about how man might fly and drew designs for parachutes, helicopters, and ornithopters (flapping wing machines)—some 150 sketches in all. However, although many of his ideas were visionary, even his great mind was clouded by a number of misconceptions about how birds fly, and his ornithopter designs would never have allowed a man to lift himself off the

ground. Sadly, the results of his obsession with flight did not inspire further research, and da Vinci's original concepts had no influence on the later history of human flight. His papers were not revealed to the world until the latter part of the nineteenth century, by which time aerodynamics had been advanced by the work of others.

Lighter Than Air

Real progress in aerodynamics had to wait until the nineteenth century, although man had managed free flight of another kind before then. It is a curious fact that several of the most significant steps

first men to travel by air were Pilatre de Rozier and the Marquis d'Arlandes, who stoked a fire of straw to keep them aloft as they flew across Paris in the course of a twenty-five-minute flight on November 21, 1783. Only ten days later, Professor J.A.C. Charles also rose from Paris in a balloon, this time one filled with hydrogen. On December 1, he was in the air for over two hours and at one stage reached a height of some nine thousand feet.

Within a very short space of time, ballooning became something of a popular craze. In spite of the unpredictable nature of balloons, which could travel only

Sharing the fate of all those who finish second, Professor J.A.C. Charles and his hydrogen balloon have been overshadowed in aeronautical history by the hot air balloon of the Montgolfier brothers. On December 1, 1783, little more than a month after the Montgolfiers' success, Professor Charles rose above Paris and improved markedly on the time and distance of his rivals. On a second flight that same day, he climbed above 9,000 ft, so startling himself that he never flew again.

in early aviation were taken by cooperating brothers. In 1783, the first of these pairs, the Montgolfiers, successfully demonstrated a number of hot air balloons, or "aerostatic machines," in France. Prudently, the Montgolfiers (like the creators of the first space vehicles two centuries later) chose not to test their aerostats themselves. The first aeronauts were a sheep, a rooster, and a duck. These creatures having survived an eight-minute flight, the

in directions chosen for them by the winds, the attraction of reaching for the clouds was such that the intrepid and wealthy rushed to experience the new adventure. Fresh achievements crowded upon one another and, just over a year after the Montgolfier success, a balloon carrying Jean-Pierre Blanchard and an American doctor, John Jeffries, left from Dover and crossed the English Channel to France. This sent a tremor through the hearts of

sign for glider

Sir George Cayley (1773-1857) was the first man to design, build , and fly both model and man-carrying gliders featuring fixed wings with dihedral, adjustable tails, and flying controls. Initially called "governable parachutes," his creations established the basic configuration adopted for aircraft of the 20th century.

those English people who saw a threat to the island nation's security in a device which could ignore the water barrier of the Channel and fly over the protecting ships of the Royal Navy.

Such fears were not entirely without foundation. Engravings exist which show a fantastic Napoleonic project for a French invasion of England by troops carried in balloons, and there are also sketches of English soldier-bearing kites intended to meet and defeat the aerial threat. Conceived in the early years of the nineteenth century, these ideas for airborne confrontation may have been premature, but they foresaw the nature of future air defense problems and foreshadowed a very real twentieth century Battle of Britain. They were not, however, by any means the first speculations on the possible use of the air for military purposes. It is a sobering thought that almost all technological advances in human history have been immediately exploited for their military potential, and the balloon was no exception. Benjamin Franklin was an eyewitness of Professor Charles's first ascent, and his subsequent comments on the event are revealing:

"Convincing sovereigns of the folly of wars may perhaps be one effect of it, since it will be impracticable for the most potent of them to guard his dominions. Five thousand balloons, capable of raising two men each, could not cost more than five ships of the line; and where is the prince who could afford so to cover his

country with troops for its defense as that ten thousand men descending from the clouds might not in many places do an infinite deal of mischief before a force could be brought together to repel them?"

The French Army was already using tethered balloons for reconnaissance of the battlefield by 1794, but in many ways it was a surprise that it had taken Western soldiers so long to take advantage of the high ground of the air. Airborne military development, after all, had been foreseen and, to a limited extent, practiced for a very long time. Man-carrying kites had been used for reconnaissance in the Far East for centuries, and offensive action was predicted as far back as 2,000 B.C. in a Hindu legend about a battle between an aerial city and a flying chariot. The chariot is said to have maneuvered above the city and destroyed it with weapons which demolished everything on which they fell. Similar destruction was later imagined by a Jesuit priest. In 1670, Francesco de Lana suggested that an airship could be borne aloft by large evacuated copper balls, but he made no attempt to construct such a vessel because, he said:

"God would not suffer such an invention to take effect, by reason of the civil disturbance it would cause to the government of men. For who sees not that no city can be secure against attack, since our ship may at any time be placed directly over it. . . . that the same it would happen to ships on the sea, for our ship . . . may overset them, kill their men, burn their

ships by artificial fireworks and fireballs. And this they may do not only to ships but to great buildings, castles, cities."

Francesco de Lana was ahead of his time and it was almost two hundred years before his warnings began to gather substance. With the United States at war with Mexico in 1846, John Wise proposed that a tethered balloon should be flown over the fortress of Veracruz to drop bombs on the defenders. The U.S. War Department did not pursue the idea, but only three years later a city actually was attacked from the air when the Austrians used unmanned balloons to drop bombs on Venice. Expectations of reducing the city to rubble were not met, but that would not be the last time in aerial warfare that prediction would exceed capability.

The value of balloons for reconnaissance did not escape the attention of American soldiers, and, in September 1861, the Balloon Corps of the Army of the Potomac was formed. This small precursor of American air power started with just two balloons under the command of Chief Aeronaut Thaddeus Lowe. His reports from the battle of Fair Oaks at the end of May 1862 suggest that his corps was a valuable addition to the army. More than once he saw enemy movements, undetected on the ground, which posed considerable threats to Union forces. Following one report of Confederate troops massing, General McClellan hurriedly brought up reserves on his army's left, and Lowe says: "Had not our forces been concentrated, it is very evident that our left . . . would have been driven back and in consequence the whole army routed."

Despite the fact that similarly useful information about the enemy was obtained on many occasions, the balloon unit was disbanded in 1863. It was not until 1892 that a balloon section was reformed as part of the Signal Corps of the U.S. Army. Even then, it was a minor affair, with only one balloon. Nevertheless, it was sent to Cuba during the Spanish-American War, and was flown under fire to spy out the land before the famous charge of the Rough Riders up San Juan Hill.

The quality lacking in a balloon was "dirigibility"—the capacity to be directed. Without it, lighter-than-air machines had to be tethered or remain at the mercy of the winds. The problem was understood from the start and, in 1784, one far-sighted French officer produced a design for a dirigible airship. Lt. (later General) Meusnier proposed a cigar-shaped balloon 260 ft long, carrying a car powered by three propellers. In the absence of a suitable power source, his proposal was dropped, but the idea was sound and, as practical power plants began to appear, it was put into practice. The French again led the way with Henri Giffard, who in 1852 steered his steam-driven airship from Paris for some seventeen miles. During the latter half of the nineteenth century, he was followed by a number of others, primarily Frenchmen, who built airships powered inadequately either by steam or electricity. Then, in 1885, events in Germany opened the door to practical manned flight. Karl Benz and Gottlieb Daimler, building on the work of Nikolaus Otto, constructed the first gasoline-fueled engines with a reasonable power-to-weight ratio. They did so for the benefit of surface transport, but engines based on their designs soon became the first choice for the aviation world.

France remained at the center of airship development, principally through the efforts of the Lebaudy brothers and the showmanship of the Brazilian Alberto Santos-Dumont, who, in the early 1900s, flew his "little runabouts" all over Paris. The most significant airship developments, however, were German. They took place at Lake Konstanz under the guidance of Count Ferdinand von Zeppelin, for whom great size seemed to be a guiding principle. From the outset, his airships were more than four hundred feet long, and the first of them (LZ1) flew successfully in 1900. In the years which followed, it seemed for a time that "Zeppelins" and their kin would prove themselves the most practical way of exploiting the air. They led the way both in airborne passenger travel and in the projection of strategic air power. Their use by Germany against Britain in WWI initiated the first sustained air offensive against a nation's population. Eventually, however, their demonstrated vulnerability in war and several well-publicized peacetime disasters, like those which destroyed the airships "Akron," "R101," and "Hindenburg," led to their general displacement by powered, fixed-wing airplanes.

Cayley and His Followers

Meanwhile, the cause of heavier-than-air flight had prospered much more slowly. After Leonardo da Vinci's speculations in the sixteenth century, nothing noteworthy was accomplished in aerodynamics until the advent of Sir George Cayley in England some two centuries later. Cayley was an extraordinarily talented and practical scientist who was intensely interested in the "whys" and "wherefores" of everything around him. He brought his powerful intellect to bear on such diverse matters as electricity, optics, architecture, railways, lifeboats, land reclamation, and artificial limbs. Among his inventions were the expansion air engine (1805) and the caterpillar tractor (1825). Cayley's insatiable curiosity was attracted to the problems of flight at an early age and he worked intermittently at finding solutions for over sixty years, until his death in 1857.

Cayley's list of "firsts" in aerodynamics is impressive. It includes the derivation of a balance of forces to explain the principles of flight, an investigation of the effects of streamlining and wing dihedral, and the realization both that it is low pressure above a wing which provides most of the lift and that a cambered airfoil gives more lift than a flat one. Before Cayley, the aerodynamics of a fixed-wing aeroplane had not been formulated, nor had bird flight been understood. His researches led him to be the first to build and fly a glider which had elevator/rudder control surfaces and succeeded in carrying a man. Cayley's coachman flew for some nine hundred feet across a valley before crashing into the slope on the far side. The man apparently was unhappy at being asked to probe the frontiers of technology. According to Cayley's granddaughter, he crawled from the wreckage unhurt and shouted: "Please, Sir George, I wish to give notice. I was hired to drive and not to fly!"

The practical results of Sir George Cayley's work in aerodynamics were invaluable, but perhaps his greatest contribution to the cause of manned heavier-than-air flight was that he took it out of the realm of fantasy and showed that it was possible. More than half a century before the engines of Benz and Daimler appeared, he even suggested that the problem of power would be solved by a form of internal combustion engine. He was an inspiration to those who followed him and deserves the title now universally bestowed—"The Father of Aerial Navigation." Wilbur Wright bowed in his direction in 1909, saying: "Sir

William Henson's "Aerial Steam Carriage" was never built, yet its visionary design strongly influenced the course of aviation history. Patented in 1843, it was a wire-braced monoplane with a recognizable fuselage and tail unit. It had a tricycle undercarriage, 150 ft cambered wings with shaped spars and ribs, and an engine which drove two pusher airscrews. It was confidently (if prematurely) advertised as being intended to carry passengers all over the world.

In 1884, Alexander Mozhaiski's square-winged monoplane (wingspan almost 75 ft) gathered speed under power down a slope near St. Petersburg and managed a brief hop of 20 or 30 meters while carrying a man named Golubev. The achievement, however, could not be claimed as sustained or controlled flight.

George Cayley carried the science of flying to a point which it had never reached before, and which it scarcely reached again during the [nineteenth] century."

In Cayley's footsteps came his disciples Henson and Stringfellow, remarkable for their promotion of the ambitious Henson Aerial Steam Carriage project in the 1840s. This was advertised as offering rapid passages to India and China. Known as the "Ariel," it never flew, but its design predicted the shape of successful aircraft in the twentieth century. A monoplane, with a fuselage, tailplane, rudder, tricycle undercarriage, and twin propellers, it was designed on an impressive scale with a 150 ft wingspan. Imaginative and farseeing though it was, it would have been doomed to failure even if built. Its designed weight was over three thousand pounds and its two ten-foot diameter, six-bladed propellers were to be driven by one 25 hp steam engine—and perhaps a great deal of wishful thinking.

European Dreamers

During the second half of the nineteenth century much of the most notable effort made in aeronautical research was French. In 1858, Felix du Temple (in another fraternal partnership with his brother Louis) tested a model monoplane which took off under its own clockwork power and hopped for a short distance, so becoming the first airplane to sustain itself in the air. He followed this with a man-carrying version powered by an expansion air engine which, in 1874, hopped forward with a young French sailor aboard after being launched down a sloping ramp. A similar hop was achieved in Russia in 1884 by a large twin steam-engined machine designed by Alexander Mozhaiski. In 1865, the French engineer Charles de Louvrie published a design for a jet-propelled airplane, which he said would be powered by "burning hydrocarbon, or better, vaporised petroleum oil" ejected to the aircraft's rear by two pipes. Alphonse Penaud then appeared on the scene and dominated the world of aeronautics for the brief period of his working life. Penaud was a brilliant man who built and flew a number of airplane and helicopter models driven by twisted rubber, an idea which has persisted and helped to foster air-mindedness among the world's youth. He later patented a design for an amphibious monoplane which embodied several remarkable innovations—a single control column to move control surfaces, retractable landing gear with shock absorbers, a glass cockpit canopy, an engine enclosed in the fuselage, and a set of flight instruments including a compass, a level, and a barometer. In 1880, disheartened by lack of capital and by the ridicule which aviation pioneers commonly endured, Penaud ended a life of great promise with a bullet in his brain.

Many other men contributed to a greater or lesser degree to the science of aeronautics during these years—among them Frenchmen like Le Bris, Renard, Mouillard, and Tatin; Hargrave from Australia; and the Englishmen Brearey, Moy, Phillips, and Francis Wenham, who was the first to build and use a wind tunnel for aerodynamic experiments. They (and others) all deserve their place in aviation history, but they are relatively minor figures compared with the men who, in the closing years of the nineteenth century, competed to be the first to achieve manned heavier-than-air flight.

The Engineers

There were two principal approaches to the solution of the problem. The first of these was taken by men who were engineers and thought the answer lay in providing sufficient power and lift to get them off the ground. They seemed to believe that they would be able to sort out the business of flying once they were airborne, and the difficulties of controlling flight were not at the forefront of their minds. To the degree that they considered control at all, they tried to devise ways of making their creations as stable as possible. In experiments with free-flying models, stability was necessarily important if flight was to be sustained, but it was not appreciated that such stability, built into a man-carrying airplane, would make it extremely difficult to fly. The more stable the airplane, the harder it is to make it deviate from its line of flight, and therefore to maneuver it in a direction chosen by the pilot. Those who took the view that power and lift came first, and that control was a subject which could be studied later, proved to be both determined and ingenious, but they were to find that they were doing their best to run before they could walk.

Clement Ader deserves inclusion in this select group if only because he is credited with building the first powered airplane to raise itself from level ground with a man on board. In every other way, his machine is something of an anachronism. Ader paid little attention to the available aerodynamic information when he built his monoplane "Eole." Completed in 1890, the "Eole" was a monoplane with bat-shaped wings and no control surfaces. It was powered by a single steam engine producing about 20 hp and flown by a pilot seated behind the boiler so that he could not see where he was going. Ader seemed to think that the only control necessary was the variation of engine power to initiate climb or descent. In 1890, he got the "Eole" to leave level ground and fly forward for some fifty yards at a height of less than a foot, so claiming a first of a kind in manned flight, although even he never went so far as to say that it had been either sustained or controlled. Ader learned little from this experience and later, in a project which made the French government the first to provide official backing to an aircraft manufacturer, he produced a larger bat-winged machine driven by two propellers and equally devoid of controls. Called "Avion III," this creation was submitted for trial in 1897, but observers noted that it could not be induced to leave the ground.

In Britain, the expatriate American Hiram Maxim, inventor of the machine gun, set himself limited objectives. He elected to "build a flying machine that would lift itself from the ground." He apparently had no intention of trying to fly it in the true sense. After experimenting with airfoils in a wind tunnel, Maxim built an enormous machine—145 ft long and 104 ft across the main wing, it had lifting surfaces totaling over 5,500 sq ft. Power was provided by two huge 180 hp steam engines, each driving an 18 ft propeller. The total weight of this colossus was over eight thousand pounds when carrying a crew of as many as four. To discourage any tendency to become inconveniently airborne, Maxim designed it to run along a set of rails six hundred yards long. Above the rails were outriggers which were intended to restrain the beast if it rose more than two feet into the air. In 1894, it did just that after running on its rails for two hundred yards. Engaging the outriggers firmly, it tore itself loose and careered on until Maxim shut off the steam, finally coming to rest after a total journey of almost 370 yards. Maxim repaired the dam-

age and did further tests, but he was no longer really interested. He brushed aside the many unanswered questions and swept on to other things, saying: "Propulsion and lifting are solved problems; the rest is merely a matter of time." Maxim's contributions were colorful and intriguing, but his work was little more than a detour in the march towards manned flight.

As the century drew to a close, the center of gravity for aeronautical research began to shift across the Atlantic towards the United States, and a number of Americans carved themselves permanent niches in aviation history. Among them was Samuel Pierpont Langley, a distinguished engineer and astronomer who became Secretary of the Smithsonian Institution, and another of those who believed that power and lift came first in the development of a flying machine. He began his aeronautical research in 1886 with the construction of a large steam-driven whirling arm which could carry models (and stuffed birds) forward at speeds up to 70 mph. This device, he said, enabled him to work out "what amount of mechanical power was requisite to sustain a given weight in the air, and make it advance at a given speed."

By 1892, Langley had started on the construction of a series of large steam-powered models which he rather oddly called "Aerodromes" and numbered in a sequence starting with "0." Numbers 0, 1, 2, 3, and 4 were all failures, but in 1896 Numbers 5 and 6 gave him encouragement. The successful design had two wings in tandem, with a 1 hp steam engine and twin propellers amidships. To Langley's delight, these unwieldy objects were launched from a houseboat on the Potomac and flew considerable distances; No. 5 managed 3,300 ft and No. 6 a commendable three-quarters of a mile. Suitably impressed, President William McKinley, under the impetus of the Spanish-American War in 1898, appointed a committee to investigate these achievements, and the War Department later gave Langley a $50,000 subsidy to build a man-carrying airplane. The United States thereby became the second nation to finance the acquisition of an aircraft in-

tended for military trials.

The full-size Aerodrome was completed in 1903. It closely resembled its smaller relations in having tandem wings closely followed by a large vertical tail. It was 48 ft from wing tip to wing tip and 52 ft long. Langley realized that steam would have to be replaced by gasoline as his power source for an airplane of this size and he set a target of an engine which would weigh about 100 lbs and produce 12 hp. His assistant, C.M. Manly, proceeded to design and build an engine from scratch and the finished article proved to be an astonishing achievement. Weighing only 125 lbs, the 5-cylinder radial produced 53 hp. With this power plant in place amidships, the Aerodrome weighed 730 lbs.

Two attempts were made to fly Langley's creation with Manly as the pilot, on October 7 and December 8, 1903. On both occasions it was intended to launch the Aerodrome from a catapult mounted on the Potomac houseboat, but each time some part of the airplane appeared to foul the launching mechanism and the intended flight became a plunge into the river. As a reporter for the *Washington Post* wrote: "A mechanic stooped, cut the cable

Samuel Pierpont Langley and his able assistant Charles Manly. In 1903, striving to become the first man to achieve sustained powered flight in Langley's "Aerodrome", Manly survived two successive dunkings in the Potomac River when the cumbersome Aerodrome "slid into the water like a handful of mortar" after being launched.

Langley's Aerodrome on its way into the Potomac River after leaving its houseboat launching ramp on October 7, 1903.

belief that man could fly and the influence that his opinion had on others. As Wilbur Wright later said: "The fact that the great scientist, Professor Langley, believed in flying machines was one thing that encouraged us to begin our studies."

The School of Gliding

As men like Ader, Maxim, and Langley showed, the direct "engineer's route" to manned flight was a blind alley. Real success was to be found only by following an apparently slower path via the art of gliding. The greatest of the gliding men, and the first human being to launch himself into the air and fly with any consistency, was the German Otto Lilienthal. (Otto is the famous one, but he was half of yet another fraternal aviation partnership with his brother Gustav.) Lilienthal began his practical experiments in 1889, when he built the first of some eighteen gliders. All of them were hang-gliders, in which the pilot's lower body hung down below the wings and was swung about to move the center of gravity and so achieve limited control. By 1894, Lilienthal had piled up an artificial hill 50 ft high near Berlin so that he could face the wind and start his glides in any direction, and he had built his most reliable glider, No. 11, with which he was regularly controlling glides of 350 yards or more. In the course of his lifetime, he carried out over two thousand glides.

holding the catapult; there was a roaring grinding noise, and the Langley airship tumbled over the edge of the house-boat and disappeared into the river sixteen feet below. It simply slid into the water like a handful of mortar."

The chorus of jeers in Congress and the press which greeted the failures of the Aerodrome forced the withdrawal of government support for the project and crushed Langley's spirit. He died a sadly disillusioned man less than three years later. His Aerodrome did eventually fly. Exten-

sively modified by Glenn Curtiss to add much needed control and structural strength, it was briefly tested as a floatplane in 1914, and it is possible that a successful launching in 1903 could have led to a sufficiently long flight to have given Langley the prize he sought so assiduously. However, without adequate control, the Aerodrome was not a practical flying machine, and, for all his efforts, Langley's technical influence on his successors in aviation was negligible. He remains an important figure nevertheless, if only because of his firm

Lilienthal's experiments included flying with wings of different span and various cambers, using biplanes as well as monoplanes, and devising several ways of control by adding movable surfaces to the wings or tail. He was inspired in his youth by the flight of birds and, if he had a blind spot, it was his conviction that experiments with fixed-wing gliders would lead to powered ornithopters. He actually built two machines designed to carry motors and be propelled by twisting slats intended to simulate a bird's primary feathers. The opportunity to test his theories was denied him, however. On a bright summer's day in 1896, he stalled a glider and fell from a height of 50 ft, breaking his spine on im-

The German gliding pioneer Otto Lilienthal conducted many of his successful flights from a conical artificial hill built near Berlin. From its 50 ft summit, Lilienthal could launch in any direction, according to the prevailing wind.

pact. He died the following day, reputedly uttering some philosophical last words: *"Opfer mussen gebracht werden."* ("Sacrifices must be made.")

Otto Lilienthal's place in aviation history is secure as the first birdman. He was a great pioneer who recorded his ideas and results carefully, and there is no doubt that his work had considerable influence on those who followed him, including the Wright brothers. His findings were widely read and highly valued by aspiring aviators, but Lilienthal's impact was also felt in a wider world because of the photographs taken of him in the air. These were the first to show that a man could be supported by wings and could truly fly, and they did much both to inspire other airmen and to popularize the idea of manned flight for the general public.

Percy Pilcher in Britain was one of those inspired by Lilienthal. Between 1895 and 1899, he built and flew several gliders incorporating original ideas of his own. He was the first to use a light, wheeled undercarriage with shock-absorbing springs, and he had his glider towed by a team of horses to achieve launches from level ground. More significantly, Pilcher's object from the outset was powered flight, and in 1896 he patented a version of his most successful glider, the "Hawk," which would have included a gasoline engine driving a pusher propeller. It was the most sensible proposal for a practical powered airplane developed up to that time, and it probably would have flown had not fate intervened. In 1899, during a gliding demonstration in which the "Hawk" was about 30 ft up, a rod in the tail assembly snapped. Pilcher crashed to the ground and was killed. With his death the progress of aviation in Britain stalled, and signs of recovery did not appear for almost ten years.

It remained for one more significant figure to forge the last link in the chain leading to the prize of manned, powered, heavier-than-air flight. Octave Chanute, a French-born American engineer, became interested in flying as early as 1855 but it was not until 1896 that, inspired by Lilienthal, he began to build gliders himself. His designs emphasized his belief that stability was all important, although he recognized that there was more to it than that. He once wrote: "A flying machine to be successful must at all times be under intelligent control," so revealing an insight which was lacking in men like Ader and Langley. Several of Chanute's gliders were flown successfully by his assistant, A.M. Herring, but it was not in the field of practical flying that Chanute made his most valuable contributions. He was, essentially, a catalyst for the enterprise of others.

In 1894, Chanute published in book form a series of articles under the title *Progress in Flying Machines.* This became one of the classics of aviation literature, a bible of flying which summarized all that was known about aviation to that date. It was read by everyone worldwide who was interested in manned flight. In the years which followed, Chanute came to be regarded as aviation's father figure, and he used his considerable prestige to ensure that information about flying was disseminated as fully and widely as possible. He relished his position at the center of the aviation world and later went so far as to hint that the Wrights had been his pupils, which was a considerable expansion on the truth and led to a period of estrangement between himself and the brothers. His influence on the Wrights was significant, nevertheless, particularly in the early stages of their work. He was very quick to see real merit in the Wrights when they began their study of flying and his constant encouragement of their efforts was no small factor in their eventual success.

At the end of the nineteenth century, Octave Chanute stood at the pinnacle of a mountain of aeronautical fact and fantasy which had been accumulating for thousands of years. In an act with which he seems almost to have been consciously tying up loose ends to set the stage for the closing acts of the preflight drama, he had compiled the first comprehensive history of aviation. That done, he turned his energies to the achievement of what he passionately believed was a realistic goal—sustained human flight—and was on hand to help and encourage the principal actors in the drama's final scene as they learned their lines, struggled through their rehearsals, and prepared themselves for a triumphant first performance at Kill Devil Hills.

Glossary

AAA
Antiaircraft Artillery

AAC
Alaskan Air Command

AAF
Army Air Forces

AAFAC
Army Air Forces Anti-Submarine Command

AAC
Armoured Column Cover

ABM
Anti-Ballistic Missile

ACC
Air Combat Command

ACSC
Air Command and Staff College

ADC
Air Defense Command

AEF
American Expeditionary Force

AETC
Air Education and Training Command

AFB
Air Force Base

AFCC
Air Force Communications Command

AFFTC
Air Force Flight Test Center

AFLC
Air Force Logistics Command

AFMC
Air Force Materiel Command

AFRes
Air Force Reserve

AFROTC
Air Force Reserve Officer Training Corps

AFSATCOM
Air Force Satellite Communications System

AFSPC
Air Force Space Command

AFSC
Air Force Systems Command

AFSOC
Air Force Special Operations Command

AFTI
Advanced Fighter Technology Integration

AIM
Air Intercept Missile

ALCM
Air Launched Cruise Missile

ALSEP
Apollo Lunar Surface Experiments Package

AMC
Air Materiel Command

AMSA
Advanced Manned Strategic Aircraft

ANG
Air National Guard

ARDC
Air Research and Development Command

ARIA
Advanced Range Instrumentation Aircraft

ARPA
Advanced Research Project Agency

ARRS
Aerospace Rescue and Recovery Service

ARS
Air Rescue Service

ARVN
Army of the Republic of Vietnam

ASTP
Apollo-Soyuz Test Project

ATC
Air Transport Command (USAAF)

ATC
Air Training Command (USAF)

AVG
American Volunteer Group

AWACS
Airborne Warning and Control System

AWAL
All Weather Airline

AWC
Air War College

AWPD
Air War Plans Division

AWS
Air Weather Service

BMEWS
Ballistic Missile Early Warning System

C3I
Command, Control, Communications and Intelligence

CAP
Combat Air Patrol

CATF
China Air Task Force

CBI
China/Burma/India Theater

C-in-C
Commander-in-Chief

COMAIRSOLS
Commander Air Solomons

CONAC
Continental Air Command

CrewTAF
Crew Training Air Force

DEW
Distant Early Warning

DMSP
Defense Meteorological Satellite Program

DMZ
Demilitarized Zone

DRU
Direct Reporting Unit

DSCS
Defense Satellite Communications System

DSP
Defense Support Program

DSTS
Deep Space Tracking System

EAC
Eastern Air Command

ECM
Electronic Counter-measures

EHF
Extremely High Frequency

EMP
Electro-magnetic Pulse

ESC
Electronic Security Command

ESM
Electronic Support Measures

FAC
Forward Air Controller

FAI
Fédération Aéronautique Internationale

FEAF
Far East Air Force

FLIR
Forward Looking Infrared & Radar

FlyTAF
Flying Training Air Force

FOA
Field Operating Agency

GATS
GPS-Aided Targeting System

GEODSS
Ground-based Electro-optical Deep Space System

GHQ
General Headquarters

GLCM
Ground Launched Cruise Missile

GPES
Ground Proximity Parachute Extraction System

GPS
Global Positioning System

H2X
Designation for WWII bombing radar

HARM
High-speed Anti-Radiation Missile

HOTAS
Hands on Throttle and Controls

IBS
India/Burma Sector

ICBM
Intercontinental Ballistic Missile

IFF
Identification Friend or Foe

IONDS
Integrated Operational Nuclear Detection System

IRBM
Intermediate Range Ballistic Missile

JAC
Joint Aircraft Committee

JATO
Jet-Assisted Takeoff

JCS
Joint Chiefs of Staff

JPATS
Joint Primary Aircraft Training System

JSTARS
Joint Surveillance and Target Attack Radar System

JSTPS
Joint Strategic Planning Staff

LANTIRN
Low Altitude Navigation and Targeting Infrared for Night

LAPES
Low Altitude Precision Extraction System

LORAN
Long Range Aid to Navigation

LRCA
Long Range Combat Aircraft

MAAG
Military Assistance Advisory Group

MAC
Military Airlift Command

MACV
Military Assistance Command Vietnam

MATS
Military Air Transport Service

MAW
Mission Adaptive Wing

MIDAS
Missile Detection and Alarm System

MIRV
Maneuverable Independently Targeted Re-entry Vehicle

MOL
Manned Orbiting Laboratory

MRBM
Medium Range Ballistic Missile

MTD
Maneuver Technology Demonstrator

NAAF
Northwest African Air Forces

NASA
National Air and Space Administration

NATAF
Northwest African Tactical Air Force

NATO
North Atlantic Treaty Organization

NAOC
National Airborne Operations Center

NEACP
National Airborne Emergency Command Post

NKAF
North Korean Air Force

NORAD
North American Air Defense Command

OKW
Oberkommando der Wehrmacht (German Army High Command)

PACAF
Pacific Air Forces

RAF
Royal Air Force

RESCAP
Rescue Combat Air Patrol

RFC
Royal Flying Corps

RHAW
Radar Homing and Warning

RNZAF
Royal New Zealand Air Force

ROK
Republic of Korea

RPV
Remotely Piloted Vehicle

SAC
Strategic Air Command

SAGE
Semiautomatic Ground Environment

SAM
Surface to Air Missile

SAMOS
Satellite and Missile Observation System

SAR
Search and Rescue

SDS
Satellite Data System

SEATO
Southeast Asia Treaty Organization

SIOP
Single Integrated Operational Plan

SPADATS
Space Detection and Tracking System

SRAM
Short Range Attack Missile

SSN
Space Surveillance Network

STOL
Short Takeoff and Landing

SUPT
Specialized Undergraduate Pilot Training

TAC
Tactical Air Command

TAF
Tactical Air Force

TechTAF
Technical Training Air Force

UN
United Nations

USAAF
United States Army Air Forces

USAF
United States Air Force

USAFE
United States Air Forces in Europe

USASTAF
United States Army Strategic Air Forces

USMC
United States Marine Corps

USN
United States Navy

USSBS
United States Strategic Bombing Survey

V-1
Vergeltungswaffe Eins (German flying bomb, WW2)

VHSIC
Very High Speed Integrated Circuits

VLR
Very Long Range

VNAF
Vietnam Air Force

WASP
Women's Air Force Service Pilots

Abbreviations of Air Force unit designations are derived from a few initial letters. Simply combining them as appropriate decodes a unit's primary role: W: Wing. G: Group. S: Squadron. AR: Air Rescue. B: Bombardment. C: Composite. F: Fighter. I: Interceptor. N: Night. P: Photographic. R: Reconnaissance. S: Strategic. T: Tactical. TC: Troop Carrier. CCT: Combat Crew Training.

Chapter 2

Flying Start-Lost Advantage

" Success four flights thursday morning all against twenty one mile wind started from Level with engine power alone average speed through air thirty one miles longest 57 seconds inform Press home Christmas. Orevelle Wright"

(Telegram, complete with errors, as received by Bishop Wright, December 17, 1903)

"The problem of aerial navigation without the use of a balloon has been solved."

(*Virginian-Pilot*, December 18, 1903)

" So easy it seemed/Once found, which yet unfound most would have thought/Impossible."

(John Milton, *Paradise Lost,* quoted by Griffith Brewer, President of the Aeronautical Society of Great Britain, to Orville Wright)

"What they had done was a miracle. . . . Without any formal training whatsoever, two ordinary Americans from an ordinary town in the state of Ohio had not only grasped and advanced the whole known science of aerodynamics—they had become its admitted masters."

(General of the Air Force Henry "Hap" Arnold)

"The side planes were operated by my feet, the rudder by my left hand, and the elevator by my right. It was very difficult, really. I don't know how we did it!"

(J.T.C. Moore-Brabazon, Lord Brabazon of Tara)

"[It is demonstrable that] no possible combination of known substances, known forms of machine, and known forms of force can be united in a practicable machine by which men shall fly long distances through the air."

(Simon Newcomb, eminent scientist, 1906)

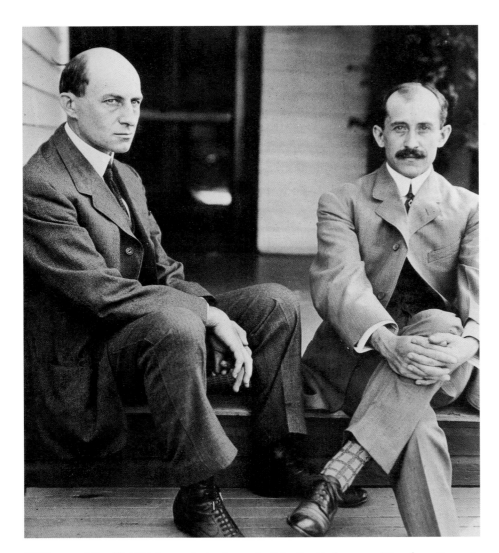

Wilbur and Orville Wright on the back porch of the family house on Hawthorn Street in Dayton, Ohio, in 1910.

Wilbur and Dan Tate launching Orville in the third Wright glider at Kill Devil Hills, near Kitty Hawk, N. Carolina, in October 1902.

The Wright Stuff

The images and models of the USAF Museum's first gallery offer a few brief highlights to suggest the epics of trial and error, abject failure, and near success which mark the long history of man's fascination with flight before the twentieth century. A visitor turning away from the evidence of all those early hopes and dreams is suddenly made aware that the heroic prelude is finally over and that the curtain is now rising on the first act of the human flight drama. The Wright brothers and their works are at center stage and the thrill of seeing full-size versions of aircraft which were among the first to carry men aloft in controlled heavier-than-air flight is heightened by the knowledge that the adventure began in Dayton, close to where the visitor now stands in the USAF Museum. The Wrights' progress from bicycle manufacturers to the world's first true aviators is traced with the aid of photographs and artifacts, and most impressively manifested by the aircraft at the heart of the display. Some of the engines which made it possible to fly are here, too, and so is evidence that Americans were among the first to give practical consideration to the military potential of flying machines.

From the letters and newspaper clippings which tell the story on the museum walls, it is possible to get some sense of the satisfaction which the Wrights felt at their success, and of the flying start their achievement gave to the United States. As the story continues, however, notes of frustration and disillusionment appear. The U.S. government is slow to recognize the promise inherent in the airplane, and the advantage passes to Europe, where the development of aircraft for military purposes is hastened by the outbreak of World War I. The Wrights themselves seem reluctant to carry their inventive genius beyond the basic ideas embodied in their first successful aircraft, and their designs are overtaken by those of others. The few efforts which are made to develop a military aviation capability in the U.S. Army are limited in scope and effectiveness. As the United States becomes committed to entering the war in Europe, American air power is almost non-existent and reliance must be placed on European aircraft designs with which to go to war. The flying start has become a stumbling run to catch up, and, having shown the world how to fly, America's aviators find themselves ill-prepared to face European airmen who have already learned the realities of war in the air.

The Wright Approach

It is probable that Wilbur and Orville Wright first became truly intrigued by the idea of human flight in 1894, after reading a magazine article on Lilienthal's gliding exploits, but it was not until 1899 that they were able to give serious consideration to the problem of how man might fly. That year, after some careful bird-watching, Wilbur came to an important conclusion. "My observations of the flight of buzzards (vultures)," he said, "led me to believe that they regain their lateral balance . . . by a torsion of the tips of the wings." Wilbur's concern with how flight was controlled was a crucial element in the brothers' eventual success. Unlike Ader, Maxim, or Langley, the Wrights thought about control from the beginning. They recognized that without control in the air, the provision of adequate lift and power to get them off the ground would be meaningless.

Circumstances had denied Wilbur and Orville Wright the benefit of the college education enjoyed by their older brothers, but there was never any doubt about their intelligence or inventive flair. They were methodical and self-sufficient by nature, and they were moderately successful. Their bicycle shop in Dayton, Ohio, had given them a solid background as light engineers and businessmen. When they turned their attention to flying, they did so with their accustomed thoroughness, first writing to ask the Smithsonian Institution for a list of all the relevant literature on the subject. They read voraciously, carefully noting the results of previous research before moving on to experiments of their own. Included in the recommended reading was Chanute's *Progress in Flying Machines,* which so impressed Wilbur that he wrote to Chanute in 1900 for advice, beginning a copious exchange of correspondence, which marked a close and often fruitful friendship.

The Wrights approached flying in ways that were markedly different from most of their predecessors. Although the accumulated wisdom of the books they read often provided a basis for their work, they took nothing for granted. Figures recorded by someone else might be used as a starting point, as were Lilienthal's for wing area and camber, but their trial results were closely scrutinized and the figures corrected where needed. These scrupulously systematic methods went hand-in-hand with a frugal practicality when it came to building a flying machine. The brothers saw no need to employ expensive materials or methods to get the job done. They used timber, fabric, and wire readily available in local stores, and they shaped spars, stitched seams, and rigged wings with their own hands. When they reached the point where they needed an engine, they designed and made their own from scratch, and, since there was then no useful existing propeller theory, they developed one and built remarkably efficient propellers on their own. Their special genius was fueled by a sincere belief that the goal of human flight was attainable and by an unshakeable confidence that they were capable of overcoming any difficulties which might appear. As each problem arose, they confronted it with logic and worked their way through to a solution. It sounds simple, yet not until the Wrights had anyone drawn all the elements of the flying puzzle together and made them into a comprehensive whole. In an age when developments affecting all of human society would generally be born from the sophistications of big business and great industries, the Wrights changed the world from the bench of a home workshop.

When the brothers built their first glider in 1900, they deliberately avoided the inherent stability that had been so avidly pursued by others, seeking instead to make the machine as responsive as possible to pilot control. As Wilbur put it: "We therefore resolved to try a fundamentally different principle. We would arrange the machine so that it would not tend to right itself." The 1900 glider also featured what the Wrights called "helical twisting of the wings," a system which they had already tried on a biplane kite in 1899. It was a method of control which was later described by Chanute as "wing-warping," a term which became the common usage. By introducing a capacity to alter the shape of the wings, twisting the trailing edge of one wing tip up and the other down, the brothers correctly interpreted the flight of vultures and at one stroke overcame the problem of controlling an airplane in roll.

Three gliders were built, in 1900, 1901, and 1902. All were flown at the Kill Devil Hills, near Kitty Hawk, on North Carolina's lonely and windswept Outer Banks. The site was chosen for its lively breezes and because the brothers preferred to conduct their trials away from the public's prying eye. With their first two gliders, simple biplanes with no tails and a forward control surface which they called a "horizontal rudder," they felt their way towards the daring conclusion that Lilienthal's figures for wing area and camber were wrong. As Wilbur wrote: "Having set out with absolute faith in the existing scientific data, we were driven to doubt one thing after another, till finally, after two years of experiment, we cast it all aside and decided to rely entirely upon our own investigations."

The Wrights' "investigations" included designing and building their own wind tunnel, capable of providing a steady wind of 30 mph or so, in which they tested a great many differently shaped wings. Their exhaustive research led them to rework Lilienthal's aerodynamic tables and thereby gave them a firm basis on which to found their future success. In 1902, using the figures they had derived, they built their third glider, with vertical tail surfaces added to the construction. They had already discovered that, although wing-warping gave them the control they were looking for, it introduced another problem. The wing that was warped down rose as it should, but it also swung back, inducing a nasty sideslip towards the down-going wing. The twin vertical tail surfaces were an attempt to stop that from happening.

Once they started flying the third glider, it was quickly apparent from its sharply improved performance that they had been right to doubt Lilienthal. In September and October 1902, it completed over 1,000 glides and flew splendidly, although initially the sideslipping problem was still there. The brothers eventually worked out that when a wing was warped down its drag increased markedly. The solution they devised was to convert the fixed tail surfaces into a single movable rudder interconnected with the wing-warping control. Whenever the pilot initiated a banked turn, the rudder was automatically applied to counter the "warp drag" on the rising wing.[1]

Now sure that they had a practical flying machine, the Wrights turned their attention to adding power. Automobile engines of the time proved too heavy, so the ever-practical brothers designed and built their own. When completed, their water-cooled engine and its accessories weighed about 200 lbs and produced 12

The third Wright glider in flight from the Kill Devil Hills in 1902. The sheds built by the Wrights to protect themselves and their aircraft from the sometimes severe Outer Banks weather can be seen in the background.

---

[1]On later aircraft the term became aileron drag.

hp. It turned over at 1,090 rpm and this was geared down through simple bicycle-style chains and sprockets to drive twin propellers. If the engine was a triumph of do-it-yourself light engineering, the propellers were works of art. They were eight feet across and made of laminated spruce, carefully shaped with a gentle twist. In the absence of any useful information on propellers other than those used on boats, the brothers determined the shape of their pro-

sary preparatory work had been completed, it was December and the weather was both cold and unexpectedly calm. For a while, the Wrights waited patiently for a suitably stiff breeze to improve their chances of success, but by December 14 they decided to wait no longer. The Flyer was taken to the crest of a gentle rise and its portable "runway" laid so that it ran down the slope into what little wind there was. This runway was part of a typically ingenious solu-

into the air, but too sharply. The large "horizontal rudders" at the front of the machine proved to be extremely sensitive and Wilbur underestimated their effect. The Flyer stalled and came down after being in the air for less than four seconds, doing some minor damage on impact. Wilbur was disappointed, but also sure that success was now certain. In writing to his family that night, he admitted his mistake, saying: "The real trouble was an error in judgement in turning up too suddenly after leaving the track," but then he later added: "The machinery all worked in entirely satisfactory manner, and seems reliable. The power is ample, and but for a trifling error due to lack of experience with this machine and this method of starting, the machine would undoubtedly have flown beautifully."

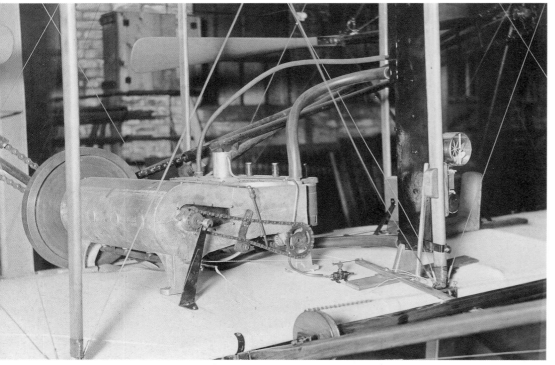

The 12 hp Wright aero-engine. Chains and sprockets are evidence that the builders had a bicycle engineering background. The strut-mounted anemometer for measuring airspeed was on loan from Octave Chanute.

pellers by viewing them as wings moving through the air along a helical path in the vertical plane. The concept was difficult to grasp but the finished propellers proved to be remarkably efficient. The way they were mounted on the aeroplane gave further evidence of the thoughtful logic which was characteristic of the Wrights' work. These propellers were "pushers" (set on the back of the plane) because it was thought that the airflow over the wings should not be unnecessarily disturbed, and they were made to counterrotate to avoid any possible difficulties from torque or gyroscopic effect.

The first Wright "Flyer" was built in the summer of 1903 and was taken to the Kill Devil Hills in September. By the time it was assembled and all the neces-

tion to the problem of launching. The Flyer had been designed with gracefully curved skids to ease its landings on the Kitty Hawk sands, but they would not do for takeoff. The skids, therefore, rested on a wooden plank which was itself lying on another board fitted with two modified bicycle wheel hubs, one behind the other. These tiny wheels ran along a sixty-foot track made out of two-by-four planks standing on edge and covered with thin metal sheet.

Success at Kitty Hawk

The toss of a coin selected Wilbur as the pilot for the first try with the Flyer. Once the engine had warmed up, he settled himself in the prone position on the lower wing and slipped the restraining cable. The Flyer surged away down the slope and rose

As the damage to the Flyer was being repaired, the wind rose and the temperature fell. On the morning of December 17, there was a cutting northerly breeze of about 25 mph, almost too strong, but the brothers made up their minds to try again. This time the track was laid on level, hard-packed sand, and it was Orville's turn at the controls. At about 10:35 a.m., he slipped the restraint and moved forward, with Wilbur running alongside steadying a wing tip. After traveling along the rail for some 40 feet, the Flyer rose into the air. Orville recorded his impressions in his diary:

"I found the control of the front rudder quite difficult on account of its being balanced too near the center and thus had a tendency to turn itself when started so that the rudder was turned too far on one side and then too far on the other. As a result the machine would rise suddenly to about 10 feet and then as suddenly, on turning the rudder, dart for the ground. A sudden dart when out about 100 feet from the end of the track ended the flight. Time about 12 seconds (not known exactly as watch was not promptly stopped)."

Apart from Wilbur, the audience on the beach was just five local men. Standing there in the icy wind, it may not have occurred to them that they were witnesses to an event which was a turning point in history. In a mere twelve seconds of undulating progress, the realization of the dream of human flight had begun and the door had cracked open on the aviation century. By the end of the day, the door was significantly further open. Alternating as pilots, the brothers made four flights in all, improving their performance with each one. On the last attempt, Wilbur remained airborne for 59 seconds and traveled 852 feet. Given the strength of the head wind, the actual distance flown through the air was much more, about half a mile. There was no longer any question that the Flyer really could fly.

For its performance on December 17, 1903, the Flyer's place in aviation history is assured, but it never flew again. Before it could be returned to its shed, it was caught by a very strong gust of wind and turned over. The damage was substantial and the Wrights left Kitty Hawk to spend Christmas in Dayton without attempting any repairs. The career of one of the world's most famous airplanes was over after it had been in the air for a total of not much more than a minute and a half.

There were times between 1899 and 1903 when the Wrights had become depressed at what they felt to be the crawling pace of their progress. In later years Wilbur wrote that, after suffering some disappointments with the 1901 glider, he had confided to Orville his opinion that "man would sometime fly, but that it would not be within our lifetime." Looking back at what was accomplished in those four years, however, a dispassionate observer must surely be astonished at the fact that the Wrights, starting from scratch and working with their innate intelligence and talent, solved a problem of the ages in so short a time. The significance of their achievement was immense, and yet it passed almost unnoticed. The withdrawn nature of the brothers and the remoteness of Kitty Hawk combined to ensure that their activities were not well reported, whereas the public failures of Langley in the heart of the nation's capital were covered by some very influential newspapers. Few people got to hear a true account of the events at Kitty Hawk, and to most who

did it seemed unlikely that an obscure pair of bicycle mechanics would succeed where a distinguished scientist like Langley had failed. The claims of the Wrights were therefore either ignored or viewed with great skepticism.

Developments at Dayton

The lack of public interest had little effect on the Wrights. They knew that their first Flyer was an imperfect machine and

Helpers and hangers-on from the nearby life-saving station with the 1903 Flyer at Kitty Hawk. The tracks in the sand tell the tale of the Flyer having just been dragged into a suitable position.

they set out to make it better. By the spring of 1904, a second Flyer was ready. Very similar in design to its predecessor, it was sturdier and had an engine capable of producing up to 16 hp. Now that they were engaged in powered flying, the Wrights were no longer so needful of the fresh breezes of the Outer Banks, so they made arrangements with a farmer to carry out their trials in an eighty-acre field near Dayton known as Huffman's Prairie. To make up for the relative lack of wind in Ohio, they erected a derrick in the field and hung 600 lbs of metal weights from a rope inside it. The rope ran from the top of the derrick, under the launching rail, to the front of the Flyer II's trolley. When ready, the pilot tripped a catch restraining the weights and their fall considerably augmented the thrust of the twin propellers

as the Flyer II surged forward to takeoff.

During 1904, the brothers made over one hundred flights in the Flyer II. None of them was very long and the series was bedeviled by a number of small mishaps. Nevertheless, a great deal was learned and, by the end of the year, both Wilbur and Orville had managed circling flights of more than five minutes. In 1905, the Wrights poured their experience into designing and building a third airplane. In

its final form, Flyer III was a more aesthetically pleasing and effective machine than either of its forebears. The front and rear control surfaces were mounted further from the wings and the link between the rudder and the wing-warping mechanism was disconnected to improve control. The result was an aircraft which was both graceful and maneuverable. By the end of the year, Flyer III had proven capable of completing tight figure-eight patterns and flying for as long as its fuel lasted, which on October 5 was for thirty-eight minutes. It was the world's first practical flying machine. All this was accomplished at a time when no other would-be aviator had succeeded in achieving any kind of controlled powered flight, and when most authorities still flatly refused to accept that such a thing was possible.

The Wrights had decided in 1904 to seek the legal protection of patents. While these were still pending, they were anxious not to allow anyone to get close to their Flyers or to watch their trials. Apart from the local farmers, few people realized what was being done at Huffman Prairie. Nevertheless, the brothers had begun to feel that the time had come to look for some return on their investment, and it had occurred to them that their airplanes had military potential, principally for reconnaissance. Accordingly they approached both the American and British governments, stating that they had produced a flying machine and offering to supply similar machines for a contracted price. The British government appeared to accept the Wrights' claims, but refused to go further without a practical demonstration, something the brothers were not prepared to give without promise of a contract. The U.S. government's rejection was even firmer. Although three separate approaches were made to Washington, no American official thought it worthwhile to visit Dayton, and the third response from the Board of Ordnance and Fortification in October 1905 seemed to represent the official blind eye at its most opaque. The letter concluded: "The Board does not care to . . . take any further action until a machine is produced which by actual operation is shown to be able to produce horizontal flight and to carry an operator."

In the circumstances, it is hardly surprising that the Wrights were both frustrated and discouraged. Since there was little likelihood of a government contract in the foreseeable future, they elected to shut up shop and secure themselves against any possible commercial espionage. They thought it necessary to keep the details of their Flyers from prying eyes until their patents had finally been approved and governments had become more amenable. They stopped all flying and did not take to the air again for two and a half years.

In the course of this interregnum, the Wrights refined their engine design and continued to build aircraft. Promise of a French contract led them to crate one Flyer and ship it to France in 1907, but the deal

Orville and Wilbur with their new Wright Flyer at Huffman's Prairie, Dayton, in May 1904.

fell through and the plane sat in its box at Le Havre until the following year. A number of air-minded men in France, alarmed by stories of the Wrights' success and the thought that France might be left behind, were working on a variety of machines, but there was no appreciation of the real problems to be confronted in making human flight practicable. The basic secrets of the Wrights had been made available through a 1903 lecture by Chanute in Paris, and by the publication of the Wrights' patents in 1906, but such vital clues were unaccountably ignored by Europeans who should have known better. No methodical program of research was undertaken and the critical problem of three-dimensional control in the air was not even considered. The Wrights took note of what was going on and rightly concluded that there were no serious rivals on the horizon.

Small successes there were, however. In 1906, the Paris-domiciled Brazilian, Santos-Dumont, managed a few barely controlled hops of up to 250 yards in a tail-first creation which was little more than a few large box kites strung together. It was entirely impractical and contributed nothing to the advance of aeronautics, but its performance was well reported and applauded with wild enthusiasm by a French

population ignorant of what the Wrights had done. Although the Santos-Dumont machine, and others which followed it in Europe, posed no real technological threat to the Wrights, it did sound an alarm about the prospects for aircraft contracts. Since there was little understanding of what the Wright Flyers represented in terms of research and development, the suggestion that the secrets of flight were about to become common property might be enough to make the negotiation of rewarding contracts difficult. With this in mind, the Wrights renewed their efforts to attract potential customers in 1907. Talks were conducted with a company interested in selling Flyers to the French government, and a new proposal was sent to the U.S. Board of Ordnance and Fortification after President Theodore Roosevelt, his attention drawn to the Wrights by the Aero Club of America, had nudged his administration into finding out more about what the brothers were up to in Dayton.

The U.S. Army Stirs

At the same time, the U.S. Army felt the tremors of the growing aviation fever in Europe and decided to revive its moribund interest in the third dimension. The balloon detachment of the Signal Corps

Alberto Santos-Dumont, a rich Brazilian living in Paris, recorded the first powered flight in Europe in 1906, coaxing his kite-like "14 bis" into the air for some 21 seconds. He later turned to monoplane designs like this, the little "Demoiselle," the first successful ultralight aircraft.

had languished after 1898. On August 1, 1907, an Aeronautical Division of the Signal Corps was established under Captain Charles Chandler to "have charge of all matters pertaining to military ballooning, air machines, and all kindred subjects." The first official step on the road to the United States Air Force had been taken.

Within months, the new Aeronautical Division had issued Signal Corps Specification No. 486 for "the construction of a flying machine supported entirely by the dynamic reaction of the atmosphere and having no gas bag." It was based on the Wrights' performance estimates and was issued for competitive bidding on December 23, 1907. The airplane was required to carry two persons weighing a combined 350 lbs, reach a minimum speed of 40 mph, and fly for 125 miles. A 10 percent bonus or penalty on the agreed price was included for each mph achieved above or below 40, and it was stipulated that the machine should be easily disassembled for transporting in army wagons, with reassembly taking no more than an hour. Other provisions were that the airplane should be able to land on an unprepared field without damage, and that it should be capable of safe descent in the

event that the propulsion unit broke down. Most particularly, it had to be "sufficiently simple in its construction and operation to permit an intelligent man to become proficient in its use within a reasonable length of time." Such was the general ignorance of what the Wrights had achieved that the American press ridiculed Specification No. 486, claiming that it asked for the impossible. Surprisingly, no fewer than forty-one bidders responded, but only three bids were thought to be worth accepting, including that from the Wrights, who set their price for meeting the contract at $25,000. In the event, only the Wrights proved capable of providing an airplane for trial.

Public Demonstrations

After doing some refresher flying at Kittyhawk in the 1905 Flyer III, Wilbur set off for France in May 1908 to collect the Flyer stored at Le Havre, reassemble it at a racecourse near Le Mans, and then show off its capabilities publicly for the first time. Wilbur's preparations were regarded with great skepticism by the French, and a critical audience gathered to view his first flights on August 8, 1908. The subsequent reaction to his mastery of the air was dra-

matic. The Flyer's easy maneuverability and soaring flight put the struggling efforts of European pioneers into perspective, and people on both sides of the Atlantic were at last forced to recognize the true magnitude of the Wright brothers' achievement. The European press lionized Wilbur, calling his performances "Marvelous! Glorious! Sensational!" And one French commentator remarked, "We are as children compared with the Wrights." In England, Major Baden-Powell of the Aeronautical Society reached beyond the collective European astonishment of the moment to comment, "That Wilbur Wright is in possession of a power which controls the fate of nations is beyond dispute."

While Wilbur widened the eyes of the Europeans, Orville stayed at home to arrange the trials of the Type A Military Flyer, which were to be carried out at Fort Myer, just across the Potomac from Washington, D.C. Like the Flyer in France, this new biplane had upright seats for a pilot and a passenger. Orville began flying on September 3, 1908, and promptly duplicated Wilbur's success, electrifying onlookers with the sureness of his control in the air. Within the next two weeks he achieved an endurance record of more than an hour, set an altitude record of 310 feet, and carried the first military observer, Lt. Frank Lahm of the Aeronautical Division. The Army was impressed and the Washington spectators wild with enthusiasm. The trials could not have gone better—until the last day. On September 17, Orville took off with Lt. Thomas Selfridge as his passenger. They were circling the Fort Myer field when a crack developed in a blade of the starboard propeller. The blade became unbalanced and was deflected sufficiently to strike and tear loose one of the bracing wires supporting the rudder. The Flyer could no longer be controlled and it dived steeply into the ground, severely injuring Orville and killing Lt. Selfridge, who thus gained the morbid distinction of being powered flight's first aerial fatality.

The First Military Aircraft

The accident did not discourage the U.S. Army. Enough had been seen in two

Lt. Thomas Selfridge seated with Orville Wright in the Military Flyer just before takeoff during the Army trials at Fort Myer on September 17, 1908. After completing four circuits of the Ft. Myer field, a cracked propeller began a series of structural failures which led to the crash of the Military Flyer. Amid the tangled mass of wreckage, Orville was conscious but badly injured, having broken a thigh and several ribs. Lt. Selfridge's injuries included a fractured skull. He died after surgery, so gaining the morbid distinction of becoming the world's first fatality in an aircraft accident.

was 42.583 mph, which was enough to secure the $25,000 contract price, plus a $5,000 bonus. On August 2, the U.S. Army officially accepted the Flyer as the world's first military airplane. Officially designated Signal Corps Aeroplane No. 1, it was reported by the Washington *Evening Star* as being "Aeroplane No. 1, Heavier-than-air Division, United States Aerial Fleet."

Competition

While the Wrights and their aircraft undoubtedly dominated the aviation world during this period, a number of rivals began to appear. Wilbur's performance in France had initially chastened and amazed the Europeans, but as the shock wore off they were inspired to greater things by his brilliant flying. Great names like Henry Farman, Hubert Latham, Louis Bleriot, S.F. Cody, and Moore-Brabazon came to the fore, showing themselves eager to learn, adapt, and develop the Wrights' methods and ideas. As they grasped the essential nature of the Wrights' system of three-axis control, they also saw value in retaining the inherent stability which had been a feature of the largely unsuccessful European machines. Reaching for a sensible compromise between the two, they made rapid progress and before long were producing aircraft which could outperform the Wright Flyers.

On the other side of the Atlantic, the Wrights faced some home-grown competition in the form of the Aerial Experiment Association (AEA), a group under the leadership of Alexander Graham Bell. Among the original members, known as "Bell's Boys," were Lt. Thomas Selfridge, who died in Orville's crash at Fort Myer, and Glenn Curtiss, who also was at Fort Myer in 1908, involved with trials of Thomas Baldwin's airship. The airship subsequently became Signal Corps Dirigible No. 1, and much of its success was due to an engine designed and made by Curtiss. A water-cooled, four-cylinder engine of 20 hp, it was a modest beginning for a long line of Curtiss engines and derivatives which would come to have a significant influence on the world of aviation.

weeks of flying at Fort Myer to convince everyone that the Wrights had a machine which was more than capable of meeting the contract specifications. An extension of the contract gave Orville time to recover from his injuries and, in July 1909, he was back at Fort Myer with a new Flyer. After a few days of false starts, Orville got into his stride and showed that the Flyer did

indeed meet the specifications. On July 27, with President William Howard Taft looking on, Orville and Lt. Lahm were airborne for 1 hour, 12 minutes, and 40 seconds, a new record for a flight with a passenger. Then, on July 30, Orville flew with Lt. Benjamin Foulois as navigator on a cross-country speed trial between Fort Myer and Alexandria. The average speed achieved

Glenn Curtiss was a young motorcycle engineer and racer who turned to aviation because it combined new engineering challenges with an adventure promising excitement and speed. He was involved with the AEA's construction of four biplanes in 1908, the third of which "June Bug" he designed and flew with considerable success. On July 4, 1908, with the Wrights otherwise occupied, Curtiss and the June Bug won the *Scientific American* magazine's prize for the first public flight in the U.S. of more than a kilometer by staying in the air for almost a mile in front of several hundred people at Hammondsport, New York. By the Wrights' standards that was not much to shout about, but it was done in public and was given far more acclaim than anything the secretive Wrights had done up to that time.

Perhaps piqued by all the fuss, Orville wrote to Curtiss, pointing out that since the June Bug had "movable surfaces at the tips of the wings, adjustable to different angles on the right and left sides for maintaining lateral balance," there appeared to be an infringement of the Wright wing-warping patents. Before the year was out, the brothers had embarked on a long and increasingly bitter lawsuit against Curtiss which set out not only to punish him for using ailerons but also to prove that their patents should be applied to all forms of lateral control on aircraft worldwide. Sadly, over the years, the implacability of the Wrights on this matter diminished their reputation. They were widely viewed as standing in the way of aeronautical progress, and the strictures of their patents were largely ignored or circumvented. Rightly recognized as men of genius who had once pointed the way to the future for the world, after 1909 they were often attacked for defending the achievements of the past as their personal property. While they expended their energies in trying to hang on to what they had, others overtook them and went on to greater things. By 1911, European designs, notably Bleriot monoplanes, were being built under license in the U.S. and sold assembled for $1,000, complete with the proud boast: "All assembled machines guaranteed to fly!"

The U.S. Army Flies

With the acquisition of an "aerial fleet," the U.S. Army needed pilots. Under the terms of their contract, the Wrights were required to train two pilots and it was arranged that this would be done from a cleared site just north of Washington, D.C., at College Park, Maryland. Wilbur gave Lts. Frank Lahm and Frederic Humphreys about three hours dual instruction each and sent them both solo at College Park on October 26, 1909. On November 5 they damaged the aircraft, and then the Army returned both of them to their regular units. For a while, therefore, the "aerial fleet" had neither an airworthy

Motorcycle racer, engine builder, and founder member of Alexander Graham Bell's Aerial Experiment Association, Glenn Curtiss became a dominant figure of American aviation's early days. Curtiss aircraft held a place in the air force front line until after WW II, and Curtiss ideas had an influence on some of the world's most successful in-line engine design.

airplane nor pilots to fly it.

The necessary repairs having been completed, the Military Flyer was shipped to Fort Sam Houston in Texas to escape the Washington winter, and Lt. Benjamin Foulois, who had managed three brief flying lessons with the Wrights, was sent with it. As Foulois later recalled, he got his orders from the Chief Signal Officer, General James Allen, in person. General Allen told him: "Don't worry. You'll learn the techniques as you go along. . . . Just take plenty of parts and teach yourself to fly."

On March 2, 1910, after some correspondence with the Wrights seeking helpful advice on "how to avoid basic disasters," Foulois got Aeroplane No. 1 airborne and completed his first solo intact. He continued to fly throughout the summer of 1910, suffering a number of minor accidents and repeatedly patching up his long-suffering airplane in the course of becoming a proficient pilot. Foulois later recalled: "The bad bucking habits of No. 1 in gusty winds, and forced landings because of the erratic temperament of the engine, kept the machine in the shop more days than it was out." The worry was that the Army did not seem to be all that interested. It was one thing to have formed an Aeronautical Division and acquired a flying machine, but it was quite another to provide the necessary operating funds. Foulois was startled to discover that his budget for the year was just $150, and he more than once was forced to put his hand into his own pocket to pay for fuel and repairs so that he could keep flying.

A case for both operating funds and new aircraft was made by the Signal Corps, and an appropriation of $200,000 was requested, but Congress was not impressed. One Congressman was driven to remark: "Why all this fuss about planes for the Army? I thought we had one." By the end of 1910, that one airplane was sadly the worse for wear and ready for retirement. The Aeronautical Division was in danger of being grounded until Robert Collier, the publisher, bought a new Wright Type B Flyer and, in February 1911, leased it to the Army for the princely sum of $1 per month. This bizarre arrangement may have helped to shame Congress into taking limited action, because only three months later the approved appropriations for the War Department included $125,000 specifically for military aeronautics, $25,000 of which was made available immediately.

This was hardly a generous allocation, and it was indicative of the general apathy being shown towards the potential of military aviation in the United States. In the eyes of the American public, flying was a great new adventure, in which daredevils broke records or entertained the crowds at the fair. The U.S. was protected by oceans and vast distances, and it seemed inconceivable that flimsy aerial machines could ever be more than marginally useful to either the army or the navy. In Europe, the picture was quite different. The smaller, more densely populated European countries were traditionally on guard against each other across notoriously porous land frontiers. Only the British had the luxury of a water barrier, and the effectiveness of that was questioned when Louis Bleriot flew his monoplane across the English Channel in 1909.

It was true that many European of-

trained by various countries before World War I. Between 1908 and 1913, both France and Germany spent well over $20 million each, Russia $12 million, and even Belgium $2 million. In the same period, the U.S. allocated less than $500,000. In terms of certified pilots, both civilian and military, the disparity was startling; in 1913 there were some 2,400 pilots in the world, and of those the U.S. could lay claim to less than one hundred.

The conservative American attitude to military aviation was emphasized when it came to anything which might improve the aircraft for war. In 1911, Riley Scott

standard Benet-Mercie, a gun of sufficient weight and size to make it entirely unsuitable for mounting in an aircraft. Lewis promptly left for Belgium, where his gun was manufactured to become a standard air-to-air weapon of the Allies in WWI.

Seen in this context, it is apparent that the first appropriations of the U.S. Congress for military aeronautics in 1911 were short-sightedly small and representative of the fact that the U.S. lead in aviation was being allowed to slip away across the Atlantic. Even so, the appropriations were a beginning. General Allen immediately ordered five new airplanes at a cost of about $5,000 each, two Curtiss Model Ds and three Wright Type Bs. The first of these to be delivered in April 1911 was a Curtiss Model D, which became Signal Corps Aeroplane No. 2 (SC2).

The Curtiss aircraft were directly descended from his successful Golden Flyer, the successor to his June Bug. In 1909, flying a modified Golden Flyer fitted with a 50 hp Curtiss engine, Glenn Curtiss won the Gordon Bennet Trophy race at the world's first international air meet near Reims, France, at an average speed of 47 mph. The Model D, which had similar performance, was a "pusher" biplane with only one seat, so trainee pilots necessarily learned to fly it without the benefit of an instructor alongside. The training was done in stages; first the student made himself familiar with the controls, then he tried some straight-line taxiing with the foot throttle tied back so that he could not exceed 15 mph. Comfortable with that, he was allowed to get off the ground in short hops no higher than ten feet, gradually progressing to free flight. Curtiss supervised these elementary operations at a flying school he had established at North Island on San Diego Bay.

In April 1911, Foulois at last lost his lonely status as America's only military pilot. He was joined at Fort Sam Houston by three graduates of the Curtiss flying school, Lts. Beck, Kelly, and Walker. The Aerial Division did not have long to enjoy its newly acquired strength intact. On May 10, Lt. Kelly got into trouble in SC2, crashed on Fort Sam Houston and became

Signal Corps No. 1, the world's first military aircraft. The Wright Type A Military Flyer comfortably exceeded the Army's contract specifications and became the basis of the "United States' aerial fleet" for $30,000. Orville Wright and Benny Foulois are enmeshed in the structure.

ficers in the older armed services sneered at the airplane. Britain's most senior soldier regarded aviation as: "A useless and expensive fad, advocated by a few individuals whose ideas are unworthy of attention." Marshal Foch of France later added: "It is good sport, but for the army the aeroplane is useless." Nevertheless, there were enough people in high places in Europe who were concerned about the airplane's military potential to ensure that it was not ignored. To put the relative attitudes of the U.S. and Europe into perspective it is useful to examine the total amounts spent on military aviation and the numbers of pilots

demonstrated a bombsight which showed great promise, but the War Department was not interested. Discouraged, he took his bombsight to Europe where it won a prize at an international competition. Colonel Isaac Lewis produced a lightweight low-recoil machine gun in 1912 and its airborne firing trials were so good that ten more guns were requested for intensive testing. The request was refused by the Ordnance Department because the gun had not been adopted as a U.S. Army weapon. It was decreed that, in the unlikely event that a machine gun should ever be needed in the air, it should be the Army's

the first pilot to be killed in a heavier-than-air flying accident. The local commander, General Carter, decided that he could no longer tolerate the hazard of having dangerous machines using his drill field for their runways and maneuvering in the air over the heads of his troops. He forthwith prohibited all flying at Fort Sam Houston and hastened the Army into moving the Aeronautical Division back to College Park, where some of the Signal Corps' new-found funds were already being used to establish facilities for a more permanent military flying school. In the hope of avoiding Maryland's cold weather problem, arrangements were made for the school to have winter quarters in Augusta, Georgia.

At College Park, Captain Chandler resumed his position as the chief of the Aeronautical Division and also served as commandant of the flying school. Up to now, even though a number of officers had been flying, none of them had been properly certified as Army pilots. In the absence of a prescribed military test, it was decided to use the regulations of the Federation Aeronautique Internationale. Two newly arrived pilots, Lts. Henry Arnold and Thomas Milling, who had just completed a flying course with the Wrights in Dayton, passed the FAI tests in July 1911 and earned certificates as U.S. Army Aviators Nos. 1 and 2. Captain Chandler and his adjutant, Lt. Roy Kirtland, became the students of Arnold and Milling and qualified soon after.

The Army now had airplanes and an embryo flying school, but none of the members of the Aeronautical Division were clear about what their military role was supposed to be. They had been told that they must learn how to operate the airplanes, but they were not at all sure how they were to be used in anger, apart from a vague idea that the machines might be useful as observation platforms. In later years, General "Hap" Arnold recalled:

"Without radio communications, the rapid delivery of intelligence still depended largely on horsemen. We, the airmen, were to jot down what we saw on brightly colored pieces of paper and drop the weighted paper to the ground, where

Lt. Benny Foulois taught himself to fly Signal Corps No. 1 at Fort Sam Houston in 1910. As seen here, landing on the drill field sometimes included the hazard of an approach over the latrines, which must have been a suitable deterrent to landing short.

a cavalryman, galloping hell for leather, would pick it up and take it back to the command post."

The pilots believed that they were not being taken seriously by senior commanders, most of whom regarded the aircraft as little more than toys, and they found the lack of positive direction from above disconcerting. They therefore decided to try defining their mission themselves, and they set out to discover what their machines were capable of and what sorts of devices might be hung on them to increase their effectiveness.

Arnold and Milling gradually increased the distances of their cross-country flights, going out as far as Frederick, Maryland, 42 miles away, and Arnold made a point of seeing how high he could coax the Wright biplanes, eventually getting one up to 4,167 feet. This was also the period when Milling flew with Scott's bombsight and the Lewis gun, only to find that the Army was not interested. Somewhat earlier, in 1910, Lt. Jacob Fickel had fired a rifle while flying and had consistently hit a small ground target, and the first trial bombs had fallen from an aeroplane when Glenn Curtiss, flying his pusher biplane, dropped tennis ball-sized dummy bombs on a target shaped like a battleship. Live bombs followed in January 1911, with Wright demonstrator Philip Parmalee piloting a Flyer near San Francisco while Lt.

Myron Crissy dropped the bombs by hand.

In September 1911, Arnold became the first pilot to carry U.S. mail when he flew a small satchel of letters five miles from the Nassau Boulevard field to Hempstead, Long Island. Night flying was tried, albeit inadvertently at first, when a pilot, delayed on his return to College Park until after sunset, was guided to a safe landing by a row of burning oil puddles set afire by his anxious comrades. Arnold and Milling also carried out experiments with air-to-ground communication by radio, and found that they could dispense with horses and bits of paper by sending coded radio messages.

Benny Foulois, Chief of the Army Air Corps in the early 1930s, seen as an Air Service captain in front of a Burgess trainer.

Hap Arnold and Thomas Milling learned to fly in 1911 in a Wright Type B Flyer. As majors, they flew Boeing P-12s at Mather Field, California, and both later became generals. Arnold went on to be appointed Chief of the Army Air Force and was the only airman ever promoted to five-star rank.

Taken individually, such small achievements may not have seemed very significant to the Army's generals, but they were slowly expanding the known capabilities of the Aeronautical Division and, since the press regularly reported their activities, establishing the fact of military aviation in the minds of the American public.

Unfortunately, the Army's aviators were discovering another way to get themselves noticed. Accidents were frequent, and too many of them were fatal. In the five and a half years from the date of Selfridge's death on September 17, 1908, to the end of February 1914, there were eleven flying fatalities in the Aeronautical Division. If that does not seem very many, it must be remembered that the number of aircrew was very small and the length of the flights quite short. The true picture is revealed by the Signal Corps' flight records. In 1911, a death was suffered for every 65 hours spent in the air, or once in 372 flights. By 1914, the rate was down to once in 125 hours or 515 flights, but it was still much too high. Added to these were the large number of lesser accidents in which aircraft were destroyed or damaged and personnel injured. "Hap" Arnold himself had more than one unpleasant incident, including one in a Wright Type C in 1912 which so alarmed him that he stopped flying for four years. He was not the only one to find that particular type difficult to

handle, and in February 1914 the Signal Corps grounded the aircraft, noting that the Type C had been involved in most of the fatal accidents. Shortly thereafter, a Board of Investigation into the problem found the Type C "dynamically unsuited for flying" and recommended that Army flying should be done on the newer Curtiss and Burgess machines, both of which were "tractors" rather than "pushers," with the engine and propeller mounted ahead of the pilot instead of behind. It was perhaps felt that it was safer to have all that weight of wood and metal in front to absorb the shock of an impact rather than in the rear from where it could rush forward and crush anyone in its path. Whatever the reason, it was clear that the days of Wright supremacy were over. When Wilbur died in 1912, the Wright biplanes were still the fragile descendants of the original 1903 Flyer—pusher biplanes with no cockpit and with wing-warping for lateral control. The aviation world born of the Wright brothers' genius had passed them by.

The growth of U.S. military aviation was painfully slow, but its gradual development and its associated dangers did bring about the realization that it deserved formal recognition as a military activity. In 1912, the Army announced that qualified officers should be rated Military Aviators and that they could then wear a badge showing an eagle in flight. For the badge

to be awarded, flying tests had to be completed which included climbing to 2,500 ft, operating in a wind of at least 15 mph, carrying a passenger to 500 ft, and landing power off within 150 ft of a chosen point. There was also a twenty-mile cross-country exercise, flown at 1,500 ft.

The following year, in 1913, a case was made to Congress concerning the daily hazards of military flying and the need to attract more aviation volunteers. Congress accepted the arguments and authorized a 35 percent pay increase for officers assigned to flying duties. This was followed in 1914 by legislation in the form of "An Act to Increase the Efficiency of the Aviation Services of the Army, and for Other Purposes." The bill included the words:

"There is hereby created an aviation section, which shall be a part of the Signal Corps of the Army, and which shall be, and hereby is, charged with the duty of operating or supervising the operation of all military aircraft, including balloons and aeroplanes, all appliances pertaining to said craft, and signalling apparatus of any kind when installed on said craft; also with the duty of training officers and enlisted men in matters pertaining to military aviation."

Provision was made for the Aviation Section to have a strength of 60 officers and 260 enlisted men, and for there to be ratings of Military Aviator and Junior Military Aviator. Both would be entitled to flying pay, but neither was expected to be other than unmarried lieutenants of the line.

As military aviation became accepted as an established element of the U.S. Army, it also began to spread to some very distant outposts. For a time between 1912 and 1914, there were flying schools in Hawaii and the Philippines. Both closed down eventually because of difficulties in keeping the aircraft serviceable in the local conditions and because no replacement aircraft were made available. They were notable if only because they were Army units regularly engaged in operating from water. At Kamehameha, Hawaii, and in Manila Bay, the Army flying was done with floatplanes, which struggled on until they were destroyed or rendered useless by repeated accidents. Having got its feet wet, the Army continued to flirt with the water, going so far as to order three Curtiss F Type flying boats in 1912.

1913 was a turbulent year for the Army's fledgling air arm. On February 25, with the bulk of the Aviation Section enduring unexpectedly unfriendly weather at their southern base near Augusta, Captain Chandler received orders to move the unit to Texas City on the Gulf coast. Relations between the U.S. and Mexico had become strained, and it was thought that aircraft might be needed for patrolling the border. As the year moved into spring the tensions with Mexico eased, but others which had arisen within the Aviation Section did not. To take account of some dissatisfaction and lowered morale, the chief signal officer, Brigadier General George Scrivens, undertook a series of corrective measures. One of the first was the recognition that the flying units needed to be properly organized to operate in the field; the 1st Provisional Aero Squadron was therefore established on March 5, 1913, consisting of a headquarters staff and two "aero" companies with a total strength of nine officers and fifty-one men, plus nine aircraft.

Other improvements followed as the Air Service established more flying schools, drew up requirements aimed at forcing manufacturers to make their aircraft safer, and began installing radios and rudimentary flight instruments. Scrivens understood the challenges faced by the Air Service and was generally sympathetic to improving matters, but he was occasionally irritated by the impatient attitude of the young airmen and once described them as being "deficient in discipline and a proper knowledge of the customs of the service and the duties of an officer." Hap Arnold later recalled seeing a letter from the pilots to Scrivens which set out a number of demands for changes in the senior personnel controlling military aviation, so it is perhaps not surprising that the chief signal officer was irritable.

The need for aircraft on the Mexican border having passed, the 1st Provisional Aero Squadron got ready to leave, but they were not ordered back to College Park. The lease on the Maryland field had expired and was not renewed. Instead, most of the squadron moved on to North Island, San Diego, which now became the Army's principal flying school and a center for Army aviation. Many famous airmen, including Carl Spaatz, were taught to fly at North Island.

Mexican Adventures

Although the border alarm came to nothing in 1913, the turbulence of the Mexican revolution continued to have its effect on the use and deployment of the U.S. Army and its Air Service. Tensions flared again early in 1914, by which time War Department General Order No. 75, dated December 4, 1913, had set out formal tables of organization for flying units and steps were being taken to remove the word "provisional" from the title of the 1st Aero Squadron. Once again, aircraft were deployed to Texas, but the danger passed and they saw no action. The struggle between the three Mexican factions of Carranza, Zapata, and Pancho Villa raged on, however, and early in 1916 it spilled across the border into the U.S. In October 1915, the U.S. recognized the government of Carranza, and Pancho Villa, angry at being denied U.S. supplies for his forces, crossed into New Mexico on March 9, 1916, and killed U.S. citizens in the town of Columbus. President Woodrow Wilson reacted by sending a force of 15,000 men under General John Pershing to punish the raiders and to capture or kill their leader. The 1st Aero Squadron was ordered to accompany the expedition.

The absence of landing fields and fuel depots on the way forced the 1st Aero Squadron to send their aircraft to Columbus by rail. They arrived on March 15, only six days after Pancho Villa had left. The squadron of eight aircraft, now under the command of Captain Benjamin Foulois, deployed with 10 pilots and 84 enlisted men, and increased to 16 officers and 122 men by May. The squadron was tasked with assisting the Army's ground forces, but it soon became apparent that it was the airmen who were in need of help. Operating from a desert strip one hundred miles south of Columbus, the eight Curtiss JN-3s ("Jennies") were incapable of getting the job done. Extreme temperatures, penetrating dust, and boisterous mountain winds combined to take their toll on aircraft which were already well-worn from a year of training pilots. Even when fully serviceable, the JN-3s could not get across the area's mountain ranges of ten thousand feet and more, and they were vulnerable to the violent weather of the mountains.

Relegated to the ignominy of carrying dispatches in good weather, the squadron still got into difficulty. Foulois and Lt. Dargue took two aircraft to Chihuahua City in Mexico to deliver dispatches to the American consul and were fired on when

A lineup of some of America's earliest military aviators. From the left: Lt. Frank Lahm, Lt. G.C. Sweet (USN), Maj. C. McK. Saltzman, Maj. George Squier, Capt. Charles Chandler, Lt. Benny Foulois, and 2nd Lt. Frederic Humphreys.

The Curtiss "Jenny" was the first aircraft to be built in quantity for the Signal Corps and the nearest thing to a combat aircraft owned by the U.S. Army before WW I. It proved sadly inadequate for the task of supporting the Army's gound operations during the Mexican Punitive Expedition in 1916. High temperatures, strong winds, and rugged terrain exposed its operational shortcomings, and the supporting facilities were rudimentary at best.

they arrived. Foulois was arrested and jailed, and an angry mob burned the aircraft's fabric with cigarettes and slashed it with knives. When Foulois was released, the two tattered JN-3s took off, but a section of Dargue's fuselage, loosened because the crowd had removed some bolts, blew off and damaged the tail. He landed and was stoned for his trouble, but held the mob off until Mexican soldiers arrived to stand guard while he hurriedly completed basic repairs and left.

By April 20, after little more than a month of operations, the 1st Aero Squadron was reduced to just two flyable aircraft. Those two JN-3s were just serviceable enough to be flown back to Columbus and condemned for scrap. The squadron collected four new Curtiss N-8s to replace the JN-3s, but they proved to be equally unsuited to the harsh conditions of the border and were junked within a year. One way or another, the unit struggled on until 1917, but it was never able to offer anything of much value to the military expedition it was supposed to support. General Pershing was not impressed with the operational performance of his air arm, but he recognized where the shortcomings lay. In acknowledging that Foulois and his men had done their best, he said: "They too often risked their lives in old and often useless machines which they have patched up and worked over in an effort to do their share of the duty this expedition has been called upon to perform."

U.S. Aerial Shortcomings

The limited capabilities of U.S. military aviation were brutally exposed during the Mexican Punitive Expedition. The First Aero Squadron represented the best that the Air Service had to offer, and by any measure it suffered in comparison with European air forces which had been in combat since 1914. By 1916, all the major combatants had air forces engaged in aerial reconnaissance, air-to-air combat, and tactical support of ground forces. Heavy bombers for strategic operations were being produced by Russia, Italy, France, and Britain, and air fighting tactics had been well developed in the hard school of combat experience. High explosive bombs and machine guns synchronized to fire through the propeller arc had been developed. The air effort was backed by large training organizations and by industries producing air force equipment in vast quantities. Confronted by the alarming shortcomings of U.S. military aviation revealed on the Mexican border, and the contrast that made with news of the air war in Europe, Congress was finally spurred into action. In August 1916, authorization was given to provide $13,281,666 for military aeronautics. It was still inadequate, but viewed against the fact that a total of less than $1 million had been spent on U.S. military aviation since the Wright brothers first flew, it was an indication that attitudes were changing in Washington. The intention was for the Air Service to be increased to seven front-line squadrons and three flying schools spread among six U.S. bases plus the Philippines and Hawaii, but with U.S. involvement in Europe becoming imminent, the fact was American air power remained shockingly unimpressive.

Early in 1917 the U.S. Army Air Service had only one front-line squadron functioning, with a second in the works. They were equipped with Curtiss R-2 and R-4 machines, which were little more than upgraded Jennies and quite unsuitable for aerial combat. At a time when the British and French each had more than 1,700 combat aircraft available, the total strength of the U.S. Army Air Service was 131 officers, 1,087 men, and less than 250 aircraft, only half of which were serviceable. None of the machines could be classified as other than a trainer, and many of them were obsolete even in that role. No bombers or fighters were in service or being procured. Worse still, the American aircraft industry was then incapable of supplying the equipment needed to support an operational air force. In the eight short years since the purchase of the first Wright Military Flyer, the U.S. had fallen to fourteenth in the world's ranking of aviation powers. With war on the horizon, it was time to start catching up.

24

A

C

26

B

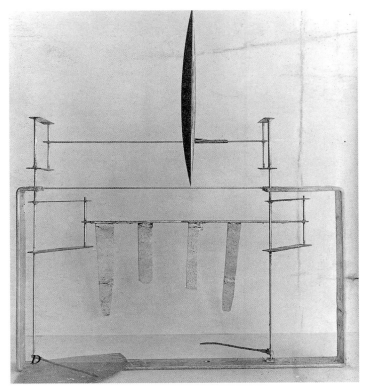

D

Previous page: The Wright wind tunnel—a 6-foot long, 16-inch square wooden box with a glass viewing window on top. The metal honeycomb straightened out air flowing into the tunnel from a large belt-driven fan. Balances measured the lift and drag of model wings placed inside the tunnel. Scraps of wallpaper are covered with the brothers' calculations.

A   At 10:35 am EST, December 17, 1903, with Orville at the controls and Wilbur looking on, the Wright brothers open the door to the aviation century. For the first time in history "a machine carrying a man had raised itself by its own power into the air in full flight, had sailed forward without reduction of speed, and had finally landed at a point as high as that from which it had started."

B   Wilbur tenses and checks as the Flyer takes to the air, the tautness of his body capturing the excitement of a moment in which the world changed.

C   In 1927, following a dispute between Orville Wright and the Smithsonian Institution, the original Wright 1903 Flyer, suitably restored, was sent overseas for long-term exhibition in London's Science Museum. Before shipping, it was photographed, minus its engine, with the controls deflected.

D   The Wrights' wind tunnel balance had an upper bar on which model wings could be mounted. The lift of a wing was compared with figures already determined for metal plates carried on the lower bar.

A   The key to success. Wing-warping was the method by which the Wrights achieved control in the air, the essential element of the puzzle ignored by so many others. Multiple exposures reveal the extent of the warping.

B   The Wright Military Flyer over Fort Myer during the Army trials in 1908. The shape of the counterrotating propellers can be seen, and it is clear from the warped wings that Orville is rolling to his right.

C   The Wright propeller, designed from first principles by the brothers. It was not easy, as Orville described: "With the machine moving forward, the air flying backward, the propellers turning sidewise, and nothing standing still, it seemed impossible to find a starting point from which to trace the various simultaneous reactions." Lubrication was supplied from the small receptacle above the shaft, which was filled before flight.

D   The USAF Museum's 1909 Military Flyer is an exact replica constructed in the Museum's workshops. In front of the pilots were rudders that the Wrights called "horizontal rudders" (elevators), here shown   deflected in the up and down positions, and small vertical stabilizers.

E   Vertical rudders to the rear were the answer to the problem of sideslipping in banked turns.

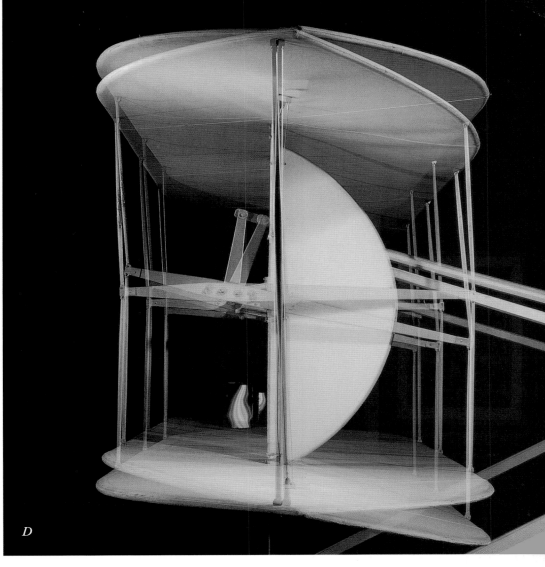

D

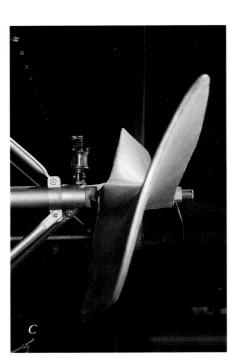

C

E

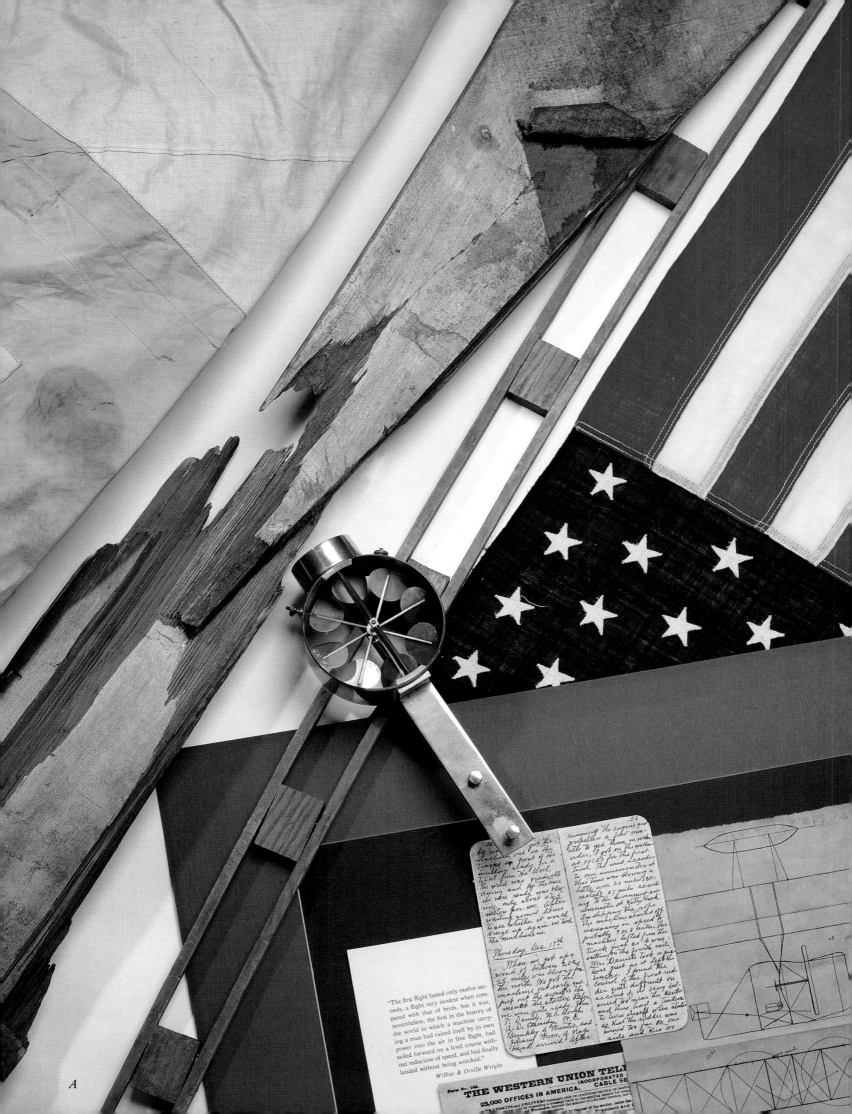

"The first flight lasted only twelve seconds, a flight very modest when compared with that of birds in the history of nevertheless, the first in which a machine carrying a man had raised itself by its own power into the air in free flight, had sailed forward on a level course without reduction of speed, and had finally landed without being wrecked."

Wilbur & Orville Wright

THE WESTERN UNION TELE...
23,000 OFFICES IN AMERICA.

A Wright brothers' relics on show at the USAF Museum include fabric from the 1903 Flyer, the splintered propeller from the 1908 accident which killed Lt. Selfridge at Ft. Myer, a wing rib made by the Wrights, a U.S. flag given to Orville by the commander of Ft. Myer in 1908, an anemometer fashioned by the Wrights, copies of the diary entry from December 17 and of the telegram sent after the first flight, and an original drawing by the Wrights.

B Intrigued, curious, and skeptical spectators gather round the Flyer between flights during the Army trials in September 1908.

C The Flyer about to lift off its launching rail at Fort Myer.

D It flies! Orville circles the Fort Myer parade ground on September 9, 1908, in the course of setting a world record of 57.5 minutes in the air.

The Dream Fulfilled © *Keith Ferris, 1986*

A   Glenn Curtiss fitted ailerons to his aircraft for lateral control, as on this Curtiss 1911 Model D replica. Although this was a departure from the wing-warping method, the Wrights sued Curtiss for infringement of patents.

B   The USAF Museum's Curtiss Model D is a replica of Signal Corps Aeroplane No. 2. The materials used in the reconstruction are essentially the same as in the original, except for the engine, which is an accurate representation in wood and plastic of the 90 hp Curtiss OX-5 engine.

Following page:
A refinement of earlier Curtiss engines, the OX-5 powered the Curtiss "Jenny." Its V-shape was to dominate liquid-cooled engine design, and a later Curtiss engine, the D-12, helped to inspire Rolls-Royce to develop the line of V-12s which led to the famous Merlin.

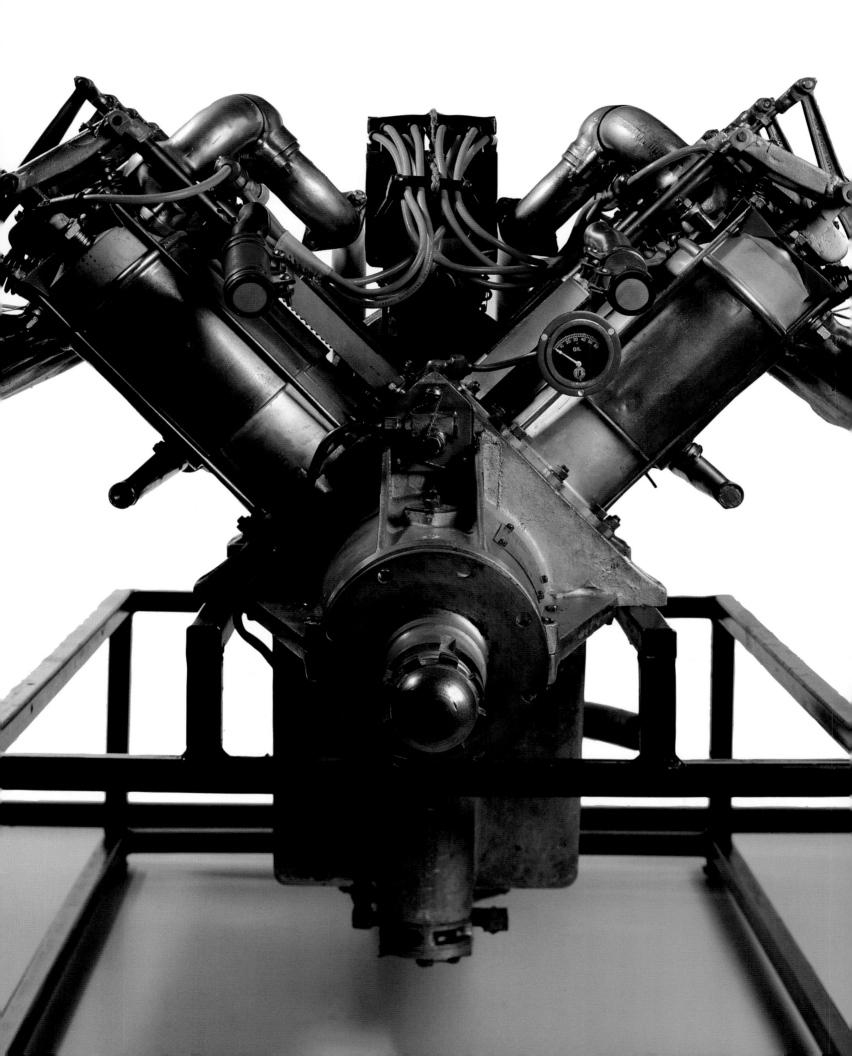

Chapter 3

The Crucible of War, 1917-18

"Rick [Rickenbacker] wasn't the best pilot in the world; . . . but Rick rarely missed. He even pulled the wing off an Albatros one time—with his tail skid."

(Major Reed Chambers, 94th Aero Squadron)

"When my brother and I built and flew the first man-carrying machine, we thought we were introducing into the world an invention which would make further wars practically impossible."

(Orville Wright, 1917)

"If you see a steady line of tracers coming near you, remember that the quickest way to change your relative position is a jerk on the stick—not too strong or you will disconcert the observer."

(Captain Stephen H. Noyes, Corps Observation Group, First Army)

"Aerial observation is neither a bed of roses nor the path to glory that the man on the ground some times imagines it to be. The wind behind a Liberty [engine] is terrific, and it taxes the strength of the strongest to fight it three hours. If the ship is rolled and tossed about very much, either by bumps or purposely to avoid shell and shrapnel, the occupants sometimes get sick . . . you lose your lunch and the wind places it in a neat layer on your goggles. The wind has blown your handkerchief from your pocket. You wipe it off on your teddy bear sleeve [airman's fur coat]. You start to write your messages and of your three pencils you have one left. You break the point on it and your knife is in your pocket under your teddy bear. . . . But I like it."

(2d Lt. W.J. Rogers, Observer, 50th Aero Squadron)

Capt. Edward Vernon Rickenbacker (1890-1973). Eddie Rickenbacker commanded the 94th ("Hat in the Ring") Aero Squadron in France during 1918. He became America's WW I "ace of aces," with twenty-six confirmed victories in the air.

War in the Air

In a famous poster of 1914, the stern, pointing figure of Britain's General Kitchener welcomes the museum visitor to the World War I gallery of the USAF Museum. The wall displays include brief reminders of the vast strides made by military aviation in Europe while the U.S. Air Service languished in the shadow of America's isolationist policy between 1914 and 1917. More significant evidence of America's not being prepared for large-scale aerial conflict is on every side—the combat aircraft standing on the museum floor and those suspended overhead in simulated flight are all of European design.

The exhibits tell a story which begins with the unrealistic expectations of U.S. military aviation following America's awakening in 1917, moves on to the struggles of U.S. industry and the Air Service to create a powerful air force, and climax with the first successful applications of U.S. air power which marked the closing months of the war. Attention is drawn to the American airmen whose impatience for combat led them to join the British and French air forces before 1917, and there are displays which single out those who particularly distinguished themselves in Europe—among them Lufbery, Vaughan, Rickenbacker, Luke, Bleckley, Goettler, and Mitchell.

The stories of the men, together with small collections of their memorabilia—uniforms, flying helmets, logbooks, medals, and awards, etc.—provide the fascinating detail which binds the WWI display together, but inevitably the eye is first caught and held by the aircraft, their engines, and their armament. A Fokker Dr1 Triplane soars inverted over Allied fighters—a Sopwith Camel, a SPAD VII, and a Nieuport 28—while the massive shape of an observation balloon floats in the background. The birth of strategic air power is represented by a Caproni CA-36 bomber, and a Halberstadt CL IV illustrates an early stage in the development of close air support for ground troops. Hovering nearby are examples of famous U.S. trainers, including the Standard J-1 and the legendary Curtiss Jenny. All fascinating airplanes, but the pride of the WWI fleet is a two-seat reconnaissance aircraft: the SPAD XVI flown by Billy Mitchell when he commanded the American air forces on the Western Front in 1918.

As visitors leave the WWI gallery, they can be in little doubt that extraordinary advances were made by the U.S. in military aviation during 1917–18. Serious shortcomings had to be acknowledged in the way the U.S. built its air strength, but the achievements eventually recorded were remarkable by any standards—in less than two years, an aircraft industry built from almost nothing, and a burgeoning U.S. Air Service with a hard core of experienced airmen who had more than held their own against determined adversaries. In the course of passing through this single gallery, visitors have moved from the depressing inadequacies of 1916 to a point where the U.S. has all that is necessary to become a formidable power in the air. The challenges of aerial warfare have been met; very different postwar challenges are to come.

The Air War in Europe

When the United States declared war on April 6, 1917, few people realized just how far America had fallen behind the European combatants in the development and application of air power. In 1914, the European powers had faced each other with the most rudimentary of air arms. There were then no aircraft which were truly military and it was generally thought (certainly by the respective armies) that the airplane might prove useful for reconnaissance or artillery spotting, but for little else. Three years later, aerial warfare had grown to encompass a wide range of specializations and was taking up more than its share of space in national newspapers. Air forces were using aircraft designed for roles as diverse as air defense, interception, interdiction, ground attack, reconnaissance, and strategic bombing. The tactics for each kind of operation were highly developed. Large training organizations had been created, both for air and ground crews, and industries had arisen which, in France and Britain, produced the almost incredible number of 50,000 aircraft for each nation in the course of the war.

The foundations of strategic bombing had already been laid, notably by German attacks on London, and heavy bombers were being operated by Germany, Russia, Italy, and Britain. The horrors of aerial warfare predicted by such writers as H.G. Wells had begun to be realized by attacks on civilian populations, yet, in the public eye, this new dimension restored chivalry to a war in which men lost their identities in the mass and were dominated by the unfeeling efficiency of barbed wire and ma-

Regarded with affection for its viceless handling qualities, the Curtiss "Jenny" was the mainstay of the Army's primary flying training program during WW I and the early 1920s.

chine guns. Aerial combat was compared to the knightly tournaments of an earlier age, the opponents facing each other as individuals in fair contest, mounted on brightly decorated, propeller-driven steeds, their silk scarves fluttering like banners in the wind. The reality of men trapped in burning machines or falling thousands of feet to their deaths was glossed over, and the names of national champions like Richtofen, Immelman, Boelcke, Guynemer, Fonck, Ball, McCudden, and Mannock became as familiar as those of celebrated actors or sporting figures.

The airmen themselves were often caught up in the chivalrous imagery of their profession, saluting each other's prowess and honoring fallen enemies. Guynemer once fought a long battle with Ernst Udet until the German's guns jammed; seeing his enemy disarmed, the Frenchman waved gallantly and flew away.[1] When Boelcke was killed, Royal Flying Corps aircraft flew over his grave and dropped a wreath with the message: "To our brave and chivalrous foe." If they came to see themselves as airborne knights, however, they also accepted the fact that they were poor insurance risks. Loss rates were high and death has no respect for reputations; few of the famous survived the war. Major John Slessor of No. 80 Squadron, RFC (later Marshal of the Royal Air Force Sir John Slessor), remembered: "The squadron's average [aircrew] strength was 22 officers, and in the last ten months of the war no less than 168 officers were struck off strength from all causes—an average of about 75 percent per month, of whom a little less than half were killed."

By 1917, the air war had become an enterprise of unforeseen scale. It had a rapacious appetite for men and machines and was demanding an increasing share of national resources; it was even beginning to change the way generals thought about strategy and tactics. By its very nature, aerial warfare stood much of military tradition on its head. It was breeding a force in which the officers were the fighting men and the men were skilled technicians rather than cannon fodder. Its public figures were junior officers rather than generals, and in

The Nieuport 28 was a later version of a type which had been a successful fighter when it was introduced in 1915. The U.S. Air Service took delivery of 297 Nieuport 28s in 1918, but the 28 was no match for the Fokker D VII and was withdrawn from operations after only four months in the front line.

its attacks on civilian populations it was opening the door to a modern concept of total war.

American Commitments

When the United States entered the war, most American leaders and military men had not grasped the extent to which war in the air had developed, nor did they fully understand the art of the possible in their proposals for the U.S. Air Service to join the fray on an equal footing. Nor did the European Allies appreciate how far the U.S. had lagged behind. They saw only the immense potential of America's resources in terms of manpower and industrial capacity. The French Premier, Alexandre Ribot, opened the bidding on May 24, 1917, with a message to President Woodrow Wilson in which he suggested a program "to enable the Allies to win supremacy of the air." A target date of spring 1918 was set and the U.S. was asked to send to the front a total of 4,500 aircraft, 5,000 pilots, and 50,000 mechanics, plus supporting services. Using the French request as a basis for planning, a group of

officers headed by Major Benjamin Foulois proposed an even more ambitious program—22,625 aircraft (12,000 of them intended for combat) supported by 80 percent spares, plus 45,000 engines. The thousands of aircrew to man this armada were to be graduated from flying schools which did not then exist. The estimated cost of this astonishing proposal was a massive $640 million.

Given that the U.S. had produced a total of less than a thousand aircraft of all types in the fourteen years since Kitty Hawk, and that the combat capability of the U.S. Air Service in 1917 was nonexistent, these were startling figures. They did nothing, however, to dampen the sudden enthusiasm of the American public for military aviation. The air war had glamorous appeal and the building of an air force was seen as the quickest way to bring the power of U.S. industry to bear. The newly formed Aircraft Production Board burst into print with a confident statement including the passage:

"Manufacturing capacity can easily be doubled in the first year. A prominent British general has asserted that America's greatest contribution to the war will be

[1]This may not have been a wise move. Udet survived the war with 62 aerial victories and went on to become one of Hitler's generals in the building of the Luftwaffe during the 1930s. He was given responsibility for aircraft development and production and committed suicide in 1941 when German aircraft production programs began to fail.

aircraft and aviators. We believe that once started upon quantity production, American mechanical genius will overcome any present obstacles to the progress of the art."

The link between quantity production and art may not have been entirely clear, but the general euphoria was emphasized by the words of the Aircraft Production Board's chairman, Howard Coffin: "The road to Berlin lies through the air. The eagle must end this war." An emotive outburst from the U.S. Army's Chief Signals Officer, General Squier, spoke in glowing (if archaic) terms of putting "Yankee punch into the war by building an army

almost without dissent, and it was signed into law by President Wilson on July 24, 1917.

With the promises made, a plan completed, and money available, it was time to start facing facts. The U.S. did not have an aircraft industry capable of building combat aircraft in the time specified or the numbers required. Even under the pressure of contracts already issued and war newly declared, American aircraft builders had delivered just seventy-eight airplanes during the month of July 1917. After the war, Secretary Baker acknowledged that eagerness for the idea had over-

cans desired that our country should appear speedily, worthily and decisively in the war."

While the industry wrestled with impossible problems, the Air Service staffs broke down the original plan into more detailed figures. In August 1917, it was announced that 345 combat squadrons would be formed (plus supporting services), 263 of which were to join the front line in France by June 30, 1918—a mere ten months away. It soon became obvious that the plans could specify what they liked, but good intentions, even when backed by unlimited money, could not make up for years of neglect. The difficulties were staggering. The existing aircraft manufacturers in the U.S. were dwarfed by the size of the task. Even the huge lumber industry was unable to meet the vast increase in demand for spruce needed in aircraft construction. The technical expertise to design aircraft capable of holding their own in combat did not exist in the U.S., and the U.S. Army had no officers serving who had much idea of the kind of aircraft needed. In part, this was the fault of the European Allies, who had exercised strict censorship of aeronautical information throughout the war, but the fault was compounded by the complete absence of any Air Service plans for building an air force capable of combat.[2]

To solve the most pressing problem, it was decided to make use of already proven European designs. A mission under Major Raynal Bolling went to Europe in June 1917 and recommended four types for production in the U.S.: the SPAD single-seat fighter, the Bristol two-seat fighter, the DH4 reconnaissance/light bomber, and the Caproni triplane heavy bomber. The Handley-Page 0/400 heavy bomber was later added to the list. During the latter part of 1917 contracts were placed with a number of companies, including Curtiss, Dayton-Wright, and Fisher Body, to build these aircraft in the thousands necessary to meet the commitments so freely given for the U.S. to have an air force in the front line by the summer of 1918.

The contracts were complicated by

Known by some aircrew as "two wings on a hearse," the Liberty-engined DH-4 was the only aircraft built in the U.S. to see WW I combat. Of 3,431 made, only 417 reached the front line before the end of the war.

in the air; regiments and brigades of winged cavalry on gas-driven flying horses." The Secretary of War, Newton Baker, announced that military aviation "furnishes our supreme opportunity for immediate service," and gave the proposal his full support. Carried along by the fervor of the moment, Congress passed a bill authorizing $640 million for the Air Service

come reason when the aviation program was approved. He wrote:

"The airplane itself was too wonderful and new, too positive a denial of previous experience, to brook the application of any prudent restraints which wise people would have known how to apply to ordinary industrial and military developments. As a consequence, the magicians of American industry were expected to do the impossible for this new and magical agency, and this expectation was increased by the feverish earnestness with which all Ameri-

[2]An insight into this lapse can be gained by examining American attitudes in the early part of the 20th century. The concept of planning for war was alien to most Americans. President Wilson himself was reported to have been outraged by the idea that the War Department was considering the need for war plans in 1916. He believed that the War Department should be concerned only with the mobilization of manpower.

the fact that the decision had already been made to modify those combat aircraft built in the U.S. to carry a standard American engine if possible. It was reasoned that although the U.S. might lag in aircraft design, Americans were among the world's leaders when it came to automobile engines, and providing a new engine suitable for combat aircraft ought not to be too difficult. Starting on May 29, 1917, prodigies of design and construction were achieved and the first 8-cylinder Liberty engine was being tested by July 4. A 12-cylinder version followed on August 25 and was soon delivering 440 hp. The Liberty was rushed into production with the major automobile manufacturers and, despite some early teething troubles and the complaint that it was too heavy for fighter aircraft, it proved to be an American success story. When the war ended in November 1918, a total of 13,574 Liberty engines had been produced and the production rate had risen to 150 per day. Modified Liberty engines continued to provide power for U.S. military flying for more than a decade.[3]

Bitter Realities

If U.S. engine production was something of a success story, most other aspects of the Air Service program continued to disappoint. The aircraft industry expanded dramatically as it tried to reach the planning goals, but the task was too great, and the industry's efforts were not helped by the confusion of constant changes of plan and uncertainty over who was responsible for what. Until the end of the war there were difficulties in coordinating the ideas and activities of the War Department, the American Expeditionary Force Headquarters, the Aircraft Production Board, and the Air Service, despite a number of reorganizations and changes of command intended to alleviate the problems.

By the end of 1917, the summer of unbounded confidence had become a winter of discontent. Widespread public disillusion at the apparent failure of the Air Service program led to some reassessments. With aircraft production lagging badly, an attempt was made to set more realistic goals. A new program both reduced the

number of operational squadrons promised for the front line and delayed the date of their arrival. The original 263 squadrons became 120, and they would be in action by January 1919, not June 1918. These were more sensible targets, but although herculean efforts were made, even these were not reached. When the war ended in November 1918, there were forty-five squadrons assigned for combat, twelve of which were operating DH-4s manufactured in the U.S. The DH-4 was the only combat aircraft made in any numbers in American factories; 3,431 of them had been delivered. Of these, some 1,200 had

arrived in France, but only 417 had reached the front.

Looking back on his experiences many years later, General Hap Arnold could not hide the bitterness he felt over the way the Air Service program had been handled in 1917–18. He wrote:

"No American designed combat plane flew in France or Italy during the

entire war. The foreign planes built in this country failed to arrive in Europe on schedule or in the promised numbers, until what had started out as a triumphant exhibition of American know-how turned into a humiliating series of Congressional and other investigations."

Eddie Rickenbacker, the celebrated American fighter ace, was equally harsh in his judgment:

"None of us in France could understand what prevented our great country from furnishing machines equal to the best in the world. Many a gallant life was lost to American aviation in those early months

The French SPAD XIII was the principal pursuit aircraft used in WW I by the U.S. Army Air Service, which took delivery of 893 during 1918. It was robust and fast, and was described by Rickenbacker as "... the ultimate aircraft in the war in which aviation developed."

of 1918, the responsibility for which must lie heavily on some guilty conscience."

Sentiments like these are understandable, especially when they are held by those who went to war, and there are endless stories and statistics which emphasize the shortcomings of the U.S. air effort in WWI. However, it should not be forgotten that in 1917 the U.S. was being invited to accelerate from a standing start to the hectic pace of an air war which had been in progress for three years. Viewed

---

[3]Between July 1917 and November 1918 the U.S. built a total of over 32,000 aircraft engines, among them some 10,000 Hall-Scott A7A and Curtiss OX-5 engines for training aircraft. Besides being the engine of the famous Curtiss "Jenny," the 90 hp OX-5 led the way to a Curtiss family of V-shaped, liquid-cooled engines which powered American fighters of the 1920s and strongly influenced Rolls-Royce when they began to design the series of engines which resulted in the Merlin, the most successful engine of WW II.

The 90 hp OX-5 powered the famous "Jenny" and led the way to a Curtiss family of V-shaped, liquid-cooled engines which were used by American fighters during the interwar years. Curtiss engines had their influence on other manufacturers, including Rolls-Royce, designers of WW II's famous "Merlin."

from that angle, what was accomplished is more commendable. The U.S. industry in 1917 was negligible, but by November 11, 1918, it had produced over 11,000 aircraft of all types, including nearly 8,000 trainers, and the production rate had risen to no less than 21,000 aircraft per year.

Training Explosion

The expansion of the aviation training organization was remarkable by any measure. Inspired by stories of the air war in Europe, there was no shortage of willing volunteers. When the U.S. entered the war, thousands of young Americans clamored for flight training and the Air Service embarked on a program which brought about a 150-fold expansion by the end of the war. Starting with 1,200 officers and men and 3 flying fields, the force grew to over 190,000 men and 43 airfields in nineteen months. Overseas, there were 4,872 officers, 46,667 men, and 16 airfields, and the 45 operational squadrons were manned by 767 pilots, 481 observers, and 23 gunners.

At the heart of the training program at the primary flying schools was the Curtiss JN-4 Jenny, powered by the 90 hp OX-5 engine. The Standard J-1 trainer was produced in smaller numbers to supplement the Jenny, but it was a more tem-peramental beast and never matched the popularity of its celebrated Curtiss rival, which proceeded to dominate the primary training program for years to come. The Jenny was neither powerful nor very quick, being "flat out" at 75 mph, but it was durable and it was not so forgiving that a student could afford to develop bad habits or be careless. Thousands of American and Canadian pilots, including many who would later make their mark on the world of aviation, flew their first solos in the Jenny and later recalled the biplane with affection.

Jimmy Doolittle, who was not very tall, trained in the Jenny in 1917, finding that his greatest difficulty was in seeing over the edge of the rather high-sided cockpit. He was sent solo after only six hours of dual instruction, and later proved himself one of the world's greatest airmen in peace or war. The Jenny went on to a life after the Armistice, too, principally as the aircraft of choice for the barnstormers of the 1920s. Many surplus Jennies were sold off as the military flying training program wound down, and they were flown by their ex-military pilots to fairgrounds and cow pastures all over the U.S. Americans who had never seen an airplane could watch the thrills of aerobatics or wing-walking, and,

if they had the nerve and a few dollars, they could climb into a cockpit and fly. The foundations of U.S. air power were laid with the help of the Curtiss Jenny. It may not have been a sensational performer, but it trained the first generation of American combat airmen, and, to the great future benefit of the U.S., it played a large part in making the American people airminded.

Although the expansion of the primary training program was quickly underway in 1917, it was realized that American airmen would reach the squadrons all the quicker if the early waves of volunteers could go to flying training schools already functioning in Europe. It was also accepted that it would not be possible to provide the new pilots with the advanced training they would need before being committed to combat. Only the European Allies had the necessary aircraft and experience. It was equally obvious that U.S.-built combat aircraft would not be available for some time. Agreements were therefore reached with Britain, France, and Italy both for flying training facilities and for the purchase of suitable aircraft.

In common with all the other aspects of the U.S. entry into the air war, almost nothing about the first phases of the training buildup went smoothly. Administrative shortcomings, language difficulties, failures of communication, and clashes in priorities all contributed to a series of delays and disappointments. Places held open at European schools in the summer of 1917 were not filled, and most of them were no longer available by the time American cadets arrived in the autumn. Cadets accumulated in the hundreds and were misemployed on guard duty or as construction workers for new American airfields. The backlog was not fully cleared until the summer of 1918, by which time a number of American schools were operating in France, notably those at Issoudun and Tours. Issoudun, in the winter of 1917–18, was not remembered with affection by the cadets. One of them described it as "A sea of frozen mud. Waiting in shivering line before dawn for the spoonful of gluey porridge slapped into outstretched mess kits, cold as ice. Wretched flying equipment. Broken necks. The flu. A hell of a place, Issoudun."

Americans in Combat

While all this was going on, a number of Americans were already in action, having found a quicker way to the war. Since 1915, there had been American volunteers flying with the French and British, and several became legendary figures. Among the first was the French-born American, Raoul Lufbery, who reached a French squadron after being a U.S. soldier in the Philippines, a mechanic for a barnstormer in India and China, and a French Foreign Legionnaire. He transferred to the French Air Service as a mechanic and inveigled his way into pilot training. By October 1915, he was flying bombing sorties in French two-seaters. The opportunity to make his name came with the formation of the Escadrille Americaine, the inspiration of a Harvard graduate named Norman Prince.

After tortuous negotiations with the French government in 1915, the Escadrille Americaine was formed on March 21, 1916, as a pursuit (or *chasse*) squadron equipped with Nieuports. By that time, several of the original aviators of fortune had become impatient with the bureaucratic delays and had joined French squadrons (*escadrilles*). Once formed, however, the Escadrille Americaine soon attracted many more Americans who wanted a chance to engage in "the knightly combat of the air," and it was not long before the unit began to build itself a reputation. Its public recognition drew a formal complaint from the German ambassador to the United States, and the name of the squadron was changed to the Lafayette Escadrille so that the diplomatic niceties might be observed.[4]

So many Americans were anxious to join the squadron that a larger organization was introduced—the Lafayette Flying Corps. This functioned as a headquarters which arranged for American volunteers to enter French flying schools and for graduates to be sent forward as replacements as necessary to the Lafayette Esca-

Aircraft in various states of repair in the hangar at Issoudun, home of an American flying school in France.

drille, and to French combat units. Frank Baylies was one pilot who served with a French squadron and scored twelve victories before being shot down on June 18, 1918. Of 224 Americans awarded French wings, 51 were killed in action. Between them, they were credited with destroying 199 enemy aircraft.

The First "Aces"

Early members of the Lafayette Escadrille included Norman Prince, William Thaw, Elliott Cowdin, Bert Hall, James McConnell, Victor Chapman, and the brothers Rockwell—Kiffen and Robert. Kiffen Rockwell scored the first victory for the Lafayettes on May 18, 1916, but it was Raoul Lufbery who became the squadron's most celebrated airman. He recorded his fifth kill on October 12, 1916, to become the first American "ace," and he added steadily to his score in the following months, reaching a total of seventeen kills before transferring to the U.S. Air Service and becoming a major in the 94th Aero Squadron in February 1918. He led the first patrol of three aircraft from the 94th to fly over the front line on March 6, 1918, choosing as his wingmen Lts. Douglas Campbell and Eddie Rickenbacker, both

of whom later became aces in their own right. Astoundingly, the patrol was flown in unarmed aircraft because although the Nieuports had been delivered, their guns had not!

Lufbery's personal victory score remained at seventeen, but he exerted considerable influence on the way the unblooded American squadron approached its combat initiation, continuing to lead patrols of the 94th, with and without guns, for another two months. On May 19, 1918, he took off alone in pursuit of a German two-seater. He was seen to open fire and then to pull away, apparently to clear a jammed gun. When he attacked again, the German gunner got off an accurate burst and the Nieuport exploded into flame. The little fighter dropped for some distance before Lufbery either fell from the cockpit or jumped to his death to avoid the flames.

Lufbery flew Nieuport 17s and 28s during most of his combat career. They were from a line of fighters which had been effective in challenging the Germans in the air when introduced to the front line in 1915, and they became the favorite mount of many great aces—Ball, Guynemer, and Fonck among them. Nieuport 17s had the advantages of being small, very agile, and fairly fast for their time, but there were disadvantages, too. The upper wing had

[4]In February 1918, the Lafayette Escadrille was transferred to the U.S. Air Service and became the 103rd Aero Squadron under the command of Major William Thaw. The squadron continued combat operations without interruption and remained under French command for a further five months, before joining the 3rd Pursuit Group on the American front in August.

the reputation of disassembling itself in a high speed dive, and the engine was a large rotary, which led to other problems. For example, the rotating mass of the engine had a considerable effect on the handling of such a small airplane. One pilot said that it was "like trying to fly a gyroscope." Another problem was the absence of a throttle, the rotary being controlled only by means of a "blip" switch, which allowed the pilot to have the engine running flat out or stopped; there were no half measures. As 1st Lt. Louis Simon of the 147th Aero Squadron reported: "The Nieuport 28 has the rotary motor and is the hardest to fly formation with because you can't regulate your speed. . . . In those with stationary motors, formation flying is easier because of not having to 'S' so much."

The American links with the French Air Service—through training, aircraft acquisition, provision of bases, service with French units, and so on—were generally more extensive than those with the other European Allies, and the scale of this association is best exemplified by the aircrew training and aircraft programs. More than 8,000 American pilots and observers received training of some sort in France, and the French delivered over 4,800 aircraft to the American Air Service during the last year of the war. The bulk of these were outdated types used for advanced training, but French machines, principally SPAD fighters, Breguet bombers, and Salmson observation aircraft, still constituted the lion's share of the U.S. front-line strength of 740 aircraft in November 1918.

RFC Connections

Cooperative arrangements between the U.S. and Britain were equally diverse if not so large. A few individuals had found ways to join the Royal Flying Corps before 1917, but it was not until the U.S. entered the war that the trickle became a flow of both air and ground personnel. Agreements between the two countries reached in December 1917 provided for the U.S. to build up a force of 15,000 mechanics in the U.K. for training on front-line aircraft and also to release British mechanics for posting to France. As

the American mechanics became proficient, they in turn would become available for France and would be replaced with newcomers to maintain the 15,000 total. In addition, a labor force of 6,200 was to be provided to work on British bases. Because of insufficient shipping space, the 15,000 figure for mechanics was not reached until August 1918, and no more than half of the 6,200 workers were ever employed. Nevertheless, at the Armistice there were over 20,000 Air Service personnel in Britain, and at least fifteen U.S. squadrons in France were manned by British-trained mechanics. Yet another sizeable

force was working on an ambitious program to equip thirty U.S. Air Service squadrons with Handley-Page 0/400 night bombers for a strategic campaign against Germany in 1919.

The first American cadets for flying training in Britain docked at Liverpool on September 2, 1917. Quickly assimilated into the RFC's program, they began their training on aircraft like old Farmans (known as "Rumptys") or DH6s, and moved on through Avro 504s to single-seater Sopwith Pups and Camels. The con-

trast with the French system was marked. Hap Arnold described the training of student pilots in France as "the gradual absorption of the knowledge of the art of flying by the pupil by his being transferred from one machine to another until he finally reached the best of its particular type," but that statement does not fully reflect the caution of the French approach. Handling exercises were begun in "*rouleurs*" (planes with wings clipped so that they could not fly), and progress was made in a series of carefully controlled steps through aircraft with increasingly demanding characteristics until a combat type was reached.

Stalwarts of the Lafayette Escadrille, a squadron of American volunteers flying with the French Air Service before the U.S. entry into the war. From left to right: James McConnell, Kiffen Rockwell, Georges Thenault (the French CO), Norman Prince, and Victor Chapman.

The process was lengthy, but the French insisted that it was justified because it saved lives. Even so, accidents were not infrequent—seventy-eight American pilots were killed at Issoudun in the course of their pursuit training.

The approach adopted by the RFC was more robust, with cadets often reaching the stage of flying combat types like the Sopwith Pup within a month or so of starting their training. It can be argued that this was too robust, since thirty-four of a little more than five hundred American airmen trained by the British died in flying accidents, most of them in single-seaters at the most advanced stage of pursuit training. By modern standards, this is a horrifying statistic, but during WWI it was accepted as one of the hazards of doing business. In his final report at the end of the war, Major General Mason Patrick, Chief of Air Service, American Expeditionary Force, acknowledged the dangers of flying training, wherever it was carried out. In recording the deaths of 218 pilots and observers at training centers in Europe, he said: "A great many can be fairly ascribed to engine failure and lack of judgement or poor flying on the part of the pilot," and

of them had served either with RFC squadrons or with two American squadrons fighting on the British front, the 17th and 148th. The two U.S. squadrons flew their first operations on the section of the front closest to the Channel coast in July 1918. As was usual with newly formed units, they patrolled a relatively quiet sector for their introduction to the battle area. Even so, it was not long before they had some success. On July 13, 1918, Lt. Field Kindley of the 148th shot down an Albatross D3 over Ypres, and one week later the 17th opened its score when Lt. Rodney Williams downed a Fokker. A natural rivalry developed between the squadrons and their

dive. One pilot claimed that "A Camel pilot had to shoot down every German plane in the sky in order to get home himself, as the Camel could neither outclimb nor outrun a Fokker." It was tricky to fly, too, because of its small size and the considerable torque from its rotary engine. In a sharp turn to the left the nose rose abruptly and had to be checked by coarse use of the rudder, or the Camel would very quickly spin without warning. On the other hand, it was extremely maneuverable in the hands of a competent pilot, and it would turn to the right quicker than any other machine. Many of its pilots came to think of it as "unquestionably the greatest plane on the front" and there is some weight behind that opinion. Between the time of its introduction in July 1917 and the end of the war, the Camel was the victor in more aerial combats than any other aircraft on either side—a total of 1,294 enemy aircraft destroyed—and so, in spite of its shortcomings, it has some claim to be considered the fighting scout supreme.

After their initial blooding, the pace of combat picked up rapidly for the 17th and the 148th, and the numbers of both victories and losses began to rise steadily, although the balance was always markedly in favor of the American squadrons. Of the two, the 17th had the most fluctuating fortunes. On August 13, 1918, the 17th took part in a devastatingly successful raid on a German airfield in Belgium, destroying fourteen aircraft and killing more than thirty pilots on the ground. Just two weeks after that dramatic success, the squadron was ambushed by several Fokker formations and had six Camels shot down, with three of the pilots killed and three taken prisoner. The shattered squadron was withdrawn from the line to refit and wait for replacements.

One of those taken prisoner was Lt. Robert Todd, who had shot down his fifth enemy just moments before. One of his combat reports is typical in its description of the aerial fighting of the time—brief, violent, and terribly final—and offers an object lesson in the dangers of a pilot concentrating so hard on his opponent that he loses track of his own position:

Raoul Lufbery was a French-born American who flew with both the Lafayette Escadrille and the 94th Aero Squadron. He recorded seventeen aerial victories before his death in combat on May 19, 1918.

he drew particular attention to "the fundamental failure to maintain sufficient flying speed." He also stressed the dangers of single-seat pursuit training in his findings on the proportion of fatalities to graduates—1 to 90 in preliminary training, 1 to 50 in advanced observation training, and a startling 1 to 9.2 in pursuit training.

American Squadrons in Action

By March 1918, the first British-trained Americans were joining their units in France, and at the end of the war 216

competition led them to compile two of the most illustrious combat records in the history of the American Air Service.

The 17th and the 148th flew Sopwith Camels on the British front. By the summer of 1918, the Camel was not quite the dominant fighter it once had been. With a top speed of 115 mph, it was among the slowest of the fighters and this sometimes proved an embarrassment when it was used on escort duty, because the RFC's DH9 bombers were faster than Camels both when flying level and in the

For many pilots, the Sopwith Camel was the supreme combat aircraft. Although not very fast, it was extremely maneuverable and a good gun platform. By the end of the war the Camel had been victorious more often than any other aircraft on either side, with a total of 1,294 enemies destroyed.

"While on offensive patrol 8–10 a.m., August 1, 1918, our formation met three triplanes and one Fokker biplane at 14,000 to 16,000 feet. The leading three of our formation dived on the EA (enemy aircraft) and when the EA turned, I dove on the nearest triplane, opening fire at about 100 yards range. The triplane pulled up, allowing me to get within 25 yards of him, and my next burst sent him down out of control. While watching him, I went into a spin accidentally and pulled out of it at about 6,000 feet. While still diving, I saw the triplane crash into a wood near Provin."

On October 28, 1918, with the war in its last days, the 148th extracted some revenge for the rough treatment given to the 17th in August when it caught a German formation in a carefully prepared ambush. Field Kindley led four Camels over no-man's land at 3,000 feet to act as the bait. Eight more aircraft from the 148th flew 7,000 feet higher and hung back in the shadow of some clouds. The bait was duly taken by seven Fokkers,

which attacked Kindley's flight from above. Timing their interception perfectly, the 148th's high cover tore into the Germans as Kindley's Camels turned to meet their enemy. Within seconds the fight was over. Seven Fokkers littered the ground within a radius of 1,000 yards and the 148th had not lost a single pilot.

When the war ended, the 148th was officially credited with 66 victories in the air, while the 17th had destroyed 52 enemy aircraft, despite taking time behind the lines to refit in late August. Casualties (killed, wounded, or taken prisoner) were 25 for the 17th and 11 for the 148th. Both squadrons had several pilots who finished the war as aces, notably George Vaughan (13), Lloyd Hamilton (9), and Howard Burdick (8) of the 17th, and Field Kindley (12), Elliott Springs (12), Henry Clay (8), and Jesse Creech (8) of the 148th.[5] Including those airmen who flew only with RAF units, American pilots on the British front had destroyed 200 enemy aircraft at a cost of 84 casualties. (Different sources claim as many as 225 destroyed for as few as 71 casualties.)

In November 1918, it was finally decided that the 17th and 148th Squadrons should come under the command of the U.S. Air Service. They moved to the

American sector of the front near Toul and began their conversion to the SPAD XIII, but the war ended before they could return to combat. On their departure from the British front, General Salmond, the Royal Air Force's commander in France, sent a letter to General Mason Patrick of the AEF:

"Now that the time has come when Nos. 17 and 148 Squadrons return to you, I wish to say how magnificently they have carried out their duties. . . . Every call has been answered by them to the highest degree, and when they have arrived with you, you will have two highly efficient squadrons filled with the offensive spirit."

Americans in Italy

The program arranged between the U.S. and Italy was on a smaller scale than those with France and Britain, but it was significant because it provided American airmen with combat experience of a quite different character. Training for U.S. fliers was centered on Foggia, near the spur on Italy's heel, and the American who managed the program was a U.S. Congressman who had volunteered for the Air Service—Fiorello LaGuardia, later mayor of New York. As an Italian-speaking politician whose family roots were in Foggia, he was a natural choice for the job.

Just over four hundred Americans graduated from the Italian school between September 1917 and the end of the war. Preliminary training was done in old Farmans, and it did not progress as quickly as had been hoped. An American cadet, Claud Duncan, later offered his comments on the system of training at Foggia, and some of them reflected the frustrations of an eager young man being taught to fly by an instructor with whom he had no common language:

"The Italians had a belief that you couldn't absorb more than ten minutes flying in a day, so you would go out and get your ten-minute hop and that was all for the day. Of course, you stayed out on the line, observed, listened, and picked up what you could. It took a long time at ten minutes a day to get any time in. . . . In our particular set-up the motor mechanic

---

[5]The question of aerial victories claimed and officially recognized is a vexed one. National authorities had different rules for keeping score. For instance, if more than one pilot had shared in shooting down an enemy aircraft, each would be awarded a fraction of the victory on the British front, but a whole kill on the French front. This explains the sometimes wide discrepancies between squadron and individual scores. (i.e., the 95th Squadron official total is 48, but the scores of the individual 95th pilots added together total 70.) It is equally the case that historians find it difficult to agree on the true figures. While the official total of victories for the 148th is 64, in various histories the squadron is credited with 71, 66, and 63.

was the one who spoke English. We would go up and fly around with the instructor and come down. He would tell the mechanic what he wanted to tell us and the mechanic would say it to us in English. . . I think we got as much information out of talking with each other as we did out of the instructors."

Duncan got his first flight with an instructor on October 10, 1917, and graduated on February 22, 1918, with only eighteen hours flying. Then came advanced training, which began in the SIA7 until it was condemned as being too fragile, and was continued in the gigantic Caproni heavy bombers. The Capronis were among the world's earliest aircraft built with the idea of being able to attack strategic targets beyond the battlefield. The huge biplanes flown by the Americans were twin-boomed machines with wingspans of over seventy feet, powered by three engines, two pulling and one pushing. Initially the total available power was 450 hp, but in later models this increased to 600 hp. Given the weight of a fully loaded Caproni (between 8,000 and 12,000 lbs), the unreliability of its engines, and the enormous drag of its angular airframe, this was not an abundance of power. As one American pilot said:

"The principal trick to flying a Caproni was getting off the ground. You had three throttles and would start opening the two side motors little by little until the plane had good speed on the ground. Sometimes the rear motor would stop without you knowing it while you were getting the side motors open—which could of course be mighty serious if you had a load of bombs in a small field."

For all its limitations, the big Caproni was an effective first step on the road to strategic bombing. It could carry almost 2,000 lbs of bombs and had a range of nearly four hundred miles. Its crews, however, acknowledged that it was slow and not very sophisticated. It was flat out at 85 mph and the absence of any trimming controls made it an exhausting aircraft to fly. All the big Capronis were tail-heavy, and it was reported that "you had literally to jam your elbow into your stom-

Sopwith Camel
(Anglais)

The slightly humped shape of the Camel's fuselage, from which the name derived, was somewhat masked by the two Vickers .303 in machine guns mounted over the engine cowling. The machine illustrated was flown by Errol Zistel, an American flying with the RFC's 148 Squadron from Dunkirk in July 1918.

ach and hold the stick forward with one hand while you operated the ailerons with the other." The instruments were pretty basic, too. One pilot remembered that:

"The air speed indicator was a rough and ready affair consisting of what we called a 'penny on a string,' a little round disc on a spring on one of the struts outside the cockpit. When the wind was blowing on it, it was blown backwards, and when the wind wasn't so strong, it came forwards. Behind it was a plate on which were the two words 'Minima' and 'Maxima.' If you let it get below 'Minima' you stalled, and if you got above 'Maxima' the wings fell off."

From June 1918 on, American pilots were assigned to Italian squadrons where they were integrated with Italian crews to fly bombing missions against Austrian targets. Almost one hundred Americans served in the battle area and took part in sixty-five raids, mostly at night. In the course of a raid on October 27, 1918, a Caproni flown by Lts. Dewitt Coleman and James Bahl was attacked by five enemy fighters. The bomber put up a terrific fight and shot down two of its attackers before being itself destroyed. The Caproni crewmen were killed, and Coleman and Bahl were awarded respec-

tively gold and silver Medals of Valor, Italy's highest decoration for courage in combat.

It had been intended that the Caproni bomber should be acquired in large numbers for the U.S. Air Service, and if the war had lasted into 1919 it probably would have been. An agreement was reached for the aircraft to be built in the U.S. and powered by Liberty engines, but only one aircraft was completed before the end of the war brought about the cancellation of the contract. Nevertheless, small and brief though the Italian program was, it was invaluable in providing the U.S. Air Service with its first combat experience in strategic bombing.

Enter Billy Mitchell

The greater part of the U.S. air effort in WWI was necessarily concentrated in France and with the French. It had begun with the arrival in Paris of Major William Mitchell only a few days after the U.S. declaration of war. Until the arrival of the U.S. headquarters under General Pershing in June 1917, Billy Mitchell used his initiative and visited French combat units, headquarters, airfields, and supply depots. He borrowed French aircraft and flew reconnaissance flights over the battle area. The result of all this activity was a series of reports to Washington commenting on everything he saw, and including copious personal observations and recommendations. Mitchell's hand could also be seen behind the text of the cable from the French Premier to President Wilson on May 24, 1917, which suggested the scale of U.S. involvement in the air war.

One of Mitchell's visits was to the British front, where he met the commander of the RFC in France, Major General Hugh Trenchard. In later years, Trenchard was to become the first Chief of Staff of the Royal Air Force and a noted advocate for strategic air power. Mitchell was profoundly influenced by Trenchard, who held that aircraft were primarily offensive weapons, that they should be used for deep penetration and bombardment of enemy territory, and that they should be operated under unified command. These ideas took root in Mitchell's fertile mind and grew into the concepts with which he later so forcefully sought to shape the development of American air power.

During the fifteen months following the U.S. declaration of war, the Air Service of the American Expeditionary Force was first formed and then underwent a series of reorganizations as General Pershing searched for the best way to provide his army with air support. As chains of command and areas of responsibility changed, disagreements among the staff officers were frequent and often acrimonious. Pershing remarked that the Air Service was "a lot of good men running around in circles." Always prominent at the center of the turbulence was Billy Mitchell. By June 1917 he was promoted to Lieutenant Colonel and made Aviation Officer on Pershing's AEF staff. While in that appointment, he recommended that the Air Service should be composed of two distinct forces, the first for strategic operations and the second to support the ground troops. Pershing appointed a board of officers (which included Mitchell) to examine the proposal and they essentially rubber-stamped Mitchell's ideas, recommending an Air Service with a strategic force of thirty bombardment groups and thirty fighter groups, plus a second air force of a

Major Fiorello La Guardia and Count Gianni Caproni in July 1918. Caproni was a pioneer in building large, multiengined aircraft, and La Guardia, an Italian-speaking U.S. Congressman with family roots in Foggia, was the ideal choice for the job of managing the training program for the U.S. Army Air Service in Italy. American airmen flew Caproni bombers on strategic missions towards the end of WW I.

size determined by the strength of the ground forces it was to support. Pershing, an old army warhorse, was not ready for such revolutionary views and accepted only the second part of the recommendations. Later, the formation of specialized bombardment and pursuit squadrons was authorized, but a separate strategic force was never accepted, much to Mitchell's disappointment.

In the months after his initial appointment as Aviation Officer, AEF, Mitchell became successively Air Commander, Zone of Advance (front line areas), and Chief of Air Service for 1st Corps, 1st Army, and finally Army Group. In the process he rose to Brigadier General and managed to annoy most of his superiors at one time or another. After one particularly difficult period, General Foulois went so far as to write to Pershing on June 4, 1918, requesting that Mitchell "be immediately

relieved from duty as Chief of Air Service, 1st Corps, and that he be sent to the United States." Pershing recognized that Mitchell's prickly temperament made him difficult to live with, but he also knew his potential as a combat commander, so he calmed things down and imposed a truce. Faced with such aggressively independent behavior in the Air Service, senior soldiers tried to make the chain of command quite clear. General Patrick said:

"The units of the Air Service are organized as integral parts of larger [army] units. . . . They are therefore commanded in the full sense of the word by the commanding generals of these larger units. . . . There is no separate chain of tactical command in the Air Service."

That may have been the official position, but the fact is that Mitchell insisted on exercising considerable independence in his use of Air Service squadrons during the closing weeks of the war.

First Blood

Although they flew their first patrols with unarmed aircraft in March 1918, American airmen did not see combat until April 14, almost exactly a year after the U.S. entered the war. On that day, Lts. Winslow and Campbell of the 94th Squadron ("Hat in the Ring") were standing by on alert duty at Gengault aerodrome. It was a misty day with low clouds and they were not expecting anything much to happen, particularly in the relatively quiet Toul sector where the American squadrons were operating. However, at 08:45 the alarm was given and the Nieuports of Winslow and Campbell roared into the air. As they cleared the airfield, they almost ran into two German single-seaters emerging from the mist, a Pfalz D3 and an Albatros D5. Taken by surprise, both German aircraft were shot down in rapid succession within sight of the cheering men of the 94th. It was a sensational start to the American air campaign and a wonderful boost for the morale of the newcomers to the front line.

Building Combat Strength

In the weeks which followed, the American buildup gathered pace as more squadrons arrived at the front and became operational. The 94th was paired with the 95th, and these two were later joined by the 27th and 147th. As more squadrons became available, they were formed into Pursuit Groups until, by November 1918, there were four groups controlling twelve pursuit squadrons. (One of these was the 185th Night Pursuit, operating as the fifth squadron in the 1st Pursuit Group.) At the same time, others were taking their place in the line. The 1st Aero Squadron, which not so long before had been dragging its Curtiss Jennies over the unfriendly terrain of northern Mexico in search of Pancho Villa, was the first to arrive in France from the U.S. in September 1917. Under the command of Major Ralph Royce, the squadron's airmen endured a lengthy conversion to the art of battlefield observation flying obsolete Dorand AR1s and finally reached the front line in April 1918. They were not very happy to find that their op-

erational aircraft was the SPAD XI, a two-seat variant of the excellent SPAD fighters which never matched its single-seat cousins. It had an unreliable engine and was uncomfortably unstable in the air, neither of which qualities endeared it to its crews.

The problem was that the expected DH-4s from the U.S. were still months from delivery, and the American observation squadrons had to make do with the castoffs from the French and the British. Those units arriving after Ralph Royce's 1st suffered aircraft which were frankly obsolete. The 12th had to use Dorand AR1s ("Antique Rattletraps") to their

crews), and the 88th was issued French-built Sopwith 12 Strutters designed in 1915. It was helpful that the Toul sector of the front was comparatively quiet and that the German air strength facing the American squadrons there was weak. Fortunately, it was not long before the squadrons began receiving new French Salmson 2A-2s, fast and rugged two-seaters powered by a reliable 260 hp radial engine. They were well armed with two Lewis guns for the observer and a forward-firing Vickers, and they were maneuverable enough to give a crew a fighting chance against German fighters. The Office of Air

Force History's *The U.S. Air Service in World War I* later recorded: "At the altitudes at which the 91st Squadron worked (five thousand meters), the Salmson had a decided advantage over [Pfalz and Albatros scouts] both in climbing and in horizontal speeds."

As with the pursuit squadrons, the observation squadrons were formed into groups as their numbers grew, with Major Royce moving up to command the 1st Corps Observation Group on May 8, 1918. At the end of the war, there were sixteen observation squadrons in eight groups serving 1st Army and seven army

Big and boxy in appearance, the Breguet 14 B2 was a reliable workhorse bomber popular with its American crews. It had dual controls and such advanced features as aluminum tube framework and automatic flaps which extended at speeds below 70 mph. As can be seen, servicing facilities on most French airfields were rudimentary.

corps, and over seven hundred Salmson 2A-2s had been delivered to the U.S. Air Service.

The number of bombardment squadrons was much slower to build up. The 96th was the first into the fray on June 12, 1918. That they were able to get into action by then was a tribute to the ingenuity of the squadron's mechanics. Their aircraft were worn out Breguet 14-B2s which had been in use at a training school since late 1917. Spare parts were impossible to obtain. Master Sergeant James Sawyer and his men scavenged the local area for pieces of discarded farm machinery and

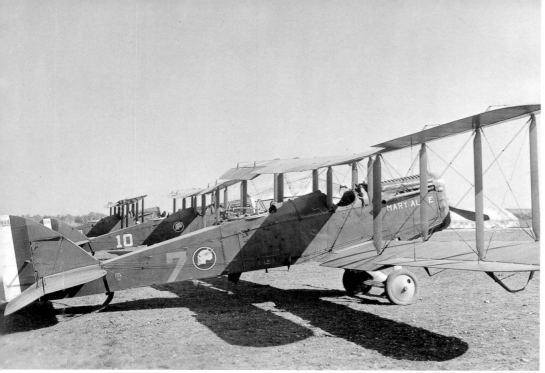

The DH-4s of the 168th Aero Squadron arrived at the front in time to take part in the Meuse-Argonne campaign at the end of September, 1918. The name Mary Alice *on the DH-4 in the foreground can also be found on a B-17G displayed at Duxford, the Imperial War Museum's airfield in the UK.*

used their imagination: "Part of a weather-beaten harvester was used for a tailpost for one of the planes; wagon tires were cut up and used for tail skids, and pieces of an ox-cart tongue were employed to reinforce wing spars. One of the planes carried brace wires which had once served on the telephone line."

The determination of the 96th to join the battle and their valiant efforts to fight on with dilapidated equipment were brought to a temporary halt by one of the most embarrassing episodes of the American campaign. On July 10, 1918, the squadron's "press-on" spirit was much in evidence as the commander led his six available Breguets on a late evening raid against German railway yards. Flying conditions were poor, with heavy clouds, and an unexpectedly strong wind blew the aircraft deep into Germany. After a fruitless search for a break in the weather, the squadron commander turned for home and eventually let down through the clouds. With their fuel almost exhausted, the six Breguets landed successfully, only to find themselves in Germany. All the American airmen were captured, and their aircraft

were taken intact. In one stroke, the only operational bombardment force had been lost. The Germans were quick to send Air Service HQ a message: "We thank you for the fine airplanes and equipment you sent us, but what will we do with the Major?" Billy Mitchell was furious. He wrote in his diary: "I know of no other performance in any air force in the war that was as reprehensible as this. Needless to say, we did not reply about the major, as he was better off in Germany than he would have been with us."

By August, new Breguet bombers were being delivered to the 96th, and September saw the arrival of more bombardment squadrons equipped at last with Liberty-engined DH-4s. The Breguet was almost universally popular with American aircrews, but the Liberty DH-4 got mixed reviews. Opinions varied widely, but in general it is true to say that the bomber crews disliked the DH-4 more than their counterparts in the observation squadrons. When loaded with bombs, the DH-4 became sluggish; its top speed was reduced and it did not climb well. Other criticisms were aimed at the length of fuselage between the pilot and observer, which made communication difficult, and the unprotected fuel tanks which occupied that space between the cockpits. Some aircrew referred to the DH-4 as "two wings on a hearse" or "the flaming coffin" because it was thought to be more susceptible than other aircraft to bursting into flames when hit by enemy fire. Observation squadrons were not always so critical. The commander of the 50th Squadron, Captain Daniel Morse, admitted that his airmen would have liked to have had protected fuel tanks, armored seats, and better pilot visibility, but he went on to conclude that: "The Liberty plane was considered the best on the front, and its excellent speed and combat power were well demonstrated in actual combat with enemy planes. . . . The Liberty, at low altitude, could outdistance and outclimb any plane the Germans had."

Serious Opposition

The period in which the American squadrons were allowed to become accli-

The American pilot Emil Zadmais seen with his Nieuport 28 in 1918.

mated to the battle area in the relatively quiet sector of Toul came to an end in the summer of 1918. On June 29, the 1st Pursuit and 1st Observation Groups moved to airfields near Chateau-Thierry, on the River Marne east of Paris. These groups, together with some French squadrons, were formed into the 1st Air Brigade under Mitchell, and positioned to help in countering German thrusts along the Aisne and Marne Rivers. As they soon found out, the opposition in their new area of responsibility was far more severe than anything they had experienced so far. The Germans had concentrated forty-six of their seventy-eight squadrons on the Western Front in this sector, and that included all three of the celebrated "Flying Circuses." It was later estimated that the inexperienced American squadrons, still equipped at first with outdated aircraft, were outnumbered four to one by German Jagdstaffeln, which were primarily battle-hardened units.

As the American squadrons moved to Chateau-Thierry, the Chief of Air Service issued a memorandum which recognized the need for young pilots to be able to keep track of their leader in the maelstrom of a dogfight, or even in the excitement of their first patrols, in the presence of the enemy or not. The memorandum established a system of marking a leader's aircraft so that it could be easily identified. There were to be streamers on the wingtips and rudder, and red, white, and blue diagonal bands behind the cockpit. It was also directed that units could mark their aircraft with distinctive badges, but only after they had proved themselves under fire. Several squadrons already met the combat requirement, and their aircraft soon wore their emblems—among them the 94th's "Hat-in-the-Ring," the 95th's "Kicking Mule," and the 103d's "Indian Head."

During the month of July, the German Army's offensive was first stopped and then driven back in a series of bloody battles which presaged Germany's final defeat. Although the Allies were successful, the Germans had generally held the advantage in the air. American casualties

mounted as their small formations were often overwhelmed by masses of enemy fighters. Even so, they usually gave as good as they got. By the time the Aisne-Marne campaign had run its course, the 1st Pursuit Group had lost thirty-six pilots and the 1st Observation Group eleven aircrew. Thirty-eight enemy aircraft were claimed destroyed. The unsung members of the Air Service balloon companies had gone through their baptism of fire, too. Eight balloons were lost to enemy aircraft and twelve observers were forced to use their parachutes.

just as eager and unknowing as the founding members had been such a short time before. The concern of squadron commanders at the brash confidence of the young newcomers could be heard in the "welcoming" remarks given to nine of them by Major Harold Hartney of the 27th Squadron. Among other things, he said:

"You are going to be surprised in the first, second, or third trip over the line and, despite all I can say right now, you will never know there is an enemy ship near you until you notice your windshield disintegrating or until a sharp sting interrupts

Captive balloons were used by both sides in WW I to direct artillery fire and monitor enemy movements. Tethered two to five miles behind the front, they reached heights of up to 5,000 ft. Being a balloon observer could be a hazardous business. In 1918, the U.S. Army Air Service lost 48 observation balloons to enemy attack. Unlike their counterparts in Allied aircraft, the observers routinely carried parachutes to allow the possibility of escape from beneath burning balloons.

In comparison with the appalling casualties suffered by the ground forces, the airmen may seem to have gotten off lightly, but there was no doubt that the losses were deeply felt by the squadrons, small groups of men with close personal relationships. Within weeks most of the original faces had gone, to be replaced by others fresh from the flying schools and

your breathing."

Hartney's prophetic warning was made fact on August 1 when the 27th lost six aircraft in one whirling dogfight with four Fokker Jagdstaffeln and a number of two-seat Rumplers and Hanoveraners.[6] In

---

[6]One of the Americans missing in the fight was Lt. Charles McElvain, who experienced a little of the chivalry which was still in evidence even at this late stage of the air war. He was unable to disengage from a lengthy duel with Lt. Alfred Fleischer of Jasta 17 and ran out of fuel. As he glided down with his engine dead, Fleischer held his fire and landed close by. Their meeting led to a close friendship, and eventually to Fleischer's son becoming an American citizen working in McElvain's company.

Billy Mitchell with staff officers in the latter stages of WW I. Once appointed Chief of the U.S. Army Air Service in France, Mitchell sought to use air power in overwhelming strength at selected points, rather than spreading his forces thinly along the front. The air offensives launched under his command made decisive contributions to the success of the Allied ground forces as the war entered its final phase.

the same fight, Lt. Donald Hudson experienced the full bedlam and blazing intensity of air combat. In just a few minutes of confusing action in a sky full of airplanes, he escaped an attack by four Fokkers, had a near collision with a stricken SPAD, spun and recovered three times, dealt with a boiling engine, and shot down a Fokker and two Rumplers.

Mitchell in Command

As the local air commander, Billy Mitchell grasped the opportunity to make his mark. At an early stage of the campaign, on July 15, 1918, with the Allies uncertain of where the German blow would fall, Mitchell borrowed a SPAD and set off on a lone dawn reconnaissance. The clouds were as low as 300 ft and he followed the River Marne, flying between its steep banks. As he rounded a turn in the river

near the town of Dormans, he came upon five pontoon bridges carrying masses of German troops. The point of the German assault was now clear. The bridges were subjected to continuous air attack and the Allied armies were forewarned. Later in the day, Mitchell made a decision which had a significant effect on the battle. He shifted the weight of air attack from the bridges to the enemy supply base behind the front, with the aim of both destroying essential supplies and forcing the German air forces onto the defensive to protect their stockpile. The plan worked, and Mitchell afterwards commented that it was, "the first case on record where we, with an inferior air force, were able to put the superior air force on the defensive and attack whenever we pleased, without the danger of the Germans sending great masses of pursuit aviation over to our side of the line."

With the blunting of the German assault, the initiative passed to the Allies and preparations began for a major offensive involving American forces. General Pershing was given the job of removing the St. Mihiel salient to shorten the front line in readiness for a subsequent general Allied offensive. Mitchell was appointed Chief of Air Service, First Army, and successfully argued for the assembly of the greatest concentration of air power ever in a single operation. General Hap Arnold later said that "The air offensive which Mitchell laid on in September 1918 was the greatest thing of its kind seen in the war. . . . the first massed air striking power ever seen." Units of the American, French, British, and Italian air forces were gathered on fourteen airfields, bringing together a total of 1,481 aircraft—701 fighters, 366 observation aircraft, 323 day bombers, and 91 night bombers. Facing them on the other side of the line, it was estimated that the Germans had between 200 and 300 aircraft of all types. The air superiority boot was on the other foot.

Mitchell planned to use his massive air force to overwhelm the opposition. One-third of the force would be dedicated to ground support, and the remaining two-thirds would be split to attack installations, communications, and troop columns be-

In the closing months of WW1, Brig. Gen. Billy Mitchell often used a SPAD XVI as his observation and command aircraft. This aircraft is now on display at the USAF Museum.

hind the lines, as well as the flanks of the St. Mihiel salient. Besides seeking to defeat the German air force, Mitchell was intent on using his fighters for "attacking his troops on the ground, and protecting our own air and ground troops." This commitment was something new in warfare. Fighters had been used before in attacking ground targets, but mostly in random fashion and not in large numbers. This time the air force was to intervene in the ground war in a big way.

The attack was launched on September 12, 1918, in foul weather with low clouds and driving rain. Major Hartney, now commander of the 1st Pursuit Group, noted the conditions and drew attention to the change in policy:

"The weather was atrocious—pouring rain, with low-hanging clouds. This, however, was perfect for part of our plan— low flying. The pilots certainly flew low that day—they could not do otherwise— and the success of this new system (low altitude strafing and bombing attacks on troop convoys and trenches) pointed the way we followed until the end of hostilities. And by low I mean low. The clouds at times formed a solid mist at 100 ft and everything had to be done below that. This low flying by an entire group was a revolution in war-time flying."

Pilots were now exposed to some of the horrors of the ground war in a very real way. Eddie Rickenbacker was among those who described the carnage which resulted when a single-seat fighter attacked a column of troops:

"Dipping down at the head of the column I sprinkled a few bullets over the leading teams. Horses fell right and left. One driver leaped from his seat and started running for the ditch. Half-way across the road he threw up his arms and rolled over on his face. . . . All down the line we continued our fire—now tilting our aeroplanes down for a short burst, then zooming back up for a little altitude in which to repeat the performance. The whole column was thrown into the wildest confusion. Horses plunged and broke away. Some were killed and fell in their tracks."

Lt. Walter Case's account was equally graphic:

"At one time we flew over a small town where there were, to my judgement, about 3,000 troops. . . . I fired on the troops in the street which caused utter confusion, a great many of them trying to enter one door at once. I concentrated my fire on that door, killing and wounding many of them, I am sure, for I could see them fall."

The poor conditions persisted and necessarily limited air activity somewhat for the first two days, but the efforts made by Mitchell's command contributed significantly to the success of the whole operation. Losses were high on both sides,[7] but the Germans were kept on the defensive by the aggressiveness of the Allied air forces, and most of the action took place on the German side of the front. During the four days of the Allied armies' assault, American airmen flew 3,300 combat sorties, fired 30,000 rounds of ammunition,

and dropped over 75 tons of explosives. General Pershing was suitably appreciative. In a letter of congratulation to Mitchell he commented:

"The organization and control of the tremendous concentration of air forces. . . which has enabled the 1st Army to carry out its dangerous and important mission is as fine a tribute to you personally as is the courage and nerve shown by your officers, a signal proof of the high morale which permeates the service under your command."

The final act of WWI began on September 26, 1918, with the start of the Meuse-Argonne offensive. American

Nieuport pursuit aircraft were aesthetically pleasing to look at, but they had some worrying structural problems. High speed dives could strip fabric from the upper wing or might even induce a Nieuport to shed a wing altogether. Airframe riggers are here doing some much-needed re-skinning of one such overstressed Nieuport 28.

troops were given the task of penetrating several defensive lines lying across the broad valley between the heights of the Argonne forest to the west and the bluffs of the Meuse River to the east. Both areas of high ground were studded with German guns, and the defensive lines took advantage of rugged features in the valley. Pershing's hopes for a rapid advance and breakout were not realized, and the American army, which rose to more than 1 million men, was forced to grind its way forward in the face of determined resistance.

---

[7] The American bombardment squadrons were particularly hard hit. On one raid, the 11th Squadron launched seventeen DH4s. One crashed shortly after getting airborne and ten failed to reach the primary target. Of the six which bombed the primary, only one survived. The ten officer casualties included the squadron commander, two flight commanders, and the lead observer. The squadron was withdrawn from operations to replenish its strength. Also driven from the battle was the bedeviled 96th, still flying its Breguets. The 96th lost sixteen officers and fourteen aircraft in five days to record the highest AEF loss rate of the war.

On October 2, men of the 308th Infantry Regiment broke through the German line only to be surrounded and pinned down by heavy fire in a deep ravine. Their exact position was unknown, and the 50th Aero Squadron was asked to find what the press was calling "The Lost Battalion." In atrocious weather, several crews took their DH4s through the area at low level without success, and by October 6, the soldiers' plight was desperate. On that morning, Lts. Goettler and Bleckley flew through a number of ravines so low that German gunners were firing down on them. There were more than forty holes in their DH-4 when they landed. Later in the day, they

to walk out.[8] Lts. Harold Goettler and Erwin Bleckley were both awarded the Medal of Honor.

Billy Mitchell, promoted to Brigadier General during the campaign, continued to trust the tactical principles which had succeeded at St. Mihiel. This time, however, his relative superiority in numbers was not so great. On September 26, he had more than 800 aircraft at his disposal, about three-quarters of which were available for operations. The Germans began the battle with some 300 aircraft but, as the offensive progressed, German air strength was reinforced, and by early November the ratio had closed to 700 against

shoot down observation balloons.

"Aces" Extraordinary

Attacking balloons was a dangerous business. They were heavily guarded by antiaircraft guns and fighters, and there was a gauntlet of fire from the infantry to run as well. The most celebrated of those who were consistently successful in this hazardous art was Frank Luke. Between September 12 and 29, Luke, flying a SPAD XIII of the 27th Squadron, shot down the incredible total of fourteen balloons and four aircraft. His meteoric and often undisciplined career ended on the evening of September 29 when he subjected the Germans on the front near Verdun to a lone assault worthy of a Wagnerian epic. As the sun was setting, he flew over the American 7th Balloon Company and dropped a note which warned them to "Watch for burning balloons." The first German balloon fell in flames at 7:05 p.m. and was rapidly followed by another. Luke was momentarily diverted by harassing Fokkers and disposed of two of them before claiming his third balloon. At some point he was hit by ground fire and seriously wounded, but he turned to strafe German troops before crash-landing his SPAD. Once on the ground, he dragged himself from the cockpit and died nearby, pistol in hand. Frank Luke was posthumously awarded the Medal of Honor.

In the early days of his meteoric career, Frank Luke flew the Nieuport 28. He is seen here leading in a flight after a balloon-busting mission.

volunteered to try again, aiming to draw enemy fire and so home in on where the battalion might be. They repeatedly flew at treetop level through the most likely ravine and were raked with gunfire again and again. Already dying, Goettler lifted the shattered DH-4 out of the ravine and crash-landed in front of some French positions. He was dead when the French reached them and Bleckley was dying. Bleckley's mission notes were intact and the search for the "Lost Battalion" was narrowed to a small area. A rescuing U.S. force reached them the next day. Of the 554 men who had entered the ravine, 194 were able

500. Whatever the circumstances, Mitchell steadfastly refused to compromise. He would not spread his forces thinly in an attempt to cover the whole area, but wherever possible operated strong formations and maintained attacks on the German rear areas. He did agree to offer protection to the forward American troops by flying patrols of five aircraft assigned to six-mile fronts. These patrols were flown at low level by the 1st Pursuit Group and had the responsibility of breaking up any German formations attacking American soldiers, while at the same time taking every opportunity to strafe German troops and

Another prominent figure to feature in the war's closing battles was Eddie Rickenbacker. He had six victories in the Toul sector before a severe ear infection grounded him for much of June, July, and August. He returned to action with the 94th in mid-September and was made squadron commander a few days later. Older than most fighter pilots, at twenty-eight he was a mature and thoughtful leader, much respected by his men. In the air, he was nerveless and calculating, taking time to maneuver the tactical situation in his favor rather than rushing headlong into combat. Like all the great aces, he believed in getting in close to his enemy, firing one solid burst, and then breaking away, ever watchful for the surprise attack from behind.[9]

---

[8]It was during this rescuing drive that then Corporal Alvin York singlehandedly defeated a German battalion, killing many of them and bringing in 132 prisoners and 35 machine guns. He was subsequently awarded the Medal of Honor.

[9]After WW II, the Luftwaffe's "Bubi" Hartmann (the supreme "Ace of Aces", with 352 aerial victories) said he regarded dogfighting as a waste of time. He, too, took care to get the tactical situation clearly in his favor before committing himself to an attack, and he usually opened fire from 100 yards or less. It was his opinion that 90 percent of those he shot down never even saw him.

At the opening of the Meuse-Argonne offensive, Rickenbacker's personal score had risen to ten enemy aircraft, and on his first day as squadron commander he gave a demonstration of his skill. He set off on a "hunting" expedition over the front and was rewarded by sighting two LVG observation aircraft escorted by five Fokkers. Placing himself above them and into the sun, he dived onto the last Fokker and dispatched it with one burst. The rest of the escorts broke up in confusion, and Rickenbacker kept his dive going for the LVGs. After exchanging spirited fire with the rear gunners and avoiding the attempt of one LVG to get behind him, he slipped out to one side of the pair and ruddered his SPAD so that the nearer LVG flew through his line of fire. As Rickenbacker himself so colorfully described it: "It burst into flames and tumbled like a great blazing torch to earth, leaving a streamer of black smoke against the blue sky." He went on to take his score of kills to a total of 26 (22 aircraft and 4 balloons) to become America's leading ace of WWI. In 1931, Rickenbacker's exploits were finally recognized formally, and he belatedly became the fourth airman to be awarded the Medal of Honor.

Although Rickenbacker achieved his early kills flying Nieuports, both he and Luke were particularly associated with the SPAD XIII. Heavier and not nearly so maneuverable as the Nieuport, nor its formidable adversaries the Fokker Dr1 and DVII, the SPAD had other signal advantages. It was powerful and so robustly built that the strains of combat flying were never a cause for concern. The sturdy airframe was a rock steady gun platform, but the controls were light and rate of roll was excellent. It climbed well and could reach over 20,000 ft, but above all, it was fast, capable of over 130 mph in level flight, and it could outdive any of its contempo-

The 91st Aero Squadron used the Salmson 2A-2 for observation duties. Powered by a 260 hp water-cooled radial, it was reliable and relatively fast, and had an advantage over most German pursuit aircraft at its usual operating altitudes above 10,000 ft.

raries. In short, it was a fighter which suited Rickenbacker's style of aerial combat perfectly. It is hardly to be wondered that he described it as "more impressive than any other airplane, any automobile, any other piece of equipment I had ever seen. . . . [It was] the ultimate aircraft in the war in which aviation developed."

Armistice and Aftermath

It was perhaps appropriate that the 94th Squadron, having led the American Air Service into combat, should bring the

fighting to a close with the last American aerial victory of WWI. On November 10, 1918, Major Maxwell Kirby in a SPAD of the 94th shot down an unsuspecting Fokker near the village of Maucourt. The guns fell silent on the following day.

In seven months of combat, American airmen claimed 781 enemy aircraft destroyed, plus 73 balloons.[10] They had taken part in over 150 bombing raids and dropped more than a quarter of a million pounds of bombs. The U.S. lost 289 American Air Service aircraft and 48 bal-

The CO of the 103rd Pursuit Squadron was Bobby Soubiran, seen here with his personal SPAD XIII.

[10]The question of claimed victories has always been a vexed one. Apart from the practice of allowing each airman a victory even when a single enemy was attacked and shot down by more than one American flier, it has been shown in every air war that claims usually outnumber actual kills by at least two to one. Accurate German records from WW I are not available, but it is reasonable to suppose that Allied victory claims are similarly inflated. On the other hand, the claims of leading aces like Rickenbacker and Luke are well documented and can be assumed to be close to accurate.

loons in the struggle. There were 569 battle casualties (164 killed, 200 missing, 103 wounded, 102 captured). In considering these figures, it is interesting to note that another 319 American airmen were killed in accidents, and 335 died of other causes, such as influenza. It is also beyond doubt that many of the men killed in action could have been saved if parachutes had been issued. However, although these live-savers were being used by balloon observers and, in the latter stages of the war, by German airmen, Allied aviators irrationally spurned parachutes apparently on the grounds that they were an implied insult to their courage and skill.

Whenever they were given the chance, American airmen fought well in WWI. Their disappointment was that they were never able to fulfill the promises made in the euphoric days following the U.S. declaration of war in 1917. As 1918 drew to its close, American manpower was flooding forward and the great wheels of U.S. industry were finally shifting into top gear. If the war had lasted into 1919, the American Air Service might have provided the legions of aircraft predicted at the outset, including several squadrons of strategic bombers intended for deep strikes against targets in Germany. Such overwhelming air power might then have become a decisive factor in the struggle, but what might have been necessarily takes second place to what was.

As things stood on November 11, 1918, it could not be said that air power had played a decisive part in the victory. However, it was apparent to many strategists that aircraft had permanently changed the face of war, and that a defining principle was emerging. In effect, the experiences of 1918 suggested that, even if air power could not of itself procure victory, its absence could ensure defeat. The most reactionary of army commanders was beginning to see that the achievement of air superiority over the battlefield was essential to success. At the strategic level, the evidence was thin, but there was enough to offer support to the revolutionary idea that air forces could leap over armies and navies, attack the enemy's heartland, and

bring about national collapse without incurring the awful carnage resulting from the clash of ground forces. In such thoughts were laid the foundations of the air power debate which raged between the wars.

WWI had roused American air power from its slumber. It was inevitable that with the coming of peace the U.S. Air Service would feel the pain of contraction as the great American military machine went into reverse, and airmen like

and there were some who were already charting a course towards an independent air force. The war had been won—the lengthier challenges of peace now had to be faced.

The Liberty DH-4 got mixed reviews from its crews. Many bomber crews thought it sluggish and vulnerable when fully loaded. Observation crews were kinder, some even claiming that it was the best aircraft at the front. Here pilot Ray Krout shows that the DH-4 could be exuberant, while his observer, Hunter MacDonald, lounges casually in the rear cockpit.

Billy Mitchell might secretly regret that the fighting had stopped before the U.S. could "darken the skies," but the genie of air power was out of its bottle and could not be replaced. Many future leaders of U.S. military aviation—Mitchell and Spaatz among them—had been in aerial combat and had strong views on how U.S. air power should develop. The U.S. aviation industry had been jerked out of its lethargy and forced to think about matching the Europeans. Perhaps even more significantly, American airmen generally had begun to develop pride in their service and to nurture the roots of an air force tradition. They had proved themselves in battle

Old Number One © *Keith Ferris, 1992*

A   The bare essentials of the SE-5A, a typical WW I scout. (Compare the simple wire-braced, box-girder wooden construction and the empty spaces of the fuselage with the cutaway of the F-86 Sabre shown at the end of Chapter 6.)

A

B   The internal structure of the Curtiss "Jenny" revealed. Wood and wires predominate, surrounding simple bucket seats.

C   The solution to the problem of cooling early aircraft engines was to keep the crankshaft still and spin the finned cylinders round it. The Le Rhone rotary weighed 308 lbs and gave 110 hp. The torque of the whirling engine helped a very small aircraft like the Sopwith Camel turn to the right very quickly.

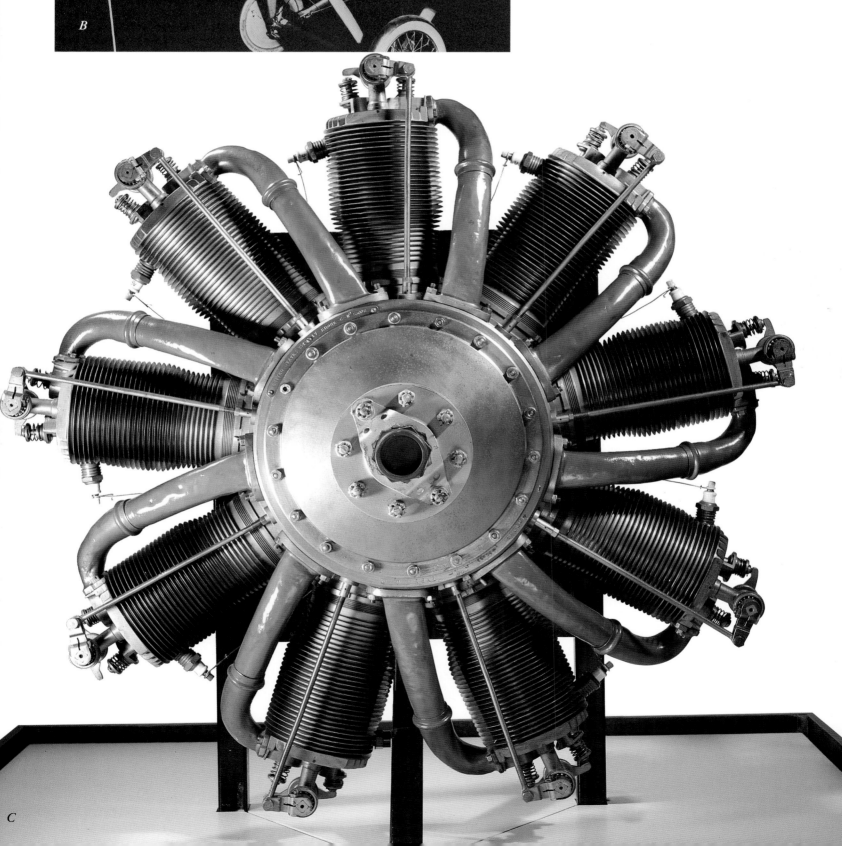

C

A   The USAF Museum has a number of items which recall the days when montage American airmen flew with the French Air Service in WW I as members of the Lafayette Escadrille. Shown here are Robert Rockwell's jacket, William Thaw's helmet and pocket altimeter, Thomas Hitchcock's service cap and logbook, and a pilot's badge of the French Air Service.

B   The SPAD VIIs of the Lafayette Escadrille lined up near their hangar in 1916. The Americans were still flying the SPAD VII when the unit was transferred to the U.S. Army Air Service in February 1918, but soon moved on to the larger and more powerful SPAD XIII.

C   Norman Prince, a founding member of the Lafayette Escadrille and a five-victory ace, seen here in the unusual Voisin "Avion Canon" fitted with a huge 47 mm cannon. The effect on so slow and apparently fragile a biplane of firing such a weapon can only be imagined.

D   The Nieuport 28 was the first scout flown in combat by American pilots in WW I, and was also the aircraft used by Lts. Winslow and Campbell of the 94th Squadron in scoring the first American Air Service victories on April 14, 1918. It was no match for the Fokker D VII, however, and had an unfortunate tendency to shed wing fabric at high speeds.

D

A

B

A   Going Home For Breakfast
© *Keith Ferris, 1975*

B   *A Halberstadt CL IV hovers above the Nieuport 28's wing tip. Halberstadts were fitted with both fixed and movable machine guns, and carried small bombs. They were intended for use principally against ground troops. This one is in the markings of Schlachstaffel 21's squadron leader at the time of the Chateau-Thierry campaign in July 1918.*

C   *Standard armament for the Nieuport 28 was two Vickers .303 in machine guns, offset to the left, firing through the propeller.*

D   *To keep the weight as low as possible, the pilot's seat in the Nieuport and other scouts was made of basketwork.*

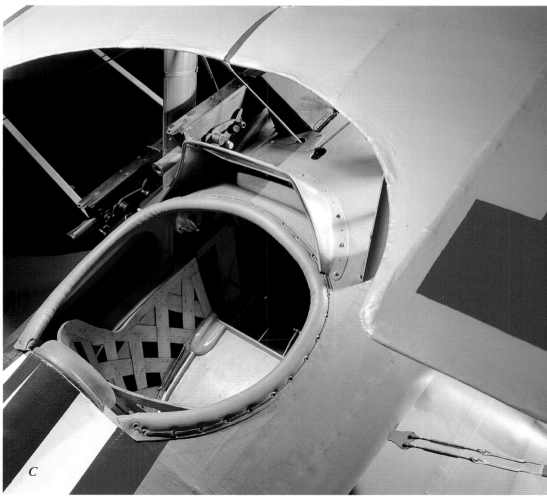

61

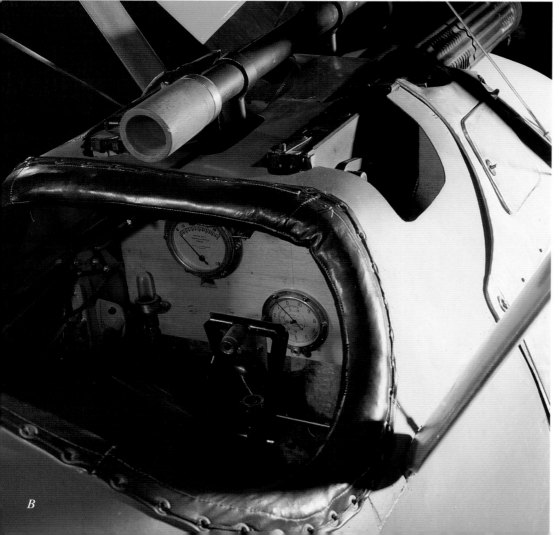

A   Just Airborne, At Sea
© *Keith Ferris, 1980*

B   *The Camel's instrumentation was not complex. (Compare fighter cockpits illustrated at the end of Chapters 7 and 8.)*

C   *Two Vickers .303 in machine guns mounted close together and synchronized to fire through the propeller helped to make the extremely maneuverable Camel WW I's deadliest combat aircraft.*

A

B

A   The most famous of all Germany's WW I fighters, the Fokker D VII was often painted in exotic color schemes. This lavender finish was favored by Lt. Rudolph Stark of Jaste 35b in October 1918.

B   The Fokker D VII had a good all-round performance and was a delightfully sensitive aircraft to fly. Its often flamboyant appearance reflected the confidence felt by its pilots, and it proved a formidable opponent for the Allies in the closing months of WW I.

C   The D VII's blunt nose hid either a 160 hp Mercedes or 185 hp BMW 6-cylinder liquid-cooled engine.

D   The cockpit of the D VII was typically uncluttered, and the two Spandau machine guns were close at hand.

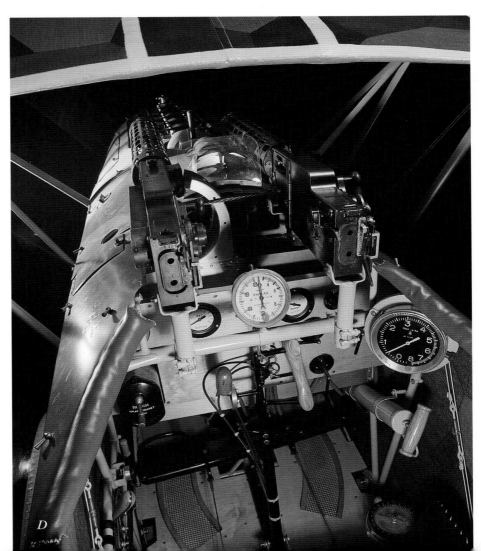

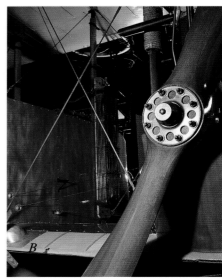

A   Two pilots sat side by side in the open cockpit nose of the bombers developed by Caproni from 1914 onwards. A gunner was exposed to the elements even further forward with a single Revelli machine gun.

B   The Caproni Ca.36 was powered by three 6-cylinder, 150 hp Isotta-Fraschini engines, two pulling and one pushing from its mount between the aircraft's twin booms.

C   The Caproni Ca.36 was a variant of the Ca.33 fitted with five-section wings for easy disassembly. The Caproni bombers were very stable and pleasant to fly, but could not be described as lively performers, the maximium speed being less than 90 mph. They carried a useful bombload of nearly 2,000 lbs and had a range of almost 400 miles.

D   Caproni Ca.3 © Bill Marsalko, 1989
Air Force Art Collection

A

C

D

A   The favored fighter of the American Air Service, the SPAD XIII, was fast and had an excellent rate of climb. The USAF Museum's example is finished in the 1921 colors of the 95th Pursuit Squadron.

B   Hauled along by a 220 hp Hispano Suiza, the SPAD XIII would do 135 mph.

C   The SPAD XIII's powerful rudder once allowed Eddie Rickenbacker to bring his guns to bear from almost alongside an enemy.

D   Still simple, the SPAD XIII's cockpit was nevertheless more complex than its predecessors. The pilot's field of vision could not have been helped by the framing of the small windscreen.

E   Eddie Rickenbacker peers intensely over the twin Vickers machine guns of his SPAD XIII.

F   The USAF Museum's display covering Eddie Rickenbacker includes his Sam Browne belt, watch, war diary, and Medal of Honor, set against a WW I airman's uniform jacket.

Medal of Honor and lapel rosette

The Mackay Trophy

Established before World War I by Clarence H. Mackay, publisher of *Collier's* magazine and aviation enthusiast, the Mackay Trophy is presented annually by the National Aeronautic Association in recognition of the most meritorious U.S Air Force flight of the year.

1912	2nd Lt. Henry H. Arnold. First successful aerial reconnaissance of U.S. Army maneuvers, Wright biplane.
1913	2nd Lt. Joseph E. Carberry and 2nd Lt. Fred Seydel. Reconnaissance exercises, Curtiss biplane.
1914	Capt. Townsend F. Dodd and Lt. Shapler W. Fitzgerald. Reconnaissance exercises.
1915	Lt. B.W. Jones. First U.S. Army officer to loop an aircraft.
1916-17	Not awarded.
1918	Lt. Edward V. Rickenbacker. U.S. "Ace of Aces," Spad.
1919	Lt. Belvin W. Maynard, Lt. Alexander Pearson, Jr., Lt. R.S. Worthington, Capt. John O. Donaldson, Capt. Lowell H. Smith, Lt. Harold E. Hartney, Lt. E.H. Manzelman, Lt. R.G. Bagby, Lt. D.B. Gish, Capt. F. Steinle. Performance in Gen. Mitchell's transcontinental endurance and reliability test.
1920	Capt. St.Clair Streett, Capt. Howard T. Douglas, 1st Lt. Clifford C. Nutt, 2nd Lt. Erik H. Nelson, 2nd Lt. C.H. Crumrine, 2nd Lt. Ross C. Kirkpatrick, Sgt. Edmond Henriques, Sgt. Albert T. Vierra, Sgt. Joseph E. English. Alaskan flight, DH-4s.
1921	Lt. John A. Macready. World altitude record of 34,509 ft, LePere biplane.
1922	Lt. John A. Macready, Lt. Oakley G. Kelly. World endurance record of 35 hrs 18 mins 30 secs, Fokker T-2.
1923	Lt. John A. Macready, Lt. Oakley G. Kelly. First nonstop transcontinental flight (Roosevelt Field, NY, to Rockwell Field, CA), 26 hrs 50 mins, Fokker T-2.
1924	Capt. Lowell H. Smith, 1st Lt. Leigh Wade, 1st Lt. Leslie P. Arnold, 1st Lt. Erik H. Nelson, 2nd Lt. John Harding, Jr., 2nd Lt. Henry H. Ogden. First flight around the world, Douglas World Cruisers.
1925	Lt. Cyrus Bettis, Lt. James H. Doolittle. Winners of the Pulitzer and Schneider Trophy races.
1926	Maj. Herbert A. Dargue, Capt. Ira C. Eaker, Capt. Arthur B. McDaniel, Capt. C.F. Wolsey, 1st Lt. J.W. Benton, 1st Lt. Charles McRobinson, 1st Lt. Muir S. Fairchild, 1st Lt. Bernard S. Thompson, 1st Lt. Leonard D. Weddington, 1st Lt. Ennis C. Whitehead. Pan-American goodwill flight, Loening OA-1A amphibians.
1927	Lt. Albert F. Hegenberger, Lt. Lester J. Maitland. First flight from California to Hawaii, Fokker C-2.
1928	1st Lt. Harry A. Sutton. Research into the spinning characteristics of aircraft.
1929	Capt. Albert W. Stevens. High-altitude photography.
1930	Maj. Ralph Royce. 1st Pursuit Group's midwinter cross-country flight from Selfridge, MI, to Spokane, WA.
1931	Maj. Gen. Benjamin D. Foulois. Leadership of the 1st Air Division.
1932	1st Lt. Charles H. Howard. Testing of cosmic rays at various altitudes, 11th Bomb Squadron, Condors.
1933	Capt. Westside T. Larson. Contributions to aerial defense; blind landings and takeoffs.
1934	Lt. Col. H.H. Arnold. Flight from Washington, DC, to Fairbanks, AK, Martin B-10s.
1935	Maj. Albert W. Stevens, Capt. Orville Anderson. World record balloon ascent to 72,395 ft.
1936	Capt. Richard E. Nugent, 1st Lt. Joseph A. Miller, 1st Lt. Edwing G. Simenson, 2nd Lt. William P. Ragsdale, Jr., 2nd Lt. Burton W. Armstrong, 2nd Lt. Herbert Morgan, Jr., T. Sgt. Gilbert W. Olsen, S. Sgt. Howard M. Miller, Corpsman Frank B. Conner. Bad weather bombing exercise, Martin bombers.
1937	Capt. Carl J. Crane, Capt. George V. Holloman. First fully automatic landing, Wright Field, August 23, 1937, Fokker C-14B.
1938	2nd Bombardment Group. Goodwill flight to Buenos Aires, Argentina, February 15-27, 1938.
1939	Maj. Caleb V. Haynes, Maj. William D. Old, Capt. John A. Samford, Capt. Richard S. Freeman, 1st Lt. Torgils G. Wold, M. Sgt. Adolph Cattarius, T. Sgt. Henry L. Hines, T. Sgt. William J. Heldt, T. Sgt. David L. Spicer, S. Sgt. Russell E. Junior, S. Sgt. James E. Sands. Earthquake relief mission to Chile, B-15.
1940-46	Not awarded.

Chapter 4

The 1920s-Debate and Derring-Do

"People have become so used to saying that Billy Mitchell was years ahead of his time, that they sometimes forget that it is true."

(General "Hap" Arnold, after Mitchell's death)

"The most necessary thing now is to educate the people as to what may be expected in aeronautics and how it affects the well-being of every citizen of this country."

(Brigadier General Billy Mitchell, 1919)

"Pilots will not wear spurs while flying."

(U.S. Air Service regulation, 1920)

"We wouldn't do it again for a million dollars—unless we were ordered to."

(Lt. Lowell H. Smith, after completing the first global flight, September 23, 1925)

"The insatiate United States Army won the race for the world's premier seaplane trophy, the Schneider Cup, on Chesapeake Bay. . . . it must have been a grievous sight to sailors when Lt. James H. Doolittle, U.S. Army, putting pontoons on his landplane, romped away with the cup."

(*New York Times*, October 27, 1925)

Brigadier General William Mitchell (1879-1936). Returning from WW I covered in glory, Billy Mitchell was thought by many (including himself) to be the ideal man for appointment as Chief of Air Service. The officers of the General Staff were not so sure they were ready for such an unquiet spirit in the post, and he had to be content with being Deputy Chief. Disappointment did not keep him quiet, however. He became "the gadfly of the General Staff and the hero of the Army's flyers," never ceasing to promote his ideas on the primacy of air power.

Higher, Faster, Farther

WWI is left behind and USAF Museum visitors move towards the promises of peace, but they are first reminded that war has its aftereffects. Wall displays tell of the Americans who could not go home once the armistice was signed, and of some who went on fighting. Photographs show that U.S. forces were needed for occupation duties in Germany, and that, in a remarkable recapitulation of the Lafayette Escadrille experience, American pilots formed the Kosciuszko Squadron and fought for Poland against the Bolsheviks.

The atmosphere created by the Museum's 1920s collection is one which suggests a period of continuous struggle and achievement. The Air Service was seeking to build on the lessons of WWI while overcoming the peacetime problem of having its manpower and funds drastically reduced. Money for new equipment was scarce and most of the aircraft on display in the Museum from the 1920s reflect their WWI ancestry. Although it had made its mark in combat and had begun to change the face of war, military aviation was still a minor element of the U.S. armed forces and some exhibits recall the fury of the arguments over its role in future conflicts, particularly the fight led by Billy Mitchell to gain pride of place for air power.

As they bent their efforts to the creation of an effective air force, leading U.S. airmen recognized the importance of making as much progress as possible through research and development, and of keeping the Air Service in public view by means of eye-catching achievements. Some of the fruits of invention from the laboratories at Dayton's McCook and Wright Fields can be seen in the Museum, among them the McCook wind tunnel, a 37 mm cannon which could be dangerous to the user, parachutes, landing lights, propellers, instruments, gyro controls, retractable landing gear, and the Wright Field research records.

The public face of the Air Service is here on show everywhere. In the 1920s, American aviators were pushing hard at the frontiers of flight, and military airmen were often in the vanguard. Around the Museum walls are stories of men who dedicated themselves to climbing higher, staying airborne longer, traveling farther, and flying faster than had been recorded before. Tales are told of many who reached their goal only through feats of remarkable endurance or while suffering severe hardship. Others tell of those who died in the attempt. Great names are here—Doolittle, Bettis, Harris, Macready, Schroeder, Spaatz, Eaker, Quesada, Maitland, Hegenberger, and the crews of the 1924 Douglas World Cruisers.

Events which captured fewer headlines, but were perhaps just as significant to ordinary Americans, are also recalled. Military aviators were encouraged to involve themselves in humanitarian aid wherever needed, and the records show that they were only too willing to help. Food supplies were dropped to flood victims, crops were dusted, and the destructive capacity of bombardment squadrons was put to good use against both ice jams and lava flows.

As the 1920s story draws to a close in the USAF Museum's gallery, it can be seen that the Air Service has gained in status in becoming the Air Corps, and that most Americans have been made aware that the nation's military airmen are capable of great achievements. Looked at closely, however, it is apparent that the promise of air power is a long way from fulfillment. The Air Corps of 1930 is still struggling to leave the shadow of WWI, and is doing its best to meet its burgeoning responsibilities with resources which are less than adequate.

Postwar Problems

Glad though they were to see the end of WWI's carnage, the signing of the armistice on November 11, 1918, left American airmen with the conviction that their potential had been unfulfilled. They had fought hard with what they had and won some notable victories, but they had not darkened the skies with fleets of American warplanes, and they had not reached a point where the strategic promise of military aircraft had been proven. Disappointment led to recrimination and a series of hearings and investigations from which criticisms spread liberally. U.S. government departments, industry, and the military were all blamed to some degree for lack of organization, indecision, and poor judgment. The Air Service defended itself and spoke up for its future with vigor. Billy Mitchell was his usual forthright self on the subject of air power, but he was not the only prominent airman to voice a strong opinion. In 1919, Benny Foulois went so far as to tell a Senate Committee:

"The General Staff of the Army—either through lack of vision, lack of practical knowledge, or deliberate intention to subordinate the Air Service needs to the needs of other combat arms—has utterly failed to appreciate the full military value of this new weapon, and, in my opinion, has failed to accord it its just place in our military family."

Whatever their convictions and aspirations, the Air Service firebrands had first to cope with the sobering realities of a peacetime army. The U.S. war machine had only just shifted into high gear, but now it went into reverse. Demobilization began immediately, and an air arm which had grown from 1,200 men to nearly 200,000 in little more than eighteen months experienced the pains of contraction as it was cut to fewer than 10,000 by mid-1920. The airframe and engine orders which were the lifeblood of the newly risen U.S. aircraft industry were summarily canceled. By 1920, 90 percent of the industry was gone, and those companies which were hanging on were doing so without military contracts. Worse still, there was a glut of cheap surplus military aircraft depressing the civil market.

Reflecting the postwar mood of the country, the attitude of Congress towards military spending was unsympathetic and budgets were parsimonious. The $460 million of fiscal year 1919 fell to no more than $25 million for fiscal year 1920. Politicians wanted very much to believe that they had just fought the war to end all wars, and they found it difficult to imagine that any nation could pose a credible threat to the U.S. The wartime expansion had provided the Air Service with thousands of aircraft and their associated spares, and, until they were used up, it was the view of Congress that there was little need to spend much money on more. It was apparent that American military airmen could look forward to a good many years in which their flying would be dominated by DH-4s and Curtiss Jennies.

The prospects for a change in the status of the Air Service were no more encouraging. In 1919, bills were presented in both the Senate and the House proposing the creation of a separate U.S. Air Force, and a commission under the Assistant Secretary of War suggested the formation of a separate Department of Aeronautics to control an independent air force. The bills died, and the War Department's generals and Secretary of War Baker rejected the recommendations of the commission. Secretary Baker added the warning that the Air Service had better not get any ideas about building up a bomber force intended for attacking cities, and General Pershing delivered himself of the opinion that "an air force acting independently can of its own account neither win a war at the present time nor, so far as we can tell, at any time in the future." In what was seen as a crushing defeat for their cause by many air officers, Congress agreed with the Secretary of War and authorized the Air Service as a combatant arm of the army with manpower limited to some 1,500 officers and 16,000 enlisted men. Disappointing though this was for men like Foulois and Mitchell, some progress had been made. The rank of the Chief of Air Service was raised to major general, and the legislation recognized the uniqueness of the Air Service by giving it control of its own research, development, and procurement, besides responsibility for personnel and training matters. Flight pay was authorized, and it was required that tactical units should be commanded by flyers.

These advances were welcomed, but the size and shape of the Air Service gave an indication of how much preaching the apostles of air power still had to do. In the front line of twenty-seven squadrons there were just four pursuit and four bombardment squadrons, only one of which was a heavy bombardment unit. The remaining nineteen squadrons were all concerned with observation, as were thirty-two bal-loon companies. The emphasis reflected the views still held by most senior army officers that aircraft were intended primarily for close support of troops on the battlefield. Control of all the tactical squadrons was given to army corps commanders, and the Chief of Air Service was left with training schools and depots.

The Unquiet Spirit

Many Air Service officers hoped that Billy Mitchell would be appointed Chief of Air Service when he returned from Europe, Hap Arnold among them. As he said later: "Above all others, [Mitchell] had the pilot. Mitchell had to be content with being number two.

If they had hoped to keep Billy Mitchell quiet by making him a subordinate, the General Staff were to be disappointed. He became "the gadfly of the General Staff and the hero of the Army's flyers." Central to Mitchell's vision of an independent air force was his conviction that air power could become a decisive strategic instrument. The total war concept which was inherent in his ideas was popular in neither military nor civilian circles. In suggesting that future wars could be decided by airmen before soldiers got in-

The DH–4 and the Liberty engine having been produced in such numbers, lean postwar military budgets ensured that the most was made of them, and they soldiered on together for many years. Repeatedly modified and improved, the DH–4 was not finally retired from service until 1932. The aircraft illustrated is the one in which Lt. Frank Patterson died during gunnery trials in 1918. His name survives in today's Wright-Patterson Air Force Base, home of the USAF Museum.

background, the reputation, the personal courage, the knowledge of air operations, to do the job." However, Mitchell's fiery reputation preceded him and the General Staff was not ready for a man who propounded such radical ideas on air power, even though some of them had proved remarkably successful in France. The first peacetime Chief appointed was, from the U.S. Army's point of view, a sensibly conservative choice—Maj. Gen. Charles Menoher was an infantry officer and not a volved, Mitchell was attacking the arguments being made by the Army to bolster its diminishing budget for ground forces, and his belief that navies were made largely redundant by air power had the sailors apoplectic. His view that modern war could no longer exclude women and children horrified almost everyone. "The entire nation," he said, "is, or should be, considered a combatant force." In the face of considerable opposition, Mitchell was persistent. He continued to speak in public frequently, testified regularly before Congressional committees, and wrote articles and a book[1] spelling out his air power gospel.

At the same time, Mitchell attacked the day-to-day business of the Air Service with relentless energy. Papers were written on countless proposals: very long-range bombers, aircraft which were amphibious or on skis, an all-metal bomber, troop-carrying aircraft, armor-piercing bombs, large-caliber cannon, aerial torpedoes, civil defense against air raids, the encouragement of private flying to provide a pilot reserve, and so on without pause. He also began to encourage eye-catching events which would generate favorable publicity for the Air Service and, wherever possible, test its

Docile though the Curtiss "Jenny" was, it sometimes trapped the unwary student pilot. "Jennies" continued to be used as primary trainers for U.S. military pilots until the late 1920s.

potential. At first, this involved no more than having military aircraft perform at county fairs and other public gatherings, but to these were soon added cross-country flights and aerial competitions. If there was a down side to all this exhibitionism, it was that the young pilots sometimes went beyond the bounds of good sense and allowed their flying to become uninhibited. The accident rate rose until it was higher than it had ever been during the rapid expansion days of WWI, and it stayed high.[2] Cases of showing off by low-flying or performing low-level aerobatics were fre-

Cross-country Hazards

Even controlled exercises could have their excitements. In the first transcontinental flight by the Air Service, Major Albert Smith led five Curtiss Jennies out of Rockwell Field, San Diego, on December 4, 1918. In the course of a flight in which Major Smith reached Jacksonville on December 18 and returned to Rockwell on February 15, 1919, via Washington and New York, two aircraft crashed, two more were wrecked in severe weather, and several major overhauls were carried out. Forced landings were common, and pilots

quent, and it was not unknown for some pilots to indulge their high spirits by hunting wild fowl with their machine guns.

got accustomed to landing in any field or relatively flat area which appeared and accepting the accompanying hazards. One pilot sent a message that he was delayed "due to cow eating wing." In his later report, he stated that the patches on his aircraft were proof that "some unprincipled bovine with a low sense of humor and a depraved appetite had eaten large chunks out of the lower wing panels and stabilizer."

At about the same time, Major Theodore Macauley of Taliaferro Field, Fort Worth, flew a DH-4 west to Rockwell and then across the continent to Jackson-

ville, before returning to Fort Worth. His first aircraft was seriously damaged in landing accidents twice, and was replaced by another DH-4 in Alabama during the return trip. The second aircraft needed lengthy repairs after being flown in heavy rain in Mississippi. Not at all discouraged by the trials of this attempt, Macauley did it again in April 1919, this time without any serious problems, completing the round trip across the U.S. in seven days with a flying time of 44 hrs, 15 mins.

In July 1919, a more ambitious exercise aimed to test the long-range capabilities of the Martin MB-2 (NBS-1) bomber and the reliability of its Liberty engines while charting air routes and locating possible landing fields. Lt. Col. Rutherford Hartz and his crew left Bolling Field, Washington, D.C., on July 24 for a flight around the rim of the U.S. After a marathon effort in which they coped with seven forced landings, numerous repairs, and the challenges of social occasions in eighteen of the outermost states, Hartz and his crew completed the circuit of the U.S. by returning to Bolling on November 9, 1919, having covered 9,823 miles in 108 days and a flying time of 114 hrs, 25 mins.

As men like Smith, Macauley, and Hartz discovered, in the pioneering days of the Air Service, lengthy absences of aircraft and crew from the home base did not seem to be a problem, and fact-finding adventures were deemed at least as important as routine training. Local commanders were given a great deal of latitude to wave the Air Service's flag as they saw fit. Accidents and outlandish escapades led to this freedom of action's being curtailed in September 1919. From that date, authorization for special flights had to be obtained from Air Service Headquarters in Washington, and participation became organized into fewer and larger events.

The most important exercise of 1919 for the Air Service under the new rules was Mitchell's "transcontinental reliability and endurance test." It was meant to be a "[field maneuver] calculated to yield a far greater profit to the Air Service and the cause of aeronautics in general than any field maneuver ever did before." Personnel, equip-

[1] *Our Air Force, the Keystone of National Defense,* William Mitchell, 1921.

[2] During the last year of the war, the Air Service suffered one death per 3,072 flying hours. In the first six months after the armistice, the rate increased to one death every 2,208 hours.

ment, communications, and organization would be subjected to the pressure of an extended exercise. Navigation, meteorology, landing fields, and other matters bearing on operations would be tested. An underlying reason for Mitchell's proposal was to gather some facts on the problems of operating an air force which had suffered savage cuts and was flying obsolete aircraft over country with inadequate facilities. To check on people's ability to respond to a challenge, the exercise was not announced until eighteen days before the start.

Any local commander could enter an aircraft and pilot, and Mitchell's "test" rapidly took on the character of a race, the prospect of which excited the interest of the American people. The chosen route lay between New York and San Francisco, and could be flown either way, but all aircraft had to pass through twenty-nine control stations on the 2,700-mile flight. No night flying was allowed. Winners would be announced for the shortest elapsed time, the shortest flying time, and the fastest flying time based on a handicap system for various machines. Fifty-eight aircraft entered to start from New York, and sixteen from San Francisco. Fifty-two DH-4s dominated the lineup, and they were joined by one DH-9, seven SE-5s, five Fokkers, three LUSAC 11s, two Martin bombers, one Ansaldo SVA-5, one Thomas-Morse MB-3, one SPAD, and one Bristol Fighter. A number of these failed to reach the starting line for one reason or another, including two fatal accidents. In the event, forty-six aircraft started from Roosevelt Field, Long Island, on October 8, 1919, and another fifteen set out from San Francisco's Presidio.

Lt. Belvin Maynard's DH-4 was the first to arrive at San Francisco, and an SE-5 flown by Maj. Carl "Tooey" Spatz[3] led the west-east group into New York. Eventually twenty-six of the New York starters reached the west coast, and there were seven finishers from San Francisco. Seventeen of these thirty-three set off immediately in a hastily authorized extension of the race into a round trip, six of which made it back to New York and two to San Francisco. The double crossing was completed by five DH-4s, two SE-5s, and one Fokker.

As the survivors were only too ready to attest, it had been a grueling ordeal for both men and machines. They had contended with rain, snow, ice, and fog, and they had suffered long stretches of severe cold. They got lost, which was hardly surprising, given the weather, the guidance of very basic magnetic compasses, and the nature of their Post Office or Rand McNally state maps. Mechanical problems included engine failures, broken landing gear, splintered propellers, frozen water pumps, blown tires, leaking radiators, and damaged wings. The overall winner, Lt. Maynard, survived a forced landing after breaking a crankshaft, and, with his mechanic, succeeded overnight in changing the Liberty engine for one retrieved from a crashed Martin bomber. There were fifty-four accidents during the exercise, and these added seven deaths and two serious injuries to the two fatal accidents suffered before the start.[4]

The price had been high, but Mitchell emphasized the lessons learned from the exercise. He pointed to the obvious need for more landing fields and for improvements to those that existed. Reliable servicing facilities, communications, airfield lighting, navigation aids, and weather information had to be provided. Not least, Mitchell drew comfort from the public interest in the Air Service generated by the publicity from competitive events. He believed that the more the Air Service could be kept in the public eye the better as the case for building a large and powerful air force was put together. The fifty-four accidents and nine fatalities of the transcontinental exercise were not

The winner of the Air Service's 1919 transcontinental reliability and endurance test was a DH–4 flown by Lt. Belvin Maynard, known to the press as The "Flying Parson." He overcame the handicaps of a forced landing and an impromptu engine change during his epic flight.

good, but even they helped draw attention to the challenges of military flying and to the hazards of flying obsolete aircraft.[5]

Mitchell vs. the Navy
If army officers often found

[4]One death in particular drew attention both to one of the basic flaws in the design of the DH–4, and to the growth of some very dangerous unofficial practices developed to overcome the aircraft's shortcomings. It was known that the main wheels on the DH–4 were set too far back, and the aircraft, therefore, had a tendency to nose over when landing, especially on soft ground. To overcome this, some regular rear seat passengers had taken to unfastening their safety belts during landing and sliding back over the fuselage to reach the tail and hold it down. Two passengers did this in the course of the transcontinental exercise, and one of these was killed when thrown off.

[5]In the absence of funds for new aircraft and improved equipment, the accident rate of the Air Service continued to run at an appallingly high level. In the twelve-month period between July 1920 and June 1921, there were 330 major accidents resulting in the deaths of 69 aircrew out of a total strength of only 900.

[3]The original spelling of the name was Spatz, with the "a" pronounced "ah." It was legally changed in 1938 to Spaatz in an effort to ensure correct pronunciation.

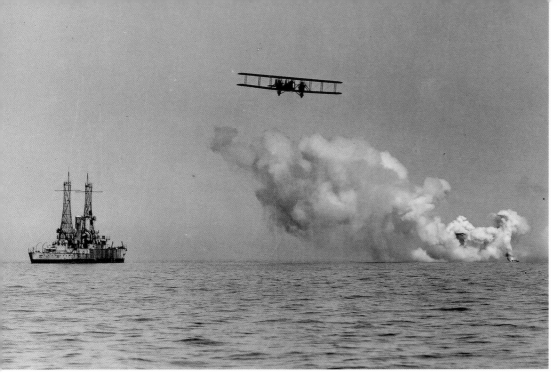

During the first phase of Billy Mitchell's exercises against the old U.S. battleship Alabama *in September 1921, Martin MB-2 bombers laid smoke screens. Later, aircraft attacked with increasingly large bombs, finally sinking the ship with a 2,000 lb weapon dropped close alongside.*

Mitchell's zeal hard to live with, their naval counterparts saw him as their mortal foe. One of the U.S. Navy's principal roles was to guard against any hostile approach to the American coasts. At the heart of this defense were the Navy's battleships, which sailors considered almost invulnerable. Mitchell was scathing in attacking what he believed to be an outdated notion, declaring that the day of the dreadnoughts was over, that aircraft could sink any ship afloat, and that the U.S. would be safer if the defense of its coastline was entrusted to the Air Service. There were naval officers who recognized that the aerial threat to their ships was real and who were keen to develop naval air power as the proper response, but many older admirals sneered at aircraft in any form. The Chief of Naval Operations actually wanted to disband the small naval air arm, saying: "I cannot conceive of any use that the fleet will ever have for aircraft." Faced with Mitchell's assault, he added: "Aviation is just a lot of noise." The Secretary of the Navy was even more intemperate. He went so far as to say that he would be prepared to stand bareheaded on the deck of any capital ship under attack from the air.

Mitchell had been asking for a test of aircraft against ships since joining Menoher's staff in 1919. In 1921, after several newspapers had picked up Mitchell's theme and argued that battleships were indeed relics of the past, his campaign finally bore fruit. A number of ex-German warships, acquired under the terms of the Versailles Treaty, were available for tests, as were some old U.S. ships. The Navy agreed to have them ready for trial by air attack fifty miles off the mouth of the Chesapeake Bay in June 1921.

A special unit known as the 1st Provisional Air Brigade was assembled for the trials at Langley Field, Virginia, and Mitchell made sure that they got as much training in the techniques of ship attack as possible. Air Service airmen began their tests against an ex-German destroyer, the G-102, in mid-July. First, a wave of SE-5s dropped 25 lb antipersonnel bombs and simulated strafing the ship from 200 ft. Sixteen Martin bombers followed, dropping two 300 lb bombs each from 1,500 ft. After the first pass by the Martins, the G-102 sank. On July 18, the cruiser *Frankfurt* got similar treatment, being sunk by Martins carrying 600 lb bombs. A more serious challenge came on July 20 in the shape of the 27,000-ton battleship *Ostfriesland.* With a four-layered hull and watertight compartments end to end, the ex-German warship was said to be unsinkable. The Martins struck on July 21, this time delivering the *coup de grace* with 2,000 lb bombs. In just twenty-one minutes, the unsinkable *Ostfriesland* was sunk.

By July 29, Mitchell was driving home some more air power points by leading his bombers in a mock raid on New York City, and then in further attacks against Philadelphia, Wilmington, Baltimore, and Annapolis. The final report on the naval tests and city attacks reached General Menoher on August 29. Mitchell's conclusions were uncompromising. The bombers had demonstrated that any ship could be sunk by bombs and that American cities were vulnerable to assault from the air. The only proper defense could be provided by aircraft, and these should be operated by an independent air force. "Aviation," he insisted, "can only be developed to its fullest extent under its own direction and control. An efficient solution of our defensive needs will not exist until a Department of National Defense is organized."

A joint Army/Navy Board acknowledged the added dangers of the air threat, and said it was imperative "as a matter of national defense to provide for the maximum possible development of aviation in both the Army and the Navy." However, the Board concluded that battleships "were still the backbone of the fleet and bulwark of the nation's sea defense." The certainty of that assertion seemed dubious after later bombing attacks on the battleship *Alabama* in September 1921, and on two more, the *Indiana* and the *Virginia,* in 1923. All three were sent to the bottom by Mitchell's bombers. On the far side of the world, Japanese naval officers took note.

General Menoher forwarded Mitchell's report to the Secretary of War, adding his profound disagreement with its conclusions. The matter might have died there if the report had not been leaked to the press on September 13, 1921. In the ensuing furor, General Menoher decided that he had had enough. He resigned, but the Secretary of War remained wary of Mitchell's reputation and he was passed over again. The new Chief was General Mason Patrick, chosen because he was a reliable part of the old army establishment; he had been the Air Service commander in France, and, most importantly, he had dealt with Mitchell before. Patrick was aware of Mitchell's single-mindedness on the subject of air power and knew that he could be a difficult subordinate, but he respected Mitchell's originality and he had seen some of his ideas succeed in the heat of combat.

Even if he was not such an uncompromising, flamboyant advocate for air power as Mitchell, Patrick agreed with his number two about the need to build up the effectiveness of the Air Service. He called attention to the improper balance among the front line squadrons, and urged a move towards fewer observation and more pursuit and bombardment squadrons. Ideally, he said, observation squadrons should constitute no more than 20 percent of combat strength. In 1923, Patrick's persistence led to the appointment of a board, headed by Maj. Gen. William Lassiter, to study his plans. The Lassiter Board accepted many of Patrick's arguments and found that the current shape of the Air Service bore "no relationship to war requirements." Disagreements between the Secretaries of War and the Navy later doomed the Lassiter findings, but the essence of Patrick's case for air power was better understood.[6]

Air Power Prophet on Trial

Mitchell was not prepared to be as patient as his Chief. In 1924, he resumed his outspoken personal campaign with more speeches, articles, and Congressional testimony.[7] As he grew more strident, he gained something of a public following but his efforts were counterproductive in most of the places where it mattered. He now not only angered the Secretaries of War and the Navy and senior officers, he antagonized President Calvin Coolidge. When his tour of duty as Assistant Chief of Air Service expired in April 1925, Mitchell was not reappointed. He reverted to his permanent rank of colonel and was "exiled"

Major General Mason Patrick, Chief of the U.S. Army Air Service from 1921-26 and first Chief of the Army Air Corps, with Ralph Royce and a Curtiss Jenny.

to Texas. From there, his frustration burst the bounds of reason. On September 5, 1925, after Navy losses of an aircraft and the airship *Shenandoah* within days of each other had prompted the Secretary of the Navy to say that the accidents proved that aircraft could not attack the U.S., Mitchell issued a statement to the press which indicted "the incompetency, criminal negligence, and almost treasonable administration of our national defense by the Navy and War Departments." The court martial which Mitchell appeared to be seeking was duly ordered by the President and was held in Washington during the closing months of 1925.

Mitchell and his supporters (including such future leaders as Arnold, Spaatz, Olds, and Eaker) knew that the verdict of the court was a foregone conclusion, but they made the best of it by treating the trial as a public hearing of the case for air power. As expected, Mitchell was found guilty of "conduct of a nature to bring discredit upon the military service," and sentenced to suspension from the service for five years without pay. On February 1, 1926, he resigned from the Air Service to continue the fight as a civilian. Unfortunately, the onset of the depression led the public to pay less attention to defense matters, and Mitchell died almost a forgotten man in 1936. Ten years later, when many

of his predictions had proven all too accurate, the farsightedness and courage, if not the diplomacy, of his principled stand were belatedly recognized when President Harry Truman authorized the posthumous award of a special Medal of Honor to Billy Mitchell, air power prophet extraordinary.

Aircraft and Engines of the 1920s

During his tenure as Assistant Chief of Air Service, Mitchell had continued to encourage both eye-catching activities and the research and development effort spearheaded by the Engineering Division at McCook Field, close to the present site of the USAF Museum. Much valuable work was done on ancillary equipment—bombsights, cannons, propellers, engines, and so on—and a number of experimental aircraft were built at McCook in the early 1920s with the help of a wind tunnel capable of providing an airstream of 450 mph. Funds were limited, however, and by 1923 experimental activities declined. Aircraft manufacturers took on the work of designing new machines to meet Air Service specifications. Progress was made, but slowly, and many products proved disappointing as ideas ran ahead of the available technology.

Efforts to develop aircraft with strategic reach were particularly disappointing. The Barling bomber (XNBL-1) was an

---

[6]Even so, lack of funds and reactionary attitudes opposed change. In 1924, the Air Service had a total of 1,364 aircraft on strength. Only 754 were in commission—and 457 of these were observation aircraft, 59 bomber, 78 pursuit and 8 attack aircraft were serviceable.

[7]On October 24, 1924, after a tour of the Far East, Mitchell submitted a report to the War Department in which he said that war with Japan was almost inevitable. In a prediction of startling accuracy, he suggested that the Japanese would strike first at Pearl Harbor: "that is where the blow will be struck," he said, "on a fine, quiet Sunday morning."

impressive monster which seemed to tackle the problem by being bigger and having more of most things than its contemporaries. In the words of one observer, it looked "more likely to antagonize the air than to pass through it." A triplane with a 120 ft wingspan, the Barling had two tailplanes and four fins, and it weighed more than 42,000 lbs. It first staggered into the air on August 22, 1923, from Wright Field, next to the present day site of the USAF Museum. Powered by six of the eternal Libertys, it later showed that it could lift its bombload off the ground, but it was then incapable of carrying it farther than 170 miles or of dragging its mass of struts and wires along at more than 95 mph. The last straw came when the Barling proved incapable of crossing the Appalachians to reach the east coast. It was hardly the creature of Billy Mitchell's air power dreams.

For the remainder of the 1920s, U.S. bombers followed more conventional lines, but none of them came close to matching Billy Mitchell's vision. The Martin MB-2 of 1920 was joined by the first of the Keystone bombers in 1923. Keystones monopolized Army bomber procurement during the 1920s, apart from a dozen Curtiss Condors ordered in 1927. Neither the Keystone nor the Condor differed in any really significant way from the WWI style of the MB-2. All three were open-cockpit, twin-engined biplanes capable of carrying bombloads of 2,500 lbs or so over ranges of up to 800 miles. Engines improved and service ceilings rose to the 17,500 ft of the Condor, but maximum speeds remained stubbornly low at no more than 130 mph. Inadequate as strategic bombers, the Keystones and the Condors at least kept the bombing force and its expertise alive while aeronautical technology struggled to catch up with strategic theory.

With bombers, both in the U.S. and elsewhere, threatening no great improvements in performance, fighters remained framed almost as badly by the WWI experience. The Air Service entered the 1920s still relying on SE5As designed in Britain in 1916, and on some Thomas-Morse MB-3s. The Thomas-Morse fighter was later developed into the more powerful MB-3A,

The Keystone series of aircraft captured over 90 percent of the U.S. Army's bomber procurement funds during the late 1920s and early '30s. As Hitler rose to power in Europe, "strategic bombers" still had open cockpits, a maximum speed of 120 mph, and a range of less than 1,000 miles. Armament was three .303 in machine guns and a bomb load of 2,500 lbs.

built under contract by a little-known manufacturer in the Pacific northwest called Boeing. In those days, it was government practice to buy the rights to aircraft designs and then to put the contract for production up for bids rather than arranging a deal with the original designer. In the case of the MB-3A the low bidder was Boeing, and the Thomas-Morse Company lost their aircraft. In the long run, although it helped companies like Boeing to get established, this policy had adverse effects. Companies generally were discouraged from expending time and effort on new research and design work for the military since they knew that they stood a good chance of failing to get a production contract even if their designs were accepted.

By the end of the 1920s, the state of the fighter art had advanced, but not by much. Boeing and Curtiss had cornered the market and had produced some very agile and attractive single-seaters, but they still bore a family resemblance to the biplanes of the western front in 1918. The Curtiss Hawk series had begun with the P-1 in 1925, which by 1929 had become the P-6E, an elegantly classic design affectionately remembered as a worthy symbol of the golden age of flight. Besides being photogenic, the P-6E had a top speed of 197 mph and could reach 25,000 ft. It was, however, still an open cockpit biplane

armed with just two .3-inch machine guns firing through the propeller arc.

As the decade drew to a close, Boeing provided a fighter with a 500 hp Pratt & Whitney radial engine. It was the P-12, and it proved reliable and popular, with over 350 being delivered to the U.S. Army Air Corps, but it represented an alternative to the Curtiss fighter rather than a noticeable improvement. The performance of the P-12 was similar to that of the P-6 and it was the last of the biplane fighters flown by the Army. Rapidly overtaken by technological advances in the 1930s, the last of the P-12s nevertheless managed to hang on until 1941 before being retired.

For all their obvious links with a bygone era of air warfare, the Army's biplane fighters did project a glamorous image of military flying for the American public to admire. Gaudily decorated in bright color schemes and unit insignia, they were a glorious sight at air shows. Leather helmets and silk scarves completed the picture and called forth memories of Rickenbacker and Luke. The aircraft were creatures of the past, but one thing about the Curtiss Hawks did point the way to the future; their cowlings hid the 450 hp Curtiss D12 engine or its 600 hp successor, the V1570 Conqueror. The D12 was a true technical watershed, an aluminum monobloc V-shaped engine which would exert its influence on aviation progress until the advent of jet propulsion. Over the years, refinements were designed to raise the overall power and the ratios of power-to-weight and power-to-frontal area, but the essential elements of the engine remained unchanged. A D12 was studied by Rolls-Royce engineers before they began the series of V12s which culminated in the Merlin, the engine powering such famous WWII fighters as the Hurricane, Spitfire, and Mustang.

A D12 derivative was also fitted to an aircraft specifically designed for ground attack. The Curtiss A-3 was a two-seater born out of the experiences of attacking troops at low-level in 1918 and the thought (perhaps even hope) that the DH-4s could not last forever. It first appeared in 1926 bearing a distinct family resemblance to the Curtiss Hawks. Armored and fitted with bomb-racks, it carried four forward-firing machine guns plus another two for the observer. Noticeably heavier than the Hawks, it was not very quick at 140 mph and would probably have been hazardous to the health of its crews if operated as intended in any major conflict. Even the A-3, however, was a marked improvement over the first attempt at a ground attack aircraft to come out of the Engineering Division at McCook Field. The GA-1 was a large, heavily armored triplane with two Liberty engines driving pusher propellers. Its three crew members directed the fire of eight machine guns and could drop a variety of bombs. There was even provision for fitting a 37 mm cannon. It did fly, but not very well, and the Army changed its mind about an extended contract. The ubiquitous DH-4, hung about with extra guns, filled in until the A-3 came along.

The remaining aircraft types on the Army's strength during the 1920s included a plethora of observation, cargo, and training machines. Notable among the observation aircraft were a series of biplanes from Douglas which began with the O-2 in 1925 and continued until the O-38 of the early 1930s, in the process developing from an open-cockpit Liberty-engined two-seater not much different from a DH–4 into a more sophisticated machine with a

cockpit canopy and a Pratt & Whitney radial. As engine power increased so did the weight, and improvements in performance were minimal, with none of them ever being capable of more than 150 mph.

Even slower but vastly more intriguing was the Loening OA-1. An amphibian built for the Army, it was a single-engined biplane dominated by a huge central float which contained retractable landing gear and was the foundation on which sat a slab-sided fuselage. To raise the propeller clear of the protuberant float, the inescapable Liberty engine was inverted. Forty-five of

these eccentricities were ordered by the Army between 1924 and 1928, primarily for deployment in the Hawaiian Islands and the Philippines, but used wherever lakes and rivers were liable to outnumber airfields.

The cargo aircraft of the 1920s were mostly civilian airliners adapted for military use. Prominent among them were two designs by the Dutchman, Anthony Fokker. The T-2 was a high-wing mono-plane built in 1921 which gave every indication of being much too large for its power plant. It was 81 ft across the wing and

The Curtiss P-6E was one of the most attractive biplanes ever built and was much loved by its pilots. Here, the 17th Pursuit Squadron from Selfridge Field, Michigan, shows off its formation skills and its Snowy Owl emblem. By the time the 17th PS took delivery of their P-6Es in 1932, bombers like the Martin B-10 were already flying and achieving higher maximum speeds.

The 12-cylinder 600 hp Conqueror engine powered the Curtiss P-6E Hawk. Splendid engine though it was, the Conqueror could not haul the P-6E through the 200 mph barrier in level flight.

nearly 50 ft long, and its uncompromisingly angular shape was hauled along by a single Liberty engine. In 1927, this was joined by the Fokker C-2, which was more reasonably provided with three Wright Whirlwind radials; other trimotors in the stable were the Fords, C-3 and C-4. In the extraordinary category was another amphibian, the twin-engined Sikorsky C-6, a sesquiplane in which ten passengers were carried in a large hull tenuously suspended beneath twin booms trailing an impossibly high wing.

Training aircraft were not nearly so exotic. Until the mid-1920s, primary flying training was completed in the Curtiss Jenny. From 1926 on the Jennies were replaced by the Consolidated PT-1, an aircraft so solid and dependable that it earned the nickname "Trusty." If it had a problem, it was that the plane was perhaps too easy to fly and so allowed some students of dubious capability to pass on to the next stage of training. The transition from primary training to operational aircraft was handled principally in DH-4Ms. (M for modernized by Boeing).

Winning Airmen

Outstanding aircraft may have been few and far between in the 1920s, but that did not stop the U.S. Army's aircrews from waving the air power flag as much as possible and recording some outstanding performances in the air in the process. Faster, farther, higher, longer—American airmen were prominent among those who struggled to push back the frontiers of flight.

Speed was always exciting and racing could be guaranteed to get the attention of the press, even if the race was bizarre. In 1921, Hap Arnold, who was commanding Crissy Field at the Presidio in San Francisco at the time, challenged a flock of homing pigeons to beat his DH-4 back from Portland to San Francisco. Since Hap neglected to warm up his engine beforehand, the result was nearly a fiasco. It was forty-five minutes after the pigeons had been released before the cranky Liberty could be induced to start. Thankfully for the Air Service's pride, he overtook the pi-

geons en route to be hailed the winner.

More serious Army involvement in racing began in 1920. Billy Mitchell fervently believed that the spur of competition and the challenge of record achievement were wholly beneficial to the air power cause. They garnered good publicity and they helped to drive forward the development of better aircraft and engines. He therefore encouraged the engineers at McCook to design an Army machine for the specific purpose of competing in air races. The aircraft, a chunky little biplane powered by a hefty Packard engine of 600 hp, was designed by Alfred Verville and given the designation VCP-R. On Thanks-

Loening OA-1A San Francisco *was one of five amphibians sent on the 22,000 mile Pan American Goodwill Tour in 1926-27. Its pilots were Capt. Ira Eaker (seen here) and Lt. Muir "Sandy" Fairchild. Both officers went on to become generals in WW II, Eaker rising to command first the 8th AF and then the Allied Air Forces, Mediterranean.*

giving Day, 1920, flown by Lt. Corliss Moseley, it won the first Pulitzer Trophy race at the disappointingly low average speed of 156.54 mph. However, success had been tasted and a pattern set. After missing the 1921 Pulitzer because of insufficient funds, Army flyers became regular entrants and were successful more often than not, winning in 1922, '24, and '25. In the 1922 race, Curtiss R-6s flown by Lts. Russell Maughan and Lester Maitland finished first and second, and afterwards Billy Mitchell used Maughan's

racer to set a new world's speed record of 222.97 mph. On the strength of that showing, Curtiss became the primary contractor for the next Air Service fighter, and the R-6 parented the Curtiss Hawk series.

The 1925 Pulitzer, held at Mitchel Field, New York, was the last because after that, Billy Mitchell was no longer there to encourage Army involvement, and it was felt that research and development funds could be better spent elsewhere. The Air Service signed off with a flourish, Lt. Cyrus Bettis winning with a Curtiss R3C-1 at 248.98 mph. Waiting in the wings as the backup pilot was a man whose record throughout his career consistently belied

his name and who was on his way to becoming one of the great air force figures— Lt. James Doolittle. In the days before the race, he and Bettis had advertised the races by flying over and through New York City. As Doolittle said later: "It was a rare thrill to fly down the city streets and look up at the tall buildings. It was also interesting to do it inverted."

Doolittle Belies His Name

Twelve days after the success of Bettis in the Pulitzer, it was Jimmy Doolittle's turn. Much to the chagrin of the U.S. Navy, he flew the same Curtiss racer, now R3C-2 because it had been fitted with floats, to leave the opposition in his wake in an overwater race, the 1925 Schneider Trophy. In winning over the Chesapeake Bay course, Doolittle, who had never flown a seaplane before being selected for the race, set world seaplane closed course speed records for 100 and 200 km, and the next day he took the outright world seaplane speed record at 245.71 mph. On his return to his home base at McCook Field, Doolittle's colleagues insisted on dressing him in a naval uniform and parading him

Once, he says: "I made a $5 bet with some friends that I could sit on the axle between the wheels while [McCullough] made a landing." He won the bet and was promptly grounded for a month when his commander, Colonel Burwell, found out. Burwell nevertheless had an eye for talent, and he was generally tolerant of Doolittle's high spirits. A short time later, Doolittle amply repaid such understanding, becoming one of the outstanding aeronautical engineering students of his day. Entering the Massachusetts Institute of Technology in October 1923, he was awarded a master's degree in June 1924, and was a

the cockpit on the outer side of the loop. In 1928 he headed a blind flight laboratory at Mitchel Field, New York, at the start of a year during which he carried out test flying of immense value to aviators everywhere. By September 1929, he had evolved a cockpit layout which included three new instruments: an accurate altimeter, a directional gyro, and an artificial horizon. Radio aids had also been developed by which an aircraft could be homed onto a runway. On September 24, Doolittle succeeded in flying a specially equipped Consolidated NY-2 through a complete flight, from takeoff to landing, while "under the hood" and unable to refer to anything outside the cockpit. "It was," he said, "the first time an airplane had taken off, flown over a set course, and landed on instruments alone." The *New York Times* greeted the achievement with prematurely euphoric headlines: "Blind Plane Flies 15 Miles and Lands—Fog Peril Overcome." Premature certainly, but the achievement was real enough. Jimmy Doolittle's work had shown the way to a reliable method of defeating the weather or flying at night, and the aviation world had become a safer place because of his efforts.

Range and Endurance

Following Doolittle's coast-to-coast success, long-distance flights by military aircraft became ever more ambitious, establishing routes and examining possibilities for the rapid deployment of aircraft both within and beyond the limits of the continental U.S. In 1922, Lts. Oakley Kelly and John Macready set themselves to fly the coffin-shaped Fokker T-2 across the continent nonstop. On their first attempt, they took off from Rockwell Field, San Diego, but could not coax the heavily laden T-2 over the hills to the west. Not wishing to waste the occasion, they settled down to break the world's endurance record. They landed over 35 hrs later, having surpassed the record by almost nine hours. After modifying the aircraft at McCook Field, they tried for endurance again in April 1923, and set a new world mark of 36 hrs, 4 mins, 34 secs. The following month, they took off on another transcon-

Jimmy Doolittle in the cockpit of the Consolidated NY-2 used to develop a practical blind flying instrument panel and reliable radio aids. On September 24, 1929, Doolittle took the NY-2 through a flight from takeoff to touchdown on instruments alone. The cockpit layout included three new instruments—an accurate altimeter, a directional gyro, and an artificial horizon.

through the streets of Dayton in a boat bearing signs saying: "Admiral James H. Doolittle."

It was not the first time Jimmy Doolittle had been in the news, and it was far from the last. Although he could be an inspired and wonderfully disciplined pilot, Doolittle himself admitted to being something of a mischief maker, too. He had bent a few rules and wrecked more than one aircraft in his early years, and been grounded for misbehavior several times.

Doctor of Science one year later.

In the air, Jimmy Doolittle made his mark in many ways. In September 1922, after several months of preparation during which his DH-4 was extensively modified to extend its range, he became the first man to cross the United States in less than a day, flying from Pablo Beach, Florida, to San Diego in 22 hrs, 35 mins, including a stop of 85 mins at San Antonio. In 1927, he used a Curtiss P-1 to become the first pilot to complete an aerobatic loop with

The first nonstop aerial crossing of the United States was achieved in May 1923 by Lts. John Macready and Oakley Kelly in a Fokker T-2. Powered by a single 400 hp Liberty engine, the slab-sided T-2 covered the 2,520 miles between Long Island and San Diego at a less than brisk average of 94 mph.

tinental flight, this time going in the opposite direction, from Roosevelt Field on Long Island. A little less than twenty-seven hours later, they touched down in San Diego, exhausted but jubilant. The Air Service acclaimed the feat, and went on to explain that Kelly and Macready had shown the feasibility of moving men, ammunition, and supplies from one coast to the other in one day during a national emergency. The statement perhaps erred towards fantasy, since the crossing was achieved by two carefully prepared pilots, and the specially modified T-2 they flew had so much trouble just lifting its own fuel it could not have carried any cargo, but at least it held a vision of the future.

The T-2's endurance record did not last long. The problem of lifting enough fuel to stay airborne for long periods had been exercising airmen's minds for some time and, Hap Arnold's engineering officer at Rockwell Field believed he had a solution. As Arnold himself reported: "There were no precedents to follow. The idea itself was simple—send up one plane and send up another when needed, carrying gas, oil, water, or food to be transferred to the duration plane." After a couple of false starts, Lts. Lowell Smith and John Richter did just that in a DH-4B on August 27, 1923. The servicing aircraft, a second DH-4, flew above trailing fuel or oil hoses, or a rope for food and messages. Richter's job

was to grab the hose or rope and take care of whatever was necessary while Smith held the aircraft steady. It was all very crude, but it worked and the DH-4B stayed in the air for 37 hrs, 15 mins. The endurance record was theirs, but more significantly they had demonstrated the basics of a technique which would be immensely important to the future of military aviation.

1924 was another year for epic distance flights. Lt. Russell Maughan had been inspired by Doolittle's coast-to-coast crossing in 1922. After his victory in the Pulitzer later that same year it occurred to Maughan that it should be possible to use the speed of a Curtiss aircraft to beat the sun across the continent from east to west. Preparatory work and false starts out of the way, he left Mitchel Field, New York, half an hour after official twilight on June 23, 1924, and, with stops at Dayton, St. Joseph, North Platte, Cheyenne, and Salduro, passed over Crissy Field, San Francisco, with just one minute to spare before the official time of dusk.

Around the World

As Maughan battled his way to the west, an even greater epic was in the making. Once the Atlantic had been conquered by the U.S. Navy's NC-4 and the Vickers Vimy of Alcock and Brown, airmen the world over thought about the possibility

of flying around the world. The competition to be the first was international. In the U.S., both the Navy and the Army had thought about the idea, but it was the Army's proposal which prevailed, primarily on the grounds of finding out more about operating over long distances and in different climates. Unspoken was the obvious point that success in such a venture would be wonderful publicity for the Air Service.

The preparation for the flight included shipping all manner of spare parts and tools to various points along the route, getting clearances from the foreign governments involved, positioning rescue ships, and dispatching officers to collect local information and arrange for supplies. It was also essential to obtain aircraft capable of getting the job done. The machines selected were designed by Donald Douglas, based on his rugged Liberty-engined DT-2 Navy floatplane. The Douglas World Cruiser (DWC) was a big, two-seat, open-cockpit biplane with a fuel capacity of 450 gallons, enough for well over 1,000 miles in still air. Since the DWC's cruising speed was not much more than 80 mph, it was clear that the Army was prepared to take its time over the venture. Five DWCs were ordered, four to make the flight plus one spare.

Led by Major Frederick Martin, the formation of four DWCs (christened *Seattle, Chicago, Boston,* and *New Orleans*) left Seattle on April 6, 1924, and headed for Alaska. There they suffered a serious blow when Martin in *Seattle* crashed into a mountain obscured by fog on the long Alaskan Peninsula. He and his mechanic survived, and the flight continued with three aircraft, now led by Lt. Lowell Smith, the aerial refueling pioneer. The route took them from Alaska to Japan, China, India, Iraq, and Turkey, and across Europe to the U.K. After refitting for the Atlantic crossing, Lt. Leigh Wade's *Boston* was lost through engine failure on the way to Iceland. Rescued by the USS *Richmond,* Wade and his mechanic were able to rejoin the flight in Newfoundland, where the spare DWC, now named *Boston II,* was waiting. On September 28, 1924, Lts. Lowell Smith and Erik Nelson succeeded in closing the circle with *Chicago* and *New Orleans*, arriving back at Seattle 175 days and over 360 flying hours after they began. Meticulous preparation combined with the professionalism and determination of the crews had brought the U.S. Army Air Service the honor of being the first to fly around the world.

Flag-waving and Fuel-burning

The late 1920s were not so rich in headlines for the Army's flyers, most of the glory going to civilian trailblazers like Charles Lindbergh (a Reserve officer), Amelia Earhart, Wiley Post, and Charles Kingsford-Smith. Even so, the Air Corps had its achievements. In December 1926, five Loening OA-1A amphibians, led by Major Herbert Dargue, went on a good-will tour of South America. It was not a trouble-free exercise. Two crew members were killed in a midair collision over Buenos Aires in which Dargue bailed out to survive, and in more than one place the crews were met by anti-American demonstrations. Dargue struggled on through breakdowns and diplomatic crises to complete the trip in May 1927, having visited most of the countries in Central and South America plus a host of Caribbean islands. It was his misfortune that he reached the U.S. just in time to have his accomplishment overshadowed by Lindbergh's Atlantic crossing.

Two other Air Corps exploits in the 1920s did attract headlines. In June 1927, Lts. Maitland and Hegenberger flew a Fokker C-2 trimotor *Bird of Paradise* 2,400 miles in 25 hrs, 50 mins, from San Francisco to Oahu. The advances in capability since 1924 were marked. Radio beacons were installed at the points of departure and arrival, and the C-2 had radios, an earth indicator compass, four magnetic compasses, and a drift sight. Lindbergh commented that it was: "The most perfectly organized and carefully planned flight ever attempted."

The Fokker C-2 also featured in a return to endurance flying in 1929. On New Year's Day, the extraordinarily talented crew of Maj. Carl Spaatz, Capt. Ira Eaker,

*One of the great milestones of aviation history was passed in 1924 when U.S. Army Air Service airmen completed the first round-the-world flight. Four Douglas World Cruisers (*Seattle, Boston, Chicago, *and* New Orleans*) left Seattle on April 6, 1924.* Seattle *crashed in Alaska and* Boston *went down in the Atlantic with engine failure.* Chicago *and* New Orleans *reached Seattle on September 28, 1924, completing their global circuit in a little less than six months.* Chicago *is seen here rigged with floats for one of the long ocean crossings.*

In June 1927, a Fokker C-2 trimotor Bird of Paradise *flown by Lts. Lester Maitland and Albert Hegenberger completed the first aerial crossing from California to Hawaii. The hazards of a 2,400-mile overwater flight to a small island were overcome with the help of radio beacons, meticulous preflight planning, and precise navigation.*

On New Year's Day 1929, a crew including three men destined to be among the great names of WW II— Spaatz, Eaker, and Quesada—took off from Los Angeles to answer a question. How long could they stay airborne? In a Fokker C-2 appropriately emblazoned with a large question mark, they flew for over 150 hrs, being refueled 37 times by a team of DH–4Bs. From a military point of view, the exercise demonstrated the feasibility of extending the range and payload of bombers by means of air-to-air refueling.

Lt. Harry Halverson, Lt. Pete Quesada, and S. Sgt. Roy Hooe got airborne from Los Angeles in a C-2A with a large question mark painted on the fuselage. The question was how long could they stay in the air? Using the crude techniques developed for the DH4s in 1923, they completed thirty-seven contacts with their refueling aircraft and stayed aloft for 150 hrs, 40 mins, landing on January 7, 1929. They were well satisfied, and Spatz noted in his report that, with refueling, a bomber's radius of action "has scarcely any limit at all." The *New York Post* said that the flight had opened "a new chapter in the history of aviation," and the *Washington Star*, with great foresight, predicted that it would lead to a nonstop flight around the world.[8] There was an immediate result to all the publicity over the *Question Mark*, and that was a rush of competitors. By the end of 1929 there had been over forty attempts on the record, and the year closed with a small private aircraft known as the *St. Louis Robin* in the prime spot, after a flight of 420 hrs, 21 mins. The contest had assumed the status of a circus act, and the Air Corps was no longer interested. Tooey Spaatz and the *Question Mark* had told them all they needed to know and offered a glimpse of the future for military aviation.

Into the Stratosphere

The efforts of American military airmen to fly faster, farther, and longer were matched by those of others aimed at finding out how high they could get. This proved to be an unusually hazardous occupation, as McCook test pilot Maj. Rudolph Schroeder found out on February 27, 1920. Flying a LePere LUSAC-11 with a supercharged Liberty engine, he ran out of oxygen above 30,000 ft and collapsed. The aircraft fell some five miles before he revived sufficiently to land at McCook Field. His eyes were frozen open. Recovering in the hospital, he learned that he had reached the world record altitude of 33,143 ft for his pains. Lt. John Macready, known for his part in the first nonstop coast-to-coast flight, took over from Schroeder and in 1921 pushed the altitude record to 34,508 ft. At the time, there was much discussion in the press about the possibility of Macready climbing so high that he ran the risk of escaping into Earth orbit![9]

In 1927, the Air Corps pursued altitude research by balloon in a program which ended in disaster. Capt. Hawthorne Gray made a number of ascents to very high altitude in an open balloon basket. On one occasion he baled out after col-

lapsing from lack of oxygen at more than 40,000 ft and then reviving only to find the balloon falling rapidly. Although his instruments showed that he had reached 42,470 ft he was denied an international record because he was not with the balloon when it came to earth. Trying again, it appears from his instruments that he once more rose to 42,470 ft, but this time died from lack of oxygen on the descent. Sadly, a world record was refused a second time because, as the Federation Aeronautique Internationale explained, on landing the aeronaut "was not in personal possession of his instruments."

In the late 1920s, high altitude research flights in aircraft continued, but lessons about the upper air seemed to be learned slowly, if at all. Altitudes of more than 35,000 ft were reached several times, but pilots still flew in open cockpits bundled up ineffectively against the ex-

---

*Thirty years later, in February 1959, a Boeing B-50 named *Lucky Lady II* circled the globe in 94 hours, refueled by KB-29 tankers four times on the way.

[9]John Macready is a largely unsung hero of the air force story. His achievements in the early 1920s were unique. He is the only man to have been awarded the Mackay Trophy three times. The trophy was established in 1912 to be awarded for the most meritorious military flight of each year. Macready won his in three consecutive years: 1921—high altitude flights; 1922—T-2 endurance record; 1923—transcontinental nonstop flight. He also represented the Air Service in the Pulitzer races, made the first emergency parachute jump at night, was the second man to fly in a pressurized cabin, the first pilot to demonstrate crop-dusting, and a pioneer of U.S. aerial photographic survey.

Loening OA-1A Detroit *seen during the Army Air Corps' goodwill tour of Latin America in 1926-27. Beset by problems, including the loss of two of the five aircraft in a midair collision over Buenos Aires, the flight nevertheless was awarded the Mackay Trophy for the most meritorious Air Corps flight of the year.*

treme cold, and they quite often collapsed and revived only when the aircraft descended into thicker air. (Jimmy Doolittle estimates being unconscious for thirty minutes on one occasion.) A thoroughly systematic method of investigation into the physiological and psychological effects of low pressures and temperatures on human beings still lay some years ahead.

Safety Measures

At the beginning of the 1920s, the hazards of flying open-cockpit biplanes with unreliable engines over all sorts of country and in every kind of weather were shrugged off by airmen as being part of the job. Steps to improve the safety of flight were at first regarded with suspicion. Flight instruments like the turn and slip indicator were a good example. Pilots proud of their ability to "fly by the seat of their pants" were reluctant to believe that an instrument could be better than their senses. Parachutes, too, were spurned by many pilots because they were thought less than manly. Reacting to a 1921 press report that thirty percent of airmen killed in accidents could be saved by parachutes, Maj. Follett Bradley wrote that "to require a pilot to wear a parachute and encourage him to employ it would foster faintheartedness." The issue came to a head late in 1922 when, within a period of three weeks, two pilots at McCook Field, Lts. Harold Harris and Frank Tyndall, became the first Air Service airmen to escape from disintegrating aircraft by using parachutes. There were two immediate results. The Air Service issued regulations requiring anyone flying in an Army aircraft to have a parachute, and the McCook Field Parachute Unit became the parent unit for a new association which would grow into an international brotherhood as the years went by. It was for people who had saved their lives by using a parachute and it was called the Caterpillar Club.

Patrols and Good Works

Behind the events which drew national headlines, the Army's airmen were kept busy in other ways. There were exercises and maneuvers to test such things as

Triple Mackay Trophy winner John Macready bundled up in high–altitude clothing before taking the LePere LUSAC-11 to unheard–of heights. In 1921, Macready pushed the world altitude record to 34,508 ft. There was much concern over the possibility of him escaping into earth orbit!

gunnery, bombing, and unit mobility. Military aircraft were routinely used to move men and supplies between bases, and the growing cross-country traffic in the air led to the establishment of airways, additional landing grounds, and weather stations. Operating from basic facilities in rough country, squadrons flew regular patrols along the Mexican border, an experience remembered by one pilot as "a life of hardship, possible death, starvation pay, and a lonely life without social contacts, in hot barren wastes, tortured by sun, wind, and sand." Some airmen joined with the Forest Service in patrolling western woodlands, looking for forest fires and directing fire fighters, and others were pioneer crop sprayers, helping the Department of Agriculture combat threats like the boll weevil. Air Service aircraft were detached to assist several U.S. agencies in mapping surveys, photographing in days areas which

might have consumed years if tackled on the ground.

Billy Mitchell was particularly enthusiastic about aerial mapping as an Air Service task, estimating that it could be done at one-tenth the cost and in one-hundredth the time required by any other method. He also believed that the Air Service should promote its public image by reacting quickly to emergencies. As a result, bombers dropped their bombs on ice jams and lava flows, and aircraft of all kinds were used on search and rescue missions, to drop emergency food supplies to flood victims, or to fly medical supplies wherever most needed. Even at a more personal level, these efforts of the Air Service were much appreciated. One pilot flew over a house in which he saw a fire developing. Since nobody appeared to be reacting, he landed in a nearby field, ran to the house, and knocked on the front door. The house-owner was surprised but grateful to be told by this ministering angel: "Mister—your house is on fire."

Air Power Debated

Mitchell, the fiery war leader and strident air power prophet, was a hero to most Army airmen, but even his closest admirers often wished he could advance his cause with methods which were less abrasive. Many came to believe that Mitchell's no-holds-barred approach had actually been counterproductive, making more enemies than friends, and that his sacrifice in the heat of political battle had occurred when he had little to show for it. While there may be a certain amount of truth behind that belief, it is equally true that Mitchell's persistence helped keep the air power debate on the political agenda. By the time of his resignation in February 1926, some of the air power seeds which he had helped plant were on their way to at least partial fruition.

From 1924 to 1925, the Lampert Committee of the House of Representatives investigated the operations of all U.S. air services, and took up where the neglected Lassiter board had left off as far as military aviation was concerned. After eleven months of hearings, the Lampert Committee included in its findings recommendations for an independent air force and increased spending on new flying equipment. However, to draw the Lampert Committee's sting and offset its supposed sympathy for Mitchell's arguments, President Coolidge ordered an inquiry of his own. Appointed by the President in September 1925, the Morrow Board reached its conclusions in less than three months, and published its findings two weeks before Lampert. The Morrow Board did not agree that air power was a decisive instrument of war, and did not recommend the formation of a separate air force. The President, and eventually Congress, generally accepted more of Morrow's ideas than Lampert's. Some of the news, but not all, was bad from the airmen's point of view. Superficially, by amending the name of the Air Service to Air Corps and creating an additional Assistant Secretary of War to

Hap Arnold seen with one of the more than 20,000 Liberty engines produced. While stocks lasted, the Liberty found its way into most American military aircraft designs, eventually becoming something of a drag on technological progress.

foster military aeronautics, the Air Corps Act of July 1926 improved the status of Army aviation, but not much had really changed in terms of how air power was to be used. On the other hand, a five-year Air Corps expansion program was authorized.

The snag was that there was no money immediately available to begin an expansion, so the program was delayed to run from July 1927 to June 1932. The goal was to reach a level of 1,650 officers; 15,000 men; and 1,800 serviceable aircraft from a starting point of 919 officers; 8,725 men; and a total aircraft strength of less

Changing an engine on a P-12 in the field was simply a matter of putting a block and tackle in the right place.

than 1,000. The Air Corps drew up hopeful plans, but money shortages persisted throughout the five-year program. The American people were not inclined to increase military spending at a time when isolationist and pacifist views were so strongly held, and there was no convincing argument to suggest that any foreign power posed a threat to national security. With the onset of the Great Depression, federal revenues declined, making it even more difficult to get adequate Air Corps funds. When June 1932 arrived, it was no surprise that the goals set in 1927 had not been achieved. The shortfalls were substantial—396 more officers and 1,940 enlisted men were needed, of whom 300 officers and 200 enlisted were missing pilots.

There were endless arguments throughout the period between politicians, the Army's General Staff, and Air Corps officers about what "1,800 serviceable aircraft" really meant. Did that figure include trainers, aircraft for the National Guard and Reserve, obsolete aircraft, those being used for research or held to cover annual wastage, or those undergoing major servicing? There were no easy answers, and in June 1932 a figure of 1,814 "serviceable aircraft" was reached, over Air Corps objections, by counting all those on hand for the Army, National Guard, and Reserve, and including 210 aircraft being overhauled. Some progress had, however, been made in altering the balance of the front line. There were now sixteen pursuit, twelve bombardment, and four attack squadrons alongside thirteen observation squadrons. The 70/30 split was not quite what General Patrick had been after, but it was noticeably better than before.

Examining the results of the five-year program dispassionately, it was clear that the Air Corps was much better than it had been at the beginning, but that left it a long way from the air force the Army's airmen had hoped to create. Disappointed by the past, they looked to the uncertain future. New politicians, new commanders, and new exciting aircraft were on the horizon, all of which could change the character of the air power debate. Perhaps the 1930s would see the promise of air power fulfilled.

Quiet and reserved though he was, Orville Wright remained involved in aviation until his death in 1948. He is seen here (left) in the early 1920s before a flight in a DH–4 with pilot Howard Rinehart.

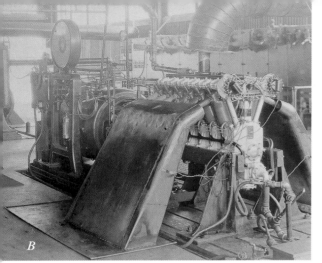

B

A A team of automobile engineers led by Jesse Vincent of Packard and J.G. Hall of Hall-Scott completed the basic design of the Liberty engine in a Washington hotel suite during one week of intense activity in May 1917. Originally conceived as an eight-cylinder engine, it went into production as a V-twelve producing 400 hp. 20,478 Libertys were built, a number large enough for them to remain the backbone of U.S. military aviation until the late 1920s. The USAF Museum's example is the last Liberty to have seen service with the Air Corps.

B A Liberty engine on a test stand at McCook Field.

A

A   The layout of the post-WW I DH–4's cockpit retains the essential simplicity typical of wartime aircraft. Since most people are right-handed, such controls as the throttle and the elevator trim wheel are placed to the left. The right hand grasps the stick and so is entrusted with the important business of maneuvering the aircraft.

B   The USAF Museum's DH–4 is painted in the colors of General Mason Patrick, Chief of Air Service during the early 1920s. Note the wing structure clearly revealed by the translucent fabric covering.

C   The selection of the de Havilland DH–4 for large-scale production in the U.S. was influenced by its capacity to mount the American Liberty engine. The combination did not produce startling performance, but the aircraft was very reliable and remained in service in a number of roles until the late 1920s.

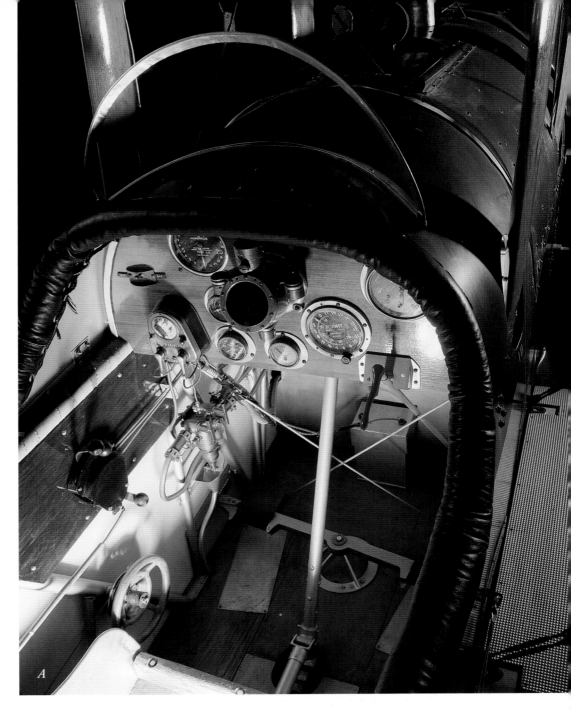

A

C

B

Douglas World Cruisers © *R.G. Smith, 1975*

Loening OA-1 Amphibian © *Keith Ferris, 1976*

A   The USAF Museum commemorates the achievement of the first round-the-world flyers in a display of artifacts left by some of the Air Corps men who took part in that epic 1924 flight. Among them are Leigh Wade's jacket, helmet, and gloves, and John Harding's bible, diary, and cigarette case. Erik Nelson is represented by a pennant given to him by a rival round-the-world airman, Anotonio Locatelli of Italy.

A   San Francisco, *the USAF Museum's Loening OA-1A, was flown by Ira Eaker and Muir Fairchild on the Mackay Trophy winning Pan-American Goodwill Tour of 1926-27.*

B   *The Loening OA-1A merged fuselage and hull as a single structure to gain the qualities of a small flying boat, but added retractable wheels to become an amphibian. The need to keep the propeller clear of the hull meant that the inevitable Liberty engine was inverted. The OA-1A had a range of 750 miles cruising at 90 mph.*

B

1921 - SINKING OF THE OSTFRIESLAND

1925-26 - US ARMY COURT-MARTIAL

GENERAL BILLY MITCHELL
1924 - BRIG. GENERAL,
ASST. CHIEF, US ARMY AIR SERVICE

A   General Billy Mitchell © *Maxine McCaffery, USAF Art Collection*

B   *The USAF Museum's Billy Mitchell collection includes his medals and the uniform jacket believed to have been worn at his court martial. Also shown are his spectacles, binoculars, and the pennant flown from his aircraft during the battleship trials.*

The Mackay Trophy

Established before World War I by Clarence H. Mackay, publisher of *Collier's* magazine and aviation enthusiast, the Mackay Trophy is presented annually by the National Aeronautic Association in recognition of the most meritorious U.S Air Force flight of the year.

1947	Capt. Charles E. Yeager. First supersonic flight, Bell X-1.
1948	Lt. Col. Emil Beaudry. Greenland rescue.
1949	Capt. James G. Gallagher and crew. First nonstop flight around the world, B-29 *Lucky Lady II,* 94 hrs 1 min.
1950	27th Fighter Escort Wing. Transatlantic deployment, F-84Es.
1951	Col. Fred J. Ascani. 100 km closed circuit speed record of 635.686 mph, F-86.
1952	Maj. Louis H. Carrington, Jr., Maj. Frederick W. Shook, Capt. Wallace D. Yancey. First jet nonstop transpacific flight, RB-45.
1953	40th Air Division, SAC. Nonstop transatlantic fighter deployment with flight refueling, F-84Gs.
1954	308th Bombardment Wing. "Leapfrog" intercontinental exercise, B-47s.
1955	Col. Horace A. Hanes. First supersonic world speed record, 822 mph, F-100C.
1956	Capt. Iven C. Kincheloe, Jr. Reaching 125,907 ft in the Bell X-2.
1957	93rd Bombardment Wing, SAC. First nonstop jet flight around the world, 45 hrs 19 mins, B-52s.
1958	TAC Composite Air Strike Force. Rapid deployment to the Far East.
1959	4520th Aerial Demonstration Team. Goodwill tour of the Far East.
1960	6593rd Test Squadron. Aerial recoveries of space capsules, C-119.
1961	Lt. Col. William R. Payne, Maj. William L. Polhemus, Maj. Raymond R. Wagener. New York to Paris in 3hrs 19 mins 41 secs, B-58.
1962	Maj. Robert G. Sowers, Capt. Robert McDonald, Capt. John T. Walton. New York-LosAngeles-New York in 4 hrs 41 mins 15 secs, B-58.
1963	Capt. Warren P. Tomsett, Capt. John R. Ordemann, Capt. Donald R. Mack, T. Sgt. Edsol P. Inslow, S. Sgt. Jack E. Morgan, S. Sgt. Frank C. Barrett. Evacuation of wounded under fire in Vietnam.
1964	464th Troop Carrier Wing. TAC. Evacuation of refugees from the Republic of Congo.
1965	Col. Robert L. Stephens, Lt. Col. Daniel Andre, Lt. Col. Walter F. Daniel, Maj. Noel T. Warner, Maj. James P. Cooney. Nine world records, including sustained speed of 2,070 mph and altitude of 80,258 ft, YF-12A.
1966	Col. Albert R. Howarth. Courage and airmanship in Southeast Asia.
1967	Maj. John R. Casteel, Capt. Dean L. Hoar, Capt. Richard L. Trail, M. Sgt. Nathan C. Campbell. Emergency multiple flight refuelings off Vietnam, KC -135.
1968	Lt. Col. Daryl C. Cole. Conspicuous gallantry in Southeast Asia, C-130.
1969	49th Tactical Fighter Wing. Deployment of 72 F-4Ds from W. Germany to New Mexico.
1970	Capt. Alan D. Milacek and crew. Destruction of targets in Vietnam with a severely damaged aircraft, AC-119K.
1971	Lt. Col. Thomas B. Estes, Lt. Col. Dewain C. Vick. Record-breaking flights, SR-71.
1972	Capt. Richard S. Ritchie, Capt. Charles B. DeBellevue, Capt. Jeffrey S. Feinstein. Vietnam War "aces."
1973	MAC aircrews. Return of POWs from Southeast Asia.
1974	Maj. Roger J. Smith, Maj. David W. Peterson, Maj. Willard R. MacFarlane. Project "Streak Eagle" test pilots, F-15.
1975	Maj. Robert W. Undorf. Outstanding performance during the *Mayaguez* crew rescue.
1976	Capt. James A. Yule. Gallantry while an instructor in a B-52D.
1977	Capt. David M. Sprinkel and crew. US/USSR energy research project, C-5.
1978	Lt. Col. Robert F. Schultz and crew, Capt. Todd H. Hohberger and crew. Airlift to Zaire, C-5.
1979	Maj. James E. McCardle. Helicopter rescue of 28 Taiwanese seamen.
1980	Crews from 644th Bombardment Squadron. Location of Soviet naval units in the Arabian Sea during nonstop flight around the world.
1981	Capt. John J. Walters. Rescue mission in Alaskan waters.
1982	Crew E-21, 19th Bombardment Wing. Emergency landing of B-52.
1983	Crew E-113, 42nd Bombardment Wing. Emergency refueling and towing of F-4E.
1984	Lt. Col. James L. Hobson, Jr. Grenada assault, MC-130.
1985	Lt. Col. David E. Faught. Emergency landing, KC-135.
1986	Crew from 68th Air Refueling Group, SAC. Emergency transatlantic refueling of Marine A-4s, KC-10.
1987	B-1B SPO. 72 record B-1B flights.
1988	Crew from 436th Military Airlift Wing. Mission to Semipalatinsk, USSR, as part of INF Accords, C-5.
1989	Crew from 96th Bombardment Wing. Emergency landing of B-1B.
1990	Crew from 16th Special Operations Squadron. Operations in Panama.
1991	Crew from 20th Special Operations Squadron. Rescue of USN F-14 pilot inside Iraq, MH-53.
1992	Capt. P.B. Eunice and crew from Air Combat Command. Emergency landing of C-130H after being severely damaged in international airspace by Peruvian fighters.
1993	Crew from 668th Bomb Squadron. Emergency landing of B-52 following loss of four engines.
1994	Crew from 56th Rescue Squadron. Rescue of Icelandic sailors from foundered merchant vessel, HH-60G.
1995	Crew from Dyess AFB. Flight around the world in 36 hrs 13 mins 36 secs, B-1B.

Chapter 5

The 1930s-Changes and Constraints

"Air power is as vital a requirement to the military efficiency of a great nation as land power or sea power, and there is no hope for victory in war for a nation in which it is lacking."

(Major General Frank Andrews, 1938)

"I will not attempt to predict what advancements will be made in the next fifty to sixty years, but I will say that I believe that in aerospace nothing, absolutely nothing, is impossible. We'll just keep moving ahead."

(Major General Benjamin Foulois, First Chief of the Air Corps)

"The best protection [for the U.S.] is to accept and build upon American tradition and not try to purchase freedom with gadgets."

(Secretary of War George Dern on the Air Corps' bid for strategic bombers, 1933)

"Independent air missions have little effect on the issue of battle, and none upon the outcome of war."

(Findings of the Baker Board, 1934)

"If [President Roosevelt] is in office when war comes he'll want to be the strategist. If he's not air-minded by that time, then God help the country."

(Billy Mitchell, 1935)

Henry H. "Hap" Arnold (1886-1950). In 1934, as a colonel, "Hap" Arnold put on a heavy flight suit and led a squadron of B-10s to Alaska. By 1938 he was Chief of the Army Air Corps, and in 1949 he became the only airman ever to be promoted to five-star rank.

The Changing Shapes of Air Power

In covering the years of the 1930s, the displays of the USAF Museum show that great changes were on hand for American military aviation. A beautifully restored Martin B-10 dominates the end of the gallery and contrasts sharply with all that has gone before. The lingering images of WWI so evident in aircraft like the P-6E are erased in the shape of this all-metal monoplane with closed cockpits, internal bomb stowage, and retractable landing gear. Here is a machine which is linked with the future rather than shackled to the past. The Air Corps' enthusiasm for their splendid new weapon is readily apparent from the account given nearby of the flight of a B-10 formation to Alaska in 1934.

In contrast is a display which tells the story of the Air Corps' ill-fated 1934 involvement in carrying the U.S. mail, a commitment which was undertaken with inadequate equipment in the teeth of appalling winter weather. Eighteen airmen were killed in four months, but their deaths drew public attention to the parsimonious funding of the Air Corps, and the resulting lack of many important capabilities.

More encouraging wall displays cover the formation of GHQ Air Force in 1935, a significant step on the road to an independent air force, and tell the saga of the B-17 Flying Fortress. Various early adventures with the B-17 are shown, especially two involving the young Curtis LeMay—a goodwill flight to South America in 1938 and the celebrated interception of the Italian steamship Rex in mid-Atlantic that same year. Mention is made also of the first of the "super-bombers," the XB-15 and XB-19. A main-wheel from the XB-19 gives an idea of the aircraft's immense size. Other technological achievements covered include the first auto-land equipment, the first pressure cabin, and the mounting of a 75 mm cannon in a B-18. As the 1930s displays come to an end, there is evidence that the U.S. was once again preparing to recover from years of neglecting and misunderstanding military aviation, and getting set to catch up with other nations in the air. Reference is made to President Roosevelt's concerns and to the approval given by Congress in 1939 to a program for building an air force of 5,500 aircraft.

American fighters of the late 1930s are represented in the chubby, gleaming shape of the only surviving Seversky P-35A. The first American single-seater with metal skin, closed cockpit, and retractable landing gear, the P-35 was nevertheless soon overtaken by events, but museum visitors should have no difficulty in making the connection, at a glance, between this aircraft and its illustrious offspring, Republic's P-47 Thunderbolt.

Now the USAF Museum's coverage of the uncertain interwar years is complete. The explosive beginnings of the bloodiest war in history lie just around the corner.

The 1930s came to America's military airmen in several conflicting guises. An Aladdin's Cave of new developments in aviation offered an air power future of great promise, one in which it looked as though the predictions of prophets like Billy Mitchell could possibly come true. Barring the way, however, was a Slough of Despond hiding in its depths the realities of a major economic depression and the stultified attitudes of the U.S. Army's "old soldiers," either of which threatened to crush hopes for the growth of U.S. air power. Even if the challenges of such a Slough were overcome, a threat of appall-

Delivery of Martin B-10 bombers went on until 1936 and they continued to serve with U.S. Army Air Corps squadrons for several years thereafter. These B-10s were photographed near San Francisco in January 1940.

ing proportions loomed on the far side—war shaped by the rise of Japanese militarism in the Pacific and Hitlerian fascism in Europe. It seemed certain that aviation's Aladdin's Cave held at least part of the answer to prevailing in this global holocaust, but U.S. airmen were to find that pulling clear of the Slough's drag to reach the treasures of the Cave would be no easy matter.

In 1931, General Benny Foulois, who in 1910 had been the U.S. Army's only pilot and who had since become a most forthright advocate for independent air power, was made Chief of the Air Corps in succession to General Fechet. His ardor for independence was in no way diminished, but he had begun to see that half a loaf was better than no bread. It seemed to him, and to a number of his senior Air Corps colleagues, that the interim arrangement of what had become known as a "GHQ Air Force" might be an acceptable compromise for a while. At the same time, the resistance of the U.S. Army's General Staff to the idea of giving the airmen a longer leash was beginning to crumble. The continuing struggle over air power was wearing, and it occurred to them that allowing the creation of a GHQ Air Force might subdue the clamor for air force independence. The seeds of the idea had taken root, but it would be some years before the airmen would taste the fruits, and they would find that some of them could be quite sour.

In November 1930, General Douglas MacArthur became the U.S. Army's Chief of Staff and almost immediately sought a way to end the bickering of the Army and Navy over who was responsible for what in the matter of operating military aircraft. On January 9, 1931, MacArthur and the Chief of Naval Operations, Admiral William Pratt, reached an agreement. A press release said: "The naval air forces will be based on the fleet and move with it as an important element in performing the essential missions of the forces afloat. The Army air forces will be land based and employed as an element of the Army in carrying out its mission of defending the coasts, both in the homeland and in overseas possessions."

The Boeing B-9, escorted here by a P-26, was a private venture development of the "Monomail" freight carrier. With an all-metal stressed skin and retractable undercarriage, the B-9 had a top speed of 188 mph and was a notable advance in bomber design when it first flew in 1931. It was, however, overshadowed by the Martin B-10, which flew only months later.

MacArthur felt that this arrangement enabled "the air component of each service to proceed with its own planning, training, and procurement activities with little danger of duplicating those of its sister service." The General may indeed have believed that his imposing presence had been all that was necessary to remove a long-standing thorn in the side of interservice relationships, but the events of later years would make his satisfaction seem a little premature.

In mid-1933, Admiral Pratt retired and his successor, Admiral Standley, could hardly wait to repudiate the MacArthur/Pratt agreement. Thereafter, the Navy proceeded to develop land-planes of its own for the defense of the U.S. coastline, but the General Staff went on planning for an Army role in airborne coastal defense. The Air Corps, adhering to the wishes of its masters in the General Staff, built up its case for aircraft capable of conducting long-range reconnaissance missions over water. It was said that these aircraft were needed to intercept and attack enemy shipping, so providing a defense for the U.S. against seaborne attack. The airmen hoped that the remarkable similarity between such "long-range reconnaissance aircraft," essentially defensive, and their Holy Grail of a

strategic bomber force, unquestionably offensive, would not be too obvious.

Metal Monoplanes

Strategic air power theory had been hampered in the 1920s by the state of the art in bomber design and construction, but the early 1930s saw the introduction of techniques which were little short of revolutionary, promising dramatic advances in aircraft performance and the steady eclipse of the biplane. Aircraft could go higher, faster, and farther than ever before. The foretaste of things to come was given by the Boeing B-9 in 1931, but even this remarkable aircraft was overshadowed by the appearance only a few months later of the Martin B-10. The B-10 embodied so many new techniques and devices that it stands out as one of the most significant single advances in the history of military aircraft. Here for the first time was a cantilever monoplane of all-metal stressed-skin construction which had wing flaps, retractable landing gear, enclosed cockpits, a glazed gun turret, variable pitch propellers, low-drag engine cowlings, and an internal bomb bay with power-driven doors. Even the underpowered prototype ran away from all the fighters in service. Its bombload of a little over one ton could have been bigger, and its combat range was only seven hundred miles, but the B-10 was rightly seen as the harbinger of an American air power spring and it was rapidly adopted as the Air Corps' front-line bomber—for aggressive long-range "reconnaissance."

The B-10 had no sooner entered service than it was used in a series of exercises to demonstrate the flexibility of air power, most notably in a deployment to Alaska. On July 19, 1934, a squadron of ten B-10s under the command of Colonel Hap Arnold left Bolling Field, Washington, DC, and flew in easy stages to Alaska. They landed at Fairbanks six days after leaving Washington, but they had covered more than four thousand miles in just over twenty-five hours of flying time without any problems. After doing a 20,000-square-mile photographic survey of Alaska, they flew back to Bolling Field just as smoothly. More than half a century later, with air travel to Alaska a commonplace event, it is easy to forget that the B-10 flight was a considerable achievement. Hap Arnold was awarded his second MacKay Trophy for the operation, with a citation which singled out the overwater leg from Juneau to Seattle with the words: "linking the Territory of Alaska with the United States by air, without a stop on foreign territory, for the first time."[1]

Such bright spots aside, the Depression of the early 1930s had its effect on the Air Corps. Annual maneuvers were abandoned, flying hours sharply reduced, and live weapons training stopped. Accident rates went up and pay was cut. On the other hand, the government's public relief programs provided money and labor for major works, such as building or improving military airfields.

Against the background of all these problems, the concept of the GHQ Air Force began to take shape. In 1933, the U.S. Army reorganized its land forces into four field armies, and it was thought that the Air Corps could respond to the de-

mands of these forces more effectively if its combat units answered directly to the General Staff, instead of to individual field commanders. As a first step in the process, General Foulois formed a headquarters unit for GHQ Air Force in Washington in October 1933, but the impetus to complete the process was lost for a few months as the Air Corps' attention was drawn in another, temporarily more pressing, direction.

Flying the Mail

Irregularities in the airmail contracts with the commercial airlines led to their

B-10 crews bound for Alaska in 1934. Hap Arnold is seen standing fourth from the right, under the aircraft's nose.

cancellation by President Roosevelt in February 1934. While new contracts were being drawn up, the Air Corps was asked to step into the breach and carry the mail. General Foulois was given ten days to create the necessary organization, assign and position men and equipment, prepare the aircraft, and begin training pilots on the routes they would be flying. Foulois divided the U.S. into three zones, setting up commands at Salt Lake City under Hap Arnold, and at Chicago and New York under Lt. Col. Horace Hickam and Major

B.Q. Jones. The rushed nature of the preparations prompted a number of observers into dire predictions, including some from Eddie Rickenbacker, then Vice President of North American Aviation. He warned that the commercial airlines were using aircraft specifically designed to do the job, and that their pilots were extremely experienced and well trained. In his opinion: "Either they are going to pile up ships all the way across the continent, or they are not going to be able to fly the mail on schedule." Rickenbacker was to be proven right on both counts.

The words were hardly out of

Rickenbacker's mouth before the first accident was reported. February 20, 1934, was the date on which the Air Corps was to take over officially as the U.S. mail carrier, but on February 16 two pilots left California in a Curtiss A-12 attack aircraft to position themselves at Salt Lake City. They were killed when they flew into a snowstorm-hidden mountain in Utah. A few hours later, the pilot of a Douglas B-7 died when he hit the ground in Idaho at night. Rickenbacker was not reticent about saying he had told them so. The next day

[1]Arnold won the first MacKay Trophy ever awarded when he used a Wright Flyer to demonstrate the reconnaissance capabilities of an aircraft near Washington in 1912. His 1934 flight was not the first to link the Alaska territory with the U.S. by air. In a perhaps even more remarkable achievement, Capt. St. Clair Streett led the "Black Wolf" Squadron of DH-4s from New York to Nome in 1920, refueling several times in Canada on the way. The DH-4s covered the 9,000-mile round trip in 112 flying hours without serious incident.

he called it: "Legalized murder!"

The weather that winter was the worst for many years, and Air Corps pilots took it on in open cockpits equipped with poor instrumentation and inadequate navigation aids. The results were almost inevitable. By the time the Air Corps was relieved of responsibility for the mail on June 1, 1934, little more than three months after it assumed the burden, there had been sixty-six crashes in which twelve men had died on mail routes and another six in training or ferrying flights. Fifteen others were in the hospital recovering from injuries.

Hap Arnold's cheerful smile for the camera could not have lasted long. Instructed to take over responsibility for delivering airmail in February 1934, the Air Corps suffered sixty-six crashes in three months. The uproar which followed was instrumental in forcing Congress to find the funds for much needed improvements in Air Corps equipment and training.

The uproar caused by the airmail fiasco focused the attention of everyone, including President Roosevelt, on the state of the Air Corps. Foulois later recalled that at one stage he and General MacArthur had been summoned to the President's bedside to endure "a tongue-lashing which I put down in my book as the worst I ever received in all my military service." When the whole unpleasant adventure was over, the recriminations dragged on for months and eventually led, in December 1935, to

Benny Foulois's resignation. There were, however, other more positive effects. Foulois himself felt that the public reaction to the airmail deaths forced the President and Congress to face the need to improve the Air Corps, basing the provision of additional funds for the purpose on the report of the 1934 Baker Board. The Board readily acknowledged the shortcomings of Air Corps equipment and the valiant manner in which military pilots had tackled an inappropriate task. Its findings suggested major improvements in all forms of equipment and recommended that aircrews should carry out more training in night and bad weather flying and radio navigation, and that they should average a minimum of three hundred hours flying a year. Foulois saw the Board's report as "the first comprehensive outline of War Department policy with respect to aviation that the Army has ever had." He felt strongly that the airmail pilots had not died in vain. Without their sacrifice, Foulois believed that the U.S. would have been as unprepared in the air in 1941 as it had been in 1917.

GHQ Air Force

While many of the Baker Board's findings were helpful to the Air Corps, the overall attitude of the committee reflected the lack of conviction of the majority of its members about the importance of air power. The report remarked on "the limitations of the airplane," and said that: "The idea that aviation, acting alone, can control the sea lanes, or defend the coast, or produce decisive results . . . [is] visionary, as is the idea that a very large and independent air force is necessary to defend our country." A lone voice on the committee recorded a dissenting view. Jimmy Doolittle, then with Shell Oil Company, told the world that most of the members of the Board knew "as much about the future of aviation as they do about the sign writing of the Aztecs." His more formal statement said: "I believe that the future security of our nation is dependent upon an adequate air force," and reaffirmed his view that such an air force would be more effective if developed as a separate arm of the military.

Boosted by the Baker findings, the move to create a GHQ Air Force resumed where it had been interrupted by the requirement to fly the mail. Other currents in the wider world lent some urgency to the need to build a more powerful and responsive air arm. By 1933 militarism was rampant in both Japan and Germany. The Japanese were flexing their military muscle in China and Hitler had pulled Germany out of the Disarmament Conference in Geneva. The American public might be understandably concerned with domestic issues and essentially isolationist, but thoughtful people recognized that the U.S. could not afford to ignore the implications of what was happening in Europe and East Asia.

On March 1, 1935, one week before Hitler announced the existence of the Luftwaffe, Brig. Gen. Frank Andrews assumed command of the GHQ Air Force and set up his headquarters at Langley Field, Virginia. It was a step in the right direction, but the organization was flawed from the outset. On the face of it, the new command and that of the Chief of Air

Corps were of equal status, both answering directly to the General Staff, with GHQAF responsible for operational affairs, but with training and logistics remaining under the Air Corps. To further complicate matters, administrative jurisdiction over the airmen's bases was given to local Army corps commanders. It was not a happy arrangement. Base commanders confronted the predicament of reporting to several different chiefs. The wrangling over responsibilities and chains of command continued throughout the tenure of Maj. Gen. Oscar Westover, Foulois's successor as Chief of Air Corps, and it was not until Frank Andrews left GHQ Air Force in March 1939 that the organization was finally changed to unify U.S. Army aviation under a single chain of command.

Troubles with Strategic Bombers

Arguments over the way they should be organized never diverted the airmen from their goal of building a strategic bomber force. In 1934, the War Department agreed to an Air Corps project to develop an aircraft much larger and of longer range than the B-10. It was justified on the grounds that an aircraft was needed which could reinforce either coast of the U.S. or its overseas possessions without refueling. Surprisingly for an old soldier, General MacArthur encouraged the move, saying: "the bombardment airplane is the most important element of the GHQ Air Force," and adding the remark that the heavy bomber "makes it possible to inflict damage on an enemy in the rear areas of his armies and his zone of interior, which no other weapon can do." MacArthur, unlike the rest of the General Staff, was apparently not too concerned that a strategic bomber might be hiding behind the screen of long-range reinforcement and reconnaissance.

The project, undertaken by Boeing, grew into a monster of an aircraft, the XB-15. Its sheer size—149 ft wingspan and 70,000 lbs gross weight—made it an experimental enterprise in every sense of the word. Boeing engineers had new problems to solve at each stage of the aircraft's construction, and it took them three and a half years to get it finished. They then found that their design had outrun the available engine technology. The XB-15 was doomed to being underpowered, and only one example was ever built. Nevertheless, the lessons learned in designing and building the XB-15 were enormously helpful in paving the way for two other Boeing bombers which were destined to leave their mark on aviation history in WWII.

Shortly after the contract for the XB-15 was let, Boeing was swept into a competition to build another bomber. With the B-10 only recently in service, the Air Corps was already looking towards its replacement. The specification said that the aircraft should be multiengine and be able to carry at least a ton of bombs over a range of 1,020 miles at 200 mph. It was added that the range and speed figures were minimums and that it was desirable for the new bomber to have a range of 2,500 miles and a top speed of 250 mph. One further point added spice to the challenge; it was now August 1934 and the Air Corps required bidders to provide their aircraft in time for them to take part in a flying competition at Wright Field in August 1935.

Three companies had aircraft at Wright Field on the appointed day. Martin appeared with the B-12, which was little more than an updated B-10. Douglas offered the DB-1, a twin-engined bomber developed from the successful DC-2 airliner. Boeing, however, stole the show with a completely new four-engined aircraft. The Model 299 flew in nonstop from Seattle, having averaged 232 mph on the way. Two months later, after exhaustive tests, the 299 was clearly the front-runner in the competition. Then, on October 30, 1935, just after takeoff for its final test flight, the 299 reared up, stalled, and crashed. The controls locks had been left engaged and the pilot could not lower the rising nose when the 299 left the ground. Boeing's hopes went up in smoke, and the DB-1, now the B-18, was declared the winner by default. Douglas received an immediate production contract for 133 aircraft.

The officers at GHQAF, however, had seen enough of the 299 to know what they wanted. The accident, after all, had not been the fault of the aircraft. Approval was given for the acquisition of thirteen 299s for flying evaluation, plus one more for static tests. This first series was designated Y1B-17 by the Air Corps[2] but the press had already coined the name by which the public would always recognize the aircraft. A Seattle reporter had been so amazed at the sight of a bomber with five gun positions that he was inspired to call

The accompanying P-26 accentuates the fact that Boeing's XB-15 was a very large aircraft, with a wingspan of 149ft. It proved too large for the engines of the 1930s and was a lumbering performer, but it was invaluable in paving the way for the later B-29.

it a "Flying Fortress." Bitter experience in combat would later reveal that the name, at least in the early versions of the B-17, was a considerable exaggeration of the truth, but it had a good sound and it stuck.

For the Air Corps, the B-17 was the answer to their prayers. It was well-mannered in the air, and it easily exceeded the requirements of the military specifications. General Andrews embarked on a persistent campaign in support of the B-17, insisting that his bombardment squadrons should be equipped only with four-engined aircraft. In a letter to General Westover in 1937 he observed: "The Air Corps until recently prided itself in securing the best equipment obtainable regardless of expense, but the recent procurement of bombers [B-18s] . . . is the first time that an inferior airplane has been produced when a superior one was available." The soldiers of the Army's General Staff, however, were not so easily convinced that B-17s were desirable. The Deputy Chief of Staff, Maj. Gen. Embrick, harped on the theme that "our national policy contemplates defense, not aggression." This shortsighted policy, adhered to slavishly since 1919 when people were rejecting armaments of almost any kind, continued to stand as a barrier to the building of effective U.S. armed forces at a time when Japan was waging total war in China and Hitler had repudiated the Versailles Treaty and declared general conscription for German youth. With German troops rolling into the Rhineland, the U.S. Army's General Staff could still say that in their preference for the B-17, the Air Corps had been led astray by "a quest for the ultimate in aircraft performance at the expense of practical military need." The B-18 remained the Army's bomber of choice.

Utterly sure of the rightness of their case, the airmen took every opportunity of showing off the B-17's capabilities to the U.S. public. Between March and Au-

gust 1937, the 2nd Bombardment Group at Langley Field, commanded by Lt. Col. Robert Olds, received twelve of the Y1B-17s. Soon after the arrival of the first, they began appearing at conventions and expositions. They flew over a number of cities in formation, and their speeds between cities were always released for publication. In January 1938, Col. Olds broke the U.S. transcontinental record by flying from Langley to March Field, California, in 12 hrs 50 mins, and then flew back again in 10 hrs 46 mins. Still more impressive were two extensive goodwill tours of South America, both completed without serious incident in a blaze of favorable publicity.

Even as these positive events were taking place, it appeared that the death knell of the four-engined bomber might be sounding. In May 1938, a memorandum from the Adjutant General to the Assistant Secretary of War included the passage: "The Chief of the Air Corps has been informed that experimentation and development for the fiscal years 1939/40 will be restricted to that class of aviation designed for the close-in support of ground

troops, and for the production of that type of aircraft such as medium and light aircraft." The note went on to emphasize that there was no military requirement for four-engined bombardment aircraft. No orders were to be placed for B-17s in 1938.

In some ways, the airmen had only themselves to blame. GHQ Air Force had compounded the problem in August 1937 by thumbing its nose at the Navy. Col. Olds's B-17s succeeded in intercepting and

Boeing's Model 299 was the most impressive entrant for the Air Corps' 1935 competition to find the next generation bomber. Clearly superior to the Martin B-12 and Douglas DB-1 in every respect, it was officially ruled out following a fatal crash on its last test flight. However, with pilot error as the cause—the controls locks had been left engaged for takeoff— an order was placed for thirteen further test aircraft, to be designated YB-17. The future of the most celebrated American bomber of WWII was thereby assured.

bombing (with water bombs) the U.S. Navy's *Utah* in an exercise off the California coast in poor weather and despite what the airmen believed to be deliberately misleading information from naval sources. An unauthorized leak to the press about the B-17's accomplishment did not improve the Navy's temper. Irritation became outrage in May 1938 when General Andrews decided to use the Italian transatlantic liner *Rex* to represent an approaching enemy fleet. Three B-17s set off from Mitchel Field, New York, to intercept a single ship some seven hundred miles out in the ocean. The weather was bad, with low clouds and rain, but General Andrews had decided to

[2]Aircraft designations can be confusing. In the case of the Flying Fortress, Model 299 was a Boeing number. When a prototype is accepted for flying by air force aircrew, it is given a military designation which it carries throughout its service life, plus the letter X for experimental. The 299 therefore should have become the XB-17, but it crashed before the designation could be changed. Test series aircraft are given the letter Y, and the first fourteen B-17s delivered to the Air Corps were YB-17s. The figure 1 was inserted merely to indicate the source of funds used to buy the aircraft, making them Y1B-17s. Production aircraft lose their prefixes, and gain series letters after the numbers — B-17A, B-17B, B-17C, etc. All B-17s were Flying Fortresses.

By May 1937, when this photograph was taken, the YB-17 test program was well underway, and the Air Corps was taking every opportunity to show off the new bombers over cities across the country, proudly announcing the point-to-point flight times.

gamble on success by taking along reporters from the *New York Herald Tribune* and the *New York Times*. To increase the tension of the crews, the lead aircraft was also carrying a commentator from NBC radio and his transmitters. It was intended that he would begin a national broadcast from the B-17 at precisely 12:25 EST. To the eternal relief of the airmen, they burst out of a squall just before the appointed time to find the *Rex* dead ahead.[3] It was a splendid achievement, and the next day it was on the front pages of newspapers all across the U.S. The *New York Times* declared that the B-17's performance was "one from which valuable lessons about the aerial defense of the United States will be drawn." Glowing from the success of the exercise,

and protesting modestly that the flight had been no more than routine for B-17 crews, the airmen were not prepared for what happened next.

The next morning, while the GHQ Air Force staff were still congratulating each other on the success of the B-17s, there was a telephone call from the Army Chief of Staff, General Malin Craig. It appeared that he was not amused. As Hap Arnold put it: "Somebody in the Navy apparently got in quick touch with somebody on the General Staff and, in less time than it takes to tell about it, the War Department had sent down an order limiting all activities of the Army Air Corps to within one hundred miles from the shoreline of the United States."

There is no evidence that this remarkably restricting order was ever written down, and its origins are hidden in a fog of hazy memories and oblique references. It seems almost certain that the U.S. Navy, perhaps at the level of the Secretary or the senior naval staff, made some sort of protest to their opposite numbers in the Army Department about Army aircraft usurping the Navy's blue water prerogatives. It may be, also, that General Craig was irked by the fact that he was on the receiving end of a naval broadside when he had not been kept fully informed about GHQ Air Force's intentions. Whatever the case, the verbal order restrained air exercise planners even though it was never spelled out in writing, nor properly understood. Months later, General Andrews sought clarification because the restriction "took a 1,000-mile weapon and reduced its operating range to 100 miles." He was told that General Craig did not object to maneuvers more than one hundred miles offshore provided that proper authority (i.e.:, General Staff agreement) was asked for well in advance. To many airmen, that pointed to the probability that the notorious one-hundred-mile restriction had been issued in a spur of the moment fit of pique. Nevertheless, because it was never formally issued, the order was never properly rescinded, and its effects bedeviled Army aviation for many months.

While the Navy's objections were real enough, underlying the one-hundred-mile restriction was the fact that many people, particularly Army officers, could see no justification for developing long-range heavy bombers. In their opinion, Army aviation should be devoted primarily to direct support of the land battle, and expensive four-engined aircraft were not required for that. Twin-engined medium and light bombers were more than adequate. More to the point, two or even three of the smaller aircraft could be bought for the price of one heavy bomber. That argument held considerable appeal

In 1938, Col. Robert Olds led a successful goodwill tour of Latin America with Y1B-17s. (In WWII and Vietnam, Robert Olds's son Robin would also make his Air Force mark.)

---

[3]It is worth noting that the successful lead navigator for the B-17s on the first South American tour, and for the interceptions of the *Utah* and the *Rex*, was Lt. Curtis LeMay. Transferred from pursuit aviation, he did not then have sufficient flying hours to become a pilot of a B-17, and so began his career in four-engined aircraft as a navigator.

for politicians. In 1938, the year of the Munich crisis, the future for the B-17 did not look bright.

The Problem of Pursuit

Aeronautical progress in the 1930s pushed the bomber into controversy not only because it raised questions about its role but also because it threatened to eliminate the performance gap between bombardment and pursuit aviation. By 1933, General Westover was reporting that bombers had enough speed and firepower to operate without support, and adding his doubts that pursuit aircraft could intercept and engage at such high speeds. General Andrews and Colonel Hap Arnold were among the airmen who believed bombers capable of penetrating any defensive system. Seeking an answer to the pursuit problem, the Air Corps considered a number of solutions, including large multiseat fighter aircraft armed with outsize cannon and carrying bombs to drop on enemy formations. Arnold actually used Martin B-12s in the role of fighters during a 1934 exercise, but without much success. Somewhat less outrageous were the Berliner-Joyce P-16 and Consolidated P-30 two-seaters, but neither remained long in squadron service. The multiplace idea found its full flowering in the Bell XFM-1 Airacuda, a twin-engined heavy fighter with a five man crew, armed with two .30- and two .50-caliber machine guns, two 37 mm cannon, and twenty 30 lb bombs. After extensive testing, sanity prevailed and the Airacuda never saw operational service.

More conventional development led to the Boeing P-26 as the standard Air Corps fighter for most of the 1930s. A chubby little monoplane with spatted, fixed undercarriage, braced wings, and an open cockpit, the P-26 could manage 235 mph in level flight, but this was a speed soon exceeded by Boeing's own B-17 and, more significantly, by the bombers of Mitsubishi and Heinkel. In the late 1930s, pursuit aviation advanced more obviously with the Seversky P-35 and the Curtiss P-36, both radial-engined single-seaters with closed cockpits and retractable undercarriages. Maximum speeds were close to 300

mph for the first time and both aircraft were rugged and agile, but neither could match the performance of fighters being produced in Europe. As WWII drew ever closer, uncertainty about the role of the fighter and the lack of a powerful in-line engine left the U.S. without an aircraft capable of ensuring superiority in the air battle.

Other Roles

Attack aviation was left similarly in the doldrums. Although the standard attack aircraft, the Northrop A-17, was beautifully constructed and popular with its crews, by the late 1930s it was clearly obsolete and was being phased into training and support roles. In the transport field, the Air Corps fared rather better. The U.S. led the world in the design of transport aircraft, and the Air Corps benefited in the shape of the Douglas DC-2 series, the various military forms being designated C-33, C-34, and C-39. However, the observation aircraft of the 1930s still reflected the thinking which produced the sort of multirole machine used in WWI. The high-wing Douglas O-46 and the elephantine North American O-47 were too slow and cumbersome to avoid enemy fighters, and too heavy to operate from unprepared fields. Both were moved to less demanding duties after enjoying a brief life with operational squadrons.

The Goodyear balloon Explorer II *which carried Captains Albert Stevens and Orvil Anderson to a world altitude record of 72,395 ft in 1935.*

In flying training, the U.S. could not have been better served. The mid-30s saw the arrival of the Stearman PT-13 and the North American BT-9, the latter the forerunner of a famous line which would endure through the remainder of the century and train the pilots of over fifty nations. Another "aircraft" which led the way in international pilot training was the Link Trainer, the grandfather of all flight simulators. Invented in 1928, it had been ignored by the Air Corps until the airmail disasters of 1934. From then on, with blind flying training being taken seriously, Link's little blue instrumented box, sporting

The Curtiss P-36 of the 18th Pursuit Group commander, over Oahu in February 1940.

stubby yellow wings, made pilots sweat in increasing numbers as they struggled to master its jerky motion and groaning idiosyncrasies. Whatever its shortcomings as a flight simulator, the Link was invaluable in raising the standard of instrument flying wherever it was used.

In the course of the 1930s, the lighter-than-air branch of the Air Corps became less and less relevant, except in the eyes of those few Army officers who still felt that the observation balloon was more to be trusted than an aircraft when it came to advising the artillery. By 1939, the lighter-than-air branch was a rump of just

A North American BT-9, the forerunner of the more famous AT-6, winging over above the distinctive circular pattern of Randolph Field, Texas. In 1939, Randolph was the most modern of the Air Corps Training Centers, which together turned out the modest total of some 300 pilots per year.

10 officers and 350 men. However, the decade did not pass without one final balloon flourish from the Air Corps, even though it was in a balloon funded by the National Geographic Society. The Goodyear Company built two "Explorer" balloons in 1935 with the joint aims of gathering information about the stratosphere and breaking the world altitude record. *Explorer II*, with Captains Albert Stevens and Orvil Anderson on board, succeeded in doing both, reaching 72,395 ft over South Dakota in November 1935.

The Arnold Era Dawns

In September 1938, Maj. Gen. Hap Arnold became Chief of the Air Corps after the untimely death of General Westover. Involved in an inspection tour of western facilities, Westover had been flying himself in an A-17. On the approach to Lockheed's airfield at Burbank, California, the A-17 was seen to stall and spin into the ground, where it burst into flames on impact. Arnold inherited an air force which was full of promise, but which was still suffering from its subservience to traditional Army ways of thinking, and from limited funding. The U.S., still inclined to be isolationist, was no higher than sixth in the world ranking of nations with combat aircraft, and the other major powers, unlike the U.S., were already building their war machines with air power very much to the fore. Change was on its way, however, and was supported from what the airmen would have believed to be an unlikely source.

President Roosevelt was known to have a particularly soft spot for the Navy. After his meeting with the President in 1935, Billy Mitchell declared: "Everything on his desk bore some relation to a ship. It depressed me. If only I could have seen one model airplane among those mementos, I'd feel a lot better about the safety of the country." It may be that the President took note of Mitchell's pleas for military aviation. If so, they were certainly reinforced by events in China and Spain in 1937, and by Hitler's use of the air power threat to get his way in Europe in the following year. Whatever the case, air power had been raised to a prominent place in the President's mind by 1938. As his adviser, Harry Hopkins, remarked after the Munich crisis: "The President was sure then that we were going to get into a war and he believed that air power would win it." When the meaning of the Hitler/Chamberlain meeting in Munich became clear, Roosevelt called a meeting of his senior military advisers and announced that the U.S. must initiate a program leading rapidly to increased military aircraft production and to a much more powerful U.S. air arm.

General Arnold could hardly believe it. He later wrote: "A battle was won in the White House that day which took its place with—or at least led to—the victories in combat later." In his determination to pursue his new enthusiasm, Roosevelt announced that he intended to ask Congress for 20,000 military aircraft, and for facilities to support a national production capacity of 24,000 aircraft per year. Such startling figures were beyond the wildest dreams of the airmen, and they were diminished in the light of reasoned assessments later. After the President's State of the Union address in January 1939, in which he said bluntly that America's air forces were utterly inadequate, Congress agreed to raise the Army's aircraft authorization to a figure not exceeding 6,000, and to provide the money for 3,251 new aircraft over a two year period. Funds to provide for additional manpower and construction were also voted. None of this was achieved without considerable opposition from those who believed that money spent on an increased defense budget was money wasted, but, viewed in the knowledge of what followed in later years, the figures which sparked such fierce debate would seem to be almost pitifully small.

The Air Corps planners aimed to have 3,300 of the authorized aircraft as combat machines, and these were to include a host of new types. Four-engined bombers rose from the dead in the shape of thirty-nine B-17Bs and seven Consolidated B-24s, a second four-engined bomber design which was still at the prototype construction stage. Among the fighters were 524 Curtiss P-40s, 13 Lockheed P-38s, 12 Bell P-39s, and 13 Republic P-43s, and 186 Douglas A-20s at last promised to give the Air Corps an attack bomber worthy of the name. North American and Martin had new medium bomber designs on the way—the B-25 and the B-26.

As the door began to open on a brighter future for American military aviation, one in which the realities of air power would begin to be faced, there were accommodating changes in organization and policy for the Air Corps. In March 1939, with the departure of General Andrews from his command, GHQ Air Force lost its apparently equal status with the Air Corps. Rather than answering directly to the General Staff of the Army, GHQAF was placed under the Chief of the Air Corps. For the first time, responsibility for all Air Corps activity would rest with one man—Hap Arnold. It was an enormously heavy responsibility, although in 1939 even he did not fully appreciate the weight which would come to rest on his shoulders, a weight resulting from the most dramatic expansion of military capability ever undertaken in the history of warfare.

The President had made it clear that the mission of the Air Corps would no longer be tied to coastlines, but would be expanded to the broader horizons of hemispheric defense. The case for the long-range four-engined bomber had been made by presidential mandate. The strategic bomber was therefore on its way, as were the other aircraft needed to make U.S. Army aviation a major player on the stage of world air power, but in the meantime it was Arnold's job to begin building an air force capable of using them. After Munich,

Always an enthusiastic aviator, Ralph Royce (third from left) joins fellow pilots by a P-26.

the Air Corps staff proposed a goal of twenty-four combat-ready groups by mid-1941, by which time the personnel strength should have risen to 48,000 officers and men. Pilot training rates would need to grow from 300 to 1,500 a year, and that meant building more training facilities.

The program had hardly taken shape when the blow fell. On September 1 ,1939, Hitler's forces invaded Poland. As the world gathered itself to face the most destructive war in history, the U.S. Army Air Corps had just 26,000 officers and men, of whom some 2,000 were pilots. The Luftwaffe had a strength of almost half a million, with over 50,000 aircrew. American squadrons in the continental U.S. were operating, according to Frank Andrews, "only slightly over four hundred fighting planes," compared to the Luftwaffe's more than four thousand, but even that numerical disparity did not tell the whole story, because the standard front-line U.S. aircraft (B-18s, A-17s, and P-36s) were no match for their counterparts in the European air forces.

In the circumstances, it was providential that the U.S. did not face immediate direct involvement in the conflict. The first moves towards expansion of the Air Corps had been made, and more capable aircraft were coming, but Hap Arnold and his colleagues now knew that would not be enough. With Hitler on the rampage and the Japanese military becoming more belligerent every day, the plans for building a twenty-four group air force were revealed as being far too modest. It was time to throw them away and start planning for

an air force which could project massive power on a global scale.

Ordered in 1935 although demonstrably inferior to the Boeing B-17, the Douglas B-18 Bolo was originally produced in two principal forms. One hundred thirty-three B-18s and 217 B-18As were delivered. This B-18A formation flew over Miami on Army Day in 1940.

A   The business end of a Boeing P-12E, the U.S. Army Air Corps' most successful biplane fighter. Powered by a 500 hp Pratt & Whitney R-1340-17 radial, the P-12E series aircraft had a maximum speed of 189 mph and a service ceiling of 26,300 ft. Introduced in 1929, some P-12s remained in service until 1941.

B   Despite evidence that some thought has been given to the needs of a P-12E pilot in the shape of a separately designed instrument panel, he still sits in an open cockpit, protected by only a small windscreen.

C   The P-12E was an early example of an aircraft with an all-metal stressed skin fuselage. Its wings were still wooden with fabric covering. The P-12E at the USAF Museum is finished in the bright colors of the 6th Pursuit Squadron, based in Hawaii during the 1930s.

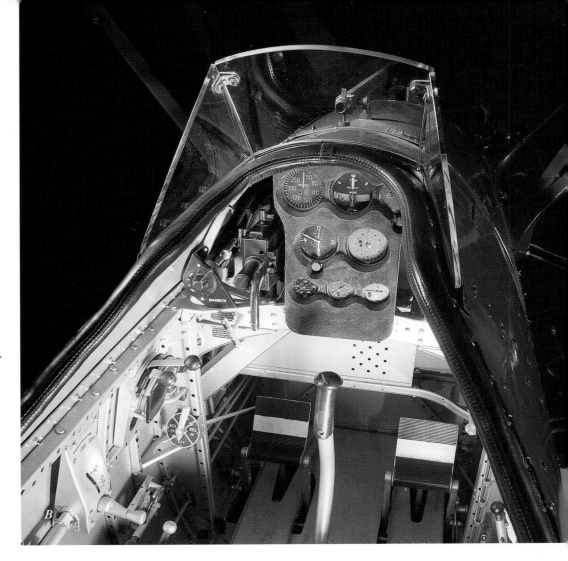

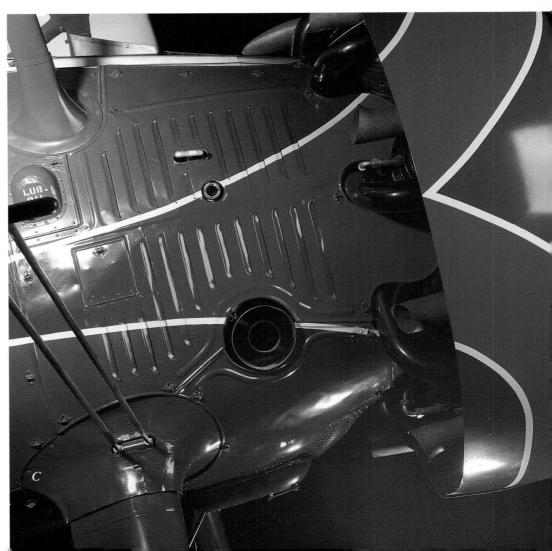

Farmer's Nightmare © *Keith Ferris, 1990.*
The artist's father, an instructor in the Pursuit section, Air Corps Advanced Flying School, is depicted in aircraft #2, with two students in Boeing P-12Bs. They are in a farmer's field practicing strange field landings in 1932.

Delivery © *Keith Ferris, 1979*

A

B

A   The B-10 was powered by two Wright R-1820 Cyclones of 775 hp each. Note the variable pitch propellers and advanced engine cowls.

B   Among B-10 innovations was an internal bomb bay with power-driven doors.

C   The Martin B-10 was one of the most significant advances in the history of military aircraft. For the first time it combined all-metal stressed skin construction, cantilever monoplane wings, flaps, and retractable landing gear. Its two cockpits and rotating gun turret were fully glazed. During trials in 1932, the new bomber proved too fast to be caught by Air Corps fighters and it was immediately ordered into production, first reaching squadron service in 1934. The USAF Museum's B-10 is the only surviving example.

A   Fitted with the 600 hp R-1340-27, a later version of the Pratt & Whitney engine in the P-12, the Boeing P-26A could manage a maximum speed of 234 mph and reach 27,400 ft. Its performance was not helped by the drag of a large radial engine, bracing wires, and fixed landing gear.

B   The instruments had improved, but the pilot of a P-26 still braved the elements in an open cockpit.

C   The P-26 was the first U.S. Army Air Corps fighter with Boeing's all-metal low cantilever wing. Important though these advances were, the P-26, first delivered late in 1933, was destined to be little more than an interim aircraft. Pretty to look at and delightful to fly though it was, the P-26 was soon overtaken by other monoplane designs on both sides of the Atlantic.

D   P-26As became standard equipment for the Army Air Corps in Hawaii and the Panama Canal Zone. The USAF Museum's P-26A is in the colors of the squadron commander, 19th Pursuit Squadron, Wheeler Field, Hawaii.

C

D

A

A   The Seversky P-35 was the first single-seat, all-metal fighter with enclosed cockpit and retractable landing gear to see service with the 146 U.S. Army Air Corps. Seventy-five were assigned to the 1st Pursuit Group at Selfridge Field, Michigan, beginning in 1937. The chubby lines of the P-35 reveal the ancestry of a later and most significant combat aircraft —the P-47 Thunderbolt.

B   The USAF Museum's P-35A is the only known survivor of the type. It carries the insignia of the 19th Pursuit Squadron based at Selfridge Field.

C   The P-35's undercarriage was only partially retracted, the wheels swinging backward into recesses, where they hid behind their streamlined fairings.

Following page: The shark-like appearance of the B-18A was the result of embodying a grotesquely modified nose which projected the bombardier's position out above and ahead of the front gunner. Slow and poorly defended, the B-18 was obsolescent almost as soon as it reached the squadrons. It is sobering to think that this was the U.S. Army Air Corps' front-line bomber at the time that Hitler's troops crossed the Polish border in 1939. The B-18A on display at the USAF Museum is marked as an aircraft of the 38th Reconnaissance Squadron in 1939.

B

117   C

Chapter 6
Air Power Unleashed- World War II, 1939-1945

"We must be the great arsenal of democracy."

(Franklin D. Roosevelt, December 1940)

Two of WW II's great leaders discuss progress in the European air war in April 1944. General "Hap" Arnold (right) met Major General Jimmy Doolittle at Bassingbourn, home of the 91st Bomb Group in England, not long after Doolittle had taken command of the 8th Air Force.

"[Americans] can make cars and refrigerators, but not aircraft.
(Hermann Goering, August 1941)

"Chennault's U.S. flyers in China fight unfairly. They zip into target areas, drop their bombs and zip right out again before we have a chance to fight back. Unless Chennault changes his tactics, the Japanese Government has warned we will take stern measures."
(Tokyo Radio, 1941)

"To have the United States at our side was to me the greatest joy. Hitler's fate was sealed. Mussolini's fate was sealed. As for the Japanese, they would be ground to powder. All the rest was merely the proper application of overwhelming force."
(Winston Churchill, December 1941)

"North American Aviation had kept their word and given us the best fighter ever designed."
(Pete Hardiman, P-51 pilot, 8th Air Force)

"Allied bombing was the dominant factor in the success of the [Normandy] invasion."
(General Feldmarschall Hugo Sperrle, Luftwaffe, 1945)

"If I didn't have air supremacy, I wouldn't be here."
(General Eisenhower, Normandy, June 1944)

To tackle the immense task of expanding Army flying training from 300 to 30,000 pilots per year, civilian flying schools were contracted to conduct primary training. Students flew some sixty-five hours in aircraft like the Ryan PT-22 before moving on to the BT-13, AT-6, and AT-9.

Glory, Death, and Destruction

The scale and impact of the most destructive war in history are reflected in the size of the USAF Museum's WWII collection, which confronts the visitor with an almost overpowering embarrassment of riches in telling the story of the years 1939 to 1945. Among the aircraft on display, a P-36 and a P-40E are representative of the fighters which U.S. pilots flew in the early days of the war. In another gallery, a gleaming but portly Douglas B-18A Bolo stands as a reminder that, with all its limitations, it was the standard front-line U.S. bomber when Hitler's blitzkrieg broke across the Polish frontier.

Wall displays cover the beginnings of the European air war, the establishment of the U.S. Army Air Forces, and the "Date of Infamy," December 7, 1941, at Pearl Harbor. Others tell of those Americans who could not wait for the U.S. to get into the war, but went to fly with the Royal Air Force in Britain or with the American Volunteer Group in China. Special mention is made of the AVG leader, Claire Chennault, and of America's first WWII aces—Albert Baumler, who scored aerial victories against three Axis powers; William Dunn, the first American ace of WWII; and Don Gentile, who became one of the most celebrated of U.S. fighter leaders. Extensive coverage is given to the Eagle Squadrons of the RAF, set off by a magnifi-

cently restored Hawker Hurricane IIA in the markings of No. 71 Eagle Squadron.

More wall displays deal with the unprecedented expansion of training facilities which was undertaken to feed the appetite of the rapidly growing USAAF front line, a training system which during the war produced nearly 200,000 pilots; over 50,000 navigators; 45,000 bombardiers; and more than 21,000 glider pilots. Some of the aircraft used in the training program are standing nearby—Stearman PT-13, Fairchild PT-19, Ryan PT-22, Vultee BT-13, North American BT-14, a Schweizer glider—and from the walls posters encourage their readers to "Remember December 7th!"; "Fly! For her liberty and yours!"; "Do your part for Duty—Honor—Country!" The Tuskegee Airmen get special mention, as do women in the AAF (WASPS), and there are displays which detail the burgeoning of the aircraft industry. We are reminded that, between July 1, 1940, and August 30, 1945, U.S. industry produced the almost incredible total of nearly 300,000 aircraft and over 800,000 engines.

A "War on the Home Front" section covers such diverse topics as radar, the Observer Corps, civil defense, ration books, and Japanese balloon bombs. Advanced trainers in the shape of the North American AT-6 and the Beech AT-11 stand in company with

examples of such famous devices as the Norden bombsight and the Link Trainer. Around a corner, the immortal poem "High Flight" by Pilot Officer John Gillespie Magee is inscribed on the wall, and nearby the Air Force song can be heard at the push of a button.

The story of the Pacific war starts with the Japanese attack on Pearl Harbor and moves through sections on the Philippines, Java, New Guinea, the Solomons, the Aleutians, the island hopping campaign, Burma, and the devastation of Japan, singling out special people and events on the way—among them the Doolittle raid on Tokyo, Medal of Honor winners Richard Bong and Thomas McGuire, and the challenge of flying the "Hump" into China.

The European combat exhibits follow the USAAF to England, North Africa, Sicily, Italy, and through the Allied invasion of the continent, covering every aspect of the air assault on Germany and the support of the ground forces. All the displays are liberally supported by historical photographs, maps, newspaper clippings, and assorted memorabilia which serve to recreate the atmosphere of a monumental struggle. Among the U.S. airmen given special mention are George Preddy, a 26.83 victory ace who once shot down six in one day and was himself destroyed by U.S. ground fire, and John Meyer, who scored 24 in the air and 13.5 on the ground (plus two more in Korea) and rose to wear four stars as C-in-C Strategic Air Command. High above is a massive painting of the Luftwaffe's senior officers in conference. Goering, Sperrle, Kesselring, Udet, and Molders are recognizable faces involved in discussion, while Adolf Galland stands in the background, peering pensively out of a window.

As visitors reach the end of the wall display gallery, they step out into the main hall of the Museum hangar and are surrounded by WWII aircraft. On one side there is a Lockheed P-38 Lightning and on the other a Bell P-39 Airacobra stands on PSP airfield matting. Suspended above are two Grasshopper spotter aircraft from Taylorcraft and Aeronca. Further on, the pugnacious silhouette of the Consolidated B-24 Liberator dominates the end of the hall. This one is *Strawberry Bitch*, which flew fifty-nine combat missions with the 376th Bomb Group.

The bridge between basic trainers and multiengine combat aircraft was the Curtiss AT-9.

Arranged between the aircraft are various engines, armaments, and war relics. An engine, nosewheel, and propeller recall the saga of the B-24 Lady Be Good, which disappeared into the Libyan desert in 1943. Contrasting exhibits suggest the sufferings of POWs at the hands of Japanese captors, and the delights of a Glenn Miller band concert. The well-known faces of Ronald Reagan, Jimmy Stewart, Clark Gable, and Joe Louis appear as "Celebrities in Uniform."

Much admired is a perfectly restored Boeing B-17G of the 91st Bomb Group, the famous Shoo Shoo Shoo Baby. Its partners are on every side—Republic's P-47 Thunderbolt, Martin's B-26 Marauder, Northrop's P-61 Black Widow, and North American's B-25 Mitchell, P-51D Mustang, and only surviving A-36. Allied aircraft are here, too, in U.S. markings—a Supermarine Spitfire and a de Havilland Mosquito. Luftwaffe aircraft include two Messerschmitts—a 109G in the markings of Gerhard Barkhorn (301 aerial victories), and a 262, the first jet aircraft to see combat. A Fiesler Storch hangs overhead. The Italians are represented by a Macchi 200 in desert camouflage, and the Japanese by a Kawanishi "George" from the last year of the war.

Enlivening the exhibition are an assortment of contemporary vehicles, weapons, and engines, notably some early guided bombs, the feared German 88 mm flak gun, and a Rolls-Royce Merlin, the engine which powered the P-51D, the Spitfire, and the Mosquito to their successes. More wall displays draw attention to the "Lend-Lease" program by which aircraft were delivered to the Soviet Union, to the history of enlisted pilots in the U.S. Army, and to glider pilots. Overhead is Little Girl, a Waco CG-4A glider used in the D-Day assault on Normandy.

The main WWII exhibition closes with the bombing campaign against the Japanese home islands. The huge shape of the Boeing B-29 Bockscar, which ended WWII with an atomic bomb on Nagasaki, takes up one corner of the hangar. Visitors can wander beside the shining silver fuselage and gaze up through the Plexiglas panels into the bomb-aimer's position. Near the B-29's tail stand copies of the atomic bombs "Little Boy" and "Fat Man." The dying spasms of Japa-

nese militarism are remembered in a display about the Kamikaze attacks. To one side of Bockscar is suspended the ultimate Kamikaze machine in the form of a piloted glider bomb boosted by rockets. The Japanese called it "Ohka" (Cherry Blossom); Americans named it "Baka" (Fool).

The USAF Museum is continually acquiring more air power history artifacts and its WWII collection has long since overflowed its original home. In other halls or on the old Wright Field taxiways outside the main buildings there are WWII aircraft and displays just as worthy of attention as those in the principal exhibition. Among them are wonderful transports (Curtiss C-46 Commando, Douglas C-47 Skytrain), rare aircraft (Douglas B-23), forgotten observers (Douglas O-46, Curtiss O-52 Owl), enemies (Junkers 52 and 88), air/sea rescuers (Consolidated OA-10 Catalina), attackers (Douglas A-20 Havoc), and many more. On the approach to the Museum is a replica of a typical WWII air traffic control tower in England, and to one side stands a group of Nissen huts of the kind so closely associated with life on an operational airfield of the U.S. Army's 8th Air Force.

Taken together, the items in the USAF Museum's collection offer visitors an unrivaled opportunity for remembering or learning about the scale and power of the U.S. Army

Air Forces in WWII. We are continually reminded that this was a citizens' air force, built up from modest beginnings to awesome proportions, in which ordinary Americans combined to accomplish extraordinary feats. With these achievements very much in mind, visitors can turn away from Bockscar and begin to examine the postwar world. As the Museum's telling of the tale of U.S. air power continues to unfold, they will see how, for America's military airmen, that world held the promise of an independent air force, the challenges of the jet era, and the unwelcome prospect of having to confront an international opponent in a nuclear armed standoff.

Part 1: America in Waiting, 1939-1941

Blitzkrieg

In the early morning hours of September 1, 1939, Luftwaffe aircraft crossed the eastern borders of Germany and attacked targets throughout Poland. Less than a month later Polish resistance had collapsed before the onslaught of the German blitzkrieg. Although France and Britain had honored pledges to the Poles by declaring war on Germany on September 3, no serious attempt was made by either nation to attack from the west and force Hitler into a two-front war. The anticipated assault on an enemy's heartland, with bombers leaping over intervening armies and navies, long predicted by air power strategists, did not materialize. Forced at last to face the limitations of their air forces and apprehensive at the possibility of awful retaliation, the French and the British,

together with the rest of the world, looked on as if transfixed by the first real demonstration of "lightning war." Hard though they fought, the Poles were crushed by the combination of racing armored columns and a powerful air force. Poland, partitioned in a cynical agreement between Germany and the Soviet Union, stood as a terrifying example of what might be expected to befall Hitler's enemies. The Luftwaffe in particular looked like a force to be feared, equipped as it was with swarms of modern aircraft flown by highly trained aircrew. By the time the fighting stopped, it had brushed aside the Polish Air Force, been prominent in the shattering of Polish Army units, and destroyed much of Warsaw.

The shock felt by the western allies and the euphoria of the Germans following Poland's fall helped to hide from both sides some Luftwaffe shortcomings which, even in 1939, hinted at problems for the future. Most significantly, the Nazi leaders were led to believe that the size and shape of the Luftwaffe were ideal for what they had in mind. Their all-conquering air force had shown that it was well-suited for fighting tactical battles in support of the army, and for engaging in short, fierce campaigns leading to rapid victories, terroriz-

ing city populations to ensure speedy surrender. Not so obvious at the time, the lack of a strategic bomber and the limitations of Germany's aircraft production plans would be among the many problems which would come to haunt the Luftwaffe when it was forced to face the consequences of being committed to endless combat in many roles on several very different fronts at once.

In 1939 it would have seemed ridiculous to suggest that the Luftwaffe was anything but all-powerful. Its success in Poland was evidence enough for most international onlookers. Even that success, however, was not without blemish. The Luftwaffe squadrons which faced the Polish Air Force outnumbered them by almost four to one, and the highly experienced German aircrews were flying aircraft of vastly superior performance. Nevertheless, by the end of September, the Luftwaffe had lost 285 aircraft, and stocks of spares and armaments had fallen to uncomfortably low levels. These very relevant facts were ignored by a jubilant German leadership and largely escaped the attention of their worried neighbors to the west.

Urged by his generals to pause for breath, Hitler reluctantly shelved a plan for an immediate assault on the West, and allowed the German forces to regroup during the winter months of the "phony war." By spring 1940, they were ready. In April, spearheaded by the Luftwaffe, the Germans occupied Denmark and Norway, and then, on May 10, opened a campaign which swept through Holland, Belgium, Luxembourg, and France. On June 4 the last survivors of the British Army's expeditionary force were driven off the continent at Dunkirk, and on June 22 the French surrendered. German forces controlled western Europe from North Cape to the Franco-Spanish border, and Britain stood alone against Hitler's ambitions. Success had come quickly, but Luftwaffe losses had been grievous. The blitzkrieg had cost them nearly 1,500 aircraft, over 1,000 of them in combat. The French and British had lost some 750 and 950 respectively, many of them abandoned as airfields were overrun by German forces. Once again, the

When the "Battle of Britain" began in 1940, Reichsmarschall Hermann Goering was a swaggering figure at the height of his powers. His Luftwaffe had been crushingly effective as an element of the German "Blitzkrieg" on the continent of Europe and it was poised to lead the invasion of Britain. At this stage, the Nazi war machine was thought to be unstoppable and Goering belittled the capacity of the U.S. to intervene effectively in the war. Here he is flanked by two of his fighter leaders, Werner Molders and Adolf Galland.

The essence of the Blitzkrieg was the Junkers 87 Stuka. Terrifying as a battlefield instrument, it proved inadequate for a strategic role in the Battle of Britain and was withdrawn from the struggle after suffering heavy losses.

pain of the Luftwaffe's wounds was forgotten in the euphoria of victory.

U.S. Reactions

News of the fall of France stunned the United States. Most Americans had thought that the combined forces of the French and British would be a match for those of Germany. Since the attack on Poland, the U.S. had viewed the European conflict with detached concern, generally sympathetic to the Franco-British cause but showing a strong desire to stay out of the struggle. On September 3, 1939, President Roosevelt announced: "This nation will remain a neutral nation, but I cannot ask that every American remain neutral in thought as well." With France defeated and Britain vulnerable, the U.S. began to look more closely at the Nazi threat. German soldiers stood on the southern shore of the English Channel singing: "Today England—Tomorrow the World!" The American people began to realize that, even from beyond the natural barrier of the Atlantic, Hitler's global ambitions would have to be taken seriously.

The possibility that British resistance could be overcome concentrated American minds wonderfully. It raised the prospect of a worst-case scenario in which Germany gained complete control of French and British assets. These could include industrial capacity, naval vessels, and colonial possessions. Taken together with those of Japan and Italy, they would present the U.S. with formidable challenges, and the probability was that many other countries, perhaps in Latin America, would see it as being in their interests to begin following the Nazi flag. In the light of these disturbing thoughts, President Roosevelt's commitment of January 1939 to the protection of the Western Hemisphere, a reaffirmation of the Monroe Doctrine, now assumed a greater significance. In May 1940, when France was on the verge of collapse, the President issued a call to action. Reemphasizing the concept of hemispheric defense, he said: "The American people must recast their thinking about national protection." To give substance to his rallying cry, he included a call for 50,000 military aircraft supported by a production capacity of 50,000 annually.

The immediate Air Corps reaction was a plan to increase its expansion program from twenty-four to forty-one groups, a goal that within two months was revised to fifty-four groups. The fifty-four group program ("The First Aviation Objective") proposed an Army air force of over 21,000 aircraft and more than 200,000 men by April 1942. In an atmosphere of national emergency, authorization for the plan was rapidly forthcoming, but such a vast increase over previous plans could not be achieved overnight. For once in its history, the Air Corps suffered the frustration of having more money than time. By December 1940, impatient airmen chafed at the fact that the aircraft industry was producing only 800 aircraft per month, up from 250 since January, but still not enough. To complicate matters, Hap Arnold's staff members were already raising their sights. In March 1941, they produced their "Second Aviation Objective," which provided for an eighty-four group air force with a personnel strength of over 400,000 by June 1942.

Sensible though these proposals were in terms of national security, they faced a number of hurdles which seemed almost insurmountable. One was the process of increasing aircraft production, another was the expansion of training facilities, and a third was the thorny problem of supporting the British in their hour of need. Prime Minister Winston Churchill pressed the point when addressing President Roosevelt in a radio broadcast, saying, "Give us the tools and we will finish the job!"

Churchill's appeal did not fall on deaf ears. As Germany's conquests mounted, more and more Americans came both to sympathize with the British people and to believe that the first line of U.S. defense lay in the United Kingdom. Self interest suggested that Britain should be helped to stay in the war. As early as November 1939, a U.S. embargo on arms sales to belligerents had been lifted by the "Cash and Carry Act," under which Allied nations could buy and collect armaments in the United States. Increasingly liberal release policies followed, culminating in the "Lend-Lease Act" of March 1941, which allowed the U.S. to transfer military equipment to an ally, requiring only that it be returned after the war. President Roosevelt characterized this unselfish act of generosity by saying it was like lending a neighbor a garden hose to "help him put out a fire." Although the legislation had been framed primarily with Britain's difficulties in mind, it had implications for the Chinese, and within months, with Hitler's imperious lunge to the East, it would apply to the Soviet Union, too. The trouble was that, given the continuing growth in the requirements of the U.S. services, the garden hose was increasingly needed at home.

By mid-1940, with U.S. industrial production struggling to move to a higher gear, the Air Corps' fifty-four group program was calling for 21,470 aircraft, and the British had outstanding orders for some 14,000 more. Recognizing that Britain was then in dire straits, it was agreed that the Air Corps should defer the delivery of 8,586 aircraft in favor of the British, a de-

U.K. by the German Army. In a savage air battle lasting until October, the Luftwaffe suffered its first defeat, losing over 1,700 aircraft to RAF Fighter Command's 950. At its outset, the Luftwaffe's leader, Hermann Goering, had revealed the limits of his strategic vision when he compared the planned invasion of the U.K. to "a big river crossing." By October, the Germans had discovered that the English Channel was no river and that, however good its tactical capabilities, the Luftwaffe was an air force neither equipped nor trained for a strategic campaign on the scale of the Battle of Britain.

Army Air Corps, the U.S. Navy's Bureau of Aeronautics, and the British Purchasing Commission. When Lend-Lease became law, the JAC took its place as an integral part of the machinery for administering the Act.

Anglo-American Cooperation

At the same time, committees representing the U.S. and British service staffs were studying the best ways in which the U.S. and Britain might collaborate if the U.S. eventually joined the war. Two reports, known as ABC-1 and ABC-2, were issued in March 1940. ABC-1 was later judged to be one of the most important military documents of the war. Its basic conclusion was that in a global conflict, "the Atlantic and European area is considered to be the decisive theater." Especially significant were comments that U.S. Army air bombardment units would "operate offensively in collaboration with the Royal Air Force, primarily against German military power at its source," and that the joint powers should achieve as rapidly as possible "superiority of air strength over that of the enemy, particularly in long-range striking forces." ABC-2 essentially recommended that aircraft production in the U.K. and the U.S. should be accelerated, and new estimates to satisfy the contingencies discussed in the report suggested that U.S. industry would need to increase its output to the undreamed of total of 60,000 aircraft per year. Skeptics were to find that American mass production techniques could accomplish almost anything, particularly with government support.

Federal money built new factories for aircraft manufacturers, who also got tax advantages and an easing of restrictions on excess profits. The expertise of the automobile industry was harnessed to the making of aircraft and components with startling results. Ford, for example, was one of the companies to confound those who claimed that large aircraft were too complex to allow for their mass production. At Willow Run, Michigan, in a factory which was then the largest in the world at a mile long by a quarter of a mile wide, Ford es-

The Lend-Lease Act of March 1941 allowed the U.S. to "lend" war equipment to an ally, an optimistic stipulation being that it should be returned after the war. Lockheed Hudsons were among the aircraft which gathered on docksides for shipment to Britain.

cision which certainly offered the hose to a friend to help with the European fire, but at the same time threatened to deny the Air Corps the flow of nourishment so essential for its growth.

The Luftwaffe Rebuffed

In mid-1940, it did indeed seem as if the British were in dire straits. Beginning in July, the Luftwaffe launched a campaign aimed at defeating the Royal Air Force, a prerequisite for an invasion of the

If anything, U.S. enthusiasm for helping Britain rose as the prospects for British survival improved. Fears that U.S. military aid might be going to a lost cause were dispelled, and more formal arrangements were made to ensure that future distributions of aircraft and engines would be systematic and equitable. In September 1940, the Joint Aircraft Committee (JAC) was established, consisting of representatives of the three principal customers of the U.S. aircraft industry—the U.S.

tablished a line which churned out B-24 Liberators at a rate to rival the production of family cars. The achievements speak for themselves. From a total military aircraft production figure of just over 900 in 1939, industry reached the astonishing number of more than 96,000 warplanes for the year of 1944, and production rates were then still rising. Such an output allowed the AAF to replace the wastage of combat losses, accidents, and obsolescence and still increase the number of aircraft on strength from about 12,000 in 1941 to almost 80,000 in 1944.

The U.S. Army Air Forces

These great events in planning and production shook the structure of American air power to its foundations. It became apparent that the old organization, with responsibilities divided between the Air Corps and the GHQ Air Force, would not be appropriate to manage the vast increases in machines, manpower, and facilities now underway. A series of organizational jugglings led, in March 1941, to the appointment of Robert A. Lovett as Assistant Secretary of War for Air, a post which had been vacant since 1933. Lovett was given the job of promoting aircraft production and streamlining Army aviation. His efforts resulted, on June 20, 1941, in the creation of the U.S. Army Air Forces, which had as subordinate elements the Air Corps and the Air Force Combat Command, which replaced the old GHQAF. Hap Arnold wore two hats as Chief of the AAF and as Deputy Chief of Staff to General George C. Marshall, the Army Chief of Staff. It was not a perfect arrangement, and other major changes would follow within the year, but it did mark a considerable advance towards air force autonomy. Advocates of independent air power were far from satisfied, but Hap Arnold was content to make progress one step at a time. He had a good working relationship with Marshall and he did not think it sensible to press for more while the AAF was in the process of both expanding and preparing for war.

Arnold's air staff was soon hard at work. The detailed U.S. plans for accom-

plishing the war tasks set out in ABC-1 were finalized in Joint Army and Navy War Plan RAINBOW 5. The Air War Plans Division of the Air Staff took account of this in producing a document known as AWPD-1. This paper reflected the now accepted view that the AAF had an offensive role, and estimated that the AAF's war mission would require 239 combat groups. For a front line of that size the AAF would need a personnel strength of nearly 2.2 million to operate a total of 26,416 combat and 37,051 training aircraft. The manpower figure included 135,000 aircrew, and among the combat aircraft were almost 7,500 heavy bombers. Prepared in less than a week by a team of brilliant young staff officers, AWPD-1 proved to be a remarkably accurate estimate.[1]

Americans in Britain

As part of the increasing collaboration between the U.S. and U.K., military missions were exchanged to serve in London and Washington. American observers had been in the U.K. for some time and

had been present during the Battle of Britain, but the arrangement was regularized in May 1941 by the formal opening of a headquarters for the U.S. mission in the American Embassy. The Army section was known as the Army Special Observer Group (SPOBS), and was commanded by Maj. Gen. James Chaney, whose chief of staff was Brig. Gen. Joseph McNarney. Both officers were airmen, which gave an indication of the expected prominence of air power in a conflict with Germany. The neutral status of the United States notwithstanding, Chaney's principal responsibility was to prepare for the establishment and control of U.S. forces in the U.K. as

The Ford plant at Willow Run, Michigan, was typical of the huge factories erected to produce war materiel. A mile long, it churned out B-24s at a rate which astonished those who thought U.S. industry could not be expected to meet the huge planned production figures. Overcoming the problems of adapting the methods of automobile mass production to large aircraft, Ford reached a peak monthly production rate of 428 B-24s in August 1944. Between September 1942 and June 1945, Willow Run produced a total of 6,791 B-24s, plus a further 1,893 "kits" which were assembled elsewhere.

laid down in RAINBOW 5.

Other Americans had been in the U.K. and ignoring U.S. neutrality for some time under less formal arrangements, but they too were leading where many would follow. When the war began, a number of young Americans had concluded that the eventual involvement of the U.S. was inevitable, but they were not prepared to wait until that happened. At least one, Jimmy Davis, managed to join the Royal Air Force

---

[1]The four authors of AWPD-1 were Lieutenant Colonels Harold George and Kenneth Walker, Majors Laurence Kuter and Haywood Hansell, Jr.

The USAF Museum has a collection of Eagle Squadron memorabilia. Among the items are Don Gentile's RAF cap, his flying jacket, and his uniform jacket with its RAF wings and Eagle Squadron shoulder badge. Dog tags are shown resting on the wingtip of a Luftwaffe aircraft shot down over England.

of the fighter force which would later dominate the skies over Europe.

Training Challenges

Meanwhile, back in the U.S., the AAF was suffering growing pains. The challenge of the aircrew training program alone was daunting. Having heard the President's statement on the need for greatly increased air power in November 1938, General Arnold had foreseen some of the problems and had begun to take action. To overcome the initial hurdle of creating more pilot training capacity, he had contracted with nine of the nation's largest civilian flying schools to take on the task of primary flight training for the Army. Just before the program began in 1939, the need was to graduate some three hundred pilots per year. As one USAAF plan succeeded another during the following months, the task grew by leaps and bounds. The First Aviation Objective raised the requirement to 30,000 pilots per year, a staggering hundredfold increase, but even that was dwarfed by the Second Aviation Objective, which proposed reaching a rate of 50,000 per year by mid-1942, little more than three years after the explosive growth began. At the wartime peak, no fewer than fifty-six civilian primary flight schools would be among those training pilots.

Primary training in the civilian schools occupied about sixty-five flying hours in a biplane like the Boeing PT-13 or 17 (the Stearman) or a monoplane like the Fairchild PT-19. In this phase the cadet completed his first solo, became accustomed to simple maneuvers, and was introduced to the basics of airmanship. Basic training came next in a closed cockpit aircraft such as the Vultee BT-13 (known universally as "The Vibrator") with seventy-five hours of aerobatics, formation, navigation, and instrument flying. The advanced training phase saw a parting of the ways, with potential fighter pilots going on to fly the North American AT-6 for seventy hours, practicing more of everything plus some aerial gunnery. Future heavy pilots went to twin-engine types like the Curtiss AT-9 and were introduced to the delights of asymmetric handling. At the

before the war began. He flew Hurricanes with No. 79 Squadron and was awarded a Distinguished Flying Cross before being killed in combat in June 1940. Seven others are listed among the famous "Few" who fought in the Battle of Britain. This small group flew and fought initially with regular RAF squadrons, and they were the vanguard of many more American volunteers. Only one of the seven survived the war.[2]

American airmen crossed the Atlantic in increasing numbers in 1940, all seeking the adventure of flying fighters and many touched by an unadmitted idealism. Chesley Peterson, later an Eagle Squadron commander, said: "Everyone wanted to fly big, fast airplanes, and the only way to do that was in one of the services. Since most

of those who joined the RAF did not have the necessary qualifications to join the U.S. Army or Navy, the only answer that readily presented itself was the RAF." Peterson also remarked that most Eagles would not admit to being influenced by ideals, but he noted that no Americans ever volunteered to fly for the Luftwaffe.

By the time the Battle of Britain was drawing to its close, the number of Americans flying with the RAF was sufficient to justify the formation of a separate unit, No. 71 Eagle Squadron. Two more Eagle Squadrons, Nos. 121 and 133, followed in May and August 1941. These three squadrons compiled a distinguished record with the RAF and the pilots who fought with them gained considerable combat experience against the Luftwaffe. This was to prove invaluable when the squadrons became the 4th Fighter Group, USAAF, in September 1942, forming the nucleus

[2]The fighter pilots who fought in the Battle of Britain were immortalized by Churchill in the words: "Never in the field of human conflict was so much owed by so many to so few." The seven U.S. citizens listed as having fought in the Battle are: Billy Fiske, Art Donahue, Ken Haviland, Shorty Keough, Philip Leckrone, Andy Mamedoff, and "Red" Tobin. Only Ken Haviland survived the war. He became a Professor of Aeronautical Engineering at the University of Virginia in Charlottesville.

end of the advanced phase, cadets were awarded their wings and most were commissioned as second lieutenants. Between July 1, 1939, and August 31, 1945, the training program graduated 193,440 pilots. The true scale of the effort can be seen from the fact that another 124,000 trainees failed to complete the course for one reason or another.

New pilots then undertook a transition phase which included an introduction to a combat type like an older model P-40 or B-18. Paul Tibbetts describes the B-18 as being "a gentle airplane," having "little value except as a trainer," but Don Lopez remembers the P-40 as being more of a challenge. Of his first takeoff in a P-40 he says: "It was fortunate that the runway was very wide, or I would have run off both sides of it." If transition was survived, it was followed by an assignment to an operational unit in the U.S. for combat training before the pilot was sent overseas. The whole lengthy process occupied about a year and gave the new pilot at least 400 hours in the air before he approached the enemy. His likely opponents were less thoroughly prepared. By 1944, Luftwaffe pilots were entering combat with about 150 hours, and the Japanese were managing 100 or less.

Matching steps were taken to ensure that the AAF had sufficient aircrew in categories other than pilots, and they were trained with equal thoroughness. Before WWII's end, 50,000 navigators and 45,000 bombardiers were graduated. There was, of course, a commensurate increase in all other training activities. For example, in 1939 about 1,500 men were graduated from the technical training schools. Two years later, the graduation rate was 42,000 annually and rising rapidly. None of this was easy. Equipment shortages forced schools to improvise as best they could, and to ensure results many moved to shift-working a twenty-four-hour day seven days a week.

To accommodate the prodigious scale of the program, new training facilities sprang up like mushrooms all over the U.S. The 1939 Air Corps operated seventy-six installations (including twenty-one

major bases). During WWII the AAF came to control a total of 2,252 installations at one time. Established bases were greatly expanded, often with solid brick construction, but newer facilities frequently used more temporary buildings, like tar-paper shacks. Some airfields were generously supplied with concrete, while others made do with hastily laid turf. By December 1941, these prodigious efforts had created an AAF of over 350,000 men and had activated seventy combat groups, but that was only a beginning. The USAAF continued to grow and ended the war with over 2.25 million people in uniform.

In such a huge and increasingly autonomous force, the old principle of the Air Corps that officers should be predominantly pilots could no longer be maintained. Besides the other aircrew specialties, there was a need for professional administrators, engineers, lawyers, public relations executives, doctors, communicators, meteorologists, educators, and many more. Arnold bowed to the inevitable and authorized the founding of an Officer Candidate School to impose minimum standards of military training on applicants for commissions and to sort the wheat from the chaff.

Gender and Race

The pressures of rapid growth soon forced Arnold to face two other prejudices of the Air Corps—the employment of women and black Americans. It must be said that best use was not made of either group, despite the conditions of national emergency which existed in WWII. The strictures of American society at the time erected too many formidable social barriers for there to be much hope of knocking

Eagle Squadron pilots scramble for their Hurricanes. "Red" Tobin, leading the charge, was one of the seven Americans to fly with the RAF during the Battle of Britain. Sam Marillo and Luke Allen run to his left.

them down overnight in such a conservative organization as the U.S. Army. The maximum wartime strength of the Women's Army Corps with the USAAF was less than 30,000, and they were principally employed in clerical duties, although some managed to break away to become mechanics. Women also performed in their traditional role as nurses, but convention was shattered by another small group known as WASPs—Women Airforce Service Pilots. Only 1,074 WASPs flew for the USAAF, serving as ferry pilots, flight instructors, and target tug pilots, but they qualified in every type of USAAF aircraft, including such demanding machines as the P-47, B-26, and B-29.

Racial segregation was an even more difficult nut to crack. In 1941 there were only five black officers in the whole of the

Racial segregation was a problem for the U.S. services in WW II. A relatively small number of black men were selected for flight training at Tuskegee, Alabama, and just over 1,000 reached operational squadrons as aircrew. Their leader was an inspiring young man named Benjamin Davis, who eventually rose to three-star rank. He is seen here on the left during primary flight training.

U.S. military, and three of those were chaplains. The vast majority of black enlisted men in the USAAF were assigned to maintenance units concerned with the upkeep of roads and buildings, or were used to manhandle supplies at depots. A select few were accepted for flight training at the Tuskegee Institute in Alabama. Inspired by the example of their leader, a young man named Benjamin O. Davis, Jr., these black airmen overcame the handicaps of racial segregation, and the Tuskegee program eventually graduated 673 fighter pilots, 253 medium bomber pilots, and 132 navigators. Davis had a distinguished career in the service both during and after the war and rose to the rank of Lieutenant General.

Changes in AAF Size and Shape

To ease the problems of controlling this large, changing, and continually growing force, four numbered air forces were formed in the U.S., together with three overseas air forces—Far East in the Philippines, Caribbean (later Sixth) in Panama, and Hawaiian. Other new organizations included Technical Training Command to direct the vast training program for mechanics and technicians, Maintenance Command to manage problems of maintenance and supply, and Air Service Command to concentrate on procurement, research, and development. The growing task of delivering aircraft to the Royal Air Force generated yet another new organization in Ferrying Command, and before long the size of the aircrew training programs forced the creation of a Flying Training Command.

In 1941, the growing power of the USAAF was becoming very obvious in materiel terms. That summer it was clear that there had also been a subtle change in status. In August, President Roosevelt met Winston Churchill on board the battleship HMS *Prince of Wales* off the coast of Newfoundland. They were accompanied by their political and military staffs, and the talks concerned the war. Since much of the discussion was about the use of air power, and a senior Royal Air Force officer was present as the representative of his independent service, Hap Arnold was there to speak for the USAAF. In this way, Arnold was accepted as a member of the Combined Chiefs of Staff, even though he was still subordinate to the U.S. Army's Chief, General Marshall.

Expanding Frontiers

With the prospect of war looming larger every day for the U.S., the AAF looked to the outer limits of its defensive responsibilities in the Western hemisphere. In September 1940, President Roosevelt announced an agreement with the U.K. which transferred fifty WWI destroyers to the hard-pressed Royal Navy in exchange for ninety-nine-year leases on airfield and base sites in Newfoundland, Bermuda, British Guiana, and a number of Caribbean islands. Other agreements with the Danish and Icelandic governments in mid-1941 put U.S. forces ashore to establish bases on Greenland and Iceland. The defining purpose of all these measures was defensive, but it was implicit that their existence secured the firm links with the U.K. which would in time be vital to the Allied cause.

The sense of urgency which marked the improvement of U.S. defenses on the Atlantic side was not so evident when it came to the business of strengthening U.S. outposts in the Pacific. Measures in the west were not at first pursued with the same vigor as those to the east. As relations with Japan deteriorated, the U.S. tried to make up for lost time, but every action was weighed against Atlantic needs.

The WASPs (Women Airforce Service Pilots) numbered little more than 1,000, but they were invaluable as ferry pilots and instructors. During WW II, WASPs became qualified on every kind of USAAF aircraft, including the most demanding operational types. Louise Thompson stands in front of a new P-38 awaiting delivery.

The policy was to do enough to deter Japan without disrupting activities aimed at keeping the door to Europe open. Most planned improvements were either incomplete or mere paper proposals by December 1941. Some reinforcement of the bases in Hawaii and the Philippines had been accomplished, and landing strips had appeared on such islands as Midway, Johnston, Palmyra, Canton, and Christmas, but many U.S. military leaders were not confident about the possibility of conducting an effective defense of either the Philippines or the farther flung outposts.

Reinforcement of Clark Air Force Base in the Philippines included the deployment of thirty-five B-17Ds. They were intended to give the AAF the capability to attack Japanese bases on Formosa and to blockade the China Sea from the air. It was also hoped that the Soviet Union might agree to B-17 shuttle operations between Luzon and Vladivostok, so that the Japanese home islands could be bombed. The air defense force at Clark consisted of one hundred P-40s, and sixty-eight obsolete fighters, a mixture of P-35s and P-26s. The forward deployment of so many B-17Ds at this early stage meant that Hawaii was left with only twelve, along with twelve A-20s, thirty-three B-18s, and a fighter force of ninety-nine P-40s, thirty-nine P-36s, and fourteen P-26s.

In Alaska, too, defensive preparations were left until almost the eleventh hour. The Air Corps had been pointing out the strategic value of Alaska for years, but work was not begun on a major base at Anchorage until 1939, and the formation of Air Field Forces, Alaskan Defense Command, did not follow until May 1941, becoming Air Force, Alaska Defense Command four months later. Several rough forward airstrips were completed in 1941, the farthest west being on Umnak Island in the Aleutians to provide cover for the U.S. Navy's base at Dutch Harbor, but the overall readiness of the Alaska Command was not impressive. The area was too remote and its weather and geography too awful for it to be given any priority over places which were more obviously accessible. By early December 1941, its front-line aircraft

The AT-6 Texan is perhaps the most famous trainer ever produced. Over 15,000 were built in various forms between 1938 and 1945, with more than 10,000 of them going to the USAAF. They were used for the advanced phase of flying training, during which a pilot polished his formation, instrument, gunnery, and bombing skills before being awarded his wings and going on to fly combat aircraft.

strength stood at twelve B-18s and twenty P-36s. Against a determined enemy, the region's fierce storms seemed a more realistic deterrent.

When the Japanese fleet put to sea on November 26, 1941, and set course for Hawaii, determined to strike the U.S. Navy a crippling blow, America was a long way from being ready for war. In the two years and more since Hitler's forces had attacked Poland, U.S. leaders had appreciated the dangers and a great many steps had been taken to enhance U.S. readiness, but the real benefits to be gained from most of those measures remained in the future. The vast resources of the U.S. in terms of manpower and industrial capacity had yet to make themselves felt. The potential was there and the machinery was in motion, but in 1941 few people on either side, including Americans, realized just how awesome U.S. power would become in the months ahead.

Considered from a short-term point of view, December 7, 1941, was not a propitious day to judge the prospects for the Western democracies. Japanese aircraft wreaked havoc at Pearl Harbor and Hitler's troops stood at the gates of Moscow. The future did not look promising. A more dispassionate observer, however, might have

seen that the Japanese attack (and Hitler's subsequent declaration of war on the U.S.) had finally released the U.S. from all restraint. Uninhibited by the shackles of neutrality, Americans became dedicated to the relentless prosecution of a global war, and the end result of the conflict was never again in doubt. The realities of U.S. power and the inevitability of the course of events escaped the leaders of the Axis powers. Not long before his careless decision to declare war on the U.S., Hitler wrote to Benito Mussolini: "Whether or not America enters the war is a matter of indifference, inasmuch as she is already helping our enemy with all the power she can muster." He must later have thought that his breezy assessment might have been a little hasty.

A

The Airplanes That Trained an Air Force

A   The Stearman Kaydet was one of the world's most significant training aircraft. A total of 10,346 Kaydets were ordered for the U.S. and the Allies in the ten years following 1935. (Boeing acquired the Stearman company in 1938.) The PT-13D at the USAF Museum carries a 220 hp Lycoming radial, but other variants were differently powered and were given separate designations—PT-17 with a Continental engine and PT-18 with a Jacobs.

B   The student sat ahead of his instructor. Note the basic fuel gauge over the PT-13's front cockpit, and the small mirror which allowed the instructor to monitor expressions of fear or delight as they appeared in the student's eyes.

B

A

B

A   The 160 hp Kinner R-540 engine of the Ryan PT-22 was only partly hidden by a cowling. Its five cylinders broke through the surface like erupting fungus and hauled the airframe along at a maximum speed of 131 mph.

B   As with other primary trainers of the 1930s and '40s, the PT-22 Recruit was a simple aircraft. With all-metal construction, it was robust but forgiving, as was required of a machine which had to suffer continually from the ministrations of student pilots.

C   Fins of cousins—the Fairchild PT-19 Cornell nestles behind the PT-22.

A

B

A Often known as the "torture chamber," the Link trainer allowed pilots to practice instrument flying procedures while fastened firmly to the floor. In the foreground is the map table and the "crab," a device which traced the pilot's wanderings during navigation exercises.

B The simple arrangement of the Link cockpit reproduced the basic instruments and controls necessary to simulate flight. The movement of the Link was often jerky and the wheezing noises it made were hardly typical, but once the hood was down the pilot could quickly become immersed in the problems he was set.

A

A   North American's AT-6 Texan became one of the world's great aircraft. Powered by a 600 hp Pratt & Whitney R-1340, the T-6 had a maximum speed of 210 mph and a range of 770 miles. In later life, the T-6 was used as a combat aircraft, notably in the Forward Air Controller role during the Korean War, and it remains the most popular of the world's "warbirds" at air shows more than half a century after its birth.

B   The tandem seating in the T-6 helped to give the student the feeling of being master of his fate even when an instructor was sitting behind him.

C   The pilots of over twenty countries got their wings by sitting in the T-6's front seat. As a trainer for introducing pilots to the art of pure flying, it is probable that the T-6 has never been surpassed.

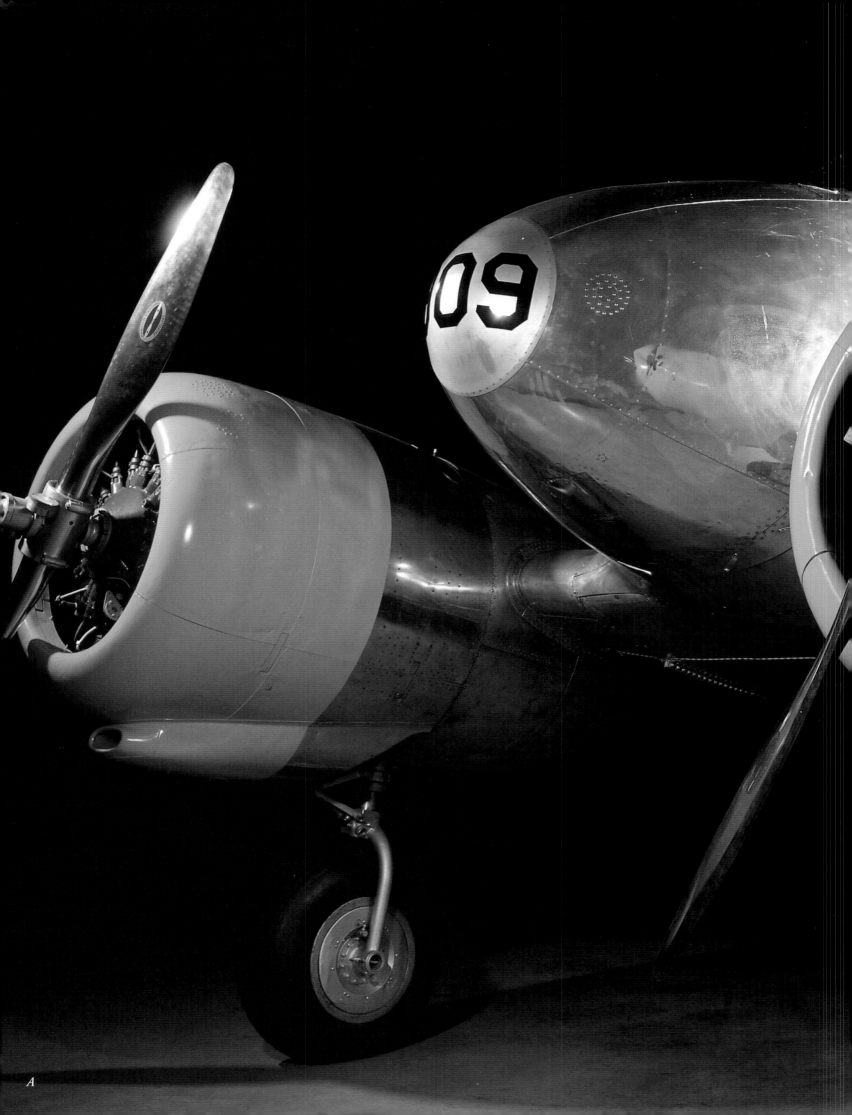

B

A   The Curtiss AT-9 Fledgling (more often called the "Jeep") was a bridge between single-engine trainers and multi-engine combat aircraft. It was not easy to fly, but its idiosyncrasies were useful in preparing pilots to take on the challenges of high performance twins like the B-26 or P-38. Two 295 hp Lycoming R-680-9 radials gave it a maximum speed of nearly 200 mph.

B   The control wheels, side-by-side seating, and central console introduced pilots to a big aircraft environment.

A

The Engines That Won the War

A   The Wright Cyclone R-1820 nine-cylinder engine developed 1,200 hp. A typically oil thirsty but rugged radial, the Cyclone was reliable and resistant to battle damage. There were many instances of it continuing to run with shattered cylinders. The engine shown is one of four powering the USAF Museum's B-17G Shoo Shoo Shoo Baby. The Hamilton Standard constant speed three-bladed propellers could drag the B-17 to well over 30,000 ft.

B   The Pratt & Whitney R-2800 Double Wasp was one of WW II's great engines. Various forms of the eighteen-cylinder twin row radial were mounted in several USAAF combat aircraft, including the Martin B-26, Northrop P-61, Douglas A-26, and Curtiss C-46. The Republic P-47D's R-2800-59 developed 2,430 hp at takeoff power.

B

A   If any engine deserves to be singled out as having done more than any other to "win the air war" it is probably the V-12 liquid-cooled Merlin. Besides powering several major RAF aircraft (Hurricane, Spitfire, Mosquito, Lancaster, etc.), it was the engine in the P-51 Mustang. Designed by Rolls-Royce, the Merlin was modified and built in the U.S. by Packard. Mounted in the P-51D, it provided 1,695 hp.

A

B

B   The Allison V-1710 engine was used in several U.S. combat aircraft, including the Lockheed P-38, Bell P-39, Curtiss P-40, and North American A-36. As fitted to the P-38L it delivered 1,475 hp.

C   Maintaining engine power at high altitude would not have been possible without supercharging. The turbo-supercharger shown here is fitted to one of the Wright Cyclones on the B-17 Shoo Shoo Shoo Baby.

Boeing B-17E

Silhouettes from the Handbook of
United States Army Air Forces Airplanes,
published September 1942.

Part 2: The Blow Falls in the Pacific

warning, when the blow fell just as he said it would, "on a fine, quiet Sunday morning."

Launched from six aircraft carriers some two hundred miles north of Oahu, Japanese airmen attacked Pearl Harbor in two waves totaling more than 350 aircraft. Surprise was complete. In the years since the attack, the repercussions of the shock felt by the American people at the news from Pearl Harbor have never ceased to

A Japanese photograph shows Wheeler Field, Oahu, under attack on December 7, 1941. To their delight, the Japanese pilots found that the airfield had almost no antiaircraft defenses, and that the resident squadrons had their aircraft parked in neat rows in front of the hangars, making their destruction all the simpler.

Pearl Harbor

As early as 1924 Billy Mitchell offered his opinion that war between the U.S. and Japan was almost inevitable. He cannot have been too surprised that his forthright views did little to concentrate American minds on the intentions of a potential enemy. In the 1920s, the horrors of the world conflict just ended had rendered the idea of global war nearly unthinkable, and the broad reaches of the Pacific lent an air of unreality to any prospect of a military confrontation involving such widely separated nations. The mood of the time was dismissive of defense issues, and Mitchell's somber prediction that the Japanese would strike first at Pearl Harbor was soon forgotten. The awful precision of his prophecy was revealed on December 7, 1941, seventeen years after his visionary

reverberate. How could the U.S. have been caught so completely off guard? How was it possible that U.S. forces could have been so thoroughly crushed while the attackers escaped almost unscathed? The answers to these questions are complex, but, in essence, they reflect the general lack of U.S. readiness to fight a Pacific war, and local convictions in Hawaii that Pearl Harbor was sufficiently remote from Japan to be unlikely as a priority target.

As the principal victim of the perfectly executed Japanese strike, the U.S. Navy suffered heavily. Most notably, all eight of the U.S. Pacific fleet's battleships were either sunk or badly damaged. In a stroke of good fortune for the American cause, their aircraft carriers were at sea when the attack took place. In concert with the assault on U.S. Navy ships, equally

damaging attacks were made on Oahu's shore installations, including the airfields. Here the Japanese airmen were presented with ideal targets. Reacting to a message from Washington on November 27 warning of deteriorating relations between the U.S. and Japan, General Short, the U.S. Army's commander in Hawaii, had judged the most serious threat to be from saboteurs. He had therefore moved all Army aircraft out of protective revetments and massed them in the open or in hangars, where it was believed they could be better protected against sabotage. Many aircraft were also kept unarmed and defueled. Standing in neat rows or huddled together under cover, they could hardly have been better prepared as targets for air attack if the Japanese had ordered the arrangements themselves.

By the time the raid was over, widespread damage had been done to Oahu's airfield buildings and support facilities by bombing and strafing attacks, and only 83 of the 234 U.S. Army aircraft on strength were flyable. Added to the local survivors were some B-17s which had left California the night before on their way to the Philippines. Their tired crews arrived over Oahu in aircraft fitted for ferrying, with neither guns nor armor in place, to find themselves in the midst of a major battle. Short of fuel and being shot at by both enemy airmen and some now thoroughly aroused "friendly" antiaircraft gunners, the twelve B-17s scattered and landed where they could, one ending up on a golf course. One B-17 was destroyed and another three badly damaged.

The American defensive reaction had been at times courageous, but pitifully ineffective and occasionally indiscriminate. Angry antiaircraft gunners fired at any planes they saw, damaging some that were American and shooting down the P-40 of Lt. John Dains. Only twenty-five sorties were flown against the raiders by USAAF pilots, who claimed ten enemy aircraft destroyed, four of them falling to the guns of Lt. George Welch's P-40. Altogether, the Japanese lost twenty-nine aircraft in combat, plus a few more in accidents during

Too Little Too Late © *Keith Ferris, 1991*

recovery to their carriers. Given the scale of their victory, it was a small price to pay. The Japanese exulted, and Americans felt anger and a desperate need to avenge, but beyond the agony and the ecstasy lay hidden ironies. In seeking to secure the eastern flank of their southerly expansion the Japanese had managed to end American isolationism and so ensure their eventual defeat, and in attacking U.S. battleships they had demonstrated the effectiveness of air power against naval vessels while failing to destroy their enemy's aircraft carriers.

Debacle in the Philippines

Farther to the west, a combination of human failings and the vagaries of the weather ensured that the U.S. would suffer another military disaster. News of the Pearl Harbor attack reached General MacArthur in the Philippines shortly after 3:00 a.m. local time. Exactly what happened in the next few hours is not entirely clear because the recollections of the principal officers involved differ considerably. It does seem, however, as if MacArthur's capacity for decisive action temporarily deserted him, and that his chief of staff, General Sutherland, denied the air com-

mander, General Brereton, direct access to the Commander-in-Chief. Brereton's request for permission to launch a B-17 strike against Japanese airfields on Formosa was passed through Sutherland, but was not immediately approved.

A little after 7:00 a.m., Brereton was contacted by General Hap Arnold from Washington and warned not to let his aircraft get caught on the ground. This was followed by a report that unknown aircraft were approaching Manila, so Brereton scrambled thirty-six P-40s to intercept and ordered the B-17s at Clark Field into the air as a precaution. When it appeared that the alarm was false, the P-40s landed to refuel, but the B-17s remained airborne. Later in the morning, Sutherland called Brereton to authorize both a photographic reconnaissance of Formosa and a late afternoon attack on the Japanese bases there once the photographs had been evaluated. Accordingly, the B-17s were recalled to be refuelled and loaded with bombs.

If Brereton displayed some anxiety over the course of events, it is hardly surprising. He had been living in constant expectation of a Japanese attack on Clark Field since first light, and his instincts were correct. The Japanese had indeed planned

to strike Clark at dawn, but they had been frustrated by thick fog covering their airfields on Formosa. They in turn had suffered agonies of apprehension as they waited for the fog to disperse, expecting the B-17s to arrive overhead at any moment. When the skies cleared, 108 bombers and 84 fighters took off and set course for the Philippines. One formation reached Clark Field soon after midday and could hardly believe their good fortune. The American aircraft were still on the ground, bunched together as they took on fuel and armaments. Mitsubishi G3M Nells and G4M Bettys bombed without opposition, and Zero fighters dropped down to strafe almost at will, leaving Clark Field a smoking shambles. All the hangars were destroyed and most of the aircraft, including two squadrons of B-17s, were reduced to scrap. Similarly catastrophic damage was done to other U.S. air bases on Luzon. At a stroke, U.S. air power in the Philippines, insufficient for its tasks at the outset, had lost over half of its strength.

Sixteen B-17s were deployed at Del Monte on Mindanao out of reach of the Japanese, and on subsequent days they and a motley collection of other aircraft did their best to counter the Japanese invasion of the Philippines. Courageous though many of these efforts were, they proved to be little more than an annoyance to the enemy. The hard facts of America's lack of preparedness for war were now bitterly revealed—aircraft were too few and often obsolete, communications facilities were unsatisfactory, airfield defenses were poor, and intelligence about the enemy was inadequate. As a result, a hard lesson about air power was administered to the U.S. forces on the first day of the conflict: air superiority is fundamental to successful military operations. Within a week, it was clear that the Japanese already controlled the air over Luzon, and that their capture of several airfields made the extension of that control over the whole of the Philippines merely a matter of time.

Shocked by the defeats in Hawaii and the Philippines, and facing the prospect of more to come, the American people needed a hero, a symbol of U.S. defiance and fighting spirit. On December 10, a suitably heroic figure emerged. Captain Colin Kelly was the pilot of a B-17C which bombed Japanese ships off the northern Luzon coast. Early reports of the action claimed that his attack had sunk the battleship *Haruna*, but it subsequently emerged that the warship was most probably the cruiser *Ashigara*, which may have been damaged but not sunk. On the return flight, the B-17 was attacked by enemy fighters and set on fire. Ordering his crew to abandon the aircraft, Kelly remained at the controls to allow them to escape. He died when the B-17 exploded in the air before he could use his own parachute. This was the first B-17 to be shot down, and its pilot was awarded a posthumous Distinguished Service Cross.[1]

On December 13, Americans had more to cheer about when, during a reconnaissance sortie, Lt. Buzz Wagner's P-40 ran into a formation of obsolescent Nakajima Ki-27s. He shot down four of them and went on to strafe other Japanese aircraft on the airfield at Aparri. Three days later, he scored another aerial victory to become the USAAF's first ace.

These brave efforts apart, there was little for Americans to savor in the Pacific. The Japanese advance was irresistible and by December 18 the last of the B-17s in the Philippines had been withdrawn to Darwin, Australia. General MacArthur was still talking stubbornly of the need for reinforcements, and spoke of having two hundred fighters and fifty dive bombers delivered to the Philippines by aircraft carrier. It was all too little, too late, however, as Japanese forces pressed through the islands with great speed and made reinforcement impossible. MacArthur withdrew his troops into the Bataan peninsula and made his headquarters on the fortress island of Corregidor. American resistance there was stubborn, but final surrender came at last in May 1942. The experience of defeat convinced the U.S. ground forces commander, General Jonathan Wainwright, of "the futility of trying to fight a war without an air force."

The Capable Enemy

The Japanese air forces were a revelation to their opponents. Their aircrew were well trained, their tactics were sound, and their aircraft were formidable. The Zero fighter in particular quickly showed that it could outfly anything the Allied air forces had. First blooded over China in 1940, the Mitsubishi A6M, Type O, known as the Zero, should not have come as a surprise to the Allies, but early reports of its performance were treated with skepticism and generally disbelieved. In fact, it was a remarkable fighter. Powered by a 950 hp radial engine, the Zero had a maximum speed of 330 mph, which was slower than some of its competitors, but it had an excellent rate of climb and was incredibly maneuverable. Saburo Sakai, the Japanese ace who scored sixty-four victories in Zeros, described it as being "a dream to fly. The airplane was the most sensitive I had ever flown, and even slight finger pressure brought instant response." Its range, too, was extraordinary—nearly two thousand miles with a drop tank—allowing Zeros to appear in areas thought to be inaccessible to Japanese fighters.

Such outstanding performance came at a price, however. It was largely achieved by keeping the weight of the Zero as low as possible, not much more than 5,000 lbs fully loaded. Japanese fighter pilots were specific in demanding that their aircraft not be encumbered with what they regarded as excessive weight. Above all, they wanted a light, agile aircraft, comparing their fighters with "master craftsmen's Samurai swords." The designer of the Zero, Horikoshi Jiro, later wrote: "As a result of our pilots' figurative demand for the blades and the arts of the old masters, the Japa-

The Mitsubishi A6M, Type 0, otherwise known as the "Zero," came as something of a shock to the Allies. It was a formidable, highly maneuverable fighter, and in the Pacific War's early stages it seemed almost unbeatable. Later, when such weaknesses as its lack of armor and self-sealing fuel tanks became apparent, Allied pilots learned to defeat the Zero by using the superior speed of their fighters and avoiding turning dogfights.

nese fighters were the lightest in weight and among the most maneuverable in the world." Armor plate was not used, nor were self-sealing fuel tanks. Once U.S. fighter pilots learned to use the superior speed and diving ability of their aircraft to advantage, and to avoid being drawn into low-speed turning dogfights, these shortcomings of the Zero were often brutally exposed.

During the first six months of their campaign to create a "Greater East Asian Coprosperity Sphere," the Japanese ran riot. Weaknesses in the Zero or in any other element of their military machine were not readily apparent. Their successes at Pearl Harbor and in the Philippines were reflected in similar victories elsewhere. By

---

[1]After the war, it was discovered that Kelly's B-17 was shot down by one of Japan's greatest aces, Saburo Sakai. In his book, *Samurai*, Sakai tells of his surprise at the ruggedness of the B-17. After a succession of firing passes from ten Zeros, the bomber seemed unharmed and full of fight. Sakai says that then "I decided to try a close-in attack directly from the rear. Greatly to my advantage was the fact that the early B-17s lacked tail turrets...Pieces of metal flew off in chunks from the bomber's right wing, and then a thin white film sprayed back.... The bomber's guns ceased firing; the plane seemed to be afire within the fuselage."

May 1942, their combat record was impressive. They had crippled the U.S. Pacific fleet, conquered the Philippines, Hong Kong, Indo-China, Malaya, Singapore, the Dutch East Indies, and Burma, and had spread out across the Pacific to seize a host of islands, including Wake, Guam, the Gilberts, and the Solomons. It seemed only a matter of time before Australia and India were added to the list. In trying to halt the avalanche, allied forces in South-East Asia had been consistently outfought and, most significantly, had suffered the consequences of facing superior air power forcefully applied.

Chennault's AVG

It was difficult to find anything to lighten the prevailing Allied gloom, but two bright spots did emerge in the first half of 1942. The first took shape in the hands of Claire Chennault, a man who had left the Army Air Corps in 1937 because his uncompromising views on the use of fighter aircraft ran counter to the accepted bomber-driven doctrine of the generals. Hired by the Chinese to improve their air force, he recruited and organized the American Volunteer Group (AVG), later known as the "Flying Tigers," to fly for China. The AVG was equipped with P-40s and Chennault made sure that his pilots knew how to take advantage of their aircraft's level flight speed, diving ability, and rugged construction. They generally operated in pairs and used hit-and-run tactics whenever possible. On December 20, 1941, the Japanese got their first taste of the AVG in action when ten Kawasaki Ki-48 Lilys attacked Kunming. Four were shot down, and a Japanese history records that the survivors turned for home, having "realized that P-40 fighters were prevailing and a difficult foe."

In the months which followed, the Flying Tigers continued to harass the Japanese at every opportunity, consistently recording a victory to loss ratio in combat of at least two to one. They were among the first to show that the Japanese military could be successfully opposed. When the AVG was disbanded in July 1942, many of its pilots transferred into the USAAF,

Duke Hedman in front of his AVG P-40 in China. He flew with the AVG's 3rd Squadron, which styled itself as "Hell's Angels." In accordance with the complex rules of air combat, Hedman was credited with 4.83 victories during his time with the AVG.

taking with them the experience of being able to fight the Japanese in the air and win.

The Doolittle Raid

The second gleam of hope in the first half of 1942 came from what might best be described as a gesture of defiance. Wars are not won by being defensive, and Americans were impatient to hear that the U.S. had demonstrated some offensive spirit by striking back at Japan. President Roosevelt wanted the Japanese home islands attacked both to bolster American morale and to give the Japanese people a sharp reminder that they were not beyond the reach of the war. The operation decided on was fraught with risk. Sixteen modified B-25 Mitchell

medium bombers, led by Lt. Col. Jimmy Doolittle, were to be launched from the aircraft carrier *Hornet* to attack Tokyo. To some, such a daring concept stepped beyond the bounds of reason. With the U.S. task force already ploughing through rough seas in the Pacific, it seemed that the enemy was of that view. Listeners heard an English language news report from Radio Tokyo describe as "laughable" the idea that American bombers could attack Japan. "It is absolutely impossible," the announcer told her audience, "for enemy bombers to get within five hundred miles of Tokyo."

On April 18, when 650 nautical miles east of Tokyo, the task force was seen by Japanese picket boats. The decision was made to launch Doolittle's aircraft immediately, some two hundred miles farther from their targets than had been intended. This meant that Doolittle's aircraft would have minimal fuel reserves for their planned recovery to Chinese airfields. All sixteen B-25s took off successfully, Doolittle in the leading bomber having a maximum of 467 ft of deck available. Thanks to the *Hornet* making twenty knots

ter were later executed as war criminals, and another died in captivity. The sixteenth B-25 landed without damage near Vladivostok, where it was appropriated and its crew interned by the Soviets.

Depressed by the sight of his aircraft's wreckage the next day, Doolittle convinced himself that the raid had been a failure and that he would face a court

members of the Japanese High Command were brushed aside and plans to strike back at the American enemy were brought rapidly to fruition. Operations which might better have been separated in time now came together in what was intended to be a massive four-pronged expansion around the extremities of Japan's huge empire. The four prongs pointed at Port Moresby in New Guinea, Guadalcanal in the Solomons, Midway Island, and the Aleutians. A dispassionate assessment of the prospects for succeeding in four such widely separated and challenging campaigns at once might have suggested that at least one of them should be delayed, but the Japanese were in no mood to be dispassionate. The Japanese Navy, in particular, needed to expunge its feeling of shame and, in any case, most Japanese at this stage of the war were infected with "victory disease." They had accomplished so much so easily that failure seemed only the remotest of possibilities.

One of the most surprising sights of the Pacific War. B-25 bombers parked on the deck of the **Hornet** *while on their way to launch a "one-way ticket" attack on the Japanese mainland in April 1942.*

into a thirty-knot wind, he later said that he was "off the deck with feet to spare." During the subsequent flight, the B-25 crews saw many Japanese ships and aircraft, and they were engaged by numerous anti-aircraft guns, but all dropped their bombs at various points in Tokyo, Kobe, and Nagoya. A providential tail wind then helped fifteen of the force to reach the Chinese coast, but from that point on things went less smoothly. Darkness was imminent, the weather was bad, fuel was low, and no radio contact of any kind could be made. All fifteen aircraft were lost when the crews were forced to either crash-land or bail out. Three men were killed and several injured in the process, and eight were captured by the Japanese. Three of the lat-

martial for the loss of the B-25s when he returned to the U.S. The reality was rather different. As the President had believed it would, the raid deeply shocked the Japanese and gave a tremendous boost to American morale at a difficult time. Jimmy Doolittle was rewarded for his efforts with a promotion to Brigadier General and the award of the Medal of Honor.

With the benefit of hindsight, it can be seen that the raid appears to have been the first small link in a great chain of strategic disasters for Japan. The Imperial Japanese Navy had suffered a crushing loss of face. The sacred soil of Japan had been desecrated by enemies, and they had come from the sea. There was an immediate emotional reaction. The views of cautious

The tremendous flurry of Japanese naval activity which followed the Doolittle raid was also a considerable boon for U.S. intelligence. Thousands of coded radio transmissions were intercepted which gave the analysts their chance to break into Japan's naval code. It became possible to read perhaps five percent of Japanese messages and that was enough to discover that the Japanese were dispersing their superior forces in a way which would allow the U.S. to concentrate its then limited strength against the threats individually. Hope began to blossom in the minds of American commanders.

After the Tokyo raid, it was perhaps understandable that Jimmy Doolittle should be depressed by the thought that he had done no more than deliver a pinprick to Japan, that he had lost all his aircraft doing it, and that the Chinese people were now suffering terrible Japanese retribution as a result. These things were so, but the raid also accomplished a great deal. It could later be seen as the first small offensive step on the road which led to the eventual defeat of Japan.

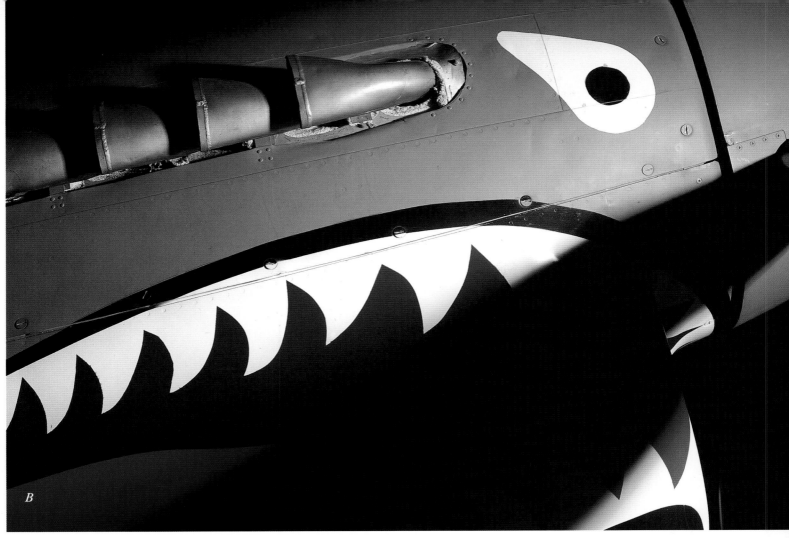

B

A   The USAF Museum's Curtiss P-40E was originally a Kittyhawk, the export model produced for the RAF. It has been restored as a Warhawk and finished in the markings of Chennault's American Volunteer Group in China, the "Flying Tigers." P-40s fought on every combat front in WW II.

B   The celebrated tiger shark's teeth on any Flying Tiger P-40 are a prominent feature.

C   The new-fangled gunsight in the cockpit was apparently not so trusted that the external ring and bead could be removed.

C

A

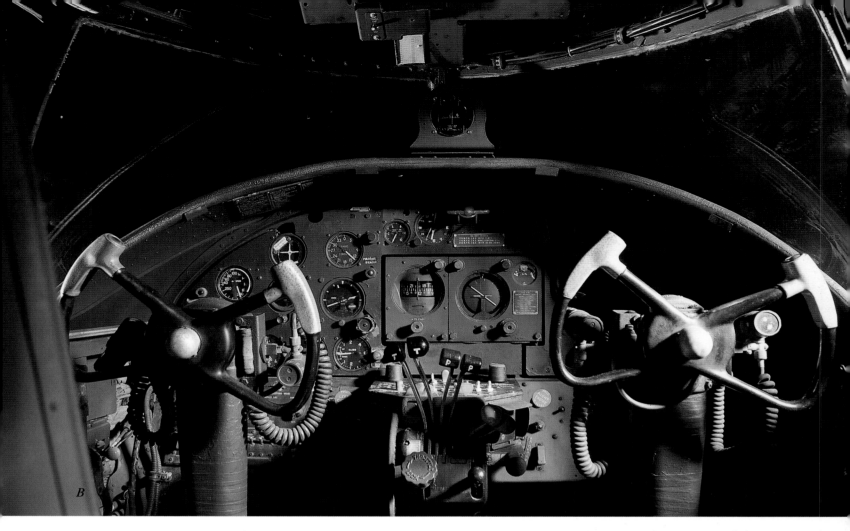

B

A   Most versatile of the USAAF's twins, the North American B-25 Mitchell made significant contributions in both the Pacific and European theaters and was flown by several Allied air forces. Heavy on the controls and something of a challenge when engines failed, B-25s were well regarded because of their resistance to punishment. The glazed nose carried a single .303in machine gun. Other .303s were in the waist positions, and twin .5s fired from dorsal and ventral turrets. The USAF Museum's Mitchell was rebuilt by North American to B-25B configuration and marked as the aircraft used by Jimmy Doolittle on the 1942 Tokyo raid.

B   The B-25's functional cockpit looks ready to go. Basic flight instruments are duplicated between the pilots' panels. Engine instruments are clustered to the right behind the copilot's control column.

C   Soon after 08:00 on April 18, 1942, Doolittle's sixteen B-25s launched from the Hornet. Tokyo was 824 miles away. All sixteen B-25s bombed Japan. Fifteen of them crashed in China and the sixteenth was impounded by the Soviets when it landed at Vladivostok.

D   Marc Mitscher, captain of the Hornet, has just handed Jimmy Doolittle some Japanese medals (presented to U.S. Navy personnel during a 1908 goodwill visit) with the instruction from Secretary of the Navy Frank Knox that they be returned to Japan "with interest." They were attached to the fin of the nearby bomb. (Navigator Tom Griffin is standing behind Mitscher's left arm.)

C

D

A   Half a century on! Tom Griffin (left) and Travis Hoover seen in the USAF Museum's B-25 more than fifty years after their epic raid on Tokyo. Hoover was the pilot of the #2 aircraft and Griffin the navigator of #9.

B   Two of the photographs taken over Japan during the Doolittle raid by Richard Knobloch, the copilot in B-25 #13. He used the camera which is among the items in the USAF Museum's Doolittle raid collection.

C   The USAF Museum's Doolittle raid collection includes a small piece of a crashed B-25, a simple bombsight, a flight jacket (Tom Griffin, navigator, aircraft #9), the camera used to take the only strike photographs of the mission (Richard Knobloch, copilot, aircraft #13), and part of a parachute canopy used to supply a sleeping bag, raincoat, and bandages (Ross Greening, pilot, aircraft #11).

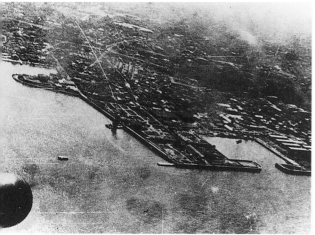

Part 3: The European Air War, 1942-45

At Pearl Harbor and in the Philippines, U.S. forces had suffered ignominious defeat. In the early months of 1942, the Japanese, in the grip of "victory disease," were sweeping all before them, and it was understandable that the focus of the American people's concern should be in the Pacific. The Japanese had to be stopped and those early defeats avenged. However, Hitler's impulsive declaration of war four days after the Pearl Harbor attack committed the U.S. to battle on two fronts, and American military leaders necessarily turned to the provisions of the Joint Army and Navy War Plan RAINBOW 5, which established the principle of "Germany first."

The War against the U-Boats

For the first few months, most USAAF activity to the east of the U.S. was limited to countering the depradations of German U-boats. By the end of 1941, enemy submarines had moved into the waters off the American East Coast and were enjoying rich pickings, often attacking at night when ships were silhouetted against the lights of coastal cities. Before long, ships were being sunk at a rate which exceeded the capacity of U.S. shipyards to replace them and the cargo-carrying capability of the Allies was under serious threat. The U.S. Navy was ill-prepared to deal with an assault of this magnitude, and an early request was put to the USAAF for aircraft to carry out antisubmarine patrols. At first, a motley collection of B-18s, B-25s, and older model B-17s was made available, but they could manage only a limited number of daily patrols between them. These were augmented by Civil Air Patrol pilots in private aircraft based all along the east coast. Few of these patrolling aircraft were armed, and those which were did not carry depth charges. Nor were many crews trained in oversea navigation, antisubmarine attack, or ship recognition. On one memorable occasion, a USAAF bomber crew aimed four bombs at a U.S. Navy destroyer in the belief that they were attacking a surfaced submarine. Thankfully, their delivery was as wide of the mark as was their identification.

Matters improved as experience was gained and became much better after USAAF aircraft began to be fitted with radar from March 1942 on. However, for all the thousands of hours flown on monotonous searches, recognizable successes were few. It was not until July 7, 1942, that a USAAF Lockheed A-29 recorded the first confirmed sinking of a U-boat. The combat report leaves no doubt that the submarine was destroyed:

"[Lt. Harry Kane of the 396th Bombardment Squadron] attacked from fifty feet at 220 mph, releasing three Mk XVII depth charges in train about twenty seconds after the target submerged. The submarine was still visible underwater as the bombs fell. The first hit short of the stern, the second just abaft the conning tower, and the third just forward of the conning tower. Fifteen seconds after the explosions, large quantities of air came to the surface, followed by seventeen members of the crew."

The rarity of attacks on U-boats was not, however, a true indication of patrol effectiveness. Submarines were keenly aware of patrolling aircraft and U-boat commanders were forced to keep their heads down more than they would have liked. In 1942, the air patrols became more persistent and the U-boats were forcibly driven from the U.S. East Coast first to the Gulf of Mexico, then to the Caribbean,

If there was a symbol of the USAAF's war against Hitler's Germany it was the B-17 Flying Fortress. From the summer of 1942 until the spring of 1945, the B-17 was in the vanguard of the assault on the enemy's homeland. Of the approximately 11,500 B-17s sent to the European and Mediterranean theaters, some 8,000 were lost either in combat or to accidents.

and finally out into the Atlantic. In October 1942 the Army Air Forces Anti-Submarine Command (AAFAC) was activated, and as the months went by the war against the U-boat was given more bite by steadily improving technology. Besides microwave radar, aircraft were equipped with magnetic anomaly detectors, sonobuoys, radar altimeters, LORAN (Long Range Aid to Navigation), and better depth charges. Obsolete aircraft were replaced by B-24s with powerful offensive capability, and the force grew to 286 aircraft. After the war, the radar-equipped B-24 was singled out by Admiral Doenitz as a decisive factor in the

aircraft on U-boats, but the considerable effort expended (and the mind-numbing boredom endured by the crews) had been worthwhile. The submarines had been robbed of their freedom of action and had been so hounded from the air that they were at last rendered operationally ineffective.

The Eighth Air Force

Meanwhile, the USAAF had been preparing for what they believed to be the main event. In February 1942, Brig. Gen. Ira Eaker was sent to the U.K. to establish a bomber command headquarters and pre-

RAF's Bomber Command headquarters at High Wycombe, some thirty miles west of London. With the RAF's assistance and encouragement, they set about the daunting process of acquiring and building airfields, establishing a logistics chain, and planning a training program. From the beginning, American and British airmen recognized the need for cooperation, and the RAF did its utmost to help its potentially powerful new neighbor to settle in as quickly as possible. The excellent relations between the two air forces were in no small part due to the character of Eaker himself. He was generally well liked, endearing himself to the British on his arrival in the U.K. with the pointed brevity of his first speech: "We won't do much talking until we've done more fighting. After we've gone, we hope you'll be glad we came."

For the first few months, it was inevitable that the infant Eighth Air Force should rely on the battle-hardened RAF for help and advice as it was readied for the fight. The British assumed initial responsibility for the defense of U.S. airfields, arranged transportation and administrative support, shared intelligence material, provided communications and weather services, trained U.S. intelligence officers and photographic interpreters, and allocated training airfields in Northern Ireland. Eaker and his staff attended the daily operations conference held at RAF Bomber Command, and it was agreed that the two forces would cooperate in the selection of targets and in the issuance of press releases. All of this activity went remarkably smoothly, and there was much mutual goodwill. In June, Eaker reported that "We are extremely proud of the relations we have been able to establish between the British and ourselves." Even so, there were still some notable differences of opinion.

To begin with, the RAF proposed that the Eighth Air Force's fighter units should cover some of the air defense sectors of the U.K. This idea was not enthusiastically received, both because it carried with it the assumption of heavy responsibility for defending U.K. national air space, and because the USAAF preferred to concentrate all of its forces for the air assault

The Lockheed A-29 Hudson was developed from the L-14 civil transport to meet a British requirement for a maritime patrol aircraft. In 1942, with the U.S. facing a serious U-boat threat along the East Coast, a number of Hudsons were delivered to USAAF squadrons. It was an A-29 of the 396th BS which scored the first USAAF success against a U-boat on July 7, 1942.

defeat of his U-boats.

Operating in concert with the U.S. Navy, and with Canadian and British forces, the AAFAC helped to turn the tide in the Battle of the Atlantic. By July 1943, it was agreed that the nature of the threat had changed to such an extent that the USAAF could withdraw from antisubmarine operations. The AAFAC units were disbanded and their equipment handed over to the U.S. Navy. The 135,000 hours they had flown on patrol had led to less than one hundred direct attacks by USAAF

pare for the arrival of combat units. At that time, General Arnold had ordered the formation of a new air force, the Eighth, to take part in Operation GYMNAST, a proposal for the occupation of French North West Africa. When GYMNAST was abandoned as impractical at that stage, the Eighth Air Force was reassigned to the U.K. Selected to command was Maj. Gen. Carl Spaatz.

During the early part of 1942, Eaker and his staff moved into a large manor house, formerly a girl's school, near the

on Germany. Spaatz made the American position clear when he defined the primary function of AAF fighters as being "To support our bombers in an effort to secure air supremacy and not for the defense of England." Nevertheless, he compromised by adding that U.S. fighter squadrons could be trained for air defense duties so that they could be used in an emergency.

More fundamentally, the two air forces disagreed on the way in which heavy bombers should be used. In the first few months of the war in Europe, the RAF had tried daylight operations and had been badly mauled. Furthermore, the RAF's

way through to targets, unescorted if necessary, and that they could ensure the destruction of those targets most effectively if they bombed them by day, when they could be seen and hit precisely. Initially, the British sought to dissuade their American colleagues by pointing out the hazards of operating by day and offering the alternative of being integrated into the night offensive. The USAAF, however, was unshakable in its determination to do what it was trained and equipped to do. As events were to show, neither air force in 1942 had the capability to undertake a strategic air offensive to match the hopes of

on July 1, bringing with it the hope that daylight heavy bomber operations could not be far behind. The distinction of being the first American bomber crews to drop bombs on a European target, however, had already been claimed. A detachment of B-24s, originally en route to the Far East via Africa, was halted in Egypt and ordered to strike a blow in Eastern Europe with the object of helping the hard-pressed Soviets against Hitler's invading armies. The chosen target was the immense Ploesti oil refinery complex in Rumania. Given Ploesti's size and the fact that only twelve B-24s were committed, this could never have been more than a gesture, and its effects were even more limited by the cloud covering the refineries on the day of the raid, June 10, 1942. Ineffective though it was, it offered a small sample of greater things to come.

The Eighth in Action

The first Eighth Air Force airmen to see European action were Captain Charles Kegelman and his crew from the 15th Bombardment Squadron. Flying a Douglas Boston (A-20) borrowed from the RAF, they were quietly added to a force striking the Hazebrouck marshaling yards in France on June 29, 1942. USAAF crews entered the fray more formally a few days later, marking July 4 by joining a British squadron in attacking German airfields in Holland from low-level. It was not an auspicious start. The enemy flak was as fierce as any of the RAF veterans could remember and two American crews were shot down. A third, Kegelman's, survived through a display of gritty determination and superb airmanship. On the run into De Kooy airfield, Kegelman's aircraft was hit in the right engine. The propeller flew off and flames erupted beneath the cowling. As the low-flying Boston slewed to the right, the right wing-tip and rear fuselage scraped the airfield surface. Dragging his crippled aircraft back into the air, Kegelman got rid of his bombs and blasted a flak tower with gunfire. The engine fire went out and Kegelman succeeded in staggering back across the North Sea to base. His thoroughly deserved Distinguished

The first 8th AF airmen to take part in active operations against German forces were Capt. Charles Kegelman and his crew from the 15th BS. On June 29, 1942, they flew with an RAF force in a borrowed Douglas Boston to attack French railway marshaling yards.

fighters had defeated the Luftwaffe's day offensive in the Battle of Britain, but had been unable to stop German bombers operating at night during the ensuing Blitz. The conclusion reached by the British was that, if they were to succeed in carrying the war to Germany, they had to do it at night. The Eighth Air Force, on the other hand, was quite determined to bomb by day. It was an article of faith with the USAAF, built on the foundation of interwar air power theories, that formations of fast, well-armed bombers could fight their

its leaders, nor would they have for many months to come. The road to be followed in building a truly overwhelming bomber force would prove to be unexpectedly long, and its hazards would be overcome only with the help of bitter experience and a host of developments, both technical and operational.

During May 1942, ships carrying the ground elements of the Eighth Air Force began docking in the U.K., and on June 18 General Spaatz assumed command. The first B-17 landed in Scotland

Apparently marshaling yards were felt to be good targets for new squadrons to cut their teeth on. The 8th AF "heavies" joined the fray on August 17, 1942, with an attack by twelve B-17Es on the railway center at Rouen. Maj. Gen. Ira Eaker was in Yankee Doodle, the leading aircraft of the second flight.

Service Cross was the first of many gallantry awards won by the Eighth Air Force.

As the year wore on into August, the impatience of American leaders for the main Eighth Air Force bombing campaign to begin became more obvious. The laborious business of creating a new air force in another country seemed unending, and even with the first bombers in place, further delays were imposed by the minimal level of training of some arriving aircrews, and by another enemy which was soon recognized as a frustratingly everpresent threat—the fickle weather of northwest Europe. At last, on August 17, the skies cleared sufficiently to allow twelve B-17Es of the 97th Bomb Group to fly their first operational mission. Escorted by RAF Spitfires, they attacked the marshaling yards at Rouen in France. Opposition was light, the visibility was good, and the bombing from 23,000 ft was reasonably accurate. The 97th's aircraft returned to base almost untouched to find that British monitors had heard a German voice reporting "twelve Lancasters heading inland." The error was perhaps understandable at this stage, but the German controllers were to have every opportunity to grow only too familiar with the shape of the B-17 as time went by.

The first B-17 raid raised American morale considerably. The Eighth was in action, even if only on a small scale, and the smoothness of the operation hinted at great things for the future. It was notable, too, for some of the prominent (or soon to be) air force figures involved. The mission was led by Colonel Frank Armstrong, with Major Paul Tibbetts in the other pilot's seat. General Eaker was in the leading aircraft of the second flight, a B-17 appropriately bearing the name *Yankee Doodle*. Congratulations to Eaker came immediately from the Commander-in-Chief of the RAF's Bomber Command, Air Marshal Sir Arthur Harris, in a message which said: "Yankee Doodle certainly went to town and can stick another well-deserved feather in his cap!"

The early promise of the Rouen raid seemed to be confirmed by eight more missions flown against other targets in France or the Netherlands between August 19 and September 5. None was large in scale nor represented a deep penetration of enemy territory, and all were heavily escorted by fighters. Nevertheless, the bombing was generally quite accurate and no B-17s were lost. The growing confidence of the bomber crews and their commanders received its first check on September 6 during a raid on aircraft factories at

Meaulte in France. For the first time, Luftwaffe fighters pressed home their attacks on the bomber formation and two B-17s were shot down. Several others were damaged and came back with casualties.

Weather restricted operations in the following weeks, but on October 9 the bombers of the Eighth again faced serious opposition. On that day, General Eaker issued his first mission tasking for over one hundred bombers, eighty-four B-17s, and twenty-four B-24s taking off with fighter escort to attack targets near Lille. Mechanical failures forced fifteen B-17s and fourteen B-24s to turn back, reducing the force to seventy-nine. Over northern France, the Luftwaffe harried the bombers continually, shooting down four and damaging most of the rest. The bombing results were poor, too, but concern over the negative aspects of the mission was overridden by the claims of the gunners that they had destroyed fifty-six fighters, probably destroyed twenty-six more, and damaged another twenty. (In intelligence officer's shorthand: 56-26-20.) Since this almost equaled the total number of Luftwaffe fighters then thought to have been in the area, it was welcomed, but with some skepticism. Further investigation eventually reduced the figures to 21-21-15, but even that was probably excessive. It had to be accepted as inevitable that in the confusion of battle, with many gunners firing at the same fighter, claims were going to be exaggerated. While this added to the problems of assessing the enemy's losses, it at least had the positive effect of boosting the morale of the bomber crews.[1]

Another problem which was to bedevil the Eighth Air Force throughout its time in England showed itself on the Lille mission. Operating large aircraft in close proximity introduced an obvious collision hazard which had to be accepted. In 1942, the problem was relatively minor since the number of USAAF aircraft in the U.K. was

[1] Postwar research showed that gunners' claims were generally about three times Luftwaffe losses. The battle of October 9, 1942, is perplexing because only two Luftwaffe losses can be traced. Equally baffling was a running battle in which "Wild Bill" Casey and his crew defied a succession of fighter attacks on November 23, 1942. Casey's gunners described shooting down seven FW-190s in twelve minutes. They "disintegrated" or "hit the sea," and more than one pilot was seen to "bale out." German records for that day indicate that one FW-190 was lost. None of this suggests that the gunners claims were anything less than genuine, but it does highlight the difficulty of remaining precise and dispassionate while under the stress of combat.

still quite small. Even so, two B-17s of the 92nd BG on their way to Lille collided over the Channel, one being stripped of its rudder and part of the fin, and the other losing two engines and rupturing a fuel tank. On this occasion, both aircraft managed to get back for emergency landings, but future incidents would not always have such happy endings. As the Eighth grew in strength, the challenge of operating thousands of aircraft in the uncertain weather and restricted airspace of eastern England sometimes proved too great, often with disastrous results for the aircrews involved.[2]

With four B-17 and two B-24 groups available and the force blooded in combat, Eaker was looking forward to further growth and to planning operations in which his bombers could penetrate the German heartland and strike the enemy with real power. So far, his crews had been gaining valuable experience but he had been limited to attacks which were little more than pinpricks. Unfortunately for Eaker, higher authorities were about to make it impossible for him to develop the bomber offensive as he would have wished.

Operation TORCH

President Roosevelt and Prime Minister Churchill had originally agreed that first priority should be given to the prepa-

[2]The collision on the Lille raid was the first of more than 100 between heavy bombers of the Eighth Air Force during the war, the vast majority of them fatal to the crews.

ration of plans for an Allied invasion of Europe, principally with the object of easing the pressure on the hard-pressed Soviets. It was thought that carrying through such a venture in late 1942 would be impractical, although a plan (code name SLEDGEHAMMER) was drawn up for that to happen if the Soviet Union appeared to be on the brink of defeat.

Much firmer was the proposal to launch an invasion of France in the spring of 1943. This operation was code named ROUNDUP, and its preparatory phase was BOLERO. The Eighth Air Force figured in the plans, both as a strategic weapon and as one to ensure air superiority for the Allied forces. With these intentions in mind, Spaatz and Eaker worked to build up the strength and capability of the Eighth as rapidly as possible. They believed, with other air force leaders, that the future status of air power in the U.S. military largely depended on the success of the strategic bomber, so they were keen to show that the Eighth Air Force could give an emphatic response to the skeptics who claimed that there were better ways to use national resources. In 1942, with so many other battles to be fought, it was by no means certain that the air war over Germany would remain a high priority. The U.S. Chiefs of Staff needed convincing, and it was up to the Eighth to provide the proof.

As the summer of 1942 progressed, tension eased somewhat in the Pacific and

the Japanese advance to the gates of India was slowed by the monsoon, but the German Army still hammered at the Soviets, and the British suffered a series of defeats at the hands of Rommel in North Africa. By July, Rommel's army stood within reach of the Suez Canal and there was talk of reviving the GYMNAST plan for a U.S. invasion of North Africa, much against the wishes of the U.S. Joint Chiefs of Staff. They still believed that ROUNDUP should take pride of place, but the two national leaders concluded otherwise, and the decision was made to invade North Africa, using the new code name TORCH. The promised second front in Europe to help the Soviets would have to be in the form of an intensified air assault against Germany. In that, of course, the Eighth Air Force chiefs were only too ready to take part, but it was apparent that, at this stage, resources were insufficient to mount a strategic air offensive and provide an air support for a major invasion at the same time.

Spaatz wrote to Arnold in August: "Regardless of what operations are conducted in any other theater, in my opinion, [England] remains the only base area from which to launch aerial operations to obtain air supremacy over Germany, and until such air supremacy is established there can be no successful outcome of the war." Arnold's chief of staff did his best to reassure Spaatz in his reply, suggesting that TORCH was to be carried out at the expense of anything *but* the bombing offensive from the U.K., but that was soon seen as an empty promise. The forces were just not available to conduct both offensives at once. On September 8, Spaatz had to order that all air operations in the European theater be subordinated to preparations for the invasion of North Africa. The Eighth Air Force was to lose a large part of its existing strength to a new air force, the Twelfth, being created for the invasion, and for some time to come, it would be the Twelfth which would be given priority for men and machines. The answers to the strategic bombing question would have to wait.

The Allied landings in North Africa took place on November 8, 1942, under

Hundreds of Supermarine Spitfires were obtained by the USAAF from the British for operations in the European and Mediterranean theaters. Among the first 12th AF units to land in N. Africa in support of Operation TORCH were the Spitfire squadrons of the 31st and 52nd FGs. Here Spitfire 5Bs of the 31st FG stand ready for action in Tunisia.

the overall command of Lt. Gen. Dwight Eisenhower. TORCH was the first Allied combined operation, and it was as complex and potentially hazardous as any which followed. Over five hundred ships from the U.S. and U.K. made their way through the dangerous waters of the Atlantic to land more than 100,000 men on the North African coast, at Casablanca, Oran, and Algiers. Air cover was provided initially by aircraft operating from carriers and from the RAF bases at Gibraltar and Malta, but it was not long before Twelfth Air Force units joined the battle against the French colonial forces resisting the landings.

The commander of the Twelfth, Maj. Gen. Jimmy Doolittle, arrived at Gibraltar on the afternoon of November 6, his B-17 bearing the scars of a brisk encounter with four Junkers 88s over the Bay of Biscay. He was therefore on hand on November 8 to order the 31st Fighter Group, waiting on the crowded airstrip, to fly its Spitfires into Tafaraoui airfield near Oran. Their arrival there was eventful, some Spitfires silencing French artillery shelling the airfield before landing, while others took on four Dewoitine fighters which shot down one of the 31st's aircraft during its landing approach. Three of the Dewoitines were destroyed. Within hours, the 52nd FG's Spitfires and the 33rd

FG's P-40s were added to the Twelfth's strength ashore. The 60th Troop Carrier Group's C-47s also arrived carrying paratroops from the U.K., although bad weather and communications failures bedeviled their efforts and scattered them all over the northwest shoulder of Africa.

By November 10, the French Air Force in North Africa had been destroyed or captured. The Twelfth Air Force had lost six Spitfires (two to friendly fire) and three C-47s. In the next ten days, the Twelfth's strength in Algeria grew to include four fighter groups (1st and 14th with P-38s, and 31st and 52nd with Spitfires), a light bomber squadron (15th with A-20s), the B-17s of the 97th BG, and two troop carrier groups. In Morocco, the buildup went more slowly, but there were still the P-40s of the 33rd FG, some B-25s of the 310th BG, and parts of the 62nd troop carrier group.

Once established ashore, the Allied forces turned east to move on Tunisia, aiming to crush Rommel's army between themselves and the British Eighth Army under General Montgomery, which was now driving the Axis armies westward out of Egypt. The Germans reacted quickly, pouring reinforcements into Tunisia and checking the forward Allied units. To make things worse, the heavy winter rains now set in, bogging down the inadequate trans-

port of the Allied armies and turning their dirt airfields to soup. The Luftwaffe was operating from hard surfaces and was not affected. The winter months proved to be a testing time for the Allied forces, with the Luftwaffe generally having the upper hand in the air. Nevertheless, Allied bombers continued to harass the enemy whenever possible, with B-17s, B-26s, A-20s, and RAF Blenheim Vs attacking airfields and port facilities. They were joined in these efforts by RAF Wellingtons based in Malta and the western desert, and by B-17s and B-24s of another recent arrival in the Mediterranean theater, the U.S. Ninth Air Force.

New Command Arrangements

Late in June 1942, Maj. Gen. Lewis Brereton had arrived in Cairo from the Pacific to command a hurriedly organized U.S. Middle East Air Force. In November, this became the Ninth Air Force, operating principally in support of General Montgomery's Eighth Army as it pursued Rommel in his westward retreat. By February 1943, the Axis armies had been driven back into Tunisia, and the campaigns of the British Eighth Army and the Allied TORCH armies merged. After some interim arrangements, the Allied air forces combined as part of a sweeping reorganization in the Mediterranean. Air Marshal Sir Arthur Tedder became Commander, Mediterranean Air Command, which had three elements—the Malta and Middle East Commands, and the Northwest African Allied Air Forces (NAAF). The NAAF was given to Carl Spaatz in a shuffle which still left him with the responsibility of commanding U.S. air forces in the European theater while accompanying Eisenhower to Africa. Ira Eaker was moved up to command the Eighth Air Force in the U.K.

The NAAF was functionally divided into three elements—a strategic air force commanded by Jimmy Doolittle; a tactical air force (NATAF) under Air Marshal Maori Coningham; and a coastal air force led by Air Marshal Hugh Lloyd. The new arrangements placed the two officers who had been most closely involved with the development of army/air force cooperation

Among the medium bombers operated by the 12th AF in the Mediterranean was the Martin B-26 Marauder. The 319th BG was one of the first to see action with the B-26 in N. Africa.

during the war in the desert, Tedder and Coningham, in command positions, and their record of success profoundly influenced their USAAF colleagues. The NAAF was a new experience for U.S. airmen. USAAF and RAF officers were intermingled at every level, and the importance of eliminating interservice rivalries and working closely with their army opposite numbers was constantly emphasized. These principles, although not always strictly adhered to, were afterwards always in the minds of USAAF officers. Functional divisions also became common, with whole air forces being designated "strategic" or "tactical." Significantly, too, the belief that air forces cooperating in the land battle should fight under a single air commander was firmly established.

The Luftwaffe Struck Down

As the winter weather eased, Coningham issued a directive to the NATAF. In it, he stressed the importance of achieving air supremacy before becoming heavily engaged in the land battle. His priorities were, first: "A continual offensive against the enemy in the air," and second: "Sustained attacks on enemy airfields." In conclusion, he emphasized that "The inculcation of the offensive spirit is of paramount importance." Concentrated offensive operations were unleashed in March 1943, and the days of Luftwaffe superiority were over. German aircraft losses rose rapidly, both in air combat and on the ground. Much to the relief of Allied troops, but probably the regret of the fighter pilots, the notorious Ju 87 Stuka had to be withdrawn from combat in Africa after crippling losses, notably on April 3, when the 52nd FG intercepted twenty Ju 87s and, brushing aside their escort, destroyed fourteen for the loss of one Spitfire.

From March 1943 until the end of the North African campaign in May, the Allied air forces kept up a constant pressure on the enemy's airfields, ports, and troop concentrations. The principal Axis line of defense in Tunisia, the Mareth Line, was broken after a relentless pounding by tactical aircraft, including the P-40s of the

57th and 79th Groups. Luftwaffe fighters became hunted creatures, moving continually from one airstrip to another and adopting extreme dispersal measures. The B-17s introduced themselves to Italy, achieving an impressive success in sinking the cruiser *Trieste* at its anchorage from 19,000 ft, besides destroying thirty acres of Palermo's docks and several ships in an explosion felt at 24,000 ft.

In April, measures were taken to sever the Axis lifeline across the straits between Sicily and Tunisia. Some five hundred enemy transports (Ju 52s, SM 82s, and Me 323s) were being used to ensure the survival of the Axis armies in North Africa. Offensive sweeps were undertaken against the Sicilian airfields mounting the enemy airlift, destroying dozens of transports on their bases, and strong fighter patrols made the straits a killing ground. Among a number of big days for the Allied fighters was April 18, the day of the "Palm Sunday Massacre." A huge formation of about one hundred Ju 52s, escorted by MC 202s, Me 109s, and Me 110s, was intercepted by four squadrons of P-40s (57th and 324th FGs) with a top cover of RAF Spitfires. Fifty-one transports and sixteen of their escorts were shot down for the loss of six P-40s and one Spitfire. Four days later, a formation of twenty-one giant Me 323s, each carrying ten tons of fuel, was caught and obliterated by Allied fighters, effectively ending the Axis airlift. Over a period of only seventeen days, the enemy transport losses in the North African campaign totaled 435 aircraft. The back of the Luftwaffe's airlift capability was broken.

Under incessant pressure from Allied ground and air forces, Axis resistance crumbled and by May 7 the German air commander in Tunisia was ordering his squadrons to fly to safety. Serviceable aircraft left for Sicily immediately, but the effectiveness of the Allied campaign against Axis airfields was revealed by the fact that more than six hundred aircraft had to be left behind because they were unfit to fly. Final surrender of all Axis units in North Africa came on May 13 when over a quarter of a million Axis troops capitulated and

In the early months of 1943 Allied aircraft effectively destroyed the enemy's capability to supply forces in N. Africa by air. Enemy transport aircraft venturing over the Mediterranean did so at their extreme peril. This giant Me 323 was caught and shot down near Corsica by a passing B-26.

passed into captivity.

The USAAF had not been enthusiastic about TORCH. The need to provide the air power for the operation was seen as an unwelcome diversion from the principal objective—the development of a bombing offensive against Germany. Nevertheless, the North African adventure had proved invaluable. Combat experience had been gained at relatively little cost, and the basic principles of air/ground cooperation had been absorbed. The lessons were quickly incorporated into Field Manual 100-20, which was forthright in declaring:

"Land power and air power are co-equal and interdependent forces. . . . The gaining of air superiority is the first requirement for the success of any major land operation. . . . The inherent flexibility of air power is its greatest asset. . . . Control of available air power must be centralized and command must be exercised through the air force commander if this inherent flexibility and ability to deliver a decisive blow are to be fully exploited."

These principles, established in North Africa, would give rise to the overwhelming tactical air power which proved so vital to the overthrow of Hitler's Fortress Europe.

The Air Assault on Germany

In January 1943, Roosevelt, Churchill, and their Combined Chiefs of Staff met in Casablanca to discuss the future direction of the war. Daylight strategic bombing was among the operations subjected to their scrutiny. The claims of its USAAF advocates were still unproven, and not a single Eighth Air Force bomb had yet fallen on Germany. The British remained of the opinion that the Eighth should become part of the night bombing offensive, and the U.S. Navy was saying that the resources needed to build up a bomber force in the U.K. would be better expended in the Pacific.

sults achieved by the Eighth were discouraging. Between mid-October 1942 and mid-January 1943, a total of just over one thousand bomber sorties had been dispatched, but over four hundred of these had failed to attack. In September 1942, the number of aircraft returning from raids with repairable battle damage was 13.3 percent of the attacking force; by December, it was up to 42.1 percent. Total losses had risen from 3.7 percent in November to a disturbing 8.7 percent in January.

One of the factors affecting these worrying figures was a change in the tactics of Luftwaffe fighters. On November 23, 1942, during a mission against St.

bombers of the Eighth and this tactic became a feature of the struggle throughout the air war in Europe. Almost immediately, countermeasures were sought. More forward-facing guns were added to the B-17s and B-24s, and new formations were devised to ensure that the bombers made the most of the benefits of mutual protection. At first, the bomber formations had flown in elements of no more than three aircraft, loosely coordinating their mutual support. By 1943, the Eighth's bombers were going to war in combat boxes of eighteen to twenty-one aircraft, with two or three boxes flying together in a defensive formation.

Only too well aware of the problems confronting the Eighth, Hap Arnold summoned Ira Eaker to the Casablanca conference to present the case for strategic daylight bombing. Eaker brushed aside past and present difficulties and concentrated on the prospects for the future, winning over Churchill by describing an offensive in which the USAAF by day and the RAF by night subjected Germany to a relentless pounding, to "soften the Hun for land invasion and the kill." Churchill's imagination was caught by Eaker's arguments, particularly one which became a slogan, pledging to bomb the Third Reich "around the clock." As a result of Eaker's persuasions, the Allied leaders were able to agree that a coordinated bombing offensive, by day and night, was the only way immediately available to carry the war to Germany, and that it was indispensable preparation for the eventual Allied invasion of Europe. A directive was issued which called for a Combined Bomber Offensive aimed at "the progressive destruction and dislocation of the German military, industrial and economic system, and the undermining of the morale of the German people to a point where their capacity for armed resistance is fatally weakened."

B-17Fs of the 364th BS in Curt LeMay's 305th BG set an example of keeping a defensive formation tight.

At this stage of the war, the USAAF could produce very little supporting evidence to defend its position. Since being ordered to give priority to TORCH, the Eighth had accomplished nothing of any great significance. The shortage of aircraft and crews, and the appalling winter weather in northwest Europe, had placed tight limits on both the strength and frequency of operations. Worse still, most of the operations flown were in response to a directive to concentrate on the U-boat pens in France, targets which were nearly impervious to attack and were well defended. From almost every point of view, the re-

Nazaire, fighters led by Oberleutnant Egon Mayer began to attack the bomber formations from the front. At that time, neither the B-17 nor the B-24 was heavily armed in the nose, and there were blind spots which the guns of the upper and lower turrets could not reach. The rapid closing rates of frontal attacks demanded considerable skill and determination from fighter pilots, but they also made the fighters more difficult targets for the gunners, presenting them with small frontal area targets and high crossing speeds. With the introduction of frontal attacks, Luftwaffe pilots began to score consistently against the

Less than a week after the end of the Casablanca conference, on January 27, 1943, the Eighth Air Force opened its long campaign against Germany with a raid on Wilhelmshaven. Fifty-five aircraft out of the ninety-one launched bombed their targets, but cloud and fighters spoiled their

aim and the bombing was not very effective. A B-17 and two B-24s were lost, but the gunners had a good day, claiming twenty-two fighters shot down. (The actual score was seven.) The first step having been taken, the offensive against German targets did not build up as had been hoped. Between the first Wilhelmshaven raid and mid-August 1943, more than six months later, there were less than twenty days when the Eighth was able to penetrate German airspace. Eaker's masters in Washington had difficulty in grasping the reasons for such slow progress, although their policies were in large part responsible for the problem. Eaker had to withstand a continual stream of criticism as the Eighth battled the enemy, the European weather, the diversion of assets to other theaters, shortages of spares, and the problems of aircrew arriving inadequately trained. There were times when half of Eaker's meager force was grounded because neither spares nor qualified aircrew were available.

Those missions which were flown into Germany included the Eighth's first attacks on Kiel, Hamburg, and the Ruhr, and with them came an inkling that unescorted daylight bombing might not be so feasible after all. Notable losses were suffered on June 13 (twenty-two B-17s of sixty attacking Kiel), July 25 (fifteen B-17s of one hundred against Hamburg), and August 12 (23 B-17s of 133 over the Ruhr). On these days, and a number of others, the absence of escorting fighters was severely felt. The P-47 Thunderbolts tasked for escort duty could not accompany the bombers past Aachen on the German border, after which the Luftwaffe took over. Not content with swarming in on the bombers from head-on (at least one head-on collision was reported between a B-17 and a Focke Wulf 190 in this period), the German fighter units tried several new tactics, including aiming bombs and salvos of rockets at the formations.[3] The determination of the Luftwaffe to oppose the USAAF was obvious, and was to become

A B-17F of the 569th BS, 390th BG, at Framlingham waits for its lethal cargo. The 390th BG was involved in one of the war's most concentrated air battles on October 10, 1943, over Munster. The group lost eight B-17s and claimed sixty Luftwaffe fighters, a record for a bomber group on one operation.

even more apparent in the latter half of 1943.

The significance of high loss rates was not lost on the bomber crews. In 1943, twenty-five missions were needed to complete a tour of combat duty. Statistically, that meant that a mere four percent loss rate would result in no crew finishing a tour. Double-figure percentages suggested that all bomber aircrew would quickly reach a point where they were living on borrowed time. As the months went by, the slow pace of the bomber offensive stretched out the accumulation of combat missions into an agony of waiting, and the number of crews who reached the end of their tours seemed frighteningly small. It was June 1943 before a crew of the 91st BG, together with their B-17F, became the first in the Eighth Air Force to complete a combat tour and fly back to the U.S. It was a sufficiently notable event for Captain Bob Morgan's crew and their B-17, *Memphis Belle*, to be sent on a publicity tour of the U.S. to promote the sale of war bonds.[4]

The 8th AF's principal heavy bomber was the B-17F until late 1943, when the first B-17Gs (B-17s with chin turrets) began to arrive. The peak front-line strength of the B-17F was about 800, reached in September 1943. By the summer of 1944, most B-17Fs had been retired.

[3]On July 28, 1943, a B-17 of the 385th BG was struck by a rocket and broke up, the pieces crashing into two other B-17s which were also destroyed.

[4]*Memphis Belle* survived the war and is now exhibited in a special museum on Mud Island, Memphis, Tennessee.

Ploesti

The directive governing the Combined Bomber Offensive, derived from plans drawn up after the Casablanca conference, was issued on June 10, 1943, and was given the code name POINTBLANK. Among the primary objectives listed were ball bearings and oil. In August 1943, the USAAF turned its attention to both of these vital products and launched two daylight raids which penetrated more deeply into Europe than the bombers had been before. The first, against the Ploesti oil refineries in Rumania, which produced almost two-thirds of the oil used by the Axis powers, was made by B-24s operating from North Africa. Two groups from the resident Ninth Air Force (98th and 376th) joined two deployed from the Eighth (44th and 93rd) and a new group from the U.S. (389th) in sending 177 B-24s across the Mediterranean on August 1, 1943. To achieve maximum impact, the raid was flown at extremely low level, and with waves of B-24s going through the target area almost nose to tail.

The B-24 was not the ideal aircraft to fly at low-level and in close proximity to lots of others. It was 110 ft across the wing and weighed 60,000 lbs, and it was often described as looking and flying like a truck. Pilot Carl Fritsche says: "To fly formation for several hours in a B-24 required endurance. The controls took so much strength to move that you didn't have to worry about getting to sleep after a long mission." The B-24's great advantage was its range. It was selected for the Ploesti mission because in 1943 it was the only bomber capable of getting there and back. The round trip to the refinery from Libya was about 2,700 miles, and some aircraft were in the air for more than sixteen hours.

For the Ploesti raid to be an unqualified success, the attack needed to be led by the best navigators, to be undisturbed by bad weather en route, to face light defenses, and to catch those defenses by surprise. Unfortunately, none of these conditions were met. As the leaders approached the coast of Greece on the outbound leg, the B-24 *Wingo Wango*, carrying the mission's lead navigator, suddenly dived

B-24s of "Killer" Kane's 98th BG fly through the smoke and flame of the 93rd BG's earlier attack on the Ploesti oil refineries. Kane was awarded the Medal of Honor for his determined leadership on this raid.

steeply into the sea. A second aircraft, this one with the deputy lead navigator, circled to investigate and was left far behind. Over Albania, severe weather disrupted the B-24 formations, splitting them into two main groups. Approaching the target area, the aircraft carrying the mission commander, Brig. Gen. Ent, turned too early and took the leading groups (376th and 93rd) towards Bucharest instead of Ploesti. Major Ramsay Potts of the 93rd and Major Norman Appold of the 376th both broke radio silence to warn of the mistake, but by this time the cohesion of the raid had been lost forever. These two groups finally turned to approach Ploesti from the south instead of the northwest, and crews were told to attack targets of opportunity. To add to their problems, the Ploesti raiders had been misled about the strength of the defenses. By August 1943, Ploesti was one of the most heavily defended areas in Europe. Nor were the B-24s blessed with the advantage of surprise, having been seen by German radar before crossing the Greek coast.

Their ordered ranks gone, the raiders attacked Ploesti in ragged flocks from

several directions, few finding their allocated targets and all of them heavily engaged in a running battle with German gunners in flak towers, on freight trains or secreted in haystacks. Within minutes, Ploesti was covered in flame and smoke as bombs found oil storage tanks and aircraft fell to the defenders' guns. B-24s hurtled between refinery chimneys and dodged other bombers coming at them head on. Aircraft attacked whatever targets presented themselves among the dense clouds of oily smoke and other B-24s flew through the blast of the resulting explosions. Colonel Leon Johnson, leader of the 44th BG, said it was "indescribable to anyone who was not there. We flew through sheets of flame, and airplanes were everywhere, some of them on fire and some of them exploding." Countless acts of heroism and grim determination marked the battle. One of the more memorable was that of Lt. Lloyd Hughes. The tanks of his B-24 punctured and streaming fuel, Hughes pressed home his attack at the Campina refinery through a wall of flame. His aircraft's liquid fuse of leaking fuel ignited and fire enveloped the aircraft, but Hughes held it level and delivered his bombs before attempting a crash landing. Two gunners survived the impact. Lloyd Hughes died and was one of five airmen to be awarded the Medal of Honor for the Ploesti raid.[5]

Escaping from the fires of Ploesti, the surviving B-24s were harassed by fighters all the way to the Ionian Sea. Several bombers diverted into Malta and Cyprus, and others struggled into Turkey, where the crews were interned. Still others crashed into the Mediterranean, leaving just eighty-eight to reach their home base in Libya. In all, fifty-four B-24s were lost, forty-one of them in combat. There were 532 men who did not return from the raid, including more than 100 taken prisoner or interned. The damage sustained by the surviving aircraft was such that only 30 or so of the original 177 were fit for combat on the following day.

The aircrews having made so valiant an effort and paid such a high price, their commanders hoped that the rewards would be equally great, but they were to be disappointed. Severe damage had indeed been inflicted on Ploesti, and total refining capacity had been reduced by 40 percent. However, the refinery had been running at much less than full capacity. Within days, idle plants had been brought on line to replace lost production, and the Allies thought it would be impractical to try adding to the destruction by repeating such a costly mission. Total loss rates of over 30 percent could not be borne. Unescorted long-range, low-level attacks by heavy bombers against defended targets disappeared from the options open to the USAAF, never to return.

Schweinfurt

On August 17, 1943, it was the turn of Germany's ball bearing industry. At that time, Schweinfurt's factories produced half the bearings needed by the Nazi war machine. It was decided to fly a maximum effort by B-17s of the Eighth Air Force against both Schweinfurt and Regensburg, site of a Messerschmitt aircraft factory. Regensburg was the deeper of the two into Germany, and it was planned for the 4th Bomber Wing groups allocated to that tar-

get to lead the way for the whole force and continue to North Africa after bombing. The idea was to time the 1st Bomber Wing's raid on Schweinfurt so that Luftwaffe fighters opposing the Regensburg mission would be on the ground refueling when the second force arrived. It was unfortunate that the English weather disrupted the plan. On the morning of August 17, fog blanketed the airfields of the Eighth and prevented the intended dawn start to the operation. The 4th BW airfields began to clear first and the Regensburg mission got airborne, but thick fog persisted over the 1st BW and the Schweinfurt force was delayed for more than a further three hours.

Fog also disrupted operations for the 4th BW's intended fighter escort of P-47s. Only one group made contact with the bombers, and even they had to turn back as they neared the German border. Colonel Curtiss LeMay, leading the Regensburg attack with the 96th BG, later remarked that the only escorts he saw "had black crosses on their wings." The 4th BW began its journey across Europe with 139 B-17s, but that number began falling before they reached German airspace. Both Luftwaffe fighters and flak left their mark while the B-17s were still over Belgium. By the time they reached Regensburg, fourteen bombers had been shot down, and three others had been forced to jettison their bombloads. There were 122 B-17s left which could attack the Messerschmitt factory. The two leading groups had never come under serious attack and were intact, but some of those further back had taken a severe beating, particularly the 100th Bomb Group which had lost six of its original twenty-one aircraft and had several others damaged. Looking back from near the front of the aerial armada, Staff Sergeant Earl Spann (390th BG) had a grandstand view:

"The trip into Germany was a bloody battle all the way. It was mostly fighter planes but also heavy flak at times. . . . From our position, I could see behind

us and there were planes falling everywhere, a lot of ours and a lot of theirs. Many trails of smoke could be seen coming up from crashed planes. A lot of brave men had died."

Lt. Col. Beirne Lay (100th BG) encapsulated the intensity of the struggle in the phrase: "Each second of time had a cannon shell in it."[6]

The final approach to Regensburg met few fighters and little flak. Visibility was generally excellent and the bombing was accurate and tightly grouped. No B-17s were lost in the target area (although three were badly damaged and would not reach Africa) and the Messerschmitt factory was heavily hit. LeMay's wing could hardly have done a better job. At the time it was thought that Messerschmitt production must be severely curtailed, and there is no doubt that several weeks of production were lost, later estimated at perhaps the equivalent of one thousand fighters. What was not then realized was that the bombs being used (500 lbs HE, plus incendiaries) were powerful enough to knock down buildings but not to destroy machine tools. Within weeks, the Germans had dispersed their production facilities and were on their way to being back in business. Nevertheless, the raid did achieve one great success which was hidden from the Allies

On April 4, 1943, the crew of Lady Be Good, *a B-24 of the 376th BG, left Soluch, Libya, to attack Naples. It was their first mission—and their last. Pushed on by a tail wind during the night return, they overshot Soluch by 400 miles. Sixteen years later, the wreckage of* Lady Be Good *was discovered in the desert, and the bodies of the crew were found at intervals up to 100 miles to the northwest of the aircraft. Here a member of the 1959 investigating team prepares to examine the interior of the aircraft's fuselage.*

---

[5]Posthumous Medals of Honor were awarded to Lt. Lloyd Hughes (389th BG), Lt. Col. Addison Baker, and Maj. John Jerstad (93rd BG). Surviving recipients were Col. Leon Johnson (44th BG) and Col. John "Killer" Kane (98th BG).
[6]Beirne Lay subsequently wrote the screenplay for the epic film about Eighth Air Force operations—*Twelve O'Clock High*.

The 361st FG took its P-47Ds to Bottisham, England, in November 1943. In May 1944, the group re-equipped with P-51Bs.

at the time. Among the items destroyed were jigs for a revolutionary new fighter—the jet-propelled Messerschmitt 262.

The 4th BW landed in North Africa some five hours later, having faced little further opposition. Not turning back from Regensburg appeared to have taken the Germans by surprise. Attrition took its toll, however, as damaged aircraft continued to fall out of formation. On landing, twenty-four B-17s were missing from the 139 which had crossed into Europe. Of those, nine had come from the 100th BG, a crippling unit loss rate of over 40 percent.

Shortly before midday, the 1st BW was finally ordered into the air. With the original plan of mutual support with the 4th BW long since abandoned, it was clear that the long flight to Schweinfurt and back would be a hazardous operation, but the decision was made to go ahead. Two hundred twenty-two B-17s crossed the Dutch coast and faced a Luftwaffe fighter force which had been reinforced and prepared to meet what they believed would be the Regensburg force on its way back to England. Almost three hundred Luftwaffe fighters were ready and waiting for the fight along the route into southern Germany.

Up to the German border, first Spitfires and then P-47s did a good job of holding the Luftwaffe at bay. Things changed dramatically as the last Allied fighters left.

Lt. William Wheeler (91st BG) recalled the scene:

"The thing I remember most vividly is that the Germans started making their initial attack almost exactly at the same time as the P-47s above us made their 180 degree turn to return to base. . . . Looking back at it now, I think that very moment . . . was the major turning point when the Air Force had it proved to them that their idea of sending B-17s unescorted on a deep penetration was not valid. It broke the back of the theories of those who were convinced that the Flying Fortress could protect itself if you had good formation discipline and that excellent fifty caliber gun."

This time it was the leading groups of the 1st BW which bore the brunt of the Luftwaffe's assault. The German fighter leaders deployed their *Staffeln* well ahead of the B-17s in line abreast, as many as fifteen fighters at a time, for waves of head-on attacks which followed relentlessly one after another. The B-17 aircrew who experienced it testify to the ferocity and determination with which the German airmen pressed home their attacks. Staff Sergeant John Thompson (waist gunner, 384th BG) spoke for many of his comrades when he recalled the battle:

"I witnessed something that mankind will never see again. It was rare to see hundreds and hundreds of aircraft in the sky at once. On one occasion our forma-

tion made a small turn and I was able to look back. It looked like a parachute invasion of Germany. . . . Planes were going down so often that it became useless to report them."

Lt. Donald Rutan (copilot, 381st BG), was mesmerized by what was going on in front of him:

"There wasn't much sense in calling out fighters that day; everything was at twelve o'clock level for what seemed like an eternity. Each time they came in you thought that it would be our turn to get it. So many of our planes had gone. This was the fiercest we ever had."

Combat losses and battle damage took a savage toll of the 1st BW on the long flight across Germany, but 184 B-17s reached and bombed Schweinfurt. Shaken and somewhat scattered by the ferocity of the running fight, many crews were then confused by the dust and smoke which soon covered the target area. The later groups, unable to identify the ball bearing factories, followed their briefing instruction to aim at the center of the city. As a result, the bombing was not well concentrated and, although the factories were damaged, they were far from having been destroyed. Some of the aircrew were only too well aware of their limited success, one navigator in particular complaining that they had suffered so much "only to come this far and miss the damned target."

By the time the 1st BW fought its way back across Germany and reached the haven of its English bases, thirty-six of its B-17s had gone down. From the combined force of 361 heavy bombers which had crossed into Europe during the day, sixty had been lost. At least eleven more were so badly damaged that they never flew again, and 162 others had lesser damage. Over 550 men had been killed or were missing. In one day, the Eighth Air Force had suffered losses equal to those of its first six months of operations.

Such alarming figures were thought at the time to have been offset by the success of the B-17 gunners. No less than 288 Luftwaffe fighters were claimed as destroyed. Postwar research revealed that the Luftwaffe lost forty-seven fighters on August 17, 1943—twenty-one to B-17s, twenty-one to escorts over Belgium, and five to accidents. Given the disappointing results at Schweinfurt, it is apparent that the laurels of the day belonged to Germany's defenses. However, the Germans took the hint about the importance of Schweinfurt. Thought was given to dispersing ball bearing production, the number of antiaircraft gun batteries around the Schweinfurt factories was more than doubled, and more fighter units were withdrawn from duties elsewhere to cover the approaches to southern Germany. Despite their defensive successes, there were signs that the Germans were beginning to worry that they could be badly hurt by the persistence and growing strength of the Eighth Air Force.

In the remaining months of 1943, the hard lessons of Schweinfurt/Regensburg were driven home whenever the Eighth Air Force struck at targets within Germany. On September 6, in a fiasco, 262 B-17s scattered bombs in the Stuttgart area through cloud, doing little damage and losing forty-five aircraft. Between October 8 and 10, 1,074 B-17s were launched at various German targets, 855 of them bombed, and 88 were lost. On these raids, well over six hundred aircraft were damaged, many never to fly again.[7]

Grimly determined that the Eighth Air Force should defeat the Luftwaffe, General Eaker gritted his teeth and sent his bombers back to Schweinfurt on October 14. Two hundred ninety-one B-17s were confronted with a Luftwaffe performance described by the official USAAF history as "unprecedented in its magnitude, in the cleverness with which it was planned, and in the severity with which it was executed." In the face of such powerfully determined opposition, the attack on Schweinfurt was remarkable. This time the bombing was accurate and the ball bearing factories were severely damaged, but the price was unbearably high—another sixty B-17s shot down, with seven more

destroyed on return to England and a further 138 damaged to some degree. Two hundred eighty-eight Luftwaffe fighters were claimed as destroyed (German records suggest only thirty-five, although many more were damaged), but even that exaggerated figure could not obscure the fact that the Eighth Air Force was taking a beating. Over Germany, the Luftwaffe was consistently imposing losses of well above 10 percent on the bombing force, and that was a rate which would lead inexorably to its destruction. It was ever more apparent that the daylight bombing offensive could not be continued in the absence of escort fighters with the range to accompany the bombers over Germany.

Wee Willie, *a B-17G of the 323rd BS, 91st BG, successfully returned from 127 operations before being hit by flak on April 8, 1945. This was the last of 197 B-17s reported as missing in action from the 91st BG.*

Changes at the Top

Nineteen forty-three had been a testing time for the Eighth Air Force and as the year drew to a close the daylight offensive was in the balance. Some experiments were even carried out in which some B-17 units joined the RAF's night offensive to gain experience in case daylight bombing had to be abandoned altogether. Unpromising as things looked, however, the persistence of the Eighth was about to be rewarded. Nineteen forty-four would bring great changes and see the scale and intensity of the air war over Europe raised to

levels unimagined in prewar years.

Among the changes was the replacement of General Ira Eaker as the commander of the Eighth Air Force. Hap Arnold's impatience with what he perceived as the slow pace of the air assault on Germany led him to initiate a shake-up among his senior commanders. With Eisenhower and Tedder moving to the U.K. to prepare plans for the invasion of Northwest Europe, Eaker was to take over from Tedder as commander of the Allied air forces in the Mediterranean. Spaatz would command the U.S. strategic air forces in Europe (coordinating the operations of the Eighth and Fifteenth air forces), and Doolittle would be the new commander of the Eighth Air Force. Eaker was not happy at this turn of events. Having seen the Eighth through its worst days, he had been looking forward to future triumphs. His vigorous protests were brushed aside, however, and he duly packed his bags and moved south. Although resentful of the change, he found his new command much changed from its days in North Africa. It was now an immense force of over two hundred Allied squadrons, and it included two numbered U.S. air forces—the Twelfth, which had evolved into a tactical force, and the Fifteenth, which had a strategic role.

Sicily and Italy

At the Casablanca conference in January 1943, it had been agreed that the defeat of the Axis forces in North Africa would be followed by an invasion of Sicily and then of Italy. As a preliminary step, the Allied air forces began to pound Pantellaria during the latter part of May and early June 1943. This heavily defended island in the middle of the Sicilian Straits boasted an airfield which could be used as a forward base from which to provide air cover for the Allied landings on Sicily. Over five thousand Allied sorties were flown against Pantellaria, with the bulk of the bombing being done by USAAF squadrons. As assault forces approached the island on June 11, it was seen that the defenders had run up a white flag. Pantellaria had been conquered by air power alone.

---

[7]Curiously, one of the most celebrated examples of daylight precision bombing took place during this period, and with minimal loss. The Focke Wulf factory at Marienburg was attacked on October 9, 1943, by a force of 96 B-17s from the 94th, 95th, 100th, 385th, and 390th BGs — 83% of the bombs dropped fell within 2,000 ft of the aiming point. Only two B-17s failed to return.

A continuous air campaign had also been carried out against Axis airfields and ports in Sicily and southern Italy, and the tempo of this rose as D-Day for the Sicilian invasion drew nearer. During June and the first ten days of July, about one thousand Axis combat aircraft were destroyed by the Allied air campaign. Many were caught on the ground when they diverted from damaged bases into one or two airfields left untouched by the Allies. These became killing grounds where Allied fighter-bombers took full advantage of a generous selection of targets for their strafing and bombing attacks.

Allied troops invaded Sicily on the night of July 9-10, 1943. The operation was massively supported by Allied air forces and opposition from enemy aircraft was negligible. Allied air supremacy had been imposed over Sicily and the surrounding area for the invasion. Nevertheless, there were aspects of the air operation which went sadly awry, notably those concerned with paratroop operations and air/naval co-operation. "Friendly fire" instances were numerous, with naval gunfire forcing covering Allied fighter patrols up to higher altitudes, and shooting down some of the twenty-three C-47s lost during paratroop operations. Alarmed by the gunfire and dispersed by bad weather, the C-47s scattered their paratroops over a wide area. Sixty-nine Horsa and Hadrian gliders fell into the sea. To make things worse, it happened again on July 13, when 124 C-47s once more flew through friendly fire to drop their paratroops. Eleven were destroyed and another fifty damaged. Investigations after these bungled affairs led to specific recommendations which benefited later airborne operations. In particular, it was emphasized that planning for such operations should be done in one nominated headquarters and that every effort should be made to ensure that associated ground and naval forces were informed of the plan well ahead of time.

By mid-August 1943, all enemy resistance in Sicily had been overcome. The Axis forces had been deprived of air cover and slowly strangled by incessant attacks on their supply lines from the north. The

The P-40 and the C-47— air support workhorses for the ground war in Italy, September 1943.

defeat and the constant pressure of air power on targets as far away as Rome helped to bring down dictator Benito Mussolini and drive Italy out of the war. By early September, all Italian forces had laid down their arms and surrendered to the Allies.

U.S. commanders had not been enthusiastic about a campaign against the "soft underbelly of Europe" after North Africa had been secured. They had feared that involvement in southern Europe might detract from preparations for an invasion of France in 1944. Now, with the fall of Mussolini, General Eisenhower pressed for immediate landings on the Italian mainland in the hope of completing a rapid occupation of Italy and acquiring bases from which to attack Germany from the south. In this the Allies were to be only partially successful. Troops landed in the toe of Italy and at Salerno, near Naples, early in September had fought their way north to occupy Naples on October 1. Soon after, worsening weather and determined German resistance stabilized the front on the prepared defenses of the Gustav Line, about halfway between Naples and Rome. For more than six months, their movement hampered by mountainous terrain and severe winter weather, the Allied armies battered themselves against this line and were denied. In the air, results were more positive. The continuous Allied air assault drew Luftwaffe squadrons south and so had a

beneficial effect on the Eighth Air Force's bomber offensive from England. Without the substantial Luftwaffe combat losses in Sicily and Italy, the near defeat of the Eighth over Germany might have developed into disaster.

Equally significant was the capture of a number of Italian airfields around Foggia on the Adriatic coast. From there, after the end of 1943, the heavies of the newly formed Fifteenth Air Force, commanded by Maj. Gen. Nathan Twining, could cover strategic targets all over northern Italy, southern Germany, Austria, and Rumania. Ploesti's oil complex was now within easy reach, and it was visited regularly by USAAF bombers operating at high level. Before Ploesti was overrun by the Red Army in August 1944, it had been attacked by some 7,500 heavy bomber sorties and oil production had almost dried up. At a cost of about 350 aircraft, Germany's capacity to fuel its forces during the final year of the war was seriously reduced. Heavies from Foggia also delivered telling blows on the German aircraft industry, particularly the Messerschmitt factory at Wiener-Neustadt.

Important though the strategic operations were, they did not typify the air war in Italy. The emphasis was on supporting ground operations. True to FM 100-20, priority was given to achieving and maintaining air supremacy, then came interdiction of enemy supply lines and direct support of ground forces. At the heart of these operations were the fighters and medium bombers—in USAAF squadrons principally A-36s, P-38s, P-39s, P-40s, Spitfires, B-25s, and B-26s—although heavy bombers were also called on to fly tactical missions as necessary. The introduction of forward air controllers ("Rover Joes") and improvements in air/ground communications allowed precise strikes to be called in on enemy positions immediately in front of friendly troops, within the area between the front line and the normal bomb line, even when bombs were dropped from medium altitudes.

In an effort to break the impasse in central Italy, Allied troops were landed at Anzio, north of the Gustav Line, on January 22, 1944. Despite having achieved complete tactical surprise, largely as a result of the Luftwaffe being denied the ability to fly reconnaissance or to operate any aircraft in strength in the battle area, the landings were not a success. Thousands of Allied sorties were flown against enemy airfields and road/rail communications before the assault. The Anzio landings were almost unopposed, but the Germans reacted swiftly and quickly sealed off the Allied beachhead. At the same time, a major Allied offensive had stalled on the Gustav Line and, as the Germans there consolidated their position, they began to move more troops to Anzio. A series of heavy attacks on the Allied bridgehead might well have succeeded in bringing about its collapse had not the Allied air forces held such marked air superiority. During this critical period, the Luftwaffe was able to fly about 150 sorties per day over the front lines, whereas the Allies consistently managed to put up almost ten times that many.

A-36s were among the aircraft prominent in harassing the German troops. The A-36 was the ground attack/dive bomber version of the P-51, and had all the advantages of the Mustang's clean design. Although fitted with dive brakes it was seldom used as a dive bomber, shallow dives and strafing runs being its usual attack profiles. Unlike most other aircraft considered for a dive bombing role it was both fast and maneuverable, and having got rid of its bombs, it could engage en-

emy fighters on equal terms at low level. Unfortunately for the aircraft's reputation, the A-36 squadrons seemed to be involved in more than their share of "friendly fire" incidents. General Omar Bradley recorded his own experience when A-36s attacked a column of American tanks:

"The tankers lighted their yellow smoke bombs in a prearranged recognition signal. But the smoke only caused the dive bombers to press their attacks. Finally in self-defense the tanks turned their guns on the aircraft. A ship was winged and as it rolled over, the pilot tumbled out in a chute. When he landed nearby to learn that he had been shot down by American tanks, he bellowed in dismay. 'Why you silly sonuvabitch,' the tank commander said, 'didn't you see our yellow recognition signal?' 'Oh, ——!' the pilot said. 'Is that what it was?'"[8]

At the heart of the Gustav Line was the town of Monte Cassino, dominated by the abbey of St. Benedict. Convinced that the enemy were using the abbey to direct their defensive operations, the Allied com-

manders ordered it bombed. On February 15, 1944, the abbey was destroyed by B-17s, B-25s, and B-26s, which dropped nearly six hundred tons of bombs during the day. One month later, with the stalemate still unbroken, the town itself was flattened by over one thousand tons of bombs. The record of the B-26 squadrons in this attack was remarkable, with close to 90 percent of their bombs falling within the target area of 1,400 x 400 yards.[9] The B-17s were not so impressive, and several of their bombs fell among Allied troops, who were positioned only one thousand yards from the edge of the town.

A direct hit by flak could be devastating. Here the left wing of a 464th BG B-24 breaks away in a sheet of flame over northern Italy.

The tremendous attack was effective in destroying Monte Cassino, but it was found that the use of bombers for close support operations was a two-edged sword. Apart from "friendly fire" hazards, the problem with wielding a bomber force as a club with which to crush dug-in enemy troops was that the concentrated bombing created obstacles in the form of craters and masses of rubble which impeded advancing infantry and made it almost im-

---

[8]Several other instances of A-36s attacking their own troops are given in Dr. Richard Hallion's book *Strike from the Sky*, p 177-178.

[9]Air Marshal Sir John Slessor was General Ira Eaker's deputy in Mediterranean Air Forces. In a letter to the RAF's Chief of Air Staff in April 1944 he commented on:"...the astonishing accuracy of the medium bomber groups — particularly the Marauders [B-26s]; I think that the 42nd Bombardment Group...is probably the best day-bomber unit in the world."

The A-36A was heavily involved as a ground attack aircraft during the Allied campaigns in Sicily and Italy. It was flown by the squadrons of the 27th and 86th Fighter Bomber Groups.

possible to maneuver tanks. The tremendous destruction also deluded ground commanders into believing that enemy resistance after such an air attack would be negligible, but that was seldom the case.

Denied by the tenacity of the Germans both on the Gustav Line and at Anzio, the Allied commanders launched STRANGLE, an interdiction operation aimed at severing supply lines in northern Italy, so starving the German war machine and forcing a withdrawal. Between March 19 and May 11, 1944, aircraft under General Eaker's command flew over fifty thousand sorties against railway lines, tunnels, bridges, and ports. It was a massive effort, but STRANGLE did not achieve the results its proponents predicted. The Germans were not forced to withdraw by the use of air power alone. However, their capacity to maintain their stocks of ammunition and food (or to move at all behind the front) was seriously diminished. When STRANGLE gave way to DIADEM, a combined Allied air/ground offensive begun in May, the Germans were unable to maintain their resistance. The Gustav Line crumbled and the Allied forces swept forward, entering Rome on June 4, 1944, and joining up with troops breaking out of the Anzio beachhead.

It had been almost a year since the invasion of Sicily. The quick Allied occupation of Italy originally hoped for had not

materialized and the Italian campaign was far from over. German resistance in Italy would persist until the last days of the war, while the Allies concentrated their efforts on other fronts. By the time Rome was taken by General Mark Clark's Fifth Army, the Allied forces in Italy had already had to accept the diversion of many units needed for the buildup of the Normandy invasion force in England (OVERLORD). Others would follow for an invasion of southern France (ANVIL). France now featured at center stage, while Italy rumbled on, almost forgotten, in the background.

The reassuring presence of their own air cover little more than a distant memory, the German army retreated northwards to form another defensive line, the Gothic, in the mountains south of the River Po valley. There the opposing armies faced each other through the miseries of a second Italian winter. Whenever the weather allowed, the Allied air forces kept up the pressure of their interdiction campaign, pounding transport routes until rail networks were a shambles and daylight travel of any kind, even by bicycle or mule, was unsafe. In the spring of 1945, when the Allied armies resumed their offensive, the Germans in Italy were no longer capable of effective resistance. They fell back across the Po, hounded unremittingly by air power, and finally surrendered on May 2, 1945.

The lessons learned by the USAAF in the Mediterranean theater were not forgotten. The ways in which air power could be used to influence the land battle had been thoroughly absorbed, and the priorities laid down in FM 100-20 confirmed. Allied air superiority had allowed the ground forces the maximum possible flexibility in their operations. Strong medium bomber forces, notably of B-25s and B-26s, had been at the heart of an interdiction campaign which had subjected enemy supply lines and airfields to an incessant pounding, seriously limiting freedom of action for the German Army and the Luftwaffe. The dramatic impact of the fighter-bomber had been repeatedly demonstrated, both in direct support of troops in contact with the enemy and in harassing movement of any kind behind the front. As General Ira Eaker wrote in February 1945: "The Mediterranean theater has been the primary crucible for the development of tactical air power and the evolution of joint command between Allies." All of these hard-learned lessons were to be carried forward and applied in WWII's climactic year, a year which began with the Allied invasion of Normandy.

The Tide Turns

As 1944 dawned, the Eighth Air Force began to feel that there was light at the end of the tunnel. The dark days of 1943 were over and the pieces were coming together which would make the Eighth the mightiest instrument of air power ever assembled. U.S. industry and the air force training system were both now in high gear, and new aircraft and crews were pouring across the Atlantic in an ever increasing flood. At the same time, new command structures were in place, designed to make the most of the lessons learned about the use of air power and to take advantage of the experience gained by senior commanders. Tactical procedures and combat techniques had been honed to a fine edge in the heat of battle, and changed policies aimed to ensure that these were used to the best possible effect. New equipments were on their way to add to the effectiveness of the force, among them H2X, an airborne bombing radar which would allow certain targets to be attacked through cloud, and—at long last—fighter aircraft capable of escorting the bombers to their targets and taking on the Luftwaffe on equal terms when they got there.

In the latter months of 1943, the burden of escorting the bomber forces over enemy territory had been borne principally by P-38s and P-47s. Extra fuel in drop tanks had made a difference, but the shorter-range P-47s had still been used principally to cover the outbound and inbound legs of a bomber mission, while the P-38s had reached out as far as such German cities as Bremen and Ludwigshaven. For all their advantages in range, however, the P-38s had some problems, too. Below 18,000 ft they were a match for the Luftwaffe's fighters, but at the heights they needed to operate as escorts they were outclassed by the Me 109s and FW 190s. The extreme cold of high altitudes induced frequent failures in the P-38's Allison engines and challenged pilot endurance in cockpits almost devoid of heating. Even so, a P-38 was the first USAAF combat aircraft to fly over Berlin. On March 3, 1944, Lt. Col. Jack Jenkins, leading the 55th FG, unaware that the bombers had turned back because of weather, reached the German capital in P-38J *Texas Ranger IV*. He recorded that he "got so cold that my crew chief had to help lift me out of the cockpit."

The solution to the long-range fighter problem was already at hand, although some air force officers did not recognize it at first. The outstanding qualities of the P-51 (A-36) airframe had been evident from the time of its earliest flights, but performance limitations at high altitude had made it seem destined for service only as a ground attack aircraft. Even when the original Allison engine had been replaced by the Rolls-Royce Merlin, transforming the P-51's performance at all altitudes, the penny did not immediately drop for some officers. Eager though the Eighth Air Force was to get hold of Mustangs, the first P-51 allocations in England went to General Brereton's Ninth Air Force, the headquarters of which had moved from the

Mediterranean and reformed in Britain in October 1943. The Ninth was now to be exclusively a tactical air force, its principal role that of supporting the Allied armies in the invasion of Europe. General William Kepner, commander of VIII Fighter Command, deplored the arbitrary assignment of P-51s as tactical aircraft, insisting that "developments in Germany [made the P-51] the only satisfactory answer." The situation was remedied and the P-51 got its chance when agreement was reached in October 1943 for all fighter units in the U.K. to support bombers engaged in Operation POINTBLANK until further notice.

The first Merlin-engined version of the Mustang to arrive in England was the P-51B. It was given to the 354th FG, which began operations on December 1, 1943, under the temporary leadership of Lt. Col. Don Blakeslee. An extremely experienced fighter pilot, Blakeslee had flown 120 fighter sweeps with the RAF before transferring to the USAAF to become deputy CO of the 4th FG, the unit he would return to command after seeing the 354th through their P-51 conversion. The 354th was soon in the thick of things, shooting down sixteen enemy fighters

without loss during a mission to Kiel on January 5, 1944. On January 11, they repeated the performance, with Major Jim Howard being awarded the Medal of Honor for his protection of a B-17 wing in an hour-long solo battle with some thirty Luftwaffe fighters. He was credited with three confirmed kills and a number of others damaged. His Mustang had a single bullet hole in the left wing.

Blakeslee rejoined the 4th FG enthusiastic about the Mustang, and he was delighted when his group's P-47s were replaced by P-51s in February 1944. It was in a P-51 that Blakeslee led the escorts for the first missions on which U.S. bombers

In November 1943, the 357th FG became the first Mustang group to join the 8th AF. Here a P-51B undergoes maintenance on its Merlin engine on the group's base at Leiston, England.

attacked Berlin, on March 4 and 6, 1944. Neither raid was particularly auspicious. On March 4, bad weather scattered the formations, only one bomber group reached Berlin, and no less than sixteen of the new Mustangs were lost, eleven of them from the inexperienced 363rd FG. On March 6, the Eighth tried again and Berlin was bombed by 672 heavies in one of the fiercest running air battles of the war. More than eight hundred USAAF fighters performed escort duty at various points in the course of the mission, but even such a strong showing could not prevent the

P.O.W.   KILLED   P.O.W.   P.O

4th FG pilots in front of one of their P-51s. From the left: John Godfrey, Don Gentile, Peter Lehman, Jim Goodson, and Willard Millikan. Gentile was withdrawn from combat in June 1944; Lehman was killed in action; Godfrey, Goodson, and Millikan were all shot down and became prisoners of war.

Luftwaffe from taking its toll of the bombers. Fifty-three B-17s, sixteen B-24s, and eleven fighters were lost. Between them, the bombers and their escorts claimed 179 of their attackers, a figure later reduced to 66 from German records. It was clear that raids on Berlin were never going to be easy, even with the help of long-range fighters, but there were differences from the deep penetrations of 1943. The Eighth Air Force

Don Gentile got into the air war early by joining the RAF and becoming a member of No. 133 Eagle Squadron. Later, he flew both the P-47 and P-51 with the 4th FG, 8th AF. He was most successful in the P-51B when teamed as a pair with John Godfrey, a partnership which Winston Churchill described as "a latter-day Damon and Pythias." Officially credited with 21.83 victories in the air and seven on the ground, Gentile is also remembered for the spectacular destruction of his P-51B Shangri-La while "buzzing the field" at Debden after his last mission. Don Gentile was killed in the crash of a T-33 near Andrews AFB on January 28, 1951.

could now count on putting more than five hundred heavy bombers over a target deep inside Germany, and they could hurt the Luftwaffe in the process. Agonizing though the losses were, the Eighth Air Force knew they would be replaced and that more units were being formed. By contrast, the Luftwaffe was finding replacement increasingly difficult, particularly of experienced pilots.

The weight of fire from a well-organized B-17 group was impressive and no Luftwaffe pilot ever relished attacking a heavy bomber formation. Now, however, they did not even have the option of braving such a daunting hazard without interference. The appearance of USAAF fighters over the Reich was disturbing, and the Mustang came as a considerable shock. Here was a fighter which could accompany the bombers to Berlin, and yet was superior to the Me 109 and FW 190 in terms of speed and turning ability. If the German aircraft had better rates of climb, they could not outdive the P-51 and could not match its zoom climb. The FW 190's only noticeable advantage was in rate of roll, and even that diminished at high speeds. To quote Major Robert Riemensnider, commander of the 55th Fighter Squadron: "[The P-51] had speed, range, and an all-round versatility that was unsurpassed by any of its contemporaries in combat service."

To add to the Luftwaffe's problems, the long-range fighters had been let off the leash. Soon after General Doolittle took over the Eighth Air Force, he visited General Kepner, his fighter commander, who had been pressing for a more aggressive fighter policy. Fresh in Doolittle's mind was General Arnold's New Year message to him: "Destroy the enemy air forces wherever you find them, in the air, on the ground, and in the factories." On Kepner's office wall was a sign which reflected the concerns of previous commanders. It read: "The first duty of the Eighth Air Force fighters is to bring the bombers back alive." Doolittle ordered the closing phrase changed to read: "is to destroy German fighters." Escorting bombers was still important, but close escort, in which the fighters were not allowed to leave the vicinity of the bomber stream, was a thing of the past. Strong fighter forces would now range ahead of the bombers as hunters, and escorts would pursue enemy fighters aggressively, seeking their destruction rather than merely chasing them away. Released from close escort duty, fighters would be encouraged to look for targets of opportunity on the way home, descending to ground level and strafing enemy airfields as they presented themselves.

Doolittle regarded the freeing of the fighters as "the most important and far-reaching military decision I made during the war." In effect, the new fighter tactics gave another role to the bombers besides that of dropping high-explosives on German targets. They were now the bait which lured the Luftwaffe into a life or death struggle with the USAAF's long-range fighters. The Luftwaffe's General Adolf Galland has acknowledged the dramatic effect of the change:

"Only now did the superiority of the American fighters come into its own. They were no longer glued to the slow-moving bomber formation, but took action into their own hands. Wherever our fighters appeared, the Americans hurled themselves at them. They went over to low-level attacks on our airfields. Nowhere were we safe from them, and we had to skulk on our own bases. During takeoff, assembling, climb and approach to the bombers, when we were in contact with them, on our way back, during landing, and even after that, the American fighters attacked with overwhelming superiority."

Big Week

In concert with the new escort fighter policy, the Allies, intent on ensuring air supremacy for the invasion of France, hatched a plan aimed at crippling the German aircraft industry. Known as Operation ARGUMENT, its principal objectives were German factories engaged in the manufacture of aircraft components and ball bearings, and in final aircraft assembly. Appalling weather prevented ARGUMENT from being launched during the early weeks of 1944, but the skies over Europe began to clear in mid-February. Between February 20 and 25, in what came to be called "Big Week," over 3,300 Eighth Air Force bomber sorties pounded Germany's aviation industry. They were joined by some 500 more from the Fifteenth Air Force in Italy, and RAF Bomber Command added another 2,750 at night. Nearly 4,000 fighter sorties were dispatched to accompany the daylight raids. By the time weather closed in to bring "Big Week" to an end, the USAAF had lost 226 bombers (6.8 percent) and 41 fighters; the RAF's losses from four major raids totaled 141 aircraft (5.1 percent).

In the fierce fighting of the first day of "Big Week," three Medals of Honor were awarded to B-17 crew members, two of them posthumously. First Lt. Walter Truemper and S. Sgt. Archie Mathies, navigator and flight engineer in a B-17 of the 351st BG, were killed trying to land their damaged aircraft at base. Their copilot already dead, they refused to bale out and abandon their badly wounded pilot, who survived the crash but died soon after. In a second incident highlighting the hazards of head-on attacks, a B-17 of the 305th BG became a straggler when its bombload failed to release over the target and it was heavily hit by fighters. Cannon shells set an engine on fire and shattered the cockpit, killing the copilot and wounding eight other crew members. The pilot, 1st Lt. Bill Lawley, seriously hurt and bleeding pro-

fusely, held the dead copilot off the controls with one hand and recovered from a steep dive with the other. Electing not to bale out because of the serious injuries to his crew, Lawley made for the English Channel, surviving another fighter attack en route which set fire to a second engine. Shock and loss of blood caused Lawley to suffer a temporary collapse on the way home, but by the time the French coast was crossed, both engine fires had been extinguished and the bombs jettisoned. Over southern England a third engine died and Lawley, by now at very low altitude, managed to belly-land the B-17 on the

The end of a formidable adversary captured on camera. A Focke-Wulf 190 goes down under the guns of an 8th AF fighter.

grass airfield at Redhill, south of London, without further injury to his crew.

The cost of "Big Week" to the bombers had been relatively high, but far from fatal. The Luftwaffe, however, staggered under the repeated blows. The material injury to the aircraft industry and the losses of fighter aircraft—355 fighters destroyed and 155 damaged—were undoubtedly serious but not disastrous in themselves. Under the organizational leadership of Albert Speer, German industry proved wonderfully resilient, dispersing its assets and actually increasing aircraft production in the months after "Big Week." The real problem was that the lifeblood of the Luftwaffe was being drained away. In fighting to protect the Reich, well over four hundred German fighter pilots were lost

in February 1944. In March, the month of the attacks on Berlin, the figure rose to nearly five hundred, among them a dozen of the greatest German aces, including Egon Mayer, the man who in November 1942 initiated the tactic of the massed head-on attacks against B-17s. During the five months before the D-Day invasion, no fewer than 2,262 German fighter pilots died. With losses like that, the Luftwaffe was irrevocably on the slippery slope to defeat. All the production in the world was of little use if there were not enough competent pilots to fly the aircraft.

During this period, when the Eighth Air Force began to impose its will on the Luftwaffe, the lion's share of fighter escort duty was still being borne by the P-47 Thunderbolt. Over three thousand of the fighter sorties in support of "Big Week" were flown by P-47s. An unusually big fighter for its time, the P-47 was powered by the huge Pratt & Whitney R-2800 radial engine of over 2,000 hp. It was heavier than its rivals by several thousand pounds, and could not match them as a dogfighter. However, it was fast, ruggedly built, and heavily armed. It was almost impossible to run away from because it could outdive any of its likely opponents (until the coming of the Me 262 jet), and a burst from its eight .50-caliber machine guns was usually decisive.

The highest scoring group in the 8th AF was the 56th FG, flying P-47s. Among the pilots were (standing) Francis "Gabby" Gabreski, Robert Johnson, Walker "Bud" Mahurin, Robert Landry; (on the wing) Walter Cook and David Schilling.

The ruggedness of the P-47 was attested to by its capacity to withstand battle damage. Its combat loss rate was a remarkably low 0.7 percent, compared with the P-51's 1.2 percent. As a pilot in the 362nd FG said: "For the low-level job we had to do, where you couldn't keep out of the light flak and small arms fire, there wasn't a better plane than the P-47. It would keep going with damage with which other types would have fallen out of the sky." These characteristics endeared the Thunderbolt to its pilots, among whom were some of the great USAAF aces of WWII. The leading P-47 group was the 56th FG, commanded initially by Colonel Hub Zemke, one of the war's outstanding fighter leaders. By the end of the war, the 56th had destroyed 664.5 enemy aircraft in aerial combat, more than any other group in the Eighth Air Force, and many leading aces had scored their victories while on its roster, among them Fred Christensen (21.5), "Gabby" Gabreski (28), Gerald W. Johnson (27), Walker "Bud" Mahurin (21), and David Schilling (22.5).

The V-weapons

The direct assault on the elements of German air power might have been even more intense if the Eighth Air Force had not occasionally been diverted from its primary task to add its weight to an Allied effort aimed at countering a new and initially puzzling enemy threat. Aerial recon-naissance revealed that the Germans were building some very large concrete structures, including a number of ramps, in northern France. Photographs gave substance to other intelligence on the development of two German "vengeance" weapons—a small pilotless aircraft powered by a pulse-jet (the V-1), and a large ballistic missile (the V-2), both armed with warheads of about a ton. By December 1943, the Allied campaign against these weapons had been given the formal title of Operation CROSSBOW, and a chain of over seventy probable launching sites had been identified near the Channel coast of France, in an area some ten to twenty miles deep and three hundred miles long. Most of the ramps on these sites appeared to be aimed at London, but there was also considerable concern over the possibility that the new weapons might be capable of causing considerable disruption to the planned Allied invasion of Normandy.

During the first six months of CROSSBOW, the Allied air forces between them dropped over 36,000 tons of bombs on V-1 and V-2 installations, with the USAAF's Eighth and Ninth air forces delivering the lion's share. They succeeded in seriously damaging all but a small number of the sites. General Doolittle and Air Marshal Harris grumbled about being asked to accept the repeated diversion of their heavy bombers from the assault on Germany, but the effort was not in vain. It was later estimated that CROSSBOW probably delayed the V-weapons program by three to four months. The first V-1 did not land in England until the night of June 12-13, 1944, and by then the Allied armies had secured their Normandy beachheads.

Once under way, the V-weapons attacks increased rapidly in intensity, with the V-2 joining the V-1 in the offensive against England on September 8. The V-1 (known as the "buzz-bomb" because of the distinctive note of its engine) was small and fast, and was not easily intercepted. The V-2, approaching from the stratosphere at supersonic speed, was immune from interception. Both weapons were impressively destructive in built-up areas, but neither could be aimed with any real accuracy and they were essentially indiscriminate. The scale of the German offensive was such that Operation CROSSBOW had to be continued, but it was not entirely successful in countering the threat. By the time the advance of the Allied armies finally brought the campaign to an end in March 1945, over three thousand V-1s and one thousand V-2s had fallen on British soil. Nearly two thousand more V-weapons fell on Allied-held territory on the continent, mostly in and around Amsterdam. Destructive though they certainly were, the V-weapons ate up an immense amount of scarce German resources and achieved very little of military value. They did, however, divert a considerable amount of Allied air power away from targets which had a more direct bearing on the outcome of the war.

By April 1944, it was apparent that the tide in the daylight bombing offensive had turned. The objectives of Operations POINTBLANK and ARGUMENT had been largely achieved and the Luftwaffe was no longer capable of holding back the flooding Allied air assault. German fighter pilot loss rates were running at 25 percent per month, and replacements from the flying training schools had a life expectancy on a front-line squadron of no more than thirty days. As the Luftwaffe's effectiveness declined, so Allied air power grew until it was irresistible. By day, the USAAF air armadas operated over Europe at will, carving out an aerial victory which had seemed only a remote possibility in the dark days of 1943.

To most airmen's surprise, it was a victory being won because of an aircraft they had thought an impossible dream—an agile single-seat fighter with the range of a strategic bomber.

The Coming of the Ninth

As the balance of the air war began to tip inexorably in favor of the Allies, an increasingly significant part was played by the newcomer to northern European skies—the Ninth Air Force. In drawing up the plans for the USAAF's role in the Allied invasion of France, the air force staffs had originally suggested that tactical air support would be provided by a greatly enhanced Air Support Command of the Eighth Air Force. By August 1943, General Arnold had decided both that the tactical air commander should be Lt. Gen. Lewis Brereton, who had proved himself in the Mediterranean theater, and that the scale of air operations envisaged for the invasion was such that a separate tactical air force was warranted. Accordingly, when Brereton moved to the U.K. in October 1943, his Ninth Air Force headquarters staffs went with him, leaving their combat and support units behind to be absorbed by the Twelfth Air Force. The nucleus of the new Ninth was formed from tactical and support units transferred from the Eighth Air Force, which from then on concentrated on operating its burgeoning front line of heavy bombers and their escorting fighters.

The primary mission of the Ninth, was to support the Allied armies in their invasion of Normandy and in their subsequent drive to defeat the enemy and occupy Germany. As its strength increased in late 1943 and first months of 1944, the Ninth was blooded against CROSSBOW targets and in operations which supported the combined bomber offensive. By the date of the invasion, it had become the most powerful tactical air force in the world, with three combat commands—IX

Fighter Command[10] (under the outstanding fighter leader Brig. Gen. Elwood "Pete" Quesada, who in 1929 had joined with Ira Eaker and Tooey Spaatz for the endurance flight of the *Question Mark*) with thirteen groups of P-47s, three of P-38s, and two of P-51s; IX Bomber Command with eleven groups of B-26 medium and A-20 light bombers; and IX Troop Carrier Command with another fourteen groups. In all, the Ninth could field some 4,500 combat aircraft plus about 2,700 gliders, and it had a personnel strength of 170,000. It was justifiable for the Ninth to claim that it could, by itself, project more power than the entire Luftwaffe.

From the time of its formation in the U.K. until the end of the war in Europe, the Ninth Air Force was continually engaged in fierce combat. In little more than a year and a half, it flew almost 370,000 sorties and lost over 2,900 aircraft, 2,139 of them fighters. In the course of these labors, 240,000 tons of bombs were dropped, 75 million rounds of ammunition expended, and 4,200 enemy aircraft claimed as destroyed. The contribution of the Ninth to the eventual Allied victory in Europe was immense.

Preparing for Invasion

In the tasking for the invasion of Normandy (Operation OVERLORD) the

Allied air forces were given the primary responsibility of preventing the Luftwaffe from interfering with the amphibious assault. The strategic bombing offensive had been working towards this end for some time. The losses inflicted on the Luftwaffe by the Eighth Air Force during the first half of 1944 had effectively broken the Luftwaffe's capacity to take the offensive. Nevertheless, there was no room for complacency. The pressure had to be maintained so that there would be no possibility of the Luftwaffe making things difficult for the Allied armies, and there were a great many other tasks which needed doing by the USAAF and the RAF in preparation for an amphibious operation of unprecedented scale against a heavily defended coastline. As D-Day drew nearer, these "other tasks"—reconnaissance, destruction of coastal defenses, and isolation of the invasion area—became increasingly important.

If there was one thing the Allied leaders agreed upon, it was that the invasion would not be a practical operation of war without overwhelming strength in the air. In just a few short years, even the most critical of prewar skeptics had grown to realize that air power had become a dominant factor in modern warfare. While it might still be unproven that the defeat of an enemy nation could be accomplished

USAAF medium bombers pounded targets in France in the weeks before the D-Day invasion of Normandy. Smoke rises from Charleroi behind B-26s of the 9th AF.

[10]Through IX Fighter Command, Quesada controlled two further burgeoning commands, IX and XIX Tactical Air Commands, both of which would play significant parts in the Allied sweep through France and into Germany.

by air power alone, there was now no denying that victory, either on the battlefield or finally in war, could not be won without it. The disagreements arose in deciding how best to apply air power in achieving the victory. As the plans for the invasion were laid, the Allied commanders split into two camps, with the heavy bombers of the Eighth Air Force and the RAF among the principal bones of contention. The debate did not easily divide along national or service lines. The bomber men, led by General Spaatz and Air Marshal Harris, believed that the best way to weaken German opposition to the invasion was to keep pounding away at the industrial heart of Germany, Spaatz specifically naming the oil industry as the most vulnerable target. Those ranged against them included Air Marshal Tedder (Eisenhower's deputy), Air Marshal Leigh Mallory (Commander of the Allied Expeditionary Air Forces), and General Brereton (Ninth Air Force). They believed that it was vital to paralyze the enemy's capacity to move by destroying as much of the rail network as possible in Belgium and northern France, and that the participation of the heavy bombers in that effort was essential. After a protracted and often passionate argument, General Eisenhower decided that the transportation plan was the one which would contribute most directly to the success of the invasion.

On April 14, 1944, to the discomfort of Spaatz and Harris, the Combined Chiefs of Staff placed the Eighth Air Force and RAF Bomber Command under Eisenhower's direction until after the Allied armies had successfully established themselves on the continent. From April 14, besides his responsibilities for huge naval and ground forces, Eisenhower commanded or directed the Allied Expeditionary Air Forces (Ninth Air Force, plus the RAF's 2nd Tactical Air Force and the Air Defense of Great Britain), the U.S. Strategic air forces (Eighth Air Force, Fifteenth Air Force), and RAF Bomber Command. On D-Day this formidable combination had available for operations from the U.K. 3,467 heavy bombers, 1,645 medium and light bombers, 5,409 fighters, and 2,316 transports. The Luftwaffe then had a front line which included some 3,200 combat-ready fighters and bombers to cover demands on several fronts. From the numbers, it had been clear to the Supreme Commander for some time that his air forces should have no difficulty in providing the air supremacy so essential over the Normandy beaches. He was encouraged to find that they were equally effective in meeting their other challenges.

In the weeks leading up to D-Day, the Allied air forces concentrated their efforts on a wide variety of targets near the Channel coast, taking care to mislead the German commanders as far as possible by hitting two targets outside Normandy for

every one in the invasion area. Airfields within 130 miles of the proposed beachhead were pounded and rendered almost untenable, while the Eighth Air Force persisted in mounting at least some raids against strategic targets in Germany, both to discourage the Luftwaffe from moving fighters forward into France and to continue with the battle of attrition which had been so effective.

Since the enemy's coastal defenses were heavily fortified, attacks on them were generally not nearly so profitable, with the notable exception of the radar stations. By D-Day, more than 80 percent of the radar coverage along the Channel coast had been destroyed, some sites near Calais being deliberately left intact so that the ingenious "spoofs" devised to mislead observers as to the objective of the main Allied landings could be detected. In effect, the enemy defenders were blinded and left vulnerable to the confusion over Allied intentions which engulfed them on the morning of June 6, 1944.

Attrition of the enemy's rail network began with attacks on rail centers and repair facilities in the hope of crippling the entire system, so making the German transport problem unmanageably chaotic. An intense campaign involving every type of offensive aircraft, from heavy bombers to fighters, achieved impressive levels of destruction. A German Transport Ministry report of May 15 admitted: "Large scale strategic movement of German troops by rail is practically impossible at the present time, and must remain so while attacks are maintained at their present intensity." Even so, the campaign was not producing the results expected by the Allied commanders. German ingenuity was countering the effects of much of the damage caused. On May 20, the campaign escalated when wide-scale fighter sweeps were authorized to attack the railways. The most spectacular of these were the "Chatanooga Choo-Choo" missions, which began on May 21 with a sweep involving 763 AEAF and 500 Eighth Air Force fighters. Locomotives, wagons, signal boxes, and maintenance sheds were attacked wherever they were found, and moving trains were hounded

Both before and after D-Day, relentless Allied attacks on transportation targets drastically reduced the mobility of German forces and their capacity for resupply. Trains venturing to move in daylight were asking for trouble, as this gun camera shot from a 353rd FG P-47 shows.

unmercifully. Similar missions were flown on several of the following days, bringing sharp reductions in the numbers of trains running in daylight.

The culminating blow in the campaign to deny the enemy freedom of movement was the destruction of the bridges over the River Seine. Until early May it was thought that the bridges might prove too unrewarding as targets. One estimate suggested that heavy bombers would have to drop as much as 1,200 tons of bombs against each bridge to ensure that it would be unusable. However, on May 7, 1944, a dramatic demonstration of fighter-bomber power offered a much cheaper solution. Eight of Pete Quesada's P-47s delivered two 1,000 lb bombs apiece on a steel railway bridge across the Seine and demolished it. Thereafter, bridge-busting became primarily a Ninth Air Force responsibility. During the last few days before D-Day, B-26s and P-47s of the Ninth conducted a spectacular series of low-level strikes which destroyed every crossing of the Seine, rail and road, between Paris and the Channel coast. As General Spaatz, a reluctant participant in the transportation plan, confessed to General Arnold: "[The campaign] opened the door for the invasion."

OVERLORD

The story of the Allied air operations flown on June 6, 1944, in support of the D-Day landings is one which points largely to the value of victories already won and emphasizes the rewards of careful preparation. Against combat sortie totals for the day of 8,722 for the USAAF and 5,676 for the RAF, the Luftwaffe managed to send less than 100 to oppose the invasion. It was a far cry from the day, less than four years before, when Goering had stood on the coast of France and, confident of victory, gloried in the power of the Luftwaffe's bomber fleets as they roared overhead on their way to England. Now Eisenhower, from the other side of the Channel, could tell his waiting troops with certainty: "If

During the buildup to the D-Day invasion, the Allies kept a close watch on German activities along the "Atlantic Wall." F-5Es (photographic reconnaissance versions of the P-38) were among the aircraft tasked with photographing enemy defensive preparations on the beaches of northern France. Sometimes the camera brought back evidence both of water obstacles and of how low the reconnaissance missions were being flown.

you see a plane, it will be one of ours."[11]

During the hours of darkness preceding the first Allied landings, RAF Bomber Command pounded the German defenses along the Normandy coast, and the transports and gliders of Brereton's Ninth Air Force assembled for the largest troop carrier operation ever undertaken. Over eight hundred C-47s, plus others towing some one hundred gliders, set out to drop troops of the 82nd and 101st Airborne Divisions on the Cotentin Peninsula, behind Utah Beach on the right flank of the Allied assault. Transports and gliders of the RAF were similarly engaged with the British 6th Airborne Division on the left flank. For most of the C-47 pilots it was their first combat mission. This lack of experience, combined with the challenge of flying at night in such large numbers, and then of having to cope with low cloud over the Cotentin and an intense flak barrage, led to the troop carrier formations becoming separated and the U.S. divisions being widely scattered during the drop. However, what could have been a disaster was redeemed by the initiative of individual American paratroopers. Lost in the dark-

ness and with their unit organization hopelessy disrupted, U.S. airborne troops engaged the enemy wherever they were encountered, spreading confusion and alarm among German forces defending the Cotentin Peninsula. As the Supreme Commander's report later said: "the success of the Utah assault could not have been achieved . . . without the work of the airborne forces."

As dawn broke over Normandy, it was the turn of the Eighth Air Force's heavy bombers. Over one thousand B-17s and B-24s attacked Omaha and the British beaches in waves, crossing the coast at right angles and dropping almost three thousand tons of bombs against the coastal defenses. Unfortunately, cloud cover forced the bombing to be done on radar and, to ensure that friendly forces would not be hit, pathfinder bombardiers deliberately delayed their drops for several seconds after the indicated release points. Most of it fell inland from the beaches, leaving the defenses largely untouched, although seriously disrupting their communications and incidentally clearing a number of minefields.

---

[11] Eisenhower's prediction may have been accurate, but to minimize the risks to friendly airmen from trigger-happy soldiers and sailors, Allied aircraft were painted with prominent black and white stripes on the wings and fuselage, and the fighters giving cover to the invasion fleet were distinctive twin-boomed P-38s, aircraft unlike any operated by the Luftwaffe.

There was no disappointment on Utah Beach, however, nor in the area immediately behind it. The German defenders there suffered the attentions of B-26s, A-20s, and P-47s of the Ninth Air Force, all of them finding ways to attack their targets visually. As a result, Utah's bunkers and blockhouses were severely dealt with, and the defenders' capacity to resist was much reduced. Not that the American airmen had it all their own way. A B-26 crew-member reported that the flak was "the most withering, heavy, and accurate we ever experienced." At least, however, the Luftwaffe was not a factor. One German officer, dragging himself from the ruins of

some power of the Allied air forces had been clearly demonstrated and the more perceptive Germans must have realized that the pattern of the war in the west had been set. One hundred seventy-one squadrons of Allied fighters had ensured that the Luftwaffe would be conspicuous by its absence, and that anything that moved among the hedgerows of Normandy would be strafed.[12] Even though over one thousand additional fighters were moved forward from Germany by early July, they accomplished relatively little. Allied air supremacy was a reality which would be made very apparent in the weeks and months which followed the invasion.

units to move forward into the battle area. On D-Day itself, the Allies were greatly helped by the indecision of the German high command. Until late afternoon, poor flying weather prevented tactical aircraft from operating freely, and three Panzer divisions which might have intervened in the battle were prevented from doing so by the hesitancy of Hitler and his general staff. By the time the armored divisions were released, the skies had cleared and the opportunity was lost. Panzer Lehr division, needing to cover only 130 miles to the front, found it impossible to make progress at more than six or seven miles per hour because of aerial attack. As Maj. Gen. Fritz Bayerlein, commander of Panzer Lehr, has recalled: "By the end of the day [June 7] I had lost forty tank trucks carrying fuel and ninety others. Five of my tanks were knocked out, and eighty-four half-tracks, prime movers and self-propelled guns."

Interdiction of the German Army's rear areas became intensified after D-Day. Attacks on bridges became more frequent, adding the crossings of the Loire to those of the Seine now that there was no need to disguise the Allies' intentions. Attacks on rail centers were continued, and systematic bombing of German supply dumps was undertaken.[13] Even more rewarding in many ways was the massive campaign of armed reconnaissance pursued by the fighters of the Ninth Air Force and the 2nd Tactical Air Force over Normandy and the surrounding region. In daylight, it became almost impossible for anything to move anywhere in the area without attracting the attention of Allied fighters. One German officer observed that: "the effect of Allied air superiority on the Normandy front and as far as Paris is so great that . . . even single vehicles are used by day only in the most extreme emergencies." As early as June 10, Field Marshal Erwin Rommel was reporting that: "Every traffic defile in the rear areas is under continual attack and it is very difficult to get essential supplies of ammunition and petrol up to the troops."[14]

Before, during, and after the D-Day invasion, the 9th AF's light and medium bombers were heavily involved in attacking point targets like gun emplacements, bridges, and road junctions. Clearly marked with the black and white Allied invasion stripes, these A-20s leave the hedgerows of Normandy behind and head for their base in England after a mission.

his concrete gun emplacement after the shattering experience of a B-26 attack, was driven to exclaim: "It looks as though God and the world have forsaken us. What's happened to our airmen?"

That was a question which German soldiers got tired of asking. By the close of D-Day, with the Allied armies tightening their grip on their beachheads, the awe-

Tactical Air Rampant

The days following D-Day were critical for the Allies, and the immediate task for the air forces was plain. Although the assault forces were ashore, the beachheads were far from secure, and it was vital that the speed of any German reinforcement should be held to a lower rate than that of the Allied buildup across the Channel. The fighters of Ninth Air Force and the RAF's 2nd Tactical Air Force had to make it as difficult as possible for German

[12] Fifteen squadrons were allocated for shipping cover, fifty-four patrolled the beaches, thirty-three escorted the bombers and conducted offensive sweeps, thirty-three undertook interdiction of the areas inland from the beaches, and thirty-six were available for direct support of the assault forces.

[13] Much of the Allies' target selection was driven by intelligence from "Ultra," which often revealed the whereabouts of significant targets and indicated which attacks were being most effective. An "Ultra" inspired air strike on June 10, 1944, destroyed Panzergruppe West HQ and killed many of its staff, thus removing the vital armored forces control center from the battle.

As the battle for Normandy dragged on, the provision of close air support to the troops became ever more important, and soldiers and airmen cooperated in developing methods of making that support increasingly effective. Radars originally designed for air defense were incorporated into a system for the control of air strikes, and, at Quesada's instigation, IX TAC began flying "armored column cover" (ACC) missions. An air support party, in a tank equipped with VHF radio, was added to each tank column, over which IX TAC aircraft flew from dawn to dusk on call and looking for trouble. As the IX TAC operation order of the time put it: "Each of the rapidly advancing columns will be covered at all times by a four ship flight . . . which will maintain a close armed recce in advance of the column. They may attack any target which is identified as enemy, directing their attention to the terrain immediately in front of the advancing column."

The contrast in the behavior of the opposing armies brought about by the Allies' aggressive use of their dominant air power could hardly have been more complete. On the German side of the line, movement by day was almost impossible and troops were forced to keep their vehicles hidden from the searching eyes of roving fighter pilots. On the Allied side, tanks and trucks often moved openly in tightly spaced columns, confident that the Luftwaffe was incapable of offering any threat worth bothering about. Later in the campaign, the Luftwaffe occasionally concentrated its forces and managed to strike back. Such leaks in the Allied air umbrella invariably drew strong protests from the ground troops, who had come to expect nothing less than complete protection. That soldiers could voice such complaints about the infrequent and generally ineffectual efforts of the Luftwaffe offered apt comment on the benefits of air supremacy. Allied soldiers had grown accustomed to the warmth of the air's security blanket. Their German counterparts could only shiver in their nakedness.

If the aircraft of IX TAC were considered to be an integral part of the Allied armies' daily operations, the use of heavy bombers in direct support of troops was more controversial. Effective though they had been during the preinvasion campaign to seal off Normandy, they had been less successful during the invasion itself, when much of the immense weight of their bombardment had fallen on empty fields. Subsequent efforts to use them to break the impasse on the Allies' left flank, in front of Caen, were also disappointing. Short bombing had caused casualties among some forward Allied troops, and the German defenses, although savagely pounded, had not been broken. Nevertheless, plans were laid to use the Eighth Air Force heavies to launch Operation COBRA, a massive blow intended to break the U.S. First Army out of the miseries of Normandy's *bocage* country.[15]

COBRA got off to a false start on July 24 because of bad weather. Only part of the force attacked and erratic bombing caused casualties on both sides of the line. With warnings about inaccuracy heavily reemphasized, the USAAF committed its aircraft to a maximum effort on the following day. Immediately to the west of the little town of St. Lo, 1,508 heavies, 380 mediums and, 559 fighters struck at the German defenses. The very sight of such massive formations inspired awe in both friend and foe, and the three-hour bombardment they unleashed was terrifying in its concentrated ferocity. The organization of many German units was broken by an experience most frequently described by survivors as "shattering." General Bayerlein of Panzer Lehr found that 70 percent of his personnel were "dead, wounded, crazed, or dazed," and, under interrogation after the war, Field Marshal von Rundstedt said that the St. Lo bombing was "the most effective, as well as the most impressive, tactical use of air power in his experience." Unfortunately, as before, there were some gross bombing errors and the U.S. 30th Infantry Division was the principal sufferer. Over one hundred Ameri-

can soldiers died, among them Lt. Gen. Lesley McNair, the highest ranking U.S. officer killed in WWII. Distressing though the friendly fire losses were, they did not discourage the U.S. ground forces for long. They surged forward, breaking through the crumbling barrier of German resistance and throwing off the straitjacket of Normandy's *bocage* at last.

COBRA confirmed the obvious truth that the heavy bomber force was more akin to an indiscriminate bludgeon than a precise rapier, especially when used tactically. Understandably, there were bitter reactions from the troops who had suffered from the waywardness of the friendly

Maj. Gen. "Pete" Quesada (right), Commander, IX TAC, and one of WW II's great combat commanders, with Maj. Gen. Ralph Royce, Deputy Commander, Allied Expeditionary Air Force, in France after D-Day.

bombardment. Many of the Army's ground commanders began to believe, along with Spaatz and Harris, that heavy bombers were better left to their strategic tasks. Nevertheless, it was generally conceded that the Eighth Air Force heavy bombers had been the keys which unlocked the German defenses at St. Lo. The U.S. VII Corps gave its opinion that "our losses would have been infinitely greater, and our success would perhaps never have materialized, if it had not been for the overall effectiveness of this heavy bombardment." General Eisenhower later said that, in spite of all the problems, it was impossible "to convince the Army that the battle of St. Lo had not been won as a result of the

---

[14] On July 17, 1944, Rommel experienced the implacable ferocity of the Allied fighter sweeps at first hand when his staff car was strafed by two Spitfires. His driver was killed, and Rommel's skull was fractured when the car plunged off the road, effectively ending his career.

[15] The *bocage* was Norman farming country made up of small fields bounded by thick hedgerows and sunken lanes. It was ideally suited for mounting a stubborn defense.

Group identification markings were introduced generally in March 1944. As seen on this P-47, the 78th FG at Duxford adopted a striking black and white checkerboard pattern for the engine cowling.

direct support given by the Eighth Air Force."

As the number of U.S. troops in France approached the million mark and control became too unwieldy for one headquarters, the ground forces split into two separate armies, the First (Lt. Gen. Courtney Hodges) and the Third (Lt. Gen. George Patton). Quesada's IX TAC continued its old association with First Army, and the newly activated Third Army was allocated an air force of its own, XIX TAC commanded by Maj. Gen. O.P. Weyland.

As the airmen of XIX TAC were to find out, they had a tiger by the tail. Swinging at the outer edge of the Allied armies' opening door under Patton's forceful leadership, the Third Army moved across France at great speed. XIX TAC had to keep up, moving its headquarters and squadrons forward continually and operating from hastily repaired or improvised airfields to ensure that soldiers always had air cover when and where it was most needed. In the achievement of this remarkable feat, the labors of the Ninth's engineers and lo-

The 361st FG began to get its P-51Ds in the summer of 1944. Tika IV *was the mount of Lt. Vernon Richards.*

gistical units were nothing short of Herculean. As time went by, Patton came to rely increasingly on having such a responsive tactical air arm to call on, and in a development which particularly revealed the level of trust and cooperation reached between air and ground commanders, he asked XIX TAC to take on the responsibility of protecting Third Army's long, exposed southern flank during its headlong advance.

By the end of the first week of August 1944, the U.S. Army had burst out of the Cotentin Peninsula at Avranches and its spearheads were sweeping both west across Brittany and east towards the Seine. In a desperate attempt to stem the hemorrhage, Hitler ordered a counterattack to be made through Mortain to the sea, aiming to sever the head of the American advance from the body of its support. Built around five Panzer divisions, and backed by a rare concentration of Luftwaffe fighters, this was a formidable enemy thrust. It was denied in one of the war's best demonstrations of interservice and interAllied cooperation. Slowed by stubborn resistance from American infantry, the German armored columns were savaged from the air. Rocket-firing Typhoons of the RAF's 2nd TAF took on the Panzers while IX TAC's fighters flew interdiction sorties and kept the Luftwaffe from interfering. To the dismay of the Wehrmacht, not one Luftwaffe fighter appeared over the battlefield and the Panzer spearhead was stopped in its tracks with heavy losses. When the German generals finally accepted that their counterattack had failed, they began a process of withdrawal which soon accelerated into the chaos of headlong rout. As a consequence of Hitler's reluctance to abandon Mortain, the orders for retreat were given too late, and the stage was set for one of the most destructive demonstrations of tactical air power ever seen.

With the British and Canadians driving south towards Falaise, and the U.S. Third Army racing to take Argentan from the south, the German Seventh Army and Fifth Panzer Army became almost completely encircled in an oval pocket which by August 14 was less than fifty miles long and not more than thirty miles across at its widest point. The one remaining path of escape to the east was then only ten miles wide and being squeezed shut under Allied pressure. The interior of the Falaise Pocket and the narrow neck of its exit became classic killing grounds for tactical aircraft as German troops struggled to find a way out. Tanks and guns were destroyed in the hundreds, soft-skinned vehicles by the thousands. Although as many as 40,000 German soldiers escaped the Falaise trap, they left most of their equipment behind, together with some 60,000 of their colleagues—50,000 as prisoners, 10,000 of them dead.

The campaign in northern France was the heyday of tactical air power. The operational statistics of XIX TAC alone for the month of August 1944 give some idea of the effort involved:

Flown: 12,292 combat sorties

Claimed: 4,058 motor vehicles, 466 tanks/other armor, 598 horse-drawn vehicles, 246 locomotives, 2,956 railroad cars, 155 river craft, 26 seagoing vessels. (other attacks on artillery, supply dumps, radars, airfields, barracks, troops, etc.), 229 aircraft (163 in the air, 66 on the ground)

Lost: 114 aircraft

Even allowing for the inevitable exaggeration associated with combat claims, these are impressive figures. It is hardly surprising that Patton felt moved to commend Weyland's XIX TAC, calling its operations "the best example of the combined use of air and ground troops I have ever witnessed."

While these heady days were passing into history in the north, the Allies struck at Hitler's fortress from yet another direction. On August 15, 1944, Allied forces invaded the south of France and, profiting from lessons learned in previous amphibious operations, they were quickly ashore. It is true that the German forces facing the invasion were inferior to the invaders both in quality and quantity, but the ground commanders were quick to acknowledge that Allied air supremacy saved them a great many lives and a great deal of time. XII TAC, commanded by Brig. Gen. Gordon Saville, operated with

the bombers of the Mediterranean Allied Air Forces at the heart of the air campaign. Persistent interdiction before the landings had disrupted enemy supply lines and counterair activity had effectively removed the Luftwaffe threat. Most of the coastal defenses were neutralized, and both the airborne assault and the landings went in under a powerful air umbrella and with plenty of close air support available. With all the benefits of effective air/ground cooperation, the Allied forces swept forward and effected a junction with the right wing of Patton's Third Army west of the Swiss border in early September. At that point, having proved its combat capabilities by destroying tactical targets by the thousand in the Italian campaign and during the drive through southern France, XII TAC left the operational control of the MAAF to add its strength to the already formidable power of the TACs controlled by Ninth Air Force.[16]

Wehrmacht Defiant

By mid-September 1944, the Allies had freed almost all of France, Belgium, and Luxembourg, and they were ready for the next great challenge—the reaching and crossing of the Rhine. General Eisenhower directed that the main thrust should be made in the north, and that the First Al-

lied Airborne Army should be used in the assault.[17] On September 17, an ambitious operation code named MARKET/GARDEN was launched in a valiant but ill-fated attempt to drive a sixty-mile-long salient through the German lines and open the way to a crossing of the lower Rhine by seizing bridges in the Netherlands near Eindhoven, Nijmegen, and Arnhem. Aircraft of the Eighth and Ninth Air Forces and the RAF prepared the way with attacks on flak defenses and German troop concentrations, and the assaulting airborne forces were dispatched in an armada of 1,546 transports and 478 gliders, reinforced the following day with another 1,306 transports and 1,152 gliders. Unfortunately for the Allies, strong German forces were well placed to resist, especially at Arnhem. Even worse, bad weather intervened to deprive the airborne troops of the sort of close support from Allied tactical aircraft they had counted on. After a

---

[16]In effect, by the end of 1944, each of the armies had its own air force. First Army—IX TAC (Quesada); Third Army—XIX TAC (Weyland); Ninth Army—XXIX TAC (Nugent). In the north, 21st Army Group was supported by the RAF's 2nd TAF, and 6th Army Group to the south had the services of XII TAC (Saville) and the First French Air Force. XII TAC and the French joined together to become the First TAF (Maj. Gen. Ralph Royce, a celebrated figure from the early days of American air power).

[17]The FAAA was formed on August 8, 1944, under the command of Lt. Gen. Lewis Brereton. It included the U.S. 17th, 82nd, and 101st Airborne Divisions; the British 1 and 6 Airborne Divisions; and the Polish Independent Parachute Brigade. The air elements were the USAAF's IX Troop Carrier Command, and the RAF's 38 and 46 Groups. Brereton was replaced as Commander Ninth Air Force by Maj. Gen. Hoyt Vandenburg.

B-26 Marauders of the Mediterranean Allied Tactical Air Force had a big part to play in softening up the enemy's defenses in southern France before Operation ANVIL, the Allied invasion of southern France in August 1944.

The ubiquitous Piper L-4 was an unsung but essential part of the Allied drive across France in 1944. Apart from their usual liaison and observation duties, L-4 pilots found themselves reconnoitering new airfield sites from the air as the battle lines raced forward, and being "horseflies" to guide fighter-bombers to their targets.

week of bitter fighting, during which armored spearheads struggled forward through Eindhoven and Nijmegen to relieve the beleaguered paratroops, it was realized that Arnhem was "a bridge too far," and the operation was abandoned.

The European winter of 1944 proved to be one of the worst in living memory. Storms and leaden skies combined to keep the Allied tactical air forces grounded at least half of the time. Taking advantage of a situation which promised freedom from aerial harassment and prevented effective reconnaissance, Hitler gathered together his reserves and ordered a massive counterattack against thinly held U.S. Army positions in the Ardennes. On December 16 eight Panzer and ten infantry divisions punched through the U.S. front, aiming to split the Allied armies and drive on to the coast, retaking the port of Antwerp and cutting the logistic chain. The Battle of the Bulge was on. For once, it seemed that the Luftwaffe was prepared to offer the Wehrmacht some real support, although for a week foul weather hampered both sides' air forces in their attempts to intervene. In that time, the enemy penetration was extended for more than sixty miles, although a number of U.S. Army units held out in surrounded strongpoints, notably the 101st Division at Bastogne.

On December 23, the skies cleared

at last, and the full fury of Allied air power descended on the German soldiers in the "Bulge" and on their supply lines. Medium bombers attacked roads and railways behind the German columns repeatedly and struck at Luftwaffe airfields. Transports parachuted supplies into Bastogne. Fighters swarmed over the Wehrmacht units, strafing and bombing guns, vehicles, and enemy-held buildings throughout the salient. In supporting operations on Christmas Eve, the Eighth Air Force heavies pulled out all the stops and launched their largest effort of the war so far. Over two thousand B-17s and B-24s took off to pound German airfields and communications, greatly hampering the German offensive.[18]

Somewhat to the surprise of Allied airmen, the Luftwaffe had gathered its reserves together too, and it rose in strength, flying as many as eight hundred sorties on December 23, challenging Allied fighters to combat and inflicting the highest losses ever on the Ninth's mediums. From a force of 624 B-26s and A-20s, 35 were shot down and over 180 badly damaged. On January 1, 1945, the Luftwaffe did even better, launching nearly 900 aircraft for a sweep against Allied airfields. They achieved considerable success, destroying over 150 Allied aircraft and damaging many others, but it was a costly exercise. Almost a third of the Luftwaffe force was lost. More to the point, 237 pilots were killed, missing, or taken prisoner, and another 18 were wounded, among them a number of experienced leaders.

It was almost the Luftwaffe's last gasp. While German industry might be able to supply new aircraft, the men were irreplaceable. Hitler's Ardennes offensive was disastrous for the Luftwaffe, which suffered catastrophic pilot losses in the course of the Battle of the Bulge. Among several bad days was December 17, when seventy-nine pilots were killed or wounded. On Christmas Day, there were sixty-two more, and on New Year's Eve, another

forty-one, besides smaller numbers on other days. In its struggle with the Allied air forces, the Luftwaffe was being bled to death.

By the end of January 1945, the Battle of the Bulge was over and the German armies were back where they had started, but considerably worse off than before. The USAAF claims for ground targets destroyed during the period were staggering—11,378 motor vehicles, 1,161 tanks/armored vehicles, 507 locomotives, 6,266 railroad cars, 472 guns, 974 rail cuts, 421 road cuts, and 36 bridges. If the claims were exaggerated by the smoke of battle, the effects were not. The enemy offensive had been defeated, and the evidence for the air's part in that defeat was plain to see on every side.

They Also Served

The overwhelming scale of the strategic and tactical air campaigns often tended to obscure the activities of some smaller but nonetheless important air force roles, two of which had significant parts to play in the advance through France and the Battle of the Bulge. Night fighters had been used throughout the campaign in Europe to intercept occasional Luftwaffe forays and to operate as intruders over enemy-held territory. By 1944, the Northrop P-61 Black Widow had added its considerable firepower (usually four 20 mm cannon and four .5 in machine guns) to the Ninth Air Force. Fast and maneuverable despite its size, the P-61 was a fearsome night fighter, but it was also used to ensure that the enemy was kept under pressure of tactical air attack around the clock. German supply columns moving at night could not be sure that darkness would shield them, nor could repair crews working on bridges destroyed or damaged during the day. Trains, barges, factories, warehouses, and troop concentrations all felt the sting of the P-61's weapons by night.

At the other end of the scale were the Grasshoppers, tiny aircraft like the Piper L-4, which proved indispensable for rapid liaison between senior commanders and their units, served as airborne observation posts, assisted in controlling ground

[18]Leading the Eighth on this raid was Brig. Gen. Fred Castle, a former CO of the 94th BG revered by his men. His B-17 was shot down on the way to the target, and he was killed in the crash, having stayed at the controls to give his crew time to escape. He is the only general officer in American history to die while directly involved in a specific act aimed at saving the lives of his subordinates. His was the last 8th AF Medal of Honor to be awarded.

forces, and even functioned as "horseflies," pointing out selected targets to the fighter-bombers. Occasionally, their presence could be decisive. One hard-pressed U.S. Army unit in the Battle of the Bulge did not have the radio channels to talk to the only tactical aircraft nearby, which were RAF Typhoons. A Grasshopper intervened and led the Typhoons into action. As Maj. Gen. Ernest Harmon of the U.S. 2nd Armored Division recalled: "It was like a butterfly leading a squadron of buzzards. The Typhoons . . . left devastation in their wake. What was left of the German column retired with our troops in hot pursuit."

The USAAF also did some leaflet dropping and engaged in clandestine operations known as "Carpetbagger" missions. Using mostly black-painted B-24s fitted with special radio aids, the 492nd BG flew night low-level sorties to parachute agents into Europe and to supply resistance groups with arms and ammunition. In the course of some very hazardous operations, the Carpetbaggers delivered over 20,000 containers, 11,000 packages, and 1,000 agents for the loss of twenty-five B-24s. With their job in France done, many of the 492nd's B-24s were used as flying fuel trucks to deliver much-needed gasoline to the racing columns of Patton's Third Army.

Final Offensive

Although they recognized that their forces were making significant contributions in direct support of the Allied armies in France, the strategic bomber commanders remained impatient with any task which deflected them from what they considered to be their primary responsibility—the destruction of Germany's war-making capacity. Fortunately for their peace of mind, Eisenhower understood the nature of the strategic campaign, and he was quite prepared for Spaatz and Harris to continue operations against German industry in the absence of more pressing requirements on the battlefields or at the V-weapons sites. After the tense early days of the Normandy invasion, this gave the "bomber barons" ample scope to develop their strategic

bombing campaigns as they thought best.

Spaatz had no doubts about the way in which his bombers should be employed. On June 8, only two days after D-Day, he issued an order to the Eighth and Fifteenth Air Forces which established that their primary strategic aim was to starve the enemy's armed forces of their oil. His clear strategic vision was never more in evidence than on this issue. Spaatz correctly assessed that his oil plan could accomplish several things at once, all of them important in pursuit of an Allied victory. Oil restrictions directly affected transportation, factories, the army's mechanized and armored units, and the Luftwaffe. Because of this, oil facilities were targets which the Luftwaffe had to defend, thereby committing itself to an ever downward spiral. Heavy losses would result from the battle of attrition with the USAAF, more replacements would be demanded from a flying training system already inhibited by lack of fuel, experience levels would fall, the Luftwaffe would become less and less effective, more fuel targets would be struck, and the Luftwaffe's capacity to respond would suffer from a shortage of fuel and of pilots. Before long, Spaatz was convinced, the Luftwaffe would be forced to its knees by a combination of falling experience levels, rising losses, and lack of fuel. In the long run, the whole German war machine would grind to a halt.

Spaatz had begun his assault on German oil even before D-Day. The Fifteenth Air Force hit the Ploesti refineries three times in May 1944, and the Eighth Air Force struck various synthetic oil plants in Germany on May 12, 28, and 29. The assumption that the Luftwaffe would fight for the oil was proved right. The raids were strongly opposed and bomber losses were considerable, but the Luftwaffe suffered as well and the oil plants were hit hard. "Ultra" intelligence intercepts soon revealed the level of concern in Germany over the effects of the raids. Fighter squadrons badly needed elsewhere were being retained to meet the threat, and large numbers of flak units were being moved into positions from which they could defend the oil industry. Albert Speer warned Hitler: "The enemy has struck at one of our weakest points. If they persist at this time, we will soon no longer have any fuel production worth mentioning." The enemy did indeed persist, with major blows falling on the oil industry unceasingly until the end of the war.

An offshoot of the USAAF's strategic offensive was a belated agreement with the Soviet government that USAAF aircraft would be allowed to use bases in the Soviet Union for "shuttle" bombing missions. Aircraft operating from England and

Soviet officers watch as Lt. Gen. Ira Eaker's 97th BG B-17G arrives at Poltava on the first of the FRANTIC "shuttle" bombing missions on June 2, 1944.

Italy would attack targets in Eastern Europe and fly on to refuel and rearm in the Soviet Union before striking at other targets on the way back. By May 1944, three bases were ready in the Ukraine, and the first of the FRANTIC missions, as they were called, was flown by the Fifteenth Air Force on June 2. The Eighth Air Force joined in on June 21, when 145 B-17s, escorted by seventy P-51s, bombed oil plants south of Berlin on their way to the Ukraine. The bombing was excellent, but disaster followed. Unseen by the B-17s, a Heinkel 177 trailed them to Poltava airfield, and that night they were surprised on the ground by the Luftwaffe. Forty-four

B-24s of the 446th BG over the Messerschmitt 110 factory at Gotha on February 24, 1944. Luftwaffe fighter opposition was determined and the attacking force lost 34 B-24s on this day. The 446th lost two bombers in combat and another which crashed on return to England.

B-17s were destroyed and twenty-six damaged. Sporadic attempts to use the FRANTIC bases were made in the months following, but the missions were not outstandingly successful. Soviet enthusiasm for the idea was never very great, and the results achieved did not match the cost. The last FRANTIC mission was flown on September 13, 1944, by which time the Soviet Army had advanced so far that bases in the Ukraine were too distant from likely targets to be of much help.

The advance of the Allied armies in

the west to the German frontier had brought all of Germany within reach of tactical as well as strategic aircraft by the beginning of 1945. In a bid to tear out the remaining sinews of the German nation and perhaps to stun the enemy population with a massive display of air power before launching troops across the Rhine, Operation CLARION was devised. It was a plan calling for every available Allied aircraft to attack transportation targets—rail, road, canal, and river—all over Germany on the same day. On February 22, 1945, the weather was favorable and the skies above Germany were filled with more than six thousand Allied aircraft, fighters hunting

and strafing at low-level and bombers attacking targets from as low as 10,000 ft or less. The Luftwaffe reaction was feeble and those few enemy fighters which did get airborne were brushed aside. Allied losses were minimal and results so promising that the operation was repeated the next day. When the dust from CLARION had settled, it was apparent that the enemy's transport system had been badly hurt. Airmen believed, with some justification, that such severe disruptions of national lifelines, together with the aerial tourniquet they

had clamped on the oil supply, had crippled the body of the Third Reich to such an extent that its final collapse must be imminent.

The change in the fortunes of the USAAF and the Luftwaffe in the space of one year had been dramatic. At the end of 1943, the Eighth Air Force had its teeth gritted as it struggled to overcome the impact of heavy losses—forty-five bombers lost from 262 sent to Stuttgart (17.2 percent); sixty out of 229 at Schweinfurt (26.2 percent); twenty-nine out of 440 at Bremen (6.6 percent); twenty-four out of 281 at Solingen (8.5 percent); and so on. In stark contrast, as 1944 drew to its close, the Eighth was nearing omnipotence in German skies. American airmen had begun to feel that they could go where they wished without fear of serious opposition from the Luftwaffe. Flak could still be intense, but loss rates among bomber crews were nowhere near as demoralizing as they had been just a year before. As the final offensive gathered pace in 1945, the statistics told their own story—one bomber lost from a force of 1,094 sent to Kassel; five out of 1,310 at Chemnitz and Magdeburg; none of 1,219 at Nurnburg.

Even when losses climbed into double figures, as on February 3, 1945, when twenty-five were lost out of 1,370 bombing Berlin, the loss rate was so low that it seemed bearable. The twenty-four from 281 at Solingen had been nearly 9 percent, a figure which gave aircrews little hope of completing a combat tour unscathed. Twenty-five from 1,370 was well under 1 percent, and that bred confidence in the prospect of survival, particularly since in 1945 it was a rate which was uncharacteristically high.

As Luftwaffe fighter pilots saw the tide of war turned irrevocably against them, they were left wondering what might have been. Now that Allied aircraft filled the skies over Germany and the Luftwaffe had neither the trained pilots nor the fuel with which to oppose them, German industry was offering aircraft production rates and new aircraft types which, had they been available in the winter of 1943-44, could have tipped the balance of the air war in

Germany's favor. Pounded though it was, the German aircraft industry, operating under the dispersal policies of Albert Speer, produced over forty thousand combat aircraft in 1944, almost five times the number made in 1939.[19] However, after an encouraging but brief period when the front-line squadrons benefited from the glut by reequipping and being brought up to strength, the relentless attrition of combat took its toll, and pilot strengths began to fall. By 1945, fighters sat in rows waiting to be delivered, but their tanks were empty and they outnumbered the end product of the Luftwaffe's flying training program. In many cases, Luftwaffe engineers found that it was no longer worth their while to repair aircraft with even minor battle damage. It was easier to push a damaged fighter to one side and pull out a new one.

The Coming of the Jets

While Speer's production miracles had little apparent effect on Allied airmen, Germany's visionary aircraft designers did manage to take them by surprise. Turbojet engines had been under development in Britain and Germany since the 1930s, but progress towards the production of operational jet aircraft had been slowed in both countries by a combination of technical problems and official skepticism. The first jet aircraft to fly was German, the Heinkel 178 on August 27, 1939, but subsequent progress was anything but swift, and it was the summer of 1944 before the first jet squadrons became operational. The Germans introduced the remarkable Messerschmitt 262[20] to the Luftwaffe's front line in July 1944, initially as a high-speed bomber, and the RAF's No. 616 Squadron started chasing V-1 flying bombs with its Gloster Meteor jets later the same month.

Boasting swept wings and two axial-flow jet engines, the Me 262 *Schwalbe*

(Swallow) could reach 540 mph and climb to 30,000 ft in seven minutes. This marked superiority in performance over any Allied aircraft was impressive, as was the Me 262's heavy armament of four closely grouped 30 mm cannon, which could destroy a heavy bomber in one short burst. At a time when the air war seemed all but over, it promised to confront Allied airmen, and particularly those in the B-17s and B-24s, with a very real renewed threat. As it was, because of problems with the Junkers Jumo engines and Hitler's initial insistence that it should be brought into service as a fast bomber for use against the Allied invasion

force, the first unit of Me 262 interceptors was not declared operational until October 1944. Even then, they were seen by American aircrew only rarely. Me 262s managed to fly more than fifty sorties in one day just once, on April 7, 1945, when the Eighth Air Force alone flew 1,261 bombers and 830 fighters over Germany.

A host of problems combined to ensure that the Me 262 would never play a major role in the air war. There were the teething troubles which were only to be expected with so revolutionary a design.

For example, the running life of the Junkers Jumo engines never exceeded twenty-five hours, and the poor-quality tires were inclined to burst under the impact of 120 mph landings. Flying training, particularly at the reduced levels of 1944-45, was soon recognized as being inadequate to prepare a pilot to cope with the Me 262, and it took longer than expected for units to become operational. Then there were the incessant attentions of the Allied air forces. Me 262s and their spares were often stranded in the ruins of the German transport system, and jet airfields became prime targets for the bombers and fighters of both

the Eighth and Ninth Air Forces.[21]

Knowing that the jets were at their most vulnerable during takeoff and landing, American fighter pilots took to patrolling over their airfields. Lt. Urban Drew of the 361st FG showed the way in his P-51 as early as October 7, 1944, when he caught two Me 262s just after they had taken off and shot them both down before

At the center of this picture, the B-17G on the right of the element leader is **Shoo Shoo Shoo Baby** *of the 91st BG. One of the few B-17s with a combat record to survive the war, a beautifully restored* **Shoo Shoo Shoo Baby** *is now on display at the USAF Museum.*

---

[19]U.S. aircraft production figures rose from 2,100 in 1939 to 96,300 in 1944. It is worth noting that the latter figure, startling enough in itself, includes such large, complex aircraft as the B-29, whereas German industry was driven to produce more and more single-seat fighters.

[20]The Messerschmitt 163 was equally remarkable, but flawed in concept. Powered by a rocket engine, it was very fast but its fuel supply was so limited that it could run at full power for only four minutes, after which it became a glider. This limited it to an operational radius of no more than twenty-five miles and rendered it helpless during its recovery to base.

[21]It is interesting to speculate on the possibilities if the Me 262 had reached the Luftwaffe just one year earlier, before the appearance of the P-51 as an escort fighter. It is conceivable that the Eighth Air Force would have had to halt its strategic campaign, and that Allied air superiority would then not have been won as it was. In that event, an invasion in 1944 would not have been possible and the war would probably have dragged on for at least another year, with who knows what long-term consequences for Europe.

As the air war in Europe entered its final months, the numbers of heavy bombers over Germany grew until their contrails sometimes formed solid sheets of cloud. On several occasions, the 8th AF alone launched over 2,000 bombers and escorting fighters against German targets.

they could accelerate away. Once up to speed, the Me 262 was a more difficult proposition and an experienced pilot could bank on being allowed to choose or refuse combat as he wished because of his jet's superior performance. Despite that advantage, even the best of them got caught by the persistent and everpresent Mustangs. The redoubtable Walter Nowotny, a Luftwaffe ace with 258 aerial victories, was killed on November 8, 1944, after attacking a B-17 formation and tangling with its P-51 escort. On April 26, 1945, the celebrated fighter leader Adolf Galland was caught napping by a P-51 and forced to put his badly damaged Me 262 down on an airfield which was under heavy attack by P-47s. This was Galland's last operational sortie and it offered sharp commentary on the Luftwaffe's problems in the closing days of the war. Even Galland, one of the world's most experienced fighter pilots, flying the most advanced fighter aircraft

in existence, could not escape the USAAF's relentless pursuit, either in the air or on the ground.

Mission Accomplished

During the final weeks of the air war in Europe, Germany was hit by a series of hammer blows from massive formations of Allied aircraft. Berlin, Hamburg, and Dresden were among cities crushed under immense bomb tonnages intended to complete the dislocation of Germany and its war machine. On April 16, 1945, General Spaatz sent a message to the Eighth and Fifteenth Air Forces which began: "The advances of our ground forces have brought to a close the strategic air war waged by the United States Strategic Air Forces and the Royal Air Force Bomber Command." In fact, it was not quite over. Strategic missions continued until April 25, when RAF Lancasters bombed Hitler's redoubt at Berchtesgaden, and Eighth Air

Force heavies attacked targets in Czechoslovakia and Southeast Germany. The last bombs of the 696,450 tons dropped in anger by the "Mighty Eighth" fell from the bomb bays of the 384th BG. That done, the battle-worn B-17s and B-24s took on the quieter occupations of leaflet dropping and delivering food supplies to the starving people of the Netherlands.

Since the ground forces were necessarily in action until all fighting stopped, the tactical air forces retained their combat responsibilities into the last day of the war, and at least some units of the Luftwaffe were ready to oppose them to the end. As late as April 26, 1944, Adolf Galland, on his last sortie, led his Me 262s in an attack on a First TAF formation in which four B-26s were shot down. The last Eighth Air Force fighter pilot victory was claimed the day before by Lt. Hilton Thompson in a P-51 of the 479 FG, and again it involved a jet. Thompson caught an unsuspecting Arado 234 jet bomber near Salzburg and sent it down in flames. These skirmishes concluded, the European air war was over. It had been a vast enterprise, too complex to allow easy summary or glib assessment. Its operations lent themselves, however, to the cold science of statistics. Figures cannot hope to tell the stories or capture the feelings of the millions of individuals who endured the ferocity of aerial combat firsthand, but they can give some idea of the scale of the conflict and its awful cost in the European and Mediterranean theater, 1942-45:

Total USAAF casualties (dead, wounded, missing, captured): 94,565

Total USAAF personnel dead (all causes): 30,099

USAAF combat sorties: 1,693,565

Bomb tonnage dropped: 1,554,463

Enemy aircraft claimed in aerial combat: 29,916

USAAF aircraft lost (all causes): 27,694 (out of 41,575 worldwide)

Behind the figures lay the facts. From the first, the Allied air forces took the war to the enemy. Until 1945, combat aircraft were the only offensive instruments available to the Allies which could strike directly at Germany. Although initially the effects were not great and the costs were sometimes grievous, the air offensive steadily gained the initiative and forced the Germans to react by diverting more and more resources to the defense of the Reich. Manpower, aircraft, guns, and scientific effort which could have made a difference to the front lines were devoted increasingly to countering the Allied bombers. At the same time, the German people were constantly reminded that they were in a war of their own making, and that their opponents were not about to give up.

As the Allied air forces grew in strength and capability, so they had more influence on the course of the war. The German aircraft industry was heavily damaged and at least put to the serious inconvenience of becoming widely dispersed. The transportation system essential for the efficient movement of German troops and

supplies was, over time, comprehensively wrecked. Perhaps most effective was the campaign against the oil industry, which by April 1945 had reduced German oil production to no more than 5 percent of original capacity. Taken together, there could be no doubting that the various bombing campaigns had crippled the German war effort and had fatally weakened the enemy's capacity for resistance.

Equally important was the Luftwaffe's defeat, a victory which can be attributed largely to the long-range fighters of the Eighth Air Force. Their efforts over Germany broke the Luftwaffe's back and led directly to the achievement of Allied air supremacy. That achievement made the invasion of Normandy possible. Subsequently, it gave the Allied tactical air forces the freedom of action necessary to ensure that the ground forces remained untroubled by the Luftwaffe and had all the air support they needed as they drove forward to occupy what was left of Hitler's "Thousand Year Reich."

If confirmation were needed of air power's decisive role in Germany's defeat, it came from those who had been on the receiving end. Field Marshal von Runstedt, C-in-C West until March 1945, listed air power first of the factors which led to the Allied victory. Field Marshal Albert Kesselring, C-in-C Italy and then C-in-C West after March 1945, gave it as his considered opinion that "it was your air force that decided the conflict." General Alfred Jodl, OKW Chief of Staff, believed that it was air supremacy which decided the war. Field Marshal Wilhelm Keitel gave the principal credit for the victory in the west to the Allied air forces, and General von Vietinghoff commented similarly about the campaign in Italy. Albert Speer, Hitler's Minister for Armaments Production, repeatedly stated that, even though there were ways in which the air offensive could have been more effectively conducted, it was Allied air power which had been the principal reason for Germany's defeat.

Even before the final aerial dramas were played out, preparations had been made to conduct an exhaustive evaluation of the air war in Europe by creating an

impartial body known as the United States Strategic Bombing Survey. By April 1945, teams of trained investigators were following close behind the Allied armies to begin collecting documents and interviewing prisoners with the aim of assessing the contribution made by air power to the defeat of Nazi Germany. The findings of the USSBS report were detailed and comprehensive. They brought out many of air power's achievements, and they were also sometimes sharply critical of the way in which the air war had been conducted. In later years, some of these criticisms were used selectively by those who wished to deprecate air power's role in WWII, but it should be remembered that the final paragraph of the USSBS report begins by stating an emphatic conclusion:

"Allied air power was decisive in the war in Western Europe. Hindsight inevitably suggests that it might have been employed differently or better in some respects. Nevertheless, it was decisive."

A

A   The Plexiglas nose of a B-17 was a spectacular and often frightening place from which to view the air war. The impression gained was of sitting not so much inside the aircraft as in front of it, the four churning radials close behind and roaring you on. The compartment was home to the navigator, with a table just below the left cheek gun, and the bombardier, who fired the remotely controlled chin turret guns when not using the Norden bombsight.

Following page: The USAF Museum's B-17G Flying Fortress, Shoo Shoo Shoo Baby, led an adventurous life. Delivered to the 91st Bomb Group at Bassingbourn, England, in March 1944, Shoo Shoo Shoo Baby survived twenty-three combat missions before flak damage forced a diversion to neutral Sweden. After the war, she served as a Danish airliner and then as a photographic survey aircraft for both Denmark and France, suffering Arctic cold and tropical heat in the process. Abandoned and left to rot in France in 1961, the B-17G was recovered by the USAF in 1972. Restoration began at Dover AFB, Delaware, in 1978, and a reborn Shoo Shoo Shoo Baby flew to her permanent museum home at Wright-Patterson AFB in October 1988.

A   The roomy cockpit of Shoo Shoo Shoo Baby. *The navigator's astrodome is seen just in front of the windscreen. Note that the primary flight instruments are in the center, with the engine and fuel system gauges on the right, in front of the copilot. On the left of the throttle quadrant is a knob controlling the output from the turbo-superchargers. The ladder arrangement of the throttle levers is unique. Individual throttles are controlled with the upper and lower rungs, Nos. 1 and 4 at the top and Nos. 2 and 3 at the bottom. All four throttles can be moved at once by using the split middle rung, preferably with the hand palm uppermost.*

B   The aircraft was originally named Shoo Shoo Baby *after a WW II popular song. The third* Shoo *was added by a crew flying later combat missions.*

C   The top of the B-17G's tail stands 19 feet from the ground, but the space reserved for the tail gunner is remarkably cramped. The white triangle with the capital "A" identifies this as an aircraft belonging to the 91st Bomb Group, 8th Air Force.

A

B

A   Circus Outbound
© *Keith Ferris, 1989*

B   Surrounded by heavy flak, B-24s of the 15th AF attacking the Ploesti oil complex from high altitude on May 31, 1944. By the time the Soviet Army arrived in August 1944, oil production at Ploesti had dwindled to a trickle.

C   The USAF Museum's B-24D Liberator, Strawberry Bitch, arrived at Soluch, Libya, in September 1943 to join the 15th Air Force. With the 512th Bomb Squadron of the 376th Bomb Group, Strawberry Bitch flew 59 missions against targets in Italy.

A   Ramsay Potts was a 26-year-old major when he took part in the low-level Ploesti raid. More than fifty years later he renewed his acquaintance with the B-24's cockpit at the USAF Museum.

B   In the months before D-Day in 1944, Colonel Ramsay Potts was CO of the B-24 equipped 453rd BG, with movie star James Stewart as his group executive officer. Ramsay Potts is seen here in illustrious 8th AF company: (left to right) Lt. Gen. Carl Spaatz, Potts, Maj. Gen. Jimmy Doolittle, and Maj. Gen. William Kepner.

C   The B-24's cluttered cockpit was a challenge for any pilot. To complicate matters, instrument panels were not standardized. Frequent modifications made it more than possible that the cockpit of one B-24 would not resemble another. Constants were the red buttons on the coaming which were used to destroy secret equipment if a forced landing was made in enemy territory. The red buttons at the top of the windscreen are feathering controls, turning failed engine propellers knife-edge to the wind, so reducing drag.

Following pages: The twin .50-caliber machine guns in the tail turret of a B-24. With more room than his B-17 counterpart, the tail gunner was still the loneliest man in the crew, physically separated from his colleagues and unable to see the hazards into which the aircraft was heading.

The deep greenhouse nose of the B-24D was modified in later models to accept a turret firing twin .50-caliber machine guns. The navigator's astrodome remained in place.

196

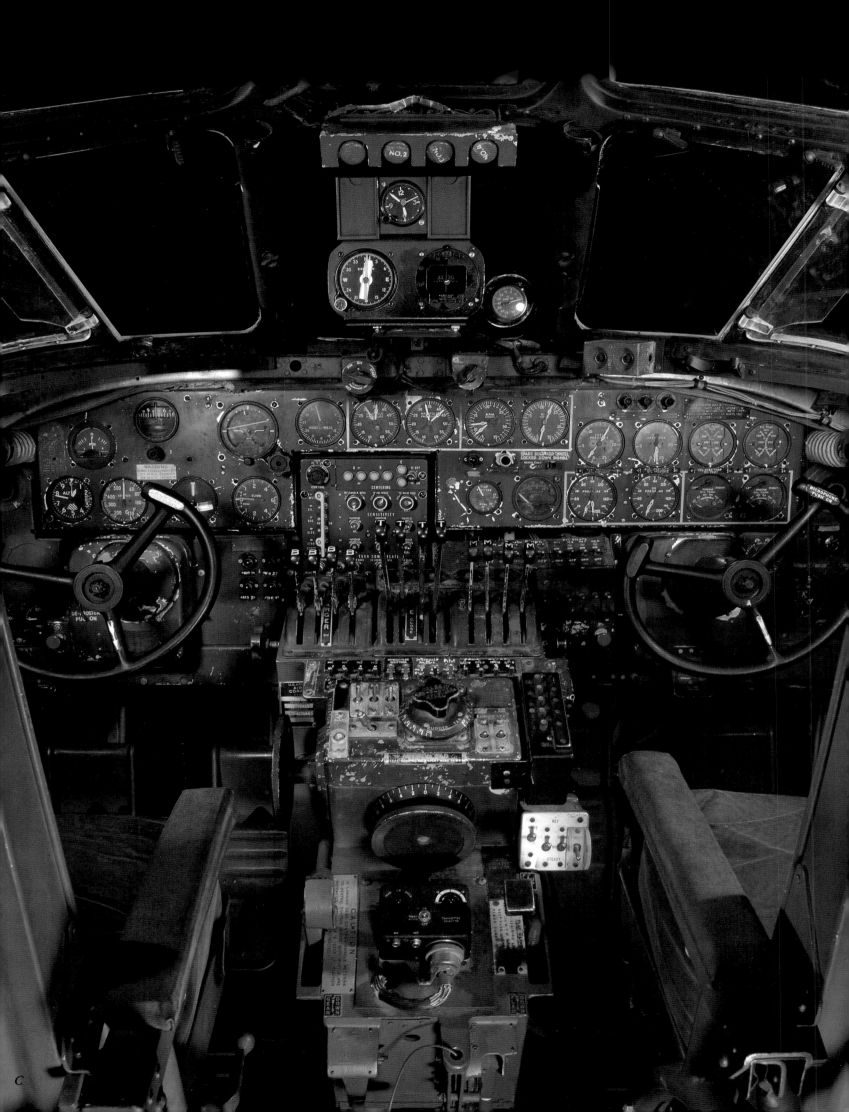

C

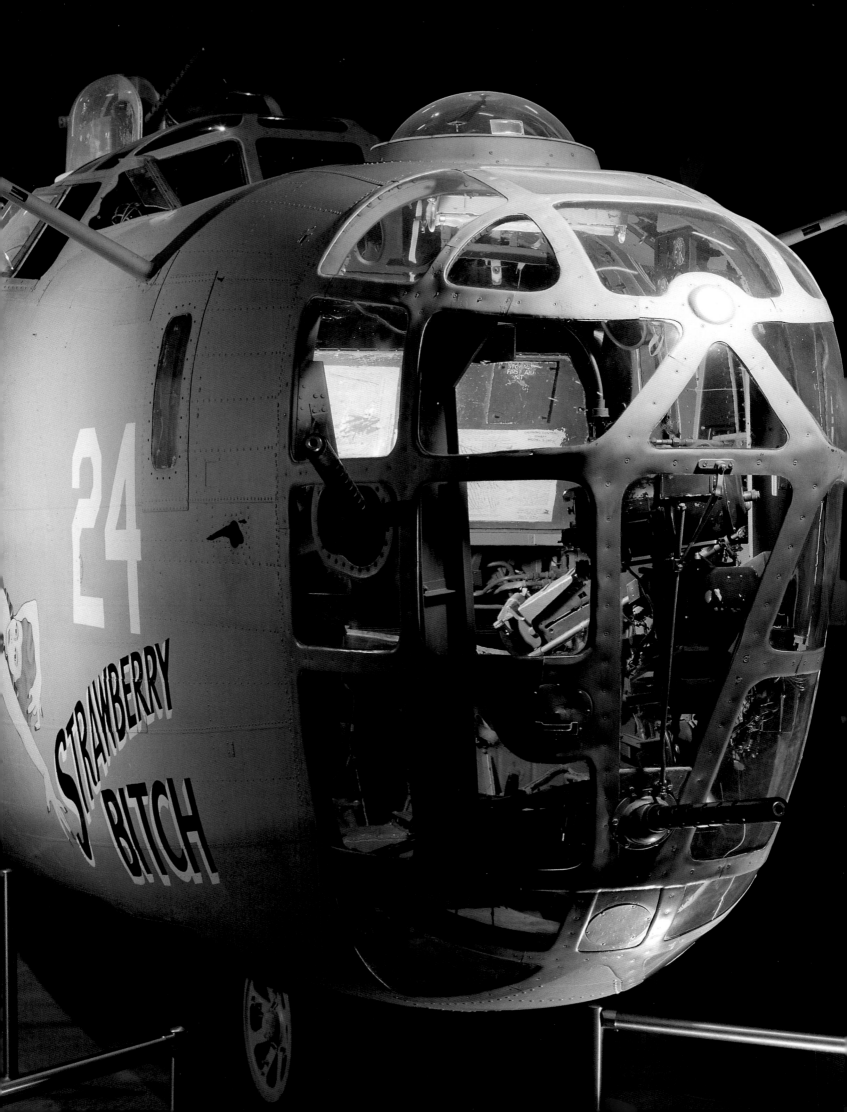

A

B

A   The high wing-loading of the Martin B-26 Marauder gave it an unjustified reputation as a "widow maker." In its early days, apprehensive units were sometimes cured of their fears when the new aircraft was delivered by a slim member of the WASPs. By the end of the war, the Marauder had recorded the lowest loss rate of any USAAF bomber and had proved itself a most effective combat aircraft. Its tubular fuselage was beautifully streamlined, and the high wing design left almost the whole mid-section available as a bomb bay. The B-26 became the chief medium bomber used by the 9th Air Force in its European operations.

B   In common with most bombers of the time, control wheels were preferred to sticks for the B-26.

C   Pratt & Whitney R-2800-43s developing 2,000 hp each were the engines for the B-26. Four-bladed propellers soaked up the power and the huge radials were neatly cowled in giant nacelles which matched the fuselage shape.

D   The upright fin of the B-26 looked out of place on such a smoothly contoured airframe. This one carries the stripes of the 387th Bomb Group, 9th Air Force.

C

2958

D

A

B

A   The enormous bulk of the 2,430 hp Pratt & Whitney R-2800-59 radial is the dominant feature of the rugged Republic P-47D Thunderbolt. It determines the portly shape of the fuselage and is a large part of the aircraft's high all-up weight of 17,500 lbs, unprecedented in a single-engined fighter. The Museum's P-47D carries the markings of the 56th Fighter Group, in terms of enemy aircraft shot down, the most successful Group in the 8th Air Force.

B   Return to Halesworth © Gil Cohen

C   Everything about the P-47 was large, but even in such a spacious cockpit the throttle lever could seem unreasonably prominent. (Compare the cockpit of this WW II Thunderbolt with that of the WW I Camel and with that of the A-10 Thunderbolt II shown at the end of Chapter 12.)

D   To begin with, P-47Ds were built with a sliding framed cockpit canopy. Not until a bubble canopy from a Hawker Typhoon was tested on a P-47 airframe in mid-1943 were clear canopies generally adopted for all P-47s. The simple bucket pilot's seat in the P-47D was backed by armor plate which reached from the floor to behind the headrest.

A   A classic symbol of the Anglo-American alliance in WW II—in the Mustang the superb aerodynamics of North American's P-51 were wrapped smoothly round the Rolls-Royce Merlin, a combination which gave the USAAF the instrument needed to ensure victory in the air war against the Luftwaffe.

B   Pressed paper drop-tanks carried additional fuel to take P-51s to Berlin and back. The barrels of the three .50-caliber machine guns in the port wing can clearly be seen.

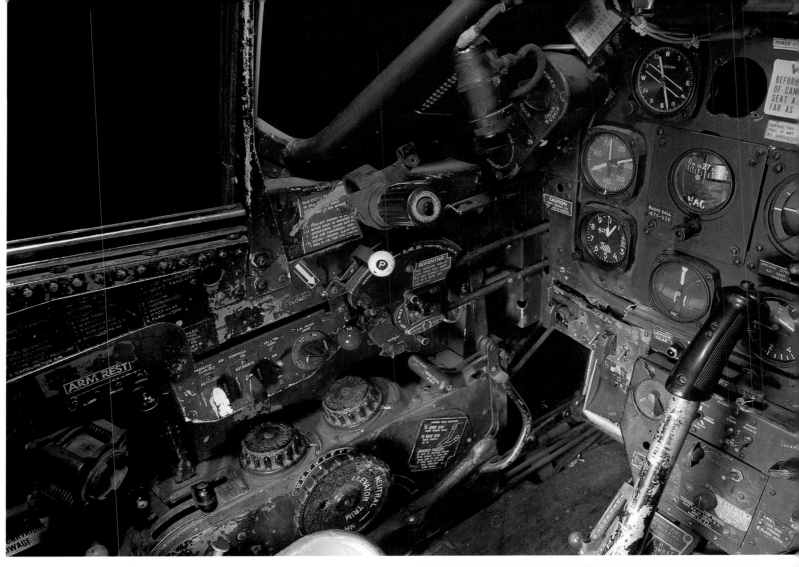

C   The cockpit of the USAF Museum's P-51D, Shimmy IV, *has a well-worn look about it. This particular airframe was the last propeller-driven fighter in service with U.S. forces. It is marked as the P-51D flown by Colonel C.L. Schluder, CO of the 325th FG, 15th AF, in Italy during 1944. Below the throttle quadrant can be seen the trimming controls. On takeoff, the rudder trim was set six notches to the right to help in counteracting the tendency of the Mustang to swing to the left.*

D   *The gun bay in the P-51's port wing. Belts of .50-caliber ammunition fed three guns in each wing. Information on loading the bays and harmonizing the guns is given on the underside of the covering panel.*

D

Nowotny's Final Encounter
© *Keith Ferris, 1980*

A   Beneath the cowling of the North American A-36 Apache was a liquid-cooled Allison V-1710 engine of 1,675 hp. This was the first version of the Mustang airframe to see service with the USAAF. It was in action in North Africa as early as June 1943. Its high-altitude performance was disappointing but it proved effective as a ground attack aircraft. The A-36A in the USAF Museum is painted as Margie H, flown by Capt. Lawrence Dye of the 522nd FBS, 27th FBG, in Tunisia, Sicily, and Italy. Aerial victories are marked by swastikas and ground attack missions with bombs.

B   Prominently featured in the A-36 were dive brakes, a much-needed restraint on an aircraft which accelerated eagerly during dive-bombing attacks. Unfortunately, frequent malfunctions led to them being kept wired shut.

A   The USAAF's need for a fast reconnaissance aircraft was met by acquiring de Havilland Mosquitos from the British under reverse Lend-Lease arrangements. The USAF Museum's example has been restored as a PR Mk XVI used for weather reconnaissance by the 653rd BS, 25th BG, 8th AF.

B   Known to the press as the "wooden wonder" because of its principally plywood construction, the Mosquito was powered by two Rolls-Royce Merlins of 1,690 hp each. The combination of lightness, clean lines, and great power made the Mosquito a formidable performer. It could achieve well over 400 mph and reach altitudes above 40,000 ft. In the reconnaissance role it was unarmed, relying on performance alone for protection.

A   The Piper L-4A Grasshopper, the military version of the Cub, is typical of the small liaison and observation aircraft used by the USAAF in WW II. Fitted with a 65 hp Continental engine, it cruised at 75 mph. This slow speed, combined with a high wing and generous "greenhouse windows," emphasized that the crew would be paying close attention to details on the ground, reporting what they saw, and calling in artillery fire or aircraft strikes.

B   Simple and cheap, thousands of Grasshoppers were delivered and saw service in every WW II combat theater. This one is marked as an aircraft flown during Operation TORCH, the Allied invasion of N. Africa.

C   The L-4 cockpit reflects its role. Sufficient instruments are fitted for safe flight but not so many as to distract the crew from looking outside!

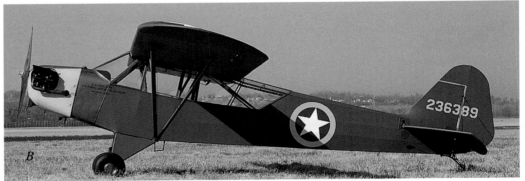

209

A

A   The Douglas C-47 Skytrain was usually called the "Gooney Bird." Over 9,000 C-47s were delivered to the USAAF. They were used in every wartime theater as general transports, and for taking troops into battle, either carrying them as paratroops or towing them in gliders. In later years, C-47s played their part in the Berlin Airlift and Korea, and added to their roles in Vietnam by becoming gunships. The Gooney Bird in the USAF Museum is a C-47A in the markings of the 88th TCS, 438th TCG, in June 1944.

B   Normandy C-47s © R.G. Smith

C   Black and white stripes were painted on Allied aircraft before the Normandy invasion in the hope that ground and naval forces would recognize them as "friendly." Added at the last minute, they were often slapped on with brooms or mops and the edges of the stripes were anything but even. In restoring the Museum's aircraft, this ragged appearance was faithfully reproduced.

D   The strengthened floor and large double doors of the C-47 turned the civilian DC-3 into the jack-of-all-trades needed by the military.   Rugged, reliable, and adaptable, the C-47 served with distinction in every corner of the world.

C

D

A

B

A   Between 1936 and the end of WW II, more than 33,000 Messerschmitt 109s were manufactured. It was a classic fighter—small, fast, maneuverable, and well armed. The USAF Museum's 109 was originally a Spanish-built HA-1112-MIL. In 1982-83, its Merlin engine was replaced by a Daimler-Benz 605 and it was restored as a 109G in the markings of Gerhard Barkhorn, the world's second-ranking ace with 301 aerial victories. Seen from the front, the aircraft reveals both strengths and weaknesses. The 20 mm cannon firing through the propeller boss gave the 109 a hefty punch, but the stalky, narrow-track undercarriage made it tricky to handle on the ground. Landing accidents were a problem throughout the war. Other features are the wide oil cooler intake beneath the fuselage, and the supercharger intake above the exhaust stubs of the DB 605 12-cylinder inverted -V engine.

B   Although Messerschmitt 109 cockpits were anything but standard, they had two things in common—they were cramped and they were covered by a heavily framed canopy, shortcomings which were never overcome.

C   The FW 190D's cockpit was typically small, but the pilot had the advantage of sitting under a blown clear-vision hood.

D   The D-9 was a formidable variant of the Focke-Wulf 190 fighter. Its nose was lengthened to hold a more powerful engine and this led to a compensating extension for the tail, resulting in a noticeably stretched appearance when compared to earlier 190s. The Jumo 213A-1 12-cylinder liquid-cooled engine, misleadingly housed under an apparently radial cowling, was rated at 1,776 hp at takeoff,

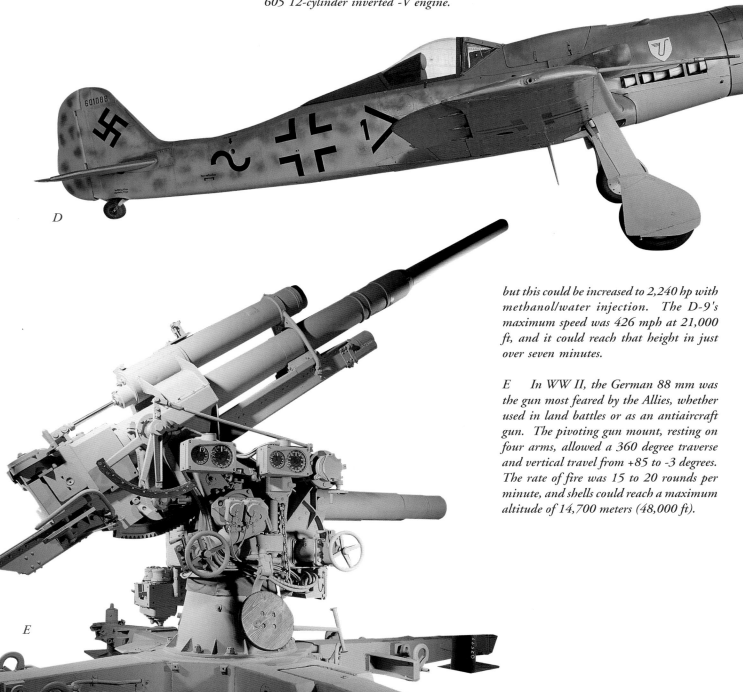

D

but this could be increased to 2,240 hp with methanol/water injection. The D-9's maximum speed was 426 mph at 21,000 ft, and it could reach that height in just over seven minutes.

E   In WW II, the German 88 mm was the gun most feared by the Allies, whether used in land battles or as an antiaircraft gun. The pivoting gun mount, resting on four arms, allowed a 360 degree traverse and vertical travel from +85 to -3 degrees. The rate of fire was 15 to 20 rounds per minute, and shells could reach a maximum altitude of 14,700 meters (48,000 ft).

E

A   Besides the normal flight instruments, the Me 262's cockpit included unfamiliar gauges, such as those measuring the critical exhaust gas temperature, and others capable of recording RPM figures as high as 9,000.

B   The Messerschmitt 262 was the world's first operational jet aircraft. Interceptions of high-flying Allied reconnaissance aircraft began in the spring of 1944. The 262 was much faster than any Allied aircraft, being capable of well over 500 mph at all altitudes. With four 30 mm cannon grouped together in the nose, its weight of fire, too, was superior. Power was supplied by the world's first successful axial-flow jet engines, two Junkers Jumo 004B engines of 1,980 lbs thrust each. Operating as they were at the outermost limits of engine technology, such early jets demanded very gentle handling by pilots. Damage or destruction could be induced by careless throttle handling.

Part 4: U.S. Army Air Power against Japan, 1942-1945

In the latter part of 1942, the 11th FS, 353rd FG, in the Aleutians was operating P-40Es. The commander was Jack Chennault, son of Claire Chennault, the celebrated leader of the AVG in China. As a tribute to his father and his "Flying Tigers," the 11th adopted a stylized tiger design for their aircraft and became known as the "Aleutian Tigers."

Stung beyond endurance by the Doolittle raid of April 1942, the Japanese military leaders launched into the next phase of their imperial expansion with more haste than good sense. To consolidate and rationalize the perimeter of their empire, they proposed a four-pronged offensive. In the south, they intended to capture Port Moresby in New Guinea, from where they could threaten Australia. At Guadalcanal in the Solomons they planned to build an airfield which would be a base for further island conquests aimed at interdicting the U.S./Australia transpacific lifeline. Further north, the Japanese believed it was vital for them to capture Midway Island, which would give them a grip on the Central Pacific while plugging a worrying gap in their far-flung defensive screen. In part as a diversion from the attack on Midway, they also proposed to invade the Aleutians. Afflicted by "victory disease," it did not seem to occur to Japanese leaders that their forces, already involved over an immense portion of the globe, might be overstretched by such a vast enterprise. Their enforced return to rationality was to prove painful in the extreme.

In early May, the hazards of the Tokyo raid and his B-25 bailout still fresh in his mind, the newly promoted Brig. Gen. Jimmy Doolittle began the long journey back to the U.S. via India and Egypt. He had hardly left China before a Japanese invasion force was on its way to Port Moresby. In the ensuing Battle of the Coral Sea, the first ever fought between aircraft carriers, the struggle was judged a tactical draw, with both sides suffering serious losses. However, since the Japanese fleet was forced to abandon the invasion and retreat, the vital strategic victory belonged to the U.S. Navy.

Before May was out, the Imperial Japanese Navy was embarked on the most ambitious of its operations, with most of its considerable strength committed to the achievement of three goals—the capture of Midway, the invasion of the Aleutians, and the destruction of the U.S. Pacific Fleet's aircraft carriers. In an epic battle on June 4, 1942, the U.S. Navy's airmen, having first stared into the abyss of defeat, dragged victory from its brink by sinking four Japanese carriers for the loss of the *Yorktown*. Once again, the enemy fleet was forced to retreat, but this time the Japanese Navy had been dealt a blow from which it was never to recover. Four large carriers were gone, as were their aircraft and many of Japan's experienced naval pi-

lots. It was a pivotal action in the Pacific War. From Midway on, the initiative in the Pacific passed to the U.S. and the Japanese found themselves almost continually on the defensive.

USAAF aircraft did play a part at Midway, but it could not be described as particularly distinguished. The principal effort was made by B-17Es of the Seventh Air Force, which flew fifty-five sorties against the Japanese ships, bombing mainly from highlevel and scoring at the most one hit on a transport. Worse yet, on June 6, six B-17s attacked what they said was an enemy cruiser. Two direct hits were claimed, and the cruiser was reported as having sunk "in fifteen seconds." Remarkable as that seemed to be, the B-17 crews would have been even more impressed if they could have seen their target unsink itself after their departure. Later that day, an indignant signal was received from the USS *Grayling* asking why it should be necessary for a U.S. submarine to crash-dive to avoid being plastered by the Army Air Force. It all begged the question of whether it was reasonable to expect heavy bombers, flying at high level, to identify and attack small moving targets like ships with any hope of success.

Jeeps and B-24s were among the machines operated in the Aleutians by the 11th AF, but Jeeps were generally better suited to the spartan conditions. Taken in 1943 at Adak, this photograph shows something of the environment endured by the men engaged in the "forgotten war." Mud and ice made servicing aircraft in the open a challenging occupation.

Aleutian Adventure

Meanwhile, far to the north, the Japanese had secured a foothold in the Aleutians, establishing troops on the islands of Attu and Kiska. Given the circumstances in which they found themselves, the troops may have come to regret their achievement. Aleutians weather is almost invariably appalling, with gales, rain, blizzards, and low cloud as expected elements of the daily experience. As one air force officer wrote: "During April and May, the weather for air operations is bad. For the rest of the year, it is worse." Campsites and airstrips were either buried in snow and ice or immersed under mud and water.

The geography and climate of the Aleutians and the North Pacific were too harsh to allow the development of a major campaign by either side, and the region was never considered to be more than a secondary theater of the war. It had not been the intention of the Japanese, however, to use the Aleutians as a launching pad for anything major, like an assault on Alaska. The detachments on Attu and Kiska were purely defensive, placed there to block any possible U.S. advance towards Japan down the Aleutian chain. Nevertheless, the Japanese had occupied U.S. territory, and this was not something which

could be treated lightly. Rather than settling for a mutual standoff, an air campaign was undertaken with the aim of making things as uncomfortable as possible for the occupying troops on Attu and Kiska. The Eleventh Air Force, commanded by Brig. Gen. William Butler, was strengthened with P-38s, B-24s, and B-25s, and persistent attempts were made to bomb and strafe Japanese positions. Bedeviled by the weather, these raids were always hazardous and often unrewarding. To give an example from the official history of the Army Air Forces:

"On the 18th [January 1943] . . . seven heavy and five medium bombers flew out of Adak with a six fighter escort. Before they reached the target, the fog closed in and the planes turned back. The mediums and the fighters were fast enough to reach Adak before the base was completely 'souped in.' Four of the slower Liberators had to seek an alternate landing field; the nearest possibility was Umnak, two and a half hours east of Adak. Two B-24s disappeared into the fog and were never heard from. A third, crash-landing on Great Sitkin, was damaged beyond repair. One reached Umnak and landed by the light of flares, but overshot the runway and crashed into two P-38s, destroying them. Six planes

were lost, no bombs were dropped, and no enemy was encountered—save fog.

"Bad luck continued. On January 21 two B-17s, out of Umnak for Adak, collided in mid-air; one disappeared, the other landed, badly hurt. A P-40, out of control, crashed into Kuluk Bay the same day. On the 23rd two B-25s tangled in a fog and went down."

Bad as they were, these losses only continued a pattern which had been set from the start. During a five-month period in the latter half of 1942, the Eleventh Air Force lost seventy-two aircraft, only nine of them in combat. Nor did matters show much improvement as time went on. Between the beginning of June and the end of September 1943, forty aircraft were lost in combat, but 174 more were written off to "operational hazards." It was only partial consolation to know that the Japanese were suffering similar problems.

Compared to other theaters of war, the numbers involved were insignificant— the Eleventh Air Force was never capable of operating more than two or three hundred aircraft—and the U.S. military in the Aleutians had every right to feel that they were clamped in the icy grip of a "forgotten war." Besides flying operations in weather which would have grounded air forces elsewhere, the airmen of the Eleventh Air Force endured poor food, miserable living quarters, inadequate airfields, and rudimentary navigation aids while pounding the Japanese whenever it was humanly possible. Much of the agony was eased in 1943, during what passed for the Aleutian summer. Attu was retaken by U.S. forces after a bloody struggle in which the Japanese defenders fought to the last man. Given that experience, U.S. commanders did not look forward to attacking Kiska, but the Japanese elected not to contest the issue and quietly withdrew.

With U.S. territorial integrity restored, the Eleventh Air Force shrank until by September it had only two bomber squadrons (one heavy, one medium), a fighter group, and one troop carrier squadron. Operations then consisted of patrolling the frigid northern waters and harassing Japanese bases in the distant Northern

Kurile Islands. Unrewarding though these activities seemed at the time, they forced the Japanese to pay attention to their back door. In 1944, there were over seventy thousand troops and more than four hundred aircraft in Japan's Hokkaido/Kuriles region, held there by the Eleventh's constant reminder that Americans posed a possible threat to the Japanese homeland from the north.

If Americans felt depressed and frustrated at the thankless nature of the fighting in the Aleutians, they could be consoled by the thought of the one priceless jewel which fell into their laps during the campaign. To be more precise, it fell into their muskeg.

One of the war's great surprises had been the Mitsubishi A6M fighter, known to the Allies as the "Zero." It was outflying everything it came up against and almost nothing was known about it. After a raid on Dutch Harbor in the Aleutians, one Japanese pilot elected to put his failing Zero down on land rather than crash into the icy sea. He saw what he took to be a flat grassy area on Akutan Island and tried to do a normal wheels-down landing. The wheels dug into boggy ground, the Zero turned over, and the pilot broke his neck. A month later, the aircraft was seen by a patrolling Catalina and recovered practically undamaged. It was shipped to California, rebuilt, and test flown. The results were used to devise tactics for countering the Zero, and they directly influenced the design of later U.S. fighters, particularly for the U.S. Navy.

New Guinea

After his escape from the rampaging Japanese in the Philippines, General Douglas MacArthur assumed command of the Southwest Pacific theater in April 1942 and set up his headquarters in Australia, initially at Melbourne, and later at Brisbane. MacArthur's appearance on the scene complicated command responsibilities, and it was never possible to reach agreement on the appointment of a Supreme Allied Commander, as was the case in Europe. The Combined Chiefs of Staff having settled that the Pacific should be an American strategic responsibility, the U.S. Joint Chiefs reconciled the differing opinions of the Army and the Navy by deciding that there should be two principal lines of advance against the Japanese, and therefore two commanders. MacArthur would rule in the Southwest Pacific and Admiral Chester Nimitz in the Pacific Ocean area. They would be responsible for developing a two-pronged assault, through New Guinea and the Solomons, with the initial goal of enveloping the Japanese main base at Rabaul on New Britain.

MacArthur's air commander was Lt. Gen. George Brett, whose assets during the summer of 1942 were a motley and scattered collection of American and Australian aircraft, described as being "pitifully inadequate for their task." The few USAAF bomber squadrons on hand were equipped with A-24s and with early models of the B-25, B-26, and B-17. Most of the available fighters were P-40s and P-400s, the latter an inferior model of the P-39 developed for export. Despite the shortcomings, efforts were made to maintain an offensive posture, with the bombers flying unescorted over very long distances against the forward Japanese bases, often suffering significant losses in the process to both the enemy and the elements. For their part, U.S. fighters tackling Japanese raids found themselves consistently outclassed, the P-400s in particular being no match for the escorting Zeros.

Many of the U.S. airmen facing these discouraging operational realities were already war-weary from having gone through painful campaigns in the Philippines and the Dutch East Indies, and they knew that their circumstances were not likely to change for the better very soon. The policy of "Europe first" would keep them at the end of the priority list for some time. Their aircraft, most of them recognizably inferior, were also poorly maintained, afflicted as they were by a perpetual shortage of spare parts and trained mechanics. To make matters worse, the units were generally deployed in surroundings which were anything but comfortable. Set in remote areas of Australia, the bases were extremely primitive, with inadequate medical facilities and food which the men found unattractive. Understandably, commanders found it difficult to maintain a high level of morale.

Things were not improved when, in July 1942, the Japanese, who were already established elsewhere in New Guinea, beat the Allies to the punch and landed at Buna, on the north coast of Papua and only one hundred miles from Port Moresby. From there they launched an overland offensive through the Owen Stanley Range, fighting their way forward in a bloody and re-

The 347th FG was assigned to the 13th AF in January 1943 and sent to Guadalcanal, from where it used its P-39s in attacks against Japanese ground forces and shipping.

lentless campaign until, in late August, overcome as much by the terrain, the jungle, and disease as by the desperate opposition of the Allies, the Japanese soldiers reached the end of their tether and began to fall back.

At about the same time, Maj. Gen. George Kenney, one of the most gifted combat commanders of WWII, arrived to take over the Allied Air Forces in the Southwest Pacific Area. He was a man with some claim to being an air power visionary, and a leader who encouraged his subordinates to use their imagination and their initiative. Under his leadership, Allied air power in the Southwest Pacific was markedly strengthened. It is true that, as the U.S. industrial machine gathered pace, more and newer aircraft became available, but that was not the whole story. Kenney's energetic influence pervaded his command, inspiring enthusiasm and determination where none had been before.

Kenney first tackled the maintenance muddle, going out to talk to the men on the line to find out what the real problems were firsthand. Always prepared to be unconventional if that would get the job done, he quickly improved matters and raised the number of aircraft available to the squadrons. He insisted, too, that maintenance facilities be kept as close to the front line as possible. Jettisonable fuel tanks were found to extend the range of his fighters, and he fostered the development of aggressive low-level attack techniques, including skip-bombing. Kenney was particularly keen on his attack aircraft being able to hit their targets very hard, and he gave one of his protégés, the appropriately named Major Paul "Pappy" Gunn, a free hand to experiment with fitting heavier armament to the A-20 and the B-25. Gunn's modifications turned moderately effective attack aircraft into truly deadly weapons. To make them even better, Kenney himself suggested the use of parachutes on fragmentation bombs so that they could be dropped during low-level attacks without endangering the bomber. Before long, Kenney had molded his air force into a fearsome instrument of war. As if these operational achievements were

A B-25H head-on was a fearsome sight. Inspired by Major "Pappy" Gunn's ideas in the 5th AF, many B-25s were modified as "strafers" with a variety of forward firing options. This B-25H carries eight .50 caliber machine guns and a 75 mm cannon. Strengthening of the skin around the guns was needed to allow the aircraft to withstand the destructive effects of its own firepower.

not sufficient, he was also man enough to be able to stand up to the imperial MacArthur and win his confidence.

In September 1942, the American air force units in the Southwest Pacific were organized as the Fifth Air Force, with Kenney assuming command at his headquarters in Brisbane. A small forward headquarters, tasked with the day-to-day conduct of operations during the New Guinea campaign, was set up at Port Moresby under Kenney's deputy, Brig. Gen. Ennis Whitehead. Soon after the Fifth Air Force was established, Kenney wrote to General Hap Arnold, setting out some of his views on air power and the way it needed to be applied in the special circumstances of the Southwest Pacific. Extracts from his letter give emphasis to the need for close cooperation with ground forces, and include some of the forceful imagery illustrative of his colorful personality:

"Tanks and heavy artillery can be reserved for the battlefields of Europe and Africa. They have no place in jungle warfare. The artillery in this theater flies."

"The Air Force is the spearhead of the Allied attack in the South West Pacific. Its function is to clear the air, wreck the enemy's land installations, destroy his supply system, and give close support to troops

advancing on the ground.

"Clearing the air means more than air superiority. It means air control so supreme that the birds have to wear our Air Force insignia. Wrecking the enemy's ground installations does not mean just softening them up. It means taking out everything he has—aerodromes, guns, bunkers, troops. Destroying his supply system means cutting him off the vine so completely and firmly that he not only cannot undertake offensive action but, due to his inability to replenish his means to wage war, he cannot even maintain a successful defense."

Kenney's actions were as good as his words during the New Guinea campaign. Allied infantry slogging up the Kokoda Trail through the Owen Stanley Range were supported whenever possible by low-flying attack aircraft, the unloved P-39 Airacobras coming into their own as strafers with their 37 mm cannon. The rapid forward movement of troops by air, urged on MacArthur by Kenney, was immensely successful. C-47s shuttled back and forth, both between Australia and Port Moresby, and further forward into areas from which Allied soldiers could surprise the Japanese and threaten their communications and main bases. By the end of

1942, the Japanese had been driven back to the north coast of New Guinea and were desperately defending Buna. Allied ground forces were able to maintain their offensive because of the C-47 lifeline over the mountainous interior, and because the Fifth was growing steadily more effective as a fighting air force. B-24s were arriving to take the load as the region's principal heavy bomber, Pappy Gunn's modified A-20s and B-25s were in action, and P-38 Lightnings were replacing the tired P-39s and P-40s.

In Europe, the P-38 was not much admired, but it came into its own in the Pacific. Its twin engines were reassuring to pilots who had to operate over wastes of jungle and ocean, and, with external tanks, it had legs long enough to cope with the scale of the Pacific theater. It was no match for the Zero as a dogfighter, but it was much faster, and it could both outclimb and outdive its Japanese opponent. The P-38 also had an armored cockpit and self-sealing fuel tanks, and its heavy armament of a 20 mm cannon and four .5 in machine guns made short work of the more lightly built Zero. When American pilots made the most of these advantages, the Zero was outclassed.

Organized Japanese resistance in and around Buna came to an end on January 22, 1943, by which time the Fifth Air Force had long since established air superiority over the Papua region of New Guinea. Among other things, this meant that the vital air transport operations into airstrips on the north coast were never seriously threatened by Japanese aircraft. This not only assured the ground forces of their supplies, but also gave the added comfort of rapid medical evacuation. Allied soldiers suffered over ten thousand casualties in the bloody struggle with their enemies, but, thanks in large part to the tireless efforts of the C-47 squadrons, only seven percent of these died.

An entry in a Japanese soldier's diary, written in December 1942, graphically underlines the Fifth Air Force's Papuan success: "They fly above our position as if they owned the skies." General MacArthur, who had been free with his criticism of the Air Force's capabilities at the time of Kenney's arrival, now gave just as freely of his praise in a statement of some architectural confusion: "To the American Fifth Air Force and the Royal Australian Air Force no commendation could be too great. Their outstanding efforts in combat, supply and transportation over both land and sea constituted the key-stone upon which the arch of the campaign was erected."

Driven out of Buna, the Japanese determined to strengthen their position further west on the north coast of New Guinea. With that intention, they began to move reinforcements from their main base at Rabaul to the Huon Gulf port of Lae. On December 30, 1942, a Lockheed F-4 Lightning reconnaissance aircraft discovered twenty-one warships and seventy merchant ships assembled at Rabaul. In a first attempt, the Japanese were successful in getting a small convoy through to Lae and landing some four thousand troops, but they lost two troop transports and over fifty escorting fighters doing it. Ten Allied aircraft were lost. In his drive to "make the birds wear our Air Force insignia," this sort of exchange rate was welcomed by Kenney. He knew that more convoys would be coming to Lae and that, since enemy fighters had to escort the ships, combat between the air forces was inevitable. The Japanese were caught in a war of attrition Kenney was sure he could win.

At the end of February 1943, five thousand troops of the Japanese 51st Infantry Division set out for Lae from Rabaul in a convoy of seven merchant ships, eight destroyers, and a special service vessel. On March 1, the convoy was seen by a B-24 and, over the next three days, the Fifth Air Force and the RAAF hit it in a series of attacks which became known as the Battle of the Bismarck Sea.

Early successes in the battle were

On September 5, 1943, the 54th TCW's C-47s dropped the U.S. 503rd Paratroop Regiment and some Australian units onto the kunai-grass plains of Nadzab in New Guinea.

claimed by B-17s and B-25s bombing from medium altitude, but most of the damage was done on March 3 by aircraft strafing and bombing from low level. The aircraft modified by Pappy Gunn to carry much heavier forward-firing armament came into their own and proved especially destructive. Gunfire from the B-25s, A-20s, and Beaufighters swept the decks of the Japanese ships, and 500 lb bombs skipped across the sea to smash into their sides. The attacks, coordinated at first, soon developed into free-for-alls as aircraft separated and maneuvered to take on one ship and then another. Aircraft crisscrossed through the convoy and competed for victims, flying at mast-head height and sometimes lower. One A-20 finished off a run by shortening a ship's radio mast with its right wing. Inevitably, attackers wound up aiming at the same target. Out of the corner of his eye, an Australian saw something flying alongside him as his Beaufighter steadied for a strafing run. It was a B-25's 500 lb bomb in mid-skip, heading in the same direction.[1]

As the low-level attackers approached the convoy, they were startled to find themselves passing through a shower

Over three thousand Japanese soldiers died, and the 51st Division was effectively destroyed.

General MacArthur later spoke of the Battle of the Bismarck Sea as "the decisive aerial engagement" in his theater of the war. Kenney's airmen had demonstrated their ability to obliterate a convoy with aircraft, and, by so doing, had created an aerial blockade of Japanese forces around the Huon Gulf. Never again did the Japanese attempt to run large ships into Lae, and the troops there were left to subsist on a meager supply from those few submarines and barges which managed to

non. Good though these were, Kenney never stopped being impatient for more of everything. To emphasize his need for troop carrier replacements, he told Hap Arnold: "The figures show that between weather and Nips a man lives longer in a P-39 than he does in a C-47 flying the troop carrier supply runs in New Guinea." He added a reminder about the scale of the Southwest Pacific theater, pointing out that the P-47s were not much good without long-range tanks, since they had no more range than was needed "to defend London or to make a fighter sweep across a ditch no bigger than Chesapeake Bay."

Whatever the limitations of their equipment, Kenney's air force did wonders with it. MacArthur now understood that New Guinea's geography defied even rudimentary maneuvers on the ground, and that victory depended on gaining and holding air superiority. The campaign settled into a pattern of using air power to hammer and neutralize enemy forces before bypassing them with troops moved forward by sea or air transport. The infantry then held the ground while airstrips were constructed, after which the process could begin again. Gradually overcome by the endless attrition of combat, the Japanese air forces in New Guinea finally succumbed in March and April 1944, when the Fifth Air Force carried out heavy attacks on three air bases in the Hollandia area. The facilities on the bases were wrecked and, counting those destroyed both in the air and on the ground, the Japanese lost more than 450 aircraft. The loss ratio in aerial combat often favored the American pilots by ten to one or more, and it was clear that the caliber of the average Japanese pilot had noticeably declined. Even so, the Fifth Air Force had not escaped lightly. In the two years following September 1942, the Fifth had lost 1,374 aircraft to all causes, and more than 4,100 airmen were listed as killed or missing.

North American B-25s © *R.G. Smith*

of long-range fuel tanks. Above the smoke and flame of the surface battle, the P-38s of the 35th and 49th FGs had lightened their load before keeping the covering Zeros occupied. Their efforts were eminently successful. By the end of the battle, more than fifty enemy aircraft had been shot down, at a cost of three P-38s and one B-17, plus one B-25 in a landing accident. More significantly, twelve ships had been sunk, including all of the troop transports.

break through. In effect, the Japanese had to accept that their hold on the eastern half of New Guinea was broken, and that, in the face of growing U.S. air power, their tenure in the rest of the island would be of limited duration.

As he turned his attention to the next phase of the New Guinea campaign, Kenney believed he could count on having greatly increased air strength, and the summer of 1943 saw several more groups join the Fifth Air Force. Among the new aircraft were the 348th FG's P-47s and yet another Mitchell variant, the B-25G, equipped with a ship-busting 75 mm can-

By mid-1944, the Thirteenth Air Force in the Solomons found itself underemployed and was moved to join the Fifth Air Force as part of Kenney's command in the Southwest Pacific area. Kenney became

---

[1] The 90th Squadron's aircraft had been modified to become B-25C1s, with forward-firing armament of eight .5 in guns grouped in the nose, plus two more in the upper turret. Almost equally effective were the A-20s of the 89th Squadron, with four .5 in guns in addition to their original armament of four .303 in, and the RAAF's Beaufighters, which carried four 20 mm cannon in the nose and six .303 machine guns in the wings.

Commander, Far East Air Forces, with Whitehead moving up to take over Fifth Air Force. The Thirteenth's original commander, Nathan Twining, had long since left for Europe, after surviving an uncomfortable six days in a life raft when his B-17 got lost and ran out of fuel. The new commander, Maj. Gen. St. Clair Streett, set up his headquarters initially at Los Negros in the Admiralty Islands, northeast of New Guinea, seized as part of the Allied encirclement of Rabaul. The resistance of Japanese ground forces continued in New Guinea until September, by which time the Fifth and Thirteenth Air Forces were preparing for the next big step—MacArthur's return to the Philippines.

The Solomons

At the same time that Japanese troops landed at Buna to start their offensive against Port Moresby, others were exerting themselves in building an airfield on Guadalcanal in the southern Solomons. This represented a major threat to the Allies' transpacific lifeline and had to be countered. As the plans for an Allied riposte were drawn up, it was clear that, since Guadalcanal was in the U.S. Navy's South Pacific area, any USAAF action would be in a supporting role.

To safeguard Army interests in an essentially naval sphere, the War Department agreed to the appointment of an airman, Maj. Gen. Millard Harmon, as commander of Army forces in the South Pacific. Operationally, Harmon's USAAF units served under Rear Adm. John McCain, who controlled all air assets in the region. Harmon arrived at his headquarters at Noumea, New Caledonia, in late July 1942. It was just a week before the U.S. Marines landed on Guadalcanal. At that time, the USAAF's presence in the South Pacific was small and widely scattered, with isolated units operating a total of thirty-three B-17s, twenty-two B-26s, and seventy-nine P-39/400s deployed on airstrips as far apart as New Caledonia, the New Hebrides, Fiji, and Tonga, covering an area not much smaller than the United States.[2]

During the early stages of the long struggle for Guadalcanal, the USAAF's B-17s supported operations by bombing Japanese bases and ships as far away as Rabaul, and flew long-range reconnaissance missions to watch for any movement of enemy warships and convoys in and around the Solomons. By the end of August, the P-400s of the 67th FS had been moved forward to Guadalcanal's Henderson Field. Their poor performance made them incapable of joining in the daily air battles with Japanese bombers and fighters over the island, but they proved useful in the close support role, using their cannon to good effect to harass enemy troops in contact with the Marines.

and to develop Henderson Field quickly into an air base capable of handling B-17s. As the weeks went by, Harmon's apprehensions were justified. In a series of spectacular naval operations involving heavy losses to both sides, the Japanese succeeded in building their forces on Guadalcanal up to thirty thousand men. The defenders of Henderson Field had to withstand ferocious ground assaults, constant air attacks by day, and frequent naval bombardment by night, but any doubts about the U.S. determination to hang on were eliminated in October 1942, when Ghormley was replaced by the fiery Admiral William "Bull" Halsey.

After the April 3, 1944, attack on Japanese airfields in Hollandia, the 5th AF effectively owned the air over New Guinea. B-25s of the 38th and 345th BGs strafed the airfield at Dagua and sowed parafrag bombs among the parked aircraft with deadly effect.

Only too well aware of the USAAF's shortcomings in the South Pacific, General Harmon badgered USAAF headquarters for more and better aircraft, only to be reminded of his lowly position on the priority list. Fearing that the American hold on Guadalcanal was tenuous and that the Japanese would be making every effort to evict the Marines, he also urged Admiral Robert Ghormley, Commander South Pacific, to reinforce the Marine lodgment

By the end of the year, the Japanese were forced to accept that the cost of supporting their attempt to recover Guadalcanal from a main base over six hundred miles away was too high. It was proving almost impossible for their ships to break through the stranglehold of the U.S. naval and air blockade, and their troops on the island were suffering greatly from their enforced isolation. Combat deaths, injuries, sickness, and malnutrition had, by November 1942, reduced the original force of thirty thousand to little more than thirteen thousand fit for duty. Early

[2]Efate, New Hebrides—5 B-17s, 26th BS. Espiritu Santo, New Hebrides—6 B-17s, 98th BS. New Caledonia—10 B-17s, 42nd BS; 10 B-26s, 69th BS; 38 P-39/400s, 67th FS. Fiji—12 B-17s, 431st BS; 12 B-26s, 70th BS; 17 P-39/400s, 70th FS. Tonga—24 P-39/400, 68th FS.

in February 1943, the Japanese bowed to the inevitable, acknowledged the growing imbalance of power, and withdrew the remnants of their Army. The grinding six-month struggle for Guadalcanal was over.

The losses at sea by the U.S. Navy attracted attention because of their severity, but the aerial conflict had been costly, too, even though the numbers involved in combat on any one day were never very great. In six months, both sides had lost over 600 aircraft each. The USAAF share, reflecting its relatively minor role, had included twenty-seven B-17s, five B-26s, ten P-40s, six P-38s, and thirty-three P-39/400s.

give the AAF both high-altitude and long-range capability. The B-24, too, had made an appearance, and one radar-equipped squadron had demonstrated that it could strike Japanese shipping through cloud or from low level at night.

For his part, General Harmon was still bothered by having so little say in the operational employment of AAF aircraft, especially now that more and better aircraft were on the way. He was particularly concerned that naval commanders viewed the B-17 primarily as a patrol aircraft, diverting it too often from its role as a bomber. As things were, he found "too little imagination being exercised in the employ-

aircraft in the South Pacific still rested with an admiral.

In most theaters of war, it was possible to distinguish service responsibilities clearly. The odd mixture of units and aircraft which had come together on Henderson Field almost by accident made this more difficult in the Solomons. Sheer necessity had driven them to work together for mutual survival, and with the end of the fighting on Guadalcanal time was taken to formalize the situation by creating a headquarters known as Air Command Solomons (COMAIRSOLS). Admiral Halsey and General Harmon were agreed that unity of command was essential and the new organization was tasked with the efficient employment of Navy, Marine, AAF, and RNZAF units operating a motley collection of types, including P-39s, P-40s, P-38s, B-25s, B-17s, B-24s, PBYs, C-47s, Lockheed Venturas, and a variety of naval aircraft. Naval officers filled the COMAIRSOLS chair until mid-1943, when Thirteenth Air Force's General Twining took over.

Faced with the fact of defeat both in Papua and on Guadalcanal, Admiral Isoroku Yamamoto tried to regain the initiative for his forces in the Solomons with a series of air raids in April. They were roughly handled and the ratio of losses greatly favored U.S. fighter pilots. With the momentum of victory building against him, Yamamoto decided to put some steel into the Japanese units by visiting them in person. Unfortunately for him, American intelligence officers were reading his mail.

The code breakers had determined that Yamamoto would be visiting Ballale, off the southern tip of Bougainville, on April 18, 1943. His detailed itinerary, complete with timings, was known. Since Ballale was just within the reach of P-38s fitted with drop tanks, Major John Mitchell of the 339th Squadron was given the job of planning an interception and an assassination. From every point of view, the operation was a longshot. The route would have to follow a curving track for nearly five hundred miles over water, flying at low level the whole way to avoid detection. With no radio navigation aids, the naviga-

Used extensively for reconnaissance, and as a minelayer and bomber, the adaptable Catalina is still remembered most for its air-sea rescue work in the Pacific. Hundreds of Allied airmen were saved from capture or a watery grave by the appearance of a lumbering "Cat."

In the course of the campaign, the USAAF in the South Pacific had undergone a number of changes and developments. Inadequate though its P-400s had been at the outset, their pilots had nevertheless integrated their operations successfully with their Navy and Marine counterparts at Henderson Field. The "Cactus Air Force," as it was known, was a splendid example of interservice cooperation under fire, and it laid the foundation for further collaborative efforts later on. As the year ended, a few P-38s were at last on hand to

ment of our Air Force." In December 1942, his pleas bore fruit when General George Marshall decreed that a new air force should be formed in the South Pacific. On January 13, 1943, the Thirteenth Air Force was activated under the command of Brig. Gen. Nathan Twining, with its headquarters on the island of Espiritu Santo. The USAAF gained from the added status of a numbered air force, but little else had changed. General Harmon retained administrative responsibility for USAAF units, but operational control of

tion would be by dead reckoning, relying on notoriously suspect aircraft compasses and primitive weather forecasting. Even if the P-38s made an accurate landfall and got there on time, it was by no means certain that Yamamoto's aircraft would be there, too. Mitchell had made a number of assumptions about the route and airspeed of the Japanese formation on the basis of the decoded itinerary, but there were no guarantees.

Eighteen P-38s, with pilots from the 339th, 12th, and 70th Fighter Squadrons, were detailed for the operation. Sixteen actually set course. Four were selected as an attack section to concentrate on Yamamoto's transport, while the rest of the P-38s took on his escort and whatever other fighters appeared from the nearby base. Much to the jubilation of the Americans and the shocked surprise of the Japanese, the sixteen P-38s ran into two Betty bombers and six Zeros at exactly the appointed time and place. In the ensuing melee, Lt. Thomas Lanphier and Lt. Rex Barber between them managed to shoot down both Bettys. The body of Japan's premier admiral, architect of the attack on Pearl Harbor, was found in the jungle the following day.

Throughout 1943, as Marine soldiers forced their way up the chain of the Solomon Islands towards Bougainville and Rabaul, the aircraft of COMAIRSOLS moved with them and maintained a relentless pressure on the enemy. Wherever possible, Japanese strongholds were pounded from the air, bypassed, and left behind to become prisons for their isolated garrisons. In November, American troops landed in a lightly held area of Bougainville, established a perimeter, built airfields, and did their best to ignore the sixty thousand Japanese elsewhere on the island. Cut off and overmatched, enemy units struggled fitfully on, some soldiers persisting until the end of the war and beyond.

Just over two hundred miles away, on their airfields near Rabaul, the Japanese steeled themselves to oppose the U.S. buildup on Bougainville, denuding several carriers and main bases to gather together a force of some 550 aircraft. It was a move

welcomed by American airmen, who relished the chance of bringing large numbers to battle. Heavy bombers from Kenney's Fifth Air Force joined the Thirteenth for raids against Rabaul and fighters harassed the Japanese unceasingly, both on the ground and in the air. By March 1944, the Japanese air forces based at Rabaul had been effectively destroyed, and Rabaul harbor had been wrecked, with many ships sunk. Few ground installations were intact, and most of the town's buildings were in ruins. Rabaul, with its 100,000-man garrison, had been rendered helpless and there was no longer any need

for a direct assault. U.S. commanders left it behind, cocooned in its uselessness, and turned their attention towards the Philippines.

Central Pacific

While the Fifth and Thirteenth Air Forces were building their combat reputations far to the southwest, Maj. Gen. Willis Hale's Seventh Air Force had remained quietly in Hawaii, regularly being asked to release units for service with its more heavily engaged cousins. In the fall of 1943, the Seventh's decline was halted by an in-

fusion of fresh units as U.S. forces prepared for their offensive in the Central Pacific, and, by November, Hale's B-24s were striking Japanese strongholds in the Gilberts and Marshalls from forward bases in the Ellice Islands.

The combat record of the Seventh is possibly the least well-known of any numbered air force. In the Central Pacific theater, the stars were the U.S. Navy's carriers. Nevertheless, the Seventh Air Force played an essential role for Admiral Nimitz as he drove his forces forward in a series of huge leaps, taking some islands and bypassing others. Nimitz knew that local air

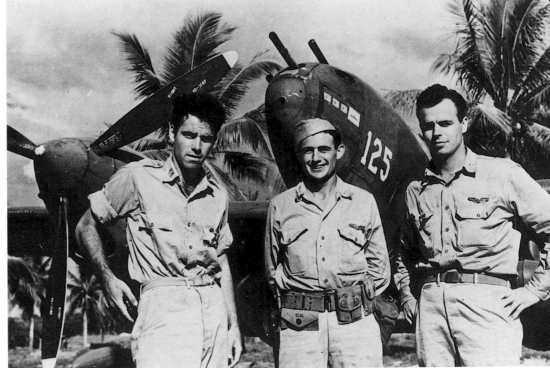

Three of the P-38 pilots from the attack section which shot down Admiral Yamamoto's "Betty" over Bougainville on April 18, 1943 —Thomas Lanphier, Besby Holmes, and Rex Barber. The fourth, Raymond Hine, was lost during the attack.

superiority was essential to the success of an invasion. The Seventh's bombers were used to batter enemy air bases in the area before an island assault, and Nimitz made it a priority to establish new bases as soon as possible for the USAAF's long-range aircraft so that they could begin reaching out to soften up the enemy for the next jump ahead. The Seventh also paid regular visits to bypassed Japanese garrisons, ensuring that they remained powerless to intervene in a war which had left them behind, frustrated and impotent.

In late 1944, P-61 Black Widows were deployed on Saipan, covering the buildup of the B-29 force in the Marianas.

In the three months following November 1943, U.S. amphibious forces swept forward through the Gilberts and the Marshalls, taking such key atolls as Tarawa, Kwajalein, and Eniwetok in fierce fighting against fanatical Japanese defenders. Moved to bases on Kwajalein and Eniwetok, the Seventh's bombers then joined the U.S. Navy in the reduction of Truk, one of the strongest Japanese naval bases in the Pacific. It was a task which occupied the Seventh until the end of the war, but long before then Truk had been rendered ineffective by constant battering from the air. Meanwhile, the Seventh also took part in the capture of the Marianas, supporting the assaults made on Saipan, Tinian, and Guam in June and July 1944. The first wave of Marines hit Saipan's beaches on June 15, and only a week later, with savage fighting still going on close by, aircraft of the Seventh were ashore, too. In a first for the USAAF, P-47s of the 19th FS were catapulted from the light carriers *Manila Bay* and *Natoma Bay* to land at Aslito (Isley) Field. Within days, they were joined by a second P-47 squadron, the 73rd FS, and the 6th Night FS, newly equipped with the P-61 Black Widow. The 333rd

FS (P-47s) arrived the following month, bringing the 318th FG up to full strength.

During the hours of daylight, the P-47s were fully occupied with standing air patrols, close support missions and fighter sweeps over neighboring Tinian and Guam, while the P-61s filled in by night. This was the first Central Pacific operation in which land-based fighters were used for close support of ground troops and they proved to be particularly versatile. From the outset, they could strafe with their .5 in machine guns, drop 500 lb bombs, and launch 4.5 in rockets. In the latter stages of the struggle they introduced a new weapon of fearful effect. Wing tanks filled with a petroleum mixture (napalm) dropped from 50 feet could each clear an area 200 feet long by 75 feet wide.

As the Marines began the first phase of the Saipan operation, the Japanese made a major effort to stop the American advance towards Japan once and for all. A formidable fleet had been gathered together, centered around three large and six smaller carriers with a total of some 450 aircraft between them. In addition, this force could be supported by over 500 land-based aircraft in the Marianas region. In

an enormous confrontation between Admiral Jisaburo Ozawa's Mobile Fleet and Admiral Raymond Spruance's Fifth Fleet, later known as the Battle of the Philippine Sea (or more colloquially by Americans as the "Great Marianas Turkey Shoot"), the back of Japanese naval air power was finally broken by the loss of three carriers and nearly 500 carrier-and land-based aircraft.

Although the last Japanese outpost on Guam did not fall until early September, the Marianas were declared secure by mid-August. American airfield construction crews were already at work building unusually long runways. The new B-29s were on the way and, from bases in the Marianas, these very heavy bombers would be able to raid the home islands of Japan. Another opportunity would be at hand to test strategic air power theories about defeating an enemy nation by bombing it into submission.

MacArthur's Return

To prepare for MacArthur's next move, U.S. forces established themselves on islands to the south and southeast of Mindanao, the southernmost main island of the Philippines. By October 1944, USAAF aircraft were operating from both Morotai and the Palaus. It had been intended that these bases would support MacArthur's invasion of Mindanao, but intelligence reports now suggested that the weakest point in the Japanese defense of the Philippines would be Leyte, in the center of the archipelago. Admiral Halsey, mixing metaphors in his enthusiasm, said that he believed the Japanese air force in the Philippines to be "a hollow shell operating on a shoestring." He suggested dropping all intermediate plans and going straight for Leyte. MacArthur seized the opportunity to bypass the large Japanese forces in Mindanao and U.S. troops went ashore in Leyte Gulf on October 20.

In spite of the awesome armada put together by the U.S. Navy for the operation,[3] General Kenney was not entirely happy. For the first time, his Far East Air Forces were based too far away to offer direct support to the landings. Air cover was provided by the carriers of the U.S. Third and Seventh Fleets, and their presence set the scene for the largest naval battle ever fought. Committing themselves once more to the "decisive battle" they had sought since Midway, the Japanese threw their ships into a desperate attempt to defeat the invasion. In the Battle of Leyte Gulf, which was actually a series of actions sometimes hundreds of miles apart, the Imperial Japanese Navy lost four carriers, three battleships, six cruisers, twelve destroyers, and all of its remaining front-line carrier-borne aircraft. As a significant fighting force, the IJN had ceased to exist.

On land, however, the Japanese were still capable of offering a serious threat. At the time of the Leyte Gulf landings, there were still some 450 Japanese combat aircraft on the island of Luzon, and reinforcements were being rushed forward from bases in Formosa and Japan. For the first few days after the U.S. troops were ashore, the beachhead was anything but secure. U.S. naval aircraft were there to provide air cover, but a horrifying new development made them understandably anxious about the protection of their own ships. Pilots from specially formed *kamikaze* units

had begun to sacrifice themselves, deliberately aiming to crash their bomb-laden aircraft into U.S. ships. In their initial operations they had already sunk one escort carrier and damaged several more, seriously reducing the U.S. Navy's capacity to provide the promised air cover over the troops. Aware of the problem, engineers opened a 2,800 ft airstrip at Tacloban by October 27. Thirty-four P-38s of the 49th FG flew in that day and were immediately in action.

Other units came in as the days went by, but until well into December 1944, when more airstrips became usable, the situation around Leyte Gulf had the USAAF men gritting their teeth. Japanese air raids on Tacloban were frequent, and they often caught U.S. aircraft on the ground. Losses to strafing attacks were distressingly high and requests for replacements commonplace. Combat also took its toll and, for a while, FEAF's front-line strength declined as losses from all causes exceeded replacements. In three months from September 1, P-38 holdings fell from 497 to 398; P-47s began with 429 in September, a figure which had become 257 plus 95 P-51s by the end of the year.

The other side of the coin was that the Japanese were much worse off. Loss rates in aerial combat invariably favored the USAAF, and FEAF fighters often wreaked havoc at enemy air bases. On November 1, for example, forty-two P-38s of the 8th FG swept over three airfields, shooting down seven enemy fighters in the air and destroying seventy-five more on the ground for the loss of three of their own. This was a period in which many Pacific fighter pilots added dramatically to their scores, with P-38 pilots leading the pack. Before the end of October, the 49th FG had claimed its five hundredth aerial victory, and by Christmas their leading ace, Richard Bong, had raised his personal total to forty.[4] Major Tommy McGuire of the 475th FG, who claimed thirty-eight before crashing during low-level combat over the Philippines, scored multiple victories on a single mission eleven times, and he was by no means unique. Robert Aschenbrenner, John Dunaway, William

Dunham, and Gerald R. Johnson[5] were among those who shot down four enemy aircraft in one sortie. Even more remarkable was the achievement of Capt. William Shomo and Lt. Paul Lipscomb of the 82nd Reconnaissance Squadron. Flying F-6s (P-51s) as a pair on January 11, 1945, they attacked a formation of twelve fighters escorting a Betty bomber. Neither had been in combat before, but when the fight was over Shomo had shot down the Betty and six fighters, and Lipscomb had added three more.[6]

With FEAF units established on Leyte, MacArthur's next move, to the island of Mindoro in mid-December 1944, followed the reassuring pattern of the New Guinea campaign, with the ground forces fighting under the umbrella of their own air forces. Even so, since the Japanese still had ships and aircraft operating in the area, they were occasionally able to make things difficult. Indeed, on December 26 the U.S. beachhead on Mindoro would have been seriously jeopardized but for the determination of the 310th Wing squadrons, which had just arrived on rudimentary strips nearby. As night fell, a Japanese naval unit comprising two cruisers and six destroyers appeared offshore with the intention of sinking the Allied transports and shelling the beachhead area. Every aircraft on strength was hurled into a low-level assault on the ships—thirteen B-25s, forty-four P-38s, twenty-eight P-47s, and twenty P-40s. Attacks in the darkness were necessarily uncoordinated, and in the glaring confusion of gunfire and bomb-bursts, pilots flashed navigation lights in the hope of avoiding collisions. By the morning, the badly mauled Japanese force was withdrawing, minus one destroyer, having sunk one transport but failing to disrupt the landing operations. A victory had been won and the troops protected, but at considerable cost to the airmen—lost during the

---

[3]Third Fleet (Admiral Halsey)—106 warships. Seventh Fleet (Admiral Kinkaid)—57 combat ships and 581 other vessels.

[4]Major Richard Bong was presented with the Medal of Honor by General MacArthur at Tacloban on December 12, 1944. After his fortieth victory, he was retired from combat and returned to the U.S. Bong was killed only eight months later while testing the new P-80 jet fighter in California.

[5]Major Gerald R. Johnson was credited with twenty-two victories and survived the war. Shortly afterwards, on October 7, 1945, he was in a B-17 on his way to Japan when it was damaged in a violent storm. He gave up his parachute to a passenger and was lost with the aircraft.

[6]Shomo was awarded the Medal of Honor and Lipscomb the Distinguished Service Cross.

action were three B-25s, seven P-38s, ten P-47s, and six P-40s. A grateful Brig. Gen. Dunckel, commander of the task force, wrote: "The action of our air units on that night will stand forever as one of the most gallant deeds to be established in the traditions of American fighting men."

Mindoro was a staging post for the later invasion of the main island of Luzon. The landing was the largest American amphibious operation of the war, with 175,000 men covering a beachhead twenty miles wide. Aircraft of the fleet's escort carriers did their best to counter the threat from *kamikazes*, but even so many got through, sinking an escort carrier, a destroyer, and ten other vessels, and damaging sixty-seven more. The *kamikaze* onslaught eased off only when the Japanese ran out of resources. Their own self-destructive methods, together with a combined USN and USAAF campaign against airfields on Luzon, reduced Japanese air power in the Philippines to impotence.

MacArthur's troops went ashore in Lingayen Gulf on January 9, 1945, with the reassuring presence of Kenney's fighters overhead. Although the struggle for Luzon proved a long and bloody one, U.S. soldiers were never again unduly bothered by Japanese aircraft. FEAF was able to concentrate on providing the ground forces with the support they needed to win the land battle. The campaign was characterized by overwhelming U.S. air power. B-24s hammered strongpoints; B-25s, A-20s, P-38s, P-40s, P-47s, and P-51s strafed, rocketed, bombed, and napalmed Japanese troops; L-5s marked targets; P-61s harassed by night; C-47s kept forward units supplied and dropped paratroops to speed the ground offensive. It was a virtuoso performance, later singled out for comment by the Joint Chiefs of Staff: "Of the many Pacific tactical air operations, we think the most striking example of the effective use of tactical air power . . . to achieve decisive results at a minimum cost in lives and materiel was the work of the Far East Air Forces in the Lingayen Gulf-Central Luzon campaign."

The embers of Japanese resistance smoldered on in the Philippines until the

Richard Bong, the American "ace of aces," with his P-38 Marge. *He was withdrawn from combat after scoring forty aerial victories. Bong was killed in a P-80 crash near Burbank, California, on August 6, 1945.*

end of the war, and many of MacArthur's troops were kept occupied in operations which, in terms of the strategic aim of defeating Japan, were not strictly necessary. Having bypassed many enemies and left them isolated, U.S. and Australian troops now found themselves turning aside to engage in bitter battles to crush the Japanese dug in on the outer islands of the Philippines and on Borneo. Savage though many of these were, they were sideshows. The eyes of the Pacific theater's commanders now turned to the north, where the curtain raisers to the main event were being prepared, with strategic air power moving towards center stage.

CBI Affairs

For reasons both geographical and political, the China/Burma/India theater of the war was not given the same priority by the Allies as Europe and the Pacific. It was the most difficult region to reach and supply, and Allied leaders did not always feel entirely comfortable in dealing with the Chiang Kai-shek regime. For the U.S., the idea of being involved in a struggle which seemed likely to return a number of colonial territories to their former European rulers was not appealing. Nevertheless, there was general agreement on the importance of keeping China in the war, and of preventing the Japanese from pur-

suing their expansionist ambitions into India.

The fall of Burma, and particularly the loss of the northern base of Myitkyina in May 1942, effectively cut China off from the western Allies. The only way of supplying the Chinese was by air from bases in India, with transport aircraft flying across the Himalayas to Kunming. With Myitkyina in enemy hands, this aerial supply route was forced further north over (and through) much higher mountains, and heavily laden aircraft were often wallowing along at heights up to 18,000 ft. The contrast between the steamy heat of the Indian plains and the freezing temperatures at altitude was hard on both men and machines, and, for much of the year, crews faced violent storms, heavy rain, and the threat of ice along the route, sometimes flying blind for hours in aircraft fitted with the most basic of instrument panels and radio aids. Icing or loss of power spelled disaster, and even a successful crossing could precede a perilous arrival if, as was frequently the case during the monsoon, the destination airfield was covered with water. Flying the "Hump," as it was known, was recognized as being among the most hazardous of occupations for a military airman.

To begin with, the airlift for the Chinese was handled by a few transport aircraft organized into what was known as the Assam-Burma-China Ferry Command, the last stage in the longest supply chain in the world, starting in Miami and traveling via the Atlantic, North Africa, and the Middle East to Karachi and Assam. By the end of 1942, the responsibility for controlling the increasing numbers of aircraft crossing the "Hump" had passed to Air Transport Command, a reflection of the dominant role of air supply in a theater of operations which lacked all but the most basic systems of communication yet exceeded by a considerable margin the size of the United States.

Meanwhile, Maj. Gen. Lewis Brereton had been ordered to India in March 1942 to establish the Tenth Air Force. It was the latest stage in Brereton's westward progress. He had spent the war so far retreating through the Philippines and the Dutch East Indies in front of the victorious Japanese and he must have felt a little discouraged at the scale of the problems he again faced in his new command. The Tenth was intended to supply the Chinese (until ATC assumed responsibility at the end of 1942), defend the "Hump" route and its airfields, and help the British fight the Japanese in Burma. To tackle this monumental task, he had an air force only on paper. The combat aircraft available were a few aging B-17s and P-40s, and there seemed little prospect of getting more in the near future. Brereton wrestled with the problem until June, when he was told to pack his bags again and move to Egypt, this time to take command of U.S. air forces in the Middle East and help the British against the Germans. He duly left, taking his B-17s with him. The Tenth reverted to being an air force without teeth.

A few teeth were inherited by the Tenth Air Force in July 1942 when Claire Chennault's AVG was transformed into a regular element of the USAAF. However, the ex-Flying Tigers added to the bite of the Tenth in name only. Although on its strength, they remained in effect independent, forming the core of a new organization called the China Air Task Force. Commander of the CATF was the AVG's Brig. Gen. Chennault, recalled to duty with the USAAF. A few of his pilots had elected to join him in the move, and they brought their battered P-40s and the benefit of their combat experience to the newly arrived 23rd FG. Seven B-25s of the 7th BG gave the CATF a little striking power.

The CATF was never very big, but the challenges and hardships it faced must have been fertile ground for developing remarkable characters, because it seems to have had more than its share. The 23rd FG was commanded by Col. Bob Scott, later author of the book: *God Is My Copilot*. Two of the squadrons were commanded by aces from the AVG, Tex Hill and Ed Rector. In 1943, Tex Hill, then commander of the 23rd FG, led one of the most successful raids of the war in China, striking Shinchiku airfield on Formosa with a force of fourteen B-25s, eight P-38s, and eight

P-51s and destroying over forty Japanese aircraft without loss. Later members of the 23rd FG included Don Lopez, who gained his first aerial victory over a Zero by surviving a head-on attack driven through to collision, and John Alison, who decided to experiment with night interceptions in his P-40 and succeeded in destroying two bombers and damaging another at his first attempt. Badly shot up and with the P-40 on fire, he lived through a night ditching in a river and swam ashore.

Chennault lost no opportunity to promote his belief that air power was the only practical way to fight the Japanese in China. This put him at odds with the senior U.S. officer in the theater, Lt. Gen. "Vinegar Joe" Stilwell, an infantryman, who insisted that the Allied cause would best be served by concentrating on a ground offensive into northern Burma. As the Allied Chiefs preferred to continue with both options, limited resources were split between the two, and neither was given what they considered adequate for the tasks at hand. However, Chennault's persistence, and his unabashed use of political channels via Chiang Kai-shek, led to the formation of the Fourteenth Air Force from the elements of the CATF, at the direction of President Roosevelt and against the advice of Generals Marshall and

Arnold. In the process, Chennault advanced to Major General.

Following the constitution of the Fourteenth Air Force in March 1943, the fortunes of American airmen in China gradually began to improve. Combat units, equipment, and supplies began to flow more generously across the "Hump." Even so, apart from the Eleventh in Alaska, the Fourteenth remained the smallest of the U.S. numbered air forces throughout the war, reaching a maximum strength of a little over seven hundred combat aircraft early in 1945. As the Fourteenth grew in size, it acquired P-38s, P-51s, B-24s, and more and newer B-25s. Chennault established a series of bases in southern China and adopted an aggressive operational policy. The Fourteenth struck at Japanese ports and bases in China and Indochina, harassed shipping along the Asian coast, mined harbors, attacked enemy airfields, supported Chinese troops, interdicted Japanese supply lines, and fought the Japanese Air Force for air superiority over China. Badly hurt by these efforts and fearing further expansion of U.S. air power, the Japanese launched a massive assault into southern China in 1944 to deny the Fourteenth its airfields and open up internal communications between Southeast Asia and Japan. By the end of the year,

Two potent symbols of the 14th AF in China. A C-46, mainstay of the aerial supply line over the "Hump," lands near a P-40 of the 23rd FG, the unit which inherited the mantle of the AVG "Flying Tigers."

Hap Arnold visited China in January 1943 and met Claire Chennault. He judged Chennault to be a formidable fighting man but a poor administrator. He also believed that the prickly "Flying Tiger" too often represented the interests of Chiang Kai-shek rather than the U.S.

they had rolled over the demoralized Chinese armies facing them and had taken thirteen of the U.S. bases, forcing the Fourteenth back towards Kunming and limiting its operations in East China. Japanese troops had suffered badly under air attack, but never enough to stall their advance.

Seriously concerned, Chiang Kai-shek appealed for help to Stilwell, who was heavily occupied with his Burma campaign. The general was reluctant to leave Burma and his intransigence led to his being recalled to Washington. His replacement as Commanding General, U.S. Forces in the China Theater, was Lt. Gen. Albert Wedemeyer. He took over at the end of October 1943, and soon agreed to return Chinese troops from Burma in preparation for a counteroffensive in the spring of 1945. From May 1945, the reorganized Chinese Army, closely supported by American tactical aircraft, first checked the Japanese and then drove them back. Napalm and the concentrated fire of .5 in caliber machine guns were the most effective methods of reducing Japanese strongpoints. By the end of July, central China and the coast were almost completely free of Japanese forces and thought was being given to continuing the offen-

sive to the north. Within days, however, the need disappeared with the surrender of Japan. As the fighting in China ground to a halt, the men of the Fourteenth were left with the feeling that they had fought their war on the fringes. Hard as they had struggled to overcome the enemy, the elements, their living conditions, the convoluted command chain, and the low priorities accorded them by their friends and allies, it was clear that they had not occupied center stage. The core of the Allied victory over the Japanese was in the Pacific. Their satisfaction came from the knowledge of a job well done, and in an accolade from an enemy soldier, General Kakuichi Takahashi, who said that, but for the Fourteenth Air Force, "we could have gone anywhere we wished."

Chennault was not there to join in the victory celebrations with his airmen. General Arnold's patience with his unconventional subordinate had come to an end. In June 1945, Arnold wrote to General Wedemeyer, saying:

"General Chennault has been in China for a long period of time fighting a defensive air war with minimum resources. The meagerness of supplies and the resulting guerrilla type of warfare must change to a modern type of striking, offensive air power. I firmly believe that the quickest and most effective way to change air warfare in your Theater, employing modern offensive thought, tactics and techniques, is to change commanders. I would appreciate your concurrence in General Chennault's early withdrawal from the China Theater."

At the same time, Arnold offered a plan for reorganizing the air forces in China. Chennault entered a vigorous protest against the whole idea, but the die was cast and he grudgingly put forward his request for retirement on July 6.

While Chennault had been creating his own air force and fighting his own kind of war, the Tenth Air Force had been wrestling with equally challenging problems. Shortly after the CATF was formed as an element of the Tenth to give Chennault his freedom of action, Brig. Gen. Clayton Bissell, the Tenth's new commander, cre-

ated a similar organization for the India/Burma region. The India Air Task Force was activated on October 3, 1942, and immediately had to face the fact that not one of its nine allocated squadrons was capable of combat operations. Several either had no aircraft or were not yet even in the theater. Matters improved very slowly, and it was not only a matter of supply. Throughout their time in the CBI, USAAF commands and units operated under a tangled web of national and service rivalries as well as suffering the handicap of being at the bottom of a long priority list. Chains of command were duplicated and tasks complicated to a degree unknown in other theaters. In 1943 it was decided by Generals Marshall and Arnold that a senior airman should be appointed to the CBI to straighten things out in the theater generally. Almost immediately, objections from Chiang Kai-shek led to the concession that there would be no interference in his direct relations with Chennault, and it had to be accepted that the new commander would have only advisory responsibility towards the Fourteenth Air Force.

In August 1943, Maj. Gen. George Stratemeyer assumed command of all USAAF units in the India/Burma sector of the CBI. At the time, this amounted to little more than the Tenth Air Force, then commanded by Brig. Gen. Howard Davidson. Recognizing the limitations of the position and the complexity of the overlapping organizational arrangements and regional politics, Arnold warned Stratemeyer: "This new command setup and your relationships . . . are somewhat complicated and will have to be worked out to a great extent among yourselves. . . If a true spirit of cooperation is engendered throughout this command, it will work. If the reverse is true, it is doomed to failure."[7]

As 1943 drew to a close, there were more organizational changes. To rationalize the operations of USAAF and RAF units in the IBS, they were integrated under a new headquarters called Eastern Air Command, with Stratemeyer as the commander. All Allied air force combat units in the IBS having been joined together, he separated them again, this time functionally under strategic, tactical, troop carrier, and reconnaissance headings. Davidson of the Tenth drew the strategic force, while the tactical aircraft, as the Third Tactical Air Force, went to his RAF opposite number, Air Marshal Sir John Baldwin. Addressing his new command, Stratemeyer emphasized the need for them to "merge into one unified force in thought and deed—a force neither British nor American, with the faults of neither and the virtues of both."

The latter half of 1943 had seen a marked increase in the number of combat units available to the Allies in the IBS. The American contribution in 1943 had risen to include five complete groups—80th FG, 311th F/BG, 7th BG(H), 341st BG(M), 5306th PRG—and four troop carrier squadrons, and more groups joined them in 1944. As Allied air power grew, so did the determination to use it to wrest the initiative from the enemy. Bombers struck at transportation targets, military airfields, ports, and supply dumps, and fighters strafed Japanese forward airfields and began to inflict serious losses in the air. The struggle in the air shifted in the Allies favor in early 1944, and by the spring Allied air superiority was an accomplished fact.

Without Allied air superiority, two major campaigns by ground forces in March 1944 would probably have had very different conclusions. On March 10, a Japanese offensive against the British Army near Imphal and Kohima on the Indian-Burmese border threatened to overwhelm the defenders. Large numbers of British and Indian troops were surrounded and were able to hold out only because reinforcements and essential supplies were flown in daily for weeks. The air transport force was augmented by troop carriers from as far away as the European theater, and a total of more than twenty thousand tons was delivered, plus the better part of two divisions of infantry. By June the British Army was strong enough to go over to the

offensive. With the constant support of EAC tactical aircraft, the British Fourteenth Army under General Sir William Slim broke out and inflicted a decisive defeat on the enemy, driving them into a retreat which degenerated into a rout. Before the assault, Slim announced that his whole plan of battle was based on Allied air support, and Japanese radio broadcasts later openly attributed their difficulties in Burma to Allied "air supremacy" and to the work of the troop carrier squadrons.

At almost the same time that the Japanese struck at Imphal, the Allies launched a very different offensive of their own. In early 1943, Brigadier Orde Wingate, a British officer who specialized in unconventional operations, had led a force of three thousand men into the jungles behind Japanese lines, causing confusion and disrupting communications for four months. The experiment was now repeated, but on a much larger scale and this time supported by aircraft. The proposal for Wingate's Long-Range Penetration Group (the "Chindits") was accepted by the Allied leaders at the Quebec conference in August 1943, and General Arnold had agreed that the USAAF would provide the necessary air power. Colonels Philip Cochran and John Alison were given a free hand to form a special air task force, and they put together the First Air Com-

mandos to operate under the control of General Stratemeyer's EAC.

The First Air Commando Force was carefully tailored for the task with a remarkably varied collection of aircraft—thirteen C-47s, twelve C-46s, 150 CG-4 gliders, seventy-five TG-4 gliders, one hundred L1/L5s, six YR-4 helicopters, thirty P-51As, and twelve B-25Hs. The operation began on the evening of March 5, 1944, when the transports and gliders took off to deliver the first soldiers to a large jungle clearing, code named BROADWAY, over one hundred miles deep into Japanese-held territory. Each transport had to act as tug for two gliders, and that led to early problems. The gliders were overloaded and the C-47 tugs struggled up to 10,000 ft to haul them over the rugged Naga Hills. Turbulent conditions compounded the difficulties and several gliders parted from their tugs, either having broken their tow ropes or been cast adrift by alarmed pilots. Less than half of the sixty-seven gliders dispatched arrived at BROADWAY, and most of those crashed in the process of making a landing after dark on a very rough surface. Of the men who got there, thirty-one were killed and thirty injured. Nevertheless, 539 men, three mules, and nearly 66,000 lbs of stores arrived safely and that was enough to get things started. Among those ready to go was John Alison, who had set aside his

An Air Commando B-25H after attacking Wunto, Burma, on March 18, 1944.

7 The limitations of his position having been revealed to him, Stratemeyer also discovered that in time no less than seven lines of command had found their way to his chair from above-Roosevelt, Marshall, Arnold, Stilwell, Chiang Kai-shek, Mountbatten (Supreme Commander, SE Asia), and Peirse (Air Commander, SE Asia) were all entitled to give him orders.

229

British M.Gen. Orde Wingate, the eccentric leader of the "Chindits" in Burma, with Phil Cochran (right), CO of the Air Commandos, and a smiling John Alison, who led the glider force into Japanese held territory on March 5, 1944.

fighter background to become a glider pilot for the operation. His cargo included the flying control equipment he needed for handling later flights and a bulldozer for leveling an airstrip. L-5s came in the next morning for the casualties, and by the following night the strip was cleared; a procession of C-47s began flying in with many more men and much more equipment. A second strip, named Chowringhee, was opened a few miles away for a while, and by March 11 the Air Commandos had delivered over 9,000 men, nearly 1,400 mules, and almost 260 tons of stores to set Wingate's offensive in motion.

By any standards, it had been an extraordinary achievement, but one which Wingate did not live to see rewarded. On March 25, he was killed in the crash of a B-25 flying from BROADWAY back to Imphal. For the next few weeks, his Chindits roamed the jungle in a number of columns and, supplied by air, harassed and confused the Japanese, cutting their supply lines to forward units. Cochran's P-51s and B-25s operated on call for close support missions and raided Japanese forward airfields, taking a heavy toll of enemy aircraft on the ground. The B-25Hs were impressive, firing their 75 mm cannon and dropping parafrag bombs on Japanese soldiers in close contact with British troops. A British patrol found a message written by a Japanese officer which recorded his despair over the relentless attentions of the Air Commandos. Unless something was done about the U.S. aircraft, he said, his operation was doomed. Flesh and blood, he insisted, could not stand up to them.

Meanwhile, Stilwell had driven his "New China Army" down the Hukawng Valley into northern Burma and a unit of U.S. special forces known as "Merrill's Marauders" had accomplished an astonishing forced march through jungles and over mountains to take the airfield at Myitkyina. For their success, both advances had been heavily dependent on air supply, a luxury not available to their often starving and poorly equipped enemies.

By mid-1944, the Japanese armies in Burma were reeling back on all fronts. Monsoon weather and the stubborn endurance of the Japanese soldier prolonged the war in Burma into 1945, but the final result was never again in doubt. In the end, the campaign was a triumph for the foot soldiers, who overcame appalling hardships to defeat their enemy. However, it was clear that their victories had been built on air power, and most notably on the achievements of the air transport force. Nowhere else had C-47s and C-46s so obviously turned the tide of battle. Allied commanders began to realize that even large forces, isolated by facts of geography or cut off by the enemy, could survive if supplied by air. When counterair operations denied the enemy the same facility, victory was only a matter of time. An entry in a Japanese officer's diary put it most succinctly:

"Enemy aircraft are over continuously in all weather. We can do nothing but look at them. If we only had air power! Even one or two planes would be something. Superiority in the air is the decisive factor in victory."

The Destruction of Japan

In the late 1930s, a few visionary air planners were already thinking of a strategic bomber which would be a generational improvement over the B-17 and the B-24. In November 1939, General Arnold formally proposed the development of such an aircraft, and in September 1942 two contenders took to the air. The Consolidated XB-32 was the first to fly, but an early crash and design difficulties prevented the B-32 from seeing combat until the closing days of the war, and then only in very small numbers. The other prototype was Boeing's XB-29, which had problems enough of its own, but was nevertheless the first step towards the production of the B-29 Superfortress, one of the war's most

The Chindit force landed at BROADWAY, a clearing 150 miles behind Japanese lines in Burma, in Waco CG-4 gliders, most of which were destroyed or heavily damaged in the process.

significant aircraft.

Urgency brought priority to development, and that forced a compression of the program, with the result that the B-29 was ordered into production with more than its share of teething troubles. Before the XB-29 even flew, 1,664 aircraft had been ordered on the strength of blueprints and a wooden mock-up. Pressurized crew compartments, new construction techniques, remotely controlled guns, and, most critically, new radial engines of unprecedented power—all were rushed into front-line service harboring problems for aircrew and mechanics to overcome in the field.

In 1940, air force planners believed that VLR (Very Long-Range) bombers would be primarily engaged in bombing Germany by 1944. Positive developments in Europe and the relatively poor situation of the Allies in the CBI brought about a shift in policy by late 1943. Japan became the more likely target for the B-29, situated as it was in a region of few bases and vast distances. As the date of the B-29's operational debut drew nearer, HQ USAAF was besieged by requests from commanders who believed that the new bomber's capabilities would be best exploited in their theater. To avoid argument and recrimination, and to prevent B-29s being wasted on missions for which they were not designed, General Arnold decided to form a new air force specifically for the B-29, and to keep it under his own command. Accordingly, the Twentieth Air Force came into being on April 4, 1944.

The organization of the B-29 front line began somewhat earlier, in June 1943, with the formation of the 58th Bombardment Wing at Salina, Kansas. XX Bomber Command followed in November, with Brig. Gen. Kenneth Wolfe, the officer responsible for the B-29 production program, as its commander. Operational deployment had to wait a while, as solutions were sought to training and logistical problems. The sheer size of a B-29 unit gave an indication of what had to be faced. A B-29 had a crew of eleven, and there were up to 180 aircraft in a wing. With a double crew allocation and its full maintenance

establishment, the total personnel in a wing reached 11,112, including 3,045 officers. When XX Bomber Command went to war, it moved with more than 20,000 officers and men. Accommodating and feeding them on the far side of the world was difficult enough, and the added challenge of operating and maintaining over a hundred very large and untried bombers from a deployment base produced a wing task which was truly monumental.

MATTERHORN was the code name given to the plan for a bombing offensive against Japan, using B-29s based in India and operating through forward airfields in China. The first of the big

B-29s of XXI BC pass Mt. Fujiyama on their way to Japanese targets.

bombers arrived at its base near Kharagpur, India, on April 2, 1944. There followed long weeks of preparing the Chinese airfields near Chengtu for operations. Fuel, armaments, and spares had to be prepositioned, and, since transport aircraft were scarce, the crews of the 58th BW (VH—for "Very Heavy") found themselves doing their own airlift. On average, it took eight B-29 "freighter" flights into Chengtu to support one operational sortie. When all was ready, the first combat mission was flown on June 5—but it did not go through China. The target was a railway repair shop in Bangkok.

The Bangkok mission was flown as a dress rehearsal for what was to follow. It

was not a polished performance. Of the ninety-eight B-29s which set out at dawn, one crashed on takeoff, fourteen aborted, and several others failed to find the target. Cloud defeated attempts to fly any sort of formation and many aircraft made their way to Bangkok separately. One hour and forty minutes went by between the passage of the first and last of the seventy-seven crews claiming to have bombed the target, forty-eight of which did so by radar. The Japanese defense was feeble and there were no combat losses. On the return trip, however, mechanical failures took their toll before bad weather and fuel shortages joined in to scatter B-29s over a wide area, two in the Bay of Bengal and more than forty at airfields other than their own. Five B-29s were lost and fifteen crewmen killed, a high cost for the placing of less than twenty bombs within the target area. XX Bomber Command put on a brave face over the results, saying that a great deal of experience had been gained from operating the B-29 under combat conditions. Any thought of becoming more critical was swept aside by an urgent message from Arnold. A maximum effort was required for a raid on Japan. It was time for the B-29 to get on with the real war.

Strenuous efforts were made by all concerned to turn MATTERHORN into a success, but the conditions under which the operation labored were too difficult. The first B-29 raid on Japan was indicative of the problem. Eighty-three bombers were gathered together at Chengtu for a mission to strike the Yawata steel works. Sixty-eight got airborne on the evening of June 15, aiming to be over the target close to midnight. Forty-seven of them bombed Yawata and seven more unloaded elsewhere. Seven B-29s were lost, only one of them to enemy activity, and fifty-five men died. Just one bomb hit the target area, and that was over half a mile from the aiming point. If concrete results were poor, there were some intangibles to consider.

and in September, Maj. Gen. Curt LeMay arrived from Europe to grip the problem of making XX Bomber Command more effective. Squadrons were reorganized, tactics were changed, and occasionally results were good, but aircraft losses continued and there were times when results were abysmal. By October 1944, airfields in the Marianas were ready for B-29s, and with that preferred alternative available it became possible to accept that the operations through Chengtu were a poor return on the investment of men and materials. Weather, geography, and logistics had limited the 58th BW(VH) to just forty-nine

Haywood "Possum" Hansell brought the first B-29 into the Marianas, landing *Joltin' Josie, the Pacific Pioneer* on the vast new Saipan base. Hansell had been one of the principal planners of the air assault on Japan, and he was now to lead XXI Bomber Command, which was being formed to spearhead the offensive. The 73rd BW (VH) provided XXI BC's cutting edge. Training missions were flown against Truk and other Japanese-held islands, and, after some preliminary photographic sorties by F-13s (a strategic reconnaissance version of the B-29), the 73rd aimed its first bombing mission at Japan on November 24. The target directive from the Joint Chiefs of Staff put aircraft assembly and engine plants at the top of the priority list, and the Nakajima engine factory in Tokyo was the first selected. As had been the case with the raids by the 58th BW (VH), weather and mechanical problems had their effect on the raid and the results were disappointing. Only two B-29s were lost, but, ominously, one of them went down after what appeared to be a deliberate ramming by a Japanese fighter pilot.

With few exceptions, the B-29 raids followed strategic bombing's conventional wisdom for the next three months. Attacks were generally made in daylight from high altitude, and they were planned as precision strikes on specific targets, usually in the aircraft industry. Reconnaissance revealed that very little damage was being done, and XXI BC reported a now familiar list of shortcomings, among them the slow buildup of the B-29 force, bad weather, poor bombing accuracy, mechanical problems leading to a high abort rate and to aircraft losses, and a lack of escort fighters. Nevertheless, the raids had disturbed the Japanese sufficiently for them to strike back at Isley Field on Saipan with aircraft from Iwo Jima, destroying several B-29s on the ground.

Impatient for better results, Arnold intervened, sending LeMay to replace Hansell as commander of XXI BC in January 1945. LeMay brought his usual energy

Maj. Gen. Curt LeMay (left) moved to Guam and took over XXI Bomber Command from Brig. Gen. Haywood Hansell in January 1945. Brig. Gen. Roger Ramey (right), who had been serving as Hansell's chief of staff, moved to India to take LeMay's place at XX Bomber Command.

American bombs had fallen on Japan for the first time since the Doolittle raid more than two years before, and the Japanese were deeply concerned. In the U.S., the news was received enthusiastically. B-29s competed with the Normandy beachheads for the front pages of the newspapers.

MATTERHORN struggled on for the rest of the year, with the B-29s striking both at Japan and at a number of targets in Southeast Asia. Wolfe, an excellent logistician and engineer, returned to the U.S. to sort out B-29 production problems,

missions, less than half of them against Japan, and an average of only two sorties per aircraft per month. Of course, there were some positive aspects to MATTERHORN. Operational lessons had been learned, crews had become familiar with the B-29, and many "bugs" had been driven from the aircraft. But the support costs had been prohibitive, and so had the loss of 147 B-29s by the end of the year, the majority of them not attributable to enemy action.[8]

On October 12, 1944, Brig. Gen.

---

[8]At least three B-29s survived emergency landings in the USSR. The aircraft were not returned and were copied as the Tu-4 bomber and the Tu-70 transport.

to making changes aimed at improving aircraft maintenance and aircrew training, but initially the operational pattern remained the same. Daylight precision attacks continued to be made, dropping high-explosive bombs from above 20,000 ft, and the results were little better than before. At the request of Twentieth Air Force, a couple of experimental raids were made with the B-29s carrying only incendiaries. These were also from high altitude and did not produce much more encouraging results, although a few promising fires were started. By the time February arrived, XXI BC was nearing a crisis. Two things happened to deflect it. The first was another island assault by the U.S. Marines some 725 miles north of Saipan, and the other was a radical change in B-29 bombing tactics.

Japanese aircraft on Iwo Jima had posed a threat to the U.S. bases in the Marianas from the start. Raids were launched from there against B-29s on the ground, and Iwo's fighters intercepted the bombers on their way to Japan or forced them to dogleg, thereby using more fuel and reducing bombloads. If no interception took place, radar on Iwo still gave early warning to the Japanese mainland of the B-29's approach. Even taken together, these threats did not amount to much and hardly justified Iwo's capture, but the benefits to U.S. forces of taking the island were considerable. Deploying U.S. fighters on Iwo's airfields would allow the B-29s to operate over Japan under escort, and the runways there would be available for emergency use by bombers either damaged or struggling home with a mechanical failure. Equally important, Iwo would be a forward base for air/sea rescue units, which had already proved to be an essential element of B-29 missions against Japan.

The Marines went ashore at Iwo Jima on February 19, 1945, setting off a bloody battle which raged until the island was declared secure in the middle of March. On March 6, P-51s of the Seventh Air Force's[9] 15th FG began arriving on Iwo's South Field, and were soon in action, often taking off under fire to give close support to the nearby Marines. Later in the month, they were followed by the 21st

FG, and by the P-61s of the 548th and 549th Night Fighter Squadrons. As it happened, the fighter squadrons did not contribute as much as had been expected as escorts for the B-29s. By the time they were ready to fly escort missions, the air defense of Japan was already deteriorating, and, in any case, the B-29s were operating much more frequently by night. Iwo's true value proved to be as an emergency way station for ailing bombers, and as such it was in frequent use.

Early in March, LeMay made a decision which defied conventional theories on how to use USAAF strategic bombers.

The B-29 had been designed to conform to the ideas of those dedicated to daylight precision bombing, and plans for its employment against Japan had naturally been based on classic AAF doctrines. LeMay himself had fought under those doctrines in Europe, but his mind was not closed to other ways of doing things, and his obser-

vations since taking command of XXI BC convinced him that B-29 operations had to change if they were to play a decisive part in the defeat of Japan. In his view, the B-29's ineffectiveness was the result of several factors, most of them attributable to flying at high altitude in daylight. If the missions went in at lower levels at night, it seemed to him probable that a number of benefits would follow. Elimination of the climb to maximum altitude would save fuel, reducing the weight of fuel carried and increasing the bombload. Operating at low altitude would save wear and tear on the engines and perhaps cure the en-

B-29s being serviced on Guam between missions. The 18-cylinder Wright R-3350s gave 2,200 hp but were temperamental, suffering repeated fires.

gine fires which were one of the B-29's greatest problems. It was also true that Japan's day defenses had been improving and the B-29 loss rate was rising. Japan's night defenses were thought to be poor, and LeMay believed that even flak would not offer a serious threat. He also felt that, in spite of the inconclusive results from the experimental raids flown so far, Japan's wood and paper cities ought to be susceptible to incendiary attack and that the quickest way to destroy many of the Japanese war industries would be to burn them

[9]During the latter part of 1944 the Army Air Forces, Pacific Ocean Areas, had been formed under the command of General Harmon, who was also Deputy Commander, Twentieth Air Force. Harmon's new HQ provided the necessary support services for XXI Bomber Command besides being the superior HQ for Seventh Air Force, the latter nearing the end of its island hopping progress across the Pacific. Harmon himself disappeared without trace into the Pacific on February 25, 1945 while on a flight to Washington. He was succeeded by Maj. Gen. Willis Hale.

B-29s in tight formation for mutual protection during a daylight raid on Japan. LeMay introduced attacks by night and from much lower altitudes.

out, since most of them were integral parts of built-up areas.

These conclusions having been reached, LeMay showed his decisiveness. He issued a field order for an operation to take place on March 9. It was to be a maximum effort, flown by night at low-level. Fuel was to be limited to take account of the new flight parameters and gun ammunition was not to be carried, so allowing bombloads (exclusively incendiary) to increase to about six tons per aircraft. The order raised expectations and pulse rates throughout LeMay's command. Even he must have felt a tremor of nervous excitement. He had turned the B-29 world upside down and the responsibility for the risks of the operation rested squarely on his own shoulders. General Arnold was not consulted; he was merely informed of LeMay's intentions on the day before the raid.

By this time three wings of B-29s were operating from Saipan, Tinian, and Guam—the 73rd, 313th, 314th BWs. A force of 334 bombers was assembled and Tokyo was attacked from altitudes between 4,900 and 9,200 ft. The first bombs fell just after midnight and fires started immediately, spreading quickly in a brisk surface wind. As the B-29s fanned out to cover unburnt areas, new fires sprang up and

merged with those already blazing. Later aircraft reported having difficulty because of flying through dense smoke and severe turbulence generated by the intense heat. The fire grew into one of the greatest urban conflagrations in history, consuming almost sixteen square miles of the city and destroying over a quarter of a million buildings. For the Japanese, the scale of the catastrophe defied belief. More than a million people were homeless and over eighty thousand dead. It was the most destructive air raid of the war, unsurpassed in the European or Pacific theaters.

Fourteen B-29s were shot down and forty-two damaged by flak during the Tokyo raid, which LeMay, remembering the severity of his European experience, felt to be a moderate price to pay for striking such a heavy blow. He felt his judgment had been justified, and he immediately ordered a similar strike against the city of Nagoya. Before the end of March, Osaka and Kobe had also been scorched by fire raids and the damage inflicted was such that LeMay knew he had been right. He had in his hand a weapon capable of realizing the apocalyptic strategic air power theories of Douhet, Mitchell, and Trenchard, one which could indeed destroy the fabric of an enemy nation.

Plans were made for the burning of

Japan to continue, and a list of cities intended for systematic destruction was prepared. The need to defeat Japan as quickly as possible was paramount and, since precision bombing had failed, it was, for the time being, set aside in favor of area attack. LeMay was impatient to get the job done, and he proposed driving his crews harder than ever, raising their combat flying hours to eighty per month, a far greater rate than had ever been attempted in Europe. His eagerness was at least in part sparked by the thought that his B-29s could ensure victory not only over Japan but also for the concept of strategic air power. In a letter to Brig. Gen. Lauris Norstad, Chief of Staff at Twentieth Air Force, he wrote:

"I am influenced by the conviction that the present stage of development of the air war against Japan presents the AAF for the first time with the opportunity of proving the power of the strategic air arm. I consider that for the first time strategic air bombardment faces a situation in which its strength is proportionate to the magnitude of its task."

During April 1945, a pause in the fire-bombing campaign was forced on LeMay. The B-29s were diverted to operations in support of the invasion of Okinawa, attacking Japanese airfields from which *kamikaze* missions were being flown against the U.S. fleet. B-29s of the 313th BW also began the specialized work of mine-laying, sowing thousands in harbor approaches and in the waterways most used by Japanese shipping. Unheralded though it was, the mine-laying was a conspicuous success, accounting for approximately half the Japanese tonnage sunk in this closing stage of the war.

In May, the incineration of Japan was resumed. Until mid-June, the B-29s worked their way through the major cities, and then started on a list of smaller urban areas with populations between 100,000 and 200,000. Towards the end of July, LeMay began adding warnings to the intended victims. On the day before raids were planned, leaflets were dropped over a dozen cities advising the population to leave or suffer the consequences. Some of the cities were then attacked. It proved to be an effective measure, later characterized by a high Japanese official as "a very clever piece of psychological warfare, as people in the affected regions got extremely nervous and lost what faith they still had in the Army's ability to defend the mainland."

By August, the B-29s were running out of large places to burn, and towns with populations of less than forty thousand were being attacked. Much of Japan's urban area lay in ruins, and some places were almost totally obliterated. Among them, reconnaissance recorded that the cities of Namaza and Fukui were almost 90 percent destroyed, and Toyama, with a preraid population of almost 130,000, had effectively ceased to exist. In all, some sixty-six urban centers were attacked, and about 178 square miles of Japan's built-up area had literally gone up in smoke.

With so much destruction already accomplished, there was no thought of reducing the scale of the bombing offensive. On the contrary, extensive plans were made to build up the USAAF's striking power in the Pacific and to restructure command arrangements to take account of a massive increase in strength. General Arnold advocated the appointment of a Supreme Commander for the final offensive against Japan, with senior and equal commanders from the army, navy, and air force responsible to him for operations in their own spheres. Given the sensibilities of the individual services, the question of a Supreme Commander could not be resolved, but agreement was reached by the JCS that General MacArthur should command all land operations, and that Admiral Nimitz should be the commander at sea. Those decisions made, it was further agreed that there should be an air commander who would take charge of land-based strategic aviation and have broad administrative and logistical responsibilities for all AAF forces in the theater. The senior airman selected to be Commander, U.S. Army Strategic Air Forces, Pacific, was General Carl Spaatz.

Spaatz arrived from Europe to set up his new headquarters on Guam at the end of July 1945. With Germany defeated, the "Mighty Eighth" was already on its way from Europe to add its strength to the air forces facing Japan. In a letter to Spaatz in May 1945, General Arnold explained his plans for the buildup of strategic air power in the Pacific, and gave some indication of the politics lurking behind the command appointment. He said that the Eighth would operate from Okinawa with 720 B-29s, and that the Twentieth would remain in the Marianas with 720 more, a combined striking force more than twice as powerful as that ranged against Japan so far. In nominating Spaatz for command of USASTAF, Arnold wrote: "I believe we need somebody who can work more nearly on parity and have more influence with MacArthur and Nimitz. . . . I can see nobody else who has the chance to save for us a proper representation in the air war in the Pacific." As these ideas were being considered and the necessary arrangements made, a revolutionary event changed the nature of global war forever and rendered any such activities superfluous.

The Coming of the Apocalypse

On June 11, 1945, some specially modified B-29s began arriving at Tinian's North Field. They were aircraft belonging to the 393rd Bombardment Squadron, the combat element of the 509th Composite Group. Externally, they were distinguished by a lack of gun turrets, apart from the two-gun position in the tail. They were parked in their own part of the airfield, a complex of heavily guarded buildings and hard standings. Once settled in, the crews followed normal practice and completed a few training missions to well visited islands like Truk before flying several more to se-

Bombs cascade from B-29 bomb bays during an attack on a Japanese target. A B-29 had the capacity to load up to 20,000 lbs of bombs internally.

lected targets in Japan. The curiosity of the other B-29 units was aroused because the 393rd never flew as part of a wing operation. They went off in small formations of their own, sometimes only two or three aircraft at a time, apparently following the discredited tactics of penetrating Japanese airspace in daylight at high level. Over the targets, however, their tactics were anything but standard. At the release point, a single bulbous bomb fell from the lead aircraft, which immediately broke into a steep diving turn, aiming to get as far away as

B-29 raids on Japan were not unopposed. Here a B-29 heads for the island sanctuary of Iwo Jima with its No. 4 engine feathered and smoking heavily.

possible before the bomb exploded. Even to the crews performing these maneuvers, it was all very strange.

During the training period, the commander of the 509th was the only member of the unit who knew that his group had been formed for the specific purpose of dropping the first operational atomic bomb on Japan. He was Colonel Paul Tibbets, an exceptional pilot with a distinguished B-17 record in Europe and North Africa, who had recently been testing B-29s in the U.S. On July 18 he received a coded message which told him that an atomic bomb had been detonated at Alamagordo, New Mexico. He was pretty certain then that his months of preparatory work had not been in vain, and that the next atomic explosion would take place over Japan with himself and his crew as witnesses.

The Allied powers issued an ultimatum on July 26 calling for the Japanese to surrender or suffer "prompt and utter destruction." President Harry Truman had decided that the "special bomb" would be used if the Japanese refused to comply, and the anticipated rejection came from Premier Suzuki on July 28. A directive had already been issued to General Spaatz on July 25 in the expectation that the Japanese would refuse to cooperate. In it, Spaatz

was instructed that the 509th was to deliver its first special bomb, visually aimed, on or after August 3, 1945, "on one of the targets: Hiroshima, Kokura, Niigata, and Nagasaki." The field orders for the attack were signed on August 2 by Lt. Gen. Twining, who in the reorganization of the Pacific air forces had become commander of the Twentieth Air Force. Hiroshima was selected as the primary target.

The fissionable material for the core of the bomb arrived at Tinian on board the cruiser *Indianapolis* on July 26, and by August 1 both the weapon and the 509th were ready to go. Weather forecasts for the period after August 3 were promising and led to final briefings being given. On August 4, the crews of the 509th at last learned that their special bombs were expected to explode with a force equal to twenty thousand tons of TNT.

At 02:45 on August 6, 1945, Paul Tibbets lifted his B-29, *Enola Gay*, off the Tinian runway and headed north. Two other B-29s, *The Great Artiste* and *No. 91*, followed with official observers on board. Approaching Japan, Tibbets received a report from weather reconnaissance aircraft indicating that the skies over Hiroshima were almost clear of cloud. By then, the weaponeer had made the bomb live and all was ready for the drop. Navigator Dutch van Kirk brought the *Enola Gay* accurately to the initial point for the attack and, at 09:11, Tibbets steadied at 31,600 ft on the final heading for the target and handed the aircraft over to bombardier Tom Ferebee. At 09:15, the bomb, a uranium device known as "Little Boy," fell from the bomb bay towards the aiming point of Hiroshima's Aioi Bridge. Tibbets immediately broke hard right and dropped the nose, gathering speed to escape the coming blast. Fifty seconds after release, "Little Boy" detonated and Hiroshima was transformed into a scene of utter devastation.

The official Japanese communiqué after the raid minimized the disaster at Hiroshima. It mentioned a new bomb which had caused "considerable damage" and "should not be made light of," but there was no hint of a Japanese surrender. The decision was therefore made to use

the second bomb, "Fat Man," which had a plutonium core. The mission was flown on August 9, this time led by Major Charles Sweeney in a B-29 called *Bockscar*[10]. The primary target selected was Kokura, but that city was saved by the weather. Complete cloud cover defied Sweeney over Kokura and *Bockscar* was turned towards the secondary target, Nagasaki. With the cloud cover persisting, the approach to the target was made on radar, but at the last moment the city was seen through a break and the bomb was released visually. The blast from the explosion caught up with the aircraft about a minute later. The crew felt "it was as if the B-29 were being beaten by a telephone pole."

At Hiroshima, the area destroyed covered nearly five square miles. Almost 80,000 people died and those injured numbered about the same. Nagasaki was to some extent protected by its hilly terrain and the area destroyed was less than one and a half square miles. The dead and injured figures could not be precisely determined, but they were approximately 35,000 and 60,000 respectively.

The Japanese were in desperate straits. Their armies had been defeated, their navy and air forces destroyed, their sea lanes closed, their cities burned, and now they had felt the impact of two frightful new weapons. As if that were not enough, on August 8 the USSR had declared war on them and Soviet armies were sweeping into Manchuria. Yet Japanese militarism remained strong and there were still those among the leadership who vehemently opposed any move for peace. Deadlocked, the Japanese government turned to Emperor Hirohito, and on August 10 he gave his view that "the time has come when we must bear the unbearable." Papers flew between Japan and the Allies, but it was August 14 before the Emperor's will prevailed. While intense internal struggles were going on in Tokyo, the USAAF resumed its conventional opera-

---

[10]Sweeney's own B-29, *The Great Artiste*, was the principal observation aircraft and was loaded with monitoring instruments. On the Nagasaki mission Sweeney exchanged aircraft with Capt. Fred Bock, whose usual B-29 was the appropriately named *Bockscar*. It is *Bockscar* which is preserved as an exhibit in the USAF Museum, Dayton, Ohio.

tions, culminating in a "1,000 plus" grand finale on August 14, when 828 B-29s and 186 escorts attacked various targets. Before the last B-29 landed, President Truman was at last able to announce the unconditional surrender of Japan.

The formalities ending the Pacific War were concluded by General MacArthur on board the battleship *Missouri* in Tokyo Bay on September 2, 1945. The Army's senior soldier and the Navy's battlewagon occupied center stage, but overhead the Air Force made its point with a flypast of 462 B-29s. In view of recent events, it was a display of strength which could hardly fail to draw the eye.

With Hindsight

Generally speaking, the Allied cause was served even more effectively by air power in the Pacific and CBI theaters than in Europe. This was possible because, for one thing, the discrepancies in strength between the two major combatants were more obvious. In terms of population and industry, Japan was greatly inferior to the United States. In the air, that was evidenced by the Japanese air forces becoming increasingly outnumbered and being unable to keep up in the race to produce not only more aircrew and aircraft, but better versions of both. One of the most extraordinary aspects of the war was the speed with which the U.S. was able to mobilize and organize its forces in the Pacific while still committing huge resources to the Allied policy of "Germany first." The growth of the USAAF's six Pacific/CBI air forces was typical of what was accomplished. In 1942, the USAAF in the Pacific was an operator of small, scattered collections of outdated aircraft. Little more than three years later, it was a mighty assembly of air power capable of dominating any confrontation anywhere in the world. The overwhelming nature of U.S. air power was emphasized when it became possible to mount an aerial offensive against the main islands of Japan. The emphasis was marked because Japanese air defenses were found to be relatively poor and the cities which housed the principal industries proved to be particularly suscep-

tible to incendiary attack. In Europe, on the other hand, the Luftwaffe was always a ferocious adversary and German industry more robust.

Another factor was the geography of the region. The vast distances and frequently rudimentary national infrastructures put a premium on the reach and flexibility of air power, and the U.S. employed its assets far more effectively than did its enemy. The Japanese understood the importance of air power, but were limited in their view of how to use it. It was primarily for the support of their Army and Navy, and those two services generally kept the

the immense amount of destruction effected during the fire-bombing campaign had reduced Japan's already declining industrial capacity dramatically. By mid-1945 Japan's production was down to about one-third of that reached during the previous year, and this was the result of both the loss of factories and a lowering of the morale of the Japanese people, who had become noticeably more defeatist and less willing to work. The evacuation of large numbers of people into the countryside was also having an effect.

The first series of incendiary attacks on the major cities in March 1945 shocked

A B-29 strike in progress. Smoke is already rising from an area near the docks. Presumably the bombardier of the photographer's aircraft is keenly aware of the one below.

efforts of their air forces well separated. The USAAF used its aircraft in every role imaginable—strategic bombing, interdiction, close support, artillery spotting, reconnaissance, air defense, fighter escort, ship attack, maritime patrol, air/sea rescue, troop and freight transport, glider assault, casualty evacuation—and became highly effective at each one. The USAAF did all these things, usually did them very well, and still found time to cooperate in operations alongside the U.S. Navy.

At the war's end, it became clear that

some of the Japanese leaders sufficiently to make them think about how they might initiate peace negotiations. Indeed, well before the dropping of the atomic bombs, the members of the "peace party" in the Japanese government were predicting that the bombing would force an end to the war by September and were arguing that further resistance was pointless. Their reaction to the immediate aerial threat was understandable, but, in its postwar examination of the air war against Japan, the United States Strategic Bombing Survey took care not to attribute Japan's defeat to any single factor, preferring to mention "the numerous causes which jointly and cumulatively were responsible for Japan's disaster." The USSBS report pointed out that the final air assault on Japan had not been feasible until bases had been secured within reach of the main islands, and that the history of the war in the Pacific was largely one of surface forces seizing territory with the support of air forces. It went without saying that the surface campaigns would have been unlikely to succeed in the absence of air support.

Of course, the USSBS comments were justified. By the time the B-29 offensive began, Japan was in decline as a result of calamitous defeats for its armed forces and the strictures of a relentless naval blockade. Nevertheless, it is interesting to speculate on how the war might have gone had there been no strategic bombing campaign. Given the nature of their society in 1945 and the military domination of their government, the Japanese would probably have been prepared to endure the sufferings of total isolation and would have fought to the death against invasion. The B-29s made such stoicism impossible by bringing the war home to the Japanese people in a form so irresistible and so horrifyingly destructive that increasing numbers of them lost the will to fight on. Even military fanatics who could not think of surrender no longer talked of victory but of "finding life in death."

In reaching the point at which they felt driven to seek the intervention of their Emperor, the Japanese leaders would undoubtedly have been keenly aware that Japan was facing inevitable defeat. Their military reverses and the naval blockade had created that situation, but had not forced them to consider surrender. They were unequivocal in testifying later that the bombing campaign had done that. Prince Konoye said: "Fundamentally the thing that brought about the determination to make peace was the prolonged bombing by the B-29s." Premier Kantaro Suzuki agreed: "It seemed to me unavoidable that in the long run Japan would be

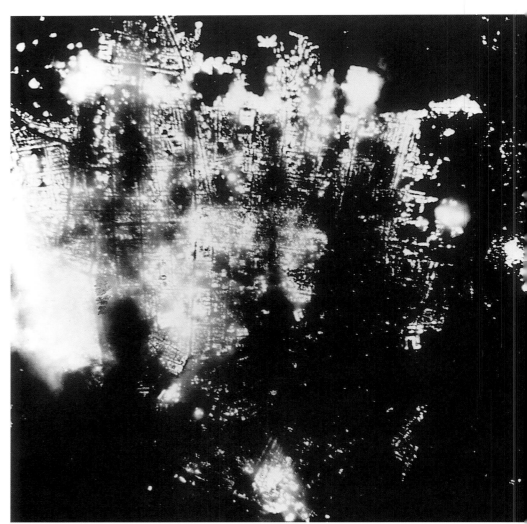

Toyama, a Japanese aluminum manufacturing center of 130,000, was subjected to a B-29 fire raid on the night of August 1, 1945. It was one of the war's most punishing attacks, destroying more than 90 percent of the city.

almost destroyed by air attack so that merely on the basis of the B-29s alone I was convinced that Japan should sue for peace."

Suzuki and others mentioned the atomic bombs and the Soviet declaration of war as additional factors, but seemed to suggest that, significant though these events were, they were not the real roots of the drive to end the war. Their catastrophic nature served to bolster the arguments of the members of the "peace party," but they had already made the difficult decision to face the terrible disgrace of surrender. At that stage, they had no idea what kind of bomb had destroyed Hiroshima and did not particularly care. B-29s had shown that they could eradicate cities just as effectively with incendiaries and the distinction between one kind of bomb and another did not seem to them significant.

By 1945, the inevitability of Japan's

defeat, with or without a strategic bombing offensive, was not in doubt. The fact remains that the blows which precipitated the end of the war, and obviated the need to consider a costly invasion of Japan, were delivered by the USAAF's B-29s. It was their demonstrated destructive capacity which most affected the states of mind of the Japanese leaders in 1945 and led them to sue for peace. Early air power strategists who had theorized that bombing an opposing nation's heartland would, among other things, "destroy the enemy's will to fight," might at last have claimed justification for the thought.

In 1947, General Carl Spaatz looked back on WWII and delivered the airmen's verdict on the role of air power in the Pacific:

"In our victory over Japan, air power was unquestionably decisive. That the planned invasion of the Japanese home islands was unnecessary is clear evidence that air power has evolved into a force coequal with land and sea power, decisive in its own right and worthy of the faith of its prophets."

The views of General Spaatz were hardly unbiased, but they were founded on a rock of solid achievement by the USAAF, and they were a rallying call for the faithful who believed that the time had come for the creation of an independent United States Air Force.

On August 9, 1945, the second atomic bomb ("Fat Man") was dropped on Nagasaki from the B-29 Bockscar *after it was found that cloud obscured the primary target, Kokura. A mushroom cloud rose rapidly towards the stratosphere, and the B-29's crew felt their aircraft shudder under the impact of five separate shock waves as they turned towards Okinawa.*

The atomic bomb "Fat Man" at Nagasaki yielded some 23 kilotons, more than "Little Boy" at Hiroshima, which was close to 15 kilotons. Destruction was just as complete near ground zero, but the area totally destroyed (2.3 x 1.9 miles) was less than at Hiroshima, being confined by the natural bowl in which Nagasaki was built. The U.S. Strategic Bombing Survey estimated casualties at 35,000 dead, 5,000 missing, and 60,000 injured.

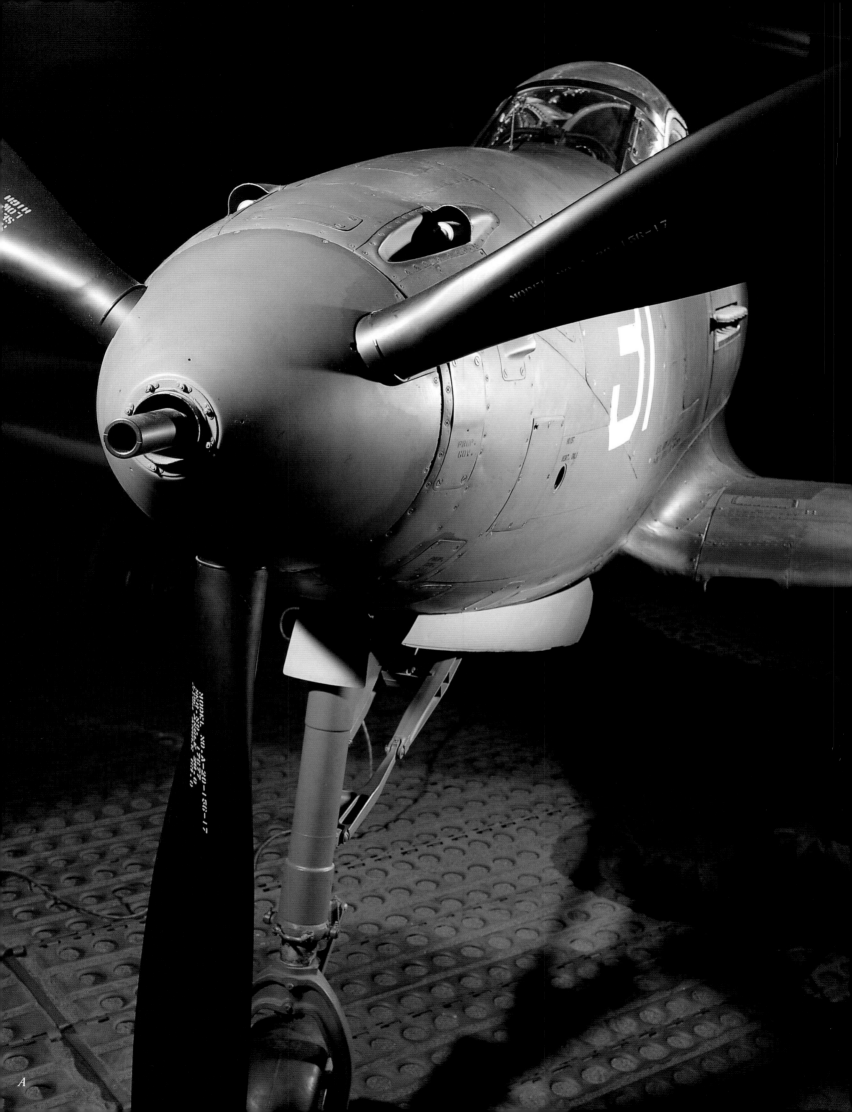

A

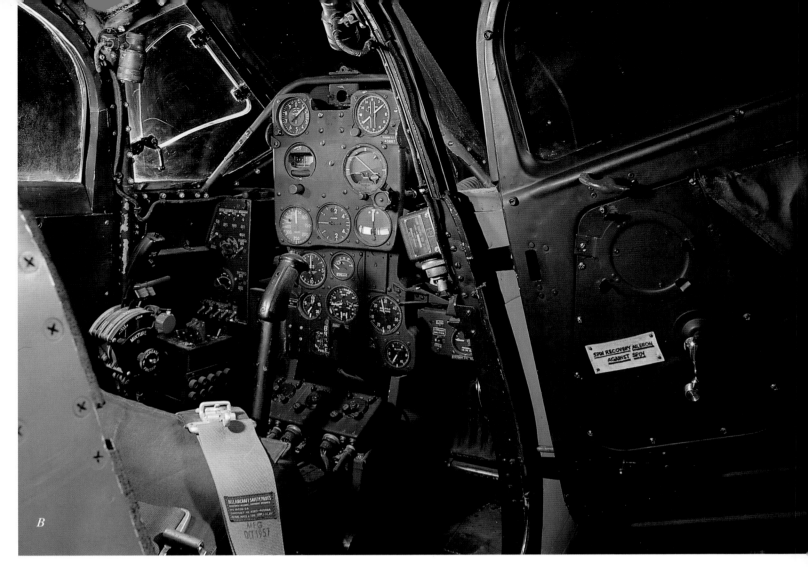

B

A   The Bell P-39 Airacobra was unusual for the 1940s in being a single-seat fighter with a tricycle undercarriage. This was possible because the Allison V-1710 engine was mounted behind the pilot. A long drive shaft ran through the cockpit to the propeller. Lacking a supercharger, the P-39 was not a good performer at altitude, but it was powerfully armed with two .50 caliber machine guns and a 37 mm cannon firing through the propeller boss. This made it most suitable for ground attack operations, and it was particularly popular with Soviet pilots for that reason.

B   Among other P-39 peculiarities was the "car door" entry to the cockpit. Once inside, the layout was reasonably typical for a fighter of the period.

C   The USAF Museum's Airacobra is a P-39Q painted as the P-39J flown by Lt. Leslie Spoonts of the 57th FS in the Aleutians during 1942.

C

A   The formidable firepower of the Lockheed P-38 Lightning is evident from this view of the nose. Four .50 caliber machine guns are grouped above a 20 mm cannon. The Lightning's unorthodox design set it apart among single-seat fighters. The fuselage pod was relatively small, serving principally to hold the cockpit and the guns. The nacelles housed the two Allison V-1710s and were extended into twin booms to carry the tail. The USAF Museum's example is a P-38L, finished in the markings of a P-38J of the 55th FS, 20th FG, serving at Kingscliffe in England.

B   The Lightning was large for a fighter, and the impression of size was enhanced by the spectacle grip provided for the pilot's flying controls, an arrangement which might have been more normally associated with a bomber or a transport.

C   A P-38 of the 475th FG parked on steel matting in the Philippines. Note the two sizes of drop tanks carried—310 and 165 gallons.

A

B

A   The Douglas A-20 Havoc was not an attack aircraft to be taken lightly. It was armed with six .50 caliber machine guns in the nose, and could carry up to 4,000 lbs of bombs. The A-20G on display at the USAF Museum is marked as an aircraft of the 89th BS, 3rd BG, in the SW Pacific.

B   A-20s of the 5th AF undergoing major servicing at the Eagle Farm depot in Australia.

C   The A-20's cockpit was neatly and conveniently arranged, with the possible exception of a few instruments hiding behind the control column. As was the case with many Douglas aircraft, the A-20 was considered to be very much a pilot's aircraft.

D   The way in and out of the A-20 pilot's seat was through the roof.

A

B

A The Curtiss C-46 Commando gained its reputation during operations to supply China from India over the "Hump" of the Himalayas. With two Pratt & Whitney R-2800 radials of 2,000 hp each, it could carry some 12,000 lbs of payload almost a thousand miles.

B The C-46D at the USAF Musum is painted as an aircraft which flew the Hump in 1944. The circular insignia is that of the Air Transport Command of the USAAF.

C   The Northrop P-61 Black Widow was the first U.S. aircraft designed from the outset as a night fighter. It therefore did not follow in the typical fighter tradition. It is a large, heavy, twin-boomed aircraft with a crew of three—pilot, gunner, and radar operator.

D   The P-61 nose was reserved for the disc antenna of an AI radar. The heavy armament was therefore located in a remotely controlled top turret with four .5 in machine guns and a belly pack of four 20 mm cannon. The USAF Museum's Black Widow is a P-61C marked as a P-61B of the 550th NFS (Moonlight Serenade) as flown in the Pacific in 1945.

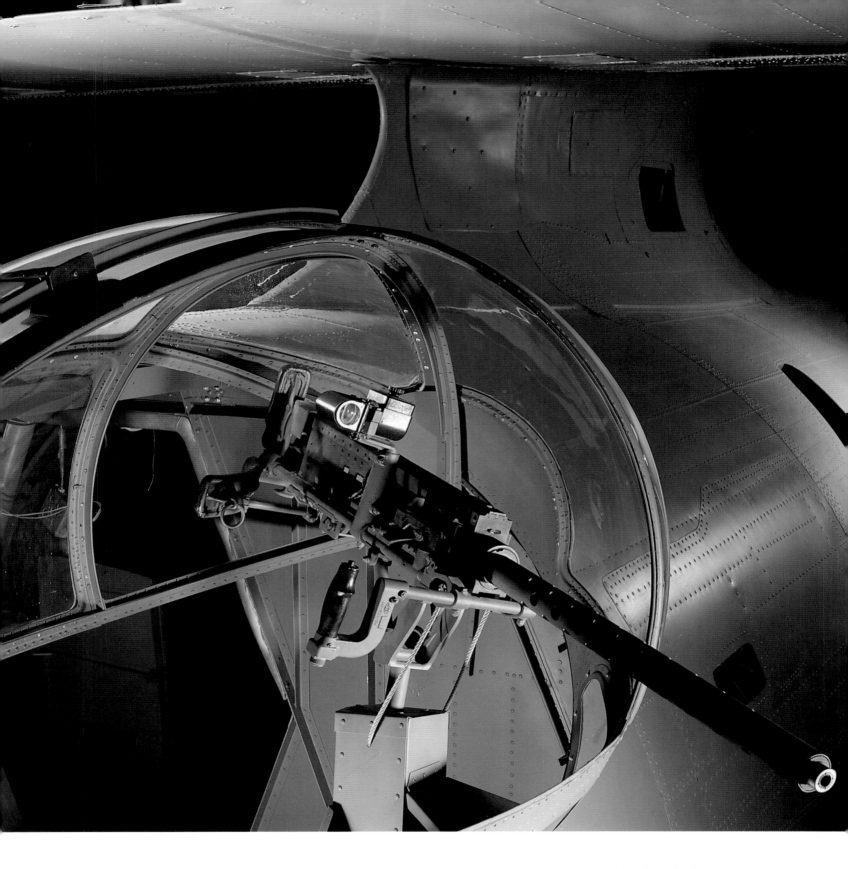

A   Bulging from the fuselage of the Catalina like frog's eyes, the gun blisters each carried a single .50 caliber machine gun.

B   The Consolidated OA-10 was the USAAF's version of the PBY Catalina series operated extensively by the U.S. Navy. OA-10s were used principally for air/sea rescue work and for long-range reconnaissance. Slow and cumbersome though it was, the Catalina was a welcome sight to many downed airmen. The USAF Museum's OA-10 is finished as *Snafu Snatchers,* an aircraft of the 2nd Emergency Rescue Squadron in the SW Pacific.

A

C

A   The nose of Bockscar, *the USAF Museum's Boeing B-29 Superfortress. It was from this position that Capt. Kermit Beahan saw a hole in the cloud covering Nagasaki and dropped the atomic bomb "Fat Man" on August 9, 1945.*

B   The B-29 Bockscar *photographed during the approach to Nagasaki, August 9, 1945.*

C   The pilot's seat in a B-29 seems almost too exposed. The general roominess is emphasized by the huge expanse of glass on every side.

D   The flight engineer's position of a B-29 was comprehensive in its coverage of the aircraft's systems. Note the throttle, pitch, and mixture control levers which duplicate those between the pilots.

A   Charles W. Sweeney piloted Bockscar over Nagasaki on August 9, 1945. More than fifty years later he once more took his place in the left-hand seat.

B   The crew of Bockscar on August 9, 1945. Charles Sweeney is standing at far right.

C   Looking aft through the hatch at the rear of the forward crew compartment of a B-29.

D   The view from inside the forward bomb bay of a B-29 looking towards the nose. The open hatch into the crew compartment is seen in the center of the picture.

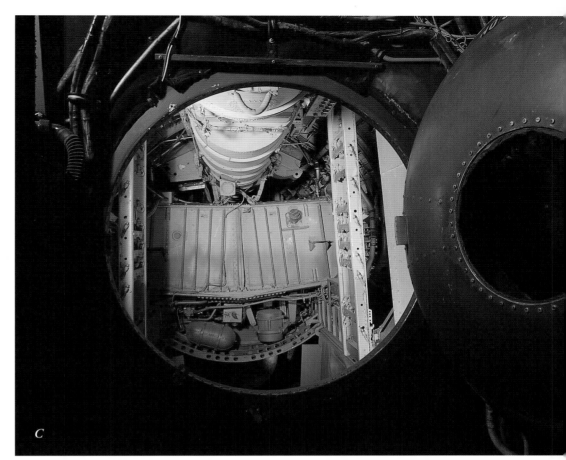

C

D

MEDALS of HONOR

World War I

Rickenbacker, Capt. Edward V.	Sept. 25, 1918, Billy, France
Luke, 2nd Lt. Frank, Jr.	Sept. 29, 1918 Murvaux, France
Bleckley, 2nd Lt. Erwin R.	Oct. 6, 1918, Binarville, France
Goettler, 2nd Lt. Harold E.	" " "

World War II

Doolittle, Lt. Col. James H.	Apr. 18, 1942, Tokyo, Japan
Pease, Capt. Harl, Jr.	Aug. 7, 1942, Rabaul, New Britain
Craw, Col. Demas T.	Nov. 8, 1942, Port Lyautey, French Morocco
Hamilton, Maj. Pierpont M.	" " "
Walker, B. Gen. Kenneth N.	Jan. 5, 1943, Rabaul, New Britain
Mathis, 1st Lt. Jack W.	Mar. 18,1943, Vegesack, Germany
Smith, Sgt. Maynard H.	May 1, 1943, St Nazaire, France
Sarnoski, 2nd Lt. Joseph R.	June 16, 1943, Buka, Solomons
Zeamer, Maj. J., Jr.	" " "
Morgan, 2nd Lt. John C.	July 28, 1943, Kiel, Germany
Baker, Lt. Col. Addison E.	Aug 1, 1943, Ploesti, Rumania
Hughes, 2nd Lt. Lloyd H.	" " "
Jerstad, Maj. John L.	" " "
Johnson, Col. Leon W.	" " "
Kane, Col. John R.	" " "
Cheli, Maj. Ralph	Aug. 18, 1943, Wewak, New Guinea
Kearby, Col. Neel E.	Oct. 11, 1943, Wewak, New Guinea
Wilkins, Maj. Raymond H.	Nov. 2, 1943, Rabaul, New Britain
Vosler, TSgt. Forrest L.	Dec. 20, 1943, Bremen, Germany
Howard, Lt. Col. James H.	Jan. 11, 1944, Oschersleben, Germany
Lawley, 1st Lt. William R., Jr.	Feb. 20, 1944, Leipzig, Germany
Mathies, SSgt. Archibald	" " "
Truemper, 2nd Lt. Walter E.	" " "
Michael, 1st Lt. Edward S.	Apr. 11, 1944, Brunswick, Germany
Vance, Lt. Col. Leon R.	June 5, 1944, Wimereaux, France
Kingsley, 2nd Lt. David R.	June 23, 1944, Ploesti, Rumania
Pucket, 1st Lt. Donald D.	July 9, 1944 Ploesti, Rumania
Lindsey, Capt. Darrell R.	Aug. 9, 1944, Pontoise, France
Bong, Maj. Richard I.	Oct. 10 - 15 Nov. 1944, SW Pacific
Carswell, Maj. Horace S., Jr.	Oct. 26, 1944, S China Sea
Femoyer, 2nd Lt. Robert E.	Nov. 2, 1944, Merseburg, Germany
Gott, 1st Lt. Donald J.	Nov. 9, 1944, Saarbrucken, Germany
Metzger, 2nd Lt. William E., Jr.	" " "
Castle, B.Gen. Frederick W.	Dec. 24, 1944, Liege, Belgium
McGuire, Maj. Thomas B., Jr.	Dec. 25/26, 1944, Luzon, Philippines
Shomo, Maj. William A.	Jan.11, 1945, Luzon, Philippines
Erwin, SSgt. Henry E.	Apr. 12, 1945, Koriyama, Japan
Knight, 1st Lt. Raymond L.	Apr. 25, 1945, Po Valley, Italy

Korea

Sebille, Maj. Louis J.	Aug. 5, 1950, Hamch'ang, S. Korea
Walmsley, Capt. John S., Jr.	Sept. 14, 1951, Yangdok, N Korea
Davis, Maj. George A., Jr.	Feb. 10, 1952, Sinuiju-Yalu River, N Korea
Loring, Maj. Charles J., Jr.	Nov. 22, 1952, Sniper Ridge, N Korea

Vietnam

Fisher, Maj. Bernard F.	Mar. 10, 1966, A Shau Valley, S. Vietnam
Wilbanks, Capt. Hilliard A.	Feb. 24, 1967, Dalat, S. Vietnam
Dethlefsen, Maj. Merlyn H.	Mar. 10, 1967, Thai Nguyen, N. Vietnam
Thorsness, Lt.Col. Leo K.	Apr. 19, 1967, N. Vietnam
Young, Capt. Gerald O.	Nov 9, 1967, Da Nang, S. Vietnam
Jackson, Lt. Col. Joe M.	May 12, 1968, Kham Duc, S. Vietnam
Jones, Col. William A., III	Sept. 1, 1968, Dong Hoi, N. Vietnam
Fleming, 1st Lt. James P.	Nov. 26, 1968, Duc Co, S. Vietnam
Levitow, A1C John L.	Feb. 24, 1969, Long Binh, S. Vietnam
Bennett, Capt. Steven L.	June 29, 1972, Quang Tri, S. Vietnam
Day, Col. George E.	POW, Hanoi, N. Vietnam
Sijan, Capt.Lance P.	" " "

Chapter 7

Liberation and Restraint

"They thought they were pretty good . . . so my first chore was to convince them they weren't."

(Curt LeMay, on taking over Strategic Air Command, November 1948)

"Air power has been developed to a point where its responsibilities are equal to those of land and sea power, and its contribution to our strategic planning is as great."

(President Harry Truman to Congress, December 1945)

"Anyone who is capable of understanding, who is aware of even the most basic truths upon which World War II was prosecuted, is fully aware that the first line of defense and the last frontiers of America lie in the sky."

(General Jimmy Doolittle to the Senate Naval Affairs Committee, 1946)

"The real barrier wasn't in the sky, but in our knowledge and experience of supersonic flight."

(Chuck Yeager, after flying faster than sound in the Bell X-1, October 14, 1947)

"It is hereby declared to be the policy of the President that there shall be equality of treatment and opportunity for all persons in the Armed Services without regard to race."

(President Harry Truman, Executive Order 9981, July 26, 1948)

General Carl Spaatz (1891-1974), first USAF Chief of Staff.

Jets, Giants, and Whirlybirds

The fiery end of WWII needs no emphasis in the Museum's displays. It is powerfully represented in the huge gleaming form of the B-29 Bockscar. In the shadow of such a dominant icon the visitor must look carefully to find the next stage of the Air Force story. The wall displays are unobtrusive but they cover a number of postwar events which held great significance for U.S. air power. Panels describing the pains of peacetime military contractions and the turbulence of subsequent restructuring are followed by others documenting the fulfillment of American Army airmen's dreams—the creation in 1947 of an independent United States Air Force.

On the floor of the Museum stands the evidence that the newborn USAF would not take shape in the image of its forebears. The first U.S. jet aircraft have arrived. Shorn of propeller disks, they squat forward on their nosewheels, staring visitors straight in the eye rather than gazing loftily over their heads in the manner of their tail-wheeled predecessors. America's first jet, the ungainly Bell P-59 Airacomet, lies alongside the sleek Lockheed P-80R Shooting Star record breaker, in which Colonel Albert Boyd reached a speed of more than 623 mph in 1947. Overhead hang aircraft from the other end of the aeronautical spectrum, the first Sikorsky helicopters.

The story told on the Museum's walls reflects the excitement of the times. Photographs proliferate of experimental jet fighters and bombers, most of which fell by the wayside before reaching production, while others formed the backbone of the USAF's postwar front line. Ideas for extending the range of combat aircraft are pictured, the more prosaic methods of in-flight refueling seen together with wilder flights of fancy, like fighters attached to bombers' wing tips or carried in cradles. The USAF's major combat commands appear, Strategic Air Command (SAC), Tactical Air Command (TAC), and Air Defense Command (ADC), with SAC as the dominant partner in the early years. The uniforms of SAC's first two commanders, Generals Kenney and LeMay, are preserved under glass, watched over by a glowering bronze bust of the fearsome Curt. A

Thomas Jefferson quote reminds visitors that Americans have always had to be watchful in the cause of freedom: "Eternal vigilance is the price of liberty."

The theme of American commitment to democratic freedoms is carried on in displays covering the Korean War of 1950–53. The story of the conflict from the USAF's point of view is told in text, maps, and photographs. Highlights feature the first USAF air-to-air victories, the B-29 bombing campaign, the contribution of the transport force, the valor of four Medal of Honor winners, and the impact of the F-86 Sabre on the air war. One section deals specifically with the F-86 aces, thirty-eight in all, and notes that six of them were already aces from WWII—Gabreski, Garrison, Thyng, Davis, Hagerstrom, and Whisner. Ohio's own John Glenn, later celebrated astronaut and Senator, is remembered as the Marine exchange pilot with the USAF who flew F-86s and recorded three victories over MiG-15s. Special mention, too, is given to Dean Hess, an ordained minister from Ohio who flew P-47s in WWII and P-51s in Korea. He was the driving force behind Operation KIDDIE CAR, which succeeded in rescuing hundreds of Korean orphans from the horrors of the war.

The hardware of the Korean War era lies on every side and includes some of the most impressive items in the Museum's collection. The aircraft which scored the first USAF victories of the war, the F-82 Twin Mustang, stands facing a shining black A-26 night intruder, dressed as Dream Girl of the 34th Bomb Squadron. A B-29 fuselage, painted as Command Decision, a bomber with five claimed victories against MiGs, is open for walk-through inspection. Passing into the next gallery, visitors are often left speechless at the sight of the gargantuan Convair B-36. With horizontal dimensions close to those of an American football field and a fin tall enough to cover the fifth story of a block of apartments, the B-36 is awesome. Alongside are some of the tools of its various trades, including one of the largest cameras ever made and a 41,400 lb nuclear bomb. The extraordinary McDonnell XF-85 Goblin parasite fighter, tiny would-be protector of its giant host, crouches nearby.

Grouped around the ten-engined monster or huddled beneath the overcast of its wings are other Korean War veterans: a Republic F-84E Thunderjet and its occasionally troublesome Allison J-35 engine, Lockheed's F-80C and F-94C, and the great air combat rivals, the F-86A Sabre and the MiG-15. This particular MiG-15 came to the U.S. by courtesy of a defecting North Korean pilot.

Elsewhere in the Museum are examples of other aircraft from the earliest days of the USAF and the Korean War period, including Sikorsky's H-5 Dragonfly, Grumman's HU-16 Albatross, Fairchild's C-119 Flying Boxcar, North American's B-45 Tornado, and Northrop's F-89 Scorpion.

With the images of Korea freshly in mind, the Museum visitor turns to consider a time of expansion for the USAF, with a host of exciting new jet aircraft leading the way into the second half of the century. In their wake trails the troubling prospect of a second and even more horrifying limited war, in which new challenges will arise for the USAF and old air power lessons must be learned again by airmen and by politicians.

Recession and Renewal

As its victorious airmen patrolled newly peaceful skies over Germany and Japan at the end of WWII, the USAAF was the most powerful military instrument ever created. It had a personnel strength of more than two and a quarter million, and nearly 70,000 aircraft of all types. The front line comprised 218 combat groups.[1] The men and women who had built this immense organization and fought its battles were, for the most part, not career professionals; 90 percent of them were civilians in uniform and, when the fighting stopped, they were only too ready to go back to what they were doing before the war disrupted their lives. The demobilization program obliged them as quickly as it could and less than two years after VJ-Day the USAAF was down to not much more than 300,000 people. Aircrew numbers had taken a 95 percent cut, falling from well over 400,000 to just 24,000. Tens of thousands of aircraft, many fresh from the

---

[1] Peak figures were as follows: Personnel—2,411,294 in March 1944; Combat Groups—243 in May 1945.

factories, had been written off and summarily junked. On paper, the front line had fifty-two groups, but only two of these were combat ready.

Desirable as all this was from the point of view of those being demobilized, the precipitous rate at which the USAAF declined alarmed many regular officers. Maj. Gen. St. Clair Streett, who was responsible for overseeing much of the rundown, warned General Arnold as early as October 1945 that "we will soon have reached a point, if it has not been reached, at which the Army Air Forces can no longer be considered anything more than a symbolic instrument of National Defense."

Streett's concern expressed a deeper reality. There could be no return to the conditions of 1939. The world had changed irrevocably since Hitler's troops burst across the Polish frontier, and the United States could no longer afford the luxury of isolationism. Having given the enormous wealth of its manpower and in-

dustrial strength in the cause of subduing Germany and Japan, the U.S. was inextricably entangled in world affairs. The economic recovery and political well-being of Western Europe and Japan depended on continued American involvement. In the immediate aftermath of the war, this included the provision of small occupation forces in the former enemy nations, but other responsibilities soon became apparent.

President Truman's hope that the western Allies would be able to cooperate with the Soviet Union to their mutual advantage in the postwar world quickly gave way to disillusionment. The headlong withdrawal of U.S. forces from most of the WWII operational theaters encouraged Communist leaders to think in terms of consolidating and expanding their influence wherever they could. Early in 1946, Stalin declared that communism and capitalism were incompatible. Another war was inevitable, he said. Churchill responded

with his "Iron Curtain" speech, and the term "Cold War" became established as part of everyday vocabulary. Events built towards the climactic year of 1947 and the declaration of the Truman Doctrine as the foundation of U.S. foreign policy. The President's words were unequivocal:

"I believe that it must be the policy of the United States to support free peoples who are resisting attempted subjugation by armed minorities or by outside pressures. . . . If we falter in our leadership, we may endanger the peace of the world, and we shall surely endanger the welfare of this nation."

President Truman's speech formally committed the United States to bearing the responsibilities of an international power. It cleared the way for the announcement of the Marshall Plan for European recovery and gave Americans notice that the considerable resources necessary for promoting the Truman Doctrine would have to be provided by the U.S. Not least

Walnut Ridge, Arkansas, was typical of the huge aircraft parks set up to deal with the problem of 50,000 surplus USAAF aircraft once WW II was over. Once essential B-17s, some of them factory fresh, were among the aircraft which stood in rows waiting for scrap metal merchants.

Stuart Symington and General Carl Spaatz seen together soon after Symington had been sworn in as the first Secretary of the Air Force on September 18, 1947. That day is recognized as the official birthday of the United States Air Force.

among the requirements would be military forces based outside the U.S. and capable of "containing" the Soviet Union.

When Carl Spaatz took over from Hap Arnold as Commanding General, Army Air Forces, in February 1946, he was already working on the problems of how best to cope with force contraction and how to reorganize the AAF for the future. Convinced by his own experience, Spaatz saw air power in global terms and believed that long-range bombers should form the core of U.S. air power. He was also an advocate of a strong Air National Guard and Air Force Reserve, and he argued the importance of a well-funded research and development program. He worked with the confidence that independence for the Air Force could not be long delayed. In March 1946, he proposed a new framework for his service which took his convictions into account. At the heart of the reorganization were three new functional commands to provide the Air Force's teeth: Strategic Air Command, Tactical Air Command, and Air Defense Command. In support were Air Materiel, Air Proving Ground, Air Transport, and Air Training Commands, plus Air University. Overseas combat strength, deployed from the functional commands, would be controlled primarily by the United States Air Forces in Europe

(USAFE) and the Far East Air Force (FEAF). Smaller overseas elements were the Alaskan, Caribbean, and Northeast Air Commands. Between them, it was intended that the combat commands would field seventy front-line groups. At a time when defense spending was not popular, they soon realized that seventy groups was an overambitious target.

While this restructuring was going on, even greater things were afoot. Independence for the air arm was not a new idea; it had been a subject for discussion since before WWI. As early as 1916, legislation for an independent department for aviation had been considered by Congress, and in the years which followed the topic was revisited on the Hill on more than fifty occasions. Proposals were still being put forward during WWII, but senior airmen were then rightly wary of taking such a major step with so many other things on their minds. Even so, as the war progressed and the importance of air power was more clearly recognized, the Army Air Force enjoyed a degree of autonomy which was very close to independent status and General Arnold was accorded the privileges of a member of the Joint Chiefs of Staff. Ideas of reorganization persisted in the background, however. A 1943 War Department paper concluded that there was a need for

a single Department of National Defense, and in 1944 the JCS ordered a study to examine alternative systems for national defense management. This study agreed with the earlier paper in recommending the creation of a single department of government controlling three service branches.

In the latter stages of the war and the months immediately thereafter, a rash of studies issued from a number of committees seeking the ideal arrangement. The trouble was that the committees generally reflected the bias of their members. Those from the War Department generally favored a Department of the Armed Forces with three single service divisions, while those from the Navy Department, although conceding the need for a separate air force, were strongly opposed to placing the services under a superior authority. Hearings on the Hill drew endorsements for a single department not only from air force men like Arnold and Spaatz, but also from such eminent soldiers as Marshall and Bradley. Always opposed were the admirals—King, Nimitz, Halsey, and Leahy. In December 1945, President Truman intervened with his request for Congress to introduce legislation which would combine the War and Navy Departments. The arguments dragged on into 1946, but the President persisted, returning to the charge repeatedly as several proposed bills failed. Eventually a compromise was reached and the completed draft of a bill entitled the National Security Act of 1947 went to Congress at the end of February 1947. It provided for a single Secretary of National Defense and a separate Department of the Air Force, but was careful to stipulate that the Navy would retain control of its own aviation units and the Marine Corps. Prolonged hearings and many amendments followed before the bill was signed into law by President Truman on July 26, 1947. Immediately after approving the National Security Act, he signed an executive order setting out the functions and roles of what were now three independent services. Appropriately enough, the papers were brought to him as he waited to leave for Missouri from Washington National Airport, and they were signed on board his official Air Force aircraft, the C-54 *Sacred Cow*.

Billy Mitchell's vision had at last been given substance. The Air Force was legally an independent service, officially tasked with performing a number of functions for the nation: gaining and maintaining general air supremacy, establishing local air superiority, operating strategic air forces, supporting land and naval forces, supplying air lift for airborne operations, and providing air transport generally for the armed services. All that was left was to consummate the act with the formal appointment of officials—Stuart Symington as the first Secretary of the Air Force, and General Carl Spaatz as the new service's first Chief of Staff. Symington was sworn in on September 18, 1947, and that date was established as the official birthday of the United States Air Force.

Jet Turbulence

If the size, shape, and structure of the Air Force as a whole were adapting to the march of organizational evolution, what was beginning to happen on air force bases was closer to revolution. In the late 1940s, the familiar sights, sounds, and smells of hangars and flight lines began to undergo dramatic change. Jet engines had arrived and they had their effects in varying degrees on everything the air force did. Operational and training concepts, engineering practices, logistics, equipment design, and all kinds of administrative functions were remolded by the hot breath of jet propulsion. Pilots had to adjust their mental gears to take account of aircraft which flew faster and higher than their piston-engined predecessors, and which guzzled fuel at frightening rates, especially at low-level.

American interest in developing a jet aircraft began before the U.S. entered WWII. In September 1941, Bell Aircraft was asked by the USAAF to design a jet fighter. Just one year later, the XP-59A was ready to fly. It was a large aircraft weighing over 13,000 lbs and, powered as it was by two General Electric-built Whittle engines of a modest 1,100 lbs thrust each, it was not the answer to a fighter pilot's

dream. Production variants, delivered from August 1944 onwards, were fitted with GE engines of 2,000 lbs thrust, but even then they were never lively performers. Nevertheless, the P-59 opened the door to the jet age for the USAF. Many useful lessons were learned and much better aircraft were not far behind.

Among the earliest was one from Kelly Johnson's design team at Lockheed. They had toyed with the idea of a jet aircraft in 1939, but had abandoned it for lack of an engine and because of bureaucratic indifference. In 1943, the USAAF asked them to try again, replacing indif-

reached Europe before WWII was over, but too late to see any action. Lockheed's basic design would prove to be one of the most enduring of the jet age. The two-seat T-33 version, universally known as the "T-Bird," became the world's best known jet trainer and was still in service with more than a dozen air forces over fifty years after the XP-80 first flew.

Few of the early bids to enter the jet race were nearly so successful as the P-80 and its offspring. In the rush to take advantage of the new technology, jet engines with limited thrust were often married with airframes which still lingered in the pis-

The Bell P-59 Airacomet was America's first jet aircraft. Its performance was not good enough to make it a front-line fighter, but it was a useful introduction to the jet age. The aircraft illustrated had shorter wings and fin than earlier models and was one of thirty P-59Bs built.

ference with urgency and stipulating a time limit of 180 days between the request and first flight. Lockheed responded by having the XP-80 ready in 143 days. It first flew on January 8, 1944, and inspired enthusiasm from the start. It was a delight to fly and, even though powered by a de Havilland engine with only 2,460 lbs thrust, it was capable of exceeding 500 mph. Production P-80s were larger and heavier, but also faster and more powerful. In April 1944, the USAAF placed orders for one thousand P-80As, and four

ton-engined era, and the resulting performance figures were disappointing. Bomber designs like the XB-46 and XB-48 were essentially conventional aircraft hung about with jet engines. So was the North American B-45, but it was ordered into production anyway as an interim measure. Orthodox airframes persisted in the fighter world, too. Republic produced the F-84 Thunderjet, a tough and reliable single-seater which later led to greater things, and Northrop followed up the successful P-61 with the F-89 Scorpion, another large, heavily armed night fighter with a shape seemingly made to encourage drag.[2]

To make the most of the jet engine's promise, a host of aerodynamic problems needed solving. Some of the answers were already on the way. Among the most important were those revealed at the end of WWII when the results of research done by German aerodynamicists and engineers fell into the hands of the Allies. Particularly significant was the work done on using swept wings as a method for delaying and diminishing compressibility drag. Designers at Boeing and North American were the first to bring the fruits of these

not register in the consciousness of many people. With the war won, the average American was content to let someone else worry about military affairs. Only days after the USAF became independent, however, an event occurred which excited public interest and pride in the accomplishments of America's professional military airmen. It was the first major achievement of the new USAF and it could hardly have been more auspicious in its promise for the future.

shaped aircraft with thin, straight, laminar-flow wings, powered by a four chamber liquid fuel rocket motor. With all four chambers burning, the maximum thrust produced was 6,000 lbs and the four tons of fuel on board disappeared in only two and a half minutes. To get the most out of each flight, the X-1 was carried aloft in the belly of a B-29 and launched into free flight at 20,000 ft or higher.

The initial proving flights of the X-1 were conducted by a Bell company test pilot, but when the aircraft had performed satisfactorily up to Mach 0.8, the Air Force took over the program. The pilot selected to fly the X-1 into regions unknown was Captain Charles E. "Chuck" Yeager, a man who had already built himself a considerable reputation with the P-51 in Europe.[3] On October 14, 1947, the X-1 was dropped from the B-29 over the California desert and Yeager fired up all four rocket chambers to climb away. At 36,000 ft he switched two chambers off again, and then:

"Leveling off at 42,000 ft, I had 30 percent of my fuel, so I turned on rocket chamber three and immediately reached .96 Mach. I noticed that the faster I got, the smoother the ride. Suddenly the Mach needle began to fluctuate. It went up to .965 Mach—then tipped right off the scale. . . . We were flying supersonic!"

Chuck Yeager's achievement of becoming the first man to fly faster than sound won him both the Mackay and Collier Trophies. He had confirmed that the "sound barrier" was no barrier at all, and pointed the way for whole families of aircraft to follow the X-1 and make supersonic flight an everyday occurrence. For the USAF, it was an inspiring start to life as an independent service.

On October 14, 1947, "Chuck" Yeager became the first man to fly faster than sound. His rocket-powered Bell X-1 Glamorous Glennis *reached Mach 1.06 at 42,000 ft after being launched from a B-29 mothership.*

discoveries into service with the USAF. Both companies had been working on jet designs with straight wings, but moved quickly to incorporate sweepback. The results were Boeing's B-47 Stratojet and North American's F-86 Sabre, two of the most outstanding military aircraft ever built.

Much of the work of modernizing and reorganizing the Air Force in the postwar years made little impact on the general public. The paradox of a shrinking service with expanding opportunities did

Brittle Barrier

During WWII, high performance piston-engined aircraft like the P-51 and the Spitfire sometimes reached very high speeds in dives and the pilots then encountered severe buffeting and control problems. To explore the unknown aerodynamic territory close to the speed of sound where these phenomena occurred, Bell Aircraft developed the X-1, a small, bullet-

Operation VITTLES

In the wider world, where the services functioned as instruments of international politics, the USAF's postwar decline was causing its leaders some concern. Implicit in the Truman Doctrine was the need for an air force which could project power globally, but at the moment of its birth in 1947 the USAF's capability for fulfilling that role was severely limited. Stra-

---

[2]The USAF replaced the P for Pursuit designation with F for Fighter on June 10, 1948.
[3]Yeager's first few flights in the X-1 took him up to Mach 0.94 where his observations on elevator control difficulties led to the discovery that a "flying tail"—a moving solid slab horizontal stabilizer—offered greatly improved control at high Mach numbers. That development later gave the F-86 Sabre a marked advantage in combat.

tegic deterrence of Soviet expansionist ambitions seemed to depend solely on the U.S. nuclear monopoly and on the B-29 as a means of delivering a nuclear weapon. Respecting the weight of such a big stick, the Soviets chose to challenge the West in ways which would emphasize their strengths while minimizing the risk of a U.S. nuclear threat. In February 1947, the Czech government was overthrown in a Communist coup and the country became a Soviet satellite. Then, in the following month, the Soviets raised the stakes in Berlin. By so doing, they ensured that the first operational test of the USAF would not feature its front-line fighters and bombers. The stars of this show were to be haulers of food and fuel.

Berlin, the prewar German capital, was deep inside the Soviet zone of occupation in Germany from 1945 on. Itself divided into Soviet, American, British, and French zones, Berlin was connected to the West by a number of air and surface corridors over and through Soviet-held territory. The Soviets proved uncooperative when it came to working for Germany's economic revival, and the Western Allies decided to proceed with proposals affecting only their occupation zones. In March 1948, angered by what they saw as an attempt to build up West Germany into a resurgent threat against them, the Soviets began harassing Allied road and rail traffic into Berlin. By June 24, surface traffic into the city had ceased entirely. On that day the Allies received a teletyped message from the Soviet zone which read:

"The Transport Division of the Soviet Military Administration is compelled to halt all passenger and freight traffic to and from Berlin tomorrow at 0600 hours because of technical difficulties."

Since blocking surface routes was a simple matter, and any attempt to force the issue on the ground was likely to be unacceptably dangerous, the Allies were left with the alternatives of withdrawing from Berlin or supplying the city by air. An airlift on that scale had never been contemplated before. It hardly seemed sensible to suggest that West Berlin, with a population of nearly two and a half million people,

could be sustained by aircraft alone. Once the city's reserves had been depleted, the estimated supply lift required was thought to be about 4,500 tons per day, a figure which included not only essential food, but also large quantities of fuel, much of it in the form of coal.

Commander, USAFE, in 1948 was Maj. Gen. Curt LeMay. Soon after the Soviets began their blockade, he was called by the U.S. Military Governor in Germany, General Lucius Clay, and asked a simple question: "Curt, can you transport coal by air?" Understandably confused, LeMay asked for the question to be repeated. His answer was confident, if a little sweeping:

General Curt LeMay in typical cigar-chewing pose at Tempelhof, Berlin, in 1948. Commander of USAFE when the Soviets blockaded Berlin, he initiated the airlift which saved the city.

"Sir, the Air Force can deliver anything!"

By scraping together every aircraft he could lay his hands on, LeMay managed to have eighty tons of supplies flown into Berlin on June 26. It was pitifully small compared with the requirement, but it was a start. The problem was that the Allies did not have many assets immediately at hand. LeMay had about one hundred C-47s and a couple of C-54s. The RAF had a few more Dakotas (C-47s). Berlin needed the equivalent of 1,500 C-47 sorties per day. Even if it were possible to fly that

many, there were only two airfields available for them to use—Tempelhof in the U.S. zone, and Gatow in the British zone. It seemed an almost impossible task, but by mid-July LeMay's transport force had built to fifty-four C-54s and 105 C-47s with a daily lift of 1,500 tons. RAF Yorks and Dakotas added another 750 tons. It was a long way from meeting the long-term need, but it was improving steadily, and it had certainly irritated the Soviets, who encouraged their fighter pilots to "buzz" Allied aircraft following the air corridors in and out of the city.

The governments of the Western Allies having determined that the Soviet challenge had to be met, the USAF reacted strongly. General Hoyt Vandenburg, who had taken over as Air Force Chief of Staff on April 30, deployed three B-29 groups to the U.K. to send the Soviets an unmistakable message, and followed up by ordering F-80s to Germany from bases in the U.S. and the Canal Zone. On July 23, the Military Air Transport Service detached eight squadrons of C-54s (seventy-two aircraft with three crews apiece) to join the airlift. Aircraft flew in from as far away as Guam and Alaska. To ensure that the growing number of transports was used as effectively as possible, an Airlift Task Force was formed, which at the end of July came under command of Maj. Gen. William Tunner, a veteran of the "Hump" airlift into China. By October, Tunner was running a Combined Airlift Task Force, which merged American (USAF and two squadrons of USN R5Ds) and British efforts.

Tunner's principal key to getting the most out of his resources was standardization of everything—training, crew briefing, in-flight procedures, ground handling, aircraft maintenance, loading and unloading, etc. What Tunner called "a real cowboy operation" was turned into an endless conveyor belt of aircraft delivering supplies with metronomic efficiency. Besides improving the organization, Tunner also pressed for bigger aircraft. The C-47s were replaced as rapidly as possible with larger capacity C-54s, an average of 300 of which became the U.S. front line for the airlift. Some 225 were usually available to fly, with another 75 undergoing maintenance. The British had more than 100 aircraft in operation on any given day. Specialization helped, too, with the USAF concentrating on coal and the British on liquid fuels.

Flights inbound to Berlin entered the air corridors three minutes apart, twenty-four hours a day, maintaining precise heights and speeds from one radio beacon to the next. Interspersing arrivals with departures, this meant that there was an aircraft movement every ninety seconds of the day or night at both Gatow and Tempelhof, so careful planning and accurate flying were essential. Aircraft that missed their approach, an occasional happening in really bad weather, were not permitted a second try. They were committed to taking their cargo back to base. Once landed and parked on the ramp in Berlin, aircrews stayed with their aircraft and were briefed for the return flight while the aircraft was unloaded, keeping the average turnaround time to thirty minutes.[4] Tight control of the aircraft was exercised both in the air and on the ground, with check pilots ensuring adherence to procedures, Ground Controlled Approach operators

Almost two-thirds of the cargo carried during the Berlin Airlift was coal. A C-54 carried over six tons of coal, but an energetic team could unload the aircraft in less than six minutes.

monitoring aircraft separation, "Follow Me" Jeeps marshaling arrivals after landing, and operations officers allocating slots for each flight.

A meticulous program of aircraft maintenance was vital to the continued success of the airlift. The C-54 had been designed by Douglas as the DC-4, an airliner intended to fly for long periods at cruising power and to land at relatively light weights. On the airlift, they were operating overloaded, flying short legs, and therefore spending more time each day at takeoff power, carrying such difficult cargoes as coal or salt which spread corrosive particles into every corner, and landing at well over the designed weight. Engines, brakes, and tires suffered excessive wear and tear. Ground crews worked wonders to keep their aircraft on the line, and ex-Luftwaffe mechanics, so recently the enemy, were hired to help out. Besides normal servicing, one of the more onerous jobs done at base was aircraft cleaning with brooms and mops to keep the grit down as much as possible. Bearing the residual scars and grime of their unexpected calling, the C-54s were withdrawn to the U.K. for major inspections every two hundred flying hours, and at one thousand hours they went back to the U.S. for a complete overhaul.

With growing confidence and expe-

rience, the Allied airlift went on without pause throughout the winter of 1948-49. Daily tonnages delivered rose above the 4,500 of the original estimate in September 1948. A third airport, at Tegel, became usable in December, and by January 1949, the daily figure was averaging more than 5,500 tons; in May it reached over 8,000. On one spectacular day of deliveries, April 15, 1949 (known thereafter as the Easter Parade), 1,398 aircraft landed in Berlin and off-loaded 12,941 tons of supplies.

Impressive as the Berlin airlift was, it contained a smaller, unofficial activity, known as "Operation Little Vittles," which generated almost as much publicity and at least as much affection. C-54 pilot Lt. Gail Halvorsen enjoyed Berlin's children and brought them candy when he could. There were always some watching the aircraft on the approach to Tempelhof, and it occurred to him that he could drop them candy as he flew by. He and his crew-chief made small parachutes from handkerchiefs, hung candy beneath them, and began throwing them out of the cargo door on finals. The small groups of children soon grew into crowds and Operation Little Vittles made news. People in the U.S. contributed handkerchiefs, U.S. servicemen gave candy, and safety equipment personnel cut time-expired parachutes into smaller editions. It was both a great kindness and a public re-

[4]Unloading could be remarkably rapid. One German team of twelve men managed to unload six and a quarter tons of coal from a C-54 in only five minutes and forty-five seconds!

C-54s at Tempelhof. By mid-winter 1948-49, the Allied airlift into Berlin had reached a daily total of 5,500 tons. Some 300 C-54s formed the backbone of the relentless delivery schedule, night and day in all weathers.

lations success. Bringing a light-hearted touch to a serious business, it was loved by Americans and watched with despair by the Soviets. If the Americans could take the time to think about throwing candy to kids, was it likely that they would find it difficult to keep the airlift going?

On May 12, 1949, the Soviets called it a day and lifted the blockade. The airlift continued until September 30 to help in building up Berlin's stocks against possible future emergencies. On that day, a USAF C-54 completed the last of the 277,804 flights which comprised the airlift. In all, the Allies flew 2,325,000 tons of supplies into Berlin, or almost exactly one ton per inhabitant; 1,783,000 tons of the total were lifted by U.S. aircraft, no less than one and a half million tons of which were coal. Given the intensity of the operation, accidents were almost inevitable, and there were losses. The USAF lost four C-47s and six C-54s, and the USN one R5D; the British another nine transports. However, the Soviets had been made to back down and had been given a graphic illustration of Allied resolve and capability. The losses were sad, but relative to the immense total of sorties flown they were a small price to pay for such a major triumph.

In monetary terms, the Berlin airlift had been an extremely good value. For the expenditure of some $200 million, the opposition had been seen off and the USAF had gained immeasurably in experience. Interservice and international teamwork could not have been better. The feasibility of extended and intensive transport operations by day and night in all weathers had been tried and proved. Air traffic and freight handling procedures had been developed to new levels of excellence. Aircrews had become expert in flying accurately on instruments for long periods and had come to trust the guidance of radio aids and approach controllers. Maj. Gen. Tunner had had his enthusiasm for large aircraft reinforced. As he pointed out, lifting a daily total of 4,500 tons into Berlin would have required a fleet of almost 500 C-47s flying three sorties per day. About 180 C-54s had done the same job, with others adding additional tonnage. If C-74s (later C-124s) had been available, only 68 could have handled the same lift, and that would have meant fewer flights, fewer men, less maintenance, and a cheaper, less hazardous operation.

For their part, the Soviets had learned that the West was prepared to be stubborn in Europe. It seemed that Communism would have to try elsewhere. It was not long before it did just that.

Confronting the Bear

The continued intransigence of the Soviets and the openly threatening nature of their behavior in Czechoslovakia and Berlin brought home to the Western powers the marked disparity in conventional military capability which had arisen in Europe since the end of WWII. The Soviet Army had, if anything, increased in strength, while the West had effectively disarmed. The only clear Western advantage lay in American nuclear weapons and it was by no means certain that this would be enough to deter a westward march of Soviet influence, either through political blackmail or direct military action. To counter the threat and provide a system of mutual support within which individual nations might build prosperous democratic societies, steps were taken which led in 1949 to the formation of the North Atlantic Treaty Organization (NATO). Twelve Western nations agreed to develop their capacity to defend themselves, and to regard an attack on one as an attack on all. There was no doubt, particularly in 1949, that the alliance depended heavily on U.S. military power, and that the USAF was a vital element of that power. The problem was that the USAF was but a shadow of its former USAAF self.

Of the combat commands, TAC suffered most from the postwar shortage of funds. By 1949, TAC had withered to a small planning headquarters under Continental Air Command (CONAC), a new organization designed to absorb the sadly diminished rumps of ADC and TAC, allocating their resources to air defense or tactical missions as situations demanded. Those previously mighty tactical air forces, the Ninth and Twelfth, could muster only eleven groups between them. It was true that the first jet fighters, F-80s and F-84s, were starting to appear, and there were twin-boomed C-82s on the troop-carrier squadrons, but the USAF's tactical air strength was generally far below what was needed for an air force with global responsibilities.

ADC was hardly any better off than TAC. The knowledge that the USSR pos-

The Convair B-36J was the last version of SAC's first global bomber. Originally conceived in WW II in response to the thought that transatlantic attacks on Germany might become necessary, at the outset of the Cold War the B-36 was the only U.S. combat aircraft which could reach Soviet targets from American bases.

sessed a B-29 look-alike in the TU-4, which could at least make one-way attacks on the U.S., concerned USAF leaders and led them to seek funds for the construction of a North American early warning radar system. By 1949, Congress had authorized only an interim measure (known as LASHUP), but the fact was that the U.S. was practically defenseless against air attack. Radar coverage was almost nonexistent, and the available fighters were inadequate for maintaining a day and night continental air defense. The piston-engined F-82 Twin Mustang, armed with 0.5 in machine guns, served on night fighter squadrons until well into the 1950s.

SAC had been the command most favored in the allocation of the USAF's scarce funds, and by 1949 changes and improvements were beginning to show. Perhaps the most notable of these came in the person of General Curt LeMay, who assumed command of SAC in October 1948. In the course of a remarkable ten-

ure of nine years, LeMay imposed his steely will on his command to a degree rarely equaled in military history and built SAC into an awesome instrument of war, the annihilating weapon he believed a strategic striking force should be. When he took over, he was appalled by the command's lack of strategic capability and poor standards. He took an early opportunity to administer a sharp shock by ordering a bombing exercise at altitudes vastly greater than the SAC crews were used to. The results were, as he expected, abysmal. His remarks to commanders were typically blunt: "What a sorry operation. I've been telling you we were in bad shape. We *are* in bad shape. Now let's get busy and get this fixed."

LeMay began by establishing the highest possible standards for every aspect of life in SAC. He was an unforgiving master and a relentless perfectionist, demanding only the best from aircrew, maintenance men, administrators, and every-

one else. It was clear, however, that he demanded the best *for* them, too. Better aircraft began to arrive and the living standards on SAC bases soon became the envy of the rest of USAF. Under the driving impulse of LeMay's personality, SAC grew steadily in power and in self-respect.

If LeMay needed added fuel to stoke the fires of SAC's expansion, it came in September 1949, when the Soviet Union detonated its first atomic bomb. The short-lived U.S. nuclear monopoly was broken and SAC's significance as an element of national security surged overnight. At this stage, the position of SAC as the nation's primary strategic military instrument was still a matter of ardent discussion, continuing a debate which had intensified in 1948. Driven by the interservice competition for limited funds, arguments broke out between the Navy and the Air Force over the respective merits of carrier task forces and long-range bombers for conducting strategic air operations. Meetings held by Secretary of Defense James Forrestal at Key West and Newport led to formal allocations of primary responsibility for strategic air warfare to the USAF and for control of the seas to the USN. Requirements for procuring both aircraft carriers and large aircraft from the funds available persisted, however, and long-term plans for a seventy-group air force were necessarily affected. By 1949, President Truman's proposed defense budget contained provision for only forty-eight groups.

Well aware of the running controversy over funds and missions, Forrestal's successor as Secretary of Defense, Louis Johnson, ordered a review of major programs. During 1949, this led to the cancellation of the USN's proposed supercarrier, and then to Congressional hearings on the USAF's new bomber, the Convair B-36. Questions were asked about whether the B-36 had the capabilities to carry out its strategic mission, and whether it had become an expensive obsession which was damaging to the USAF's other roles. It was suggested that there had been corruption in the aircraft's selection process. Beyond that, the debate broadened into an indictment of the USAF's strategic bombing doctrine as a whole. When the dust had settled, the USAF had successfully defended both its procurement of the B-36 and its doctrine, and naval leaders had to accept that long-range bombers were going to take a large share of the defense budget in the years ahead.

The B-36, impressive as it might be, was a holdover from WWII thinking. It had been planned originally for attacks on Germany from the U.S. in the event that Britain was overrun by the Nazis. It met a requirement for an aircraft to operate over a five-thousand-mile radius of action carrying a 10,000 lb bombload. Since it did not fly until 1946 and was not in regular squadron service until 1948, its intended purpose was overtaken by events, but with the onset of the Cold War, it was the only aircraft capable of reaching strategic targets in the USSR from U.S. bases. It was gigantic—230 ft across the wing and with an eventual maximum loaded weight of 410,000 lbs (B-36J). Power came from six

3,500 hp P&W radials, later augmented by the addition of four GE jet engines of 5,200 lbs thrust each. Over a radius of 2,300 miles, the B-36 could deliver the incredible total of 72,000 lbs of bombs—far more than the B-17's maximum loaded weight.[5]

Such startling figures aside, however, the B-36 was something of a dinosaur. Heavily armed with multiple cannon in turrets though it was, it was difficult to imagine such a lumbering monster penetrating Soviet airspace with impunity. Fighters could not be expected to escort the giant on intercontinental missions, and it was only its capacity to deliver nuclear

The Lockheed P-80A Shooting Star was the first jet fighter ordered in large numbers by the USAAF. Deliveries of 677 P-80As began in December 1945.

weapons which made it a credible threat. An attempt was made to provide an escort by hanging one on the B-36 itself. The McDonnell XF-85 Goblin was a tiny parasite fighter designed to be carried in one of the B-36's bomb bays and released when needed. The XF-85's instability and limited endurance doomed the project, although a few reconnaissance versions of the B-36 (GRB-36F) did later succeed in

operating for a while with RF-84Ks carried in a cradle. In this role the bomber stayed in international airspace, while the RF-84K was launched on a high-speed dash mission and then retrieved for the ride home.

By the end of 1949, there were three heavy bombardment wings of B-36s in service. Their arrival had demoted the existing B-29s to the medium bomber category, where they were joined by newly delivered B-50s, essentially greatly improved B-29s. There were eleven B-29/50 wings, plus two fighter and three reconnaissance wings. SAC organized these assets into three numbered air forces: Eighth (heavy/medium bombers); Fifteenth (medium bombers); and Second (reconnaissance). Now with well over one thousand aircraft, SAC set about making itself into a strategic force to be reckoned with, working on professionalism and readiness, and looking for ways to improve its global reach.

Overseas bases in the U.K. and Greenland began the process of constructing a worldwide network, and, in a return to ideas pioneered by DH-4s in 1923, SAC initiated a program to make all of its bombers capable of in-flight refueling. In an early

<hr>

[5]Reporting their aircraft type to air traffic controllers, B-36 pilots took to announcing:"Six a-burnin', four a-turnin'!" A contemporary piece of doggerel left no doubt about the B-36's purpose:
"How dare Convair try to scare the bear-With this colossus which crosses-The globe to probe-Those gremlins in the Kremlin."

demonstration of this force multiplying technique, the B-50A *Lucky Lady II* remained airborne for ninety-four hours between February 26 and March 2, 1949, covering almost 24,000 miles and completing the first nonstop flight around the world. Refueling was completed four times from B-29 tankers based in the Azores, Saudi Arabia, the Philippines, and Hawaii. With the passage of time, in-flight refueling would become ever more important to USAF operations, and the tanker force would grow to impressive proportions, using at first only flexible hose systems but soon moving to a fleet in which the more efficient Boeing flying boom system predominated. Operating with tankers, SAC could reach targets anywhere in the world.

As the USAF prepared itself for the long confrontation of the Cold War, it was changing in other ways, too. President Truman's Executive Order 9981 of July 26, 1948, attacked discrimination and fostered the principle of equal opportunity in the armed services. The Air Force had already done some studies on the problem, but it was still a segregated service in 1948. The celebrated 332nd FG had been deactivated at the end of WWII, but the 99th FS had been retained and assigned to the 477th Composite Group at Lockbourne, Ohio, equipped with B-25s and P-47s. Later, this all black unit lost its B-25s and regained its number as the 332nd FW. Following the President's order, the Air Force led the way in writing an integration plan and was the first of the armed services to issue revised rules and procedures for training, employing, and accommodating personnel. Air Force letter 35-3 of May 11, 1949, set out the new policy, and included the sentence: "It is the policy of the United States Air Force that there shall be equality of treatment and opportunity in the Air Force without regard to race, color, religion, or national origin." Just three weeks later, on June 1, 1949, the 332nd FW was disbanded and its personnel reassigned to a variety of units all over the Air Force.

In a move which was almost as significant, the USAF at last took the step which most visually symbolized separation

F-82s and F-80Cs, seen here sharing the ramp at Itazuki, Japan, were the first American fighters to see action in Korea. On June 27, 1950, just two days after the Communist invasion of S. Korea began, both types were involved in air battles with the N. Korean Air Force. Three Yak-9s and four IL-10s were destroyed without loss to the USAF.

from its parent service. On January 25, 1949, airmen said an official good-bye to their Army uniforms. From then on, Air Force blue would be the dress of the day. On June 2, there was a powerfully symbolic gesture of another kind. President Truman recognized Hap Arnold's achievements as "Father of the Air Force" by awarding him the permanent rank of General of the Air Force. It was just reward for a man who, more than any other person, embodied American military aviation. Six months later, the only USAF officer ever raised to five-star rank was dead. General Arnold died of a heart attack in Sonoma, California, on January 15, 1950.

Surprise, Surprise!

In the closing days of WWII, Soviet forces invaded Korea and accepted the surrender of the Japanese in the northern half of the country. Ignoring prior agreements with the Allies, the Soviets refused to allow the North to take part in the free elections of 1948. Instead, they created the People's Democratic Republic of Korea, dividing the country into two states at the 38th parallel. It was across this arbitrary partition that the Communist world next chose to challenge the democracies. At first light on June 25, 1950, in the wake of several border incidents, North Korean armed

forces swept across the frontier, intent on conquering the South and reuniting Korea under a Communist government.

The attack achieved complete strategic and tactical surprise. Ten Communist divisions, amply provided with armor and artillery, brushed aside the inadequately armed Republic of Korea (ROK) Army and raced southwards. During these early hours of the war, the North Korean Air Force (NKAF) was active and effective. It operated almost two hundred aircraft, mostly Russian of WWII vintage, including seventy Yak-9 fighters and sixty-two IL-10 ground attack bombers. Unimpressive by Western standards, it was formidable compared to the pitifully few T-6 trainers owned by the South Korean Forces.

Response to the invasion was led by the United States. Reacting to pleas for help from South Korea, President Truman pledged support, and the U.S. took the matter to the Security Council of the United Nations. In the fortuitous absence of the Soviet Union, whose delegation was boycotting the Security Council at the time, a vote was taken to support the South against the aggression of the North. Member nations were encouraged to "render such assistance to the Republic of Korea as may be necessary to repel the armed attack." General MacArthur was appointed Supreme Commander, Allied Powers, and the U.S. set about rallying democratic nations to the flag.

As a first step, MacArthur was instructed to ensure the evacuation of U.S. citizens from Korea, covering the operation with fighter aircraft flying from bases in Japan. Once again, U.S. transport aircraft were to lead the charge in meeting an emergency. The first USAF aircraft lost in the Korean War was a C-54, strafed and burned by a Yak-9 on the first day at Seoul's airfield, Kimpo. On June 27, the NKAF hit Kimpo again, but this time there were F-82Gs from the 8th FBW overhead. Three out of five Yak-9s were destroyed, Lt. William Hudson of the 68th FS claiming the first U.S. air victory. Later that day, eight IL-10s tried their luck and were met by F-80Cs of the 35th FBS. Four IL-10s were destroyed, and the rest fled. Although these encounters suggested that USAF crews and aircraft were clearly superior, it was apparent that the NKAF did pose a threat and that it would be sensible to counter it at source. On June 30 President Truman authorized the USAF to strike targets above the 38th parallel and, within a month, attacks on airfields in the north by B-26s[6] and B-29s had helped reduce the NKAF to a handful of aircraft, rendering it impotent.

Air supremacy over the whole of Korea having been so easily established, Allied army commanders may have hoped that the situation would come to resemble that in Western Europe after the Normandy invasion. If so, they were to be disappointed. The circumstances of the two conflicts were so vastly different that many of the lessons learned in WWII offered misleading guidance for combat in Korea. Most significant was the fact that the resources committed to the war were never on the unlimited scale of WWII, nor was it possible for those available to be used without restraint.

By the time of the D-Day landings in Normandy, the U.S. had been fighting an all-out war for over two years. The nation was committed to a maximum effort, and supplies of both men and materiel were virtually endless. There were almost no restrictions, political or otherwise, on the way U.S. and allied forces could fight the enemy and, whenever possible, massive force was applied using the best available equipment. Air supremacy had been achieved and was maintained over Western Europe. Free of effective opposition, the Allied air forces were able to inflict severe damage on German industry and to disrupt the sophisticated system of road and rail communications on which the enemy was heavily dependent.

None of these conditions existed in Korea. American forces went into action in Korea without preparation at a time when the U.S. military was at a low ebb, surviving on minimal funding and with its units often understrength and poorly equipped. Things would improve, but massive force, as it was understood in Europe, was never available. Air supremacy over Korea was achieved at the outset but would not last, even though the USAF was invariably able to gain local air superiority when necessary. Perhaps most significantly, political restrictions seriously limited the way in which the Korean War could be fought, reducing the effectiveness of air strikes and offering the enemy safe havens.

Enemy industries supplying the war from outside Korea were permanently out of reach, and the effective interdiction of surface communications proved almost impossible, given the USAF's limitations and the undeveloped nature of Korea. The enemy was always ready to use pack animals and manpower to keep supplies flowing over trails to the front. In short, the U.S. found itself involved in a limited war, a phenomenon which was to become disturbingly familiar as the twentieth century progressed.

Gaining air supremacy in the first month of the war was one thing; checking the onrushing North Korean Army was quite another. Neither the soldiers of the broken ROK Army nor the lightly equipped U.S. Army infantry units were capable of imposing anything more serious than temporary delays on their rampant opponents. By the end of July, the Allies had been driven back into a small pocket no more than about seventy miles across in any direction, centered on the port of Pusan. Here General Walton Walker, U.S. 8th Army commander with responsibility for U.N. ground forces, took his stand, warning his troops that: "There will be no more retreating, withdrawal, readjustment of lines, or whatever you call it." Until early September, the Allies hung on, enduring an almost endless series of

A Douglas B-26 Invader harmonizing its formidable battery of guns before a night interdiction sortie in Korea.

[6]These aircraft were the Douglas A-26 Invaders introduced towards the end of WW II. In 1948, when the original B-26, the Martin Marauder was phased out, the A-26 inherited the designation B-26, to the eternal confusion of aviation historians.

At the beginning of the Korean War, F-51s, overdue for retirement but better able to cope with the primitive conditions of Korean airfields in 1950, were hastily restored to front-line service. Two 18th FG F-80C squadrons transitioned back to the F-51. One of them was the 12th FBS at Chinhae, near Pusan, its Mustangs recognizable from their grinning sharks' mouths.

crises as the North Koreans hurled themselves against the defenses of the Pusan perimeter. During the desperate weeks of August, U.S. and ROK soldiers withstood numerous fierce assaults, buying time for reinforcements and supplies to build up through Pusan. At times, North Koreans broke through the lines, but were stopped by judicious use of reserves and of air power. On September 3, Maj. Gen. William Kean of the 25th Division reported: "The close air support strikes rendered by the Fifth Air Force again saved this Division, as they have many times before."

At the heart of the Allied air effort in Korea was the USAF's Far East Air Force (FEAF), commanded by Lt. Gen. George Stratemeyer. The largest of its subordinate commands was the Fifth Air Force, described by its commander, Lt. Gen. Earle Partridge, as "a small but highly professional tactical-type air force." It comprised three F-80C wings, one understrength

light bombardment wing of B-26s, and two all-weather fighter squadrons with F-82s. One wing of FEAF's B-29s was drawn from the Twentieth Air Force in Okinawa, and a further two wings were detached from SAC. The three B-29 wings were formed into FEAF Bomber Command under Maj. Gen. Emmett O'Donnell.

Initially, the F-80Cs were something of a problem. Their combat radius was limited and there were no airfields in Korea capable of handling jets. As an interim solution, many F-80 pilots found themselves reconverting to F-51s taken from storage. The Mustangs could be based in South Korea, had the endurance to allow them to fly extended armed reconnaissance sorties, and could carry bombs and napalm, which the F-80Cs could not. At a time when the ground forces were so hard pressed and close air support was vital, the born-again F-51s proved invaluable, repeatedly blunting enemy thrusts until army

reserves could be brought into action.

Throughout August, the priority for the airmen was close support of the beleaguered Allied troops. A breakdown of the operations flown during that month shows that there were 7,397 close support sorties, compared to 2,963 interdiction and 539 strategic bombing sorties. Even the B-29s were sometimes used against battlefield targets, counter to Stratemeyer's advice and with disappointing effect. For the most part, however, the Bomber Command's B-29s pounded industrial and transportation targets north of Seoul, and did a good job. By September, there was little left of the North's steel plants, oil depots, railway yards, and harbor facilities.

Interdiction targets south of Seoul were tackled by the Fifth Air Force, but they were more difficult. After the first few days, when some enemy convoys were caught in the open in daylight and severely dealt with, the North Koreans learned to move at night. Thereafter, FEAF's lack of an adequate night tactical capability proved to be an embarrassment. The night intruder role fell to the B-26s, but they were far from ideal since they were not fitted with radar altimeters, short-range navigation radar, or blind-bombing radar. Nor were they particularly maneuverable, which was a distinct disadvantage for an aircraft which sometimes needed to operate at low-level by night through Korea's rugged terrain. Although the B-26s tried to overcome their failings by operating in pairs, with one aircraft dropping flares and the other strafing, results were not encouraging. It was too difficult to find the elusive enemy in the darkness.

Interdiction of static targets by daylight was much more successful. By mid-September, FEAF claimed that, with the help of naval aircraft, 140 bridges had been destroyed between Seoul and the Pusan perimeter, and forty-seven cuts had been made and maintained in rail lines. Another ninety-three bridges around Pusan had been rendered unusable, and hundreds of locomotives, railway cars, and motor vehicles had been destroyed. Impressive though these figures were, it was never possible to stop the flow of North Korean supplies entirely. Pack animals, including humans, helped to keep them trickling through. Nevertheless, it is clear that the interdiction campaign against the lengthening enemy logistic chain played an important part in the eventual defeat of the North Korean offensive. The records of one North Korean infantry division show that it received 166 tons of ordnance between June 25 and July 15, but only 17 tons from August 16 to September 20. At the same time, the average daily ration of a soldier fell from a mixed diet of 800 grams to 400 grams, almost all rice. It is significant that North Korean prisoners taken in September admitted that the morale of their units, extremely high at the start of the offensive, was now very low. Reasons for the decline were sought during interrogation and two emerged as by far the most important—shortage of food and fear of aircraft.

MacArthur Strikes Back

When it came, the collapse of the North Korean Army was rapid. On September 15, MacArthur loosed his masterstroke, landing the 1st Marine Division at Inchon, close to Seoul and 150 miles behind the fighting around Pusan. Strongly supported by Allied carrier aircraft, the Marines advanced rapidly and within two days had recovered Kimpo airfield. The day after the Inchon landing, the 8th Army broke out of the Pusan pocket and drove north under the Fifth Air Force's umbrella. No longer capable of withstanding American firepower and hounded from the air, the North Korean Army disintegrated and by the end of the month had been driven from South Korea.

MacArthur made it clear that he intended to seek the final destruction of the North Korean Army by continuing to advance beyond the 38th parallel. He was quite sure that the risk of Chinese intervention was minimal. On October 7, 1950, euphoria brought on by success encouraged the U.N. General Assembly to approve a resolution that "all necessary steps be taken to ensure conditions of peace throughout the whole of Korea." Under this thin cloak of authority, the U.N. troops set off for the Yalu River, the boundary between Korea and China.

If anything, Fifth Air Force support for U.N. soldiers was now even better than before. With the utility of Forward Air Controllers (FACs) on the ground limited by the terrain, North American T-6s drew an unexpected and often hazardous combat role, flying close to the battle lines with FACs on board. Known as "Mosquitoes," they kept in radio contact with both ground units and supporting fighters, marking targets with 2.75 in rockets and

In Korea, July 1952, an LT-6G "Mosquito" of the 6147th Tactical Control Group rolls in to mark a target with smoke rockets. Waiting fighter bombers will follow up.

controlling air attacks as necessary. Air transport came into its own, too; C-119s and C-47s of General Tunner's new Combat Cargo Command dropped 2,860 paratroopers across enemy escape routes north of P'yongyang, the North Korean capital, on October 20. It was one of the most effective paratroop operations ever carried out, sealing the fate of the enemy forces leaving the city.

North Korean resistance quickly crumbled all along the front and, by the end of October, some U.N. units were on the banks of the Yalu. MacArthur was triumphant. The war would soon be over, and he would have brought about the unification of Korea, having given the Communists a bloody nose in the process. Such unbounded confidence was sharply checked in November, when the Chinese showed that they were not prepared to sit idly by while North Korea was forcibly gathered to the bosom of democracy.

Chinese Intervention

American forces first felt the heat of Chinese anger towards the end of October. Some forward positions were overrun

Bombed up F-84Es of the 8th FBS on their way to a target in Korea.

by Chinese troops and, on November 1, a patrolling F-80C was shot down by anti-aircraft guns firing across the Yalu. Chinese aircraft began "trailing their coats" over North Korea and, on November 8, 1950, the world's first all-jet combat took place when F-80Cs of the 51st Fighter Interceptor Wing were jumped by MiG-15s. In a brief exchange, the USAF scored first blood when Lt. Russell Brown shot down one of the attackers. That early success was no indication of relative capabilities, however. It was quickly apparent that F-80Cs were no match for MiG-15s. Designed

with the benefit of German swept-wing aerodynamics and powered by a copy of a British jet engine, the MiG-15 was some 100 mph faster than the F-80C, could climb to 50,000 ft, and was heavily armed with one 37 mm and two 23 mm cannon.

By the end of November, the U.N. forces were in trouble. Chinese ground forces estimated at more than half a million men had crossed the Yalu and the U.N. forces were in disorderly retreat. Overwhelmed by sheer numbers, many units broke and ran under the shock of the massive Chinese assault. In the air, the U.N. air forces had nothing to match the

MiG-15 and air supremacy close to the Yalu River could no longer be guaranteed. It was fortunate that during this period, as the USAF moved to meet the threat, the Chinese Air Force was not particularly aggressive.

By mid-December, a measure of balance was given to the air war with the arrival in Korea of the 4th FIW, equipped with North American F-86A Sabres. A classic fighter beloved by its pilots, the F-86 was not quite as good in the climb or at very high altitude as the lighter MiG-15, nor did its six 0.5 in machine guns have

the hitting power of its opponent's cannon, but it was just as fast and was more stable as a gun platform at high Mach numbers. It also had the advantage of being fitted with a radar-ranging gunsight. Just as important, the Sabre was a joy to fly and had no vices, whereas the MiG-15 had a tendency to flick savagely if driven too hard in high-G turns.

Another, less glamorous, American jet arrived in Korea in December. The 27th Fighter Escort Group brought their F-84E Thunderjets to the war. The F-84 was an aircraft which inspired more respect than affection in its pilots. It was a rugged, workmanlike machine, but it was underpowered for the fighter-bomber job it had to do, and it was not very lively. Fully loaded with bombs, rockets, and fuel tanks, the F-84 weighed over ten tons. Its spidery, wide-stanced undercarriage had to cope with punishingly long takeoff runs on the rough airfields of Korea and the J-35 engine of the earlier models was apt to shed turbine blades when shaken too hard. Nevertheless, for all its minor shortcomings, the F-84 proved to be a fearsome fighter-bomber and the champion hauler of bombs and napalm in the Korean War. If there were people who viewed the F-84 with affection, they were the hard pressed U.N. soldiers its heavy punch supported.

It was not long before the new American arrivals were in action. On December 17, Lt. Col. Bruce Hinton of the 4th FIW gained the first F-86 victory over a MiG-15, the first of four achieved by his unit that day. The welcome intervention of the F-86 in the air war was short-lived, however. The Chinese ground offensive forced the U.N. armies back south of Seoul, thereby denying airfields to the F-86s, which retreated temporarily to the safety of Japan. With his demoralized troops facing an apparently inexhaustible Chinese Army, MacArthur was suggesting that Korea could not be held unless mainland China was attacked, and he was advocating the use of nuclear weapons. During this unpromising phase of the war, the F-84s imposed themselves on the battle, hammering the advancing Chinese incessantly and giving desperate units of the 8th

Army the chance to escape destruction. In the eastern half of Korea, salvation for the Marines also came with wings—their own close air support aircraft and FEAF's transports. Cargo aircraft kept the troops supplied during their fighting withdrawal from the Chosin Reservoir, flew out their wounded from hastily prepared landing strips, and dropped a sixteen-ton, eight-section Bailey bridge to aid their escape across a deep gorge. Eventually the transports completed an aerial evacuation of over four thousand men from the Hamhung area under the noses of the Chinese.

As the bleak winter days of January 1951 passed into history, the resistance of the U.N. ground forces stiffened under the inspiring new leadership of General Matthew Ridgway. By the middle of the month, facing a more determined foe and with extended supply lines relentlessly attended by Allied aircraft, the seemingly irresistible Chinese Army slowed to a halt. U.N. counterattacks led to the recovery of Seoul, and the F-86s were back in Korea by the end of February to resume their confrontation with the MiG-15s.

Though the standard of training of the American pilots was probably better than that of their Chinese counterparts, they were still at a disadvantage operationally. Based near Seoul, the F-86s had to fly up to "MiG Alley"—the region of northwest Korea between the Yalu and Ch'ongch'on Rivers—to meet their enemy. There they were close to the limit of their range and could not spend long in combat. They were forbidden to cross the Yalu into Manchuria. Their opponents, on the other hand, often operated within sight of their bases and could stay on their side of the Yalu until they chose to engage, timing their attacks to advantage. The F-86s were also heavily outnumbered. During 1951, the number of MiGs available rose to over five hundred, as opposed to one hundred or so F-86s, although only about half of either force might be combat ready at any one time. The figures made little difference to the consistent combat superiority of the F-86. As the air superiority war resumed in 1951, the Sabres began to

hit their stride, shooting down three MiGs in March and fourteen in April. In May, Capt. James Jabara became the first jet ace when he downed his fifth and sixth MiGs.[7]

June saw the appearance in combat of Soviet instructors, but they had little effect on the trend; forty-two MiGs were claimed destroyed in the month for the loss of three F-86s.

The Chinese Army realized that they could not succeed against the U.N. forces without effective air support and they set about preparing airfields in North Korea which would allow them to move fighters south of the Yalu. Reconnaissance aircraft

hundred MiGs kept the escorts busy, while fifty more broke through to attack eight B-29s which were on their way to bomb airfields. Three of the bombers were shot down and the rest so severely damaged that they never flew again.

The B-29s had experienced similar problems when attempting to destroy the Yalu bridges earlier in the year. The Yalu bridges were difficult anyway, because heavy flak kept the bombers above 20,000 ft, and bombing runs had to be along the river because of the prohibition against entering Chinese airspace, making the attacks predictable and presenting the B-29s

The F-86A Sabres of the 4th FIG arrived at Kimpo, S. Korea, in December 1950. This aircraft, gun panels open, is the mount of Glenn Eagleston, the 4th's commander in 1951, who went on to add two MiGs to his WW II total of eighteen and a half aerial victories.

kept an eye on the work being done until it neared completion in April 1951. B-29s were then launched on a series of raids which destroyed the Chinese airfield facilities and cratered the runways. This sequence of events was repeated at intervals, and the Chinese never did succeed in operating MiGs regularly from North Korea. Important as this achievement of the B-29s was, it was not without cost. On October 23, 1951, for example, about one

with the narrowest possible targets. MiGs made a poor situation very much worse. On April 12, all three bomber groups were sent against bridges at Sinuiju and were attacked by as many as one hundred MiGs. The escort could not ward off the attack and three B-29s were lost and seven damaged.

Soon after the series of losses in October, the B-29s were finally restricted to night operations to escape the attentions of the MiGs. The loss of the daylight option reduced the B-29 sortie rate and lim-

[7]Jabara went on to become the second-ranking ace of the Korean War, registering fifteen victories. (He also had one and a half in WW II.) The leading scorer in Korea was Capt. Joseph McConnell with sixteen. Eleven pilots reached double figures.

Fast, maneuverable, and heavily armed, the MiG-15 nevertheless proved to be no match for the F-86 during the Korean War. One major reason for the claimed 10 to 1 kill ratio in favor of the Sabre was the superior training given to USAF pilots.

ited the weight of effort which could be directed against the Chinese transportation system. Restrictions of this kind, forced by enemy action, brought the USAF to the realization that air supremacy was beyond its reach over North Korea.

Stalemate

On the ground, the war congealed into stalemate by mid-1951. Both sides now recognized that there could be no easy victory and armistice talks were proposed. After a false start in July at Kaesong, the talks settled into a tedious and frustrating pattern at Panmunjom in October. The chief North Korean delegate, General Nam Il, paid the U.N. air forces a bitter tribute:

"Without the support of the indiscriminate bombing and bombardment of your air and naval forces, your ground forces would have long ago been driven out of the Korean peninsula by our powerful and battle-skilled ground forces."

As the talks assumed the character of a propaganda war and U.N. delegates found themselves embroiled in endless argument over minor details, the fighting continued.

Although the ground war had frozen into an almost static confrontation at about the 38th parallel, the aerial struggle carried on much as before. High on the

list of priorities for FEAF was the interdiction of the enemy's supply lines with the object of preventing the Chinese Army from building up stocks for a future offensive. Efficiently done, interdiction might even force the Chinese to think about withdrawing northward to shorten their logistic chain and put their front line within range of MiG-15 cover. Starting with Operation STRANGLE in May, and continuing with the Rail Interdiction Program, U.N. aircraft kept up a persistent day and night assault on roads and railways in North Korea throughout 1951. That it caused the Communist forces discomfort and inconvenience is certain. It did not, however, accomplish either of its main aims. The enemy was not prevented from accumulating supplies, nor was there any sign of withdrawal. On December 28, an intelligence summary from Fifth Air Force acknowledged defeat: "The enemy's highly developed repair and construction capability of both bridges and rail lines has broken our blockade of P'yongyang and has won for him the use of all key rail arteries."

There were a number of reasons for the failure of the interdiction campaigns. First, the daily consumption of Chinese divisions was small; perhaps only a tenth of that needed by their Western counter-

parts, particularly when they were not on the offensive. Second, the enemy's large labor pool allowed for quick repair of damaged routes and the alternative of carrying supplies over primitive tracks. Third, the USAF's global commitments ensured that FEAF would have insufficient aircraft for the task. Just as serious was the USAF's inability to replace losses quickly, especially once the enemy's defenses improved and FEAF's fighter-bomber loss rate rose to more than twenty a month.[8] Fourth, the fighter-bombers were forced by increasing flak to resort to dive-bombing, which halved the effectiveness of their strikes. Fifth, the USAF did not have an aircraft capable of undertaking effective night interdiction, especially in an under-developed country like Korea.

The frustrations of trying to fight an enemy so ready to use low-technology countermeasures did not end there. The Communist air forces, incapable of launching a major campaign against the U.N.'s airfields, began night nuisance raids using Polikarpov Po-2 biplanes to drop small bombs or hand grenades. Only occasionally did these "Bed-check Charlies" cause any real damage, but they were intensely irritating. No sensible response was ever found to their nightly raids, although a few were brought down, usually more by luck than judgment. Modern aircraft found it hard to cope with a wood and fabric biplane flying at 90 mph or less in the dark. One was shot down when it happened to fly in front of a B-26 preparing to land, and another was flown through by a pursuing F-94; since both aircraft were destroyed, it was a poor exchange. F-94s, only recently arrived to replace the F-82s, were equipped with the most advanced airborne radar then in existence. The Po-2 incident appeared to confirm the radar's accuracy but carried a warning about attempting radar interception of an aircraft with a maximum speed less than the interceptor's landing speed.

At the other end of the performance scale, the MiG-15s changed tactics and

---

[8]In August, Fifth Air Force lost thirty fighter-bombers and had another twenty-four damaged. In September, the figures were thirty-three and 233; in October, thirty-three and 239; and in November, twenty-four and 255.

began to impose themselves more forcibly on the air war. Now fitted with drop tanks, they expanded their area of operations and were seen as far south as P'yongyang. "Trains" of MiGs, sixty to eighty strong, crossed the Yalu at high altitude and flew down the center of the peninsula, elements peeling off at intervals to challenge the patrolling F-86s. The main body continued south, converging over P'yongyang with a similar formation coming from the east coast. The resulting force of one hundred or so then dropped down to medium altitude and searched for U.N. fighter-bombers on interdiction sorties. Losses to the MiGs were few, but the fighter-bombers often had to jettison their weapon loads under attack and, by September 1951, they were forced to restrict their hunting to areas south of the Ch'ongch'on River.

Towards the end of 1951, another pattern of MiG-15 activity was noticed. Large groups of MiGs maneuvered south of the Yalu, staying at maximum altitude and keeping well clear of F-86s. Over a six- week period, the formations became steadily bolder. Then the cycle started again. It appeared that courses were being run to provide a gentle introduction to combat for new pilots. The fighter strength in Manchuria rose to over one thousand MiG-15s. Neither the increase nor the innovations seemed to make much difference in the way aerial battles went. It remained true that USAF pilots were better prepared. During 1952, MiGs were claimed at an average rate of one per day. F-86 losses averaged one per week. The introduction of the F-86F with a redesigned wing and more powerful engine made the disparity even wider. The F-86F left the MiG-15 (even the improved 15bis) without any real advantages. In the last months of the war, from March through July 1953, there were 225 claims for MiGs shot down, while FEAF lost just ten F-86s.

In mid-1952, it was decided to use U.N. air power to break the stalemate at the Panmunjom talks. The "Air Pressure" campaign, as it was known, was directed against selected targets in North Korea with the aim of making the conflict as costly as

A dramatic shot of an F-80C attacking N. Korean positions at low level.

possible for the enemy. For three days at the end of June, attacks were concentrated on North Korea's capacity to generate electricity. Ninety percent of the system was destroyed and industry was crippled all over the country. For the rest of 1952 and the first part of 1953, FEAF's bombers continued to pound at military and industrial targets, but, though North Korea was badly hurt, the peace talks remained deadlocked.

Two events, one political and one military, then influenced the discussions. In March 1953, Joseph Stalin died in Moscow, after which Chinese Premier Chou En-lai let it be known that he wished to bring the talks to an end. Progress remained glacial, however, until U.N. aircraft attacked the North Korean irrigation system. It was a decision not taken lightly. Lt. Gen. Otto Weyland, commander of FEAF since

A C-119 of the 314th TCG dropping some four tons of supplies to U.N. troops in Korea.

Combat Cargo Command's transpacific supply line kept the U.N. effort in Korea going. Three of the types involved are seen here at a Japanese base in June 1952-a C-47, a C-54, and a C-124. The Globemaster proved capable of operating into basic landing strips and could offload five times the cargo of any other aircraft in the theater.

June 1951, said that he felt himself morally compelled to rule that North Korean dams could not be attacked for the sole purpose of destroying the people's rice crops. Strikes were permitted against only those dams which, when breached, would release waters to wash away railways and military supplies.

On May 13 and 16, fighter-bombers struck and breached several dams. General Mark Clark, now the U.N. commander, reported that the results were "as effective as weeks of interdiction." The Communists were suitably impressed and responded with vitriolic propaganda statements. Within two months, however, agreement on a cease-fire was reached at Panmunjom. During those two months, the Communists strove to improve their position and inflict military defeat on the U.N. Major ground offensives were launched and repulsed under the cover of massive air support. As the ground fighting subsided, FEAF's bombers hit the North Korean airfields hard to render them unusable. Under the terms of the cease-fire, Chinese aircraft were forbidden to

enter North Korea once it took effect, and Weyland wanted to make sure that there could be no last-minute move across the Yalu.

They Also Served

The greater part of the USAF's burden during the Korean War was borne by units flying fighters and bombers, but the conflict was an all-roles effort. Reconnaissance played a vital part and it involved a wide variety of aircraft, beginning with the RB-17G and the RF-80A. It was quickly apparent that the RB-17G was outclassed and it was replaced by the RB-29, but that aircraft also was found to be inadequate for the more dangerous missions. The solution came with the arrival of the 91st Strategic Reconnaissance Squadron (SRS), which was a unit operating six different types of aircraft: RB-29s, RB-50s, and RB-36s for assorted strategic tasks, WB-26s for weather reporting, and RB-45Cs for reconnaissance over the Yalu. The sixth type was the KB-29 tanker, which offered flight refueling support to various missions.

After a poorly organized start, tacti-

cal reconnaissance was centralized under the control of the 67th Tactical Reconnaissance Wing (TRW) at Taegu. Although results improved, the limitations of the RB-26 and RF-80 remained, and it was not until F-86As, and later F-86Fs, were modified to carry cameras that photographic cover of the Manchurian bases could be guaranteed.

The U.N. could not have sustained the war at all without the transport force. Initially using the C-54 and C-47, the fleet expanded to acquire the C-46, C-119, and, from mid-1952 on, the huge C-124 Globemaster. Critical supplies were flown all the way from the U.S. throughout the war, and the troops were supported by continuous resupply into forward airstrips and by air-drop to units in combat. Inbound flights carried replacement personnel, and those outbound took troops on leave and evacuated casualties. By the end of the war, Combat Cargo's aircraft had carried 2,650,000 passengers, evacuated 314,500 wounded, lifted 697,000 tons of freight, and airdropped 18,000 tons. By any standards, it was a monumental effort.

Evacuation of wounded personnel from forward areas was also undertaken by aircraft of the Air Rescue Service (ARS), although their principal task was the recovery of downed airmen. The waters of the Yellow Sea and the Communist forces could be almost equally unfriendly, and the knowledge that the ARS was there gave a considerable boost to the morale of U.N. aircrew. A wide variety of aircraft was used. SB-17Gs and SB-29s covered the coasts and the open sea, carrying lifeboats instead of bombs. L-5s and SC-47s managed evacuation from the front lines. Grumman SA-16 Albatross amphibians went almost anywhere, including rivers deep behind enemy lines, to recover airmen. The Korean War also saw the introduction of helicopters on a large scale, with H-5s and H-19s going everywhere on rescue missions. Two celebrated USAF aces, "Boots" Blesse and "Mac" McConnell, were returned to combat after being rescued from the Yellow Sea, Blesse by an Albatross and McConnell by an H-19. The helicopters often engaged in clandestine operations, too. Agents parachuted into enemy territory from VB-17Gs were later recovered by ARS helicopters.

Cease-Fire

The Korean War ended at 22:00 hours on July 27, 1953. In the final acts of the air war, an IL-12 transport was shot down by a 4th FIW F-86 at twilight on the last day, and a B-26 of the 3rd BW dropped its bombs just twenty-four minutes before the cease-fire went into effect. These minor events brought to a close a struggle which had begun as President Truman's "police action" and developed into a dangerous and punishing conflict between major powers.

The U.N. air forces flew over one million sorties during the Korean War and lost 2,670 aircraft on operations. The USAF's contribution was an impressive share of that total. More than 720,000 sorties of all kinds were flown, including over 340,000 by fighters and more than a quarter of a million by fighter-bombers. Nearly half a million tons of ordnance were delivered. In aerial combat, 954 enemy aircraft were claimed as destroyed, 792 of them MiG-15s. Compared to WWII, the air forces in Korea were never very large, but, at the end of more than three years of warfare, the cost to the USAF, often described as "amazingly light," was certainly not negligible. Before it was all over, 1,466 FEAF aircraft of all types were lost and 1,144 aircrew were killed in air operations. Of the aircraft total, 605 were fighters lost to enemy action, and that included 78 F-86s downed in aerial combat. The MiG/Sabre combat ratio was encouragingly large in favor of the F-86. Only 17 B-29s were recorded as shot down, but perhaps ten times that many either crashed on landing or were damaged beyond repair as a result of combat.

Those who fought in the Korean War were left with feelings of deep dissatisfaction and disquiet when it was over. The battle had raged from the tip of the peninsula to the Yalu, but all the effort and sacrifice had left the combatants facing each other across the 38th parallel, close to where the struggle began. Many bitter lessons had been learned about confronting the Communist powers in a limited war. Unfortunately, most of them would have to be learned again in Vietnam. One fact was driven home, however. The position of the United States as a global power was now unquestioned, and the American people realized that strong armed forces were essential elements of the "Cold War" policy of containment of communism. For the first time in U.S. history, Americans accepted that, during a period when they were technically at peace, they would have to raise and maintain a large military establishment. This time, at war's end, the U.S. services would not be run down, and the future trend would be for increases in the military and for improvements in equipment and professionalism. For the USAF, in particular, the changes would often be dramatic.

A

B

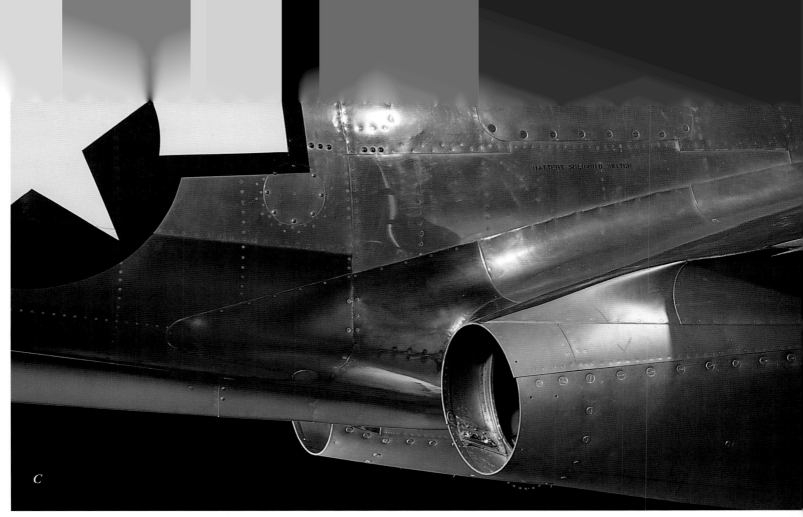

C

A   On October 1, 1942, the Bell P-59 Airacomet became the first American jet aircraft to fly. It was powered by two General Electric I-16 (J-31) engines constructed from designs by the British jet pioneer, Frank Whittle. Since each engine produced only 1,650 lbs thrust, the conventionally shaped P-59 was not a spectacular performer. Nevertheless, it paved the way to the jet age in the U.S. and provided the foundation on which more dramatic advances were later built.

B   This head-on shot of the P-59 shows how the engines were buried in the wing roots and suggests a small frontal area and clean lines. However, the wings are quite thick, and the picture reveals neither the aircraft's considerable weight nor the limitations of its first-generation jet engines.

C   The combined thrust emerging from the P-59's jet pipes at full throttle was no more than 3,300 lbs, but it was sufficient to push the straight-winged Airacomet along at a maximum of 410 mph at 30,000 ft. (In 1942, the Me 262 was achieving well over 500 mph at any height above 20,000 ft.)

D   The P-59 cockpit seemed almost as conventional as its airframe, but the throttle lever needed very careful handling. First generation jet engines were intolerant of rapid throttle movements.

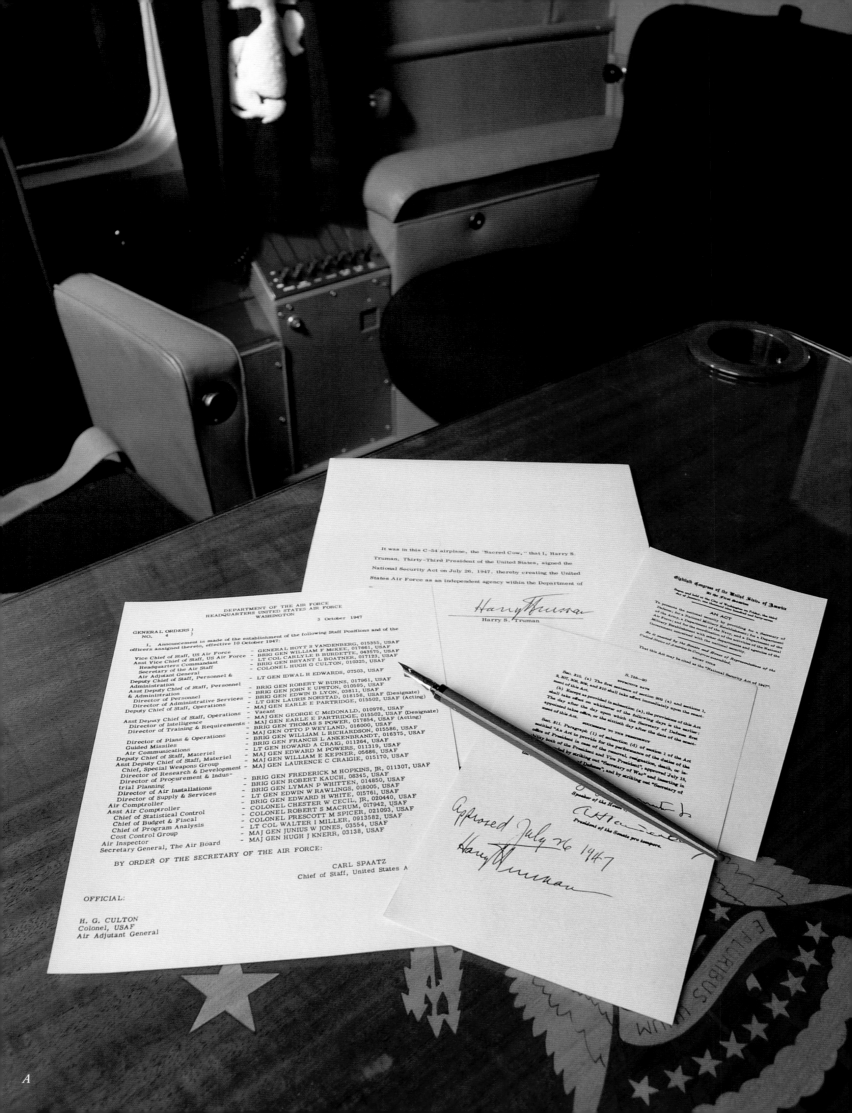

A   On July 26, 1947, President Truman sat at his desk aboard the Air Force C-54 *Sacred Cow,* waiting for the final version of the National Security Act of 1947 to be brought to him before flying to Missouri and the bedside of his dying mother. He signed the bill into law at a few minutes after noon, so creating a single Department of Defense and an independent United States Air Force. *Sacred Cow* is on exhibit at the USAF Museum, where visitors can walk through the aircraft and look into Truman's compartment. Copies of the documents with the President's signature, together with the pen he used, lie on the desk.

B   President Truman's C-54, the *Sacred Cow,* on board which the bill creating the USAF was signed.

C   Relics of the Berlin Airlift at the USAF Museum include coal and flour sacks, bags of beans, and packets of POM, potato in dehydrated form.

D   Berlin Airlift © R.G. Smith

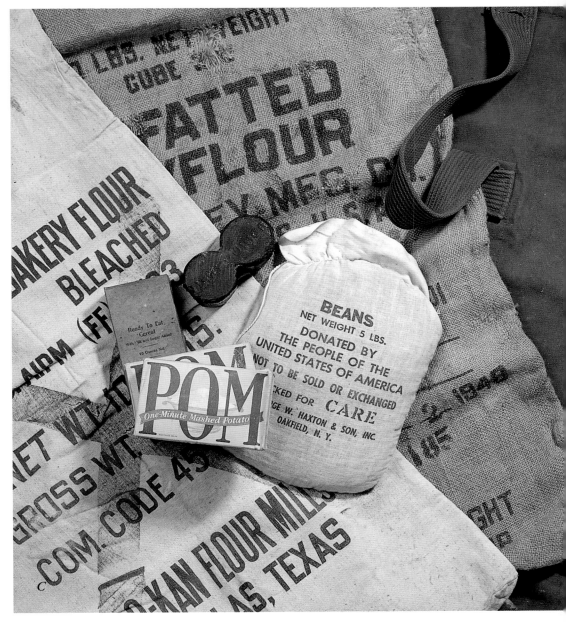

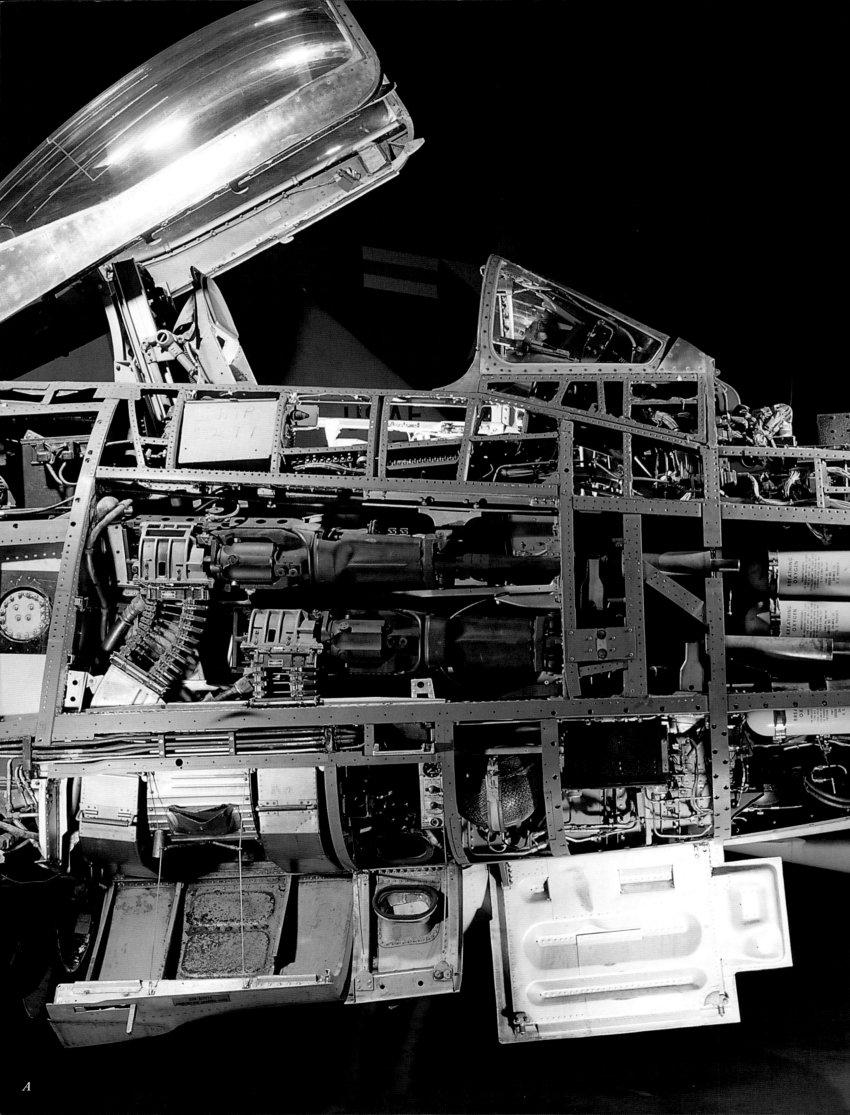

A

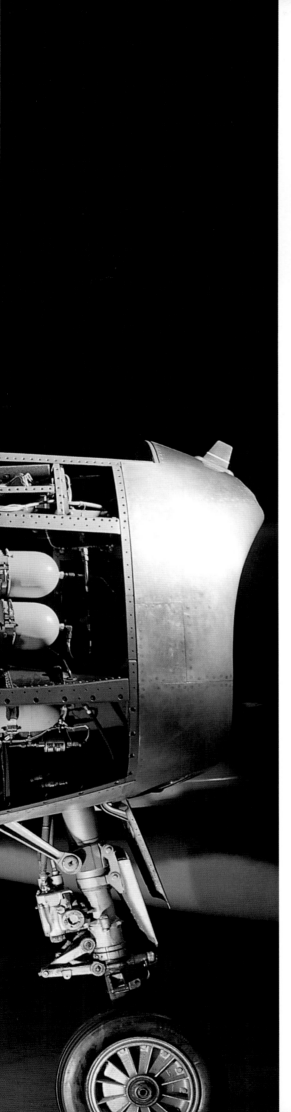

B

A   *The often dense construction of jet combat aircraft is demonstrated by the USAF Museum's F-86H Sabre, which is displayed without its skin and with its internal organs revealed. Among the most recognizable items are the H-model's 20 mm cannons and their ammunition bays. (Compare the emptiness of the SE-5 cutaway illustrated at the end of Chapter 2.)*

B   *The Allison J-33 jet engine produced 4,600 lbs of thrust and was used to power the Lockheed P-80 and T-33. It was directly descended from Frank Whittle's original centrifugal-flow design.*

A

WARNING

THIS AIRPLANE CONTAINS SEAT &
CANOPY EJECTION CATAPULTS
CONTAINING AN EXPLOSIVE CHARGE
SEE T.O. 11-1-93 & T.O. 11-1-99
FOR COMPLETE INSTRUCTIONS

EMER HYD TANK
FILL HERE USE
OIL SPEC MIL-0-3606

NO STEP

EMERGENCY CANOPY
JETTISON HANDLE
PULL TO JETTISON

FT

B

FT-696

CONDUCTING PLASTIC
DO NOT PAINT

A   As can be seen from the warning sign, the exterior of the F-80's sculptured intake was delicate. A custom-made ladder was provided to allow heavy-booted pilots to reach the cockpit.

B   The Lockheed F-80 Shooting Star was the first USAF aircraft to exceed 500 mph in level flight and, during the Korean War, the first to see combat. On November 8, 1950, Lt. Russell Brown, flying an F-80C, shot down a Soviet MiG-15 in the world's first all-jet air battle. The F-80C on display at the USAF Museum flew combat missions in Korea with the 35th FBS, 8th FBG.

C   As befitted an operational aircraft, the F-80's cockpit was more complex and well organized than that of the earlier P-59. Note the ejection seat handle at lower left, and the pad on the gunsight, placed there in the hope of protecting pilots' good looks during accidents.

D   The T-33A Shooting Star advanced trainer was derived from the P-80 by adding a little more than three feet to the fuselage. The two cockpits were arranged in tandem and covered by a long and very heavy single-piece canopy, hinged at the rear to ensure clean separation if it was ever jettisoned. The ejection seats protruded well above the cockpit rails. Warning signs left no doubt that explosive seats should be treated with respect.

A

A	The North American F-86 Sabre was the USAF's first swept-wing jet fighter. It was a delight to fly and was capable of becoming supersonic in a dive. During the Korean War it was the only Allied fighter which could meet the MiG-15 on equal terms. The USAF Museum's F-86A is in the markings of the aircraft flown by Bruce Hinton of the 4th FG when, on December 17, 1950, he became the first F-86 pilot to shoot down a MiG.

B	The F-86 cockpit was typical of a 1950s jet fighter. The flight instruments in the center and to the left of the panel included (moving clockwise from the vertical speed indicator in front of the stick on the bottom row) turn and slip, altimeter, Mach meter (reading from 0.5 to 1.5), radio compass, airspeed, compass, and artificial horizon (with gyros toppled). The white handle to the right of the stick is an emergency hand pump for the hydraulic system.

C	The small beak overhanging the engine intake on the F-86A housed the antenna for the radar gunsight. Six .50–caliber machine guns were mounted in the fuselage, and the gun camera recorded the action through the small hole visible beneath the intake.

D	John Glenn and his F-86, Mig Mad Marine, during his tour of exchange duty with the USAF. The future astronaut and senator shot down three MiGs while in Korea.

B

D

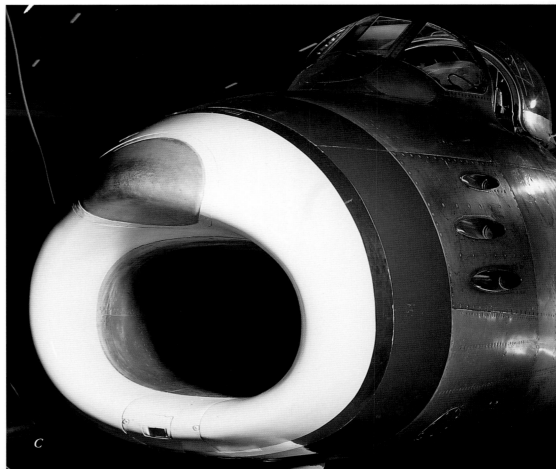

C

First Swept Wing Encounter
© *Keith Ferris, 1977*

A   In the Korean War, the principal opposition in the air came in the shape of the MiG-15. Lighter and more maneuverable than the F-86, it was also more heavily armed with two 23 mm and one 37 mm cannon. It was powered by a 6,000 lbs thrust centrifugal-flow engine copied from a Rolls-Royce "Nene." The MiG-15 in the USAF Museum is the aircraft flown to South Korea on September 21, 1953, by Lt. Kim Sok No, a defector from the North Korean Air Force.

B   The cockpit of the MiG-15 has a familiar look to it, but there are differences from its Western counterparts. Some instruments are marked in Russian, but a Chinese message written in red can be seen over the top of the stick. The English word "fuel" is taped to the gauge near the bottom of the stick, and a U.S. "G" meter sits on top of the coaming, presumably added during trials by Western test pilots. The protective pad on the gunsight is a dome rather than a cushion. (Compare the F-80 cockpit photograph.)

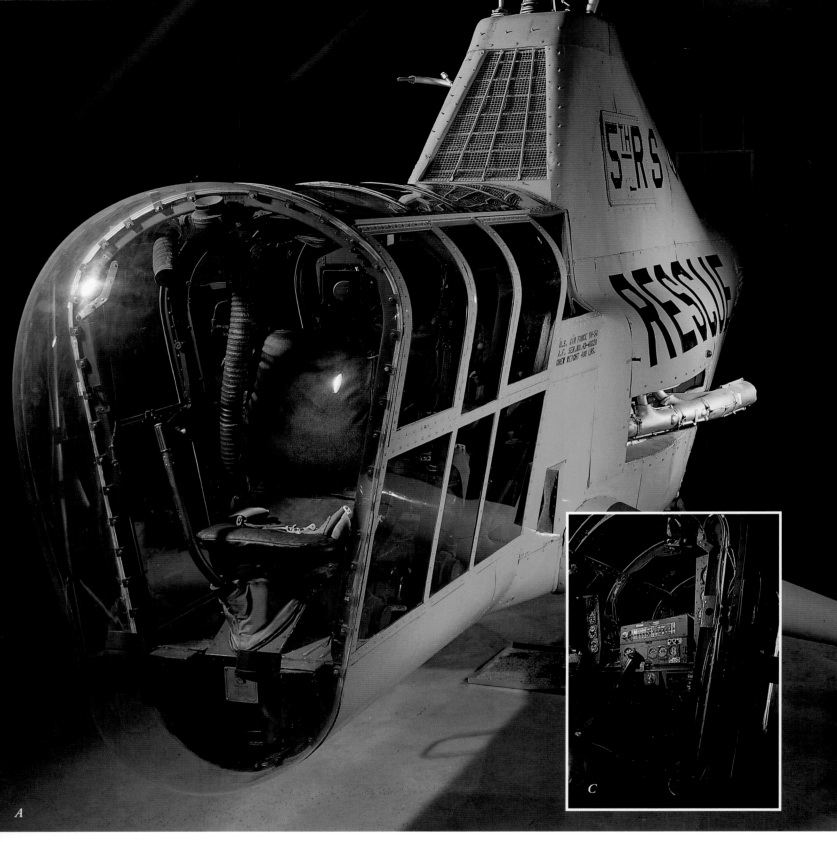

A   The Sikorsky H-5 Dragonfly (originally R-5 for Rotorcraft) was one of the earliest really practical helicopters. The example shown at the USAF Museum is a YH-5A, one of twenty-six ordered in 1944.

B   Limited though it was, the H-5 gained a considerable reputation during the Korean War, when it was involved repeatedly in rescuing downed pilots and in evacuating wounded personnel from the front line.

C   The seating arrangement in the YH-5A was, from the pilot's point of view, less than ideal. The crew of two sat in tandem, with the observer ahead in the clear bubble of the nose, and the pilot behind, with far less visibility. Looking in through the starboard door at the pilot's position, he appears to be hemmed in by the control panel and instruments in front of him.

A   Northrop's F-89 Scorpion was not the prettiest aircraft ever built. Its bulky airframe could reach maximum weights of over 45,000 lbs, a startling amount even for an all-weather interceptor in the 1950s. However, with two Allison J-35s offering 7,200 lbs thrust in afterburner, the F-89 could be coaxed up to 45,000 ft or better, and several variants were equipped with nuclear-tipped Genie missiles, making them formidable propositions for any aircraft attempting to penetrate American airspace with evil intent. The USAF Museum's F-89J is marked as an aircraft of the 449th FIS serving at Ladd AFB, Alaska.

B   The F-89's cockpit seems well-ordered when compared with that of the F-94. The radar scope has been assimilated into the layout and flight and engine instruments are in their proper place. Note the comprehensive warning signs drawing attention to the horrors of explosive seats and high pressure pistons.

Following page:
A   The Lockheed F-94 Starfire series of all-weather interceptors was developed from the F-80, but they were essentially completely redesigned. The F-94C had a higher thrust engine (P&W J-48, 8,750 lbs thrust with afterburner), redesigned wing, swept tail surfaces, radar, new fire control and navigation systems, and air-to-air rockets instead of guns. Some of the rockets were carried in wing pods, and twenty-four were mounted in a ring round the radome, protected until fired by retractable shields. The F-94 in the USAF Museum has the shield retracted to show the rocket tubes.

B   A clue to the F-94C's increase in power over the F-80 lies in the girth of the respective tail pipes. The contrasting swept tailplane and upright fin are also evident, as are the markings of the 60th FIS, Otis AFB, in the 1950s.

C   The arrival of a radar scope left the F-94 cockpit looking less well organized than many others. Two engine instruments are stranded at the top of the panel, randomly surrounded by assorted warning lights. The flight instruments are in anything but a standardized arrangement. Windscreen wiping and de-icing have been relegated to a spot near the floor. Note the red canopy rails; the F-94 canopy could crush careless fingers on closing.

Chapter 8
SAC and the Centuries

"We intend to have a wider choice than humilia-tion or all-out nuclear action."

(President John F. Kennedy, July 25, 1961)

"We must secure our nation by developing and maintaining those weapons, forces, and techniques required to pose a warning to aggressors in order to deter them from launching a modern, devastating war."
(General Henry "Hap" Arnold to General George Marshall, 1943)

"I am unable to distinguish between the unfortunate and the incompetent."
(General Curtis LeMay on his intolerance of failure to meet his standards)

"We must impress Mr. Khrushchev [with the fact] that we have [an airborne alert] and that he cannot strike this country with impunity."
(General Thomas Power testifying before Congress, February 1959)

General Curt LeMay's jacket, impressively decorated, is fronted by his bronze image, its severe gaze challenging Museum visitors as they pass by.

Supersonic Progress

Up to the time of the Korean War, the Museum's telling of the Air Force story takes an easily followed path through the display galleries. From then on, visitors may find themselves searching more widely in the Museum's newer halls or annexes to pick up the thread. Restrictions imposed by floor space or by recent acquisitions have placed some artifacts of the 1950s and '60s among their much younger successors. This arrangement can often be an advantage, offering a chance to see more easily by direct comparison the leaps in technology made between one generation and another.

After dealing with Korea, the wall displays cover the explosive growth of Strategic Air Command into a mighty instrument of Cold War deterrence, and the initially slower buildup of Tactical Air Command. There are photographs which show the deployment of TAC's Composite Air Strike Force in response to emergencies in the world's trouble spots, and recall the complete mobilization of the command during the Cuban crisis of 1962. The importance of having good reconnaissance is emphasized by the shots taken of Soviet missile sites in Cuba, and the hazards of the reconnaissance task are demonstrated by tales of a few of those aircraft shot down during the Cold War—an ERB-47 over the Barents Sea; U-2s over Cuba and Sverdlovsk.

The hunt for the hardware of the period begins in the shadow of the B-36. The ubiquitous Lockheed T-33 Shooting Star trainer stands next to Convair's F-102A Delta Dagger, this one among the first to intercept and escort a Soviet Tu-95 Bear inside the Arctic circle. Nearby are two of the aircraft which formed the backbone of TAC from the mid-1950s—a Republic F-84F Thunderstreak and a North American F-100 Super Sabre, the world's first combat aircraft capable of exceeding the speed of sound in level flight; the one displayed, a C model, was involved in a ceremony in England commemorating the 350th anniversary of the founding of Jamestown, Virginia. The F-100's streamlining contrasts with the angular shape of a Sikorsky H-19 painted in the colors of one called Hopalong which, in five easy stages from Massachusetts to Scotland, made the first transatlantic helicopter flight in 1952.

The trail now leads to the Museum's newest hangar, known as the Modern Flight Gallery. The aircraft exhibited here show facets of air power history from WWII to the Gulf War, but selective viewing reveals the exciting story of the 1950s. The somber tone of the older galleries is gone, their dark walls and shaded illumination replaced by a brilliant overarching whiteness under which the aircraft gleam and glisten, every detail sharply etched. Here is the revolutionary Boeing B-47 Stratojet, the one on display having served as a Wright-Patterson test bed for "fly-by-wire" controls. The Convair B-58 Hustler in the corner was a record breaker, earning the Bendix and Mackay Trophies for a blistering round trip between Los Angeles and New York in 1962. Appropriately hung high above is a U-2A, the "spy in the sky" created by the genius of Lockheed's "Skunk Works."

Among the most impressive indoor exhibits is the several storied Douglas C-124 Globemaster, known colloquially as "Old Shaky." Its great jaws agape to receive visitors in the way that it swallowed tanks, its slab sides tower over its smaller WWII cousins. By contrast, the little Kaman H-43 Huskie rescue helicopter is less than visually dominant, but in the 1960s the one on display established seven world helicopter records for rate of climb, altitude, and distance traveled.

Scattered about the Modern Flight Gallery are representative fighters of the 1950s. The North American F-86D Sabre introduced radar fire-control systems to single-seaters, and the Convair F-106A Delta Dart advanced the concept almost to the point where the pilot became unnecessary. The Museum's F-106A took the superfluous pilot idea to unheard-of limits. When its pilot ejected during a flat spin in 1970, the aircraft took over and survived a gentle belly landing in a snowy Montana field.

The North American F-100D in the gallery is shown in the stars and stripes of the USAF aerobatic demonstration team, the Thunderbirds, with whom it flew in the mid-1960s. Not far away is "the missile with a man in it," the Lockheed F-104C Starfighter. A dramatic performer, the F-104 was not the fighter the USAF was looking for, but the one on show did its best by winning the William Tell Fighter Weapons Meet competition in 1962. The Museum's McDonnell RF-101C Voodoo was another star. Before the B-58 stole them away in 1962, this RF-101 held the round-trip records between Los Angeles and New York. More significantly, it also flew some of the low-altitude reconnaissance sorties over Cuba in 1962 which confirmed the presence of Soviet missiles on America's doorstep.

The Modern Flight Gallery is also home to the aircraft which trained the pilots of the new jet age. The piston-engined Beechcraft T-34 Mentor and North American T-28 Trojan are complemented by two later jets—Cessna's T-37, commonly called the "Tweety-bird," and the supersonic Northrop T-38 Talon, a two-seat version of the F-5 Freedom Fighter.

Further research into the aircraft of the 1950s leads the visitor away from the Museum's main buildings. The hangars known as the Annex, on the other side of Wright Field, are a treasure house often overlooked by visitors, but they are well worth the excursion, packed as they are with artifacts of all kinds. Here is the little known L-17A Navion, designed by North American, built by Ryan, and flown in the Air Force ROTC program. Another rarity is the Vertol H-21 Workhorse, a twin-rotor helicopter in the shape of a banana, used by the USAF for rescue and capable of carrying twelve stretcher cases. In complete contrast is a McDonnell F-101B decorated with the markings of the 142nd Fighter Interceptor Group, Oregon Air National Guard.

Outside, braving all weathers on the ramp near the Museum, are some larger aircraft. A Boeing KC-97 Stratotanker, the "flying gas station" which transformed SAC, stands in the colors of the Ohio ANG. This one is a powerful L model, fitted with two additional podded jet engines, and it carries the name Zeppelinheim, having been named by the mayor of that German town in 1973. Dwarfing almost everything in sight is a Douglas C-133A Cargomaster, the first *transport capable of taking ballistic missiles in its hold. The Museum's C-133 is another world record holder; on December 16, 1958, it carried the then astonishing load of 117,900 lbs to a height of 10,000 ft. A different kind of celebrity belongs to the Lockheed EC-121D Constellation a little farther on. Named* Triple Nickel *because of its airframe serial number, this "Connie" was the first aircraft ever to direct an interception which led to a USAF fighter destroying an enemy. On October 24, 1967, over the Gulf of Tonkin, a MiG-21 fell victim to the beams of the EC-121's radar.*

Mention of the EC-121's success reminds the Museum visitor that the next stage of the Air Force story involves further conflict, a return to armed confrontation with a Communist regime which would bedevil American politics for most of the 1960s and '70s, and would lead the USAF down paths of development and doctrine as yet untrodden.

When the B-47 appeared in the late 1940s, it was a herald of the future. Sleek and elegant, the Stratojet shattered preconceptions of what bombers should look like with its dramatically futuristic design. Thin, swept surfaces, podded axial-flow engines, and a fighter-type cockpit were among the most obvious evidence of a break with the past.

Before America's involvement in the Korean War, the USAF had been caught between the nirvana of newly won independence and the perdition of shrinking defense budgets. Senior airmen knew what they wanted to do to build a global air force but there was never enough money to do it. Chinese intervention in Korea changed all that. The USAF's strength increased rapidly during the war and, with Americans generally accepting that confrontation with communism had become a fact of life, expansion continued even after the shooting stopped, albeit at a slower pace.

In 1950, before the North Koreans surged across the 38th parallel, the USAF's front line consisted of forty-eight combat groups. In 1951, a reorganization began which phased out the group level in the chain of command and left the wing as the principal combat unit. By June 1951, the USAF had eighty-seven wings, an increase made possible by the recall of many reservists to duty. A target of 143 wings had been set for mid-1955. At the end of the Korean War, the front line was up to 106 wings, and policy discussions followed which eventually led to a new target of 137 wings by mid-1957. Although numerically less ambitious than the earlier aim of 143 wings, it was still almost three times the size of the force in 1950 and was to be accompanied by substantial improvements in capability.

LeMay's Air Force

If any command exemplified the face of the new Air Force, transformed by technological advances and determined leadership, it was Strategic Air Command (SAC). In 1950, SAC had 71,490 personnel and 868 aircraft. The backbone of its striking force consisted of 390 B-29s. Five years later, the personnel strength was 196,000, and there were 3,068 aircraft, including well over 1,000 B-47s backed by a tanker fleet of more than 700. At the same time, standards of performance rose dramatically, driven by the implacable LeMay. Besides the impact of his steely personality, he brought fresh ideas to encourage his command to new heights. The SAC bombing and navigation competitions were established as annual events, and he introduced a system of spot promotions to reward outstanding performance. Temporary promotion could be awarded to ranks between technical sergeant and lieutenant colonel, but a return to the previous grade followed failure to maintain high standards. Failure by one member of a "select" crew could mean loss of rank by them all.

SAC's first Boeing B-47s were delivered in October 1951. This was a force which had inherited practices learned the hard way in WWII, when heavily armed piston-engined bombers with large crews operated in formation, preferably with fighter escort. The B-47 brought with it revolutionary changes in operational doctrine and in aircrew attitudes to the bombing mission. It was an extraordinary technical achievement, bearing almost no resemblance to its predecessors and pointing the way to the future for large aircraft in both military and civil aviation. The loaded weight of a B-47 was half again as great as the B-29, but its size was disguised by slender lines and the novelty of a fighter-type cockpit. The normal crew of a B-47 was only three—two pilots in a tandem cockpit and a navigator hidden in the nose. Its shoulder mounted wings were razor-edged and remarkably thin, and were swept back at the then startling angle of thirty-five degrees. To retain the aerodynamic advantages of thin airfoils, the conventional practice of housing the engines, fuel, and wheels in the wings was abandoned. The axial-flow turbojets were in pods hung below the wings, and fuel was stored in the fuselage, above and at each end of the bomb bay. The landing gear was a pair of two-wheel trucks placed fore and aft on the fuselage center line, with small outriggers under the inner engine pods to keep the aircraft stable on the ground. To help with the landing speeds associated with the high wing-loading (which was twice that of a B-29), a large brake-chute was installed. Defensive armament was limited to a remotely controlled tail turret housing a pair of 0.5 in or 20 mm guns.

The B-47's principal limitation was its practical radius of action on internal

weapon. Each B-47 wing had a complement of forty-five bombers and was supported by a KC-97 squadron of twenty tankers.

The capabilities of the B-47 were amply demonstrated in a series of record flights in the 1950s. On its first overseas deployment, the 306th Bomber Wing recorded a best time of five hours and twenty-two minutes from Maine to Fairford, England, an average speed of 575 mph. During an intercontinental bombing trial, a B-47 flew nonstop from Hunter AFB, Georgia, to Morocco and back in twenty-four hours and four minutes, refueling four

a strategic weapon to be reckoned with.

Remarkable though it was, however, the B-47 was only an intermediate step towards SAC's long-term future. In 1955, SAC began taking delivery of the aircraft which would come to symbolize U.S. strategic air power for generations of bomber aircrew—Boeing's B-52 Stratofortress, commonly known as the "Buff." (In genteel translation: Big Ugly Fat Fellow.) In 1946, Boeing's design team had begun work on a very large bomber, sketching out what was in effect a stretched B-29 with six engines. By 1948, the design had evolved to include four turboprop engines hung on swept-back wings.[1] The USAF wanted higher performance, however, and Boeing finally produced the immense B-52, powered by eight jet engines hung in four underwing pods. Originally intended to penetrate enemy defenses at high subsonic speeds and altitudes above fifty thousand feet, the B-52 has shown enormous capacity to absorb technological developments and to adapt to changes in role and tactics. Its unrefueled radius of action of well over four thousand miles becomes almost unlimited with flight refueling support. Over the years its maximum loaded weight has risen to nearly half a million pounds as it has taken on more internal fuel, increased its weapon carrying capacity, and accumulated various navigation and electronic defensive systems.

As with the B-47, it was not long before SAC showed the world what the B-52 could do. In 1956, within a year of its arrival in the front line, a B-52 dropped a thermonuclear weapon with a yield of almost four megatons at Bikini Atoll. The global reach of the huge bomber was demonstrated in January 1957, when three B-52s of the 93rd BW, supported by KC-97 tankers along the way, flew from California via Labrador, Morocco, Ceylon, the Philippines, Guam, and Hawaii to complete a nonstop round-the-world flight of 24,325 miles in forty-five hours and nineteen minutes. Captain of the leading B-52, *Lucky Lady III*, was Lt. Col. James

Air-to-air refueling gave the B-47 a much longer reach, but it was not easy when the tanker was a KC-97. Usually the tanker had to be in a descent at high power to hold a speed which was acceptable for the B-47.

fuel, some 1,500 miles, which would not allow adequate coverage of targets in the Soviet Union. Again, Boeing had the answer. Three months before the first B-47 joined the 306th BW at MacDill AFB, the 306th Air Refueling Squadron (ARS) on the same base took delivery of its first KC-97 tanker. The KC-97 could fly fast enough, if necessary in a slight dive, to match a throttled back B-47, and its efficient flying boom refueling system turned the bomber into an intercontinental

times from KC-97s. Even more remarkable, a B-47 flown by Colonel Burchinal of the 43rd BW was caught in the air by bad weather covering the whole of Western Europe and North Africa. Burchinal elected to wait between the U.K. and Morocco until the weather cleared and called for tanker support. He finally landed at Fairford after nine refuelings, having been airborne for forty-seven hours and thirty-five minutes. These and other demonstrations left no doubt that the B-47 was

[1]This design, Boeing's Type 464-35, bore a striking resemblance to the Soviet strategic bomber, the Tupolev 95 "Bear," which entered service in 1956 and seems set to continue into the 21st century. Like the Boeing design, the Tu-95 is also a four turboprop swept-wing aircraft, developed by the builders of the Tu-4, the Soviet copy of the B-29.

Morris, who had been the copilot of the B-29 *Lucky Lady II* on SAC's 1949 global epic. In just eight years, Morris had seen the round-the-world record reduced by better than half.

As General LeMay approached the end of his nine-year reign at SAC, the imminence of his departure did not signal any slowing down of the drive to expand the command's capabilities, nor was there a change of pace in July 1957 when General Thomas Power took over as SAC's Commander-in-Chief. Responsibilities and challenges grew with every year. In 1955, SAC had been directed to work closely with Air Research and Development Command (ARDC) in establishing an operational capability for intercontinental ballistic missiles (ICBMs), and from then on, it was clear that SAC was assured of a primary role in the USAF's increasingly important missile program. SAC extended its reach in another way when it acquired the newly formed Sixteenth Air Force in 1957 to control bases in Spain and Morocco. In the same year SAC Headquarters moved into its permanent home, a massive building at Offutt AFB, Nebraska, which included an underground control center built to withstand anything but a direct hit by a high yield nuclear weapon. In 1957, too, alarmed by the Soviet Union's progress in developing missiles, SAC started working towards a system of ground alert duty in which one-third of the strategic force would be maintained at readiness, with weapons loaded and crews standing by.

After a surprisingly short operational career, some elements of the B-47 force began phasing out in 1957, but B-52s arrived at a rate of more than ten a month during the year, and the command took delivery of its first jet tanker, the Boeing KC-135. In November, LeMay, now Vice-Chief of Staff, USAF, returned to the cockpit to show off the new aircraft, flying it to Buenos Aires for Argentina's Aeronautics Week and establishing world point-to-point records in the process. The nonstop return flight from Buenos Aires to Washington, D.C., averaged 471 mph over

5,204 miles. In the months which followed, KC-135s compiled an impressive list of world records for point-to-point speed, closed circuit speeds with payload, weight lifting, and straight line distance flown without refueling. The KC-135 proved to be a powerful force multiplier for the USAF, offering greatly improved tanker performance and growing to be an indispensable part of everyday operations worldwide for aircraft in a wide variety of roles.

Other SAC records followed when the Consolidated B-58 Hustler made its appearance in 1960. The B-58 was about

numerous world records had been set and a very public tragedy recorded. On May 10, 1961, a new mark for sustained speed was set when a 43rd BW aircraft flew 670 miles in just over half an hour, averaging 1,302 mph. On May 26, a B-58 covered the 4,612 miles from New York to Paris in three hours, nineteen minutes, and forty-one seconds, about a tenth of the time taken by Lindbergh. Sadly, that aircraft was destroyed in an accident at the Paris airshow only a week later. Though in many ways the most advanced bomber of its time, the B-58 had a short operational career. Expensive to operate and maintain,

The partnership between the KC-135 Stratotanker and the B-52 Stratofortress was the basis for the air-breathing element of the U.S. deterrent triad. The jet-powered KC-135 eliminated the problems associated with the earlier KC-97. It could operate at the same speeds and altitudes as the jet bombers, and it had a fuel capacity more than three times as great as the piston-engined tanker.

as different from previous bombers as was possible. It was a true delta, with a slim area-ruled ("Coke bottle") fuselage, and the USAF's first supersonic bomber, capable of Mach 2.1 at over 60,000 ft. Beneath the slender body hung a sixty-two foot long payload pod, part fuel tank and part weapons bay, which was expendable when empty. The three man crew—pilot, radar navigator/bombardier, and electronics officer—sat in separate escape capsules. Within the first year of B-58 operations,

it claimed too large a share of SAC's budget, and its high-altitude penetration role was overtaken by events. The B-58 was phased out of service at the end of 1969.

Under General Power's leadership between 1957 and 1964, SAC continued to enhance its capabilities. In 1958, airborne alert force trials were conducted which led to the regular practice of keeping part of the SAC bomber fleet constantly armed and in the air, and the following year saw the creation of special air corridors in the U.S. where SAC bombers could train to fly low-level missions. The growing nuclear strength of the U.S. armed services brought with it the need for closer coordination of target planning, and in 1960, that led to the formation of the Joint Strategic Planning Staff (JSTPS) under C-in-C SAC's direction, and the preparation of a Single Integrated Operational Plan (SIOP). That same year, tests were carried out, using specially modified KC-135s, on the feasibility of maintaining an airborne command post which could assume control of SAC's combat forces if the ground command centers were destroyed. In 1961, SAC went to a ground alert posture for fifty percent of its force, and airborne command post operations (code-named LOOKING GLASS) began, each EC-135 equipped with comprehensive communications and carrying a staff headed by a general officer. LOOKING GLASS shifts remained on watch in the air for eight hours before handing over to another team, ensuring twenty-four hour coverage every day of the year.

From 1957 on, SAC maintained a ground alert system to allow for rapid reaction to an emergency. Here crew members abandon their car and run for their already cocked and bombed-up B-58.

TAC and ADC—Born Again

While SAC was making such marked progress in the strategic arena, tactical aircraft were not entirely forgotten. At the end of 1950, Tactical Air Command and Air Defense Command were reestablished as separate commands, and major efforts were made thereafter by TAC to enhance the capabilities of its fighter-bombers and to establish them overseas. Even as preparations were underway to send F-84s to Korea, there was a large deployment of F-84Es in the opposite direction. In September and October 1950, 180 of the fighter-bombers were ferried in two huge waves from Bergstrom, Texas, to Furstenfeldbruck, Germany, stopping five times en route for fuel. Within two years, fighters equipped for in-flight refueling were making similar deployments to Europe and Japan much more quickly with the aid of tankers. At the same time that tactical aircraft were making such gains in global flexibility, they were becoming far more powerful offensive weapons. Rapid

progress in nuclear weapons design allowed the production of nuclear warheads small enough to be carried by fighters. With each weapon having a yield approximating that of "Fat Man," the bomb which leveled Nagasaki, the deployment of a fighter-bomber wing represented a fearsome projection of potential destructive power.

These fighter-bomber developments were not entirely the result of the natural evolution of the role. Even as war raged in Korea, Air Force leaders were looking to the future and working to expand the capabilities of tactical aircraft so that they would be ready for a "real" war against the Soviet Union. The limited Korean struggle was widely regarded as not at all typical as an air power experience, and HQ USAF's attention continued to focus primarily on deterring the Soviet Union by preparing for a large-scale war in Europe.[2] With that in mind, some tactically minded USAF officers saw a need to emphasize global deployment and nuclear weapons for tactical aircraft as the only way to challenge

SAC for a bigger share of the Air Force budget. Others feared that the U.S. Navy would usurp the overseas tactical air mission by promoting the claims of its own nuclear-armed fighters. Whatever the reason, from the mid-1950s on, straight-wing F-84Gs and swept-wing F-84Fs began waving the USAF's tactical flag by crossing the Atlantic as a matter of routine and standing nuclear alert on European bases. TAC, it was said, had come to resemble a sort of bush league SAC.

The nuclear emphasis was continued as the next generation of tactical aircraft appeared. Agility, particularly at altitude, might have been desirable for fighting MiGs in Korea, but it was not a characteristic notable in the designs of the North American F-100 Super Sabre and the other "Century Series" fighters. The F-100 was not agile. Although ostensibly designed to meet a requirement for an air superiority fighter to replace the F-86, the F-100 was built in the mold of a rugged ground attack aircraft. It was heavy and very fast, the first production fighter to be

---

[2] The air war in Korea was generally thought of as unique and of limited value as an influence on operational doctrine for any kind of conflict. Thomas K. Finletter, Secretary of the Air Force during the Korean War, wrote: "[The Korean War] was a special case, and air power can learn little from there about its future role in United States foreign policy in the East."

supersonic in level flight. On August 20, 1955, Col. Horace Hanes took the official world speed record beyond the speed of sound in an F-100C, at 822 mph. The F-100C, with its strengthened wings and points for external stores, confirmed the USAF's intention to use the aircraft primarily in the ground attack role, and the F-100D, the definitive variant, added the capacity to deliver nuclear weapons.

The later Century Series fighters continued the fast and heavy trend, and most variants, including those used as interceptors, were nuclear capable. McDonnell's F-101 Voodoo was originally conceived as a long-range escort fighter for SAC, but became an ADC interceptor and served in TAC both as a fighter-bomber and a reconnaissance aircraft. Powered by two afterburning Pratt & Whitney J-57s of nearly 15,000 lbs thrust each, its considerable size did little to slow it down. On December 12, 1957, Maj. Adrian Drew raised the world speed record to 1,207 mph in an F-101A.

Two other members of the Century Series were unashamedly of the "very fast in a straight line" persuasion, so much so in the case of Lockheed's F-104 Starfighter that it was referred to as the "missile with a man in it." Supposedly the result of talks with fighter pilots in Korea, the F-104 was offered as an air superiority fighter, but the design ensured its unsuitability for that role. Its dimensions were outrageous, fifty-five feet long and only twenty-two feet across the wing, and it was powered by a 15,000 lb thrust General Electric J-79, which gave it a startling performance—Mach 2.2; 50,000 ft/min rate of climb; zoom capability to over 90,000 ft. The Starfighter was the first aircraft to be supersonic in the climb, and the first to hold world records for speed and height simultaneously.[3] Unfortunately, the tiny, razor-edged wings restricted both weapon load and maneuverability, problems which limited the F-104's production run and its operational life with the USAF.

No such reservations were applied

to Republic's F-105 Thunderchief. It was proposed in 1951 as a high-speed, long-range hauler of conventional or nuclear weapons, and it did just that extremely well. It had an internal bomb bay, which could accommodate an extra fuel tank, and five pylons for a variety of external stores. Known colloquially as the "Thud," the F-105 was the largest single-seat, single-engine combat aircraft made, the loaded weight of later variants reaching 54,000 lbs. From the beginning it was an outstanding performer, the YF-105A exceeding the speed of sound on its first flight. Development problems held up the "Thud's" arrival in the front line until 1958, but it eventually proved itself operationally invaluable. The F-105D had all-weather capability and its external load for a combat sortie was impressive, typically eight 750 lb bombs, an ECM pod, and an external fuel tank. A 20 mm rotating-barrel cannon was fitted, and other armament could include "Bullpup" air-to-surface missiles, rocket pods, napalm, and AIM-9 air-to-air missiles.

The remaining pair of Centuries to become operational originated from the urgent need to improve the defense of the United States. At the time of the Soviet takeover in Czechoslovakia, North America was essentially undefended against air at-

tack. During the 1950s, strenuous efforts were made to rectify matters by building immense transcontinental radar screens facing north across the Arctic and by acquiring jet interceptors equipped with air-to-air radar. Interim designs, such as the F-86D, F-94C, and Northrop's F-89D Scorpion served well enough for a while but were clearly inadequate as long-term solutions to the problem. The Convair F-102 Delta Dagger and F-106 Delta Dart were almost identical twins designed to meet a 1949 request for a "1954 interceptor." Aerodynamic problems and performance shortcomings delayed their introduction to service until 1956 and 1959 respectively, but both eventually performed well, the F-106 in particular proving itself a formidable Mach 2 interceptor for ADC, armed as it was with both conventional and nuclear-tipped air-to-air missiles. The F-106 almost literally deserved to be called a missile with a man in it. It was the closest thing to a manned robot flying. Fitted with the Hughes MA-1, a radar developed as an automatic fire control system which could be coupled to an autopilot, it could be flown hands off to interception and missile launch.

As Convair's Deltas were received by the air defense squadrons, so the supporting ground organizations became opera-

[3]On May 7, 1958, Maj HC Johnson reached 91,243 ft in an F-104A. Nine days later, Capt. W.W. Irwin recorded 1,404 mph. On December 14, 1959 Capt. J.B. Jordan, in an F-104C, raised the height record to 103,389 ft. Rocket boosted F-104s were flown higher at the astronaut training school, Edwards AFB, "Chuck" Yeager reaching an unofficial 108,000 ft in 1963.

The F-100 Super Sabre was the first USAF fighter to reach supersonic speeds in level flight. Designed as a replacement for the F-86, it proved to be an outstanding ground attack aircraft. This one stands under guard at Tan Son Nhut, Saigon, in May 1966.

tional. By the end of the 1950s, three vast radar chains stretched across North America to provide warning in depth of air attack: the Pinetree Line in southern Canada, the Mid-Canada Line, and the Distant Early Warning (DEW) Line inside the Arctic Circle. Lockheed RC-121 Constellations acted as airborne radar stations and added wings to the system both to the east and west. The Semi-Automatic Ground Environment (SAGE) system had been accepted as the first computerized method of handling air defense information, and a joint North American Air Defense Command (NORAD) was function-

first flight of the F-100. The following decade saw fighter pilots move from general acceptance that they were confined by parameters of 40,000 ft and subsonic speed to everyday expectation of 50,000 ft plus and Mach 2. Reaching for the edge of the performance envelope had led to some sacrifice in the realm of maneuverability, and that was something the USAF would learn to live with until the next generation of fighters arrived. Fighters were growing in other ways, however. Radar was being recognized as increasingly essential to their effectiveness as weapons systems, as were guided missiles, and the additional role of

ning to feature the practical forms which would predominate for the rest of the century: high wings, cavernous box-shaped interiors, unobstructed flat floors, and full fuselage rear doors which lowered to become ramps. Lockheed's incomparable C-130 Hercules and its smaller cousin, Fairchild's C-123 Provider, transformed the business of hauling military cargo and later proved to be superbly adaptable multirole aircraft.

The rebirth of TAC might be said to have been largely accomplished by 1957. By then, the Centuries were either established or on the way, as were the new transports, and the interdiction role was being flown in Martin B-57 Canberras rather than B-26s. The Douglas B-66 Destroyer was also being introduced as a light bomber. SAC had finally relinquished its remaining fighter squadrons to TAC. To manage its remarkably wide range of capabilities, TAC controlled three numbered air forces: Ninth, Eighteenth (primarily troop carrier), and Nineteenth (mobile HQ for army support). The Nineteenth AF was used as the headquarters for what was known as the Composite Air Strike Force (CASF), a combination of fighter, light bomber, tanker, and transport units ready at any time to move overseas. The CASF was deployed to cover such emergencies as the 1958 U.S. intervention in Lebanon, the Chinese threats to Qemoy in the mid-1950s, and the Berlin Wall crisis of the early '60s.

An F-102 Delta Dagger of the 317th FIS is accompanied by an EB-57 Canberra of Alaskan Air Command near Mt. McKinley. The EB-57s were used to provide electronic countermeasures training.

ing at Colorado Springs to control all U.S. and Canadian air defense forces. The Ballistic Missile Early Warning System (BMEWS), with radar sites in Greenland, Alaska, and the United Kingdom, was added in 1961.

Whatever the merits or shortcomings of the individual Century Series fighters, as a group they marked a dramatic expansion of the combat aircraft's performance envelope. The P-51D made its first appearance less than ten years before the

ground attack had become a necessary consideration in the design of almost every fighter.

Although TAC's image was popularly associated with that of its fighter squadrons, there was much more to the command than that. At the end of the Korean War, TAC controlled some 1,100 aircraft, no less than 60 percent of which were transport types, with the Fairchild C-119 steadily replacing the aging C-46. By the mid-1950s, tactical airlift was begin-

Haulers

The turbulent currents of technological change began reaching out to the other USAF commands, too, in the 1950s. Halfway through the decade, the Military Air Transport Service (MATS) fleet of over 1,400 aircraft included 610 four-engined transports. Most were still C-54s, but the Douglas C-124 Globemaster, known to its crews as "Old Shaky," had added significantly to the lifting capacity of the command. The huge clamshell doors in its nose made it possible to carry such bulky cargo as tanks or bulldozers, and it was capable of taking two hundred fully equipped troops in its double-decked cabin. However, it was not very speedy, and long-range deployments depending on the support of C-124s needed the luxury of not being in immediate need of what it was transporting. The solution to that failing was in sight, since the C-124 was the last piston-engined transport ordered for MATS. Douglas sought to retain their prime position as supplier of large military transports with the C-133 Cargomaster, a four turboprop monster capable of swallowing the Atlas and Titan ICBMs through its rear-loading door. Useful as it was, the C-133 was never a great success, principally because of unexpected engine and fatigue problems. A little later, the Boeing C-135 and the Lockheed C-141 Starlifter added pure jet speed and much greater reliability.

Besides having responsibility for the operation of its global route system, MATS included such specialized functions as the Air Weather Service (AWS), the aircraft of which tracked and penetrated severe weather areas, and the Air Rescue Service (ARS), which carried out worldwide search and rescue activities over both land and water. The ARS of the 1950s was equipped with a broad range of aircraft: SB-17Gs, SB-29s, SC-54s, SA-16 Albatross amphibians, and helicopters like the Kaman H-43A, Sikorsky H-19 Chickasaw, and Vertol H-21 Workhorse.

Teachers

The demands of the new USAF, emphasized by the Korean War and the accelerating shift to a jet-powered front line, created considerable problems for the training organization. After WWII, recruiting into a declining military was difficult, and the USAF was no different from the other services when it came to attracting suitable candidates. In 1950, the flying training machine was designed to produce 3,000 pilots, but managed only 2,200. Numbers increased with the Korean War, causing Air Training Command to create two subordinate organizations, Flying Training Air Force (FlyTAF) and Technical Training Air Force (TechTAF). When the 143-wing Air Force was approved, it

was thought that pilot training should reach an output of twelve thousand per year by 1956, but the number graduated was actually less than seven thousand, an adequate figure for the slower buildup envisaged after the Korean War was over. To do the job, ATC was operating ten primary, eight basic, and nine advanced flying schools, and using aircraft like the Beech T-34 Mentor, North American T-28 Trojan, and Lockheed T-33 Shooting Star. By the end of the 1950s, these had been joined by a new twin-jet primary trainer with side-by-side seating, the Cessna T-37; the more advanced Northrop T-38 Talon was on the

The monster Douglas C-133 Cargomaster added new dimensions to the USAF's airlift capacity. It was capable of swallowing both the Atlas and Titan ICBMs.

horizon to replace the T-33.

The introduction of more sophisticated electronic equipment in aircraft continually raised the standards required in other crew members and made the training more complex. In the early '50s ATC created another organization, the Crew Training Air Force (CrewTAF), to mold newly graduated aircrew into effective combat teams. Besides the Convair T-29 "flying classroom," ATC owned a sampling of front-line aircraft from the operational commands which they used to ease the

passage of the inexperienced newcomers on to their squadrons.

If the training of aircrew was becoming ever more difficult, the problem of ground trades often seemed worse. To make recruits into skilled men was not a simple matter, and competition with civilian industry for those who were expensively trained led to a turnover which was discouragingly high. In 1956, nearly 126,000 airmen failed to reenlist after serving only one four-year term. To keep the front line properly manned in the mid-1950s, the USAF's technical schools were consistently graduating over 100,000 tech-

nicians per year.

From the beginning, the leaders of the USAF were aware of the need to provide a solid foundation of professional training for officers. Before the Korean War, most new USAF officers came from aviation cadet or officer candidate schools, the Air Force Reserve Officer Training Corps (AFROTC), or were drawn from a 25 percent allocation from each graduating class at West Point or Annapolis. It was not until 1954 that the USAF obtained authorization for its own academy. As a

An RF-101 Voodoo of the 363rd RS flies over Shaw AFB, S. Carolina. Low-level reconnaissance by RF-101s provided proof that Soviet missiles were being sited in Cuba in 1962.

temporary measure, the USAF Academy opened its doors in 1955 at Lowry AFB, near Denver, and moved the cadets to its magnificent 18,000 acre permanent site in the foothills of the Rocky Mountains near Colorado Springs in 1958. The first graduates were commissioned in 1959. Postgraduate education, at such schools as the Air Command and Staff College (ACSC) and the Air War College (AWC), was established at the Air University, Maxwell AFB, Alabama.

Eyes in the Sky

Providing trained personnel and supplying adequate combat power for the containment of communist expansion were vital aspects of Cold War confrontation, but it was equally important to know what the other side was doing. There was a continual need for strategic reconnaissance of potential enemies and their activities. Immediately after WWII, surveillance of the Soviet Union began with modified B-29s (F-13A; B-29F) of the 72nd Reconnaissance Squadron at Ladd Field, Alaska.

Later, other units expanded the role with RB-50s, RB-36s, RB-45s, and RB-47s. It was a risky occupation, involving a limited number of high-altitude overflights for photographic coverage, but soon including sorties in which electronic sensors derived information from the opposition's radio and radar transmissions.

To gain maximum value from electronic surveillance, "ferret" missions were flown. "Ferret" aircraft flew close enough to Soviet airspace to provoke a reaction. At first, search and height-finding radars would sweep the "ferret." If the "threat" persisted, missile guidance and ground-controlled interception radars joined in, accompanied by increased radio transmissions and message traffic, all monitored and recorded by the "ferret." Occasionally, the Soviet reaction to the "ferret" was aggressive and the information hunter became the hunted. In the decade of the 1950s some two dozen aircraft of the western powers were lost on strategic reconnaissance missions, and several others were attacked and damaged.[4] At least eight of the

losses were suffered by the USAF, including an RB-50 and four RB-29s, and an ERB-47H of the 55th SRW shot down by MiG-19s over the Barents Sea on July 1, 1960.

In an attempt to remove the risk from strategic reconnaissance, aircraft were sought which were of such high performance that they could operate anywhere in the world with impunity. In the 1950s and '60s, two remarkable aircraft came from Lockheed's famous "Skunk Works" to meet the need. The first, the U-2, looked like a jet-powered sailplane. Even in its earliest form, the U-2 could operate up to 70,000 ft; later versions have pushed this up to 90,000 ft. For a while, 70,000 ft seemed to put them out of reach of the Soviets, and in the late-1950s USAF pilots temporarily released to the CIA flew over the Soviet Union and gained much invaluable information about such things as bomber deployment, air defense systems, and submarine development. However, on May 1, 1960, a U-2 flown by Francis Gary Powers was shot down near Sverdlovsk by

---

[4]The American aircraft came from the USAF, USN, and CIA. Also lost were a number of British, Swedish and Chinese Nationalist aircraft.

Rows of T-33 jet trainers on the ramp at Reese AFB, Texas. Some 4,000 T-33s were delivered to the USAF alone, and they formed the backbone of the USAF's pilot training program during the 1950s-60s.

SA-2 missiles. Chairman Nikita Khrushchev used the incident to embarrass President Dwight Eisenhower and wreck a summit meeting, and penetrations of Soviet airspace were brought to a halt, at least for the time being. At Lockheed, the "Skunk Works" was already at work on an aircraft capable of presenting the Soviets with a still greater challenge. By the mid-1960s, the U.S. had the SR-71 Blackbird, a strategic reconnaissance vehicle which could match the U-2's performance for range and altitude while adding the ability to sustain flight at more than three times the speed of sound.

Missiles on the Doorstep

When Fidel Castro seized power on January 2, 1959, Cuba joined the list of countries which were under occasional surveillance by the strategic reconnaissance eyes of the U.S. After the fiasco of the Bay of Pigs invasion by U.S.-based Cuban exiles, the Soviets stepped up the supply of arms to their client, Castro, and by 1962 it was clear from photographs taken by U-2s that these included surface-to-air mis-

siles (SAMs). Further, it seemed that the SAMs were placed to defend other sitesintended for mobile medium-range ballistic missiles (MRBMs). Comprehensive high-altitude U-2 coverage of the island confirmed the assessment and revealed other sites being prepared with fixed launching pads for intermediate-range ballistic missiles (IRBMs). With these in place, nuclear warheads could be launched against U.S. targets from the east coast to Wyoming. In mid-October, American fears were confirmed when a U-2 mission photographed a site with MRBMs deployed. Low-level reconnaissance by RF-101s and USN RF-8s followed, and President Kennedy was handed incontrovertible photographic evidence of both the presence of missiles and Soviet involvement. On October 22, Kennedy reported to the American people on the threat and the countermeasures being taken, and announced a blockade of Cuba. Three days later he warned the Soviets directly against continuing to deploy missiles.

Meanwhile, USAF bases in Florida were being packed with combat aircraft—

F-100s, F-104s, F-105s, and F-106s. In SAC, B-47s went to their dispersal bases, B-52s adopted a nuclear-armed airborne alert, and missile crews came to instant readiness. Tension rose on October 27 when Major Rudolf Anderson's U-2 was shot down over Cuba and he was killed. Matters worsened even further the next day because a U-2 on an Arctic mission inadvertently strayed over Siberia's Chukotka Peninsula and Soviet missiles were readied. A U.S. apology for the transgression was accompanied by a steely assurance that American forces were now ready to take military action in Cuba and elsewhere, if necessary. Khrushchev took the hint and agreed to withdraw both the offending missiles and a number of IL-28 bombers already delivered to Cuba. The Cuban Crisis was over, and a salutary lesson had been given on the value of strategic reconnaissance in an age of global confrontation. One fire had been put out, but another was already smoldering on the other side of the world.

A   Half a century after its first appearance, the sheer size of the Convair B-36 Peacemaker is still impressive. A crew of fifteen (including a relief team of four) was housed in two pressurized cells in the nose and tail, connected by an 85 ft tunnel. Those in the nose compartment worked on three levels, the pilots sitting some twenty feet above the nose wheel. The USAF Museum's B-36J was the last of the giants to fly, arriving at Wright Field in April 1959. It is prominently marked with the badge of Strategic Air Command, whose majestic symbol it was in the period following USAF independence.

B   The cockpit of a B-36 does not immediately suggest the size of the monster following behind. One clue lies in the width of the throttle quadrant and the positioning of the throttles. Six in the familiar place close to the captain's right hand are for the huge Pratt & Whitney radials, but there are four more in the roof controlling GE jet engines. This is the combination which gave rise to the B-36 radio call: "Six a-turning and four a-burning!"

C   A dazzling array of dials, switches, buttons, and levers confronted the B-36 flight engineer. From his seat he had his finger on all of the systems which brought the B-36 to life. A handily placed clip over his head allowed notes and checklists to be readily available.

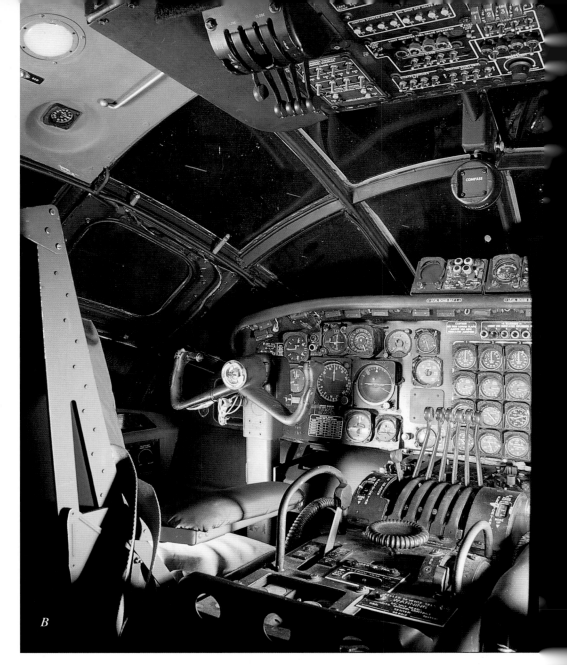

B

C

A

B

A   The extraordinary McDonnell XF-85 Goblin was to have been the B-36's defender. A trapeze would have launched and recovered the little fighter from a section of the bomb bay during operations. The hook on which this daring act depended sprouted from just in front of the XF-85's cockpit. The effort was a dismal failure, with the two XF-85's built achieving only 2 hrs 19 mins flying time between them before the program was terminated in 1949.

B   From the D model on, B-36s carried the extra power of four podded General Electric J-47s of 5,200 lbs thrust each. On the wing's trailing edge were six 3,800 hp Pratt & Whitney R-4630s driving 19 ft pusher propellers.

C   The cavernous four-section bomb bay of the B-36 could accommodate up to 84,000 lbs of conventional bombs. Alternatives included such giants as the Mark 17 nuclear weapon, seen to the right in this photograph, which alone weighed 41,400 lbs. The Goblin crouches close by on the left. More usual defensive armament consisted of no less than sixteen 20 mm cannon fired from nose and tail positions and from six retractable turrets.

D   The navigator sat in the bowels of the machine, unable to see out, relying on radar and navigational equipment to keep the B-36 on track.

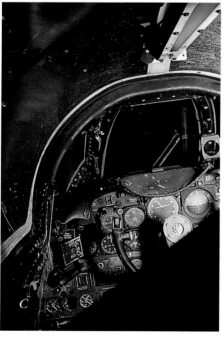

A   Boeing's B-47 Stratojet was a revolutionary design. It was the world's first sweptwing bomber and the first developed specifically to deliver nuclear weapons. A crew of three was carried — in tandem under the canopy were the pilot and copilot (who fired the tail guns by remote control); the navigator/bombardier occupied a dark space beneath in the nose. The B-47E at the USAF Museum was the first USAF aircraft used for trials of a "fly-by-wire" flight control system.

B   The B-47E was powered by six General Electric J-47s of 7,200 lbs thrust each. The podded engine installation was novel in 1947.

C   A peek over the B-47's cockpit rail reveals a typical bomber wheel control in a fighter-sized space.

D   Developed at a time when defense budgets were tight, the Republic F-84F Thunderstreak put swept surfaces on what was essentially a re-engined version of the straight-wing F-84 design. Although it had a number of problems, including occasionally unpleasant handling characteristics, the F-84F filled the fighter-bomber gap until the arrival of the F-100. The USAF Museum's Thunderstreak is one of 200 which deployed transatlantic in November 1961. It is in the markings of the 178th TFG, Ohio National Guard.

E   Note the yellow emergency handles on either side of the F-84F's seat. One jettisons the canopy and the other fires the ejection cartridge.

F   The business end of a KC-97 tanker. Boeing's "flying boom" allowed greatly increased rates of fuel transfer to thirsty combat aircraft.

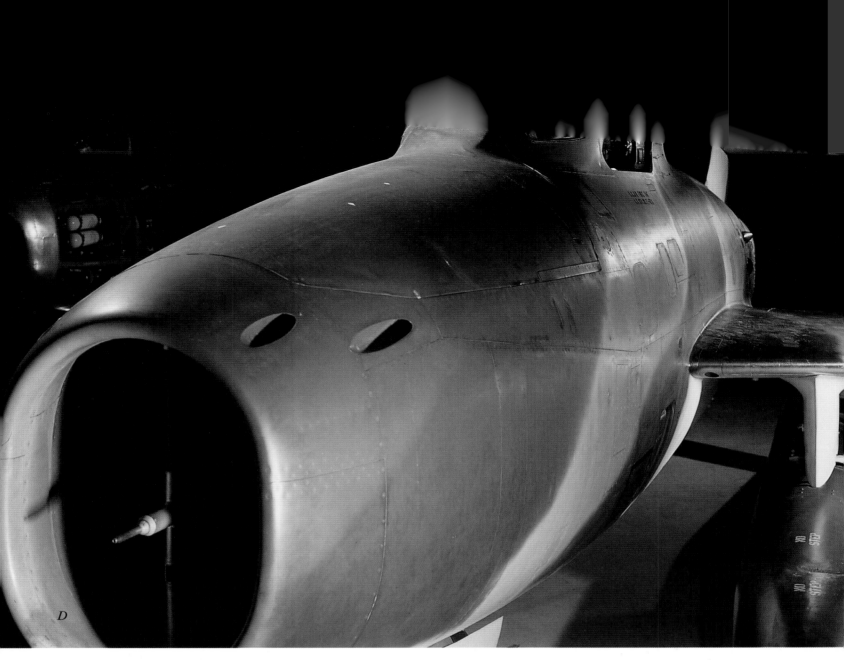

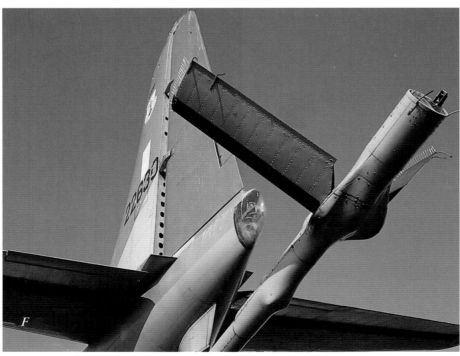

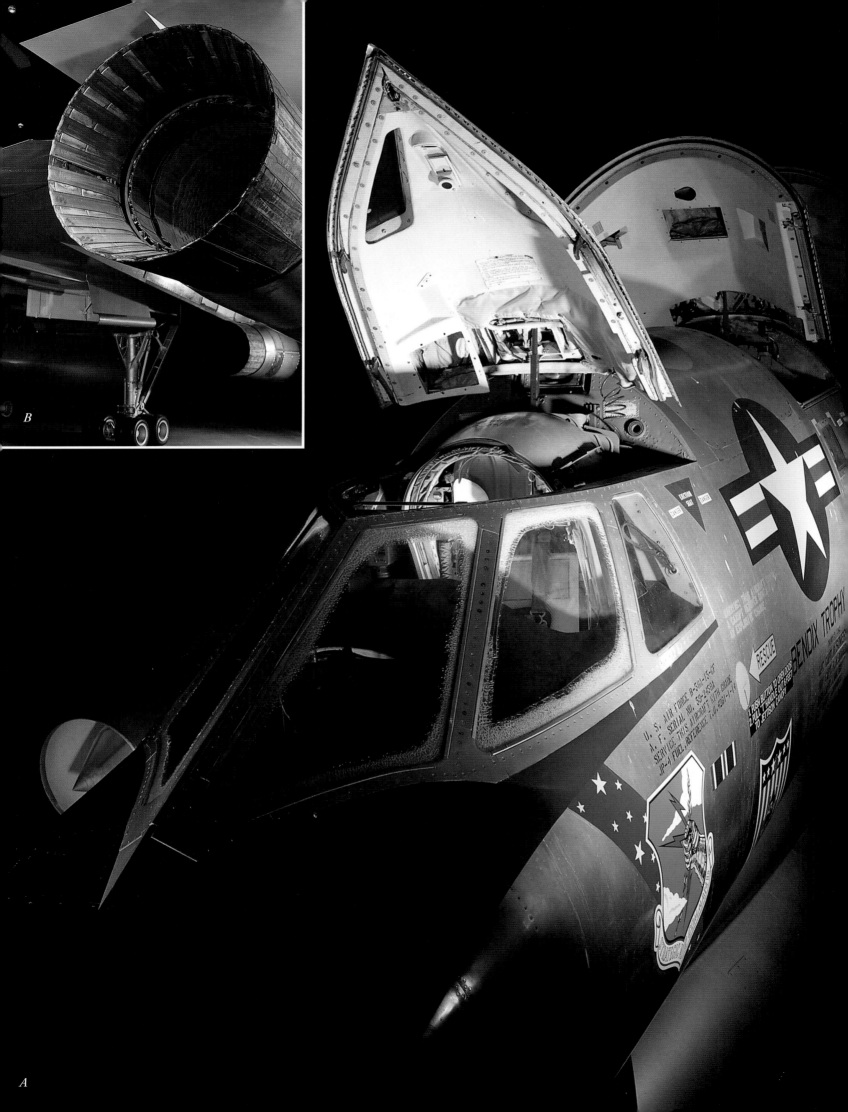

B

A

C

A   Convair's B-58 Hustler was the first supersonic bomber to go into production and was capable of exceeding Mach 2. Among its many astonishing design features was a payload pod carried beneath the slim fuselage. Pilot, navigator, and defense systems operator were sealed in separate cockpits, each capable of being ejected in a capsule in an emergency. The B-58A at the USAF Museum is a record breaker, its exploits earning the Bendix and Mackay trophies for 1962.

B   The B-58 was powered by four separately podded General Electric J-79-5 afterburning turbojets of 15,600 lbs thrust each. The streamlined shape of the finned underfuselage payload pod can be seen between the stalky undercarriage legs.

C   Faster Than a Speeding Bullet
© Mike Machat, 1996

D   Besides its other unconventional features, the B-58 defied bomber tradition in having a fighter-type stick for the pilot. The cockpit was also equipped with the most effective air conditioning system yet designed for an aircraft.

D

A   The F-100 demonstrates the conventional fighter cockpit layout established in the post-WWII period. Principal flying instruments are in the center of the panel, with engine instruments over to the right. Radios and navigation aids are along the right console, while red indicators warning of various failures are fitted at odd points, roughly at eye level. The standard control stick is shaped to the hand, and a number of services are operated by the pilot's fingers. Depending on the aircraft, buttons were used to transmit radio messages, or to drop weapons or fuel tanks. The trigger fired guns or rockets, and the "coolie hat" on the top of the stick set the aircraft's trim.

B   The North American F-100 Super Sabre was the USAF's first fighter capable of becoming supersonic in level flight. Its extra fuel tanks and flight refueling capability also gave it transoceanic deployment capability.

C   The sharply swept surfaces of the F-100 set the pattern for the rest of the Century series fighters. The USAF Museum's F-100C is marked as an aircraft of the 452nd FDS, 322nd FDG, and was named Susan Constant in a 1957 ceremony celebrating the 350th anniversary of the founding of Jamestown, Virginia.

Following pages:

A   The distinctively flat camera nose identifies this McDonnell Voodoo as an RF-101C. This particular aircraft used its cameras to good effect during the Cuban Missile Crisis, keeping an eye on the Soviet missile sites and helping to confirm that they were being dismantled.

B   The second of the USAF Museum's Voodoos is the two-seat all-weather interceptor variant, the F-101B. With the radar fire-control system entrusted to the radar operator behind, its front cockpit is relatively uncluttered. As with all aircraft fitted with ejection seats, prominent red tags warn that safety pins must be removed before flight.

C   The broad expanse of the RF-101C's tail is topped by sharply swept tail surfaces, and sits above the heavy shielding designed to protect the aircraft's skin from the blast from the afterburning J-57s. In 1957, this aircraft was flown by Capt. Ray Schrecengost in breaking the existing trans-U.S. speed records.

U.S. AIR FORCE
41753

LIFT
VERTICAL STAB. ONLY

FUEL VENT OUTLET

PUSH FIRE
FIGHTING ACCESS

DANGER
STAY CLEAR

BEWARE OF
BLAST

VOID STARTER TURBINE
WHEEL PEAKS DURING
STARTING CYCLE

C

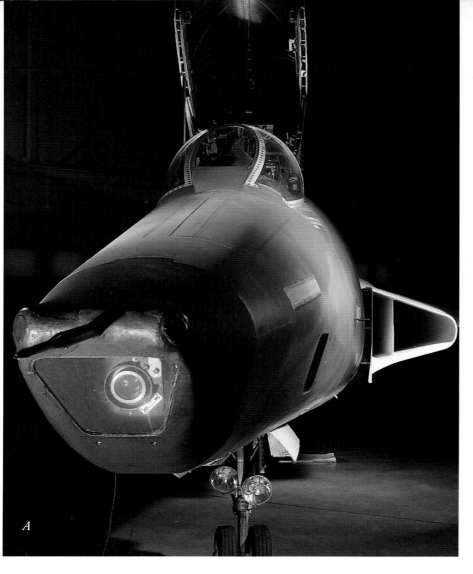

A

B

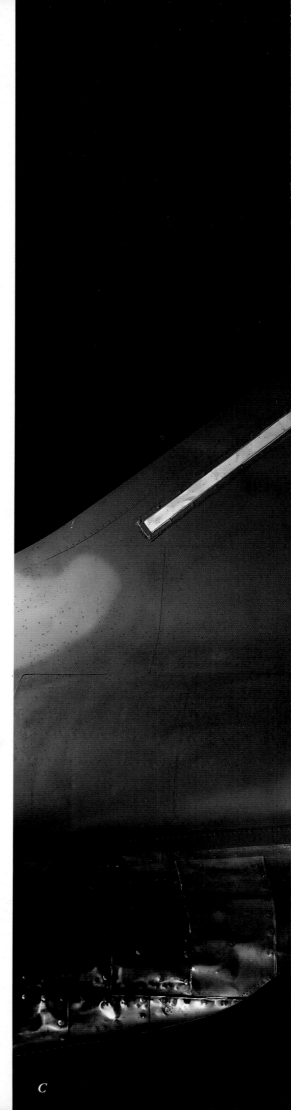

C

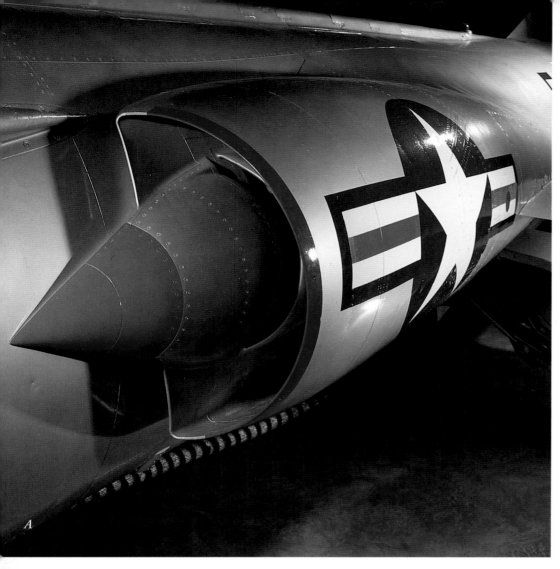

A   A sleek, almost wingless aircraft — "the missile with a man in it" — the Lockheed F-104 Starfighter was a dramatic performer. Fed by enormous quantities of air through cheek intakes, its afterburning J-79 produced up to 15,800 lbs of thrust and could propel the F-104 to speeds well in excess of Mach 2. In the center of each intake can be seen a fixed shock cone, surrounded further back by a boundary layer bleed slot.

B   The cockpit of the F-104C was snug and well arranged. Note that the throttle lever is vertical rather than horizontal, and that a rearview mirror is clinging to the open canopy rail. A yellow handle beside the footwell jettisons the canopy, and ejection (including canopy jettison) can be initiated by pulling up on the larger handle at the front of the seat pan.

C   Tactical Air Command's winged sword decorates the F-104C's fin. This particular Starfighter, 60914, was the mount of the winning pilot in the 1962 "William Tell" fighter meet.

C

A The Convair F-106 Delta Dart first flew in 1956 and was a natural progression from the F-102 Delta Dagger. It was an extremely powerful and sophisticated interceptor for its day. Its P&W J-75 produced 24,500 lbs of thrust in afterburner and it could accelerate to Mach 2. Fitted with a Hughes MA-1 guidance and fire-control system, it could carry out "hands-off" interceptions, firing its nuclear-tipped air-to-air Genie missiles when required and recovering to base afterwards.

B Not all F-106 pilots had pointed heads, but it probably helped! Note the linear instruments on the panel and the radar scope in front of the pilot.

C The F-106 was a true delta, with no separate tail surfaces. The eagle's green tail partly covers the air-brake panels, and the two small tubes on the fin's leading edge are the pitot intakes for the aircraft's artificial feel system. The USAF Museum's F-106A is an aircraft which took its "hands-off" capabilities to extremes. During a sortie from Malmstrom AFB, its pilot ejected when he found himself locked in a flat spin. The F-106 subsequently recovered and made a gentle belly landing in a snow-covered Montana field and was later put back into service.

316

Plans and Operations

Period/Event	Name	Description
WWII	ANVIL/DRAGOON	Allied invasion of Southern France, August 15, 1944
	ARGUMENT	Air attacks on industries supporting the Luftwaffe
	BOLERO	Planning and build-up stage for Allied invasion of France
	CLARION	Allied air attacks on communications in Germany, February 22-23, 1945
	COBRA	Break-out of U.S. forces from Normandy, July, 25 1944
	CROSSBOW	Allied air attacks on V-1 launching sites
	DIADEM	Allied offensive in Italy, Spring 1944
	FRANTIC	USAAF "shuttle" missions against distant European targets, turning round on Soviet bases
	GYMNAST	Proposed Allied invasion of North Africa
	MARKET/GARDEN	Operations aimed at capturing Rhine bridge at Arnhem, September, 1944
	MATTERHORN	USAAF bombing offensive against Japan
	OVERLORD	Allied invasion of Normandy, June 6, 1944
	POINTBLANK	Combined Bomber Offensive against Germany
	RAINBOW	Pre-war U.S. operational plans
	ROUNDUP	Proposed 1943 Allied invasion of Northern France
	SLEDGEHAMMER	Proposed Allied landing on coast of Northern France in late 1942
	STRANGLE	Air attacks on enemy communications in Italy, March 1944
	TORCH	Allied invasion of North Africa, November 8, 1942
Berlin Airlift	VITTLES	Supply of W. Berlin by air during Soviet blockade, 1948-49
		"Little Vittles" Delivery of candy to children during the Berlin Airlift
Korean War	STRANGLE	Interdiction of enemy communications in N. Korea, 1951
		"Kiddie Car" Airlift to rescue Korean War orphans
Vietnam War	ARC LIGHT	B-52 bombing missions against the Viet Cong
	BANISH BEACH	C-130 missions to start forest fires by dropping oil drums
	BARRELL ROLLUSAF	Campaign in support of Laotian ground forces
	BOLO	F-4 decoy mission aimed at bringing MiGs to battle, January 2, 1967
	COMMANDO VAULT	C-130 missions aimed at blasting out helicopter landing areas in heavy jungle with weapons weighing up to 15,000 lbs.
	FARM GATE	USAF training detachment to VNAF, 1961
	FREEDOM TRAIN	Strike operations against N. Vietnam below 20th parallel, 1972
	FREQUENT WIND	U.S. plan for emergency evacuation from S. Vietnam, 1975
	LINEBACKER	Comprehensive bombing campaign against N. Vietnam, 1972
	LINEBACKER II	Intense aerial assault on N. Vietnamese targets, December, 1972
	MULE TRAIN	Tactical airlift support in S. Vietnam, 1962
	NIAGARA	Air support for U.S. Marines at Khe Sanh, 1968
	RANCH HAND	Defoliation operations
	ROLLING THUNDER	Campaign of limited air attacks against selected military targets in N. Vietnam
	STEEL TIGER	Limited interdiction of Ho Chi Minh Trail in S. Laos
	TIGER HOUND	Extensive operations against Ho Chi Minh Trail
Grenada	URGENT FURY	Operation against Marxist forces on Grenada
Panama	JUST CAUSE	Operation against Panama Defense Force troops of dictator Manuel Noriega
Libya	ELDORADO CANYON	Air strike against targets in Libya
Iraq	DESERT SHIELD	Build-up of forces in the Persian Gulf region following Iraqi invasion of Kuwait
	DESERT STORM	Campaign against Iraqi forces aimed at restoring independence to Kuwait

Chapter 9

Cold War—Hot Combat

"I won't let those air force generals bomb the smallest outhouse without checking with me."

(President Lyndon Johnson on his control of Operation ROLLING THUNDER, 1965)

Air Force Col. Robin Olds Commander, 8th Tactical Fighter Wing
Fred Mason, USAF Art Collection

"We are swatting at flies when we should be going after the manure pile."
(General Curtis LeMay on the targeting restrictions in North Vietnam)

"The pilot hit by a surface-to-air missile whose site he was not permitted to bomb does not fall *halfway* out of the sky or spend seven years as a *limited* prisoner of war."
(Admiral U.S. Grant Sharp, CINCPAC, on tactical bombing restrictions, 1968)

"The amount of firepower put on that piece of real estate exceeded anything that had ever been seen before in history by any foe and the enemy was hurt, his back broken by air power."
(General William Westmoreland, U.S. Army, on the role of B-52s at Khe San, 1968)

"I have determined that we should go for broke. . . . I intend to stop at nothing to bring the enemy to his knees."

(President Richard Nixon to Secretary of State Henry Kissinger, March 30, 1972)

"Thank God for the U.S. Air Force!"
(U.S. Army survivor rescued under fire by an HH-53 helicopter at Quang Tri, 1972)

Potent symbols of air power in the Vietnam War —F-4Cs taking their turn to refresh themselves from a KC-135 tanker in 1966.

Veterans of an Asian War

Fanatics for logical progression who follow the trail of the USAF in the 1950s into the Museum's Modern Flight Hangar and then outside onto the ramp now have to retrace their steps to stand again in the shadow of the B-36. It is here that the story of the Vietnam War begins. Among the aircraft found overhead, flying in formation with the SAC monster's tail, are a couple too often overlooked. Lacking the speed and power of their more exotic jet cousins, the Cessna O-1 Bird Dog and O-2 Skymaster nevertheless deserve respectful attention; their Forward Air Controller role was among the most hazardous of the Vietnam War. Beneath the O-1 is another in the Cessna family, the YA-37A, an example of an early attempt at producing a counterinsurgency (COIN) aircraft.

In a pugnacious stance nearby is a rare bird indeed. Aircraft in which the nation's highest gallantry award is won seldom survive the experience, but this is the Douglas A-1E Skyraider flown by Major Bernard Fisher in 1966 when he landed under fire in South Vietnam to rescue a fellow pilot and so earned the Medal of Honor. The Skyraider is mightily hung about with a typical weapons load and surrounded by an impressive collection of other possibilities—"Bullpup," "Rockeye," and an assortment of cluster bomb units dispensing such varied items as tear gas

bomblets and land mines. Almost unnoticed on a corner of the display the slim shape of the opposition reaches upward—the Soviet SA-2 "Guideline" surface-to-air missile.

On a wall close by, the progress of the Vietnam War is traced year by year. Beginning with the activities of U.S. advisers in South Vietnam, the story unfolds in words and pictures, showing the changing fortunes of the opposing combatants and their allies from 1961 to 1973. Displays of rescue and survival gear, uniforms, and unit flags and insignia lie alongside Viet Cong booby traps. There are tales of courage, such as the one telling of Captain Merlyn Dethlefsen's Medal of Honor, and of achievement, like those about the USAF's Vietnam aces. In more somber mood is the section dealing with prisoners of war, their near starvation diet, and primitive medical treatment. The ingenuity of POWs is brought out by a display of items manufactured during their incarceration. Perhaps the saddest Medal of Honor is here—Captain Lance Sijan died in captivity after torture in 1968. An epilogue section tells of treaties ignored by the North Vietnamese in their Southeast Asian conquests and sets out the bald figures of the cost of the Vietnam War to the U.S. The story ends with a display of the last USAF flags flown in Southeast Asia. Tucked away at the bottom is a U.S. flag which was carried by an American who served with the Royal Flying Corps in

WWI, and was subsequently flown in a Lancaster over Germany in WWII, in a B-29 over Korea, and in a MAC aircraft into Vietnam. Before moving on, the visitor may notice that, in what is undoubtedly an unconscious gesture, the rest of the USAF Museum has turned its back on what happened in Vietnam. All the aircraft in the gallery are facing away from the story on the wall.

The majority of the aircraft associated with the Vietnam War are in the Modern Flight Hangar. The walk there is interesting in itself. There are numerous small displays on the way which are worth the visitor's attention. The evolution of the USAF's aircraft insignia is shown in color, and reveals that the first national identifying mark, from the Jennies of 1916, was a single red star! Cases containing a comprehensive aircraft model collection are followed by an area in which aviation art is hung, changed at intervals. Further on, aeroengine spark plugs and jet engine igniters are arranged in patterns to delight the eye. The corridor leading to the Modern Flight Hangar is lined with the uniforms worn by members of the USAF and their predecessors.

The Modern Flight Hangar is a very large building, as it needs to be to accommodate its outsize treasures. The floor area here is greater than the other two hangars (the Early Years and Air Power galleries) combined, yet it contains far fewer aircraft. Many of them are at the imposing end of the aircraft scale. Imposing to say the least and making an impact on visitors as soon as they enter the hangar is the massive shape of a Boeing B-52D. As the representative of a design rapidly approaching its half century and still in service, this aircraft is an example of a phenomenon in military aviation. That it saw considerable action in Southeast Asia and survived a close encounter with an SA-2 missile makes it even more remarkable.

Looking around, it becomes apparent that the B-52 is in good company. It is surrounded by others who bear the scars of combat in Vietnam. There are two Republic F-105 Thunderchiefs, D and G models. The F-105D carries nose art naming it Memphis Belle II. It shot down two MiGs in battle, and like its illustrious B-17 predecessor, it proved to be a combat survivor. The

F-105G served as a "Wild Weasel" in Vietnam, and went one better than its brother, claiming victories over three MiGs. A tiny enemy, dwarfed by the Americans, is in the shape of a MiG-17 nearby. Those anxious to see its more potent cousin, the MiG-21, must cross the airfield to the Museum Annex. While there, they should note the Fairchild C-123K, a tubby old warrior which flew defoliant missions in Vietnam and received more than one thousand holes in its skin for its trouble. Understandably, it earned the nickname "Patches," and it carries seven Purple Hearts as a reminder that seven crewmen were wounded during its many operations.

The Museum's Martin B-57 is in disguise as an EB-57B. Before its conversion to electronic countermeasures, it flew in combat as a tactical bomber for over two years. An aircraft which did regular electronic countermeasures duty in Vietnam is the Douglas RB-66B skulking in the background. Menacing in its dark camouflage, the General Dynamics F-111A sits with wings partly swept, looking much as it did for its part in LINEBACKER II, the campaign which closed the Vietnam War. Some of its associated hardware is represented—a Pave Tack laser designator, a 20 mm Vulcan cannon, AGM-130A standoff weapons, and a 3,000 lb smart bomb. Around the hangar walls and clustered among the aircraft on the floor are other examples of smart weapons.

The smaller aircraft of the Vietnam War in the Museum's collection include the North American Rockwell OV-10A Bronco, the Air Commandos' Helio U-10D Super Courier, and a Bell UH-1P Iroquois (more commonly "Huey") helicopter which was used in Vietnam for psychological warfare. Even smaller than these is the Teledyne Ryan AQM-34L Firebee drone, which has the distinction unique in the Museum's collection of having been shot down over North Vietnam. At the other end of the hangar are two unusual aircraft. The Grumman HU-16B Albatross was a welcome sight to downed airmen in the Gulf of Tonkin, and the one on show became a star when it set an amphibian altitude record of 32,883 ft in 1973. Ominous in its all-black paint scheme, the Sikorsky CH-3E close by is typical of the big helicopters so beloved for their "Jolly Green

Giant" rescue work, but this one is black (and named Black Maria) because it was used for clandestine operations.

Scattered about the hangar are a number of special displays. An F-105 sits inside a typical revetment, and the canvas "Lyles Poison Pub Cookhouse" is handily placed alongside. USAF humor of the Vietnam era is celebrated in cartoons, and there is a USAF "Misery" communications intercept van, which earned its keep by monitoring U.S. transmissions to ensure that not too much of value was offered to the enemy. There is an F-4 cockpit for visitors to sit in, and a display describing the work of Spooky, the AC-47 gunship. Part of the story covers the Medal of Honor earned by Airman First Class John Levitow in an AC-47 hit by a mortar shell on February 24, 1969.

Three more "fast movers" round out the Vietnam era. Northrop's YF-5A is a prototype of the Freedom Fighter, a few of which saw brief service with the USAF in Southeast Asia. The Museum's LTV A-7D Corsair II is one flown by Major Colin Clarke on November 18, 1972. On that day he was airborne for nine hours on a rescue support mission for which he was awarded the Air Force Cross. Finally, there is the McDonnell Douglas F-4C Phantom in which Colonel Robin Olds and Lieutenant Stephen Crocker, his back-seater, shot down two MiGs in one day on May 20, 1967. It had been over twenty years since Robin Olds had gained his string of victories in WWII.

The First Small Step

When the North Koreans burst across the 38th parallel in June 1950, the invasion engaged the attention of the world in general and the U.S. in particular, but the American government still managed to find the time to become involved in events some twenty degrees farther south. The French attempt to regain their colonial grip on Indochina after WWII had not been smiled upon by the U.S., but the threat of Communist expansion in the area was seen as a greater evil. The Communist leader Ho Chi Minh had established himself in North Vietnam and was engaged in a guerrilla war with the aim of uniting all of Vietnam under a Communist government. In

American eyes, that was only the first stage. According to the "domino theory," success by Ho Chi Minh in Vietnam would lead inevitably to Communist domination of Laos and Cambodia, with Burma and Thailand following soon after. Resisting the fall of the first domino was seen as essential, and, in July 1950, a few U.S. military personnel arrived in Saigon to form a Military Assistance Advisory Group (MAAG) offering help and advice to the beleaguered French. It was a first small and deceptively innocuous step on the increasingly slippery slope of the Vietnam War's bottomless pit.

The French will to persist in Southeast Asia was effectively broken by their defeat at the hands of Viet Minh troops at Dien Bien Phu in May 1954. At an international conference in Geneva, France accepted the inevitable. Vietnam, Cambodia, and Laos were recognized as independent countries, with Vietnam temporarily divided at the 17th parallel pending nationwide elections to be held in 1956. A demilitarized zone (DMZ) partitioned North and South. Meanwhile, separate administrations were set up by Ho Chi Minh in Hanoi and Ngo Dinh Diem in Saigon. The U.S. emphasized its partiality by offering the Saigon regime economic and military assistance, and by sponsoring the eight-nation Southeast Asia Treaty Organization (SEATO) to be the region's cloak of security against Communist expansion. President Dwight Eisenhower supported Ngo Dinh Diem's plans to strengthen South Vietnam's military, and from 1955 on the U.S. MAAG took over training responsibility for most South Vietnamese forces, although USAF instructors for the Vietnamese Air Force (VNAF) did not arrive until 1957. When 1956 came, President Diem chose to ignore the requirement for a national election on the grounds that the solidly Communist vote in the North would be overwhelming and could only lead to a Ho Chi Minh government for Vietnam.

In 1957, Communist guerrillas in South Vietnam stepped up their overt activities and civil war broke out. The weight of their attacks increased during 1958 and 1959, and in April 1959 the South Viet-

A RANCH HAND UC-123 spraying defoliant on Vietnam's jungle in an attempt to uncover the trails used by the Viet Cong.

F. Kennedy became President of the United States and made it clear that he was determined to meet the Communist challenge head on. U.S. involvement in Southeast Asia now began an inexorable climb towards a major regional war and the longest armed conflict in American history.

For the USAF, the air war fell broadly into five phases. The first, from 1961 until mid-1964, was ostensibly covert, with the USAF flying reconnaissance sorties over Laos, and sending whole units with their aircraft to undertake combat training duties with the VNAF. Aging F-8 Bearcats of the VNAF were replaced by A-1 Skyraiders and T-28s. Phase two, covering the five years from mid-1964 on, saw the large-scale deployment of USAF units into Southeast Asia and their continuous engagement in air operations over South Vietnam, with frequent forays into the North and Laos. The third phase, from mid-1969 until spring 1972, was a time of retrenchment, with the USAF withdrawing many units and handing over bases to the VNAF. During the fourth phase, following the 1972 North Vietnamese spring offensive and lasting until early 1973, the USAF conducted intense strike operations, including concentrated attacks on the Hanoi/Haiphong areas. In phase five, the two years ending in May 1975, the USAF was concerned with final withdrawal from Vietnam.

namese Communist Party (Lao Dong) was formed, its armed members being known as the Viet Cong. From May 1959, after Ho Chi Minh announced his intention of unifying Vietnam by force, the Viet Cong were openly supported by the North. The U.S. reacted to this escalation initially by sending Saigon more advisers and military equipment. Special Forces teams arrived in the South to train Army of the Republic of Vietnam (ARVN) rangers in counterinsurgency operations. As 1960

ended there were some eight hundred or so U.S. servicemen on duty with the MAAG in South Vietnam.

By 1961, the Communist insurgency in the South had grown to critical proportions and public support for Ho Chi Minh's efforts had come from the Soviets. President Nikita Khrushchev announced that the Soviet Union was wholeheartedly behind "wars of national liberation," including "the armed struggle waged by the people of Vietnam." Two weeks later, John

The Covert USAF

Regular USAF units were operating in Southeast Asia before the end of 1961. RF-101Cs of the 15th and 45th Tactical Reconnaissance Squadrons began flying missions over Vietnam and Laos from Tan Son Nhut Air Base near Saigon in October, and F-102As were later detached from the Philippines to carry out occasional patrols against unidentified intruders over the border between South Vietnam and Cambodia. Operational missions though these were, the first experience of actual combat was reserved for other detachments of a different kind.

Responding to President Kennedy's expressed concern about the U.S. military capability to fight limited wars or to en-

An RF-101C seen over Vietnam in 1967, after camouflage requirements had led to a reduction in size of the U.S. national symbols. As part of their tactical reconnaissance responsibilities, RF-101s in Vietnam provided pathfinder and damage assessment services for the strike forces.

322

gage in counterinsurgency operations, in April 1961 General LeMay arranged for the establishment of the 4400th Combat Crew Training Squadron at Eglin AFB, Florida. Nicknamed "Jungle Jim," the unit was to develop tactics and select aircraft for the counterinsurgency role. By November, a Jungle Jim detachment was deployed under the code name FARM GATE to Bien Hoa near Saigon, and directed to train the VNAF. Their first aircraft in Vietnam were four suitably modified T-28s, four SC-47s adapted for rough field operations with strengthened landing gear and JATO rockets, and four B-26 Invaders taken out of storage. For diplomatic reasons, the aircraft were flown in VNAF markings and American pilots were allowed to take part in operational sorties only if accompanied by Vietnamese. In effect, the USAF "instructors" trained their students by example while flying the missions. The official line put out for the benefit of the press was: "No USAF pilot has ever flown in tactical missions except in the role of tactical instructor." These cosmetics did not entirely hide the fact that before the end of 1961 a USAF unit had become involved in a shooting war.

Two other USAF units moved to Vietnam early in 1962, both of them equipped with C-123 Providers. Operation MULE TRAIN brought the 346th TCS to Vietnam to provide tactical airlift support. More controversial was Operation RANCH HAND. UC-123Bs of the Special Aerial Spray Flight arrived at Tan Son Nhut to see whether they could defoliate the tropical jungle which hid the Viet Cong and their trails. On February 2, 1962, RANCH HAND gained the morbid distinction of suffering the first USAF casualties of the war when a UC-123B crashed without survivors.

As the FARM GATE detachment acquired more B-26s and T-28s, it became apparent that these aircraft were showing their age. Corrosion was among the problems to be faced in elderly airframes now carrying far more than their originally designed weights of ordnance. In February 1964, a B-26 lost a wing during a combat sortie, and a T-28 suffered the same fate

soon after. In recognition of its increased establishment, the FARM GATE detachment became known as the 1st Air Commando Squadron, and its disintegrating aircraft problems were dealt with by providing ex-USN A-1E Skyraiders as replacements. At first sight, the choice of one aging prop-driven aircraft to replace another did not seem sensible. However, the venerable A-1E proved to be ideal for its role. Pilots praised its capacity to absorb battle damage and swore by the accuracy of its weapons delivery. Troops were gratified to find that the A-1E could answer calls for support in weather which grounded the jets, and they admired both its weight of fire and its ability to loiter overhead for long periods. Valuable though these piston-engined warriors were, however, by 1964 it was becoming clear that the jets could not be long denied.

Overt Steps

From the beginning of the U.S. involvement in Vietnam, intelligence gathering was an important activity. A variety of aircraft operated regularly out of Tan Son Nhut and Bien Hoa from mid-1962. EC-54s, EC-97Gs, RB-57Ds and Es, and U-2s photographed likely targets and tracked Viet Cong radio traffic. U.S. Navy reconnaissance aircraft were also active, and, when a Vought RF-8A was shot down by North Vietnamese AAA over Laos on June 6, 1964, and an F-8D was lost in the same area the following day, it was decided to retaliate. On June 9, eight F-100Ds of the 511th TFS, supported by tankers, struck at AAA targets in Laos. The gloves had finally come off, and the action had been taken which acknowledged that the U.S. was effectively engaged in open warfare with the Communists in Southeast Asia, albeit limited and selective.

U.S. Navy ships were part of the intelligence operations, too, deployed in the Gulf of Tonkin. On August 2, 1964, the destroyer *Maddox* was attacked by North Vietnamese torpedo boats while cruising in international waters, and two days later, the destroyer reported a repeat performance. Immediate retaliatory U.S. air strikes against the torpedo boat bases were followed by firm political action in Washington. President Lyndon Johnson sought sweeping powers to use U.S. forces

F-100Ds and Fs of the 90th Pair o' Dice TFS flew from Bien Hoa Air Base from 1965 to 1970. A total of 186 F-100s were shot down during operations over South Vietnam, all by antiaircraft artillery or small arms fire. Of these, ten came from the 90th TFS.

in Southeast Asia and won near unanimous support from Congress. On August 7, the Gulf of Tonkin resolution was passed, giving the President authority to use armed force as necessary to assist South Vietnam against aggression and to repel attacks on the U.S. military. Within days, the U.S. forces in Southeast Asia were massively reinforced. TAC deployed a Composite Strike Force and SAC sent more tankers. The aircraft included B-57s, F-100Ds, and F-105Ds. A U-2 found that MiG-15s and -17s had been moved forward to Hanoi from training bases in China, which prompted General Hunter Harris, Com-

stability in South Vietnam[1] encouraged the Viet Cong to intensify their efforts, and the flow of men and supplies down the Ho Chi Minh Trail through Laos from North Vietnam steadily increased. On November 1, the Viet Cong were confident enough to strike directly at the USAF with a mortar attack on Bien Hoa airfield. Five B-57s were destroyed and fifteen others damaged. The USAF withdrew some of its deployed units to PACAF bases for safety. The U.S. Joint Chiefs of Staff urged that the riposte should be swift and tough. They had no faith in State Department arguments that the U.S. should follow a

more to come if negotiation was refused.[2] The JCS agreed. The President rejected the JCS proposals, preferring the State Department's "tit-for-tat" option. However, in view of the deteriorating political and military situation, he agreed that some limited action should be taken immediately. Operation BARREL ROLL, begun in December 1964, was less than direct. It allowed bombing missions over Laos with the principal aim of assisting Laotian forces against Communist insurgents. President Johnson felt that the strikes would serve to signal his determination to counter mounting Communist aggression against South Vietnam.

Far from being countered, the aggression was further increased, and often targeted specifically at Americans. On Christmas Eve, 1964, a bomb exploded in the Brink Hotel, Saigon, which was being used as U.S. officers' quarters, killing two and wounding over seventy. On February 7, 1965, Viet Cong infiltrated a U.S. Army base and raided a nearby U.S. advisers compound at Pleiku, in the central highlands. Army aircraft were destroyed and there were over 130 American casualties, including 8 dead. Washington reacted by ordering raids on North Vietnamese barrack areas, President Johnson remaining concerned about "sending the right signal to Hanoi." In his turn, Ho Chi Minh signaled the Viet Cong to increase their efforts, and on February 10 they blew up another American hotel, this time in Qui Nhon. Twenty-three Americans were killed and twenty-one wounded. Further retaliatory strikes on North Vietnamese barracks followed, but this time there was more to come.

U-2s were invaluable in SE Asia because their high-altitude capability and excellent passive defense systems allowed them to fly their reconnaissance missions almost unmolested over even the most difficult areas.

mander of the Pacific Air Forces (PACAF), to request permission to destroy the new threat. At the same time, General Maxwell Taylor, now U.S. Ambassador to South Vietnam, was recommending "a carefully orchestrated bombing attack" against North Vietnam. The ideas were rejected. At this stage, President Johnson still hoped that a mere show of force would be sufficient and that further escalation of the conflict could be avoided.

The "show of force" had little effect on the Communists. Serious political in-

scale of graduated response, believing that an escalating campaign would be taken by the North Vietnamese as a sign of weakness and would hand them the initiative, allowing them to choose the time and place of the next step. General LeMay, the USAF Chief of Staff, believed that North Vietnam should be subjected to a punishing bombing campaign, with the promise of

---

[1]President Diem had been assassinated in November 1963 and a continuing struggle for power had ensued.

[2]During Pentagon war games on the situation in SE Asia, General LeMay was reported to have complained about civilian-imposed restraints on military action. It was his opinion that the U.S. should use every available resource against North Vietnam. With typical bluntness, he summed up views by saying that, if necessary "... we should bomb them back to the Stone Age."

The direct attacks on Americans had been accompanied by a sharp rise in the pace of the Viet Cong offensive elsewhere. Viet Cong forces were now often found operating as large, organized units, and they were achieving notable successes against the ARVN in the field. In the face of these unpalatable facts—the weakness of the Saigon regime, the consistent success of the Viet Cong, and the willingness of Hanoi to meet U.S. challenges head on—the mood in Washington hardened and a turning point was reached. Any talk of negotiated U.S. withdrawal was swept aside by warnings that U.S. prestige was at risk and by demands that military deployments to Southeast Asia should be increased. Bombing the North was seen as essential to halting Communist erosion of the South, and the JCS persisted in advocating a short, unrestrained air campaign to force Hanoi out of the war. President Johnson remained fearful of the possible consequences of such a drastic step, believing that it might bring Chinese or Soviet forces into the struggle. His authorization was for limited air operations against the North, which he intended to be conducted within well-defined and closely controlled parameters. The decision was announced in a cable to Ambassador Taylor: "We will execute a program of measured and limited air action against selected military targets in North Vietnam remaining south of the nineteenth parallel. . . . These actions will stop when the aggression stops." The campaign was to be carried out under the evocative code name ROLLING THUNDER.

ROLLING THUNDER

The method of conducting the air war against North Vietnam was always a source of intense frustration to those local U.S. commanders responsible for carrying out operations. President Johnson insisted on retaining such close control of the campaign that no significant target in the North could be struck without his personal approval. His targeting decisions were passed through Secretary of Defense Robert McNamara to the JCS, and were then issued as directives to CINCPAC, who allocated targets and routes to the USAF, USN, and VNAF. Local air commanders responded to these orders, but had also to be aware of their responsibilities to the Commander, Military Assistance Command, Vietnam (MACV), and to the U.S. ambassadors in Saigon and Vientiane. The system was necessarily inflexible and incapable of reacting quickly to developing situations. It also created safe havens for the North Vietnamese within which their assets could not be attacked.

Initially, ROLLING THUNDER objectives were selected from a fixed list of ninety-four targets, principally bridges, railways, and roads. Notification was given of those which could be struck during a given week, and the number of sorties to be flown was specifically authorized. The restrictions were copious. Paramount was a concern for local civilian casualties, but it seemed that Soviet and Chinese citizens were equally sacrosanct. Hanoi and Haiphong were protected areas, as was a buffer zone along the Chinese border. Ports could be neither bombed nor mined because of the danger to neutral (including Soviet) shipping. To avoid damage to crops, the dikes around the rice paddies could not be struck, a rule which led to their becoming favorite sites for antiaircraft batteries. Worse still, for fear of hurting Soviet and Chinese advisers, MiG bases and SAM sites could suffer nothing more intrusive than reconnaissance while they were being built and equipped. USAF pilots had to watch as they were completed and their crews trained, knowing that they would soon become lethal threats.

ROLLING THUNDER began on March 2, 1965, with an attack delivered just thirty-five miles north of the DMZ. Forty-four F-105Ds, forty F-100Ds, twenty B-57Bs, and seven RF-101Cs, supported by tankers and rescue helicopters, struck at the Xom Bong ammunition storage area. In postflight debriefing, aircrew suggested that the force's 120 tons of bombs had been dropped on target, but indicated that the antiaircraft fire had been unexpectedly fierce. Many of the attacking aircraft bore scars of battle and six had been shot down. Sterling work by helicopters had saved five of the pilots, but one, Lt. Hayden Lockhart, had ejected from his blazing F-100 to become the first USAF prisoner of war in Vietnam.

The F-105 Thunderchief was the primary strike aircraft used against North Vietnam from 1965 until 1970, and it suffered nearly 20 percent of the USAF's total wartime fixed wing losses in the process. F-105D 58-1173, here loaded with sixteen 500 lb bombs, was used for armament trials in 1962.

As the weeks went by, the pace of ROLLING THUNDER increased and the North Vietnamese air defenses stiffened. The U.S. strikes moved farther north and on April 3 an attack was launched on the "Dragon's Jaw" Bridge across the Song Ma River at Than Hoa, halfway between Hanoi and the start of the Ho Chi Minh trail. It was North Vietnam's sole north/south road and rail bridge and the only available route for the rapid movement of military supplies to the South. As such, it was understandably high on the U.S. pri-

Giving early warning of approaching MiGs was the primary role of the Lockheed EC-121 Warning Star in SE Asia. Other duties, undertaken by the EC-121R, included tracking likely targets through sensors sown along the Ho Chi Minh Trail.

ority list of interdiction targets. This attack was to be the first of many in a frustrating series lasting through seven years, until 1972.

The mission, led by Lt. Col. Robbie Risner of the 67th TFS, was intended to be decisive. The force was composed of forty-six F-105s, twenty-one F-100s, two RF-101s, and ten KC-135 tankers. The F-100s were to provide top cover and flak suppression for the main strike force of F-105s, sixteen of which carried "Bullpup" missiles, while the rest were loaded with eight 750 lb bombs each. Well planned and executed though it was, the mission was the first of many failures. Good hits were scored on the bridge, but the 250 lb warheads of the Bullpups appeared to bounce off and the bombs merely punched easily repairable holes in roads and rail lines. The robust main structure of the bridge was unaffected. To suffer this disappointment, pilots faced intense flak, which claimed an F-100 and an RF-101 besides damaging many others.

A restrike was ordered for the following day. This time the lightweight Bullpups were left behind and all forty-eight F-105s carried eight 750 lb bombs. It was estimated that the bridge and its approaches were hit by over three hundred bombs, but still it stood, badly scarred but basically intact, a massive monument to overengineering. One F-105 was lost to flak before MiGs claimed their first victims of the war. In a high-speed attack, four MiG-17s burst out of low clouds and swept through a formation of heavily laden F-105s waiting their turn at the bridge. Firing their 20 mm cannon, the MiGs shot down two on the first pass and kept going to ensure their escape.

The unwelcome intervention by the MiGs on a murky day suggested two things—that they intended to use hit-and-run tactics, and that they were under radar control for interceptions. U.S. countermeasures included the positioning of EC-121s over the Gulf of Tonkin to control traffic and to warn of approaching MiGs, and the deployment to Southeast Asia of McDonnell F-4C Phantoms. For their part, the North Vietnamese understood the importance of bridges as choke points and quickly made the approaches to each of them a briar patch of antiaircraft guns. Nevertheless, by late April, USAF and USN attacks had destroyed twenty-six bridges and seven ferries. The U.S. leadership was encouraged to believe that such disruption in what was a rudimentary transportation system must have a crippling effect on the struggle in the South and must weaken the determination

of the North to continue the war. The bitter lessons of Korea seemed already to have been forgotten.

In March 1965, U.S. Marines were landed at Da Nang to secure U.S. installations there. This deployment of U.S. troops to South Vietnam and the ROLLING THUNDER attacks on the North served to heighten public nervousness about the conflict both internationally and in the U.S. To allay these fears, President Johnson made a speech in which he promised to engage North Vietnam in unconditional discussions and offered Ho Chi Minh a one billion dollar economic development program for his country if he would stop the aggression in South Vietnam. Hanoi's strident response left no doubt that they were not interested, and suggested that not only had their attitude been hardened by the bombing, but that they had taken note of the increasing public criticism of government policy in the U.S. They insisted that there must be an American withdrawal from Southeast Asia and that Vietnam's problems should be settled by the Vietnamese people alone.

In Washington, it was felt that such obduracy could be met only by an intensification of the bombing and the commitment of more U.S. combat troops to South Vietnam. However, it was also thought that there should first be a pause in the bombing to pursue the possibility of negotiations, if only, in Secretary of State Dean Rusk's words, "to meet criticisms that we haven't done enough." On May 10, the President cabled Ambassador Taylor, telling him that the forthcoming bombing pause was intended to "clear a path toward peace or toward increased military action."

A halt in the bombing was announced on May 12 but the North Vietnamese were not to be tempted. A series of diplomatic rebuffs led President Johnson to order the bombing resumed and the second phase of ROLLING THUNDER opened after a pause of only five days. New targets were authorized, including some as far north as the rail lines linking Hanoi with China. Offensive sortie rates against the North rose steadily, reaching four thousand for the month of May. Armed reconnaissance missions were more frequent, with the aim of harassing targets of opportunity, such as trains and trucks. As had happened in Korea, this soon became an unrewarding operation, since the North Vietnamese increasingly abandoned movement by day or on main roads.

The first USAF loss to a SAM occurred on July 24, 1965, when an F-4C flying MiGCAP (top cover) for some F-105s northwest of Hanoi was struck by what one of the pilots described as " a flying telephone pole." It was a Soviet SA-2, a two and a half ton missile guided by a "Fan Song" radar. The SA-2 could reach 60,000 ft and travel at Mach 2.5. By the end of 1965, 180 missiles had been fired to shoot down eleven U.S. aircraft, five of them from the USAF. Although not the most destructive of North Vietnam's defensive systems, the SAMs did force the U.S. attackers into taking a number of countermeasures. Violent evasive maneuvers were devised to defeat the missile's ability to correct its tracking, and missions in SAM areas were flown at low-level to stay below the SA-2's effective envelope. Unfortunately, low-flying aircraft came within reach of the often lethal light antiaircraft guns which proliferated everywhere in Vietnam. Technological measures against SAMs included the introduction of Douglas EB-66s to detect and jam enemy radar, and the more aggressive response of finding, engaging, and destroying SAM sites with specially equipped fighter-bombers, a method which came to be known as "Wild Weasel."

Four two-seat F-100Fs initiated the seek and destroy operations. Using aircraft fitted with the Radar Homing and Warning (RHAW) system, a detachment from the USAF's Tactical Warfare Center arrived in Vietnam and began flying combat trials alongside F-105s. They were not only able to warn strike aircraft of imminent SAM firings, but also to home in on the Fan Song radar's signals and either carry out or direct strikes against the enemy site. Later, modified EF-105F/Gs took over as the principal Wild Weasels in missions during which they sought deliberately to draw SAM fire. They then reacted with AGM-45 Shrike missiles which followed the Fan Song beam to its source.

In their turn, the North Vietnamese showed their adaptability. They built SAM sites in profusion, many of which were either unoccupied or fake. They showed how quickly they could move from one site to another after a reconnaissance aircraft had seen them, and they developed sophisticated camouflage to make the sites look like villages or clumps of trees. Fake sites, equipped with dummy missiles and transmitting Fan Song signals to draw in U.S. pilots, were surrounded by dense concentrations of guns known as "flak traps." On September 16, 1965, a flak trap claimed the F-105 of one of the USAF's most celebrated airmen, Robbie Risner, condemning him to over seven years as a prisoner of war. Sadly, Risner's rank and reputation[3] ensured that he would be singled out by his captors for special treatment. He was forced to endure the pain of physical torture and the deprivation of solitary confinement during his long incarceration.

By the end of 1965, so-called "fastmover" squadrons of the USAF in Southeast Asia were spread among bases at Takhli, Korat, Ubon, and Don Muang air-

[3]Lt. Col. Risner had been featured on the cover of *Time* magazine just a few months before he was shot down.

port in Thailand, and Tan Son Nhut, Da Nang, Bien Hoa, and Cam Ranh Bay in South Vietnam. Six squadrons had F-4Cs, which had begun to make their presence felt in the air-to-air war on July 10, 1965, when the combination of Phantoms and "Sidewinder" heat-seeking missiles accounted for two MiG-17s in a brief dogfight. Five more squadrons were equipped with F-105s, four with F-100s, one with F-102s, one with B-57s, and one with F-5As. Other jet aircraft operating in support included RF-101s, KC-135s, RB-66s, and the Wild Weasel F-100s. Special detachments were flying the RB-57E and the U-2C. Added to all these were the USN squadrons flying from three carriers stationed in the South China Sea.

The increasingly hazardous air environment of Vietnam was revealed in the rising numbers of aircraft being destroyed. Of 273 U.S. fixed wing aircraft lost to enemy action in 1965, 158 belonged to the USAF. No fewer than 139 of the USAF's losses, including fifty-four F-105s, were attributed to AAA and small arms fire, a reflection in part of the fact that there were now more than two thousand radar-directed AAA guns in North Vietnam.

On December 24, 1965, President Johnson ordered a cease-fire over the Christmas period. For air operations, this

A Douglas EB-66 Destroyer acts as ECM escort for an F-105 formation as bombs are released over N. Vietnam. EB-66s provided threat warnings and jamming protection against gun-laying radars and SAMs.

A pair of thirsty F-4s waits for a drink off the wing of a KC-135.

was extended into a prolonged bombing pause. A "peace offensive" was launched, offering the withdrawal of U.S. forces from Vietnam but refusing to accept the participation of the Viet Cong in a coalition government in Saigon. Ho Chi Minh's rejection of the offer denounced it as "deceitful," and on January 31, 1966, President Johnson opened the third phase of ROLLING THUNDER. Unwilling to accede to JCS requests for a marked increase in the tempo of the bombing and for the mining of enemy harbors, and still wanting to leave the door open for the North Vietnamese, the President kept a tight grip on air operations, and phase three was less intense than phase two had been. However, by the end of March, the intransigence of Hanoi led to a recommendation from Secretary McNamara that the bombing should be intensified and that the target list should be widened to include oil. Reluctantly, the President agreed, and phase four of ROLLING THUNDER began in June 1966, now under the operational control of Seventh Air Force, commanded by General William Momyer.

For the remainder of 1966, U.S. aircraft flew extended armed reconnaissance missions throughout the North (always excepting the Hanoi/Haiphong sanctuaries), attacked the rail links with China, and made a determined effort against oil tar-

gets and the infiltration routes north of the DMZ. The pace of the air offensive was sharply increased, with U.S. aircraft reaching a peak of twelve thousand sorties over North Vietnam in September. In spite of frequently poor weather and concentrated defenses, the damage done by the campaign was clearly substantial. Countless trucks and railway wagons were destroyed, and cuts made everywhere in road and rail networks, with hundreds of bridges demolished. It was estimated that two-thirds of the North's oil storage capacity no longer existed. These considerable efforts forced the North Vietnamese to improvise. Oil was stored in barrels rather than large tanks, and dispersed in hundreds of minor dumps. Perhaps 300,000 people were diverted into repair work and into moving supplies, on foot or by bicycle if necessary. This they were evidently prepared to do, and the ground war in South Vietnam gave no sign of slackening.

By the end of 1966, there were at least 150 SAM sites operating in North Vietnam, and the first MiG-21s had made their appearance carrying infrared homing missiles. They could be seen flying from five airfields in the Hanoi area, but the bases were not on the list of targets for U.S. aircraft. A typical execution order of the time included the instruction: "Not, repeat not, authorized to attack North Viet-

namese air bases from which attacking aircraft may be operating." At least a partial answer to the MiG problem came in Operation BOLO. Colonel Robin Olds, commander of the 8th TFW flying F-4Cs, planned a mission to lure the MiGs into battle. On January 2, 1967, a force composed predominantly of F-4Cs approached the Hanoi area in a formation normally associated with a standard F-105 strike package. Cloud covered Hanoi and Olds had to trail his coat over the enemy airfields three times before MiG-21s began popping up on all sides. In the frenetic combat of the next few minutes, seven MiGs were shot down for no loss. An extract from Colonel Olds's report of the action describes one success:

"[I] fell in behind and below the MiG-21 at his seven o'clock position at about .95 Mach. Range was 4,500 ft, angle off 15. The MiG-21 obligingly pulled up well above the horizon and exactly down sun. I put the pipper on his tail pipe, received a perfect growl, squeezed the trigger once, hesitated, then once again. The first Sidewinder leapt in front and within a split second turned left in a definite and beautiful collision course correction. . . . The missile went slightly down, then arced gracefully up, heading for impact. Suddenly the MiG-21 erupted in a brilliant flash of orange flame. A complete wing separated and flew back in the airstream, together with a mass of smaller debris. The MiG swapped ends immediately, and tumbled forward for a few instants. It then fell, twisting, corkscrewing, tumbling, lazily toward the top of the clouds. No pilot ejection occurred."

The determined enemy air defense efforts in 1966 led to a sharp rise in U.S. fixed wing combat losses to 465, of which 296 were USAF. AAA and small arms accounted for 265 USAF aircraft, and again the F-105 had suffered most heavily—no fewer than 103 Thunderchiefs had fallen to the guns.

A six-day truce on the occasion of the 1967 Lunar New Year (Tet) marked the end of ROLLING THUNDER, phase four. Phase five began on February 14 and lasted until Christmas 1967. During the

Skyraider Attacks Viet Cong Camp © *R.G. Smith*

year, the target list was expanded to take in the previously forbidden Hanoi/ Haiphong area. Among the most significant new items was an industrial complex at Thai Nguyen where the country's only steel mill was situated. Ringed with ninety-six AAA batteries and several SAM sites, it was a formidable challenge. Leading the first raid on March 10 were four F-105s, two of them equipped as Wild Weasels. On the run in, the lead aircraft was shot down and his wingman severely damaged. The remaining pair, led by Capt. Merlyn Dethlefsen, set about the job of eliminating a SAM site which would threaten strike aircraft bombing the steel mill. MiGs closed and attacked; Dethlefsen dived into the intense flak barrage to brush them off. The F-105s were hit repeatedly, but turned back into the flak twice more to drop bombs and finish off the site with 20 mm cannon. Dethlefsen's fierce determination was rewarded with a Medal of Honor. He made light of his gritty persistence under fire: "All I did was the job I had been sent

to do," he said. "I expected to get shot at a lot."

Following a similarly courageous action only a month later, the Medal of Honor was awarded to a second F-105 Wild Weasel pilot. On April 19, 1967, Major Leo Thorsness braved heavy flak to hit two SAM sites, shot down one MiG and damaged another while covering F-105 crewmen who had been forced to eject, and engaged the attention of several other MiGs before lack of ammunition and almost dry tanks dictated a high-speed escape at low level and diversion to a forward base.

Other targets hit successfully by U.S. aircraft in and around Hanoi/Haiphong in 1967 were power plants, the provoking MiG airfields, and the Paul Doumer bridge across the Red River in Hanoi. Several spans of the bridge were dropped at the first attempt with the help of 3,000 lb bombs. Elsewhere, strike operations expanded into the buffer zone with China, and mining was begun of rivers, but only

south of the 20th parallel. As offensive operations were stepped up, the air-to-air war moved increasingly in favor of the U.S. The F-4D model of the Phantom and the AIM-4 "Falcon" missile arrived and were delivered to the 555th TFS, the combination scoring its first victory over a MiG on October 26. By the end of the year, seventy-five MiGs had been shot down for the loss of twenty-five U.S. aircraft (USAF ratio fifty-nine to twenty-two), and American airmen had gained virtual air supremacy over North Vietnam. The year as a whole had seen U.S. fixed wing combat losses peak at 515. Of that number, 325 were USAF, with 252 of those attributable to AAA and small arms fire.

Nineteen sixty-seven was a year in which the results of ROLLING THUNDER were subjected to close scrutiny in a number of studies. The bombing campaign was credited with having hurt Hanoi's military-industrial base (such as it was) severely. Nevertheless, the conclusions drawn in Washington were that Ho Chi Minh's strategy appeared to be unwavering, that there was every indication that the North Vietnamese people would continue to resist, and that the ability of the North to carry on the war remained little changed. What was more, in the balance account terms of Secretary McNamara, the bombing was costing the U.S. at least ten dollars for every dollar of damage inflicted. Even so, the factor in the equation which might conceivably have made the difference, the severance of North Vietnam's principal lifeline to the Soviet Union by the mining of Haiphong and other harbors, was still denied to U.S. military leaders by President Johnson because he believed the possibility of damaging Soviet shipping to be an unacceptable risk.

Following the 1967 Christmas bombing pause, ROLLING THUNDER entered its sixth phase. It did so without McNamara, who was replaced as Secretary of Defense by Clark Clifford early in 1968. On March 31, 1968, Lyndon Johnson suspended all bombing north of the 20th parallel and announced that he would not be seeking a second term as President of the United States. To almost everyone's surprise, the North Vietnamese reacted by announcing that they would be willing to engage in peace talks. Later in the year, with the talks underway in Paris and on the eve of the Presidential elections, Johnson halted the bombing of North Vietnam altogether. Forty-four months and over 300,000 sorties after it began, ROLLING THUNDER rumbled away into history.

The "In-Country" War

As the U.S. moved inexorably towards open involvement in Vietnam in 1964, the requirement for VNAF personnel to fly on all USAF operational sorties was reconsidered. On February 18, 1965, it was rescinded, and the government of South Vietnam officially requested the USAF to fly "in-country" combat missions. B-57s struck at a guerrilla concentration the next day, and other U.S. combat aircraft became engaged in operations soon thereafter because a threatened coup in Saigon kept the VNAF otherwise occu-

pied, standing by to intervene. By March 6, Washington accepted the inevitable and removed all restrictions on the use of U.S. aircraft for combat in South Vietnam.

With the restrictions lifted, USAF aircraft poured into the country and a crash program of airfield construction was undertaken. By the end of 1965, the USAF had more than 500 aircraft and 21,000 men stationed at eight major air bases in South Vietnam. American ground forces in the country had risen to over 200,000. The command arrangements for this massive military influx were labyrinthine. The general conduct of the air war in the South

fell under the aegis of General William Westmoreland, the MACV commander, but, as 1966 dawned, the management of the air units was the direct responsibility of Maj. Gen. Joseph Moore, MACV's air deputy and commander of the 2nd Air Division of the Thirteenth Air Force. (Later in the year, the 2nd AD became Seventh Air Force.) Moore answered to MACV for air operations over the South, but also looked after out-of-country missions for CINCPAC. Not infrequently, the two superior headquarters had urgent needs for

the same squadrons at the same time. Answering to Maj. Gen. Moore's Tactical Air Control Center in Saigon for operations within South Vietnam were four USAF/VNAF manned Direct Air Support Centers, one to each of four corps areas, which did their best to cooperate and assign air assets for tasks in support of the ground war. Complicating the picture was the fact that Moore's system had no control over aircraft belonging to either the Army or Marines.

Whatever juggling of air units was going on at staff levels, the control of combat aircraft once airborne was often in the

Low-level FAC missions in the slow, unarmored Cessna O-1E Bird Dog were hazardous operations, but the presence of a FAC to call in air strikes was often the difference between life and death for U.S. or S. Vietnamese ground forces in contact with the enemy.

hands of a forward air controller (FAC). Mostly former jet pilots, the FACs spent much of the war flying the Cessna O-1 Bird Dog, a single-engined light plane capable of 115 mph flat out and unarmed except for target-marking rockets. Bird Dogs lacked even the minimal protection of armor and self-sealing fuel tanks. Since it was necessary to make visual contact with the enemy, and then to hang around marking targets and directing strikes, FAC missions were among the most challenging flown by the USAF. Later, the O-1 was supplemented by the larger, twin-engined Cessna O-2 and the more capable North American OV-10, which had both armor and self-sealing tanks and carried powerful armament of its own. The job, however, was always hazardous. As one Skyraider pilot put it: "You've got to hand it to those guys. . . . Just a light plane, a pair of good eyes, and guts." During the war, 122 O-1s, 82 O-2s, and 47 OV-10s were lost in combat. Two FAC pilots, Capt. Hilliard Wilbanks and Capt. Steven Bennett, were awarded posthumous Medals of Honor for persistence and self-sacrifice in the face of heavy fire.

troops. If the ground forces had a favorite aircraft, it was not among the jets. It was the prop-driven A-1 Skyraider. It could carry an incredible amount of ordnance, over four tons on fifteen attachment points beneath the wings and fuselage, and it could stay in contact for long periods while its thirsty jet cousins came and went. Four 20 mm cannon made for lethal strafing attacks, and heavy armor-plating made the A-1 resistant to small arms fire. It was particularly suited for giving covering fire during rescue missions for downed aircrew, a task known as Rescue Combat Air Patrol (RESCAP) and operating under the call

AAA and small arms fire coming from the valley slopes, they heard radio calls saying that the camp was being overrun. As they strafed the attackers, two of the Skyraiders were hit hard by enemy fire. One pulled up and made for home, but the other, piloted by Maj. "Jump" Myers, lost its engine and burst into flames. Myers bellied the aircraft onto the camp landing strip, exploding his external fuel tank in the process. He leapt clear into a ditch as flames enveloped his A-1E. Seeing that Myers was alive, Fisher called for a rescue helicopter before joining his wingman and two other newly arrived Skyraiders in strafing enemy troops trying to reach the downed pilot. However, the helicopter was at least twenty minutes away, the A-1Es were out of ammunition, and Fisher realized that the North Vietnamese would probably reach Myers before he could be rescued. Rather than run that risk, he decided to do the job himself. As the others made dummy runs overhead to distract the enemy, he landed his aircraft under fire on the shell-torn strip. Myers sprinted out of the ditch and dived into the cockpit as Fisher opened up and roared away, dodging debris on the runway and climbing into the safety of the clouds. Fisher's Skyraider bore the scars of many hits, but made it back to base. For this breathtaking exploit, Bernard Fisher was awarded the Medal of Honor.

F. Bernie Fisher and "Jump" Myers after the astonishing rescue under fire in S. Vietnam's A Shau valley on March 10, 1966 for which Fisher was awarded the Medal of Honor.

FACs controlled a formidable array of strike aircraft and weapons. Fast movers like F-100s, F-4s, and B-57s could between them respond to calls for support with general purpose bombs of up to 2,000 lbs, fragmentation bombs, cluster bomb units, a variety of rockets and missiles, gunfire, and the ground forces' weapon of choice—napalm. Soldiers liked napalm not only because it could be guaranteed to penetrate thick jungle foliage, but also because, since it created no shrapnel, it could be used very close to hard-pressed friendly

sign "Sandy." By the end of the war, "Sandies" had assisted in the rescue of over one thousand airmen.

On March 10, 1966, an outpost in the A Shau Valley manned by 375 Montagnard irregulars and 20 U.S. Green Beret advisers called for help against a force of 2,000 North Vietnamese. Close air support was made extremely difficult by thick, low clouds covering the rugged terrain, but four A-1Es led by Maj. Bernard Fisher found a way into the valley through a gap in the overcast. Running the gauntlet of

On countless occasions, close support aircraft answered desperate calls for help from besieged troops and made the difference between survival and destruction. However, more than half of the operational sorties flown over South Vietnam were planned attacks on suspected guerrilla strongholds and supply routes. Such strikes were intended to deny the Communists safe havens and storage areas, and they were carried out by both day and night. In 1966, the ground-based "Combat Skyspot" MSQ-77 radar was introduced, which could guide bombers to a precise release point, so allowing tactical strikes to be made on selected targets at any time and in any weather.

The firepower for tactical operations was vastly increased in June 1965 when SAC's B-52s were made available to MACV

The devastating rain of bombs which fell from high-flying B-52Ds made the "Buff" the USAF weapon most feared by the Viet Cong.

to fly combat missions under the code name ARC LIGHT. It was a surprising shift, but one which underlined the flexibility of air power. Strategic operations were conducted against the North by fighter-bombers, while aircraft designed to promote the strategy of nuclear deterrence were tasked to meet tactical needs in the South. The B-52Fs which flew the first ARC LIGHT missions from Guam were modified to enable them to carry twenty-seven 750 lb bombs internally and twenty-four more on external racks. Later, B-52Ds went through a "Big Belly" modification which allowed them to load the astonishing number of eighty-four 500 lb bombs in the bay, while retaining the external capacity for twenty-four 750 lb bombs. It was often claimed that such profligate use of air power was wasteful, since the intelligence which selected targets for the B-52s was in many cases less than certain and, in view of the B-52s' understandably slow reaction to a situation, seldom timely. Nevertheless, although the raids sometimes struck at empty forest, captured Viet Cong usually reported that B-52s were what they most feared. The destructive power and scale of B-52 bombing patterns was awesome, and morale suffered because it was never known where or when the earth would next erupt. With the bombers op-

erating at 30,000 ft, nothing was seen or heard before hundreds of bombs arrived, obliterating everything over a huge area. For those who had seen the results of a B-52 raid, or had survived the experience, wondering when the heavens would open again could concentrate the mind and weaken the spirit.

In 1967, part of the B-52 force was moved to Thailand, from where they could reach their targets much more quickly and without having to refuel. By then, the B-52's contribution to the war had become considerable. A little less than two years after ARC LIGHT began, the ten thousandth B-52 combat sortie was flown, and the big bombers were being increasingly relied on to break up enemy troop concentrations threatening U.S. bases. For example, at the time of the enemy's Tet offensive in 1968, a major assault was launched on the U.S. Marines' base at Khe Sanh, six miles from the Laotian border and fourteen miles south of the DMZ. General Westmoreland believed that "the enemy hoped at Khe Sanh to obtain a climactic victory such as he had done in 1954 at Dien Bien Phu." The U.S. base was attacked and surrounded by twenty thousand North Vietnamese regulars in January 1968 and remained under siege for seventy-seven days. Operation NIAGARA was

devised to provide the Marines with air support and the USAF's General Momyer was given temporary command of all U.S. air assets operating at Khe Sanh. Hundreds of sorties every day were flown against enemy concentrations, with a C-130 command center handing off incoming fighter-bomber sorties to one of up to thirty FACs in good weather and letting Combat Skyspot radar guide them in when clouds were heavy.

Vital though these missions were, it was the B-52s which most impressed the enemy. Missions were arranged so that a formation of three B-52s arrived over Khe Sanh every ninety minutes to bomb at Combat Skyspot's direction. Initially, a buffer zone was established which allowed the B-52s to bomb no closer than three thousand yards from the forward Marine positions. However, when it became apparent that the enemy troops were developing extensive bunker complexes much closer in, the Marine commander nervously agreed to reduce the buffer to as little as one thousand feet. Ensuing close-in strikes devastated enemy positions and gave an exhilarating lift to the spirits of the Marines. A captured North Vietnamese soldier estimated that one strike alone had killed 75 percent of an 1,800 man regiment. There was ample reason to believe his story. By the time the siege was broken, the countryside around Khe Sanh had been transformed into a lunar landscape, scarred as it was by endless overlapping bomb craters. During NIAGARA, U.S. aircraft had dropped almost 100,000 tons of bombs, and two-thirds of them had fallen from B-52s. Intelligence estimates suggested that two North Vietnamese divisions had been effectively destroyed as fighting units. It was hardly surprising that General Westmoreland later gave credit to the B-52s for preventing the large-scale buildup of forces needed by the enemy to overrun Khe Sanh.

On the Trail

Although combat operations against the enemy's fighting forces, both North Vietnamese and Viet Cong, were an essential part of the war, they did not strike at the root of the problem—how to deprive the Communist insurgency in South Vietnam of its lifeblood. From the outset, the vast network of rough roads and tracks through Laos, known collectively as the Ho Chi Minh Trail, was used to sustain the Viet Cong with a flow of supplies which grew steadily over the years to the proportions of a flood. The prime movers employed on the trail were thousands of Soviet ZIL-157 trucks. Stopping the movement of these trucks became a paramount concern of U.S. leaders.

Supplies from North Vietnam usually crossed into Laos and entered the Ho Chi Minh Trail system through two passes: Mu Gia, about seventy-five miles north of the DMZ, and Keo Neua, which was twice as far. Much of the trail offered its users the natural concealment of a thick forest canopy, but there were open spaces which provided opportunities for movement to be detected by reconnaissance and for tactical aircraft to make visual attacks. Once U.S. aircraft began operating over the trail, traffic moved at night through these vulnerable areas. The first operations aimed specifically at interdicting the Trail in southern Laos were code-named STEEL TIGER. They began in April 1965, using roving F-100s and F-105s by day, and B-57s accompanied by C-130 flareships by night. The poor flying weather associated with the monsoon badly restricted operations until October, but over one thousand STEEL TIGER sorties per month were flown, nevertheless. Even with the help of covert ground reconnaissance teams to plot traffic on the trail, results did not match the effort expended and it became obvious that greatly improved interdiction methods would have to be developed.

The first step was the preparation of a systematic campaign against the Ho Chi Minh Trail in the areas of Laos contiguous with South Vietnam. The plan, code-named TIGER HOUND, combined U.S. Air Force, Navy, Marine, and Army air resources with those of the small Royal Laotian Air Force. UC-123s sprayed defoliants on the forest obscuring the trail, and an airborne command post was established using C-47s/C-130s to control strike operations. FACs roamed the area, and RF-4Cs, equipped with infrared sensors and side-looking radar, combed the trail for targets. F-100s, F-105s, B-57s, A-1Es, U.S. carrierborne aircraft, and Laotian T-28s were on call for strikes; night operations added C-130 flareships and Army OV-1 Mohawks. Later, a few resurrected A-26Ks took on the night interdiction role, just as they had in Korea, and there were even some C-123s carrying special detection devices and dispensing cargo-hold loads of bomblet canisters. By 1966, the B-52s had joined in, operating with the aid of Combat Skyspot radar, and later came the sophisticated B-57G, fitted with low-light television, infrared sensors, forward-looking radar, and laser target-marking.

Aircrews were sometimes aided in their search for targets by an electronic anti-infiltration system. It used small air-dropped sensors which were sown along the trail and could detect the movement of troops and trucks. The information was transmitted to a monitoring aircraft, like the EC-121R, which made assessments and recommended targets. Some of the weaponry used on the trail was also unusual. Besides the conventional array of bombs, rockets, and guns, there were land mines, incendiary clusters, fuel-air explosive munitions, and even canisters of riot control gas.

This remarkable combination of air power instruments seemed impressive enough, but the most effective truck killers were found elsewhere, drawn from the unlikely ranks of the tactical transports. They were transport aircraft modified into forms that Admiral Nelson would have understood; "gunships" capable of firing broadsides of terrifying destructiveness. The first of the gunship line was the AC-

Rearming an AC-47 Spooky. A broadside from the three Gatling guns was spectacular, with each firing at rates up to 6,000 rounds per minute.

47, Douglas's venerable "Gooney Bird" in yet another role. Known to the media as "Puff, the Magic Dragon" but to ground forces by the call sign "Spooky," AC-47s were armed with three 7.62 mm miniguns which fired sideways from the cargo door and windows. Targets were attacked simply by flying an orbit around them and holding them centered in a sight placed to the left of the pilot in the cockpit window. Later, more sophisticated gunships included the AC-119K Shadow, and several variants of the C-130 Hercules, the most advanced of which was the AC-130E Spectre. The Spectre was heavily armored and equipped with a multitude of sensors, including one which could detect running truck ignition systems. Its battery consisted of paired miniguns and Vulcan 20 mm cannon, a 40 mm cannon, and a 105 mm howitzer, all fired with the aid of a computer. A broadside from a Spectre was memorably devastating.

Gunships were as useful in South Vietnam against the Viet Cong as they were on the trail, giving timely aid to hard-pressed ground units on many occasions, their murderous fire destroying the cohesion of countless enemy attacks on army bases and outposts. Impressive as the statistics of their destructive powers were, however, with literally thousands of trucks wrecked each year, even the mighty gunships could not bring the flow of supplies along the Ho Chi Minh Trail to a complete halt, and the Viet Cong resolutely continued to increase their capability to operate in the countryside of South Vietnam throughout the 1960s.

Fetchers and Carriers

As is always the case in war, it was the men and machines engaged in front-line combat which took the eye and monopolized the headlines. Behind them and their activities there were a host of specializations without whose services the armed warriors could not have operated.

The contributions made by transport aircraft in WWII and Korea were essential to the conduct of the various campaigns, but in Southeast Asia their work was perhaps even more significant. The air bridge built across the Pacific by the Military Air Transport Service (Military Airlift Command from 1965) was massive. In the absence of adequate ports and infrastructure in South Vietnam, it needed to be. In the early days, the bulk of the transoceanic traffic was handled by C-124s. MATS had twenty-one squadrons of them, backed up by three squadrons of C-133s, seven of C-130s, and three of C-135s. The limitations of this force were soon exposed, and were emphasized by the fact that MATS still had to provide a service for the U.S. military elsewhere in the world. Only the

C-124s and C-133s had the capacity to cope with such large items of equipment as tanks and bulldozers, but the C-124s were agonizingly slow and the C-133s technically temperamental.[4] Although help came from aircraft of the Air Force Reserve and Air National Guard, mostly aging C-97s and C-119s, the air bridge did not gain enough strength to take the strain fully until the appearance of the Lockheed C-141 Starlifter in 1965. The C-141A's ability to carry its maximum payload of 67,000 lbs for 4,000 miles cruising at 440 knots was a quantum jump over the C-124's 25,000 lbs for 2,300 miles at 200 knots. Even so, the C-141's cargo bay was neither as high nor as wide as the C-124's, and it was not until Lockheed's giant C-5A Galaxy started operations into Southeast Asia in 1971 that the U.S. had a true strategic airlifter capable of handling the bulkiest military loads.

MAC's airlift capacity improved in other ways besides that of acquiring better

---

[4]The C-124 took almost two weeks to make the round trip between the U.S. and SE Asia, accumulating some ninety-five flying hours in the process.

From 1965, Lockheed C-141s played a major role in the airlift of personnel and supplies within SE Asia and across the Pacific. Between 1965 and 1972 they flew over 6,000 medical evacuation missions out of Vietnam. Here a C-141 loads a medical vehicle at Cam Ranh Bay in April 1969.

aircraft. The demands of the Vietnam War forced the development of a whole new air transport system. Established transpacific routes grew from one to more than a dozen, and airfields both en route and in Southeast Asia gained longer runways and sophisticated facilities. Aircraft utilization rates rose and freight priority categories were introduced; the "Red Ball" Express system guaranteed shipment of vital spares within twenty-four hours of receiving the request. MAC also demonstrated an impressive capacity to react quickly in an emergency. For example, in 1967 C-141s and C-133s moved 10,335 paratroopers of the 101st Division, plus 5,118 tons of equipment (including thirty-seven helicopters), from Fort Campbell, Kentucky, to Bien Hoa between November 17 and December 29. The average aircraft unloading time for this operation was just seven and a half minutes. Even faster overall was the response to the Tet offensive in February 1968, when a brigade of the 82nd Airborne at Fort Bragg, North Carolina, and a regiment of the 5th Marine Division at Camp Pendleton, California, together with 3,500 tons of equipment, were deployed to South Vietnam in only twelve days.

Outbound from Vietnam, MAC's transports performed services which were equally essential. They took troops on rest and recuperation leave, evacuated the wounded, and carried the sad coffins of the dead. When it was all over, they went back to fetch those who had survived as prisoners of war and flew them home.

For tactical transports, employed within the theater of operations, war had always held its hazards. In Vietnam, the risks were vastly more severe. In a country where there were no front lines and the enemy could appear almost anywhere, the tactical transports operated all the time in a combat zone. U.S. and ARVN troops in scattered outposts relied on them for supply. They carried men and equipment quickly into areas for search and destroy operations, and they were involved in paratroop assaults. To keep the soldiers supplied, they landed on makeshift airstrips under fire, or delivered loads using either the Low Altitude Parachute Extraction

A C-123 disgorges U.S. Marines at Calu, S. Vietnam, in June 1968.

System (LAPES) or the Ground Proximity Extraction System (GPES) while flying through just above the runway. Deliveries could also be made by parachute, even when the drop zone was obscured, using either on-board or ground-based radar.

At first, the aircraft used were C-47s and C-123s, but the immensely capable Lockheed C-130 Hercules began to appear in 1964, and in 1967 the U.S. Army transferred its force of de Havilland C-7 Caribous to the USAF. Small as it was, the C-7 proved to be invaluable. It was simple and rugged, and it could get in and out of very short, rough strips. Its sortie rate under primitive conditions was remarkably high—in the seventy months after its transfer from the U.S. Army in January 1967 the Caribou flew over 773,000 sorties, an average of more than 11,000 per month. (Monthly averages for other types in theater during the same period: C-123s— 6,651; C-130s—8,597.) In terms of lifting capacity, however, the C-130 had no competition. It was the most important theater transport aircraft for bulk movement, registering a high figure of 69,499 tons transported in one month. (The highest totals for other types were: C-123— 16,643; C-7—10,264.) The ubiquitous C-130 was also involved in many other missions. Besides its gunship and aerial command post roles, it was used to start forest fires by dropping oil drums (Operation

BANISH BEACH), for sowing antipersonnel mines during the interdiction of the Ho Chi Minh Trail in Laos, and for clearing instant helicopter landing zones in the forest with huge weapons like the 15,000 lb BLU-82 bomb (Operation COMMANDO VAULT).

On May 12, 1968, Lt. Col. Joe Jackson answered a call for help from a Special Forces camp at Kham Duc. An evacuation of the garrison had been carried out under heavy fire earlier in the day by C-130s and C-123s. Two C-130s had been lost and a third badly damaged in a desperate operation. Unfortunately, three members of a USAF control team had inadvertently been left behind and were in imminent danger of being overrun by enemy infantry swarming over the camp. Joe Jackson was flying a C-123 unsupported by attack aircraft. However, he judged that the Americans on the ground could not afford to wait. Approaching at 9,000 ft, he made a steep descent and slammed the C-123 down on the runway. Braking to a halt, he reversed the props and backed up to a point opposite where the men were taking cover. Guns, rockets, and mortars engaged the aircraft, but the control team managed to scramble aboard and Jackson took off without once being hit. For the daring rescue Joe Jackson was awarded the Medal of Honor, a rare recognition of a "trash hauler" pilot.

A low-flying C-123 over S. Vietnam in 1965, escorted by a watchful AC-47 Spooky.

Joe Jackson's exploit was extraordinary, but it was not unusual for unarmed "trash haulers" to face dangers, nor to brave enemy fire. During the siege of Khe Sanh, the surrounded Marine garrison was supplied entirely by air, the C-123s and C-130s making 601 parachute drops and 460 landings between them. Transport crews operated daily into the besieged base, knowing that they would be exposed to antiaircraft fire on the approach and over the field, and to mortar fire on the ground.

To reduce the exposure time as much as possible, even those aircraft which had to land were often unloaded on the move, resulting in an average touchdown-to-take-off time of three minutes. Including those shot down or destroyed in attacks on Khe Sanh and other bases, the USAF lost fifty-five C-130s, fifty-three C-123s, and twenty C-7s during the Vietnam War.

Other Helping Hands

The combat aircrew who delivered the weapons and fought the enemy directly were only too well aware of the debt they owed to those in supporting roles, without whom their task would have been much more difficult and their chances of survival considerably reduced. The labor of the technicians who serviced the aircraft was especially close to their hearts, but the work of logisticians, air base defense teams, medical personnel, and many others was equally essential, though not often fully recognized. In the air, there were reconnaissance crews who sought out enemy defenses and likely targets, those who detected and countered enemy electronic transmissions, the ever present tankers with their life-saving fuel, and the courageous men of the search and rescue squadrons.

Throughout the war, the USAF gathered copious information from many sources—visual observation, aerial photography, electronic surveillance, and infrared detection. The aircraft used were as varied as their intelligence activities. At one extreme was the Lockheed SR-71 Blackbird, and at the other was the Cessna O-1. In between were jet aircraft like RF-101Cs, RF-4Cs, RB-57Es, RC-135s, and U-2s, plus an assortment of Remotely Piloted Vehicles (RPVs). Even for the faster aircraft gathering information was not a risk-free exercise. In all, thirty-three RF-101s and seventy-six RF-4s were lost in combat. Nor was the task a simple one. Visual and photographic reconnaissance were often foiled by triple-layer jungle, bad weather, and the preference of the enemy for movement by night. During emergencies, such as the siege of Khe Sanh, the demands placed on the reconnaissance forces were overwhelming. As a measure of the effort, less than ninety days of Operation NIAGARA at Khe Sanh involved the flying of almost 1,400 reconnaissance sorties.

Much valuable reconnaissance work was done by units like 4025 RS, which was responsible for a variety of RPVs, or "drones," such as the Ryan AQM-34 series. Launched from a C-130, they were capable of covering a very wide range of missions, including photography, television (with real-time transmission), elint, sigint,

Troops and vehicles of the 1st Cavalry Division with a C-130 of the 834th Air Division. C-130s showed incredible versatility during the Vietnam War, filling roles as strategic and tactical transports, tankers, gunships, command posts, rescue aircraft, drone controllers, and occasionally even as specialized bombers.

jamming, and leaflet dropping. Although programmed for a particular profile, their progress was monitored and could be adjusted by the controller in the C-130 as necessary. On return to a friendly area, the drone deployed a parachute and was snared by a recovery helicopter. A total of 3,435 drone missions was flown, and 578 RPVs lost.

Electronic Support and Electronic Countermeasures (ESM and ECM) aircraft became increasingly important as the war went on. As the North Vietnamese defenses became more electronically sophisticated, so the U.S. services responded with more competent electronic warfare systems. Most specialized of the USAF's aircraft in this role were the EB-66s, which were large enough to have four radar receiver positions for detecting and identifying enemy signals, and nine jammers for deceiving and disrupting enemy defensive systems.

If there had ever been any doubt about the value of having a tanker force, it was entirely dispelled in the skies over Southeast Asia. Whenever there were combat aircraft in action, there were tankers on station. They proved their worth repeatedly both as force multipliers and as aerial lifeguards. In the knowledge that a tanker would be waiting, aircraft could be given maximum weapon loads for takeoff and then filled up with fuel at the top of the climb. On the way home after a strike, the tankers would refresh those who might otherwise die of thirst.

The KB-50Js which were originally in Southeast Asia were permanently grounded at the end of 1964. From then on, SAC took over the aerial refueling responsibility and deployed its KC-135s in support of PACAF. Some tankers were positioned in Okinawa, Guam, Taiwan, and the Philippines, principally to look after deployments from the U.S. and to aid B-52 operations. Others were moved forward into Southeast Asia to support the fighter-bombers. Since the tankers were such highly valued assets, it was not thought wise to have them in South Vietnam, and they were based in Thailand. The peak KC-135 strength, spread across the

Air operations on the scale of those conducted by the U.S. services during the Vietnam War would not have been possible without the KC-135 tanker. Apart from making it possible for offensive operations to carry the maximum amount of ordnance to their targets, KC-135s were on hand to save countless aircraft leaving the combat area with low fuel or battle damage. Here a tanker streams a drogue from its boom in preparation for receiving a customer equipped with a probe.

region between Kadena and Bangkok, reached 172 in 1972, and there were then twenty-eight regular refueling stations established over the countries of Southeast Asia, with seven more tracks in the area of the Philippines. In a little more than nine years of operating in support of the air war in Vietnam, SAC tankers gave away almost nine billion pounds of fuel in the course of 813,878 refuelings.

Spectacular though these figures are, they cannot begin to tell the whole story. On countless occasions, tankers were there to aid damaged or fuel-starved aircraft which would otherwise have been lost. Pilots often left the tanker with the heartfelt message: "Thanks, tank, you can count this a save." Some of the saves were dramatic, with fighters losing fuel so fast from battle-damaged fuel systems that they had to stay hooked up and be towed back to base on the end of the tanker's boom. Others were stunningly complex, particularly one flown by a crew from the 902nd Air Refueling Squadron off North Vietnam on May 31, 1967. While engaged in refueling two F-104Cs, the tanker crew was asked to help a number of USN aircraft which were in dire straits. The first to arrive were two A-3s, both themselves equipped as tankers but desperately short

of fuel. As the A-3s each took a quick drink, two F-8s arrived, equally poorly placed. One latched on to the first A-3, while the other, so short of fuel that he could not afford to wait, hooked up with the second A-3, which was still attached to the KC-135. Further refuelings from the KC-135 took place in a complicated shuffle, including more for the original pair of F-104Cs, before two Navy F-4s were taken on. The KC-135's own fuel supply was now so depleted that it was forced to divert into Da Nang, having transferred nearly 50,000 lbs of fuel in fourteen contacts and saved eight aircraft in one sortie. In recognition of this remarkable achievement, Maj. John Casteel and his crew were awarded the 1967 Mackay Trophy for the most meritorious USAF flight of the year.

There were other airmen who regularly saved lives, but in a different way. The motto of the search and rescue (SAR) squadrons was "So That Others May Live." In pursuing this goal they routinely risked their own skins for anyone downed in enemy territory. In the course of the war, it grew to be generally understood by all aircrew that, if they were shot down, SAR teams would make every effort to get them out, regardless of the location or the risk. Such a policy did wonders for the morale

Oil, dirt, noise, and plenty of punch. Stained with the grime of many combat missions and loaded with assorted weaponry, an A-1E Skyraider of the 1st SOS at Nakhon Phanom RTAFB rumbles forward on another escort and fire suppression sortie in support of rescue helicopters.

of crew members being asked to face some of the most effective air defense systems in the world. Unfortunately, once the opposition recognized what was happening, it also meant that any downed flier was used by the enemy as a lure around which they could gather a flak trap. Rescue missions therefore tended to increase in danger as time went by. Before it was all over, three Medals of Honor were earned in the course of rescue operations, two by helicopter pilots (Capt. Gerald Young and Lt. James Fleming) and one by the pilot of a RESCAP A-1H (Lt. Col. William Jones III).

In the early days, the few helicopters available for rescue in Southeast Asia were provided by Air America. It was not until mid-1964 and the open commitment of U.S. forces to combat that the USAF deployed twin-rotor Kaman HH-43Bs and a few Grumman HU-16B amphibians specifically for rescue duties. Designed for local rescue in the U.S., the HH-43B was not ideal for a combat area. It lacked armor, armament, and self-sealing fuel tanks, and it was short-ranged. As an interim solution, armored HH-43Fs were introduced, but the range problem remained. In 1965, matters improved considerably with the arrival of Sikorsky HH-3Es, large, well-armored helicopters with a range of

over six hundred miles. Fitted with a refueling probe, they could reach anywhere in Southeast Asia. Before long, the jungle camouflage of the HH-3E had gained it the nickname, "Jolly Green Giant." Two years later, the even more capable HH-53C Super Jolly Green made its debut and proved to be one of the great successes of the war. Nearly twice as large as the HH-3E, the Super Jolly was also faster, more heavily armored, and formidably armed with three 7.62 mm miniguns.

As it developed, the SAR business became a highly organized operation. In 1967 it was renamed the Aerospace Rescue and Recovery Service (ARRS) and missions into enemy territory were conducted by a rescue package of aircraft. By 1969, the mission commander was usually flying in an HC-130P equipped as a tanker and carrying an aerial tracker system for locating downed airmen. Escort was provided by A-1E/H Sandies (later A-37Bs or A-7Ds could be included) and top cover by F-4s. Additional help in the shape of gunships might be added. The Jolly Green Giant carried a pararescue jumper, trained as a scuba diver and medic, who was ready to jump or be winched down to the assistance of grounded aircrew. The helicopter's winch had 240 ft of cable ending in a heavy jungle penetrator, so that

rescues could be accomplished through the jungle canopy.

The crowning glory for the helicopter crews should have been a daring rescue of POWs from a camp outside Hanoi on November 21, 1971. The raid was well planned and brilliantly executed. One HH-3E full of U.S. Rangers deliberately crash-landed inside the prison compound while five CH-53Cs waited outside. Sadly, the cupboard was bare. The prisoners had been moved to another site some time before. Out-of-date intelligence had led the rescuers to a rare failure. However, in this attempt and in more conventional rescues, it was clear that the rescue teams were dedicated to their task. An example of their determination not to abandon aircrew to their fate was the rescue of Lt. Col. Iceal Hambleton, the sole survivor from an EB-66 shot down on April 2, 1972. Hambleton avoided capture by the enemy for twelve days under an umbrella of A-1Es, OV-10s, and an assortment of jet fighters and helicopters. Before he was recovered, concern for Hambleton's safety had cost several more aircraft, but there was never any consideration of giving up the effort as long as he was free.

From almost any point of view, the creative innovation demanded by the rescue challenge and the massive effort expended were worth it. No service was more respected, and perhaps none more rewarding. By the end of the war, the ARRS had successfully recovered 3,883 men. It was not done without cost. In the process, forty-five rescue aircraft were lost and seventy-one men gave their lives.

The Beginning of the End

The bombing halt ordered by President Johnson as he came to the end of his term of office in 1968 was confirmed by President Richard Nixon in January 1969. At that time, the personnel strength of the U.S. force in Vietnam had reached 536,000. Before the year was out, Nixon announced a program of "Vietnamization" and initiated a steady U.S. withdrawal from Southeast Asia. In April 1970, U.S. troops joined with the South Vietnamese in an invasion of Cambodia to attack enemy bases and supply routes, but within months the U.S. Congress had banned the use of U.S. ground forces in Laos or Cambodia. All of these steps gave great encouragement to North Vietnam. In addition, for more than three years after taking office, Nixon maintained the ban on bombing the North, and the North Vietnamese took advantage of the respite to build up their forces and prepare for an invasion of the South. Industries revived and power stations were rebuilt. Bridges, roads, and railways were repaired. Soviet and Chinese supplies poured into the country and the NVA undertook exhaustive training exercises. All this was watched by U.S. reconnaissance aircraft, which continued to fly over North Vietnam and continued to suffer losses, in spite of agreements made at the Paris talks supposedly guaranteeing them safe passage. Tit-for-tat strikes were made by U.S. tactical aircraft, which targeted air defense sites. A series of strikes carried out at the end of 1971, aimed at airfields, SAM sites, oil storage areas, and truck parks, was intended to deter the buildup of Hanoi's forces, but it had little effect.

On March 30, 1972, the North Vietnamese invaded the South, sending large forces across the DMZ and developing other thrusts out of Laos and Cambodia with the aim of cutting the country in half. With U.S. military strength now down to less than 100,000, Hanoi hoped to overwhelm Saigon's forces, and banked on Nixon's reaction being limited by antiwar feeling in the U.S. Really effective response from the U.S. air forces was no longer possible. Less than 100 USAF combat aircraft remained in South Vietnam, and the total in the whole of Southeast Asia was down to 375. In any event, the invasion was launched during the cloudy northeast monsoon, and the weather kept most aircraft from interfering with the ground battle. Those pilots who did make contact with North Vietnamese troops found that they were well covered by antiaircraft systems. Large numbers of AAA guns and mobile SAMs were evident, and there was a new threat in the form of the shoulder-launched SA-7, a portable heat-

seeker which could reach out to 8,000 ft. FACs and the A-1s of the VNAF, operating at relatively slow speeds and low levels, were particularly vulnerable.

Since there was no possibility of returning ground forces to Vietnam, it was clear that U.S. assistance to South Vietnam in repelling the invasion would have to come from the air. Accordingly, the USAF, USN, and USMC redeployed substantial numbers of aircraft to Southeast Asia. By mid-year, the USAF had almost 900 strike aircraft available, and the total from the three services was up to 1,380. To begin with, strikes against the North, code-named FREEDOM TRAIN, were restricted to areas south of the 20th parallel, but the alarming success of the invading forces led President Nixon to abandon the peace talks in Paris and to authorize operations on a much more ambitious scale. Mines were at last laid in and around North Vietnam's harbors, and a comprehensive campaign against a wide range of targets in the North was cleared by Nixon on May 8, 1972. It was called LINEBACKER.

LINEBACKER was not ROLLING THUNDER revived under a different name. It is true that there were still some

restrictions on target selection. Deliberate attacks could not be made on sensitive targets, such as anything close to the Chinese frontier, or in densely populated areas of Hanoi, for instance. However, U.S. air power generally was no longer micromanaged from the White House. Air Force commanders were allowed to use their judgment in seeking to destroy the transportation system, air defenses, and stocks of military supplies in the North. Immensely adding to the weight of the campaign, B-52s were allowed north of the 19th parallel for the first time, and, from September, F-111s were available to add their twenty-four-hour all-weather capabil-

The North American/Rockwell OV-10 Bronco was the third generation FAC aircraft in SE Asia. Unlike its predecessors, the much faster OV-10 was fitted with armor plating, self-sealing fuel tanks, and carried substantial firepower.

ity. Operationally, the crews of the fighter-bombers were greatly aided in their offensive by "smart" bombs which markedly increased the effectiveness of their strikes.

Systematic attacks were made on the bridges of North Vietnam by F-4s carrying Mk 84 2,000 lb and Mk 118 3,000 lb bombs fitted with laser-seeking heads and control surfaces. The results were spectacular. On May 13, sixteen F-4s delivered twenty-four smart bombs between them against the infamous Than Hoa bridge, wrecking a target which had defied U.S.

Linebacker in the Buf(f) © *Keith Ferris, 1990*

airmen for years.[5] By the end of June, more than four hundred bridges in North Vietnam had been destroyed or badly damaged. North Vietnamese use of more basic forms of transport, such as bicycles and small boats, ensured that their supply system did not grind to a complete halt, and it was never possible to achieve an irreparable break in their logistical chain. Nevertheless, the flow south became a trickle and, together with the effective mining of North Vietnam's harbors, it was apparent that LINEBACKER was hurting the enemy's attempts to maintain the scale and pace of the offensive in the South.

For the USAF, the LINEBACKER campaign provided a serious challenge. The air defenses of North Vietnam had stiffened in the years since ROLLING THUNDER, and by 1972 the Hanoi/Haiphong region was one of the best defended areas in the world, bristling with AAA and SAM

[5]By contrast, during the attack against the Than Hoa bridge on April 3, 1965, 638 750lb bombs were dropped and 298 rockets fired, but the bridge remained standing.

sites. Nearby, the VNAF had a force of well over two hundred MiG-17s, -19s, and -21s, and many of the pilots were old hands who had survived earlier battles. By contrast, USAF aircrews were generally younger than they had been in the 1960s, and the majority had never been in aerial combat. The MiGs now represented a formidable threat and, for a while, the kill/loss ratio swung in their favor. During ROLLING THUNDER, 85 percent of the U.S. aircraft downed were lost to AAA fire. Of the forty-four USAF aircraft lost on LINEBACKER operations, twenty-seven were shot down by MiGs.

Instrumental in turning the situation around was the establishment of TEABALL, a control center based in Thailand which coordinated all the information available on current VNAF operations from radar and an assortment of intelligence-gathering sources. This was passed via various command aircraft to airborne missions to give them up-to-the-minute warning of the enemy's activities. Thus

prepared, USAF crews began to give a better account of themselves, positioning their aircraft to meet approaching threats, and using the F-4's radar and its greater speed and power to advantage in countering the MiG's superior agility. In this environment, the USAF gained its only aces of the war. On August 28, 1972, Capt. Steve Ritchie of the 555th TFS, piloting an F-4E, shot down his fifth MiG-21. In the weeks which followed, two weapons systems officers, both F-4 back-seaters, also became aces. Capt. Charles de Bellevue of the 555th TFS raised his score to six MiGs (four with Ritchie), and Capt. Jeffrey Feinstein of the 13th TFS claimed five.

The offensive against the North was massive. Between April and October 1972, 155,548 tons of bombs fell on North Vietnam. Technology ensured that most of them were delivered with considerable accuracy. Successful though it was in the end, the campaign did not have any immediate effect on the invading North Vietnamese forces in South Vietnam. They had built up huge stockpiles of supplies to ensure that the invasion could be sustained. For the first few weeks, the NVA maintained relentless pressure on its ARVN opponents, threatening to provoke their complete collapse and so succeed in overrunning the country. Quang Tri fell, and the cities of Hue, Kontum, and An Loc seemed about to follow. On all fronts, it was air power which blunted and then smashed the Communist offensive, giving the ARVN time to recover and launch its own counteroffensive. Besieged garrisons were reinforced and repeatedly supplied by the tactical transports, and thousands of fighter-bomber and gunship sorties were flown against the NVA forces. The number of fast-mover sorties flown jumped from 247 in March to 7,516 in May. However, it may have been the B-52 attacks which proved decisive. Unlike the elusive Viet Cong, the NVA offered plentiful, recognizable targets in the shape of concentrations of troops and armor, and lengthy truck convoys. On numerous occasions, B-52s caught the enemy in the open and effectively destroyed whole units, sometimes breaking up attacks less than half a mile in front of friendly forces. General John Vogt, Commander 7th AF, said that facing regular mechanized army units "permitted air to put firepower in on good worthwhile targets instead of little huts in the jungle and a few scattered guerrilla bands. . . . After a good dose of [U.S. air power] for several months, the enemy ranks were so badly decimated that they lost all their offensive punch."

By the middle of June it was apparent that the North Vietnamese invasion had stalled. The ARVN went over to the offensive, and on July 13 the Paris talks were resumed. The last U.S. ground forces left Vietnam in August, and, on October 8, after the North had suffered a particularly concentrated period of bombing, Hanoi's representatives in Paris put forward new proposals. Within days, the prospects for an agreement seemed promising, and on October 23 President Nixon terminated LINEBACKER. All bombing north of the 20th parallel was brought to a halt. Unfortunately, it was soon seen that North Viet-

nam was once more engaged in delaying tactics and using the time to restore its forces. When the North Vietnamese walked out of the talks on December 13, Nixon ordered a resumption of the bombing. There followed an eleven-day campaign, code-named LINEBACKER II, which was the most intense aerial assault of the war. It was intended to bomb North Vietnam back to the negotiating table.

The Way Out

From December 18 to 29, 1972, by day and night, U.S. aircraft pounded airfields, military bases, oil storage, power stations, rail yards, and port facilities in and around the Hanoi and Haiphong areas. Most significantly, B-52s joined the attacks on the North Vietnamese capital. For the first time, Hanoi's leaders felt the crushing weight of conventional strikes from the big bombers for themselves, and the B-52s were exposed to the serried ranks of SA-2s defending the city.

Ahead of the first B-52 raid, F-111s hit the MiG airfields and F-4s sowed chaff corridors to screen the bombers. The protective effort was not entirely successful. High winds dispersed the clouds of chaff and the SAM sites fired over two hundred missiles, shooting down three B-52s and damaging three more. After three days, the B-52 squadrons had flown three hundred sorties, but had lost nine aircraft. Although 3 percent was a figure which was judged acceptable in WWII, it could not be long supported in a limited war, especially when the aircraft being lost were such valuable assets as B-52s. It was also ominous that six aircraft had been shot down on the third night, suggesting that worse might be to come. SAC took a close look at the tactics being employed and realized the need for a change. B-52Gs, not yet fitted with the upgraded ECM of the B-52Ds, were to be kept away from Hanoi. The raids were to be more concentrated in time, and B-52s would bomb from varying heights and different directions. Steep escape turns after bombing were to be avoided, because they produced large radar returns, and crews were authorized to make random altitude changes to confuse the SAM operators.

Using these new tactics on the four remaining nights up to Christmas Eve, only two more B-52s were lost.

After a pause for Christmas Day, it was decided to make an all-out attack on Hanoi's air defenses. With most other targets already hard hit, but the North Vietnamese still giving no indication that they were ready to sign an agreement, it was thought that they might be hoping to shoot down more B-52s and so make the cost of continuing too high for the American public to bear. Destroying the air defenses would remove that possibility and leave them vulnerable to whatever further operations U.S. air power chose to undertake. On December 26, B-52s and F-111s blasted the MiG airfields, SAM and radar sites, and command and control centers, but perhaps the decisive blow was finally struck by F-4s, which used the Loran technique to destroy the main SAM assembly area in Hanoi. At the end of the day, the North Vietnamese condemned the "extermination bombing" but let Washington know that they were ready to resume the

A boomer's eye view of a 17th BW B-52 taking on fuel. Endlessly repeated in SE Asian skies during the Vietnam War, bringing two very large aircraft close together became routine, but was always a challenge, demanding steadiness and high levels of skill from the crews involved.

The F-4 Phantom II was all brute power and awkward angles. In aerial combat with MiGs, U.S. Phantoms scored 145 kills and achieved a kill-to-loss ratio of 3.73 to 1. The USAF lost 33 F-4s to MiGs, 17 of them in 1972.

talks. The bombing continued until the arrangements were finalized, but on December 29 LINEBACKER II was over. The B-52s had flown 729 sorties in eleven days and had dropped over fifteen thousand tons of bombs. Another five thousand tons had been added by the fighter-bombers. The North Vietnamese had fired 1,242 SAMs and the USAF had lost twenty-six aircraft, including fifteen B-52s.

There can be little doubt that the

LINEBACKER campaigns together were instrumental in bringing the North Vietnamese back to the conference table in a frame of mind to sign an agreement. Peace talks were resumed on January 8 and the cease-fire document was signed on January 23, 1973. That took care of U.S. combat activities in Vietnam, but not in Laos or Cambodia. USAF bombing operations against Communist forces continued there in response to requests from the belea-

guered governments. The last sorties were flown in Laos in mid-April and in Cambodia in mid-August, when Congress reacted to an escalation of the bombing by cutting off all funds for the air war.

The sad aftermath came in April 1975, when North Vietnam brought a whirlwind campaign of conquest in the South to its conclusion, and the U.S. set in motion its emergency evacuation plan, FREQUENT WIND. On April 1, USAF C-130s and C-141s began airlifting Americans and South Vietnamese refugees out of Tan Son Nhut airport, Saigon. Load restrictions were removed on April 20, and the transports began setting records. A C-141 recorded 316 people on board, and C-130s took as many as 260. (Normal limits were ninety-four and seventy-five.) As the airfield came under fire during the final days, the operation shifted to helicopter evacuation from the U.S. Embassy compound. Fighters and gunships provided escort, and were forced to attack enemy radar and gun batteries to preserve the American lifeline. With the triumphant North Vietnamese on the doorstep, the last helicopter lifted away from the Embassy on April 30, ending an operation in which U.S. aircraft had brought out over 57,000 people from Saigon.

The Final Cost

In terms of the expenditure of national treasure, the air war in Southeast Asia was an expensive exercise for the U.S. Combat over Southeast Asia between 1962 and 1973 cost the USAF alone 1,679 fixed wing aircraft and 58 helicopters. A further 495 fixed wing aircraft and 18 helicopters were lost in accidents, bringing the total USAF loss to 2,250 of all types.[6] Over six million tons of air munitions were expended, which was about three times the amount for all theaters in WWII.

By far the most successful of the enemy's defenses were AAA and small arms fire, which accounted for 1,459 of the USAF aircraft. SAMs took down 112, and 63 fell to MiGs. A further 103 aircraft were

On February 23, 1968, Capt. Bernard Flanagan of the 355th TFS had to eject from his F-100 after being hit by ground fire over S. Vietnam. Within an hour, he was rescued by an HH-3E helicopter of the 3rd ARRG.

---

[6]The fixed wing loss for all U.S. services in combat was 2,561, with another 1,158 lost in accidents. Helicopter losses for all services were a dramatic 4,869, a figure reflecting in part the hazards of the U.S. Army's operations in support of troops. However, it should be noted that 2,282 of these were recorded as "operational (non-combat) losses."

USAF Museum artifacts from the Vietnam War include many items contributed by POWs — manufactured sandals, a T-shirt, a bowl and spoon among them. Shown with them here are an airman's shirt and dog tags (Airman 1st Class Pitsenbarger gave his life for comrades in Vietnam and was awarded a posthumous AFC) and Steve Ritchie's jacket. Ritchie scored five aerial victories over Vietnam while flying the F-4 Phantom.

lost during enemy attacks on air bases. Of the USAF aircraft involved, the fast-movers understandably provided most of the combat losses, with 379 F-4s (plus 76 RF-4s) and 334 F-105s at the top of the list. Some way behind were 198 F-100s and 153 A-1s.

Given that more than five million sorties had been flown, it could be claimed that the casualties suffered were not too excessive. Casualties included 2,118 airmen known to have been killed and 3,460 wounded. The number of prisoners was never established with such precision. At the end of the war, there were 588 Americans acknowledged by the North Vietnam-

ese as being held in captivity, plus another 3 in China. Of those, 472 were airmen from all services. A longer list of airmen fell into the "missing" column, leaving an open wound of uncertainty which has never satisfactorily healed.

The living conditions of the U.S. prisoners had been stark and their treatment often barbaric. It was a tribute to their collective spirit that so many survived their ordeal and emerged unbroken. To them, the sound of B-52s over Hanoi in 1972 was a message of hope. Col. Robbie Risner, incarcerated for over seven years, felt that his lengthy trial was about to end: "We saw a reaction in the Vietnamese that

we had never seen under the attacks from fighters. They at last knew that we had some weapons they had not felt, and that President Nixon was willing to use those weapons to get us out." Col. Jon Reynolds agreed: "For the first time, the United States meant business. We knew it, the guards knew it, and it seems clear that the leaders of North Vietnam knew it."

A

B

DANGER
DO NOT WALK IN
FRONT OF POD

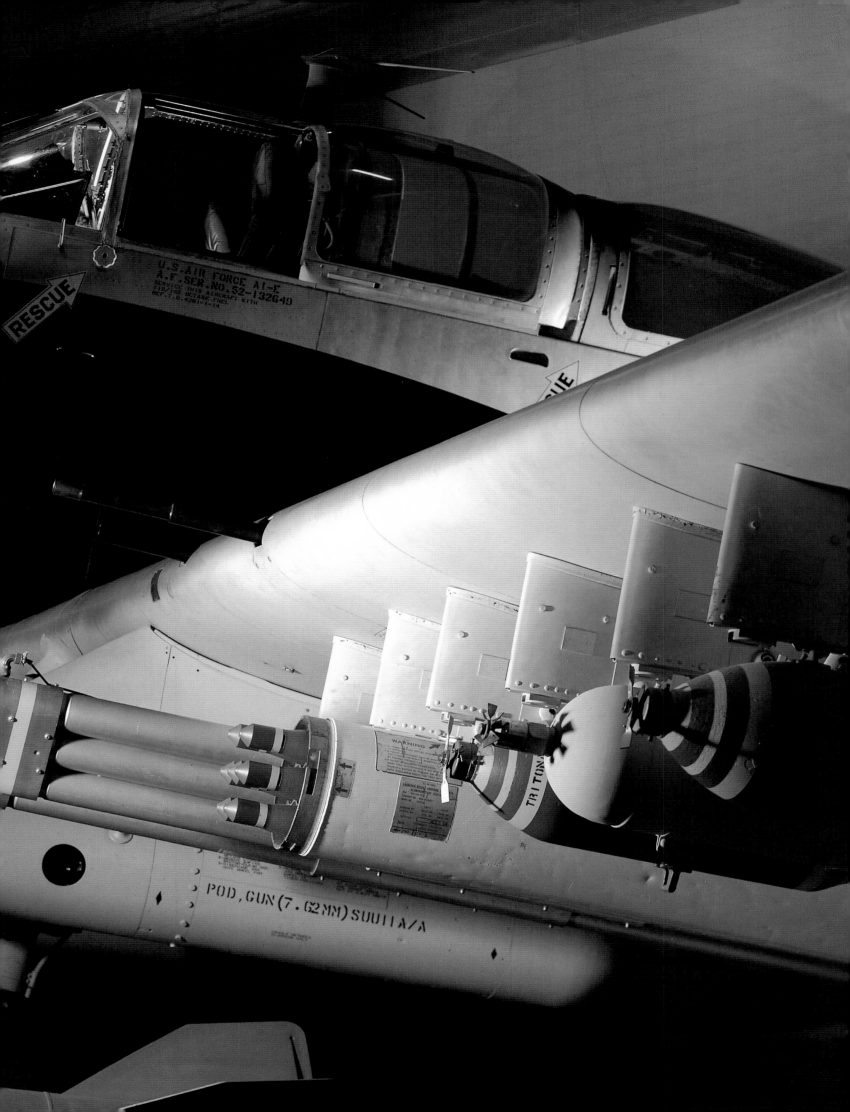

BLADE SER.NO.153044
BLADE ASSY M20A2-162-0
ANGLE LOW AT 42 IN.STA.27.5
ANGLE HIGH AT 42 IN.STA.67.5
TOTAL OPPERATION HRS.2354.3

HUB SER.NO.37352R

A

B

Previous pages:

A   Viewed from almost any angle, the Douglas A-1E Skyraider (commonly called the "Spad") is an impressive sight. Its uncompromisingly muscular lines are the epitome of a rugged warplane and its array of ordnance can be fearsome. Note the message on the light gray underwing unit which suggests that it is not a good idea to walk in front of a 7.62 mm gun pod. The A-1E exhibited in the USAF Museum is the one flown by Bernie Fisher in South Vietnam when he rescued a fellow pilot and earned the Medal of Honor.

B   The A-1E had seats for two but was often flown solo. Note that the "important" instruments are clustered in front of the left seat.

These pages:

A   Leading the A-1E into the fray was a monster Wright R-3350 18-cylinder two-row radial of 2,700 hp. It gave the Skyraider a maximum speed of over 300 mph, but more importantly, it gave it the strength to lift four tons of external stores.

B   Major Bernard Fisher's A-1E Skyraider on the ramp at Bien Hoa, S. Vietnam.

C   The hard nose A-26 could deliver a powerful punch with both guns and bombs. Here, eight .50-caliber machine guns are mounted in the nose, but other variants fitted four 20 mm cannon. Six .30-caliber machine guns fired from the wings, and bombs could be carried on wing pylons or internally.

D   The Douglas A-26 Invader was one of the piston-engined aircraft resurrected by the USAF for the Vietnam War. Its long legs and its weapons carrying capacity made it the ideal instrument for interdicting the Ho Chi Minh Trail.

E   The unmistakable triple fins of the Lockheed EC-121 Constellation, with the additional shark's fin of the upper radome in the background. The USAF Museum's EC-121D, named Triple Nickel *because of its 555 serial number, was the first ever to direct a successful aerial attack on an enemy aircraft — a N. Vietnamese MiG-21 on October 24, 1967.*

C

D

E

347

A   The intakes on the Republic F-105 Thunderchief were unique. Their narrow reverse-angle openings were designed to provide a double shock wave at supersonic speeds, so slowing the air entering the compressor to an acceptable velocity. The P&W J-75 could produce 24,500 lbs of thrust in afterburner, hurling the "Thud'" along at speeds above Mach 1 at low-level or Mach 2 at 40,000 ft. The USAF Museum's Thunderchief served with the 357th TFS, 355th TFW, based at Takhli, Thailand, in 1969. The two red stars record two aerial victories against MiGs, and Memphis Belle II nose art is painted below the cockpit. The original Memphis Belle, a B-17, could not have carried the 12,000 lbs of bombs of an F-105.

B   The second Thunderchief at the USAF Museum is an F-105G. It served in SE Asia from 1967 until the end of the Vietnam War, in the process flying numerous "Wild Weasel" missions and claiming three aerial victories over MiGs. It has two rear-view mirrors, possibly so that the pilot could keep an eye on the back-seater acquired by this late model aircraft, and uses the linear flight instruments fashionable at the time. The radar provided air search, automatic tracking, and terrain avoidance information.

C   Aerials and electronic equipment caused the F-105's fin to grow small lumps and irregularities on its smoothly swept surfaces. A ram air unit at the base of the fin provided cooling air for the rear end of the aircraft. Cloverleaf air brakes form the last three feet of the fuselage before the jet pipe.

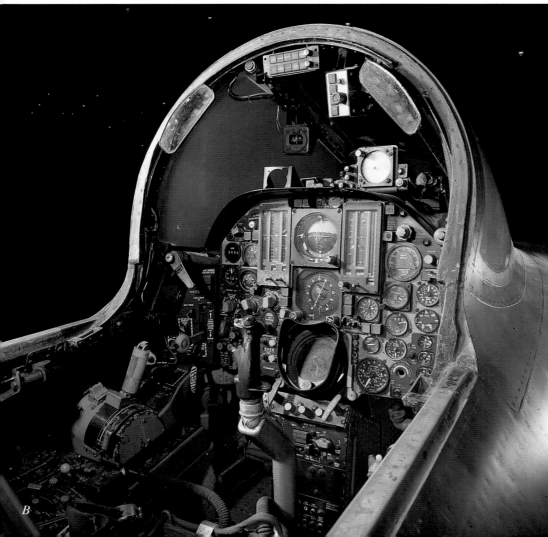

RU
AF 504
60

C

COL OLDS

SCAT XXVII

U.S. AIR FORCE F-4C-24-MC
A.F. SERIAL NO. 64-829A

SERVICE THIS AIRCRAFT WITH GRADE
JP-4 FUEL REF. T.O. 42-01-1-14

DANGER
EJECTION
SEAT

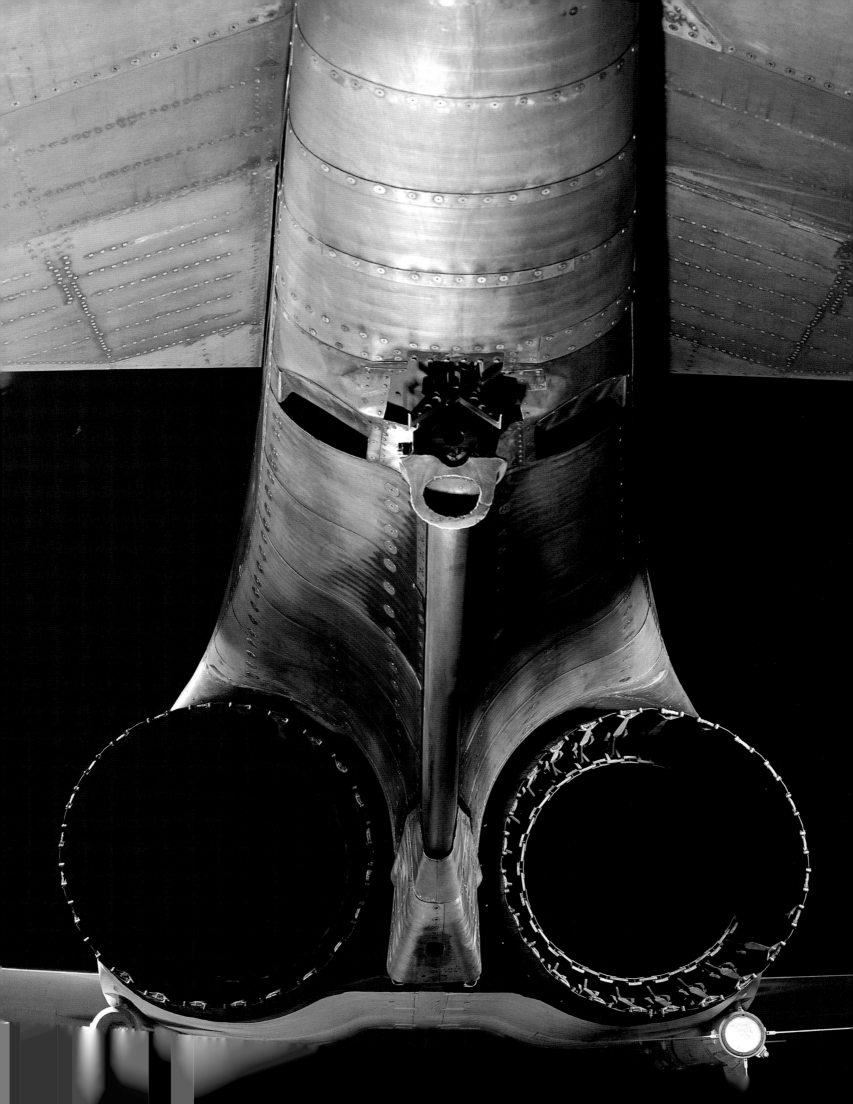

Previous pages:

A Nothing about the McDonnell Douglas F-4 Phantom II is subtle. It is big, weighing up to 58,000 lbs loaded, and powerful, urged along by two GE J-79s producing 17,000 lbs of thrust each in afterburner. It was the most significant Western combat aircraft to appear in the 1960s and was used to great effect during the Vietnam War for air superiority, strike, reconnaissance, and "Wild Weasel" missions. The USAF Museum's Vietnam veteran F-4C stands ready for air-to-air combat with a load of AIM-9 Sidewinders. Its two red stars identify it as the aircraft flown by Col. Robin Olds (CO, 8th TFW) and Lt. Stephen Crocker on May 20, 1967, when they destroyed two MiG-21s.

B In October 1996, Brig. Gen. Robin Olds once more sat in the cockpit of the F-4 in which he scored two MiG kills on May 20, 1967.

These pages:

A The huge jet pipes of the F-4's J-79s contrast with the small Sidewinder tails strapped alongside. Between the exhausts is an arrester hook — a reminder of the F-4's naval heritage.

B The pilot's scope for the APQ-100 radar peeks out from beneath the shroud at the top of the F-4's front-cockpit instrument panel. The main flight instruments are centrally placed below that, with engine instruments paired to the right. Weapons switches are hidden off to the left. To the right of the seat can be seen the hoses which carry air for G-suit inflation and oxygen.

C Robin Olds's two victory stars decorate the plate which prevents turbulent boundary layer air from entering the engine. Bombs and Sidewinders cluster under the port wing.

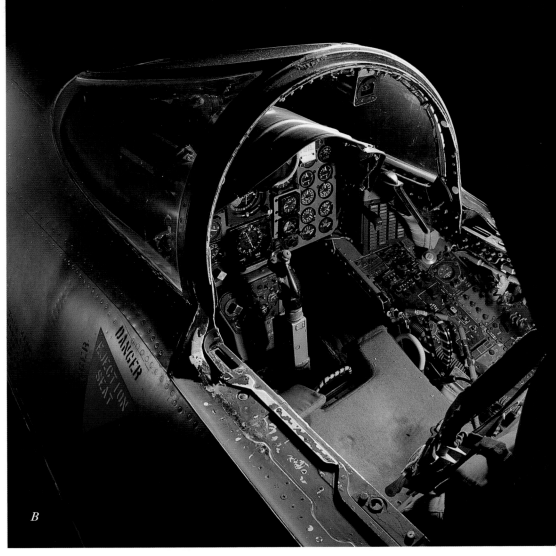

B

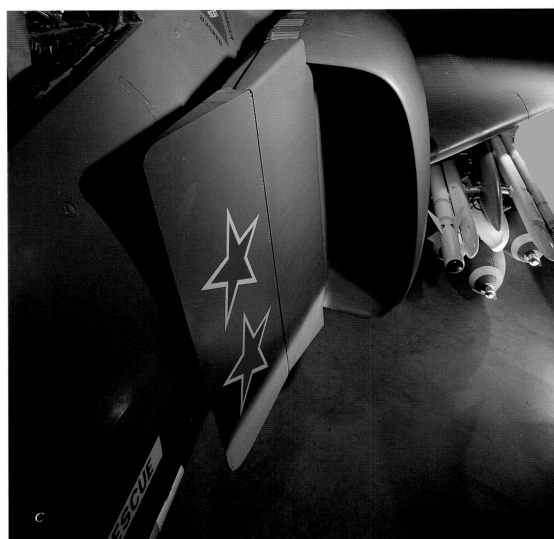

353

C

A   The MiG-21 Fishbed was the most potent enemy aircraft facing the U.S. in SE Asia. Short-ranged, but fast and agile, the MiG-21 was armed with Atoll air-to-air missiles. The intake for its Tumansky turbojet includes a fixed conical center-body containing the airborne intercept radar.

B   Apart from the turquoise surroundings, the interior of the MiG-21's cockpit bears a marked similarity to its Western counterparts. Note that the canopy is unusual in being hinged at the forward end.

C   Although recognizably a MiG-21F (which flew with the Czech Air Force), the USAF Museum's Fishbed is marked as a MiG-21PF of the North Vietnamese Air Force.

354

A   The combat record of this CH-3 is written in bullet hole patches.

B   The Sikorsky CH-3 is a big helicopter, with an all-up weight of more than 22,000 lbs. Powered by two 1,500 shp GE T-58 engines, it had a maximum speed of nearly 180 mph. In one form (HH-3E) it became the "Jolly Green Giant" of Vietnam rescue missions. The USAF Museum's black CH-3E was used by the 20th Helicopter Squadron in SE Asia for clandestine operations, acquiring the nickname Black Maria in the process.

C   A vital resource for any combat helicopter is its winch. The CH-3 had a winch of 2,000 lbs lifting capacity. Beyond can be seen the rear cabin, which could accommodate up to thirty troops or 5,000 lbs of cargo.

D   The hint that this is the cockpit of a big helicopter (a CH-3) is given by the glimpse of a cyclic control lever, just showing between the seats.

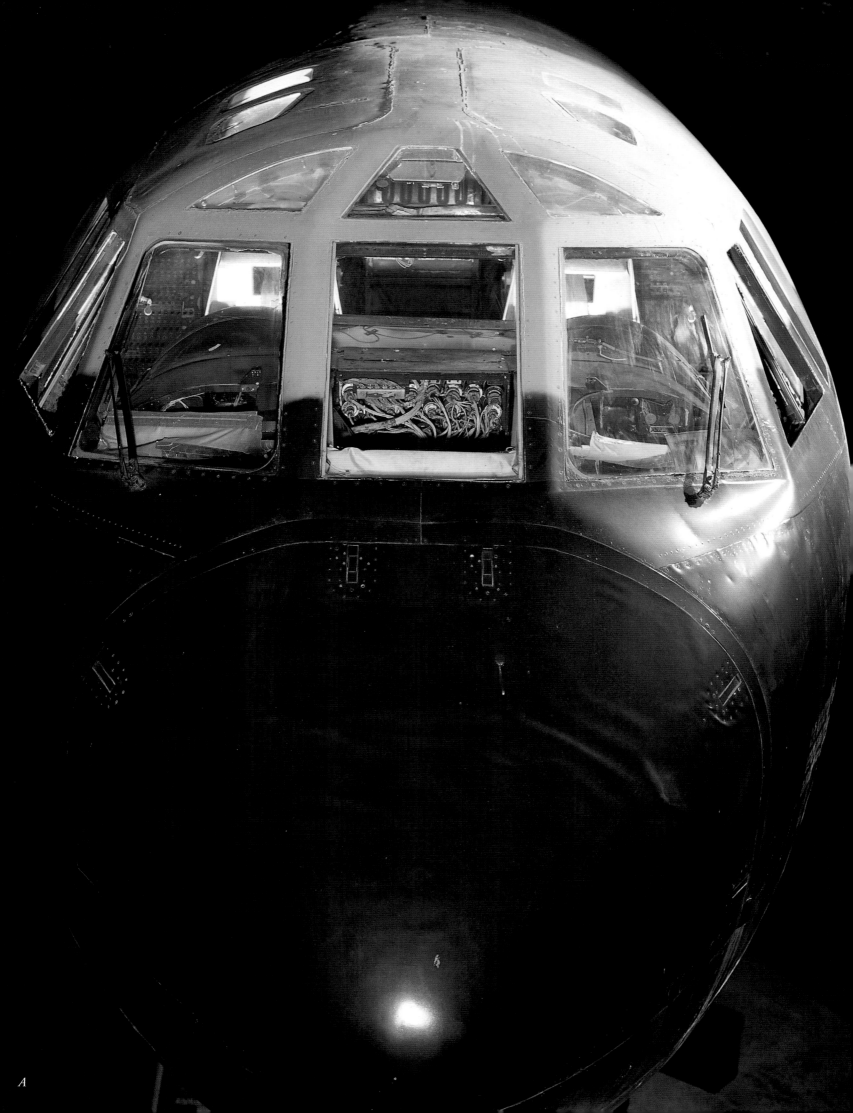

A

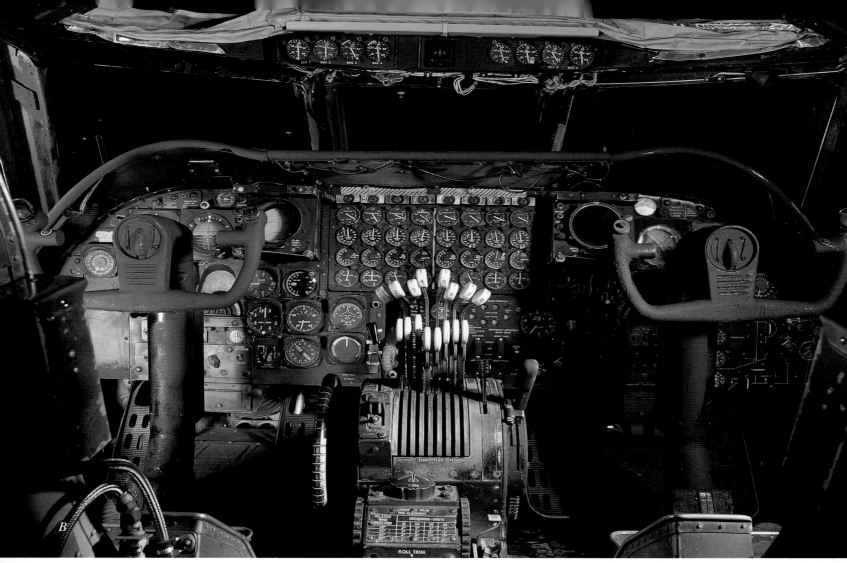

A   The looming presence of a Boeing B-52D Stratofortress (more commonly known as the "Buff") dominates the USAF Museum's Modern Flight Gallery. The longest-lived combat aircraft design ever produced, the B-52 has been in the front line since 1955, and is set to continue well into the 21st century. In Vietnam, the B-52 was the weapon most feared by the enemy, particularly the "big belly" B-52Ds, with their internal capacity for carrying eighty-four 500 lb or 750 lb bombs. The "Buff" in the USAF Museum saw action over Vietnam and was severely damaged by a SAM on April 9, 1972.

B   For all the complexity of the B-52, the cockpit is neatly and simply arranged. Flight instruments and radar scopes are in front of each pilot, and engine instruments run down the center in rows. At the top of the panel red warning light buttons signal engine fires and initiate extinguishers.

C   A fistful of throttles. Each engine's throttle lever has two white knobs, making it easier to control engines singly once the general setting for all eight has been made. To the left of the quadrant is the elevator trim wheel, and in front is the rotary control which allows the main undercarriage trucks to be offset before landing in a crosswind.

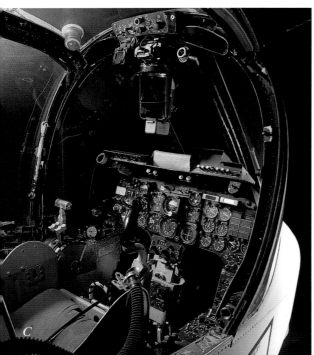

A   The North American Rockwell OV-10 Bronco was acquired by the USAF for use primarily as a forward air control aircraft. The large cockpit gave exceptional all-round visibility to both pilot and observer, who were placed in tandem on ejection seats. The additional fuel in the center-line tank allowed the OV-10 to offer an extended time on station.

B   Sponsons project from each side of the OV-10 with weapons attachment points. In this case, a rocket pod is fitted. The OV-10's power comes from two 715 ehp Garrett T-76 turboprops, which were enough to make the Bronco a lively and extremely maneuverable aircraft.

C   The seat pan sits level with the cockpit rail, giving the pilot of the OV-10 the maximum amount of canopy to look through. A gunsight hangs down above the instrument panel.

358

Chapter 10

The Professionals

"Far better it is to dare mighty things to win glorious triumphs, even though chequered by failure, than to take rank with those poor spirits who neither enjoy much nor suffer much, because they live in the grey twilight that knows not victory nor defeat."

(President Theodore Roosevelt)

"Our superiority in the latest types of technology is a fact, comrades, and one cannot escape facts."
(President Leonid Brezhnev, USSR, July 1968)

"The Soviet Union has military superiority over the United States. Henceforth the United States will be threatened. It had better get used to it!"
(N. Ogarkov, USSR, to U.S. Congressman, 1979)

"Our principal adversary, the Soviet Union, disposes military power to a dangerous degree, but otherwise is adrift in a sea of troubles."
(Alexander Haig, *Caveat*, 1984)

"All of a sudden a 130 exploded. It was one hell of a fire—a huge, mammoth fireball."
(Colonel Charlie Beckwith, U.S. Army, after the disaster at DESERT ONE, April 1980)

General Charles A. Gabriel, eleventh Chief of Staff, USAF, 1982-86. General Gabriel flew combat missions both in Korea (F-51 and F-86) and in Vietnam (F-4), and was Chief of Staff during the critical re-equipment period of the early 1980s.

359

Awesome Capabilities

After seeing the flood of material dealing with the Vietnam War, the USAF Museum visitor enters drier territory in seeking the artifacts of the 1970s and '80s. The relative drought is in part an indication that the present is on the horizon. More treats await, but the journey through the history of air power is approaching its final stages. The story of the post-Vietnam era is both important and interesting, but many of its characters have outlived its challenges and continue to perform in the front line. Their future place in the USAF Museum may be assured, but they still have many miles to travel before retirement.

Among the most dramatic exhibits in the Museum's Modern Flight Hangar is the Lockheed SR-71 Blackbird, a strategic reconnaissance aircraft spectacular both in appearance and achievement. Although a product of the 1960s, it still reigned supreme in the 1990s, its accomplishments unsurpassed. In 1976, an SR-71 established world records for speed (2,193 mph) and for height in sustained horizontal flight (85,069 ft). The aircraft on display flew the first operational SR-71 sortie in 1968, and went on to accumulate 2,981 flying hours—more than any other SR-71.

Another aircraft with its design genesis in the 1960s is the Rockwell B-1A Lancer. It is the direct ancestor of the B-1Bs now in operational service, and so can claim that its test flying laid the foundation for a strategic bomber force of awesome capability. Nevertheless, it stands as a reminder that vacillations in defense policy and operational requirements can bedevil the production of major military aircraft. This B-1A, the fourth and last built, represents the midway point in a turbulent span of more than twenty years which stretched between the origin of an idea for an aircraft and its appearance as an operational reality.

The USAF's new age dawned with the appearance of the McDonnell Douglas F-15 Eagle. First flown in 1972, the F-15 was the answer to a Vietnam fighter pilot's prayers. The value of the Eagle to the modern USAF is such that few can yet be retired from operational service. The Museum's example is

a special preproduction aircraft, with basic differences in systems and structure from those which went to equip fighter squadrons. Named the Streak Eagle, it was used as a record breaker. In 1975, flying from Grand Forks, North Dakota, it set eight time-to-height world records on the way to reaching 98,425 ft (30,000 meters) just 3 min 28 sec after brake release. The flight profile, flown by Maj. Roger Smith, read as follows:

"Release from hold-down cable at full afterburner with 7,000 lbs of fuel.

Gear up and rotate at 70 knots—3 seconds after release.

At 420 knots, rotate into an Immelman and hold 2.65G.

Expect to arrive level, upside down, at 32,000 ft and Mach 1.1.

Rotate to right side up and accelerate to 600 knots while climbing to 36,000 ft.

Accelerate to Mach 2.25 and pull 4G to a 60 degree climb angle. Hold 60 degree climb.

Shut down the afterburners when they quit.

Shut down the engines when they flame out.

Ride ballistically over the top at 55 knots and 103,000 ft.

Descend at 55 degree dive angle. When below 55,000 ft, try to start the engines.

Go home."

The Museum does not, on the USAF's fiftieth anniversary, own a truly representative General Dynamics F-16 Fighting Falcon. Fighter squadrons still have too much to gain from hanging on to their F-16 assets. The one on display is an early preproduction F-16A sheep masquerading in the colors of a DESERT STORM wolf. It is painted to represent an F-16A of the 169th Tactical Fighter Group, South Carolina Air National Guard, which took an active part in DESERT STORM.

The USAF came out of the Vietnam War with mixed feelings. The belief that the Air Force generally had performed well and done the job it was asked to do was offset by the conviction that more could have been done, that a truly effective use of air power had been frustrated by politi-

cal constraints. At an individual level, the American serviceman generally experienced relief and pleasure at the war's being over, but those sweet sensations were soured by others. There was resentment that a large proportion of the American people had turned their opposition to the war into a lack of sympathy for those who had done the fighting. Even more uncomfortable was the realization that so many lives and so much effort had been expended over more than a decade to achieve political and diplomatic defeat for the U.S. in Southeast Asia.

The open wound of Vietnam was slow to heal, but the pain and irritation it engendered forced the U.S. services into a critical examination of the nature of the war they had fought and the way they had fought it. Doctrine, methods, and equipment all changed in the aftermath of Vietnam, but perhaps no transformation was more profound than the move which led to the creation of all-volunteer services backed by strong reserves. Terms like "conscription" and "the draft" were cast aside, and the standing forces of the U.S. were made professional in every sense of the word. For an increasingly technical service like the USAF, it was especially welcome. Rates of pay increased to match more closely those of the civilian world, and talented people could be attracted by the prospect of a rewarding career. The resulting air force might be smaller, but it brought the promise of being better trained and more competent than ever before.

The USAF in particular was active in evaluating its performance in Vietnam and thereby seeking radical improvements in equipment, organization, and training. Not all the news was bad, and a great many lessons had been learned, ranging from how (and how not) to use an air force as a political instrument to the inestimable value of "smart" weapons. The USAF had shown that it had the power to stop determined ground assaults in their tracks and, during LINEBACKER II, to influence an opposing leadership decisively. Gunships had been developed, and an understanding gained of operating aircraft in high-threat environments. The vital importance

Teeth for the USAF of the 1980s. The McDonnell Douglas F-15 Eagle and the General Dynamics F-16 Fighting Falcon, immensely capable successors to the F-4, both superb as air superiority or ground attack aircraft.

of teamwork had been emphasized, whether it was in "strike packages," working with FACs, attempting rescues, or carrying out any other mission in the face of the enemy. Notably, a new generation of USAF officers and men had been blooded in combat and had come away with firm ideas about the way the Air Force should meet the challenges of the future.

In the first instance, recoiling from its open conflict with communism in Vietnam allowed the USAF to focus all its attention on its principal concern—the direct Cold War confrontation with the Soviet Union. While contributing its B-52s to Southeast Asia, SAC had not forgotten its deterrent role, nor had USAFE dropped its guard in Europe. It was well that it was so, since the Soviet Union seemed to be gaining in strength and expanding its influence in the world at a time when the U.S. was depressed by failure in Vietnam and upset by political turmoil at home. In Asia, Africa, and Central America, Soviet interests were prospering, and they were backed by impressive military power. The

armed forces of the USSR had a personnel strength of 3.5 million, and their front-line equipment appeared to be a match for anything produced in the West. Over 1,500 land-based ICBMs, 600 submarine-launched missiles, and 600 IRBMs targeted the NATO countries. The Soviet Union was defended by some 10,000 SAMs and 3,000 manned interceptors operating under comprehensive radar coverage. Moscow was ringed by an ABM system. There were 600 medium-range and 140 long-range air force bombers, and news of a supersonic, swing-wing strategic bomber (Tu-160 Blackjack) close to operational service. The Soviet Army's massive and heavily armored ground forces were supported by 4,500 tactical aircraft. Added to these were more than 6,000 aircraft of various types operated by the Soviet Navy. As time went on, Soviet weaponry got even better, with an apparently endless succession of new missiles, and combat aircraft from the Mikoyan and Sukhoi factories which posted remarkable performance figures. In the 1970s, Kruschev's earlier boast

that the Soviet Union would bury the West held the frightening prospect of becoming reality.

Confronted by the Soviet challenge, the USAF's leaders had to find ways of providing an effective counter while coping with a post-Vietnam reduction in strength and the fact that personnel costs in their all-volunteer force would consume some 40 percent of a shrinking budget. It is to their considerable credit that they recognized the importance of maintaining spending on research and development, and saw to it that so much of the effort to improve the USAF was directed at weapons and aircraft systems, and at services supporting the operational squadrons. It was recognized that even aging airframes could have their useful life extended by the incorporation of new radar, avionics, and weapons, and that new aircraft would be hamstrung if their state-of-the-art aerodynamics could not be matched by equally advanced systems. The 1970s saw explosive developments in electronics. Computers and software began to make a real im-

The 388th TFW at Hill AFB, Utah, was the first unit to be equipped with the F-16A in January 1979.

pact on the USAF's equipment, with aircraft essentially becoming powerful computers surrounded by engines, fuel, and weapons—and the crew. Some unstable fighters could not be flown by the pilot without the computer's aid, but the electronic brains were quite capable of flying an operational profile, at night and in all weathers, untouched by human hand. At the same time, with opposing air defense systems posing a much greater threat, the science of ECM became ever more important.

To make best use of new equipment, air force training had to ensure competence at every level, and to improve the "teeth-to-tail" ratio, logistics administration had to become much more efficient, reducing staff and avoiding the trap of keeping in stock more spares and supplies than were absolutely necessary.

Aircraft Made to Measure

In reviewing its combat power, the USAF had to take account of the need both to deter (and, if necessary, to fight) the USSR and to retain a capability to intervene in small wars affecting U.S. interests wherever they might occur. Here, at least in part, the lessons of Vietnam were invaluable. Aircrew who had been in combat usually had specific ideas about what

was needed in the front line. Much as they had appreciated the capabilities and toughness of aircraft like the F-4 and A-7, they knew their limitations, too. When the F-4 first appeared in Southeast Asia, it was fast, but it was also large, not very agile, gunless, and trailed the signature of smoking engines. A strap-on cannon and the later addition of leading edge slats had helped a bit, but something better was needed. (Besides, it was time the Air Force had really capable fighters which had not been designed for the Navy!)

The perfect answer came in the shape of the McDonnell Douglas F-15 Eagle, an aircraft intended to make the most of the electronics revolution of the 1970s and designed from the outset as an air superiority fighter. The F-15 first flew in 1972 and reached squadron service by the end of 1974. Even larger than the F-4, the F-15 is immensely powerful, its two 24,000 lb thrust Pratt & Whitney turbofans giving a clean aircraft a thrust-to-weight ratio of better than one at sea level. Its astonishing agility is born of this great power and the generous area of its delta-shaped wing. Pilots revel in the splendid all-around visibility from the high bubble canopy, and in the systems which simplify the business of flying and fighting the Eagle—notably the head-up display and

the "hands-on throttle and stick" (HOTAS) arrangement of essential switches. The F-15's size allows the space for installing the most comprehensive of avionics and weapons control systems, and for an integral Vulcan cannon plus a wide variety of external stores. It also made the Eagle an obvious candidate for development as a long-range, all-weather interdiction aircraft—the two-seat F-15E, capable of carrying 24,500 lbs of ordnance.

If the F-15 has a drawback it is unit cost. Even while the Eagle was still being developed, proposals were made for a lighter, cheaper fighter to complement the F-15 and to allow the building of a larger front line. It was important to have enough aircraft to meet emergencies wherever in the world they occurred. After a fly-off with the Northrop YF-17 (subsequently produced for the USN as the McDonnell Douglas F/A-18), General Dynamics' YF-16 was selected for development as the USAF's lightweight fighter. In the course of the years which followed, the F-16 Fighting Falcon grew in capability until it was neither as light nor as cheap as had been hoped, but there is no doubt that it has become a superbly adaptable fighter. It is an electronic masterpiece, evidence of which can be seen in the head-up display and in the sidestick controller operating "fly-by-wire" flying controls.

The computer-driven cockpit features a reclining seat, the better to help the pilot cope with the stresses of sustained 9-G turns, and the wings are equipped with an array of hard points which allow for the carriage of over 20,000 lbs of external stores, a load exceeding the original empty gross weight! The F-16's dramatic performance, advanced systems, and its capacity to handle a wide range of weapons have made it an admirable all-weather, multirole aircraft, capable of excelling in roles as diverse as air superiority, close air support, or deep interdiction.

Overshadowed though it was by its younger cousins, the F-4 was too valuable an asset to waste. In a classic example of extending the life of an aging airframe by incorporating new systems, the Phantom was considerably modified and updated, and continued to give sterling service in the specialized roles of reconnaissance and defense suppression.

In Vietnam, the problem of taking on guerrillas in rugged, forested country was only partly solved by reaching back to resurrect the A-1 Skyraider. Intense debate on the requirement for a modern, specialized counterinsurgency/close support aircraft led to the production of the brutally angular Fairchild Republic A-10. Officially called Thunderbolt II, it quickly acquired a name more suited to its looks and personality—"Warthog." Flying at speeds not much greater than its piston-engined predecessor, the A-10 is extremely maneuverable and built to withstand a high degree of battle damage. The pilot sits in what is effectively a "bathtub" of titanium armor, all systems are protected and duplicated, and the aircraft is designed to survive after having half its tail and an engine blown away. Eleven pylons give the Warthog the capacity to carry many different combinations of external stores, but the most memorable feature of its offensive armament is "the gun." A seven-barrel 30 mm GAU-8A Avenger, this mighty cannon can fire at rates up to 4,200 rounds a minute and its depleted uranium ammunition is capable of destroying battle tanks.

At the other end of the offensive scale, the B-52 outlasted efforts to find a replacement. Since the Buff had been flying since 1952, it seemed only rational from time to time to propose its retirement. Well before the Vietnam War, plans were made more than once to let the B-52 fade away, but the essence of a great military aircraft lies in its adaptability. As new threats appear, it is found that there is life left in the old airframe and, with a little modification, it rises to the challenge and soldiers on. The exotic B-58 and B-70 proved too specialized and died in their evolutionary blind alleys, while the Buff changed its spots and kept going. However, a determined effort to find a new strategic bomber began in the mid-'60s under the Advanced Manned Strategic Aircraft (AMSA) program, and in 1970 the USAF chose a Rockwell International proposal for development.

Few aircraft can have had such an agonizing period of gestation as the Rockwell B-1. Specification changes, vacillation over the future of the manned bomber as the third element of the deterrence triad, and abrupt shifts in the direction of defense policy resulted in more than twenty years passing between the initiation of the project and the delivery of the first B-1B Lancer to an operational squadron. A major stumble occurred in 1977 when President Carter canceled the B-1A on the grounds that it was too expensive, that there were doubts about its ability to penetrate Soviet defenses, and that Air Launched Cruise Missiles (ALCMs—carried by the B-52) would be a better bet. Use of the prototypes for test flying continued, however, and President Ronald Reagan agreed to revive the B-1 in 1981. One hundred bombers were ordered under the Long-Range Combat Aircraft (LRCA) program. Advantage was taken of the years of flight testing to produce a much improved aircraft, slower than the B-1A but much more capable. Principles of stealth technology were applied to give the B-1B a radar cross section only 1 percent that of the B-52, and its variable geometry helped to produce an aircraft which, with its wings swept back, is very much at home at high speed and low-level.

Advanced terrain-following radar, sophisticated navigation equipment, and comprehensive defensive avionics make the Lancer a formidable all-weather bomber, capable of penetrating enemy defenses and delivering a massive nuclear or conventional blow. The 4,000 lb average combat load of a B-17 in WWII seems pathetic when compared to the B-1B's enormous capacity—internal carriage of eight ALCMs, twenty-four SRAMs, or eighty-four 500 lb conventional bombs, plus eight external hardpoints for an additional fourteen ALCMs/SRAMs, or another forty-four 500 lb bombs.

By the beginning of the 1980s, the character of the post-Vietnam USAF had taken shape. All of the major new items of equipment were on hand or well on the way, and old stalwarts like the B-52 were still performing effectively in their roles. The swing-wing FB-111, christened the "Aardvark," had survived a difficult baptism of fire in Southeast Asia and was serving as a potent interdiction aircraft, with the capacity to fly missions blind at 200 ft and high subsonic speeds, placing its weapons automatically within yards of the target. Strategic reconnaissance was being carried out by updated U-2/TR-1s, and by Mach 3 SR-71s, a listening and looking combination unmatchable elsewhere. In air

There is no doubting the ability of the A-10 Thunderbolt II to deliver a hefty punch. The awesome seven-barrel 30 mm cannon is backed up by the capacity to deliver up to 16,000 lbs of assorted ordnance from eleven pylons.

MILITARY AIRLIFT COMMAND

Beset by notably serious wing cracks at the start of its service, the C-5 Galaxy was christened "FRED" (Fantastic Ridiculous Economic Disaster) by its crews. With the problems overcome, the C-5 developed into a transport indispensable for major rapid deployments of U.S. forces. It offers the most ton-miles at the fastest speed of any U.S. airlifter and its cavernous hold accepts even the bulk of the Army's M1 tank.

transport, the invaluable C-141 was enhanced by a rebuilding program which extended the fuselage and doubled the usable cargo-hold volume, and the immense Lockheed C-5 Galaxy added the ability to lift a quarter of a million pounds of cargo and move such awkward loads as the Army's biggest tanks by air. The McDonnell Douglas KC-10 Extender gave the USAF a tanker of enormous capacity. Equipped with both the boom and probe-and-drogue refueling systems, it proved able to fly a round trip of 2,200 miles each way, transferring 200,000 lbs to receivers in the process. In the complex arena of command, control, and communications (C3), Boeing aircraft held the reins. The E-3 Sentry Airborne Warning and Control System (AWACS), sprouting an outsize mushroom from its back, became the ultimate airborne military command post. In many ways even more sophisticated, the larger E-4B, originally operated as the National Emergency Airborne Command Post (NEACP, or "Kneecap") and flown by USAF crews, was provided to carry the President during an emergency. Now known as the National Airborne Opera-

tions Center (NAOC), it is hardened against the effects of nuclear explosions, and has the mystic ability to contact almost anyone available to listen, reaching out to military agencies or breaking into telephone networks and media frequencies at will.

Smaller But Stronger

In addition to all this, there were missile and space assets to be taken into account. There was no doubting that the USAF, even before the Reagan boom years of the 1980s, was a tremendously powerful and capable force. It was also smaller than it had been since the early 1940s. In WWII, aircraft strength had risen to nearly 80,000. Just after Korea, it was 28,000, and during the Vietnam War it hovered around 12,000. By 1980, it was down to less than 7,000. The WWII figure of almost 2.5 million personnel contrasted with 900,000 in 1968, and 560,000 in the diminished USAF of 1980. In the process, the advance of technology had allowed the Air Force to do far more with much less,

although at steadily rising cost.[1] At the same time, rates of airframe procurement and replacement slowed dramatically. Almost twenty thousand B-24s were produced in WWII, and most of those served the Air Force between 1941 and 1950, an operational life of only nine years. The production run of the durable B-52 was 744; it entered service in 1955 and will be operational into the twenty-first century, having successfully absorbed extensive modifications in the course of its long career. Similarly, the P-40 was in the front line for nine years and even the outstanding P-51 lasted only fourteen. The F-4 joined the USAF in 1963 to begin well over thirty years of operational service.

With its major aircraft programs already underway, the USAF took advantage of President Reagan's defense buildup of the 1980s to acquire more of the most modern types, so ensuring that all aircraft systems and weapons were as close to state-of-the-art as possible. Training and support services were not forgotten, and living conditions for Air Force personnel and their families were improved. It also became evident that the Air Force Reserves and the Air National Guard were undergoing a remarkable transformation which raised them from their former status of "second-class citizens," flying USAF castoffs and operating outdated equipment, to a position of equality.

In 1970, Secretary of Defense Melvin Laird promulgated the "Total Force Policy," which set out the requirement for Reserve and Guard units to be combat-ready forces, immediately available for mobilization in support of the regular air force and equipped accordingly. By the early 1980s, the modernization program was readily apparent. The last F-100s and F-101s (which many of the world's air forces might have been delighted to have) were gone from the Guard's squadrons, and the aircraft inventory was little different from that of the USAF, including such aircraft as F-4Ds, RF-4Cs, A-10s, F-16As, KC-135Es, C-130Hs, and C-5As. F-15As began joining the Guard from the mid-'80s. The Air Force Reserve was similarly blessed, flying an equally impressive line-

[1]The $80,000 P-47 of WWII had become the $12 million F-15 by the late-'70s.

up. In celebration of their elevation to the premier league, AFRes and Guard squadrons excelled themselves by consistently gaining high marks in USAF Operational Readiness Inspections and in such exercises as "Red Flag" and "Maple Flag." Guard units recorded several successes in air-to-air and air-to-ground gunnery meets, and tactical reconnaissance competitions, flying against USAF squadrons.

In taking a long, critical look at the lessons of Vietnam, the USAF concluded that more should be done to prepare aircrew for combat. Believing that there was no substitute for actual experience, General Robert Dixon (Commander, TAC, 1973–78) thought that crews should undergo combat training which was as close as possible to the real thing. The first few sorties under fire were when the probability of aircrew being shot down was at its highest. If these could be replicated in training, initial combat effectiveness should improve and losses should decline. This line of thought led to the establishment of the Red Flag exercises, the first of a series of similar "Flags" simulating combat conditions for air and ground personnel in a variety of roles.

The "Flags"

Nellis AFB, Nevada, home of the USAF's Weapons and Tactics Center, was chosen as the base for Red Flag. With its combat ranges, totaling some 3.5 million acres, and an associated area of twelve thousand square miles lying under military airspace, Nellis was ideal. USAF squadrons, and those of the other U.S. services and NATO air forces, were invited to deploy to Nellis in rotation to join in six-week wars, flying against a convincing enemy and attacking realistic targets. A permanent enemy air force (the "Aggressors") was formed, initially flying F-5s to simulate MiG-21s, to provide an air superiority challenge over the battlefield, and to assist visiting air defense squadrons in opposing strike missions. The ground environment was designed to simulate enemy radar, SAMs, and AAA, and the targets included airfields, aircraft, tanks, SAM sites, and guns—some genuine and some mock-ups.

B-1 Bomber Edwards AFB *by Rob Sprattler USAF Art Collection*

From the start, live ordnance was used by the attackers. An Air Combat Maneuvering Instrumentation system was developed which would record aerial combats and allow them to be reviewed in three dimensional detail on the ground. The benefits of Red Flag (and other "Flags") were almost immediately apparent. Standards of professionalism rose perceptibly, and the tendency to uninformed arrogance among inexperienced fighter pilots was curbed, often being tempered to confident enthusiasm and justified self-assurance in the heat of Red Flag's fiery combats.

Skirmishes

Regional disturbances and Cold War skirmishes involved the USAF in relatively limited ways at intervals during the 1980s. It was unfortunate that the first of them, a joint operation with the other U.S. services, should carry the same sense of unnecessary failure which lingered after Southeast Asia. In November 1979, Islamic militants in Iran, protesting the sanctuary being given the deposed Shah in the U.S., occupied the U.S. embassy in Teheran and took sixty-six hostages. As tedious and fruitless diplomatic negotiations dragged on, plans were made for U.S. forces to attempt a rescue.

After a period of planning and train-

ing, special forces were assembled on two principal operating bases—the aircraft carrier USS *Nimitz* at the mouth of the Persian Gulf, and Masirah Island airfield, off the coast of Oman. The operation began on April 24, 1980, when eight USN RH-53D helicopters left the *Nimitz* for an abandoned airstrip southeast of Teheran, code-named DESERT ONE. There they were to join six USAF C-130s[2] bringing the 132-man rescue team and all the necessary equipment from Masirah. Ill luck dogged the mission from the start, with only six helicopters managing to reach DESERT ONE more than ninety minutes late after struggling through a sandstorm. Of the missing two, one made it back to the carrier, but the other had to be left in the desert. Another helicopter then developed hydraulic failure at DESERT ONE, leaving five for the operation. Since it was judged that six was the minimum number required, the mission was aborted. The five serviceable RH-53Ds began refueling for the return flight from the EC-130H tankers. In lifting away to make room for the next in line, one helicopter allowed its rotor to strike a tanker's rear fuselage. Fire and explosions followed, and flying debris damaged the remaining RH-53Ds. Eight men were killed and a number of others burned. The survivors boarded the C-130s and withdrew, leaving the helicopters behind. At a cost of seven RH-53Ds, one

---

[2]MC-130Es with the special forces, AC-130Es for fire support over Teheran, and EC-130Hs to provide communications and helicopter refueling.

EC-130H, eight dead, and many wounded, it was a failure dearly bought and a savage reminder that the unexpected can defeat even the best equipped forces. The hostages were not released until the following year.

Division, and U.S. forces moved out to capture enemy strongpoints and ensure the safety of some one thousand American students at the university. AC-130Hs and naval attack aircraft were in frequent use to suppress enemy fire. At the same time,

Mediterranean in early 1986, a bomb was exploded in a Berlin discotheque used by U.S. servicemen. There was evidence of Libyan involvement, and President Reagan decided to retaliate. Operation EL DORADO CANYON was planned as a

The Lesson © *Keith Ferris, 1988*

Another joint operation was undertaken with more success in October 1983 on the Caribbean island of Grenada. Reacting to a blatant attempt to usurp the government and turn Grenada into a Cuban satellite and transit base for Soviet aircraft, the U.S. intervened to eject Cuban forces and restore democratic rule. On October 24, Operation URGENT FURY began with MC-130Es dropping small detachments of SEALS and Delta Force into Grenada to reconnoiter key areas. In the early hours of October 25, more MC-130Es dropped two Ranger battalions onto the main airport at Point Salines under covering fire from AC-130H gunships. With the airfield secured, C-141s and C-130Es brought in elements of the 82nd Airborne

C-5As were flying into nearby Barbados with heavy equipment, including the Army's UH-60A helicopters. An E-3A and an EC-130E cruised over the Caribbean to monitor the situation. Although resistance was often stiff, the Cuban headquarters at Calvigny was overcome on October 27. Minor mopping-up operations continued for several more days. URGENT FURY proved to be more costly than had been hoped, with 19 U.S. servicemen dead, 116 wounded, and at least 7 Army helicopters lost, but it was a success. The U.S. military had prevailed, Cuban prestige had suffered, and Communism had been handed a setback in the Caribbean.

After a series of incidents between Libyan forces and the U.S. Navy in the

combined USAF/USN strike against military and terrorist targets in Libya, the USAF being responsible for those near Tripoli and the USN for others in the Benghazi area. Initial USAF intelligence sorties were flown by SR-71s, TR-1As, U-2Rs, and RC-135s operating from bases in the U.K., Greece, and Cyprus.

On the evening of April 14, 1986, eighteen F-111Fs of the 48th TFW, based at Lakenheath in England and led by Lt. Col. Arnie Franklin, set off for Libya. An exhaustingly circuitous route via Gibraltar had to be flown because the French authorities had denied the USAF aircraft the right to fly over France. Support was provided by KC-10 and KC-135 tankers, an E-3A AWACS, an EC-135E tactical command center, and EF-111As for electronic suppression of Libyan defenses. After four refuelings on the outbound leg, the F-111Fs crossed the Libyan coast west of Tripoli just before midnight to sweep around and approach their targets from the south. Using their "Pave Tack" laser marking system, they aimed their 2,000 lb "Paveway" bombs at the military side of Tripoli airport and at Al Aziziyah barracks, where the Libyan leader Muammar Qaddafi had his quarters. Considerable damage was done to the barracks and a number of Libyan aircraft destroyed. Unfortunately, several Western embassies also suffered. One F-111F was lost in the Mediterranean after the attack. Although at the time EL DORADO CANYON was judged only a qualified success, the performance of the USAF crews was acknowledged as praiseworthy. Completing a round trip of 5,500 miles with multiple refuelings to attack pinpoint targets at night was a considerable challenge, and the achievement gained respect from military aviators worldwide. As time passed and Libya's terrorist excesses were seen to have been restrained, the accomplishments of the operation were seen in their true light.

Confrontations between warring factions in Central America attracted a good deal of U.S. concern in the 1980s, but American involvement was generally limited to providing military assistance in the form of training and equipment to those opposing the spread of Communism, whether they be governments or rebels. USAF reconnaissance aircraft kept a close watch on events in Nicaragua and El Salvador, and AC-130Hs occasionally set out to track down arms smugglers, but overt intervention by U.S. forces in the region did not occur until 1989, when Manuel Noriega went too far to be ignored in Panama. In December 1989, after Noriega had installed himself as dictator and directed some bellicose remarks at the U.S., Panamanian soldiers murdered a U.S. Marine Corps officer. Operation JUST CAUSE was launched in response. Before dawn on the morning of December 20, USAF AC-130 gunships attacked Panamanian positions in support of an assault by

Navy SEALS and Army Rangers. Other USAF aircraft used were MC-130s and two very capable helicopters—the MH-53 Pave Low and the MH-60G Pave Hawk, both fitted with all the electronic magic necessary to operate in all weathers, by day or night, at low-level. Later, when the first dust had settled, C-141s flew in troops of the 82nd Airborne Division. Effective resistance was ended within forty-eight hours. Noriega sought sanctuary in the Vatican Embassy for a while, but surrendered on January 3, 1990. A USAF MC-130 crew had the pleasure of flying him to Florida to stand trial on drug charges.

fice in 1981 with the firm intention of increasing the size of the defense budget. More money for the military had a dual purpose. In the first place, it was a deliberate escalation of the Cold War, meant to challenge the Soviet Union to an armament race which could leave the loser facing bankruptcy. As an additional benefit, it was aimed at reversing the decline in the status and perceived competence of the U.S. armed forces following the depressing experiences of Southeast Asia and the attempted hostage rescue in Iran. It was perhaps serendipitous that the name of the Chief of Staff for the USAF during much

At the outset of Operation JUST CAUSE in December 1989, MH-53 Pave Low helicopters were used to drop U.S. Navy SEALS into Panama.

Almost unnoticed, an extraordinary aircraft made its operational debut during JUST CAUSE. Rio Hato airfield was attacked by a pair of Lockheed F-117 Nighthawks. Their efforts were not particularly noteworthy, but the mission provided merely a muted prelude. The complete Nighthawk work with full fortissimo orchestration was to follow only two years later in the Middle East.

Winning Combination

President Reagan and his Secretary of Defense, Caspar Weinberger, took of-

of this resurrection was Gabriel. General Charles Gabriel was an officer who had flown hundreds of combat missions in both Korea and Vietnam. While he was Chief, he oversaw the introduction of all manner of new weapons and systems into service, including those belonging to the revolutionary world of stealth technology. With the arrival of the F-117 in the front line in 1983, the USAF took a leap forward in the science of air power which could not be matched elsewhere. It is a measure of the scale of the achievement to note that, unlike other great developments which

An LTV A-7 of the 23rd FG wings over, showing its load of AGM-65 Maverick missiles.

have influenced aviation, such as metal monoplanes, jet engines, radar, swept wings, and missiles, all of which quickly became international, U.S. stealth technology remains unmatched as the twenty-first century approaches.

By the mid-1980s, the Reagan defense buildup had brought about an increase in USAF strength to over 8,200 aircraft and 630,000 personnel. It also led to the historic period of the late-1980s and early-1990s, a time of unparalleled change in international relations, with such tumul-

tuous events as the fall of the Berlin Wall, the collapse of the Warsaw Pact, the defeat of the Soviet Communist Party, the disintegration of the Soviet Union, and the decline of communism worldwide.

In organizing itself for this final triumphant chapter of the Cold War, the USAF retained in its structure much that was familiar, but added and adjusted elements and commands as necessary to meet the demands of new circumstances and challenges. Much had changed, yet much had stayed the same since the days of Tooey

F-16s of the USAF's aerobatic display team in arrowhead formation, showing off their celebrated Thunderbird paint scheme.

Spaatz and the birth of the USAF. As the decade of the 1980s ended, the combat commands of TAC and SAC still dominated the front line, with TAC owning by far the largest aircraft inventory of almost three thousand. When reinforced by ANG and AFRes aircraft in an emergency, the total rose to over four thousand, or some 44 percent of all USAF aircraft.

TAC (Langley AFB, Virginia) commanded three numbered air forces and three other units. The First Air Force was principally concerned with the air defense of the continental United States (F-15s), the Ninth AF with tactical fighter operations (F-15s, F-16s, F-4s, A-10s, OV-10s, EC-135s, UH-1s), and the Twelfth AF for an assortment of roles, including air superiority, interdiction, reconnaissance, and close air support (F-15s, F-16s, F-4s, F-111s, F-117s, A-10s, OV-10s, OA-37s). The direct reporting units were the 28th Air Division (E-3s, EC-135s, EC-130s), the Tactical Warfare Center at Eglin AFB, Florida, and the Tactical Fighter Weapons Center at Nellis AFB, Nevada. Besides playing host to "Flag" exercises, Nellis was also the home of a unique TAC squadron, the USAF's Thunderbirds aerial demonstration team. First formed in 1953, the team began by flying the F-84G, and then moved successively to the F-84F, F-100, F-105 (briefly), F-4, T-38, and F-16. Demonstrations were given in more than fifty countries, but the primary responsibility of the Thunderbirds lay in public relations at home, reinforcing the confidence of the American people in their Air Force, and supporting USAF recruiting and retention programs.

SAC (Offutt AFB, Nebraska), outnumbered by TAC in terms of aircraft, was still the USAF's largest command, controlling two elements of the U.S. strategic triad. It had a personnel strength of 119,000, with another 15,000 gained from the ANG and AFRes. The striking force consisted of one thousand ICBMs (Minuteman, Peacekeeper) and over four hundred bombers (B-52, FB-111, B-1), supported by more than six hundred tankers (KC-135, KC-10). Reconnaissance and airborne command aircraft completed the lineup (U-2/TR-1, RC-135). Most of SAC's assets were organized under two numbered air forces, the Eighth and Fifteenth, both with WWII backgrounds in strategic bombardment.

MAC (Scott AFB, Illinois) was a command with a role which hardly varied from peace to war. It was constantly involved in lifting people and supplies around the world, and was on call to help in natural or man-made emergencies. It comprised some 90,000 people and 1,000 aircraft, and was massively supported by the ANG and AFRes, gaining an additional 71,000 people and 400 aircraft from them when needed. MAC was organized into three air forces and several separate units. The Twenty-First and Twenty-Second Air Forces were the combat-ready theater and strategic airlift elements of MAC, flying a vast and varied array of aircraft, such as the C-5, C-141, C-130, C-9, C-12, C-20, C-23, C-135, C-137, C-140, T-39, T-43, and UH-1. The Twenty-Third AF undertook special operations with such exotic machinery as variously equipped AC-130s, MC-130s, HC-130s, MH-53s, and MH-60s. Other units included the Air Rescue, Air Weather, and Defense Courier Services. It was part of MAC's tradition that its aircraft were always available for humanitarian purposes. Starting with the shining example of the Berlin Airlift, there was hardly a time when MAC was not involved somewhere with bringing relief to hardpressed people. In the U.S., MAC's aircraft had delivered snowplows to Buffalo to aid recovery from blizzards, airlifted water filtration systems to Harrisburg after the Three Mile Island nuclear emergency, and rescued victims of the Mt. St. Helens eruption and a cruise ship sinking in the Gulf of Alaska. Earthquakes, hurricanes, floods, drought, and famine drew MAC assistance year after year, in the U.S. and worldwide. The Command's unique ability to react quickly and provide immense airlift capacity, together with its unrivaled professionalism, earned the respect and gratitude of countless thousands of people on every continent.

"Top Cover for North America" was the motto of the Alaskan Air Command

A C-9A Nightingale lands past a pair of 52nd FW F-16Cs based at Spangdahlem, Germany.

(Elmendorf AFB, Alaska). A relatively small command with little more than nine thousand personnel, its principal responsibility was the defense of Alaska, and its fighter squadrons flew F-15s and A-10s. AAC answered to North American Air Defense Command for air defense purposes, and its F-15s frequently escorted probing Soviet aircraft north of the Arctic Circle. A large part of the Command's hardware was in the form of minimally attended radar sites, linked into a highly automated warning system feeding information back to the operations center at Elmendorf AFB.

Overseas, the USAF ran its affairs through the Pacific Air Forces (Hickam AFB, Hawaii), and the United States Air Forces in Europe (Ramstein AB, Germany). PACAF covered almost half the globe, with an assigned area stretching from the U.S. west coast to the east coast of Africa, and from the Arctic to the Antarctic. Almost three hundred fighter aircraft were on PACAF's strength, with support coming as necessary from the other major commands. Resident aircraft in the region included the F-15, F-16, F-4, A-10, and EC-135. Three numbered air forces, the Fifth, Seventh, and Thirteenth—all with historic links to the Pacific—served PACAF, with headquarters based in Japan, Korea, and the Philippines. USAFE was the air component of U.S.

European Command and a vital part of NATO, with the Commander-in-Chief also wearing the hat of Commander, Allied Air Forces Central Europe. USAFE consisted of three air forces, the Third in the U.K., the Sixteenth in Spain (with units in Italy, Greece, and Turkey), and the Seventeenth in Germany (plus a base in the Netherlands). Their combat assets included various models of F-111s, F-15s, F-16s, and A-10s, as well as a number of ground-launched cruise missiles in the U.K., Italy, and Germany. Aircraft of the other commands were constantly rotated through USAFE's bases in Europe.

Behind the combat commands were ranged a series of others without which the front line would have found it difficult to survive. Air Training Command (Randolph AFB, Texas) provided the foundation on which the Air Force built. Besides flying training, it was responsible for all basic and technical training, plus recruiting and most specialized military education. In the USAF's world of training and education, only the Air Force Academy in Colorado Springs, Colorado, and the postgraduate schools of the Air University at Maxwell AFB, Alabama, did not fall under ATC's wing. The scale of ATC's daily task can be seen from the fact that, in 1989, over 46,000 Americans joined the USAF, seeking training in specializations as var-

The Cessna T-37B Tweet was first brought into service at the end of 1959. It will still be training the USAF's pilots at the start of the 21st century.

T-38A Talons began arriving at their USAF units in March 1961. Structural renewal and avionics upgrades will extend their useful life until 2020. After over half a century of being handled by students, they should by then have more than earned their retirement. This Talon is seen over Randolph AFB, San Antonio. (Compare the background in the photograph of the BT-9 at the end of Chapter 5.)

ied as aircrew, nurse, supply clerk, computer operator, or various kinds of technician. Ongoing career training brought the total figures up to 300,000 students graduating from 2,800 courses annually. Pilot training was a forty-nine week course, including 500 hours of ground instruction and 175 hours of flying, 74 in the T-37 and 101 in the T-38. Basic navigator train-

ing took twenty-eight weeks, with the flying being done aboard T-37s and T-43s.

The business of Air Force Systems Command (Andrews AFB, Maryland) was delivering the future to the USAF. AFSC was charged with identifying and acquiring emerging technologies to help in defining future USAF systems. It developed and tested high-technology hardware rang-

ing from aircraft and avionics to spacecraft and missiles. Among its more exotic assets were the Air Force Flight Test Center at Edwards AFB, California, the Electronic Systems Division at Hanscom AFB, Massachusetts, the Armament Division at Eglin AFB, Florida, and the Aeronautical Systems Division at Wright-Patterson AFB, Ohio.

The Air Force Logistics Command (Wright-Patterson AFB, Ohio) aimed to buy, supply, maintain, repair, and transport everything necessary to keep the Air Force both combat-ready and satisfied. The Command stocked or managed nearly 900,000 individual items, processing about 5 million requisitions each year, including articles as diverse as nuclear weapons and light bulbs, or jet engines and church organs. The combined floor space of the AFLC Logistics Centers was said to exceed the area of Rhode Island. Two unique Air Force establishments belonged to AFLC. One was the Military Aircraft Storage and Disposition Center at Davis-Monthan AFB, Arizona, more commonly called the "Boneyard," where over three thousand aircraft retired from front-line service were mothballed in case of future need. The other was the USAF Museum at Wright-Patterson AFB.

Two other commands, newly raised to that status in 1979, linked all the others with their global services. The Air Force Communications Command (Scott AFB, Illinois) provided all kinds of communications for the USAF. In peace or war, whether telephone or radio, cable or satellite, it was AFCC's business to see to its engineering, installation, maintenance, and evaluation. AFCC was also responsible for the USAF's computers and for the air traffic control service.

The Electronic Security Command (Kelly AFB, Texas) was formed to look after electronic warfare. ESC concerned itself with such esoteric subjects as cryptology and computer security programs, but its principal responsibilities were in both offensive and defensive electronic warfare. The Command fielded equipment to confuse, jam, or destroy enemy C3, and provided protection for the

Kitten and the Bears © *Mike Machat*

USAF's equivalent systems. Working with the combat commands, ESC's divisions took particular interest in the jammers, protective equipment, and weapons carried in such aircraft as the EF-111A—intended primarily for close-in jamming and escorting attack aircraft in enemy airspace—and the EC-130H Compass Call, designed to stand off and disrupt enemy C3 over large areas. ECM pods for combat aircraft and EW RPV drones also came under ESC's scrutiny.

The story of the USAF's interest in the military uses of space and the hardware to exploit it had its roots in WWII, and its subsequent growth and development involved more than one Air Force command. However, the various threads were at last drawn together in 1982 with the birth of another member of the Air Force family—Space Command at Peterson AFB, Colorado.

With this proven framework in place and functioning well, the USAF celebrated the end of the Cold War and set itself to face the new challenges of the 1990s.

U.S. AIR FORCE F-15A-6-MC
SERIAL NO. 72-119A

A   The USAF Museum's McDonnell Douglas F-15 is not a representative operational aircraft. It is the Streak Eagle, a special preproduction aircraft used as a record breaker. It set eight time-to-height records in 1975, including a peak of 30,000 meters (98,425 ft) reached 3mins 28 secs after brake release. Mach 2 was exceeded during the climb as the two 25,000 lb thrust P&W F100 turbofans gulped air in huge quantities through its sharply angled engine intakes. The intake ducts stand clear of the fuselage to avoid turbulent boundary layer air, and pitch up and down through a limited range to adjust airflow to meet the requirements of the engine at various speeds.

B   The F-15's two huge raked fins reach a height of eighteen and a half feet above the ramp. They are topped by various ECM aerials.

372

AF 119
72

B

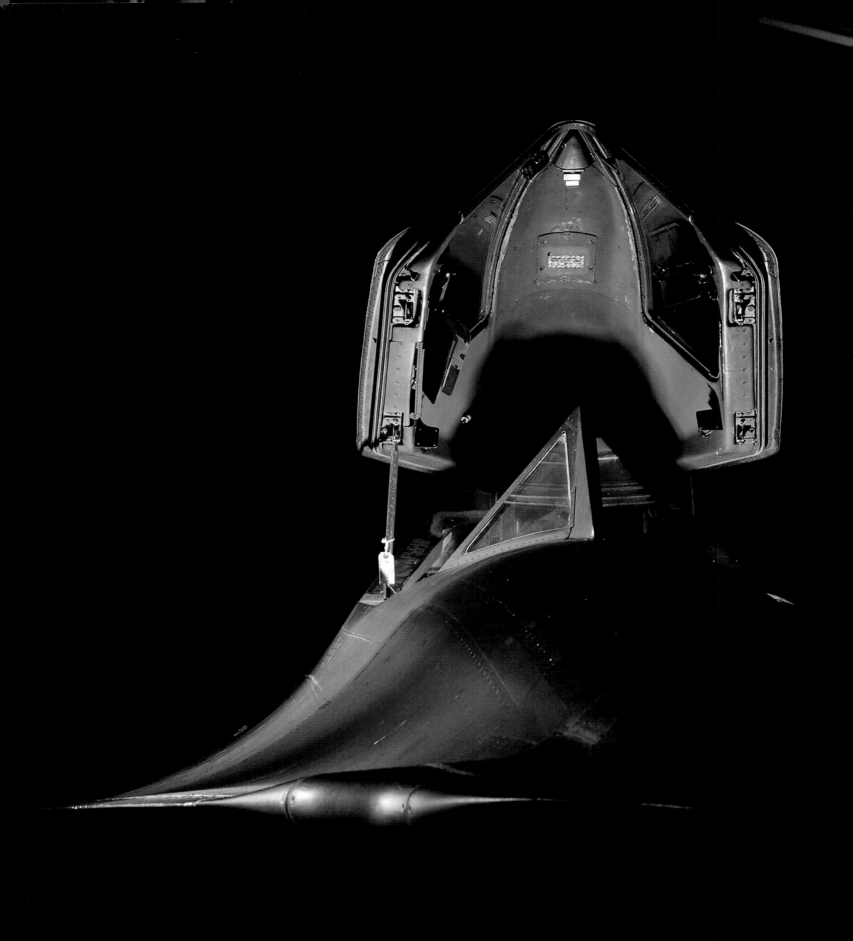

A

B

A   The Lockheed SR-71A Blackbird combines sculptured lines with dramatic performance. Heights up to 85,000 ft and speeds above Mach 3 were part of its operational reconnaissance profile. Equipped with a variety of sensors, the Blackbird could monitor an area of 100,000 sq mls in an hour. (At its cruising speed, the SR-71 was covering a mile in less than two seconds, about the same velocity as a round fired by the A-10's cannon.) Skin temperatures reached 280-300 degrees Centigrade in flight, causing the 107 ft long aircraft to stretch by almost a foot. The pilot and reconnaissance systems officer sat in separately hatched tandem cockpits, their small windows made of heat-resistant glass. The SR-71's fuel was JP-7, a special kerosene which doubled as a heat sink to absorb excessive heat loads.

B   The SR-71 was a "stealthy" aircraft long before the term was commonly used. It was designed to keep the radar cross-section as low as possible and was covered with a paint containing billions of microscopic iron balls which reduced radar reflectivity. The power required to provide the SR-71 with its stellar performance came from two P&W J-58 afterburning turbo-jets of 32,500 lbs thrust each. The large inlet cones were computer controlled, steadily retracting as Mach increased.

C   A ring of "suck-in" doors cooled and reduced the size of the tail pipes of the SR-71 at low speeds. At normal flight speeds, the tail pipes were the hottest exterior part of the aircraft, glowing white hot. The whole airframe was built almost entirely of titanium and its alloys to withstand the heat of Mach 3 cruising. Even so, the skin crinkled. The sharply canted fins were solid flying surfaces with no separate rudders.

375

C

A   The area of glass allowing a forward view to the SR-71's pilot was not generous, and, although made in heat-resistant layers, it became noticeably warm during flight. Towards the top of the pilot's instrument panel the artificial horizon is backed up by another immediately above. To the left of the standby horizon is an angle-of-attack indicator, and a combination instrument near the compass shows a read-out of airspeed, altitude, and Mach number. On the console to the pilot's right are the autopilot controls, and at center-left in front of him is a yellow handle for deploying the drag-chute and a red warning light bearing the comforting message "RSO ejected."

B   The USAF Museum's SR-71A (here arriving at the Museum in March 1990) is the aircraft flown by Majors Jerome O'Malley and Edward Payne on the first operational SR-71 sortie on March 21, 1968. It became the most productive of the SR-71 fleet, flying 942 sorties, of which 257 were operational missions.

Chapter 11

At the Leading Edge

"We crashed not because we ran out of gas, but because we ran out of knowledge."

(Inscription on a cup awarded to survivors of accidents, McCook Flight Test Section, 1920s)

"Attempt the end, and never stand to doubt. Nothing's so hard, but search will find it out."
(Robert Herrick, 1591–1674)

"To strive, to seek, to find, and not to yield."
(Alfred, Lord Tennyson, 1809–1892)

"In research the horizon recedes as we advance."
(Mark Pattison, 1813–1884)

"Engines of war have long since reached their limits, and I see no further hope of any improvement in the art."
(Frontinus, 90 A.D.)

Major General Albert Boyd, "the test pilots' test pilot." He accumulated over 23,000 flying hours in more than 700 types and models of aircraft.

377

The "Xs" Mark Their Spots

From the moment visitors enter the USAF Museum, they are surrounded by the fruits of research and development. The majority of the artifacts on display are the end products of painstaking calculation and persistent trial and error. In a number of places, attention is drawn to the research and development process—the work of Leonardo da Vinci, Langley, and the Wright brothers, for instance, or the interwar experiments with air-to-air refueling and stratospheric flight. For the most part, however, the topic is so vast and all-encompassing that it is merely hinted at or taken for granted. Nevertheless, although most of the aircraft in the galleries are either seasoned veterans of front-line service or have been dressed up to look as if they are, there are a few which were produced for the benefits of research alone, or which led down evolutionary blind alleys and were overtaken by events. Others are prototypes or testbeds which gave birth to greater things. It is worth taking time to seek them out.

Among the more bizarre of the Museum's offerings are some of the "X" plane series. Several of them are clustered together at one end of the Modern Flight Gallery. They huddle in the protective shadow of the largest member of their exotic fraternity, the North American XB-70 Valkyrie, an elegant Mach 3 monster conceived in the days when high-altitude penetration of Soviet defenses was believed to be a feasible proposition. Nearly 200 ft long and more than 30 ft high, it would have weighed well over half a million pounds when fully loaded. The one on show is the sole survivor of the breed, its only sibling having been destroyed in a midair collision in 1966.

Several of the X planes are rocket-powered and were dependent on a "mother ship"—a bomber such as the B-50 or B-52—to carry them aloft. Once released at high altitude, the pilot lit the rocket engines and surged away, often to heights and speeds previously undreamt. The Bell X-1B was one of a series specifically intended to probe the realm of transonic and supersonic flight. A much improved version of the X-1 immortalized by the first supersonic flight in 1947, the X-1B was capable of reaching twice the speed of sound and was instrumented for research into the effects of kinetic heating during high-speed flight. It flew just twenty-seven times before being retired to the museum in 1959.

Nearby are three of the later X planes, all designed to study different solutions to some of the aerodynamic problems posed by the coming of the jet age. With its long, blade-like fuselage and improbably stubby wings, the Douglas X-3 was aptly named "Stiletto." Its airframe was supposed to be capable of sustained supersonic speeds, but the engines then available were not up to the task and the Stiletto achieved Mach 1 only when thrust downwards in a dive. Hung above the Stiletto are Northrop's X-4 and Bell's X-5. The X-4 gave convincing evidence that the transonic stability problems of swept-wing aircraft without tailplanes were too difficult to be overcome by the technology of the time, and the X-5 became the first aircraft in the world to vary the sweep of its wings while in flight.

Most awesome of the Museum's aircraft in terms of being "highest and fastest" is the North American X-15A-2. This was the second of three X-15s built to meet a requirement for an aircraft which could reach an altitude of fifty miles and a speed approaching Mach 7. It was, however, the first of them to feel the thrust of a rocket engine, and it became the fastest of the three. Rebuilt after a landing accident and modified

Curtiss Jennies dominate the floor of the McCook Field hangar in 1918.

to give improved performance, it was flown to Mach 6.72 by Major Pete Knight, USAF, on October 3, 1967. Going very fast with rockets is one thing; coming to a stop is another. The Museum owns Northrop's "Gee Whiz" deceleration sled, which could accelerate on rails to 200 mph and then come to rest in forty-five feet, simulating the forces encountered in some aircraft crashes. Compared to later achievements in deceleration research, these are not excessive figures, but they certainly bugged the eyes of those brave enough to endure the brief ride.

The USAF Museum has two "lifting bodies," wingless rocket-powered vehicles used to simulate the unpowered approach and landing of a space shuttle after reentry. They are a confusing pair. The Martin X-24B near the XB-70 was originally the X-24A, but was redesignated after being rebuilt in 1972 to improve its handling characteristics. The X-24A (in the Space Gallery under the port wing tip of the B-36) was originally known as the Martin SV-5J, but was never flown and has been converted to the appearance of the X-24A for display purposes. In a glass case at the end of the Space Gallery are items calling for a much greater flight of the imagination—models of the proposed X-30 National Space Plane are shown soaring clear of Earth's atmosphere.

Experiments with vertical fixed-wing flight are represented by three quite different aircraft. Two of them are on show in the Museum Annex hangars on the other side of Wright Field. The Hawker Siddeley XV-6A Kestrel vertical takeoff and landing fighter, forerunner of the better known Harrier, was one of six received from the U.K. for testing in the U.S. The LTV XC-142A is at first sight little more than a chubby, medium-sized transport. However, its four huge (15 ft 6 in diameter) propellers give a clue to its true nature. It is a tilt-wing, intended to behave both like a conventional aircraft and a helicopter. First flight of the XC-142A was in 1964, and in its prime its portly body achieved some startling results, managing to record speeds of 400 mph forwards and 30 mph backwards. It also succeeded in operating from an aircraft carrier. Impressive though all that was, the program was canceled before the end of the 1960s.

A lighter-than-air intervention draws a crowd at McCook Field in 1921. The assembly hangar is on the right, and the test hangars of the Airplane Engineering Division are on the left.

The third member of this vertical flight group is the Ryan X-13 Vertijet, shown in its unnatural pretakeoff attitude, its nose pointed hopefully at the roof of the Modern Flight Gallery. The X-13 on display is the one which made the first full cycle through vertical takeoff to horizontal flight to vertical landing on April 11, 1957.

Hidden away in one corner of the Museum Annex is an aircraft which probably deserves to be. The ungainly Fisher P-75 Eagle was an unlovely hybrid from its conception, and it did not improve with age. Although not exhibited with an X designation, it was certainly an experiment, and one which failed. Designed by the Fisher Body Division of General Motors in 1942, it was an attempt to create a fighter by making use of an assortment of readily available parts from existing aircraft, overcoming any resulting shortcomings by hanging them around a 2,885 hp Allison engine and dragging them along behind an impressive pair of contrarotating propellers. With WWII production fever raging, an order for 2,500 P-75s was placed before it was discovered during testing that the project was a disaster. The USAAF canceled the P-75 after only six had been built, three of which were lost in crashes, two of them fatal.

Far more attractive and deserving of success was the North American YF-107A, the last fighter to bear its famous maker's name. Originally designated the F-100B, it was an all-weather fighter-bomber development based on the F-100. Supersonic on its first flight and apparently trouble free, it nevertheless lost out in competition with the F-105 and the program was canceled after only three YF-107As had been built.

The Museum's remaining X aircraft are a diverse lot. A Republic XF-91 Thunderceptor stands in the Annex, loaded with unusual features. It has inverse taper on variable-incidence wings, and it is powered by both an afterburning jet engine and a rocket motor. It was the fastest thing around in 1950, but it had a problem staying airborne for even half an hour. Eventually determined to be impractical as an operational aircraft, the XF-91 was retired in 1951. Further along the flight-line, in the Museum's restoration area, are the makings of a Convair XF-92A, the world's first jet aircraft with a delta wing and a useful test-bed for the later F-102. Two more X planes can be found back in the Museum's Air Power Gallery, both from the creative minds of the McDonnell Corporation—the ugly little XF-85 Goblin parasite fighter squats beside its intended B-36 host, and the world's first ramjet helicopter, the spidery XH-20 Little Henry, hovers not far away.

Outside on the Museum's ramp there is a fascinating blue and white F-4 Phantom. This particular aircraft (62-12200) had

A McCook test pilot and record breaker in the 1920s, Jimmy Doolittle poses beside one of his favorite aircraft, a Curtiss Hawk.

a varied career as a prototype and test-bed. Taken from the U.S. Navy's production line, it became a USAF prototype, first as a YRF-4C and later as a YF-4E. In later life, it served in the "Agile Eagle" program to test leading edge slats, evaluated a "fly-by-wire" system with a sidestick controller, and was the principal agent in the Precision Aircraft Control Technology (PACT) program, which involved the fitting of canards below the rear cockpit.

Most recent of the Museum's acquisitions from the research world is an aircraft known as "Tacit Blue." Slab-sided and with a dull gray finish unrelieved by markings of any kind, Tacit Blue is not an appealing sight. It does not even seem likely that such a creature could have flown. Nevertheless, uncompromisingly unattractive though it is, Tacit Blue was a considerable success story. It proved the concepts of stealth technology and laid the groundwork for its operational offspring, the F-117A Nighthawk and the B-2 Spirit.

USAF Research in the 1990s

At the beginning of the 1990s, the responsibility for research and development in the USAF rested with Air Force Systems Command (AFSC). The Command tested and developed everything from aircraft and air-to-air missiles to avionics and spacecraft. This vast range of activities was spread among a number of divisions. The lion's share of AFSC's budget went to the Aeronautical Systems Division at Wright-Patterson AFB, Ohio, which had oversight of all development work on aircraft, their engines and avionics, as well as missiles and such supporting systems as flight simulators.

The Air Force Flight Test Center at Edwards AFB in California's Mojave Desert looked after the evaluation of manned and unmanned aircraft and spacecraft for the USAF and a number of other agencies. At Eglin AFB, Florida, the Armament Division tested and procured all of the USAF's non-nuclear weapons and related equipment.

The Electronics Systems Division at Hanscom AFB, Massachusetts, was the primary agency for the Air Force's command, control, communications, and intelligence (C3I) systems. Among other AFSC subordinate formations were Space Division, the Ballistic Missile Office, the Directorate of Laboratories, the Aerospace Medical Division, and the Arnold Engineering Development Center, which managed the world's largest complex of wind tunnels, engine test cells, and space simulation chambers.

The efforts of all these divisions were interwoven with work done by the other services and by the corporations of the commercial aerospace industry to maintain the USAF as the world's premier air force. It had not always been so organized nor so comprehensive.

Links with Dayton

In the earliest days, aviation research was largely a matter of individuals proceeding "by guess and by God." It was not until the Wright brothers turned their minds to the challenge of manned flight that a genuinely systematic approach was devised. They read and thought a great deal about the problem, and they worked things out methodically, calculating and experimenting as they went along and recording their results for further study. Much of their work was done on Huffman Prairie, near Dayton, Ohio, an area now part of the present Wright-Patterson AFB, which can therefore lay claim to being the birthplace of aeronautical research and development.

The U.S. Army did not become formally involved in aeronautical research until after the U.S. had declared war on Germany in April 1917. Realization that the European powers had left the U.S. far behind in terms of military aviation forced the issue. In July 1917, the Army decided to open an aeronautical research and development facility at North Field, just north of downtown Dayton. Renamed McCook Field after a renowned Civil War family, the installation began operations in December 1917. It was a principally grass airfield with a 1,000 ft long hard-surface runway available for use when the ground was wet. Testing at McCook was at first a fairly basic affair, instrumentation being rudimentary and results depending almost entirely on the penciled jottings made by pilots during flight. Just how basic a business it was may be judged from a remark made by one of McCook's most celebrated pilots, Jimmy Doolittle, who recalled : "I never flew without a pair of pliers, a screwdriver, and a crescent wrench in my pocket so I could fix things on the airplane."[1]

The work at McCook grew quickly to encompass everything which excited the curiosity of airmen—engines cooled by liquid or air, fuel systems, turbosuperchargers, variable pitch propellers, machine guns, self-sealing fuel tanks, night flying techniques, aerial cameras, radio beam navigation, parachutes, and very much more. Two wind tunnels were built to test aircraft characteristics on the ground with models. Aircraft were designed and built at McCook, too, including the Packard-Le Pere LUSAC-11 flown to over 33,000 ft by Shorty Schroeder in 1920 during supercharger tests.[2] Schroeder's narrow escape from death on that occasion was generally accepted as part of the job. Accidents were frequent, and a number of McCook test pilots were killed when they pushed their aircraft through the boundaries of aviation as they were known at the time.[3] Acknowledging the hazards of what they were doing, the pilots created several "idiot" awards for survivors of crashes. There were the Alibi, Bonehead, Dumbbell, and Flying Ass trophies, and an award introduced by Schroeder himself—the Cup of Good Beginnings and Bad Endings.[4]

Basic and hazardous it might have been, but the volume of test flying grew quickly to the point that McCook airmen sought an overflow at Wilbur Wright Field, some eight miles away and next to the Huffman Prairie area used by the Wrights. Tests on the disappointing Barling bomber were among those conducted from Wilbur Wright Field. As McCook's small airfield and wooden buildings proved ever more constricting, however, the Air Service looked around for a more permanent home for their testing operations. A site to the northeast of Dayton was selected and on October 12, 1927, it was dedicated as Wright Field, in honor of both brothers. Wilbur Wright Field was absorbed, and by 1930 the last of McCook's operations had been transferred to the new installation.

From its inception, the pioneering work carried out at Wright Field covered an enormous range of activities. Airframes, engines, and instruments, and their inter-

A smiling John Macready in riding breeches with the Flight Test Section at McCook Field in 1926. From the left: R.G. Lockwood, George Tourtellot, William Amis, Jimmy Doolittle, H.A. Johnson, Macready, Hoy Barksdale, James Hutchinson, R.C. Moffat, and Louis Meister. In front of Macready are two of several trophies awarded for misdemeanors - the Quacking Duck and the Flying Ass, the latter carrying the inscription "Trophy of Stupidity."

action, were examined, and the conflicting demands of range, speed, and load-carrying capacity were investigated. Standards and specifications for the new aeronautical technologies were derived. Testing methods were worked out for aircraft both on the ground and in the air, and all innovations were exhaustively screened before being cleared for flight. In the 1930s, the evolution of American air power could be followed by watching what went on at Wright Field. More prototypes came and went during this period than at any other time in American military aviation; some,

like the B-17, moved on to far greater things, and others disappeared into well deserved obscurity. As aircraft went higher and faster, the problems of coping with the effects of aviation extremes on the human body needed solving, and Wright Field acquired a Physiological Research Laboratory, complete with pressure chambers which could simulate altitudes up to 80,000 ft.

Despite the almost limitless nature of the military aviation interests pursued at Wright Field, pre-WWII restrictions on expenditures meant that the installation

DH-4s soldiered on behind their Liberty engines throughout the 1920s. Lt. Frank Patterson was killed during gunnery trials in the DH-4 illustrated.

[1]Instructions to test pilots were pretty basic, too. Among those issued by the commander of McCook Field, Colonel Thurman Bane, was the following: "Pilots will make sure that they thoroughly understand the operation of all controls, especially the motor controls, before taking off."

[2]See Chapter 4.

[3]Lt. Frank Patterson died in the crash of a DH-4 during gunnery trials in 1918. Patterson Field was later named in his honor, and his name survives in today's Wright-Patterson Air Force Base.

[4]See the quotations at the beginning of Chapter 12.

The most striking post-WWII bomber design was the Northrop XB-35, here chased by a P-61 in 1946. Northrop never abandoned the flying wing idea, and it reappeared when the B-2 took to the air more than forty years later.

was still fairly modest in scale by 1940, with about sixty buildings on site. WWII changed all that. By 1945, there were over three hundred buildings and the former grass airfield now boasted a triangle of three hard-surface runways. The largest wind tunnel in the world was in operation, and there was a structural test building capable of handling a complete fuselage and wing section of a B-36.

Wartime urgency almost eliminated prototype testing. Instead, early production models of each type were put through their paces by both test and squadron pilots, who flew them through every conceivable maneuver in a concentrated program intended to reveal weaknesses and suggest improvements while the production of the aircraft was getting under way. Wright Field's failures under this method, like the unlovely and inaptly named Fisher P-75 Eagle, were more than offset by aircraft which went on to compile illustrious combat records (B-24/25/26/29 and P-38/39/40/47/51/61, among others), plus a host of worthy transport and training aircraft. Notable milestones included one set by Lt. Col. Laurence Craigie, Wright Field's

Aircraft Projects Branch chief, who was the first Air Force pilot and second American to fly the XP-59A, the first U.S. jet, when it made its 1942 debut in the California desert. Later the XP-59A arrived at Wright Field, and, in October 1944, Ann Baumgartner, a Women's Air Force Service Pilot, flew it to become the first U.S. woman jet pilot.

The continued increase in the range and scale of testing required for military aircraft once more led the Air Force to look for other places to do it. Wright Field was too close to Dayton's expanding metropolitan area for comfort. Besides the fact that space was limited, safety and security were concerns which could be dealt with satisfactorily only in a more remote area. For this reason, beginning in 1942, some flight testing was moved to Muroc, California, so laying the foundations for the later Edwards AFB. A man who was instrumental in building up what would become the Air Force Flight Test Center at Edwards, Col. Albert Boyd, arrived at Wright Field in 1945 to become Chief of the Flight Test Division. His appetite for flying was insatiable and, besides testing nearly every air-

craft that came to Wright Field, he found time in June 1947 to fly the Lockheed P-80R Shooting Star to a new world speed record of 623.7 mph over Muroc's wide open spaces. In 1949, Boyd moved to Muroc to take over as commander and was there to see the base renamed in honor of Capt. Glenn Edwards, who had been killed in the crash of a YB-49 the year before.

As the facilities at Muroc/Edwards expanded, so the flight testing in the Dayton area was increasingly confined to more specialized areas, such as the testing of components, systems, and instruments. One very important exercise was the bad weather flying undertaken by the All Weather Flying Group after its establishment in 1945. Later designated a division, this unit operated what became known as the "All Weather Air Line" between Clinton County Army Airfield (a satellite of Wright Field) and Andrews AFB, Washington, D.C., from August 1946 to September 1948, providing a regular air transport service on five days every week. Flying a regular scheduled service, the AWAL completed 1,128 flights in all weathers without cancellation or accident, and with an average error in takeoff and landing times of less than one minute. The lessons learned from this operation about the use of radar in air traffic control brought great rewards during the Berlin Airlift of 1948-49.

After 1950, testing activities at Wright Field (and later at Wright-Patterson AFB) remained specialized, but nonetheless invaluable to the USAF. Weather projects ranged from examining the effects of icing and lightning strikes on aircraft to the removal of rain from windshields and improving traction on slippery runways. Other tasks investigated sonic booms, found weightlessness in zero-G maneuvers, tried an air-cushion landing system, refueled helicopters in flight, mated low-light television sensors with a Gatling gun hung under a B-57, and so on in bewildering diversity.

From the 1970s, the 4950th Test Wing at Wright-Patterson AFB concerned itself primarily with the operation of large research aircraft, mainly variants of the C-135 and C-141. Among the first were bulbous-nosed EC-135Ns, which became the Advanced Range Instrumentation Aircraft (ARIA), used to support worldwide missile and space testing. Activities in other aircraft later on included testing Identification Friend or Foe (IFF) systems, tail warning radar, infrared seekers, electronic countermeasures (ECM) equipment, laser weapons, and satellite navigation systems. Testing in the Dayton area may have changed in character and scope since the days of the Wrights, but the urge to solve the problems associated with manned flight has remained as strong as ever.

Research in the Desert

The remote airfield at Muroc, deep in the Californian desert, began its long association with flight testing in December 1941, when a full-scale mock-up of the proposed Curtiss XP-55 first took to the air. It was not an auspicious start. An ugly little flying wing with canard foreplanes and a pusher propeller, neither the mock-up nor the XP-55 ever overcame serious stability problems and only three XP-55s

were made, two of which were destroyed in crashes. Matters improved the following year when Muroc saw a top secret project unveiled. On October 2, 1942, Bell test pilot Bob Stanley coaxed the XP-59A off the surface of the dry lake bed and so ushered the U.S. into the jet age. Lt. Col. Laurence Craigie from Wright Field flew the aircraft later that same day.

For most of WWII, the urgent need for aircrew in the front-line squadrons meant that most flying done at Muroc was concerned with crew training. However, flight testing continued also, and a number of first flights were recorded, among them Northrop's XP-56 and XP-79, both early elements of the flying-wing tradition that would see its culmination in the B-2 nearly fifty years later.[5] Testing programs were also completed on such exotics as Lockheed's XP-58 Chain Lightning (a massive escort and antishipping fighter), Bell's diminutive XP-77 (an all-wood lightweight fighter), and Convair's XP-81 (a compound jet and turboprop fighter), but none of these went further than the experimental stage. More significant was Lockheed's XP-80, nicknamed "Lulu Belle," which first flew at Muroc in Janu-

---

[5]The XP-79 Flying Ram was unique in that it was intended to be both rocket-powered and capable of slicing off parts of enemy aircraft with its sharp and extremely strong wing.

ary 1944 and was an instant success, quickly establishing itself as the progenitor of a line of "Shooting Star" fighters and trainers which would survive to the end of the century.

The post-WWII period saw a rush of activity at Muroc as the technologies of the jet age offered dramatic improvements in performance. Republic's XP-84 Thunderjet, the USAF's first 600 mph fighter, which flew in February 1946, was followed by the Hughes XF-11 reconnaissance aircraft and a succession of bombers. Douglas produced the prop and jet XB-42 Mixmaster and its pure jet cousin, the XB-43, the first U.S. jet bomber. From Northrop came a huge flying wing, the prop-driven XB-35, later modified for jets as the YB-49, and Consolidated delivered the immense and more successful XB-36. These were trailed by the North American XB-45 Tornado (the first operational USAF jet bomber), the Convair XB-46 (one of the most aesthetically pleasing aircraft ever built), and the revolutionary Boeing XB-47 Stratojet. In the late 1940s, the list of aircraft designed for the USAF and tested at Muroc/Edwards grew to include a string of fighters—the McDonnell XF-85 Goblin parasite, the Curtiss XF-87 Blackhawk all-weather interceptor and its rival the Northrop XF-89 Scorpion, the

The XP-55 was an imaginative 1940s Curtiss attempt at a pusher-driven fighter. It never overcame serious stability problems and development was cancelled in 1945 after a fatal crash at a Wright Field airshow.

Martin's XB-51 first flew in October 1949 and proved to be an impressive performer. However, it was overtaken by political events and Martin was left with a license to manufacture the British-designed Canberra instead.

McDonnell XF-88 and Lockheed XF-90 "penetration fighters," the Republic XF-91 Thunderceptor and the Convair XF-92A, the world's first piloted true delta. Of all the fighters tested, the most successful was the North American XP-86 Sabre, first flown on October 1, 1947, by the same George Welch who had distinguished himself six years earlier by shooting down four Japanese aircraft during the attack on Pearl Harbor. The Sabre was a winner from the start, and over seven thousand were built in seven major variants before production ended in 1956.

The long association of Muroc/Edwards with the highly specialized X-series aircraft began in 1946 with a whisper, when the Bell X-1 was first air-launched without power. It picked up pace with a bang in October 1947 as Chuck Yeager fired all four rocket chambers to push the X-1 *Glamorous Glennis* beyond the speed of sound for the first time.[6] One other X-plane program was underway before the Korean War broke out. In December 1948, the Northrop X-4 Bantam began an investigation of the characteristics of semitailess aircraft at transonic speeds. In a quite different approach to the challenges of the transonic region, a sled with a 4,000 lb rocket motor was built and mounted on a track with a hydromechanical brake

[6]See Chapter 7.

at the end. In 1951, Maj. John Stapp rode this sled and another at Holloman AFB, New Mexico, in a series of tests aimed at finding out just what forces the human body could withstand. Before he was finished, Stapp had been brought to a halt from over 620 mph in just 1.4 seconds, experiencing peak decelerations of over 40G and exposing himself to a wind blast which approached Mach 1.

Air Force Flight Test Center

On June 25, 1951, an official ceremony formally activated the Air Force Flight Test Center (AFFTC) at Edwards AFB. The motto of the new unit was particularly appropriate—*Ad Inexplorata* ("Towards the Unknown").

During the 1950s several other X planes made their mark at Edwards. Bell's X-5 probed the secrets of wings which could be variably swept in flight, and the Douglas X-3 Stiletto promised blazing speed but had an airframe which had outrun the capabilities of its engines. Designed for sustained supersonic flight, the X-3 could exceed Mach 1 only in a dive. Even so, it provided valuable data for such later aircraft as the F-104 and the X-15. The X-1 series (three X-1s, plus the X-1A, 1B, 1D, and 1E, the latter a modified X-1) did much better and continued to push back the boundaries of manned flight. Before

the program ended in 1958, Chuck Yeager had taken the X-1A to Mach 2.435, and demonstrated conclusively that it could not be flown any faster. At that speed, Yeager said, the aircraft went "divergent on all three axes" and tumbled down through 51,000 ft in less than a minute before he regained control. Bell's swept-wing successor, the X-2, went still higher and faster than the X-1, reaching 126,000 ft and Mach 3.2 in 1956. Capt. Milburn Apt was the first man to fly at more than three times the speed of sound, but he did not live to enjoy his celebrity. Just after Apt had set the record, the X-2 succumbed to the inertia coupling which had overtaken Chuck Yeager. Apt attempted to eject from the tumbling aircraft but was fatally injured.

Capt. Apt was not the only Air Force test pilot at Edwards to pay with his life in the 1950s for the privilege of operating at the limits of aeronautical knowledge. On May 9, 1952, Maj. Neil Lathrop died when a Martin XB-51 came apart during a high-speed structural test. The second Bell X-5 failed to recover from a spin in October 1953 and Maj. Raymond Popson was killed in the crash. One year later, North American's chief test pilot, George Welch, paid the penalty for taking an F-100A to its G-limit at Mach 1.4. The aircraft suffered the dreaded inertia coupling phenomenon and disintegrated. Although not a serving officer at the time, George Welch was well known in the Air Force as a WWII ace with sixteen victories to his credit. Such losses were grievous, but, considering the amount and nature of the testing done at Edwards during the 1950s, the number of serious accidents was lower than might have been expected. At the same time, there was little doubt that the achievements of the AFFTC had made it the world's leading aviation testing and research facility. Thus established at the forefront of aeronautical research, AFFTC sought new frontiers and, before the decade was out, a program was initiated which carried manned flight to the edge of space.

The North American X-15 was built to meet a 1952 specification for an aircraft which could reach an altitude of fifty miles and speeds up to Mach 7. Such figures presupposed an airframe with the capacity to withstand an extraordinary range of temperatures, from a friction-induced 650 degrees to an ambient minus 180 degrees Centigrade. North American therefore built the aircraft principally from titanium and stainless steel, covering the whole with a skin of nickel alloy steel. In March 1959, the first of three X-15As made a captive flight from Edwards under the wing of its "mother," a specially modified B-52A. Between that date and October 24, 1968, there were 199 X-15 flights. In the course of the program, the X-15 became the first aircraft to fly above 200,000 and 300,000 ft, and the first to exceed four, five, and six times the speed of sound. The pilot when each of these marks was passed was Maj. Bob White, USAF. The X-15 went on to record maximum figures of 354,200 ft (Joe Walker, NASA, August 22, 1963) and Mach 6.72 (Maj. Pete Knight, USAF, October 3, 1967).[7]

While the B-52 assisted flights of the rocket-powered X-15 were the most obviously spectacular of those conducted from Edwards in the 1960s, they were a small proportion of the tests actually completed. Jet aircraft, taking off under their own power, made great progress, expanding their performance flight envelope enormously. At the outer edge came aircraft like the Convair B-58 Hustler, a Mach 2 bomber which in 1962 lifted a payload of more than 11,000 lbs to over 85,000 ft, and the amazing Lockheed YF-12A, the predecessor of the SR-71 Blackbird, which showed that it could sustain Mach 3 plus at 80,000 ft. Just as astounding was the North American XB-70 Valkyrie, a bomber weighing half a million pounds which achieved Mach 3 at 70,000 ft in 1965. Overtaken by developments in Soviet radar and missile technology, only two XB-70s were built and both were flown in the interests of pure research. Sadly, the Valkyrie was at the center of one of the worst tragedies ever experienced at Edwards. In 1966, during a public relations photographic flight in formation with four fighter aircraft, the second XB-70 was

Rocket-assisted Lockheed NF-104As could be boosted to heights above 120,000 ft. They were used as part of the astronaut training program.

struck by NASA pilot Joe Walker's F-104. Al White, NASA, ejected from the stricken Valkyrie, but Walker and Maj. Carl Cross, USAF, were killed and both aircraft destroyed. In 1969, the surviving XB-70 was flown to the USAF Museum.

Other projects of the 1960s included several which led to major acquisitions for

Aptly named "Stiletto," the Douglas X-3 never lived up to its appearance. It could be induced to go supersonic only in a dive.

[7]Mach 6.72 equals a ground speed of 4,534 mph or 6,650 ft per sec, which is a velocity approximately twice that of a shell from the GAU-8 cannon in the A-10 Warthog.

the USAF's front line. The McDonnell YF-4C Phantom II (formerly the YF-110A Spectre) began flying from Edwards in 1963, and was followed by the reconnaissance version (YRF-4C) the following year. Intensive evaluation of the General Dynamics swing-wing F-111A started in 1965, and by the end of the decade Lockheed's gigantic C-5A was undergoing tests, demonstrating its huge capacity by setting a world takeoff weight record of 789,200 lbs in 1969.

Among more specialized programs there was a study of boundary layer control, completed in the Northrop X-21A (a modified Douglas WB-66D). The future demands of space flight were met with astronaut training in Lockheed NF-104As, which were rocket assisted to boost them to heights above 120,00 ft, and, from 1963 on, with tests on a series of lifting bodies from Northrop and Martin-Marietta, wingless aircraft which examined the problems likely to be encountered by space shuttles returning from orbit for unpowered landings.

Post-Vietnam

The 1970s and '80s saw the Edwards test pilots becoming less involved in pushing at the outer edges of the performance envelope in terms of sheer height and speed, and more taken up with the possibilities of exploiting both old knowledge and new systems technologies to develop more capable aircraft. After Vietnam, the USAF was sorely in need of new equipment and Edwards was necessarily at the forefront of the program. In 1972, the competition began between Fairchild Republic's YA-10A and Northrop's YA-9A to find a successor to the venerable A-1 Skyraider, with the Warthog eventually coming out on top. That same year, the McDonnell Douglas F-15A Eagle made its debut, impressing everyone from the start. Testing progressed rapidly and, a year later, the Eagle was flying at Mach 2.5 and 60,000 ft. It was also quickly apparent that it was the most powerful and agile fighter aircraft yet built, and that it would have no difficulty in meeting the USAF's need to field an unmatched air superiority fighter.

Anxieties about the F-15's size and cost led to another fierce competition in the mid-1970s, this time for a lightweight fighter. The contest was fought out between the General Dynamics YF-16 and the Northrop YF-17 Cobra. The YF-16's first flight at Edwards was in 1974, and it subsequently went on to win selection by the USAF and so initiate the long production run of the F-16 Fighting Falcon, the world's first fly-by-wire fighter. Disappointment in the YF-17 camp was eased somewhat by its subsequent success as the USN's F/A-18 Hornet, and by the fact that a significant milestone was passed at an early stage of the flight test program. On June 23, 1974, the YF-17 became the first jet aircraft to exceed the speed of sound in level flight without the help of afterburning.

Prominent among the larger aircraft tested at Edwards during this period were the Rockwell B-1A, which arrived in 1974, and a pair of Advanced Medium STOL (short takeoff and landing) Transports (AMST)—the McDonnell Douglas YC-15 and the Boeing YC-14. None of these managed to get past the testing phase, but at least some of the work done bore fruit some years later in the B-1B Lancer and the C-17A. The McDonnell Douglas KC-10A Extender made its first appearance at Edwards in 1980 and went on to enjoy a successful career in its own right.

Much of the significant work done at Edwards in the 1980s involved the investigation of new concepts and technologies. Test aircraft acquired add-on designations which described their special functions—or hid them in confusing acronyms. There was the "fly-by-light" A-7D, which had fiber-optic links to the flight controls, and the Advanced Fighter Technology Integration (AFTI) F-16, one of the most capable research aircraft ever constructed. As it developed, the AFTI F-16 incorporated such diverse and sometimes strange attributes as direct lift and pitch-pointing control, direct sideforce and yaw-pointing control, digital flight control, an advanced cockpit with multifunction displays, a voice-actuated command system, integrated weapons firing/flight control, an au-

tomated maneuvering attack system, and an enhanced night attack, helmet-mounted display.

Another aircraft involved in the AFTI program was the F-111. In 1985, it was flown fitted with Boeing's Mission Adaptive Wing (MAW). By operating leading and trailing edge flaps, a computer adapted the camber of the wing to ensure that its shape was always optimal for varying phases of flight. Further studies into improved performance and maneuverability were undertaken by the laboriously captioned F-15 Short Take Off and Landing/ Maneuver Technology Demonstrator (STOL/MTD). This was an F-15B modified with thrust-vectoring nozzles, canard controls, and rough-field landing gear. During intensive testing, it demonstrated dramatic improvements in landing and takeoff distances, and impressive controllability at high angles of attack. It also used an Autonomous Landing Guidance system to make precision night landings on a blacked-out Edwards runway without the help of ground-based aids.

Among other notable newcomers to the Edwards flight line as the 1980s ended was the Grumman X-29, designed to probe the possibilities of forward-swept wings. It was followed by an aircraft which drew the mind back irresistibly to the early days of desert flight testing. Northrop's B-2 seemed to be a resurrected YB-49, back at center stage after waiting in the wings for forty years.

By 1989, Edwards had long been unparalleled as a flight test center, but in September of that year its capabilities were increased even further. The Air Force Anechoic Facility was opened to allow the USAF to test the integrated avionics systems of large aircraft within a protected and secure environment. The shielded central chamber measures some 264 ft by 250 ft, with a 70 ft-high ceiling, and was first used to assist in the development of the B-1B's defensive avionics system.

Flight testing at Edwards has never stopped moving forward in its pursuit of improvements in aerospace vehicles. As the 1990s dawned, the continued program of development with the B-2 Spirit, with its remarkable stealth technology and its complex systems, was accompanied by the introduction of state-of-the-art aircraft in both transport and fighter roles. The McDonnell Douglas C-17 Globemaster III promised to simplify the handling of heavy cargo and to be the only transport capable of carrying the largest U.S. Army equipment into restricted runways in severe weather. The fighters of the twenty-first century appeared in the forms of the Lockheed/Boeing YF-22 and the Northrop/McDonnell Douglas YF-23. At the end of another close competition, the YF-22 was selected to meet the USAF's requirement for an advanced tactical fighter to replace the F-15.

Flair and imagination have never been in short supply at Edwards. More aviation milestones have been set in its airspace than anywhere else on earth. Even more dramatic creations than those already seen can be expected to arrive for testing during the USAF's second half century. Among them new multiservice aircraft may be prominent, and the hydrogen-fueled X-30 may succeed in demonstrating air-breathing single-stage-to-orbit flight, and in bringing Mach 25 speeds into the realm of the routine. Whatever possibilities come to fruition, one thing is for certain—Edwards will remain at the forefront of aerospace research, establishing new frontiers with each passing year.

Grumman's remarkable X-29 is a forward-sweep technology demonstrator made largely from parts of other aircraft, among them the forward fuselage and nose gear of an F-5 and the engine and main gear from an F-16. As with many modern fighter-type aircraft, the X-29 is so unstable that it cannot be flown by human hand alone, and must rely on computers to sense and correct almost instantaneously deviations from a chosen flight path.

A   Early wind tunnels were often considerable works of art and craftsmanship. The tunnel designed and built at McCook Field, Dayton, in 1918 was wonderfully shaped in wood. Its sixty-inch fan has twenty-four blades which can propel air through the fourteen-inch throat at speeds up to 450 mph.

B   Access to the throat of the McCook wind tunnel is gained through a small window. Airfoils and models placed in the throat could be observed here during test. Smoke released into the tunnel revealed the streamlining (or otherwise) of the airflow around the model at various speeds.

C   Engineers at McCook Field devised static stress tests for aircraft which involved placing bags of shot or lead bars on the structure. Here a LUSAC 11 is subjected to the shot bag treatment and droops under the strain.

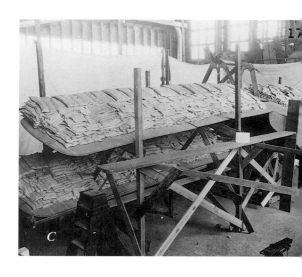

388

To the Airforce Museum
40 800 feet
John A. Macrandy
July 9, 1971

A

A LUSAC 11 Over McCook Field
Robert E. Carlin USAF Art Collection

B The LUSAC 11 was designed in 1917 by Georges LePere, a French aeronautical engineer working for the U.S. (The acronym LUSAC stands for "LePere U.S. Army Combat.") It was originally intended as a combination fighter and reconnaissance aircraft, carrying a crew of two.

C Powered by a Liberty engine, the LUSAC 11 proved to have a remarkable performance. Suitably modified, it was used as a high-altitude research aircraft at McCook Field during the 1920s, several times breaking the world altitude record.

A   The Bell X-1 rocket-powered aircraft were designed to investigate flight at transonic and supersonic speeds. The USAF Museum's X-1B was instrumented to research the effects of kinetic heating in high-speed flight. X-1s were carried aloft by a "mother" B-50 and dropped at 25,000 ft or more before lighting up the rocket engines and surging away. The subsequent dash to supersonic flight was invariably followed by a "dead-stick" landing.

B   For the pilot of the X-1, perhaps the most significant difference from more conventional aircraft cockpits was the absence of a throttle. All power came from the four switches at the top left of the instrument panel which controlled the rocket motor chambers, and they were either on or off. In the X-1B, the Machmeter just below the rocket switches reads only to Mach 1, which is ungenerous for an aircraft known to be capable of far more.

C   The power for the X-1B was provided by a Reaction Motors XLR-11 rocket engine. Four chambers of 1,500 lbs of thrust each could be fired separately or together as required. A pressurized system used gaseous nitrogen to force alcohol and liquid oxygen into the burners, but they did not burn for long. At full power, thrust was available for two and a half minutes.

D   The tail end of the X-1B. This aircraft made just twenty-seven flights in all before being retired in January 1959, with its assorted components still in the "almost new" category. A conventional elevator is fitted, but Chuck Yeager's comments about longitudinal control at transonic speeds had been heeded, and the tailplane incidence has been made adjustable in flight.

E   Lake Bed Liftoff © Mike Machat, 1989

A

A   The uncompromisingly blunt end of the X-15A-2. The exhaust cone is on the receiving end of a throttled Thiokol XLR-99 liquid-propellant rocket engine with a rated thrust of 57,000 lbs at 45,000 ft. Above it towers the foot-wide trailing edge of the wedge section dorsal fin, pivoted for directional control and fitted with split air-brakes. The spherical tank contains helium to pressurize the liquid hydrogen tanks. A conventional nosewheel was used, but the rear of the X-15 was supported on landing by steel skids.

B   In the two years starting October 1963, Joe Engle flew the X-15 sixteen times, reaching Mach 5.71 on his tenth flight and an altitude of 271,000 ft on his fifteenth. He later joined the Space Shuttle program, commanding Columbia in 1981 and Discovery in 1985.

C   The X-15A-2 on display at the USAF Museum is the aircraft flown by Major "Pete" Knight to Mach 6.72 on October 3, 1967. The three-layered windscreen includes a fused silica outer pane and a middle pane of alumino-silicate, and the airframe is covered with a skin of nickel alloy steel. A spherical device in the nose is designed to sense angles of attack and sideslip during upper atmosphere flight. Around the nose are eight of the twelve small rocket nozzles used to control aircraft attitude above the effective atmosphere. One of the two 22 ft-long tanks attached to the fuselage contained anhydrous ammonia, and the other liquid oxygen. This allowed the engine to be run for 150 seconds or more, up from less than 90 seconds on internal fuel. (The X-15A-2 burned almost sixteen tons of fuel in two and a half minutes.) The tanks were jettisoned and recovered by parachute.

D   Flying in the atmosphere, the X-15 was controlled by means of the normal stick in the center of the cockpit. However, since there were no ailerons, pitch and roll were induced by the all-moving tailplane, the two halves of which could be moved together or differentially. The small rockets which controlled the aircraft outside the atmosphere were operated by a small stick hidden from view beneath the left cockpit rail. On the panel, instruments are almost outnumbered by red warning captions.

C

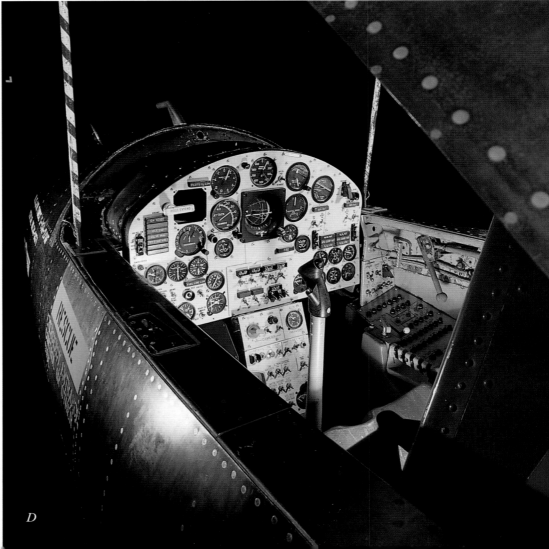

D

393

Dance of the Valkryie
© *Mike Machat, 1990*

A The intakes area of the XB-70 suggests a machine which could have been created for a futuristic movie. The "flying wedge" shape under the fuselage kept boundary layer air from spilling into the intake ducts, which themselves were sensitive to shock wave formation and were adjusted automatically to ensure that smooth airflow reached the engines. The intakes are situated almost halfway back along the underside of the almost 200 ft-long fuselage.

B Over 180,000 lbs of thrust hurl the half-million pound XB-70 into the air. Note that the folding tips on the 65-degree sweep delta wings are set level for takeoff, and that the Valkyrie appears to need the help of extended "ears" to lift its nose skyward.

C A retractable visor was used to smooth out the slight bump of the XB-70's cockpit for flight at high speeds. In the cockpit area, the fuselage was built mainly of titanium. The two-man crew sat on seats which became pressurized ejection capsules in an emergency, so pressure suits were not worn, despite the very high operating altitudes.

B

C

A

A The XB-70 cockpit is orderly. Engine instruments and controls dominate the center. The throttle levers control six GE YJ-93 engines producing 31,000 lbs thrust each in afterburner, sufficient to drive the half-million pound XB-70 forward at more than Mach 3 at altitudes above 70,000 ft. Just above the throttle quadrant are the landing gear lever and a rotary control for the movable wing tips, which could be drooped as much as 65 degrees to ensure stability for Mach 3 high-altitude flight.

B Two from the imposing row of six huge tail pipes at the rear of the XB-70. Note that the outer one is angled away from its neighbor to reduce the mutual disturbance of jet exhaust shock waves.

399 B

A

A   The LTV-Hiller-Ryan XC-142A was designed in the mid-'60s as a transport with vertical takeoff and landing capability. Four GE T64 turboprops of 3,080 shp driving four-bladed propellers of 15 ft 6 in diameter were hung on wings which could be tilted through 100 degrees. A tail rotor ensured longitudinal control during vertical and hovering flight. All engines were interconnected by cross-shafting. The main cabin could hold thirty-two troops, and the aircraft had a speed range of plus 400 mph to minus 35 mph. Of the five XC-142As built, only the one at the USAF Museum is left.

B

B   The Martin Marietta X-24A Pilot (PIloted LOw-speed Test) was one of a series of lifting-bodies which examined the problems of developing manned reentry vehicles able to perform as spacecraft and conventional aircraft. The X-24A was launched from a B-52 and accelerated under rocket power to Mach 2 and 100,000 ft before completing a rapid "glide" recovery to Edwards AFB. It completed twenty-eight powered flights. The USAF Museum's aircraft was originally the SV-5J, a jet-powered derivative of the X-24A, which never flew. It has been restored for display as an X-24A.

C   Looking more like a Greyhound bus with wings than a flying machine, the Tacit Blue is a unique aircraft which was used to validate many of the concepts of "stealth" technology. The $165 million program, which ran from 1978 to 1985, provided information which was invaluable to the design teams developing the B-2 and other stealth systems.

401   C

Leaders of the
United States Air Force

Secretaries of the Air Force

Stuart Symington	September 18, 1947 - April 24, 1950
Thomas K. Finletter	April 24, 1950 - January 20, 1953
Harold E. Talbott	February 4, 1953 - August 13, 1955
Donald A. Quarles	August 15, 1955 - April 30, 1957
James H. Douglas, Jr.	May 1, 1957 - December 10, 1959
Dudley C. Sharp	December 11, 1959 - January 20, 1961
Eugene M. Zuckert	January 24, 1961 - September 30, 1965
Harold Brown	October 1, 1965 - February 15, 1969
Robert C. Seamans, Jr.	February 15, 1969 - May 14, 1973
John L. McLucas (acting)	May 15, 1973 - July 18, 1973
John L. McLucas	July 18, 1973 - November 23, 1975
James W. Plummer (acting)	November 24, 1975 - January 1, 1976
James W. Plummer	January 2, 1976 - April 6, 1977
John C. Stetson	April 6, 1977 - May 18, 1979
Hans Mark (acting)	May 18, 1979 - July 26, 1979
Hans Mark	July 26, 1979 - February 9, 1981
Verne Orr	February 9, 1981 - November 30, 1985
Russell A. Rourke	December 9, 1985 - April 7, 1986
Edward C. Aldridge, Jr. (acting)	April 8, 1986 - June 8, 1986
Edward C. Aldridge, Jr.	June 9, 1986 - December 16, 1988
James F. McGovern (acting)	December 16, 1988 - April 29, 1989
John J. Welch, Jr. (acting)	April 29, 1989 - May 21, 1989
Donald B. Rice	May 22, 1989 - January 20, 1993
Michael B. Donley (acting)	January 20, 1993 - July 13, 1993
Merrill A. McPeak (acting)	July 14, 1993 - August 5, 1993
Sheila E. Widnall	August 6, 1993 -

USAF Chiefs of Staff

Carl A. Spaatz	September 26, 1947 - April 29, 1948
Hoyt S. Vandenberg	April 30, 1948 - June 29, 1953
Nathan F. Twining	June 30, 1953 - June 30, 1957
Thomas D. White	July 1, 1957 - June 30, 1961
Curtis E. LeMay	June 30, 1961 - January 31, 1965
John P. McConnell	February 1, 1965 - July 31, 1969
John D. Ryan	August 1, 1969 - July 31, 1973
George S. Brown	August 1, 1973 - June 30, 1974
David C. Jones	July 1, 1974 - June 20, 1978
Lew Allen, Jr.	July 1, 1978 - June 30, 1982
Charles A. Gabriel	July 1, 1982 - June 30, 1986
Larry D. Welch	July 1, 1986 - June 30, 1990
Michael J. Dugan	July 1, 1990 - September 17, 1990
John M. Loh (acting)	September 18, 1990 - October 29, 1990
Merrill A. McPeak	October 30, 1990 - October 25, 1994
Ronald R. Fogleman	October 26, 1994 -

Chapter 12
Wild Black Yonder

"The Earth from orbit is a delight—alive, inviting, enchanting—offering visual variety and an emotional feeling of belonging 'down there.'"

(Michael Collins, Apollo 11 astronaut)

General Bernard Schriever, Commander, Air Force Systems Command, 1961-66. No officer was more responsible for the creation of the second (land-based ballistic missile) leg of America's strategic triad.

"It is difficult to say what is impossible, for the dream of yesterday is the hope of today and the reality of tomorrow."
(Dr. Robert Goddard, American rocket pioneer)

"Our national space effort represents a great gain in and a great resource of our national strength."
(President John Kennedy)

"Intercontinental air power and missiles are the new double-edged sword of destruction, hanging by a hair over us all."
(Trevor Gardner, Asst. Secretary of the Air Force, 1956)

"We are confident that weapons like the ICBM and IRBM will help the Air Force to enable the free world to maintain deterrent forces which no aggressor in his right mind would dare to challenge."
(Maj. Gen. Bernard Schriever, USAF, 1958)

"'Sputnik' came along in October of 1957 and all hell broke loose!"
(General Bernard Schriever, USAF)

"Several decades from now, the important battles may be . . . space battles, and we should be spending a certain fraction of our national resources to ensure that we do not lag in obtaining space supremacy. The mission is to maintain the peace."
(General Bernard Schriever, USAF)

"They really wanted to send a dog, but they thought that would be too cruel."
(Alan Shepard, before becoming the first American in space, May 1961)

Jovian Thunderbolts, Olympian Views

Tucked away in one corner of the Museum's Air Power Gallery, with the port wing tip of the giant B-36 serving as a partial roof, is the Space Gallery. Entering from the Air Power Gallery end, the visitor leaves behind the familiar wings and engines of atmospheric flight and confronts a world dominated by the intertwining tubes and flaring nozzles of rocket engines. Gondolas, capsules, and space suits combine to create an impression that space can be an inhospitable and uncomfortable place. Judging from an Aerojet Aerobee rocket exhibit near the entrance, some of the earliest space travelers certainly seem to have found it so. A cutaway nose cone shows the less than generous accommodations provided for monkeys Patricia and Mike, and white mice Mildred and Albert, when they were launched into space as part of the preparations for manned space flight. It is encouraging to learn that all four survived the experience apparently none the worse for wear.

Nearby is a display covering balloon ascents made during the 1950s and early '60s. The champion of the high altitude balloons was Capt. Joe Kittinger, who rode in both of the gondolas on show, reaching a height of 82,200 ft in Stargazer and 101,516 ft in Manhigh II. Photographs show that in August 1960 he also rode an open gondola named Excelsior to 102,800 ft and then stepped out of it! His free-fall descent of 84,700 ft lasted more than four and a half minutes, during which he reached Mach 0.93. Slowed by the atmosphere to less than 200 mph before his parachute opened, he reached the ground thirteen minutes and forty-five seconds after leaving the gondola.

The exposed plumbing of various rocket engines can be seen on both sides of the Space Gallery. There is the XLR-99 motor from an X-15, and there are engines from rockets like the Jupiter IRBM and the Titan II ICBM. The story of rocket propulsion—from the experiments of Robert Goddard and the V-2s of Wernher von Braun to the Saturns which launched men to the Moon—adorns the walls. Above hang research satellites designed by Lockheed and Northrop. The X-

Kettering Bugs, built by the Dayton-Wright Company in WWI, the nearest two on detachable trolleys. The Bug was intended to carry a 180 lb warhead for 40 miles at 55 mph. Mission range was determined by the number of propeller revolutions turned. At that point, cams withdrew bolts attaching the wings and the fuselage became a bomb.

24A lifting body is banked over against one wall, near an experimental boost-glide reentry vehicle and a display about the manned orbiting laboratory. Photographs of the USAF's astronauts are mounted above examples of the Mercury and Gemini spacecraft, and a little farther on is the Apollo 15 capsule which in July 1971 carried the USAF crew of Col. David Scott, Lt. Col. James Irwin, and Maj. Alfred Worden to the Moon. A piece of moon rock offers evidence of their visit.

Ranged around Apollo 15 are various exhibits of space impedimenta. Several figures, their visored helmets staring blankly at the visitor, reveal the evolution of the space suit, beginning with one from 1958, which carries more than a hint of an ancestry in medieval armor. There is a space sled intended for expeditions away from the parent craft, and the more practical maneuvering unit finally chosen for use by the astronauts on space walks. Space foods are there to tempt the curious palate. The hardware of space on show is prolific. There are magnetic boots, a space can opener, and a zero-G razor. Items which have bestowed added benefits on the more earthbound population include cordless drills, solar-powered calculators, thermal blankets, Velcro fastenings, computer chips, and compact disks. It is all useful as a reminder that the human adventure in space has already changed the way we live on Earth.

The Cold War was an agent of change,

too, and some of its most powerful implements stand outside the Museum buildings. Slim, metal shapes in gleaming silver and white, some towering skyward, others straining forward on launching ramps, all seemingly eager for release—a sculpture park dedicated to deterrence. Dominating the display are the ballistic missiles, many of them named in recognition of their awesome power—Atlas, Thor, Titan, Jupiter. The names of later weapons chose to emphasize peaceful intent allied with instant readiness—Minuteman I and III.

Joe Kittinger taking the biggest step of his life from more than 102,000 ft above the Earth on August 16, 1960.

Elsewhere, both inside and out, the Museum has a variety of winged missiles, ranging from strategic weapons with intercontinental range to very high speed interceptors. Boeing's CIM-10A Bomarc was the world's first active-homing surface-to-air missile, and it was as fast as it looks, achieving speeds of Mach 3 plus. At the other end of the scale, the Northrop SM-62 Snark was the first U.S. intercontinental nuclear missile. It plugged the gap in the late 1950s and early '60s until ICBMs became available. Tactical cousins of the Snark are two Martin pilotless aircraft, the TM-61A Matador and its successor, the CGM-13B Mace. A U.S. replica of the weapon which inspired the Matador, the German V-1 "Buzzbomb," hangs in the Air Power Gallery.

In the mid-'50s, the future of U.S. strategic striking power appeared to lie with very fast cruise missiles and North American Aviation began development of the Navajo. To prove the concept of cruise missiles and solve some of the problems, several smaller pilotless aircraft designated X-10s were built and flown. The one in the Museum is the only X-10 survivor. Examples of two later cruise missiles bring to mind strong images of their respective operational deployments. The General Dynamics/McDonnell Douglas ground-launched cruise missile (GLCM) became notorious for generating fierce localized opposition when based in Europe, while the Boeing air-launched cruise missile (ALCM), carried by B-52s and B-1s, served as the very essence of deterrence with Strategic Air Command.

The stories which trace mankind's early steps in the exploitation of space and the development of missiles as weapons of war are inextricably interwoven. For both enterprises, rockets, guidance systems, complex avionics, and a host of other particulars had to be perfected. The technology which built deterrence with ICBMs also placed satellites in orbit around the Earth and carried men to the Moon. These dramatic achievements were not born of new ideas. The Chinese are known to have had rockets around 1,200 AD and the Greeks were speculating about peaceful

voyages in space nearly two thousand years ago. In more modern times, it was perhaps inevitable that the first measures in practical rocketry would be initiated with military aims in mind.

The Rockets' Red Glare

American military aviators first showed a serious interest in guided missiles in WWI. Beginning in 1917, experiments were conducted in the U.S. with pilotless aircraft known as Bugs. These efforts were continued only fitfully between the wars, but the whole business became much more serious in June 1944, when the Germans launched the world's first operational strategic guided missile against London. The Fieseler 103 (the *Vergeltungswaffe Eins*, or V-1) was a small pilotless "flying bomb" powered by a pulse jet engine. It was inaccurate and could be caught by the better Allied fighters. Militarily of little consequence, it was politically significant because of the alarm it caused civilian populations. Worse followed in September 1944 in the shape of another German first, the A-4 (V-2) ballistic missile. Although no more accurate than the V-1, the supersonic V-2 rocket was immune from interception and added the psychological impact of a "bolt from the blue" weapon to the destructive force of its one-ton warhead. Answering the cry for the U.S. to match the enemy's technology, the USAAF funded the JB (jet bomb) series of studies. From these came the JB-2, an American copy of the V-1 manufactured by a consortium of automobile companies. Northrop developed a pilotless flying wing, produced as the JB-1/JB-10. None of the JB weapons generated great enthusiasm, however, and the programs did not long survive the war.

By the end of WWII, General Hap Arnold had become convinced that technological and scientific advances, particularly in atomic energy and guided missiles, would revolutionize military doctrine, and he believed that the future of the Air Force depended on how well it adjusted to the new realities. In the immediate postwar period, however, it was generally felt that guided missiles were many years away from

A Northrop SM-62A Snark blasts away from its launching ramp.

becoming practical as weapons, and that there were more pressing problems in need of solution. This attitude, combined with a shortage of funds and endless interservice bickering over the issue of who would do what with which missile, reduced progress in U.S. missile technology to a crawl.

The first practical U.S. intercontinental missile program was Northrop's SM-62A Snark, begun in January 1946. Its progress was not pressed with any urgency, and it did not reach the flight test stage until 1951. The Snark was a pilotless aircraft in the mold of the V-1, but it was a much more powerful and capable weapon. It cruised at high subsonic speeds and had a range of over six thousand miles. Inertial guidance was updated by a star tracker, ensuring reasonable accuracy, and the warhead was multimegaton, which effectively took care of any lingering errors at the receiving end. Even more impressive was the North American Navajo, another winged vehicle. Begun in 1947, the Navajo flew successfully in June 1958. It was an imposing size—nearly 100 ft long and weighing 290,000 lbs when launched. Hurled off its ramp by rocket engines delivering 415,000 lbs of thrust, Navajo climbed to over 60,000 ft before the rockets were jettisoned and ram jets took over to drive it

Two weapons with significant teeth — a Martin Matador and a German Shepherd guard dog tasked with keeping inquisitive intruders at bay.

to Mach 3.25. Impressive though that was, the missile never became operational. By the time it was ready, Navajo (and Snark) had been overtaken by events.

Attempts were made in 1946 to initiate an ICBM program in the U.S. Commissioned from Wright Field, Convair undertook Project MX-774B to develop an ICBM which could carry a 5,000 lb warhead over a distance of five thousand miles to strike within one mile of its target. So soon after WWII, this was a startling requirement, given the one ton for two hundred miles or so of the V-2. Funding soon became a problem, and in July 1947 the project was canceled, programs like Snark and Navajo being given a higher priority because they were expected to reach operational status more quickly. Some Air Force officers were not particularly enthusiastic about missiles, anyway. General Curt LeMay, CinC SAC, was among the skeptics. Until he could be shown that missiles performed reliably and accurately, he believed that they were useful only as "political and psychological weapons," and perhaps as "penetration aids" for his manned bombers.

Handicapped by a lack of urgency and direction in its missile development, the U.S. received a series of wake-up calls in the 1950s. The shocks of the Soviet atomic bomb test of August 1949 and the

Korean War were followed by news in 1953 that the Soviets had detonated a hydrogen bomb and by alarming intelligence reports that they were developing rockets of enormous power. By 1955, the Air Force had a crash program running to produce an ICBM (Atlas), and had appointed the dynamic Brig. Gen. Bernard Schriever to drive it forward.[1] Projects had been added to develop another ICBM (Titan) and an IRBM (Thor). However, the problem of limited funding had returned and the missile programs were already suffering severe cuts when the Soviet Union took the world by surprise again. On October 4, 1957, a small artificial satellite named *Sputnik* was launched into orbit from the Baikonur Cosmodrome in Kazakhstan. The effect of its persistent beeping signals on the U.S. was electrifying.

Soon after WWII, Stalin had approved an ambitious long-term program of rocket development in the Soviet Union with the aim of deploying an ICBM force. By the time *Sputnik* was launched, it was known that the Soviets had successfully fielded several ballistic missiles, and that they posed a distinct threat to NATO forces in Europe. In 1957, it was suspected that

the latest addition to the Soviet arsenal was an immense rocket (later designated SS-6 in the West) with much greater range and lifting power than anything conceived in the U.S. The suspicions proved correct, and it was an SS-6 which was used to place *Sputnik* in orbit. Within a month, another SS-6 had carried a dog named Laika into orbit inside a capsule weighing more than half a ton. The military implications were obvious, and there was much talk in the U.S. about a technological lead having been conceded to the Soviets and of the emergence of a "missile gap." Spending cuts in the U.S. missile programs were deferred and missile development work accelerated.

Alarm over the missile gap subsided relatively quickly as the U.S. programs gathered speed and had largely evaporated by the time of the 1962 Cuban confrontation between the Soviet Union and the U.S. By then, 126 Atlas and 54 Titan I ICBMs had been deployed, and squadrons of both Thor and Jupiter (inherited from the Army) IRBMs were operational in Europe. Also on alert in 1962 were 10 Minuteman Is, the first of the solid propellant rockets which would come to form the backbone of the U.S. land-based nuclear deterrent. In the mid-1960s, the liquid propellant Atlas and Titan I were phased out of service, leaving only 54 of the more powerful Titan IIs in the front line with the Minutemen.[2] By the end of the decade, the Minuteman force had grown to twenty squadrons of 50 missiles each (450 Minuteman IIs/550 Minuteman IIIs), scattered across the plains states and along the northern rim of the U.S.

As ICBMs go, Minuteman in all three of its forms is a small missile, less than 60 ft long and with a launch weight of under 80,000 lbs.[3] Its small size was part of its appeal, as was its relative simplicity, the stability of its solid propellant, and the speed of its reaction time. Most importantly, Minuteman was cheaper to acquire, deploy, and operate than liquid propellant

[1]General Bernard Schriever was a visionary for the USAF in the fields of ballistic missiles and space. In 1957 he appeared on the cover of *Time* as the man who directed the nation's research and development of ballistic missiles, and who was instrumental in providing the launching sites, tracking facilities, and ground support systems. No single officer was more responsible for creating the second leg of America's strategic triad than was Schriever. When Air Force Systems Command was formed in 1961, he was promoted to four-star general and became AFSC commander.

[2]Titan IIs used storable liquid propellants and were more easily handled than the Titan Is.
[3]This compares with 103 ft/330,000 lbs for Titan II, and approximately 121 ft/485,000 lbs for the Soviet SS-18.

missiles. At first, SAC envisaged placing at least some Minutemen on trains, and successful trials were conducted, but agreement on the details of such a mobile version was never reached and deployment was limited to silos. Here, too, Minuteman held a clear advantage over Atlas and Titan, its silos being little more than simple holes in the ground, with no efflux ducts and none of the plumbing associated with liquid propellants. Every Minuteman fired is preceded out of its silo by a distinctive smoke ring, followed soon after by the flame and smoke of the first of its three stages and then by the missile itself, rising unharmed through rolling clouds. In its most potent form, Minuteman is capable of striking targets up to 8,000 miles distant with deadly accuracy, and its destructive power has been varied to include a single warhead in the megaton range (Minuteman II), and three Maneuverable Independently-targeted Reentry Vehicles (MIRVs) of 335 kilotons each (Minuteman III)[4]. Ten of these terrifying weapons are controlled from each two-man command bunker, which is a manpower-to-destructiveness ratio of impressive proportions.

The enormous buildup in strategic striking power represented by the ICBMs was not achieved easily. The development work was at the frontiers of technology, the costs strained defense budgets, and the missile debate between the services was often acrimonious. The USAF saw missiles of all kinds as aerial vehicles which were essentially air power components, and therefore as natural extensions to the responsibilities of the Air Force. The older services did not agree, but the USAF persisted in promoting itself as the principal aerospace agent for the employment of air-breathing aircraft (manned and unmanned), ballistic missiles, spacecraft, and satellites. Once the USAF was assigned responsibility for land-based ICBMs in 1950, and for IRBMs in 1956, this view came in large part to prevail and the USAF was forced to reexamine its role as a major element of national defense. The integration of missiles into the service entailed considerable reorganization and some hard thinking about Air Force doctrine, which

Liquid-fueled Atlas ballistic missiles were rushed into service during the late 1950s to provide an interim deterrent capability while more capable systems were developed. By the mid-'60s, the Atlas was being phased out of the front line, but has since been useful as a launch vehicle for satellites.

now had to expand to include concepts of warfare both within and outside the atmosphere. New bases, new training programs, new career paths, and new logistic problems all added to the turmoil, and everyone had to adjust to the sobering thought that air power had finally matched the apocalyptic notions of the early theorists. Once launched, these ICBMs were bombers which really would "always get through,"[5] and with dreadful effect.

Since the deployment of Minuteman, only one other ICBM has reached operational status with the USAF. In the 1970s, missile guidance in the USSR advanced to the point where the newer Soviet ICBMs could kill hard targets. This made Minuteman increasingly vulnerable,

and a more survivable U.S. system was called for. Work on a new missile (MX) was begun and a number of elaborate schemes devised for making the weapon as invulnerable as possible. Proposals included an underground rail system to keep the MX both hidden and mobile, a "Shell Game" in which three hundred missiles moved about among 8,500 shelters, and "Dense Pack," which put all the missiles in one vast field with the hope that some would survive an onslaught. In the end, none of these was found acceptable, and the MX Peacekeeper was deployed in former Minuteman silos beginning in 1986. Much larger than Minuteman at a launch weight of 195,000 lbs, the Peacekeeper has the capability to carry ten half-megaton MIRVs. In response to the dramatic changes in the world situation, President Bush announced in his 1992 State of the Union address that MX production was

<hr />

[4]In his 1992 State of the Union address, President Bush announced the planned removal of two of the three warheads from each Minuteman III.

[5]"I think it is well for the man in the street to realise that there is no power on earth that can protect him from being bombed. Whatever people may tell him, the bomber will always get through." (Stanley Baldwin, British Prime Minister, 1932).

being halted. Only fifty Peacekeepers reached the front line to become operational with the 90th Strategic Missile Wing at Francis E. Warren AFB in Wyoming.

Gaining Space

The 1957 beepings of *Sputnik* did more than warn the U.S. about a potential missile gap. There were other effects, both positive and negative. On the positive side, the Soviet Union had done the U.S. a favor by unilaterally establishing the concept of "freedom of space." Moscow had not sought permission from the U.S. (or any other nation) for a satellite to pass over non-Soviet territory, but the Eisenhower administration was happy to keep quiet and accept the international precedent. On the other hand, there was something disturbing about having the opposition's hardware passing unhindered over the U.S. at regular intervals, even if it was little more than a simple transmitter. Doubtless more capable vehicles would follow. President Eisenhower was quick to pursue the possibility of placing a U.S. reconnaissance satellite into orbit.

Considerable efforts had been made since the onset of the Cold War to unravel the secrets of military strength and nuclear capability which lay hidden in the vastness of the Soviet Union's interior. Aerial reconnaissance missions around the periphery of the Soviet empire began immediately and yielded useful information about ports and coastal areas, but deeper intelligence could come only from overflights. In early 1956, camera-carrying balloons were launched and allowed to drift across the USSR on the prevailing winds. Over four hundred balloons were released, of which forty were recovered, some snatched in mid-air by specially modified C-119s before they could splash into the Pacific. Over thirteen thousand photographs resulted, but the operation irritated the Soviets and was not very successful in terms of intelligence gained. Since they meandered over endless fields and forests at the whim of the weather, the balloons did little more than add frustration to ignorance.

From July 1956, the U-2 overflights

of the USSR were vastly more successful, but they came to an abrupt end when Gary Powers was shot down near Sverdlovsk in 1960. It was more obvious than ever that the only satisfactory solution to the problem of surveillance of the Soviet Union lay with satellites. It may have been less immediately apparent that competition in the field of satellites was the first stage of a struggle for leadership in space.

Studies into possible uses for satellites were conducted throughout the 1950s, though thinly funded. Weather forecasting, communications, and navigation applications were all considered, but the Soviet threat drove reconnaissance to the top of the priority list. In 1956, the USAF awarded Lockheed a contract (WS-117L) to provide a reconnaissance satellite with cameras which could "detect objects no more than twenty feet on a side." The launch vehicle was to be an Atlas fitted

with a Lockheed Agena upper stage. Lack of an adequate budget ensured that the project would proceed at a sedate pace. *Sputnik* changed all that, agitating the smooth waters of American complacency and sweeping U.S. policy along in its wake. In January 1958, the National Security Council assigned the highest priority to the development of an operational reconnaissance satellite, and by October, President Eisenhower had introduced the National Aeronautics and Space Administration (NASA) to oversee a national space program. An Advanced Research Project Agency (ARPA) was also created, through which the services reported on military space matters.[6]

Within the new framework, the USAF was instructed to drop the WS-117L

---

[6]In early 1958, the President also approved a secret project for a reconnaissance satellite known as CORONA, with management entrusted to a select CIA/USAF team.

A 330,000 lb Titan II stands in its silo at McConnell AFB, Kansas. Since their retirement from service as ICBMs, Titans have retained their importance as launch vehicles for many military space programs.

(Weapon System) designation for its satellite. According to ARPA, the change was intended to "reduce the effectiveness of possible diplomatic protest against peacetime employment." Development continued under the title "Sentry," and later as the Satellite and Missile Observation System (SAMOS). Since SAMOS, designed to take pictures and radio them back to a ground station, could not become operational until the early 1960s, an interim system was called for. This was Eisenhower's Project CORONA, known publicly as "Discoverer," a simple satellite using Thor as the launching booster and intended to return its film to Earth in reentry capsules.

In a sequence of discouraging perversity, the first twelve Discoverers failed—boosters exploded, satellites tumbled out of control, film turned brittle and broke, and reentry (if achieved) occurred at anywhere but the planned time and place. The capsule from *Discoverer 13* was recovered after a successful reentry on August 12, 1960, and six days later *Discoverer 14* delivered the first images of Earth taken from space. From then on the system steadily improved. When SAMOS arrived, it had an almost equally painful birth, as did another satellite known as the Missile Detection and Alarm System (MIDAS). In the light of CORONA's continued success, SAMOS was canceled in 1962. Failures were commonplace, and years were to pass before the word "reliable" could be used with any assurance in connection with satellite operations.

Under the Kennedy administration, the USAF's part in the U.S. space program became more closely defined. Among its principal responsibilities, the Air Force embraced the defense support missions of early warning and space defense. The first of these demanded automated satellites equipped with infrared sensors to spot Soviet missile launches, and the other included the development of satellites which could detect nuclear explosions on Earth or in space. Associated activities involved the launching of satellites and the tracking of them (both friendly and hostile) from ground bases. Then there were other

Minuteman I was the first of the solid propellant ICBMs to go into service, in 1962. Much smaller than its predecessors, Minuteman was more reliable and easier to handle.

established defense support tasks, such as the provision of satellite communication facilities, weather information, and navigation aids.

In the 1970s and '80s, the disappointments and poor performances of earlier years faded to little more than distant memories. Electronic intelligence and photographic reconnaissance were routinely carried out, the latter by such large satellites as those commonly called "Big Bird," combining high-resolution pictures with area coverage. The "Keyhole" camera in Big Bird, which could resolve objects as small as one foot across, returned its film to Earth by capsule, but area images could also be transmitted to ground stations via a twenty-foot dish antenna. Later digital systems do not use film at all. Images are scanned by computers which look for signs of change and the results are then transmitted to the surface by radio. This successful program was brought to the edge

of impotence in 1985-86 by the failure of two Titans in succession, and the loss of the space shuttle as a launch vehicle following the *Challenger* disaster. The U.S. was left with a single reconnaissance satellite in orbit, a precarious situation which lasted for eighteen months. In the event, the USAF chose to order more Titan launchers and abandon the use of the space shuttle for military missions. By the late 1980s, the crisis was over.

For the detection of Soviet missiles, the temperamental MIDAS system was succeeded by the far more capable and reliable Defense Support Program (DSP) satellites. At the heart of the DSP was a large infrared telescope which proved to be remarkably sensitive to the flare of rocket launches, be they ICBMs from land or sea, or much smaller vehicles. Hovering in geosynchronous orbit, DSPs gave instant warning of launch events and provided information from which could be determined the number of missiles, their azimuth and projected impact points. DSP satellites eliminated the possibility of an undetected surprise ICBM attack against the U.S.

The problem of detecting nuclear explosions in the atmosphere was tackled with a series of Project Vela satellites. These were placed in orbits 70,000 miles above the Earth and, replaced at intervals, served successfully from 1963 to 1984. Since then, similar but improved detection devices, known as the Integrated Operational Nuclear Detection system (IONDS), have been carried aloft as passengers in other

netic Pulse (EMP) damage. Another development was the provision of Air Force Satellite Communications System (AFSATCOM) channels on board a number of USN and Satellite Data System (SDS) satellites in both equatorial and polar orbit. This was to ensure efficient transmission of messages between strategic bombers and missile silos on the one hand, and ground and airborne command posts on the other. The even more advanced Milstar satellites followed in the 1990s. Operating in the Extremely High Frequency (EHF) bands, the Milstars were designed to avoid the prolonged radio black

Panama, and Libya, and in the equally challenging missions of SR-71s, U-2s, and space shuttles.

In the early 1970s, the USAF acquired the additional responsibility of leading the development of a space-based navigation system. Known as the Navstar Global Positioning System (GPS), it quickly showed that it was capable of giving positional information to an accuracy of thirty feet or better. Even so, funding was delayed in favor of other items, and GPS satellites were not launched with any urgency. By 1991, only sixteen were in operation, and the originally planned constellation of twenty-four satellites was not in place until 1994.

The construction of a system to track all satellites (and space debris) in orbit was a complex business. It involved combining the efforts of units from the USAF, USN, and Canadian Armed Forces into a network called the Space Detection and Tracking System (SPADATS), operated by North American Aerospace Defense Command (NORAD) at Colorado Springs. The sensors feeding SPADATS were scattered around the world. They included radar from the Aleutians to Turkey, and Baker-Nunn cameras as far apart as New Zealand and Norway. Later, in the 1980s, the system's name was changed from SPADATS to the Space Surveillance Network (SSN), and it was upgraded with the Ground-based Electro-Optical Deep Space System (GEODSS), with sites in New Mexico, Hawaii, South Korea, and Diego Garcia. Other improvements were the passive receivers of the Deep Space Tracking System (DSTS), and a number of upgraded radar, including those of the BMEWS and Pave Paws systems. The result of combining all this data was that NORAD was able to ensure that the growing numbers of objects in Earth orbit were identified and constantly tracked. Among the thousands regularly watched, only about 5 percent are operational satellites. The rest consist of mere spacecraft debris or inactive payloads, enduring orbital monotony while awaiting the merciful release of blazing reentry to the atmosphere.

The main battle staff position in the Combat Operations Center, North American Aerospace Defense Command (NORAD).

vehicles, notably the Navstar satellites.

Following several false starts and changes in policy, the Defense Satellite Communications System (DSCS, or "Discus") appeared in the 1960s. It was intended to provide a military communications network with the capability of handling voice, imagery, digital data, and teletype information. The DSCS I satellites were linked to fixed bases, but the more flexible DSCS II and III series were capable of orbit repositioning and communication with small portable ground stations. DSCS III was also more survivable because of its resistance to Electro-Mag-

out experienced after high-altitude nuclear explosions.

The development of weather satellites was originally entrusted to NASA, but in the early 1960s the USAF designed one to meet specific military needs. Polar orbiting, low altitude Defense Meteorological Satellite Program (DMSP) vehicles gave vital service during the Vietnam War. General Momyer at the time was unstinting in his praise, saying: "This [satellite] weather picture is probably the greatest innovation of the war." Subsequent, even more capable DMSP satellites proved just as important in combat operations like Grenada,

U.S. efforts to exploit space for military purposes came together and paid off handsomely during the Gulf War. This was the first conflict in which information from communications, weather, early warning, navigation, and reconnaissance satellites was regularly employed at all levels of planning and operations. In curious confirmation of an ancient principle of battle, U.S. space systems gained the Coalition forces the "high ground" during the struggle against Iraq. Satellites were invaluable, and their services were often combined to get the job done quickly and effectively. A particularly dramatic demonstration of the immense reach and swiftness of satellites was given in response to the menace of the Iraqi "Scuds." DSP satellites, designed to catch much bigger fish, were equally capable of detecting a Scud lift-off. In Colorado Springs the impact point was determined, and warning messages flashed via communications satellites to the Middle East. Alarms were sounded and Patriot missile batteries alerted before the Scud could complete its seven-minute flight. It was a far cry from the "bolt-from-the-blue" experience of Londoners under V-2 attack in 1944.

Although the complete Navstar constellation was not in place in 1991, and there were times during each day when GPS information was limited in the Gulf area, the navigational advantages of the system were wonderfully apparent. Coalition aircraft were guided accurately to their targets day and night in all weathers, and artillery fire was directed with invariable precision. Special forces roamed deep behind enemy lines, confident that they knew their position exactly. When the Coalition ground forces finally advanced, they did so secure in the knowledge that units on either side of them were navigating along planned routes and that there was little chance of conflict, even though they were all moving through flat, featureless terrain in the dark. The weather satellites, too, proved their worth repeatedly. The Gulf region suffered the worst recorded weather in fourteen years during DESERT STORM, and the DSMPs eased the problems of target selection and prevented the launching of many sorties which would

have been aborted or recalled. When DESERT STORM was over, Lt. Gen. Donald Cromer, Commander of Space Division, said that the operation would be seen as "a watershed for recognizing that space is as much a part of the Air Force and the military infrastructure as airplanes, tanks, and ships. All future wars will be planned and executed with that in mind."

Air Force Astronauts

In the early 1950s, it was apparent that manned space flight was only a matter of time. To the USAF, it was only reasonable to assume that when it came it would do so as a logical extension of Air

The Ballistic Missile Early Warning System (BMEWS) station at Clear, Alaska.

Force activity, following an unbroken line of progression from the Wright Flyer to the stars. While the U.S. Army took an interest in the German V-2 and busied itself with large rockets, the USAF held to more traditional forms which could be flown by pilots and operated like conventional aircraft, at least within the atmosphere. The X-15 was a step along that road and was the first aircraft to break through the arbitrary frontier of space fifty miles up. In doing so, it earned astronauts' wings for many of its pilots, including the USAF's Bob White, Bob Rushworth, Joe Engle, and Pete Knight.

The X-15, however, was not a spacecraft. In 1958, the USAF moved closer to the goal of flying its own space-plane when Boeing was commissioned for "Dyna-Soar," a program later designated X-20. As expressed by the USAF, the X-20 project was intended to produce an aircraft capable of performing space-based reconnaissance and bombing missions. Political discomfort with the idea of offensive weapons in space and competition for funds with NASA's programs eventually doomed the X-20. Much to the chagrin of the USAF, Secretary of Defense McNamara announced its cancellation in December 1963, just as the first aircraft was nearing completion.

The blow of the X-20's cancellation was somewhat softened by the allocation of the Manned Orbiting Laboratory (MOL) program to the USAF. The intention was to deploy small orbiting space stations which could be serviced by using Gemini space capsules produced for the USAF by extending the existing McDonnell production line. After a great deal of effort had been expended on the project, however, the MOL followed the X-20 into the graveyard of promising ideas. It was canceled by Defense Secretary Melvin Laird in June 1969, when U.S.

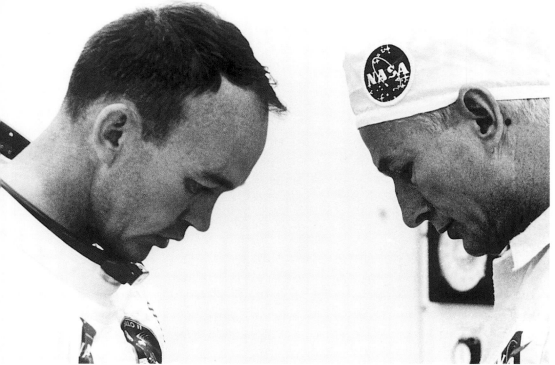

Michael Collins (left), the Command Module Pilot for Apollo 11, *the first Moon landing mission, is helped into his pressure suit.*

priorities were being set by the Vietnam War and, in space, by NASA's drive to land men on the Moon. The official reasons given for terminating the MOL were the need to trim the defense budget and the improving reliability of unmanned vehicles. The USAF's dream of creating a separate Air Force manned space program died with the MOL's demise.

While suffering through the failures of its X-20 and MOL projects, the USAF had necessarily become involved in NASA's space capsule program. President Eisenhower was satisfied that the plans for

manned space flight should remain under civilian control, but he directed that potential astronauts should be drawn from the existing ranks of military test pilots. In 1959, the seven men chosen to endure the rigors of riding in the cramped confines of Mercury space capsules were announced. There were three USAF captains (Deke Slayton, Virgil Grissom, and Gordon Cooper), three USN lieutenant commanders (Walter Schirra, Alan Shepard, and Scott Carpenter), and a USMC lieutenant colonel (John Glenn). On May 5, 1961, Shepard became the first American in

space, just three weeks after Yuri Gagarin had been successful for the Soviet Union. Grissom went next, like Shepard, fired down range into the Atlantic in a suborbital shot, and Glenn made the first Earth orbit for the U.S. in his Mercury capsule *Friendship 7* on February 20, 1962. In the last of the six manned Mercury missions, the USAF's Gordon Cooper spent over thirty-four hours in space and then gave the lie to insinuations that the astronauts were mere passengers in the capsules. An electrical failure forced Cooper to control the reentry manually, which he did with precision, bringing the capsule to a splashdown in the Pacific only four miles ahead of the recovery ship.

As the U.S. space program developed into the Gemini and Apollo series, more astronauts were selected, nine in 1962 and fourteen more in 1963. From 1963 on, the requirement that candidates should be test pilots was dropped, but most of those successful were still military personnel. USAF pilots were involved in many of the most memorable events, both intrepid and tragic, during the rush to honor President Kennedy's pledge to land a man on the Moon before the end of the 1960s. In June 1964, Ed White climbed out of *Gemini IV* to become the first American to "walk" in space. The world's first space rendezvous was achieved in December 1965, with Tom Stafford and Frank Borman as members of the crews of *Gemini VI* and *Gemini VII*. In a sharp reminder that the technology of spaceflight was far from perfect, a fire on board an Apollo spacecraft at the Kennedy Space Center in January 1967 killed all three astronauts, including Virgil Grissom and Ed White. Frank Borman and William Anders were aboard *Apollo 8* for the first manned orbit of the Moon in December 1968, and Mike Collins and Buzz Aldrin were teamed with Neil Armstrong for the climactic *Apollo 11* mission which put the first man on the Moon in July 1969.

The Moon landings continued until *Apollo 17* in December 1972. With the exception of the near disaster of *Apollo 13*, the complex and hazardous enterprise was

The Apollo 15 *mission, with an all-USAF crew, landed the Lunar Module* Falcon *on the Moon on July 30, 1971. Next to* Falcon *is the Moon's first car, a Lunar Rover which was driven some 17 miles at speeds up to 8 mph.*

Apollo 15's *crew after their safe return to Earth — David Scott (Commander, saluting), Alfred Worden (Command Module Pilot), and James Irwin (Lunar Module Pilot).*

brought to an almost flawless conclusion. Astronauts spent longer on the Moon's surface with each landing, conducting experiments and collecting rock samples. The *Apollo 15* crew was all USAF—David Scott, James Irwin, and Alfred Worden. The lunar module *Falcon* moved away from the relatively safe flat areas previously used and touched down in the more rugged Hadley-Apennine region of the Moon in July 1971, after which Scott and Irwin spent a total of more than nineteen hours outside on the Moon's surface, deploying an Apollo Lunar Surface Experiments Package (ALSEP) and accumulating nearly 169 lbs of rocks. Scott also had the privilege of becoming the first to drive a four-wheeled vehicle, the electric-powered Lunar Rover, on the Moon. The California Institute of Technology subsequently paid tribute to *Apollo 15* as "one of the most brilliant missions in space science ever flown."

Later Apollo contributions to the space program involved the "Skylab" missions and, in 1975, the remarkable Apollo-Soyuz Test Project (ASTP) cooperative venture with the Soviet Union. Commander for the ASTP mission was Tom Stafford and, at last, a place was found for Deke Slayton, the only one of the original seven Mercury astronauts not to fly. Grounded in the early 1960s because of a suspected heart condition, Slayton had been medi-

cally reinstated and, at forty-eight, was the oldest man to have been selected for spaceflight. It was noticeable, however, that experience counted for more than youth on missions like the ASTP. All five members of the U.S. and Soviet crews were more than forty years old. With the successful joining of American and Soviet hands in space in July 1975, the U.S. entered a "long winter" of absence from space. Americans did not leave the Earth's atmosphere again until April 1981.

The Space Shuttle was planned to do much more than take up where previous space programs left off. It was conceived as being sufficiently flexible to undertake an almost limitless variety of space operations and thereby to serve as a universal (and reusable) replacement for all that had gone before. Although the Shuttle was a NASA program, the USAF helped fund the effort and therefore had an influence on the design of the spacecraft, taking account of the fact that military operations in space would be dependent on its capabilities. While it was still on the drawing board, it was confidently predicted that the Shuttle would perform like a space age DC-3, a workhorse running regular missions to and from space and handling its multifarious tasks as routine. In the event, it was not like that. There were the inevitable unforeseen problems and delays,

and a backlog of missions soon accumulated. The first Shuttle did not get into space until April 1981, and thereafter the four Shuttle fleet, consistently unable to meet its scheduled launch rate, concentrated on research and development projects. Once started, NASA had planned for one hundred launches up to the end of 1985, but only twenty-three actually took place.

As was the case for the Mercury, Gemini, and Apollo programs, USAF personnel were regularly involved as Shuttle crew members, and it was originally intended that up to a third of the Shuttle's missions would be devoted to military tasks. In 1983, with such slow progress being made, the USAF sensibly renewed its interest in expendable boosters, which were under threat of being phased out. By early 1985, the Titan 34D (later Titan IV) had been selected as the system to back up the Shuttle. That year, the first military Shuttle missions were successfully flown, and several more were planned for 1986. Then, in January 1986, just as things appeared to be going well, they were stopped dead by the *Challenger* disaster, in which seven astronauts were killed in an explosion shortly after lift-off from the Kennedy Space Center. Two Titan failures and the loss of a Delta booster during the same period effectively grounded the whole U.S. space program for many months.

Although the Titan and Delta losses suggested there were problems to solve, it had become obvious that relying solely on the Shuttle for military space missions was unwise and the idea of using expendable launch vehicles returned to favor. Several post-*Challenger* military Shuttle flights were undertaken to help in making up ground lost while the program was in abeyance, but the emphasis for the future had shifted to unmanned launches. The seventh military mission after the Shuttle returned to space in September 1988 was flown in December 1992. It was the ninth and last military Shuttle mission overall and its successful conclusion marked the end of the USAF's direct involvement with manned space flight.

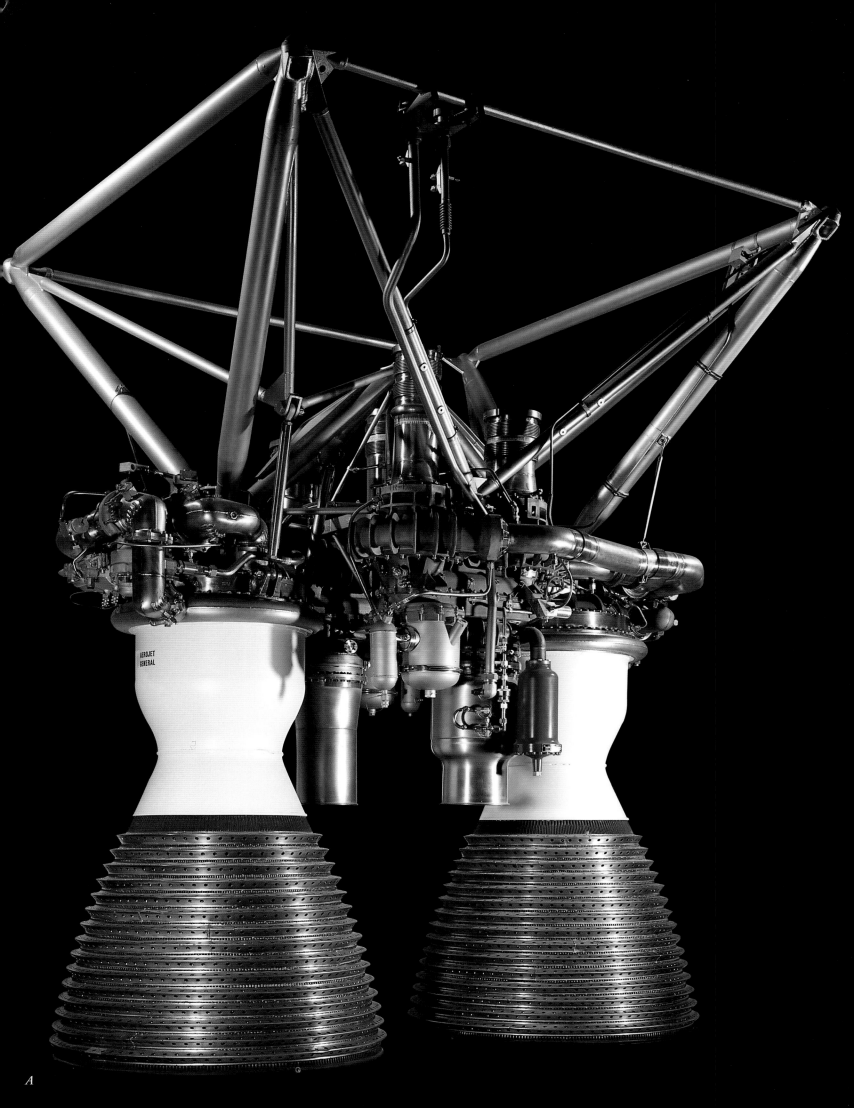

A

A Given the job it has to do, the Aerojet General LR-87 rocket engine which provides first stage power for the Titan II ICBM and launch vehicle is surprisingly small. Burning liquid propellants, the twin nozzles of the LR-87 project a massive 430,000 lbs of thrust to hurl the Titan clear of Earth's atmosphere. They are gimbal mounted to control the trajectory of the Titan during the boost phase of flight.

B The front entrance to the USAF Museum framed by Missile Row.

C Visitors to the USAF Museum must pass along Missile Row on their way to the main entrance. Seen here are Minuteman III, Minuteman I, Jupiter, and Titan I.

415

A   Minuteman launch control centers are sunk approximately 50 ft underground. The blast-resistant, shock-mounted capsules are manned by two officers who usually are responsible for controlling ten Minuteman launch sites. On display at the USAF Museum is a Minuteman launch control center training facility. Note that the two officers are seated at consoles placed well apart from each other. Since two keys must be used to launch a missile and they must be turned almost simultaneously, it is not possible for one man to initiate a launch.

B   Matador (left) and Bomarc, two early U.S. winged missiles, silhouetted against the skyline outside the USAF Museum. Matador was the first U.S. "unmanned bomber," and Bomarc was a pilotless interceptor. A time capsule buried near the foot of the sunlit flagpole is due to be opened in the year 2076.

Chapter 13

Air Power

"We were allowed by the national command authorities to conduct the war the way the war was supposed to be conducted."

(Col. Tom Lennon, F-111F, 48th TFW)

Lt. Gen. Charles A. Horner, Commander, Central Air Forces, during the Gulf War, 1990-91.

"The fireball from my kill was incredible. It completely lit up the sky and I could see the [Iraqi Air Force Mirage] break up or explode into millions of pieces. . . . There was AAA everywhere, SAMs were being shot. . . bombs were dropping, and the Wild Weasels were shooting their HARMS at all the SAM sites. Needless to say, it was very stressful."

(Capt. Steve Tate, F-15C, 1st TFW, January 17, 1991)

"Air technology has finally caught up to air theory."

(Lt. Gen. Charles Horner, USAF, Joint Force Air Component Commander, DESERT STORM)

"You cannot lose a war with air supremacy, and you cannot win one without it."

(Carl Vinson, Chairman of the House Committee on the Armed Services)

"By God, we've licked the Vietnam syndrome once and for all."

(President George Bush on the conclusion of DESERT STORM)

"The military has the best and brightest people it has ever had, the highest quality equipment, and the best training. The dollars spent in the 1980s made all this possible. For the future, we need to fund the right tools for the next century."

(Lt. Gen. Charles Horner, USAF, Joint Force Air Component Commander, DESERT STORM)

Smart and Stealthy Hardware

Having followed the story of American air power from its earliest days through to the end of the 1980s, visitors to the USAF Museum at Dayton now near the end of their journey. From this point on, most of the aircraft to be featured among the stars of the Museum's galleries in the twenty-first century are better seen still doing their jobs in operational squadrons or performing at air displays. F-15Es, B-2s, KC-10s, C-5s, C-17s, C-141s and their like will be serving in the front line for many years to come and are unlikely to grace Dayton's halls in the near future. However, representatives of the dramatic events of 1990-91 in and around the Persian Gulf are to be seen at Dayton. There are two, both prominent in the combat arena of DESERT STORM.

The F-111F version of the swing-wing Aardvark thoroughly deserves its place in aviation's hall of fame. Among the least publicized of the Gulf War's performers, it was perhaps the most successful in terms of sorties flown and ordnance delivered on target. The type was showing its age as the twenty-first century approached but, in the 1990s, it could still be argued that it had a claim to being the best all-around attack aircraft in the world.

More obviously fascinating and with much greater star quality in the public eye is the startling Lockheed F-117A Nighthawk, generally referred to as the "stealth fighter." As the visitor enters the Museum's Modern Flight hangar, its magnetic personality demands attention. It stands slightly off to the left, in front of the monstrous B-52 but not at all overawed by the looming shape of the "Buff." For an aircraft designed to escape detection, it assumes astonishing prominence as an exhibit. Its multifaceted blackness absorbs the visitors' gazes and compels their presence. Wonder and astonishment are not inappropriate reactions to its menacing weirdness. Questions hover in the air around it— "Is that a real warplane?"; "Does it really fly?"; "Can it actually make itself invisible?" Iraqis who experienced the Nighthawk's capabilities firsthand in 1991 might have little difficulty in answering all three questions in the affirmative.

As the Iraqi troops discovered, the GAU-8 Avenger multi-barrel cannon is a mighty instrument of destruction. The gun fills the lower forward fuselage of the A-10, with the rear of the ammunition drum reaching nearly 21 ft back from the muzzle. A GAU-8 fully loaded with 1,350 rounds of 30 mm ammunition weighs nearly two tons.

As might be expected, the F-117A on display is not a combat aircraft. It is the second of the type built and was used exclusively for testing. Nevertheless, its angular otherworldly appearance is genuine enough, and it really did fly.

Another little-known aspect of the DESERT STORM epic appears in a corner of the Modern Flight hangar in the display covering the activities of the Aerospace Rescue and Recovery Service. In telling of a desert rescue, it offers a glimpse of the often harsh realities of war. Lt. Devon Jones of the U.S. Navy, an F-14 pilot, was shot down deep inside Iraq in January 1991. He has every reason to be grateful for the determined professionalism of the USAF's rescue teams, who saved him from capture by plucking him from the desert in the face of his enemies. Visitors will be rewarded if they spend a few moments to read the story of the Aerospace Rescue and Recovery Service, a vital but largely unsung element of the USAF.

The Cold War was over and there was much to celebrate, but, as the USAF entered the 1990s, it was made uncomfortably aware that postwar fruits often bear the seeds of other problems. With the principal adversary no longer able to take the field, the solid template against which the USAF's force structure had been designed and shaped over many years faded to insubstantial shadow. Consequently it became less simple to define the Air Force's role for the post-Cold War era. Given the previous experiences of politically limited war in Korea and Vietnam, predictions of possible future employment in trouble spots around the world were not encouraging. However, the USAF was equipped to meet any global challenge, and, in 1990, it was ready when the world witnessed blatant aggression on the shores of the Persian Gulf. Saddam Hussein of Iraq launched an invasion of Kuwait, thereby setting the scene for a limited conflict in which air power advocates would see their cherished convictions amply vindicated.

DESERT SHIELD

Early in the morning of August 2, 1990, the Iraqi Army burst across the frontier with Kuwait in considerable strength. More than 100,000 troops and several hundred tanks brushed aside such little resistance as they encountered and within hours the tiny Gulf emirate was firmly in Saddam's grasp. The world's fourth largest army now stood on Saudi Arabia's doorstep, and Saddam Hussein appeared poised to become the man dominating Middle East oil.

Reverberations from Iraq's action shook the world's economic foundations and international reaction was immediate. The U.N. Security Council condemned the invasion and President George Bush ordered U.S. Navy units into the region. By August 6, the U.N. had authorized worldwide economic sanctions against Iraq, and President Bush had announced the movement of U.S. Army and Air Force units to the Middle East in Operation DESERT SHIELD. Initially, the aim of the U.S. forces was to defend Saudi Arabia against the further ambitions of Saddam Hussein. Communications and surveillance satellites were maneuvered into positions from which they could better support any U.S. operations, and Military Airlift Command got ready to undertake the largest airlift in history.

On August 7, within eighteen hours of the President's order, MAC's C-141s and C-5s had begun the deployment of the 82nd Airborne Division's "Ready Brigade" and the supporting elements of the 1st TFW's F-15 squadrons. The forty-eight F-15Cs of the wing were on their way, too, flying nonstop from Langley AFB, Virginia, to Dhahran, Saudi Arabia, refueling seven or eight times during a flight averaging some fourteen to fifteen hours. In welcome confirmation of allied solidarity, the U.K. deployed RAF Tornados on the following day. By the middle of the month, other USAF squadrons of F-15C/Es, F-4G Wild Weasels, A-10s, and F-16s had joined these trailblazers in Saudi Arabia, and E-3 AWACS aircraft had begun a continuous patrol over the troubled area. On August 21, twenty-two F-117 Nighthawk stealth aircraft took off from their base in Nevada to exchange the desert surroundings of one continent for those of another. While all this was happening, USAFE F-111s and F-16s arrived at bases in Turkey, and SAC deployed its U-2R/TR-1A reconnaissance assets and moved B-52s forward to Diego Garcia in the Indian Ocean.

In terms of scale, rate, or distance, the U.S. military buildup in Saudi Arabia was impressive. The air bridge was particularly remarkable. Once established, it spanned nearly half the globe and saw a cargo aircraft landing somewhere in the Middle East every ten minutes or less. By the end of the campaign, the USAF's strategic airlift had recorded 20,500 missions (a mission being a completed movement from origin to destination, regardless of intermediate stops), carried 534,000 passengers, and hauled 542,000 tons of cargo. The airlift totaled 4.65 billion ton/miles, which compared to just under 700 million for the sixty-five weeks of the Berlin Airlift in 1948.

From the USAF's point of view, the operation was a timely vindication of the case for maintaining a truly balanced air force, capable of accomplishing tasks across the whole wide spectrum of air power and of responding swiftly to an emergency anywhere in the world. The projection of global power could not have been done without the fleet of large capacity cargo and tanker aircraft in the USAF's inventory, nor without the ready availability of well-trained Reserve and National Guard personnel to fill gaps in the front line. Given Iraq's considerable forces and their aggressive intent, good reconnaissance was essential too, and, on the assumption that Saddam was not going to back down and withdraw from Kuwait, aircraft were needed for every combat role, from air superiority through conventional bombing to tank-busting. Behind this aerial armada there had to be the supporting services which enabled it to fight—command and control facilities, maintenance, armaments, food, accommodation, medical services, administration, etc. During the months following the President's launching order, the personnel and equipment to make such a force function were uprooted from their U.S. bases, transported many thousands of miles to work in unfamiliar (and often basic) surroundings, and asked to create an air force which was instantly combat ready and capable of defeating any opposition it met. That all this was done, and done superlatively well, is a tribute to the professionalism which had been achieved in the USAF during the 1980s.

After August, the momentum in the Gulf changed hands. From posing an offensive threat to Saudi Arabia, the Iraqis had become more concerned with the defense of their ill-gotten gains. By mid-January 1991, they were well dug in, but the coalition of forces opposing them had built up to the point where an assault to recover Kuwait could be undertaken with confidence. The U.N. call for troops had been answered by twenty-two nations, and the U.S. contingent had risen to more than 400,000. The overall commander of the Coalition forces was Gen. Norman Schwarzkopf, U.S. Army, although all Arab

Stretched C-141s were vital elements of the strategic airlift during DESERT SHIELD/STORM, 265 of them flying the routes between the U.S. and the Persian Gulf region.

The whole of the USAF's C-5A fleet was committed to the DESERT SHIELD/STORM strategic airlift. On their own, the Galaxies exceeded the achievements of the entire 1948 Berlin Airlift in the first three weeks.

national forces remained under the operational control of the Saudi Chief of Staff, Prince Khalid. Deputy to Schwarzkopf, and theater air forces commander, was Lt. Gen. Charles Horner, USAF. From the beginning, it was apparent that the mistakes of Vietnam were not going to be repeated. There would be no micro-managing from Washington. The President, the Secretary of Defense and the Chairman of the Joint Chiefs of Staff would decide policies and set goals, but the planning and execution of operations would be left to the discretion of the theater commander.

On November 29, 1990, a U.N. resolution was adopted which approved the use of "all necessary means" to remove Iraqi forces from Kuwait if they did not leave voluntarily by January 15, 1991. Saddam remained recalcitrant. He would not leave what he now called his nineteenth province, and he assured the Coalition that he would order the use of chemical weapons in repulsing any attack on his forces. On January 12, with the U.N.'s deadline approaching and Iraq's leaders still unmoved

by universal condemnation of their aggression, the U.S. Congress gave President Bush the authority to go to war. In the desert, nearly one million soldiers and airmen faced each other and prepared themselves for what Saddam had promised would be the "mother of all battles." The Coalition's generals had every reason to believe that he was right, and that the recovery of Kuwait was not going to be an easy matter. The Iraqi forces had spent five months preparing a defensive line in Kuwait which included bunkers, berms, minefields, masses of razor wire, and oil-filled ditches ready for burning. Gen. Tony McPeak, USAF Chief of Staff, described Iraq's protection against air attack as "a first class air defense, not a featherweight opponent." It was indeed formidable, with advanced aircraft like the MiG-29 among those equipping the Iraqi Air Force's thirty-nine fighter squadrons, and ground defenses which included some 9,000 AAA guns and perhaps 17,000 SAMs, all backed by modern radars and computer data links.

If Saddam Hussein had hoped for an early commitment of ground forces in an assault on his fortress, he was disappointed. The first blows, and most of those which followed, were struck from the air. By mid-January 1991, the 690 combat aircraft of the Iraqi Air Force were outmatched in both quality and quantity by those of the Coalition air forces. Ten countries had contributed units to raise the front line strength of the Coalition in the Gulf region to almost 2,500 fixed-wing aircraft. Of these, the USAF provided 50 percent, the USN 16 percent, the USMC 7 percent, and allied air forces 27 percent. The air plan of campaign was split into four phases. In Phase 1, Coalition airmen were to gain air superiority over Iraq and Kuwait, destroy Iraqi strategic attack capability, and disrupt the enemy command and control system. Phase 2 would suppress the air defenses around Kuwait, and Phase 3 would see the weight of attack shifted to the Iraqi Army deployed around Kuwait, while continuing to pursue the objectives of Phases 1 and 2 as necessary. Phase 4 was concerned with air support for ground operations as and when they took place.

F-15Cs dominated the skies over Iraq during DESERT STORM. USAF Eagles shot down 31 of the 35 Iraqi aircraft destroyed in aerial combat.

As it happened, the air strength available to the Coalition commanders was such that it was possible to run the first three phases concurrently.

DESERT STORM

To Iraqi early warning radar operators, the returns they saw on their screens during the early morning hours of January 17 at first looked no different from those they had grown used to seeing for months. AWACS aircraft and F-15 combat patrols were orbiting just inside Saudi Arabian airspace as usual. But this would not be just another quiet night for Iraq. What the operators could not see were hundreds of aircraft forming into strike packages outside the range of their early warning cover. Nor did they realize that their units were at the top of the Coalition target list. The first shots of the DESERT STORM campaign were fired at two radar sites by a special team of U.S. Army AH-64 Apache helicopters, led into position by MH-53J Pave Low helicopters of the USAF. Hellfire laser-guided missiles and 2.75 in rockets from the Apaches destroyed the sites, punching a hole in the Iraqi air defense screen through which the initial waves of strike aircraft could flow unseen.

At about 1:00 A.M. local time, as the Apaches were making their way to their targets, tankers from the USAF, USN, and RAF got airborne to establish their refueling stations. Combat air patrols were strengthened with more F-15s, USN F-14s, Canadian CF-18s, and RAF Tornado F-3s. Strike aircraft began taking off from bases in Saudi Arabia and Turkey, and from aircraft carriers in the Persian Gulf and the Red Sea. At 3:00 A.M., all hell broke loose over Iraq. From the ships in the Gulf came the first of a barrage of Tomahawk missiles, which led the attack on Saddam Hussein's capital of Baghdad. Seven B-52Gs reached the climax of a thirty-five hour mission from Barksdale AFB, Louisiana, the longest bombing raid ever, launching AGM-86C ALCMs at power stations and communications facilities. Confusing the issue for the defenders in the early stages of the attack were almost

two hundred pilotless decoys. These drew the attention of antiaircraft radars, which thereby exposed themselves to the HARMs (High-speed Anti-Radiation Missiles) of predatory Wild Weasels.

At about the time that the Apaches were turning away from reducing their targets to rubble, the F-117A Nighthawks made their surreptitious entrance, first attacking radars close to Baghdad and then a communications center in the city itself. Before the night was out, the Nighthawks had hit thirty-four targets, using a variety of laser-guided bombs with dramatic effect. The F-117A's low observable technology (commonly called "stealth") allowed it

The surreal shape of modern air warfare was unveiled in Iraq when F-117A Nighthawks led the attack on command and control facilities in Baghdad. Making the most of their stealthy design and smart weapons, the F-117As struck with impunity and with great precision.

to operate in Iraqi airspace at night with impunity. It was used to attack high-value targets, especially those in heavily defended areas where it might be necessary to orbit while identifying the aiming point because precision was vital. Command centers, control bunkers, chemical/nuclear facilities, critical bridges, and the like were almost invariably struck with startling accuracy. The contribution of the F-117As on the first night of DESERT STORM was remarkable. Flying only 2.5 percent of the Coalition's sorties in the first twenty-four hours, they took on over 30 percent of the

targets and achieved hit rates of better than 80 percent.

As the follow-up raids approached their targets, it was apparent that Iraq's defensive system was crumbling from the effects of the earlier strikes. F-111s, F-15Es, F/A-18s, and RAF and Saudi Tornados went after air bases, Scud missile sites, and more radars. They were supported by EF-111 Ravens, jamming whatever electronic emissions survived the onslaught. One EF-111 scored a defensive victory after dodging a missile fired by an Iraqi Mirage. The Raven's tight diving turn behind a screen of chaff and infrared decoys finished just above the desert, but the chasing Mirage did not pull out. As the EF-111's crew reported: "We got so low, he couldn't hack it and smeared into the ground behind us." It was the first Iraqi aircraft destroyed during DESERT STORM air combat.

The first conventional air-to-air kill was achieved by an F-15C pilot, Captain Steve Tate of the 1st TFW. Alerted by AWACS to the presence of a "bogey" approaching his flight, Tate confirmed it as "not friendly" and fired an AIM-7 Sparrow at twelve miles range. The weapon struck an Iraqi Mirage, which disappeared in a huge fireball. It was a rare encounter.

Not many Iraqi Air Force aircraft got airborne and contacts with those which did were few and far between. For their part, the ground-based defenders fired copious quantities of AAA and SAMs, but got little return for their efforts. Over 670 sorties were flown by Coalition aircraft that first night, without loss.[1]

By midnight on the first day, Coalition aircraft had flown over 2,100 sorties and the Iraqi air defenses were severely degraded. During the hours of daylight, the Coalition had suffered its first losses—an F/A-18 and an A-6E of the USN, a Kuwaiti A-4, and three Tornados, one Ital-

by one of the victorious F-15C pilots, Capt. Charles Magill, a Marine exchange officer flying with the 33rd TFW: "When you get down to the bottom line, everything was incredibly basic. Weapons system set up just right, shoot your ordnance at the first opportune moment, watch the MiG blow up, and get the hell out."

Unable to withstand the Coalition's aerial onslaught, Iraq hit back in the only way guaranteed to cause international alarm. After dark on January 17, a Scud ballistic missile was fired at the Dhahran air base, but was claimed destroyed by a U.S. Army Patriot SAM before reaching

Coalition would break up, since the Arab allies would not wish to be seen fighting on the same side as their traditional enemy. Intense U.S. political pressure and the rapid deployment of Patriot batteries to Israel defused the crisis, and Israelis gritted their teeth to suffer in silence through a barrage of forty Scuds in the course of the conflict. Forty-six more Scuds were fired at Saudi Arabia, one of which demolished a U.S. barracks, killing twenty-eight Army reservists.

The political danger from the Scuds was such that considerable effort was devoted to finding and destroying them, diverting Coalition strike aircraft from other tasks and effectively forcing the extension of the planned period of DESERT STORM air operations from thirty to thirty-nine days. Fixed Scud sites were quickly dealt with, but mobile launchers were more difficult. The "Great Scud Hunt" began on the night of January 18. The principal USAF hunters were F-15Es of the 4th TFW from Seymour Johnson AFB, North Carolina. They flew in pairs at about 15,000 ft, generally with the leader carrying four GBU-10 laser-guided bombs and the wingman armed with six CBU-87 cluster bombs. Sweeping ahead with their LANTIRN night vision equipment, they searched for signs of mobile Scud missile launchers, attacking in sequence when a site was found.

Another significant weapon against the Scuds was Boeing's E-8A Joint STARS, two prototypes of which were rushed to the Gulf to boost the Coalition's surveillance effort. Still involved in the development stage of the J-STARS battlefield control system, the E-8As were a great success. Their huge side-looking radars could detect stationary armored vehicles and provide an accurate plot of slow-moving objects. Besides being much in demand as a controlling agency for tactical aircraft generally, the E-8As were particularly valuable in locating mobile Scuds for the roving F-15Es.

Up to January 26, the Coalition's air offensive was principally concerned with ensuring air supremacy and with the destruction of Iraq's command and control

The EF-111A Sparkvark, an extremely sophisticated electronic warfare aircraft, was a vital factor in the DESERT STORM air war, using its powerful avionics to jam and confuse Iraqi defenses.

ian and two British. Since the Iraqi Air Force had flown only twenty-four fighter sorties, it was not surprising that none of the Coalition losses came in air-to-air combat. The Iraqis, however, lost eight fighters, five of them to the F-15Cs of the 33rd TFW from Eglin AFB, Florida. The almost clinically impersonal nature of late twentieth century air warfare was summarized

the ground. Soon afterwards, however, several more Scuds were fired at Tel Aviv and Haifa in Israel, causing casualties and some local damage. Militarily, the Scud was of little consequence. With its small warhead, limited range, and lack of accuracy, it was a minimal threat to the Coalition's operations. Even used with chemical warheads, it could not have affected the outcome of the struggle. However, fired at noncombatant Israel, the ineffective Scud became a political instrument of disturbing power. If Israel could be provoked into striking back, it was Saddam's hope that the fragile

[1]Initially, the Iraqis claimed considerable success, reporting that over 100 Coalition aircraft had been shot down. It transpired that their claims might not have been entirely imaginary. Over 100 decoys went down in or around Baghdad and might have either fallen or been shot down. It was not the first time that small aircraft falling to earth in the middle of an intense antiaircraft barrage had been claimed by the defenses. The same thing happened during the first night of the German V-1 attack on London in 1944. It was not initially understood by the gunners that the V-1 was accomplishing its mission if it fell to earth.

system, with the Scud hunt as an unlooked for complication. Some USAF strikes against Iraqi troop concentrations had been made in the early stages with A-10s and B-52s, but after January 26 these were stepped up, with other attack aircraft joining in. F-16s and A-10s were the most numerous types deployed to the Gulf, some 200 of each seeing combat, and they were heavily employed against Iraqi troops and vehicles. In close encounters, the A-10s used their awesome 30 mm cannon to fearsome effect. One pair of "Warthog" pilots from the 23d TFW claimed twenty-three tanks between them in one day, and two others, from the 10th TFW and the 926th TFG, AFRes, destroyed enemy helicopters, claiming the first ever air-to-air successes for the A-10.

Initially, the B-52s missions were flown from the island airfield of Diego Garcia in the Indian Ocean, but other bases in the U.K., Spain and Saudi Arabia came into use during the conflict. All of the bombers were B-52Gs, carrying loads of fifty-one 750 lb bombs. These were used in saturation bombing of soft targets, paying particular attention to the Republican Guard troop concentrations in the desert west of Basra. Flying in flights of three, they achieved coordinated releases of 153 bombs at a time, carpeting an area one and a half miles long by a mile wide. Apart from the damage done by such a weight of explosive, it had a marked psychological effect on troops. The morale of many Iraqi units was shattered by the B-52 attacks, which were probably instrumental in persuading large numbers of soldiers to surrender as soon as the Coalition ground offensive was launched.

As well as carrying out direct attacks on Iraqi Army units, Coalition aircraft turned their attention to military storage areas and to the interdiction of supply routes, aiming to weaken the enemy's fighting capability before the ground offensive. This did not mean that earlier targets were left untouched. Raids were still made deep into Iraq, searching out command and control centers and ensuring that the comatose air defense system did not get a chance to rise again. Many of the surviv-

ing elements of the Iraqi Air Force were fleeing to safe havens in Iran, but the occasional contact was still made with enemy fighters in the air. On January 27, two F-15Cs of the 36th TFW from Bitburg AB, Germany, were vectored towards an enemy formation by a patrolling AWACS. In the hectic seconds after making contact and closing to firing range, the USAF pilots launched a rapid combination of AIM-7s and AIM-9s to shoot down three MiG-23s and one Mirage F-1.

On the night of January 27, the USAF struck an important blow for environmental causes. The Iraqis had seriously damaged Kuwait's oil fields, and were deliberately allowing two pumping stations to spill large quantities of oil into the Persian Gulf. Three F-111Fs of the 48th TFW, RAF Lakenheath, U.K., made a precision attack on the pumping stations involved. The weapons used were GBU-15 laser-guided bombs, tossed from two of the F-111Fs flying supersonic at 20,000 ft. The third Aardvark, tracking parallel with the coast some 50 miles out to sea, guided the bombs onto their targets. Direct hits were scored on both stations and the flow of oil

stopped. Success in such a newsworthy effort offered a rare moment of recognition to the crews of the F-111Fs. Dogged by their sometimes checkered past and overtaken in the public eye by younger and more glamorous types, the Aardvarks in the Gulf quietly went about compiling the most impressive record of any strike aircraft in the war. By the time it was over, F-111Fs had been everywhere and attacked everything. They flew some 2,500 combat sorties and provided video-tape confirmation that they had destroyed 2,203 targets, including at least 920 tanks, 252 artillery pieces, 245 hardened aircraft shelters, thirteen runways, and twelve bridges (with

Boeing E-3 Sentry AWACS aircraft were involved in the 1990-91 Persian Gulf confrontation with Iraq from the beginning. Their all-seeing eyes closely monitored Iraqi activity during DESERT SHIELD, then maintained a continuous picture of the battle zone throughout DESERT STORM, warning and controlling Coalition aircraft as necessary.

another fifty-two seriously damaged). Of the more than 8,000 precision guided munitions dropped by USAF aircraft, no fewer than 4,660 were entrusted to F-111Fs.[2] As if to confirm their status, the Aardvarks finished the war in style, winning a fly-off with the F-15Es for the distinction of delivering the special GBU-28/B "Deep Throat" bomb, a weapon capable of penetrating over 100 ft of earth or 22 ft

[2]It was reported that one senior U.S. commander said during a raid briefing: "I want this target hit — give it to the F-111s."

of reinforced concrete. On the last night of the war, two F-111Fs guided their new bombs into the hardened high command bunkers north of Baghdad, sending a message to Iraq's leaders that they were at personal risk even deep below ground.

As the days of February passed by and the Coalition kept up its relentless aerial assault on the structure of Iraq's military machine, the aircraft which formed the backbone of the USAF's front line flew combat sorties by the thousand, and some of the more specialized types got the chance to demonstrate their true value. Among them were a number of variants of the ubiquitous C-130. The EC-130H Compass Call added the final touches to the campaign to close the Iraqis' eyes and ears. With their batteries of communications jammers and their computerized frequency scanning ability, Compass Call aircraft swamped the airwaves throughout Iraq, rendering reliable radio communication almost impossible for the enemy. First cousins to the EC-130H are the EC-130E PsyWar aircraft flown by the Pennsylvania Air National Guard. They have the ability to transmit over both commercial and military radio and television frequencies, and during DESERT SHIELD/STORM they blanketed the Iraqis with broadcasts intended to demoralize both troops and civilians, simply by telling the truth about what was happening. Like the B-52s, their missions made an impact, and they also were credited with convincing large numbers of the enemy to surrender.

"Hail Mary"

With the Iraqi Air Force reduced to impotence, and the enemy incapable of monitoring Coalition activities, General Schwarzkopf was able to set the desert stage for the final act of the Gulf War drama, secure in the knowledge that Saddam's forces were blind and deaf to his preparations. While maintaining a strong presence in front of Kuwait and trailing the coat of the U.S. Marines assault ships as a distraction offshore, Schwarzkopf moved a huge force of U.S., British, and French armored units westward into the desert, setting up a monstrous left hook to outflank the Iraqi

The combat record of the F-111s from the 48th TFW at Lakenheath was among the most impressive of any in the Gulf War. Aardvarks delivered over half of the precision guided weapons aimed at Iraqi targets.

Army and cut across its escape routes. As this was happening, the Coalition air forces continued to pound away at targets of all kinds, although attacks on enemy airfields were intensified for a while to insure against the possibility that the Iraqi Air Force might make one desperate concerted effort to respond to a ground offensive with chemical weapons.

At 4:00 A.M. on the morning of February 24, 1991, strong Coalition ground forces, backed up by overwhelming air support, thrust forward from their holding positions into Kuwait and southern Iraq. It was the largest combined offensive since WWII, involving as it did more than half a million troops. The frontal assault on Kuwait engaged the attention of the bulk of the Iraqi Army while the Coalition's armored columns raced across the desert far to the west. A-10s, helicopter gunships, and Marine AV-8B Harriers really came into their own, playing havoc with the enemy's armor, and in the west the inestimable value of plentiful tactical airlift was emphasized. The wettest weather for many years had turned extensive areas of the desert into a morass, and the army's supply convoys often got bogged down. C-130s, which had been heavily occupied already in moving troops and equipment to forward staging areas, now air-dropped tons of supplies to the rapidly moving spearheads, enabling them to maintain the

momentum of their advance deep into enemy territory.

Their defensive plans unhinged by the crushing weight of the air campaign and by the speed and power of Schwarzkopf's armored left hook, most Iraqi troops either withdrew from their positions in confusion or surrendered in thousands. Those few who chose to stand and resist were comprehensively outgunned and outfought. Flushed from their carefully prepared bunkers and revetments, Iraqis attempting to scramble out of the battle area and escape were harried unmercifully by the Coalition's ever-present close air support. The road from Kuwait to Basra became a river of death and destruction, with the wreckage of hundreds of vehicles of all kinds scattered along it and in the desert nearby. By February 27, Coalition ground forces had advanced to place themselves across the escape routes from Kuwait and the Iraqi Army's resistance had effectively ceased. President Bush declared a cease-fire starting from 8:00 A.M. Baghdad time on February 28, exactly one hundred hours after the ground assault began.

The Air Power Achievement

The Gulf War had lasted six weeks, all but four days of which was taken up by an air offensive against Iraq which was unrelenting in its severity. The Coalition air forces had flown 110,000 sorties, with the USAF claiming the lion's share. Losses had been remarkably light, totaling only thirty-five fixed-wing aircraft, fifteen of which came from the USAF. All were attributable to ground fire.[3] The Iraqi Air Force also lost thirty-five fixed wing aircraft during combat sorties, but all of them were shot down in air-to-air engagements, thirty-one of them by F-15s of the USAF. Many more Iraqi aircraft were destroyed on the ground by air attack, and well over 100 others fled to the dubious haven of Iran.

DESERT STORM was a crushing military victory, built on the often spectacular achievements of Coalition air power. From the speed of the initial response to Saddam's aggression and the creation of an air bridge thousands of miles long, to the imposition of air supremacy over Iraq and the effective destruction of the Iraqi Army as a fighting force, the Coalition's air forces demonstrated that air power *properly used* is a dominating factor in any major clash of arms. The USAF shouldered by far the greatest burden of any of the air forces involved in the Gulf War, and saw its dedication to advanced

technologies justified in the performance of its newest and most complex systems. Teamed with AWACS, the untried J-STARS provided unprecedented airborne battle control capabilities. The F-117As, F-15Es and EF-111As proved to be both effective and, to the surprise of some, extremely reliable, with serviceability rates approaching, and occasionally exceeding, an average of 90 percent. Precision guided munitions revolutionized the air campaign. Less than 8 percent of the 88,500 tons of bombs dropped were "smart," but they accounted for almost 80 percent of the targets known to have been destroyed by bombing. The Navstar Global Positioning System (GPS) and the Low Altitude Navigation and Targeting Infrared for Night (LANTIRN) equipment were prominent among those which enabled USAF attack aircraft to maintain a round-the-clock, all-weather campaign against Iraq with astonishing (and, for their enemies, disturbing) accuracy.

None of this would have led to the remarkable results achieved if the available air power had not been properly used. The USAF's post-Vietnam insistence on recruiting the right people and giving them the

best possible training paid off handsomely. In DESERT STORM, the USAF's personnel were notable for their professionalism. Perhaps just as significant was the political decision which, more than any other, exorcised the ghosts of Vietnam—once it was determined that it was necessary to commit the military to action in the Gulf, the conduct of the campaign was left to the theater commander. He, in turn, had the advantage of dealing with a single air commander, who was able to use his air assets to the best possible effect. For once, it all came together for the airmen, who grasped their advantage and laid the foundations of a great victory. Wherever he is, Billy Mitchell must have been smiling.

---

[3]Two F-15Es, one F-4G, five F-16Cs, five A-10s, one EF-111A, one AC-130H. A total of twenty aircrew killed, fourteen of them in the AC-130H. Non-combat fixed-wing USAF accidents during the period of DESERT STORM claimed a B-52G and two F-16Cs.

MH-53J Pave Low helicopters led the Gulf War's first strike, guiding Army Apaches to two vital radar sites in the Iraqi defensive screen.

A

A   The word "conventional" does not apply to the Lockheed F-117A Nighthawk. Even its "F" designation is surprising, since it is in no sense what is generally understood as a fighter. Seen from directly in front, the many-faceted exterior of this arrowhead shaped aircraft is readily apparent, made so to reflect inquisitive radar signals at a variety of angles. The few raised edges are jagged for the same reason. To make the enemy's problems even more difficult, much of the F-117A's surface is manufactured from radar-absorbent materials. The intakes for the two GE F404 engines (10,800 lbs thrust; no afterburner) are on either side of the nose, on the upper surface, and each is covered by a grill with strips which are closer together than the opposition's radar wavelengths. Directly in front of the cockpit, a fine mesh covers a forward-looking infrared sensor. The USAF Museum's F-117A is the second one built. It was specially modified as a test aircraft and was retired when the program was completed in 1991.

B   GBU-12 Paveway II 500 lb bombs were used to great effect by various U.S. attack aircraft against Iraqi targets during DESERT STORM.

C   High-explosive bombs have been vastly increased in effectiveness by fitting the Paveway series of laser-guidance units to their noses. Internal bays keep the F-117A's "smart bombs" hidden away until just before release. During the Gulf War the Nighthawks used the GBU-27 (a modified form of the third generation GBU-24, called Paveway III) as the guidance system for their bombs with considerable success. Note the jagged radar-dispersing edges on the weapons bay and nosewheel doors.

B

C

A

A Commonly called the Warthog, Fairchild Republic's A-10A was more formally named Thunderbolt II. It was specifically designed as an in-fighter, a highly maneuverable aircraft which could give effective close support to troops. Besides the crushing power of the mighty multi-barrel GAU-8 cannon, the A-10 has the capacity to carry up to 16,000 lbs of all kinds of ordnance on eight hard points under the wings and three more under the fuselage. (Note that the nosewheel is offset to make room for the gun on the aircraft center line.) Heavy armor, multiple aircraft systems, and widely separated engines set high above the fuselage increase the A-10's probability of survival when exposed to intense ground fire. The A-10 displayed at the USAF Museum was flown by Capt. Paul Johnson during Operation DESERT STORM. For his performance during an eight-hour rescue support mission, Johnson was awarded the Air Force Cross.

B The inside of a bathtub is not usually like this. The A-10 cockpit sits within a protective titanium bathtub shield capable of withstanding a 23 mm shell. The windscreen is bulletproof glass, and the pilot sits on a "zero-zero" Douglas ejection seat — one which could eject a pilot safely with the aircraft stationary on the ground. The trigger on the stick fires the GAU-8 cannon and releases 30 mm depleted uranium rounds at a rate of up to 4,200 per minute, the heaviest weight of fire ever from an aircraft gun.

C The business end of the GAU-8 rotary cannon.

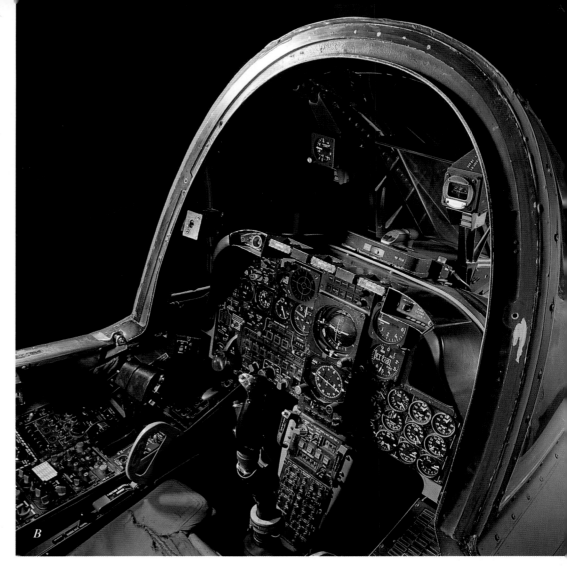

A

B

A   The "F" model was the most potent all-weather attack version of the General Dynamics F-111, commonly known as the Aardvark. In 1967, the F-111 was the first variable geometry combat aircraft to enter service. The wing sweep (here fully swept) could vary between 16 and 72 degrees, reducing the span from 63 to 32 feet. The snout of the F-111F covers nav/attack and terrain following radars, and the most common combat load included ECM and Pave Tack laser designation pods, plus four 2,000 lb LGBs.

B   The main wheels of the F-111 retracted into the fuselage and were covered by a single door which could be extended as an airbrake in flight. The "F" model was powered by two 25,100 lb thrust P&W TF30 turbofans, a considerable improvement over previous variants. Full-span slats and flaps adorned the wings; the all-flying tail surfaces moved symmetrically or differentially to provide both elevator and aileron functions.

C   In the F-111 the crew stayed together whatever happened. Emergency escape was via a McDonnell Douglas "zero-zero" module fired from the aircraft by a 40,000 lb thrust rocket. A parachute lowered the module to the ground with the crew still strapped in their seats. Airbags cushioned the impact and acted as flotation gear in water. (The module's rocket could be fired underwater, too.) The module was also a survival shelter.

D   The F-111F at the USAF Museum was the first fixed-wing combat aircraft to penetrate the opposition's airspace both in Libya and Iraq. Then an aircraft of the 48th TFW at Lakenheath, England, it now carries the markings of the 27th FW, Cannon AFB, New Mexico, the unit with which it flew until the end of its career.

C

D

A   Lockheed's C-130 Hercules is one of the most adaptable and durable aircraft ever designed. First flown in 1954, it has served in many roles — transport, freighter, maritime patrol, mine-layer, ECM, command and control, special operations, weather reconnaissance, search and rescue, tanker, capsule recovery, and airborne hospital. On display at the USAF Museum is the prototype AC-130A gunship which operated in SE Asia during 1967 to test the system. From front to rear, on the left side of the fuselage, AC-130As carried AN/ASQ-5 "Black Crow" vehicle ignition sensor, AN/ASQ-24A stabilized tracking set, two M-61 six-barrel 20 mm cannon, AN/AAD-4 FLIR, two 7.62 mm machine guns, two 40 mm Bofors guns, AN/APQ-133 beacon tracking radar, and an AN/AVQ-17 searchlight.

B   Azrael, Angel of Death is the USAF Museum's AC-130A.

C   Above are the square-ended blades of the Hamilton Standard propellers on the port engines. Four 4,050 ehp Allison T56 turboprops gave the C-130A a range of almost 2,000 miles with an eighteen-ton payload. At shorter ranges, the AC-130A could spend many hours on call over the battle area. The 40 mm muzzles reach out under the wing.

Chapter 14

21st Century Air Force

"The air ocean and its endless outer space extension are one and indivisible, and should be controlled by a single homogeneous force."

(Alexander P. de Seversky)

United States Air Force Academy cadets on parade at the Colorado Springs campus.

"Our real problem is not our strength today; it is rather the vital necessity of action today to ensure our strength tomorrow."
(President Dwight D. Eisenhower)

"Don't hit at all if it is honorably possible to avoid hitting, but never hit soft."
(President Theodore Roosevelt)

"If a nation values anything more than freedom, it will lose that freedom; and the irony of it is that if it is comfort or money that it values more, it will lose that, too."
(Somerset Maugham)

"Forces that cannot win will not deter."
(General Nathan Twining, USAF)

"Air power has become predominant, both as a deterrent to war, and—in the eventuality of war—as the devastating force to destroy an enemy's potential and fatally undermine his will to wage war."
(General Omar Bradley, U.S. Army)

433

In 1991, the USAF was on the crest of a wave, carried along by a surge of euphoria in the wake of a Gulf War victory solidly built on the achievements of air power. After such a crushing demonstration of professionalism and effectiveness, it might have been thought best to leave well alone. It was widely held that a service which had performed so efficiently and served the national interest so capably must

As might be expected in such a long-serving aircraft, the B-52 carries elements of old and new technologies. Video displays sit alongside instruments from an earlier generation. Some grandfathers of today's B-52 pilots would find that the cockpit was recognizable and that the throttle levers felt familiar under their hands.

surely have reached a state approaching perfection in its personnel, organization, equipment and training. However justified that view may have been, it was overrid-

den by a number of other, more pressing realities, in response to which the USAF was already being committed to a process of fundamental change even as the Gulf

Old and new work together even in the B-52's bomb bay. The conventional bomb racks would not be out of place in a WWII B-17, but the rotary mechanism is provided for more modern weaponry, such as ALCMs.

B-52 navigators of earlier generations would not find it so easy as pilots to roll back the clock. While the airframe has remained much the same over the years, the avionics have been constantly updated, and so have navigational techniques.

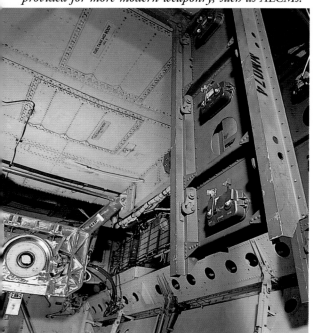

War was being fought.

Faced with the need to rethink national defense policy in the aftermath of the Cold War, and with having to tackle the problem of recurring budget deficits, the U.S. government chose to cut defense spending and reduce the size of the armed forces to levels not seen since the brief period of massive demobilization following WWII. Before the Berlin Wall came down, the USAF's uniformed personnel strength approached 600,000 and there was a total active inventory of more than 6,700 aircraft. As it prepared to celebrate its fiftieth anniversary as an independent service in 1997, those figures were down to below 400,000 and fewer than 4,700. At an early stage of the shrinking process, it was recognized by the Air Force leadership that, if the operational ability of the USAF was not to be seriously impaired, such a rapid reduction of one third in size could not be accomplished without considerable force restructuring and redeployment. Commitments in various parts of the world might continue to arise, but the costly option of manning and maintaining numerous overseas bases was no longer feasible. Although a few major facilities, for instance in Europe and Korea, would remain outside the U.S., the leaner USAF would have to feature the idea of composite task forces—multirole packages able to deploy quickly from home bases to wherever they were needed in an emergency.

Before the alarms and diversions of the Kuwait crisis, Secretary of the Air Force Donald Rice was already engrossed in tackling the challenge of shaping the USAF to operate within a diminishing budget in a world of great instability and only one superpower. In 1990, he issued a paper entitled "Global Reach—Global Power," which broke out of the mental straitjacket imposed by the words "strategic" and "tactical," and concentrated attention on some key attributes of air power—speed, range, flexibility, precision, and lethality. "Global Reach—Global Power" emphasized the extraordinary capabilities of a force which was equipped with state-of-the-art jet aircraft, precision weapons, massive air refueling and airlift capacity, and space-based information, communications, and navigation systems, and suggested that these technological developments had revolutionized the ability of the U.S. to influence world events and to project military power when necessary.

Not everyone agreed with the views of "Global Reach—Global Power." There were those who argued that the USAF's expensive systems could no longer be afforded, and there were even questions about whether a separate air force was needed at all in the post-Cold War world. Lengthy debate on the subject was overtaken by events when Iraqi troops invaded Kuwait. In a dramatic demonstration of what a modern air force could accomplish, the USAF silenced the doubters and confirmed its long-term future while assuring victory in the Gulf War. In mid-1991, taking account of the lessons learned, USAF leaders resisted the temptation to rest on their laurels, accepted the inevitability of change, and began to build an Air Force for the twenty-first century.

The most traumatic restructuring measure undertaken was the merging of the long-established Strategic and Tactical Air Commands. Since the USAF's birth, the service had been characterized by the contrasting identities of its combat arms. At its most basic level, this resolved itself into a simple rivalry between "bomber" and "fighter" pilots, but it had gone deeper than that. In Curt LeMay's time, SAC had grown into an almost independent service, an air force within the Air Force, and the "strategic" mission dominated USAF policy and doctrine. Then, and in later years when "tactical" concerns became more ascendant, the USAF was not the "single homogeneous force" promoted by air power theorists. Its various arms cooperated, but they did not always share common points of view nor accept each others' priorities. The 1992 merger of the "tactical" and "strategic" worlds under one roof at what had been TAC HQ therefore came as something of a shock to traditionalists.

Air Combat Command

The new Air Combat Command (ACC), established at Langley AFB, Virginia, absorbed the assets of TAC and SAC and became the headquarters of by far the largest USAF organization. Problems of scale were eased somewhat by recognizing that SAC's tanker aircraft should be classed as support aircraft and therefore moved to the second new command, Air Mobility Command (AMC), which replaced the old MAC. Later, ACC was further reduced by allocating responsibility for ICBMs to Air Force Space Command (AFSPC). In its final form, ACC comprises four numbered air forces (1st ANG, 8th, 9th, and 12th) and a direct reporting unit (the Air Warfare Center). Between them, they are primarily concerned with combat aircraft, ranging through the inventory from B-2s to F-16s. It is ACC's task to train its units in peacetime so that they are fully prepared for combat, but in an actual emergency ACC assets would normally be transferred as required to the Commander-in-Chief of the forces selected to tackle the problem.[1]

Although the threat from a mono-

---

[1] Just as in Desert Storm the USAF's combat came under General Schwarzkopf's command.

Seen from head on, the smooth blending of the Rockwell B-1B's wings and small cross-section fuselage contrasts with the boxy engine pods, which appear to have been added almost as an afterthought. Nevertheless, the radar cross section of the B-1B is a fraction of the B-52's, and the four General Electric afterburning turbofans can together produce the very respectable total of 120,000 lbs of thrust, enough to give the 400-ton Lancer a low-level penetration speed in excess of 600 mph.

The surreal sawtooth boomerang shape of the stealthy Northrop B-2 Spirit embodies a host of sophisticated technologies, notably those intended to minimize the possibility of detection by an enemy. Engine intakes and exhausts are hidden on the wing's top surface, masking infrared emissions. The flying wing planform also deceives the eye. The B-2 is larger than it looks — 172 ft across the wing and weighing up to 400,000 lbs at takeoff.

of-intercept radar, and a GPS-Aided Targeting System (GATS). At takeoff, the B-2 might weigh up to 400,000 lbs, and its armament could include a wide variety of nuclear or conventional weapons. The GPS Aided Munition (GAM), used in combination with GATS, gives the B-2 the ability to strike multiple targets on a single pass. Adding flight-refueling to its already considerable range, the bomber has a global reach. The extraordinary capabilities of the B-2 are managed by a crew of only two, who sit side-by-side in a cockpit smoothly blended into the wing's center section. If any aircraft, by its appearance alone, can be said to epitomize the USAF for the twenty-first century, it is surely the B-2. The enormous cost of the futuristic bomber necessarily limits the number acquired for front-line service, but, in terms of precise destructive capacity per unit, the B-2's power is unprecedented.

lithic Soviet Union has faded into history, nuclear arsenals remain which pose a threat to the U.S. ACC's heavy bombers therefore retain their nuclear strike capability as one leg of the U.S. strategic triad. However, the new command is a more flexible force than its predecessors, better able to respond easily and rapidly to threats and contingencies at all levels and in any region of the world. Composite wings have been created, "mini-air forces" equipped with several aircraft types, together comprising a self-sufficient rapid deployment force with a mix of the combat tools which might be needed to contain burgeoning emergencies or defeat an aggressor. Alternatively, the Air Expeditionary Force concept has been gaining favor. AEFs have put together and deployed on several occasions to the Middle East since the Gulf War.

At the level of nuclear deterrence, the long-established strategic role of ACC's heavy bombers remains unchanged. Delivery of nuclear weapons would be achieved either by penetrating enemy defenses or by standing off to fire air-launched cruise missiles (ALCMs). The venerable B-52 is still extremely valuable in the latter role, carrying up to twenty ALCMs for launching as much as 1,500 miles from the target. Penetration is bet-

ter performed by B-1B Lancers, now the backbone of the bomber fleet, and the relatively small force of B-2A Spirits.

Northrop's B-2 is a unique "flying wing" advanced technology aircraft, employing stealth techniques in its construction and powered by four nonafterburning turbofans. Included in its sophisticated design are digital flight controls, a new electronic warfare system, a low-probability-

Although the B-2 is capable of carrying as many as eighty 500 lb high-explosive bombs, it is difficult to imagine so valuable an asset being risked on a "tactical" mission. If used with conventional weapons, the B-2's remarkable precision and destructive powers would surely be aimed at gaining strategic objectives. As became apparent both in Vietnam and the Gulf, however, the formerly simple sepa-

More than thirty years after it first flew, the astonishing SR-71 remains the fastest, highest flying manned reconnaissance vehicle in existence. Originally retired because of their demanding maintenance requirements and high operating costs, three were brought out of storage in the mid-1990s and restored to the front line.

ration of aircraft into "strategic" and "tactical" roles, more or less arbitrarily by size, is no longer appropriate. B-52s were used "tactically" against Iraqi troop concentrations, for example, while the "fighters" took on "strategic" targets, like national command centers. This blurring of the distinctions between roles will continue, with weapons systems being allocated to tasks for which they are most suited, depending on the circumstances.

The bulk of ACC's front line consists of aircraft which impressed themselves on the public consciousness during the Gulf War. Their designs are no longer new, but they are far from being outdated. The newest of them, the F-117A Nighthawk, first flew in 1981, while the oldest, the B-52, dates in its earliest form from the mid-'50s. Even so, in the mid-'90s, all of them are either preeminent or among the best in the world for their particular roles. As strike/attack aircraft, the F-117A and the F-15E Strike Eagle are equipped to deliver precision-guided munitions in any weather, day or night, and to operate in dense threat environments.

The "stealthy" F-117A is nearly impossible to detect on radar and the F-15E retains the superior air-to-air combat capabilities of its breed once its external load is dropped. Indeed, the F-15E may be the twentieth century's ultimate all-around combat aircraft. Equipped with the APG-70 synthetic aperture radar and a full all weather/night fit, including infrared sensors and terrain-following radar, the Strike Eagle can attack targets with over 24,000 lbs of assorted ordnance, including Maverick missiles, CBUs, and both "dumb" and "smart" bombs. While doing so it retains the ability to destroy enemy aircraft beyond visual range with its AIM-120 missiles or in closer combat with either AIM-9M missiles or a six-barrel 20 mm cannon. Given its proven capacity to accept new systems and new weapons, the F-15E will remain ACC's premier strike/attack aircraft well into the twenty-first century.

As the first decade of the twenty-first century reaches its midpoint, the F-15's primacy will be challenged as a new generation of combat aircraft begin making

The U-2R of the 1990s is a much larger and more capable aircraft than the original Lockheed Dragon Lady of the 1950s. Intelligence gathering systems can include synthetic aperture radar, a SIGINT suite, infrared sensors, optical cameras, and PLSS (Precision Location Strike System). The detachable nose cone of the U-2R helps to make it a most adaptable vehicle, allowing variously equipped alternative cones to be fitted when a reconnaissance role change becomes necessary.

Upgrades for the MH-53J Pave Low helicopter improve its already impressive capabilities, blending the information gained from on-board systems (FLIR, terrain-following radar, GPS, INS, secure communications, comprehensive ECM, etc.) with graphically displayed over-the-horizon intelligence. The MH-53J and MC-130P partnership gives the USAF a formidable capability for rescue and special operations.

their appearance. The Lockheed Martin F-22 will be able to penetrate enemy airspace and engage multiple aircraft targets simultaneously at long range and before being detected. It will take advantage of stealth technology and will be highly maneuverable when either subsonic or supersonic. Two Pratt & Whitney engines, rated at 35,000 lbs thrust each in afterburner, will have vectored thrust to allow maneuvering at high angles of attack. All that thrust will not be needed for supersonic flight, however, and a cruising speed of Mach 1.5 will be achievable without afterburner. The

F-22's superb aerodynamics will be backed up by avionics systems of astonishing capability feeding information to the pilot via a head-up display and six flat multi-function cockpit display panels. Very High Speed Integrated Circuits (VHSIC) and fiber optics data transmission will be used, and a voice command facility will be included. The F-22 is not a small aircraft, weighing as it does up to 60,000 lbs at takeoff, a reflection of a twin-engined design which provides weapons storage and ample fuel internally. Already planned to have the capability to handle a wide range

Sikorsky M/HH-60G Pave Hawk helicopters are used by the USAF for special operations and combat search and rescue duties.

The clown's nose on this Hercules identifies it as an MC-130H Combat Talon II variant, developed for use with special forces. The enlarged radome contains a multimode radar which enhances low-level navigation and provides terrain following and avoidance.

Bearing its post-Gulf War Air Mobility Command label on its visor, a C-5 Galaxy gapes to swallow another outsize load.

of both air-to-air and air-to-ground weapons, the F-22 will also have the capacity for development as a multirole aircraft, adding in time strategic strike, interdiction, reconnaissance, and defense suppression to its air supremacy function.

Although not quite as capable as the F-15, the smaller and cheaper F-16 has proved itself to be an extremely adaptable multirole fighter and its all-around cost-effectiveness has made it the most numerous aircraft in ACC's front line. It will retain that distinction for many years to come. Specialized variants include the F-16 ADF (Air Defense Fighter), the F-16CG (LANTIRN capable), and the F-16CJ with the HARM Targeting System (HTS) for air defense suppression missions. Some squadrons are already using F-16C/Ds modified for the close air support and air defense suppression roles. A-10 Warthogs soldier on, giving way gradually to F-16s over the battlefield, but still with contributions to make in OA-10 form as elements of air rescue teams and as the mounts of FACs.

The defensive responsibilities of ACC are met by the First Air Force, which is an administrative command possessing no aircraft of its own. All U.S. air defense commitments for the foreseeable future will be entrusted to F-15/F-16 squadrons of the Air National Guard, which is required to train its crews in peacetime for their combat roles. In the event of an air threat developing to the U.S., ACC becomes the gaining command for ANG's air defense assets.

ACC's other aircraft include the unmatched EF-111 for electronic warfare, HH-60 Pave Hawk helicopters, and an assortment of C-135 variants used for command and control duties, range instrumentation, intelligence gathering, and weather reconnaissance. E-3B/C Sentries and E-8 J-STARS bring their all-seeing eyes to the battlefield, and the E-4B NAOC (National Airborne Operations Center) is always ready to serve the U.S. leadership should the threat of nuclear war become real. In peace or war, ACC's strategic reconnaissance aircraft are engaged in actual operations daily. RC-135s and U-2Rs keep watch on the world's trouble spots, helped out by three of the incomparable SR-71 Blackbirds, brought out of premature retirement in 1995 to give the USAF back its capability for wide-area reconnaissance at speeds above Mach 3.

Air Mobility Command

In the 1992 reshaping of the USAF, Military Airlift Command (MAC) rearranged more than its initial letters when it became Air Mobility Command (AMC). The headquarters remains at Scott AFB, Illinois, but units and equipment have been reshuffled. AMC controls two numbered air forces, as did MAC—the 15th (a SAC number) and 21st, the 22nd having gone to the Air Force Reserve. Losses of assault transports to ACC in 1992 were more than offset by the acquisition of the tanker force, and, in any event, in 1996 it was decided that the transports should be returned.

The newest aircraft in the AMC fleet is the McDonnell Douglas C-17 Globemaster III, which was declared operational in 1995 and is destined to be at the core of USAF airlifting for decades to come. Designed to provide both inter- and intratheater lifting capacity for all classes of military cargo, the C-17 owns a hold roomy enough to carry as much as four times the maximum payload of a Hercules and to handle loads too awkwardly bulky even for its strategic partner, the gigantic C-5A. Primarily intended to replace the most aged of the C-141 fleet in the long-range strategic airlift role, the C-17 is nevertheless, like the C-130, able to operate tactically from small, austere airfields.[2] The normal crew is three, two on the flight deck plus a loadmaster, and they operate the aircraft with the benefit of state-of-the-art systems, ranging from the first fly-by-wire controls and head-up displays seen in a military transport to powered equipment which greatly simplifies the problem of handling large cargo items.

Air Force Materiel Command

Recombining functions which were

Air Combat Command C-130Es lined up and ready to go on a paradropping exercise. The long-serving Hercules, in its multifarious variants, is set to continue serving as the USAF's premier tactical transport well into the 21st century.

separated in the 1950s, Air Force Materiel Command (AFMC) was formed in 1992 from the merger of Air Force Systems Command and Air Force Logistics Command. AFMC's responsibilities can be summed up as developing, testing, acquiring, delivering, and sustaining the USAF's weapons systems and equipment. From its headquarters at Wright-Patterson AFB, AFMC oversees the work of a network of four major product centers, four superlaboratories, three test centers, five air logistics centers, and five specialized centers. Among them, these units employ more than 100,000 military and civilian personnel, and they are concerned with obtaining and managing equipment used in every aspect of Air Force life, from B-2s to kitchen sinks.

Air Force Space Command

In 1993, as a follow-up to the major reorganizations of 1992, Air Force Space Command (AFSPC), Peterson AFB, Colorado, acquired the ballistic missile force from ACC, so adding operational responsibility for nuclear weapons (530 Minuteman IIIs and fifty Peacekeepers) to the command's other, wide-ranging duties in the fields of radars and satellites. The Command splits its responsibilities between two numbered air forces, the 14th and 20th. In an era of increasing world turbulence, the value of Space Command's daily work cannot be overstated. Since the breakup

of the Soviet Union, the importance of the nuclear deterrent may have become less starkly obvious, but maintaining the credibility of the ultimate deterrent as an element of national policy is just as vital as it ever was. As was demonstrated during the Gulf War, the specialized field of Command, Control, Communications, and Intelligence (C3I) is hardly less significant. Mastery of C3I is an essential part of combat readiness today and is likely to be more so tomorrow, accentuating the crucial nature of the role to be played by AFSPC and its satellites in the years ahead.

Air Force Special Operations Command

Air Force Special Operations Command (AFSOC), Hurlburt Field, Florida, was formed in 1990 from the forces of 23rd Air Force in MAC. It serves as the Air Force component of the U.S. Special Operations Command, working in the fields of unconventional warfare, clandestine operations, and counterterrorism with a unique collection of aircraft, including exotically equipped C-130 variants and heavily armed helicopters of great sophistication. Besides its units in the U.S., AFSOC controls special operations groups based in the U.K. and Japan. In a crisis, AFSOC is the gaining command for additional EC/AC-130As from the Air National Guard and Air Force Reserve.

---

[2]A C-17, operating with a payload of 44,000 lbs, close to the maximum for a C-130, has taken off and landed in less than 1,400 ft.

Air Education and Training Command

In the restructuring of 1992, Air Training Command was given both ACC's crew training task and the Air University at Maxwell AFB, becoming in the process Air Education and Training Command (AETC). Two numbered air forces answer to AETC—the 2nd at Keesler AFB, Mississippi, and the 19th at Randolph AFB, Texas. With a staff of 60,000 and responsibilities which include recruiting and training all new Air Force personnel, as well as conducting career education for those of all ranks already established in the service, and training foreign air force personnel in assorted skills, AETC is both complex and large, with units spread across the U.S. from coast to coast.

The aircraft operated by AETC for flying training are among the longest-serving in the Air Force, most of them being at least a quarter of a century old. Prospective pilots, however, get their first taste of Air Force flying in a new aircraft. The little Slingsby T-3A Firefly was selected in 1992 to replace the T-41 Mescalero for the preliminary job of weeding out those candidates judged unsuitable for pilot training. After successfully surviving the T-3A, student pilots move on to primary training in the Cessna T-37B, which has been giving yeoman service since 1959. Nearly 500 T-37Bs are still flying and have been modified to extend their service life into the next century. From 1999 on, they will be progressively replaced by the winner of the Joint Primary Aircraft Training System (JPATS) competition, a turboprop–powered trainer based on the Swiss Pilatus PC-9 and built in the U.S. by Raytheon. No such replacement is envisaged for the next step in the training program, at least for those intended to fly combat aircraft. The T-38 Talon has been the USAF's advanced trainer since 1961, and has undergone major structural renewal and avionics upgrades which together should extend its service life to the year 2020. By then, the T-38 will have outlived many of those who earned their wings in its cockpit during the 1960s and will have thoroughly earned retirement.

Until 1993, all USAF pilots in advanced training flew the T-38. After that, the Air Force changed to the Specialized Undergraduate Pilot Training (SUPT) scheme and those selected for transport and tanker types moved from the T-37B to the new T-1 Jayhawk, a version of the Beechjet 400A, a twin-engined executive aircraft specifically modified for military multiengine pilot training. USAF navigator training is completed in the Boeing CT-43, derived from the 737-200 airliner. AETC also has units operating some of the newer aircraft in the USAF inventory, including the F-15, F-16, and C-17.

The USAF Overseas

The United States Air Forces in Europe (USAFE) are mere shadows of their former selves. USAFE's three numbered air forces (the 3rd in U.K., 16th in Italy, and 17th in Germany) had twelve wings operating their own aircraft when the 1990s began. Reflecting the dramatic change in the political situation, this shrank to five operational wings by 1996, equipped among them with 108 fighters (F-15C/D, F-16C/D), sixty attack aircraft (F-15E, A-10), six observation aircraft (OA-10), and an assortment of forty-seven others (tankers, reconnaissance, transports). The 17th AF was inactivated in September 1996, leaving 3rd AF responsible for operations north of the Alps, and 16th AF covering everything farther south.

The Pacific Air Forces (PACAF) have always been generously provided with numbered air forces, and the 5th (Japan), 7th (South Korea), 11th (Alaska), and 13th (Guam) have all survived with a total of eight wings operating aircraft—246 F-15/F-16/A-10 fighters/attack aircraft, four E-3 AWACS, eighteen OA-10s, fifteen KC-135 tankers, thirty-eight transports, and eleven helicopters. All of which is little enough to cover an operational area which extends from the west coast of the U.S. to the east coast of Africa, and from the Arctic to the Antarctic.

The reductions in strength experienced by USAFE and PACAF in the 1990s were the inevitable result of the post-Cold War defense cuts. The realities of the draw-down serve to emphasize the importance of the principles embodied in the "Global Reach—Global Power" paper which underpinned the Air Force reorganization. While the forces in place overseas may be sufficient to maintain a presence and perhaps cope with minor contingencies, the twenty-first century USAF must be able to react to a serious crisis by deploying from its home bases in numbers and with speed. If necessary, it must also be capable of imposing itself decisively on the situation once it arrives.

The Agencies

The restructuring of the USAF did not stop with the major commands. Many supporting functions were realigned and others disestablished entirely. Those which remained, including a few which had previously had command status,[3] were formed into functionally arranged Field Operating Agencies (FOAs) reporting to offices in USAF Headquarters. Three Direct Reporting Units (DRUs) were retained to report directly to the Chief of Staff—the USAF Academy; 11th Wing, which is largely concerned with ceremonial functions and includes the USAF Band and Honor Guard; and the Air Force Operational Test and Evaluation Center, which undertakes testing of such critical items as the B-2, C-17, and many command and control systems. Among them, the twenty-seven FOAs cover the myriad supporting activities which ensure the smooth day-to-day running of the Air Force machine. Their titles give an indication of the enormous range of their interests—auditing, flight standards, civil engineering, real estate, special investigations, personnel management, news, legal services, environmental excellence, weather, and many more—including Air Force history.

Reserve Forces

Listed among the USAF's FOAs are the Air Force Reserve (AFRes) and Air National Guard (ANG), although as operators of combat aircraft they bear little resemblance to the other twenty-five. The AFRes has the primary responsibility of providing the USAF with immediately available, combat ready forces in a national emergency. It is organized into three numbered air forces—the 10th (Bergstrom ARS, Texas), which looks after fighters and tankers; and the 4th (McClellan AFB, California) and 22nd (Dobbins ARB, Georgia), which are primarily responsible for transports. Close to 80,000 personnel serve thirty-seven flying wings, which operate almost 500 assigned aircraft in all roles, including F-16s, B-52s, KC-135s, C-5s, C-141s, and a varied collection of C-130s and helicopters. Reserve crews are also employed under an associate program in which they gain experience with regular USAF units in front line aircraft like the KC-10 and C-17.

The ANG inherits an honorable tradition closely linked with the birth of the United States as an independent nation—that of the volunteer, the Minuteman, willing to fight for the country in times of national crisis. Every one of the fifty states, plus the District of Columbia and Puerto Rico, has at least one ANG unit assigned, all of which operate under state government jurisdiction except in times of national emergency. With a personnel strength of over 111,000 operating eighty-eight flying wings with more than 1,200 modern aircraft, the ANG represents an increasingly important element of U.S. air power. In the USAF's fiftieth anniversary year, the ANG provides 100 percent of the air defense fighters, 33 percent of the multirole fighters, 43 percent of KC-135 air refueling, 28 percent of air rescue, 45 percent of tactical airlift, and 8 percent of strategic airlift. In other duties, the ANG's tasks include 100 percent of aircraft control and 80 percent of Air Force communications. ANG units have made major recent contributions to operations in Central America, the Gulf region, and Bosnia, and have been identified on many occasions with disaster relief both worldwide and in the U.S. after hurricanes, floods, and earthquakes.

In the years ahead, as the USAF is compelled by budgetary constraints to meet its global responsibilities while re-

³   For example, Air Force Intelligence Command is now an agency, and Air Force Communications Command became the Air Force C4 Agency. (C4 = Command, Control, Communications, and Computers.) Where there were thirteen major commands before 1992, there are now only eight.

Hardships and discomfort are commonplace in warfare, and modern war can be particularly demanding. Helicopter technicians find out what it is like to work while encumbered with clothing designed to protect them from the effects of nuclear, biological, and chemical warfare.

The sun is far from setting on the career of the magnificent F-15 Eagle. In its various forms, the F-15 provides the USAF with superlative performance in the air defense, mission escort, intercept, battlefield support, defense suppression, interdiction, and nuclear strike roles.

The KC-10 Extender is a tanker of remarkable capacity, able to transfer 200,000 lbs of fuel at a radius of 2,200 miles from base. On overseas deployments, it doubles as an escorting tanker for combat aircraft and as a transport carrying personnel and ground equipment. Large as it is, the KC-10 is still dwarfed by the E-4 National Airborne Operations Center. Four E-4s are operated by Air Combat Command and based at Offutt AFB, Nebraska. All four now carry a dorsal hump housing a satellite communications antenna.

The Lockheed Martin F-22 will become established as the USAF's air superiority aircraft with the dawn of the 21st century. State-of-the-art avionics and superb aerodynamics will combine to make the F-22 a combat aircraft of extraordinary capabilities.

stricting the size of its front line, being able to call on additional forces of the size and professionalism of the ANG and the AFRes will be a considerable advantage. U.S. military intervention in any future world crisis would not be practicable without their involvement.

The Twenty-first Century

The USAF begins its second fifty years and will enter the twenty-first century as the world's most powerful air arm. Although its strength in both personnel and aircraft has fallen significantly in recent years, the effectiveness of the force has nevertheless increased dramatically. In terms of simple numbers, the USAF may actually be smaller than the air forces of Russia and China, but in its ability to as-

sure air supremacy, strike hard and precisely, and move aircraft, people, and heavy equipment quickly to anywhere in the world, the USAF has no rivals.

The U.S. lead in aerospace technology has been growing, and is likely to continue to do so for the foreseeable future. No other nation, or group of nations, has yet demonstrated a capacity to produce military aircraft which might match the F-117A, the B-2, the C-17, and the F-22—or much of their weaponry and equipment. In space, the U.S. is equally dominant, particularly from the point of view of its exploitation for such military purposes as navigation, communications, and intelligence gathering of all kinds. This should remain the case provided that the challenges of the future are anticipated and the

U.S. continues to invest in further developing its capabilities. Space is the high ground of the twenty-first century battlefield and the USAF's preeminent place there needs to be secured.

If the USAF's superiority in aerospace technology is unparalleled, it is equally the case that the quality of its personnel is better than it has ever been. The Air Force has the most highly educated work force in its history, and advantage is being taken of its professionalism by ensuring that decision making and accountability are delegated to the lowest practicable level in the service. The size and number of headquarters staffs has been sharply reduced and responsibility for the day-to-day running of the USAF has been placed more firmly in the hands of its operators. It is true that the Air Force of the future may have to ask fewer people to tackle more tasks, and that U.S.-based units will face the prospect of an even greater number of overseas deployments than in the past, but given the caliber of the men and women involved, there is no reason to suppose that the challenges will not be met.

At various times in this first century of air power, the U.S. allowed its strength or its technological advantages in aviation to evaporate as the attention of the American public was drawn to problems which seemed more immediate than those of national security. Somerset Maugham's penetrating observation on freedom at times appeared to fall on deaf ears. The priceless lead gained by the achievements of the Wright brothers was squandered before WWI, and the funding for America's air force was cut back to recklessly low levels after both WWI and WWII. In the aftermath of the Cold War and the disintegration of the Soviet Union, it was inevitable that there would be a similar inclination to reduce defense spending and that a technologically advanced (and therefore very expensive) service like the USAF would have to justify its existence to people searching for a "peace dividend." From that point of view, the Gulf War may have been providential in that it allowed the USAF to demonstrate to the American public the

Symbols of the USAF's "Global Reach — Global Power." The power and stealth of a B-2 linked with the force-multiplying capability of the tanker force.

value of a modern air force in countering the dangers of the post-Cold War world. Having created a positive image for itself, the USAF was able to complete its reorganization and look to the future with confidence.

The foundations for a twenty-first century air force have been laid. Plans, structure, personnel, aircraft, weapons, and supporting equipment are in hand as the USAF celebrates its fiftieth anniversary. Americans can be assured that they have invested wisely, and that the USAF will indeed be a force with "Global Reach— Global Power" in the years to come.

The United States Air Force Museum

The chapters of this book are each preceded by a passage describing what a visitor might expect to see (and perhaps feel) when walking through the various galleries and annexes of the USAF Museum. Not covered in the main text is a brief history of the Museum itself, the work it does, and its aims for the future.

In 1923, the Aeronautical Engineering Center at McCook Field, Dayton, set up a small display in the corner of a hangar. Known as the Engineering Division Museum, its aim was to collect and exhibit both U.S. and foreign aviation technology from WWI. The intention was laudable, but the execution less so. By 1927, the collection had been much reduced by a combination of natural deterioration, pilferage, and fire. The remnants were then moved, as the Army Aeronautical Museum, to a new home at Wright Field, where they occupied about 1,500 sq ft of a laboratory building. More securely housed though it was, the collection was so severely cramped that most aircraft had to be shown without wings. Even then, the fuselages were often placed so close together that it was difficult to get a clear view.

In 1935, the need for a separate and properly organized Museum was finally given formal recognition when the collection was moved into a new structure which had been specifically designed to house and display aviation artifacts. The new Museum opened to the public in 1936 with an array of some 2,000 items. With WWII on the horizon, however, other priorities arose and the new building was needed for other things. In 1940, therefore, the exhibition was closed to the public and the collection placed in long-term storage.

After the Allied victories over Germany and Japan in 1945, it was some months before the Museum program began to revive, but in 1946 Mark Sloan was appointed as the Curator of the Air Force collection. An engine overhaul building at Patterson Field was set aside as the Museum's new home and Mark Sloan began to collect artifacts both for the National Air Museum of the Smithsonian Institution and for what was then described as the Air Force Technical Museum.

It was April 1954 before the collection was once more opened to public view, and at first there were no complete aircraft on display. When aircraft did arrive, they were mostly left outside to suffer the vagaries of the weather. The interior of the Museum building was hardly ideal. It was neither fire-proofed nor air-conditioned, and it had supporting pillars every sixteen feet in one direction and every fifty feet in the other. By the early 1960s, even the outdoor area was overcrowded and it was clear that an alternative solution was needed to the problem of housing the USAF's uniquely valuable and growing collection.

Help came from the Air Force Museum Foundation, chartered in 1960 by a group of private citizens led by Eugene Kettering. Launching a fund drive in 1964, they raised over $6 million for the construction of a new museum complex. Work began in 1970 and the USAF Museum opened its doors in August 1971. A large building, offering a floor space almost 800 ft long and 240 ft wide, allowed more than eighty aircraft to be displayed inside, ranging from an original Wright Type B Flyer to Century series jet fighters, and including a Convair B-36, surely the largest aircraft on display anywhere under cover.

In 1976 a building expanding the administrative center and adding various visitor facilities was opened, and in 1985 ground was broken on a third, much larger hangar, which was completed by April 1988. By then, the total floorspace available for exhibits had grown to over ten and a half acres, making the USAF Museum the largest aviation museum in the world. Its storage areas included thousands of drawings, photographs, magazines, books, microfilm images, tape recordings, press clippings, and films. Annexes on the other side of Wright Field held additional aircraft and an area in which major restoration projects could be undertaken, together with shelves and cabinets for artifacts of all kinds. Outside the main buildings, large missiles and aircraft still looking for shelter clustered on extensive concrete aprons, adding their nostalgic appeal to the Museum's surroundings.

In the 1990s, all of this still holds true, but aviation museums must live with the pressure of constant and appreciable growth. As the USAF celebrates its 50th anniversary, aircraft and equipment from the 1980s are already included among the USAF Museum's exhibits and more will be added with each decade that passes. With that in mind, plans are being laid for further extensions to allow space for both new acquisitions and restorations, and to accommodate some of the aircraft at present braving the weather. Amenities have been improved by remodeling the restaurant and by adding a 500-seat IMAX theater where visitors, confronted by a six-story-high screen and wrapped in sound from dozens of speakers, can experience vicariously the thrills and enjoyment of flying powerful aircraft or walking in space. Gifts and books can be bought in the excellent shops operated by the Air Force Museum Foundation near the entrance to the main buildings.

There have been other developments in the area surrounding the main Museum. An air traffic control tower and a group of Nissen huts have been built, recalling the great days of the 8th Air Force in Europe during WWII. A Memorial Park has been laid out commemorating the service of well over 250 units and individuals. The memorials — simple plaques, granite monuments, trees — have been donated by family members, group associations, and other benefactors. While so honoring the past, there has also been a nod in the direction of the future. For the benefit of generations yet unborn, a time capsule, filled with documents, prints and microfilm of aircraft developed at Wright-Patterson AFB, and with articles covering contemporary events, lies buried in front of the Museum.

Comprehensive though its coverage of air power history is, the interests and responsibilities of the USAF Museum do not have their being only at Wright-Patterson AFB. Air Force and Department of Defense Museums in every part of America are supported from Dayton, as are numerous other aviation museums, both in the U.S. and abroad. Vast quantities of items are on loan to these museums, including thousands of aircraft.

As it approaches the 21st century, the USAF Museum is a far cry from the relatively minor affair of the 1920s and '30s. The 2,000-item collection has mushroomed to more than 50,000 objects, from the minute to the colossal, not much more

than 10 percent of which can be exhibited at any one time. This prodigious escalation in size has been matched by an equally impressive growth in international status and in popularity. Annual attendance in the 1950s was only about 10,000 visitors. In the 1990s, that figure regularly exceeded one million. To look after the rising flood and to ensure that the collection is maintained in impeccable condition, the Museum employs a professional staff of almost 100, and is able to rely on the dedicated service of more than 300 volunteers.

Besides their duties connected with the daily operation of the Museum as a public facility, the staff and volunteers are deeply concerned with the shape of things to come. Plans for new buildings and exhibits are constantly being considered, and the need to acquire, restore, and display significant aircraft is always kept in mind.

Everyone connected with the Museum is keenly aware of its leading international position as a repository of air power history. In 1971, Secretary of the Air Force Robert Seamans was present for the dedication ceremony of the new Museum buildings, as were President Richard Nixon and members of the Wright family. In his speech, the Secretary summarized the purpose of the USAF Museum, and his words still ring true today:

"The new Air Force Museum will serve as a tribute to all Americans who have contributed so much to the field of aviation. It will also serve as an inspiration to future generations of Americans to increase their knowledge and awareness of the United States Air Force and the history of flight."

Previous page:

Visitors to the USAF Museum are welcomed by the impressive presence of the Rockwell B-1A Lancer. In the background, the F-15 Streak Eagle stands in front of the Museum entrance hall, with a display hangar on the left and the IMAX theater on the right.

On the far side of Wright Field from the USAF Museum's main buildings is the Museum Annex, consisting of two hangars open to the public. These house a varied display of aircraft, including three used by Presidents. *Sacred Cow* is the C-54C aboard which Harry Truman signed the bill which made the USAF an independent service. The VC-121E *Columbine* carried Eisenhower, and *Independence* is a VC-118 which saw service with both Presidents. *Independence* flew Truman to Wake Island in 1950 for his meeting with MacArthur.

The contrast in types to be seen in the Museum Annex is exemplified by the C-133 Cargomaster and its neighbor, a WWII Macchi C-200 Saetta.

The Museum's red, white, and blue F-16 is no stranger to admiring crowds. It is instantly recognizable as an aircraft which once flew with the internationally recognized USAF aerobatic display team, the Thunderbirds.

The USAF Museum grounds hold a host of memories. Among them, a 52nd Fighter Group memorial has a Spitfire and a Mustang curving upward, while a bronze eagle honors American prisoners of war. WWII veterans have no difficulty recognizing the 8th AF control tower with two uniformed figures at its rail, or the corrugated Nissen huts in which so many were billeted during their operational tours in England.

Whenever possible, original parts are refinished to exhibition standard, but where necessary missing or badly worn items are manufactured, preferably from company drawings. The photographs show the restoration of the Museum's Boeing P-12 and give some idea of the extremely high quality of the work done, even on pieces of the aircraft structure which are never seen by the public.

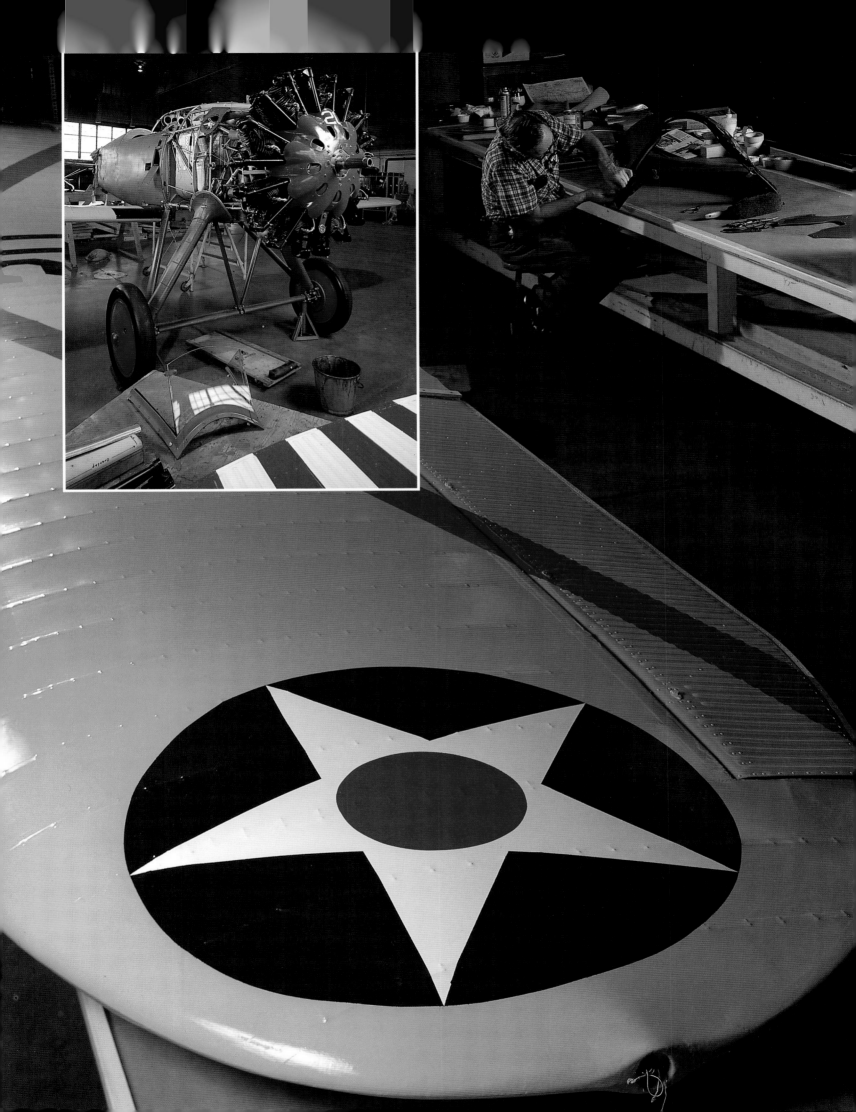

Bibliography

Air Force Museum Foundation. *United States Air Force Museum*. Wright-Patterson Air Force Base, Ohio: The Museum, 1993.

Ambrose, Stephen E. *D-Day*. New York: Simon & Schuster, 1994.

Anderson, Clarence "Bud" and Joseph Hamelin. *To Fly and Fight*. New York: St. Martin's Press, 1990.

Anderton, David A. *Aggressors, Vol. 3*. Charlottesville, VA: Howell Press, 1991.

_____. *History of the U.S. Air Force*. New York: The Military Press, 1981.

Angelucci, Enzo. *The Rand McNally Encyclopedia of Military Aircraft*. New York: The Military Press, 1983.

_____. *The World Encyclopedia of Civil Aircraft*. New York: Crown Publishers, 1982.

Apple, Nick and Gene Gurney. *The Air Force Museum*. Dayton, OH: Central Printing, 1991.

Arnold, H.J.P. *Man in Space*. New York: Smithmark, 1993.

Avery, N.L. *B-25 Mitchell*. St. Paul, MN: Phalanx Publishing, 1992.

Aymar, Brandt. *Men in the Air*. New York: Crown Publishers, 1990.

Ball, Jr., John. *Edwards: Flight Test Center of the U.S.A.F.* New York: Duell, Sloan and Pearce, 1962.

Beck, Alfred M. *With Courage: The U.S. Army Air Forces in World War II*. Washington DC: Air Force History and Museum Program, 1994.

Bendiner, Elmer. *The Fall of Fortresses*. New York: G.P. Putnam's Sons, 1980.

Berger, Carl. *The United States Air Force in S.E. Asia*. Washington, DC: Office of Air Force History, 1977.

Biddle, Wayne. *Barons of the Sky*. New York: Simon & Schuster, 1991.

Bidwell, Shelford. *The Chindit War*. New York: Macmillan, 1979.

Bilstein, Roger and Jay Miller. *Aviation in Texas*. San Antonio, TX: Texas Monthly Press, 1985.

Bodie, Warren M. *Lockheed P-38 Lightning*. Georgia: Widewing Publications, 1991.

Bowen, Ezra. *Knights of the Air*. Alexandria, VA: Time-Life Books, 1980.

Bowers, Peter M. *Boeing B-17 Flying Fortress*. Seattle, WA: Museum of Flight, 1985.

Boyne, Walter and Donald Lopez. *The Jet Age*. Washington, DC: Smithsonian Institution Press, 1979.

Boyne, Walter. *Boeing B-52*. London: Jane's, 1981.

_____. *Clash of Wings*. New York: Simon & Schuster, 1994.

_____. *Phantom in Combat*. Washington, DC: Smithsonian Institution Press, 1985.

_____. *Silver Wings*. New York: Simon & Schuster, 1993.

_____. *The Leading Edge*. New York: Stewart, Tabori, & Chang, 1986.

_____. *The Smithsonian Book of Flight*. Washington, DC: Smithsonian Books, 1987.

Braybrook, Roy. *Air Power: the Coalition and Iraqi Air Forces*. London: Osprey, 1991.

Bryan, C.D.B. *The National Air & Space Museum*. New York: Harry N. Abrams, 1979.

Caine, Philip D. *Eagles of the R.A.F.* Washington, DC: National Defense University Press, 1991.

Calvorcoressi, Peter and Guy Wint. *Total War*. London: Pelican Books, 1974.

Campbell, Christy. *Air War Pacific*. New York: Crescent Books, 1990.

Christy, Joe. *American Air Power - the First 75 Years*. Pennsylvania: TAB Books, 1982.

Clancy, Tom. *Fighter Wing*. New York: Berkley Books, 1995.

Cloe, John Hailie. *Top Cover for America*. Missoula, MT: Pictorial Histories, 1985.

Coffey, Thomas M. *Decision over Schweinfurt*. New York: David Mackay, 1977.

_____. *Hap*. New York: Viking Press, 1982.

Coffman, Edward M. *The War to End All Wars*. Wisconsin: University of Wisconsin Press, 1986.

Cole, Goldberg, Tucker, and Winnacker. *The Department of Defense, 1944-78*. Washington, DC: Secretary of Defense, Historical Office, 1978.

Comer, John. *Combat Crew*. London: Leo Cooper, 1988.

Constable, George. *World War II*. New York: Prentice Hall Press, 1989.

Cooling, Benjamin Franklin. *Close Air Support*. Washington, DC: Office of Air Force History, 1990.

Copp, DeWitt S. *A Few Great Captains*. New York: Doubleday, 1980.

_____. *Forged in Fire*. New York: Doubleday, 1982.

Cornelisse, Diana. *Against the Wind*. Washington, DC: Aeronautical Systems Center, 1994.

Cortesi, Lawrence. *Pacific Siege*. New York: Zebra Books, 1984.

Costello, John. *Pacific War 1941-45*. New York: Quill, 1982.

Craven, W.F. and J.L. Cate. *The Army Air Forces in W.W.II*. Washington, DC: Office of Air Force History, 1983.

Cross, Robin. *The Bombers*. London: Bantam Press, 1987.

Davis, Larry. *Air War over Korea*. Carrollton, TX: Squadron/Signal Publications, 1982.

_____. *Wild Weasel*. Carrollton, TX: Squadron/Signal Publications, 1986.

Dean, David J. *The Air Force Role in Low Intensity Conflict*. Maxwell Air Force Base, AL: Air University Press, 1986.

Dear, I.C.B. and M.R.D. Foot. *The Oxford Companion to W.W.II*. New York: Oxford University Press, 1995.

Donald, David. *U.S. Air Force Air Power Directory*. London: Aerospace Publishing, 1992.

Doolittle, James and Carroll Glines. *I Could Never be so Lucky Again*. New York: Bantam Books, 1991.

Dorr, Robert F. *Vought A-7 Corsair II*. London: Osprey, 1985.

Dorr, Robert F. and David Donald. *Fighters of the U.S.A.F.* New York: Military Press, 1990.

Drury, Richard S. *My Secret War*. Fallbrook, CA: Aero Publishers, 1979.

Duerksen, Menro. *The Memphis Belle*. Memphis, TN: Castle Books, 1987.

Dupuy, Trevor, Curt Johnson, and David Bongard. *The Harper Encyclopedia of Military Biography*. New York: Harper Collins, 1992.

Dyson, Emma, Dean Herrin, and Amy Slaton. *The Engineering of Flight*. Washington, DC: U.S. Department of the Interior, 1993.

Edmonds, Walter D. *They Fought with What They Had*. Washington, DC: Center for Air Force History, 1992.

Ellis, John. *Brute Force*. New York: Viking Press, 1990.

Elstob, Peter. *Bastogn*. London: MacDonald & Co., 1968.

Ethell, Jeffrey & Alfred Price. *Target Berlin*. London: Jane's Publishing, 1981.

Ethell, Jeffrey and Robert T. Sand. *Fighter Command*. Osceola, WI: Motorbooks International, 1991.

Finney, Robert T. *Air Corps Tactical School 1920-40*. Washington, DC: Center for Air Force History, 1992.

Fletcher, Eugene. *Fletcher's Gang*. Seattle, WA: University of Washington Press, 1988.

Flintham, Victor. *Air Wars and Aircraft*. London: Arms & Armour Press, 1989.

Ford, Daniel. *Flying Tigers*. Washington, DC: Smithsonian Institution Press, 1991.

Foxworth, Thomas G. *The Speed Seekers*. Newbury Park, CA: Haynes Publications, 1989.

Francillon, Rene J. *The United States Air National Guard*. London: Aerospace Publishing, 1993.

_____. *Vietnam - the War in the Air*. New York: Arch Cape Press, 1987.

Frank, Richard B. *Guadalcanal*. New York: Random House, 1990.

Frankland, Noble. *Bomber Offensive*. New York: Ballantine Books, 1970.

Freeman, Roger. *The Mighty Eighth War Diary*. Osceola, WI: Motorbooks International, 1990.

_____. *B-17 Fortress at War*. New York: Charles Scribner's Sons, 1977.

_____. *Combat Profile: Mustang*. London: Ian Allan, 1989.

_____. *The American Airman in Europe*. Osceola, WI: Motorbooks International, 1991.

_____. *The Mighty Eighth in Color*. Stillwater, MN: Speciality Press, 1992.

_____. *The Mighty Eighth War Manual*. Osceola, WI: Motorbooks International, 1991.

_____. *The Mighty Eighth*. New York: Doubleday, 1978.

Fricker, John. *Air Forces of the World*. New York: Hanover House, 1958.

Futrell, Greenhalgh, Grubb, Hasselwander, Jakob, and Ravenstein. *Aces and Aerial Victories*. Washington, DC: Office of Air Force History, 1976.

Futrell. *The U.S.A.F. in Korea*. Washington, DC: Office of Air Force History.

Galland, Adolf. *The First and the Last*. London: Methuen, 1955.

Garfield, Brian. *The Thousand Mile War*. New York: Bantam Books, 1982.

Gibbs-Smith, Charles H. *Aviation*. London: H.M.S.O., 1985.

_____. *Early Flying Machines 1799-1909*. London: Methuen, 1976.

Gilster, Herman L. *The Air War in S.E. Asia*. Maxwell Air Force Base, AL: Air University Press, 1993.

Glines, Carroll V. *Compact History of the U.S.A.F.* New York: Hawthorn Books, 1963.

_____. *Round the World Flights*. New York: Van Nostrand Reinhold, 1982.

Glines, Carroll V., Harry M. Zubkoff, and F. Clifton Berry. *Flights*. Montgomery, AL: Community Communications, 1994.

Goldberg, Alfred. *A History of the United States Air Force*. Princeton, NJ: Van Nostrand, 1957.

Graham, Dominich. *Cassino*. New York: Ballantine Books, 1971.

Green, William. *The Complete Book of Fighters*. New York: Smithmark, 1994.

Green, William. *Warplanes of the Third Reich*. New York: Galahad Books, 1986.

Greenwood, John T. *Milestones of Aviation*. New York: MacMillan, 1989.

Greer, Thomas H. *The Development of Doctrine in the Army Air Arm, 1917-41*. Washington, DC: Office of Air Force History, 1985.

Grinsell, Robert. *Aces Full*. Granada Hills, CA: Sentry Books, 1974.

Grintner, Lawrence E. and Peter M. Dunn. *The American War in Vietnam.* New York: Greenwood Press, 1987.

2Gunston, Bill. *American Warplanes.* New York: Crescent Books, 1986.

_____. *Chronicle of Aviation.* Liberty, MO: J.L. International, 1992.

_____. *Rockets and Missiles.* New York: Crescent Books, 1979.

_____. *The Illustrated Encyclopedia of Aircraft Armament.* New York: Orion Books, 1988.

Hall, Jr., Grover C. *1,000 Destroyed.* Fallbrook, CA: Aero Publishers, 1978.

Hallion, Richard P. *On the Frontier.* Washington, DC: N.A.S.A., 1984.

_____. *Strike from the Sky.* Washington, DC: Smithsonian Institution Press, 1989.

_____. *D-Day 1944.* Washington, DC: Office of Air Force History, 1994.

Halpern, John. *Early Birds.* New York: E.P. Dutton, 1981.

Hammel, Eric. *Aces Against Germany.* New York: Pocket Books, 1995.

_____. *Aces Against Japan.* New York: Pocket Books, 1995.

Hansen, Chuck. *U.S. Nuclear Weapons.* New York: Orion, 1988.

Hart, B.H. Liddell. *History of the Second World War.* London: Cassell, 1970.

Hastings, Max. *The Korean War.* New York: Simon & Schuster, 1987.

_____. *Overlord.* New York: Simon & Schuster, 1984.

Haugland, Vern. *The Eagle Squadrons.* New York: Ziff-Davis Flying Books, 1979.

Haulman, Daniel. *The High Road to Tokyo Bay.* Washington, DC: Center for Air Force History, 1993.

Hawkins, Ian L. *B-17s over Berlin.* Washington, DC: Brassey's, 1990.

Hennessy, Juliette. *The U.S. Army Air Arm, 1861-1917.* Washington, DC: Office of Air Force History, 1985.

Hess, William N. *American Fighter Aces Album.* Dallas, TX: Taylor Publishing, 1979.

Hess, William N. and Thomas G Ivie. *P-51 Mustang Aces.* Osceola, WI: Motorbooks International, 1992.

_____ *Fighters of the Mighty Eighth.* Osceola, WI: Motorbooks International, 1990.

Higham, Robin and Abigail Sidall. *Flying Combat Aircraft of the U.S.A.A.F./ U.S.A.F., Volumes I & 2.* Ames, Iowa: Iowa State U. Press, 1975-1978.

Howard, Fred. *Wilbur and Orville.* New York: Alfred A. Knopf, 1987.

Hoyt, Edwin P. *War in the Pacific.* New York: Avon Books, 1991.

Hudson, James J. *Hostile Skies.* Syracuse, NY: Syracuse University Press, 1968.

Hughes, Thomas Alexander. *Over Lord.* New York: Free Press, 1985.

Huttig, Jack. *1927 - Summer of Eagles.* Chicago: Nelson-Hall, 1980.

Inoguchi, Rikihei and Tadashi Nakajima. *The Divine Wind.* New York: Bantam Books, 1978.

Jablonski, Edward. *Air War.* New York: Doubleday, 1979.

_____. *America in the Air War.* Alexandria, VA: Time-Life Books, 1982.

_____. *Flying Fortress.* New York: Doubleday, 1965.

Jenkins, Dennis R. *McDonnell Douglas F-15.* Arlington, TX: Aerofax, 1990.

Jerram, Michael F. *Incredible Flying Machines.* London: Marshall Cavendish, 1980.

Johnson, J.E. *The Story of Air Fighting.* London: Hutchinson & Co., 1985.

Josephy, Alvin M. *The American Heritage History of Flight.* New York: American Heritage, 1962.

Kaplan, Philip and Andy Saunders. *Little Friends.* New York: Random House, 1991.

Karnow, Stanley. *Vietnam.* New York: Viking Press, 1983.

Keegan, John. *The Second World War.* New York: Viking Press, 1990.

_____. *The Times Atlas of the Second World War.* New York: Harper & Row, 1989.

Kelsey, Benjamin S. *The Dragon's Teeth?* Washington, DC: Smithsonian Institution Press, 1982.

Kennett, Lee. *The First Air War 1914-1918.* New York: Free Press, 1991.

Kinzev, Bert. *The Fury of Desert Storm.* Pennsylvania: TAB Books, 1991.

Knaack, Marcelle Size. *Encyclopedia of U.S.A.F. Aircraft and Missile Systems, Vol. 1.* Washington, DC: Office of Air Force History, 1978.

Lande, D.A. *From Somewhere in England.* Osceola, WI: Motorbooks International, 1991.

Larrabee, Eric. *Commander in Chief.* New York: Harper and Row, 1987.

Leuthner, Stuart and Oliver Jensen. *High Honor.* Washington, DC: Smithsonian Institution Press, 1989.

Longstreet, Stephen. *The Canvas Falcons.* New York: Barnes & Noble, 1995.

Lopez, Donald S. *Fighter Pilot's Heaven.* Washington, DC: Smithsonian Institution Press, 1995.

_____. *Into the Teeth of the Tiger.* New York: Bantam Books, 1986.

Lucas, Laddie. *Wings of War.* London: Hutchinson & Co., 1983.

Macksey, Kenneth, David Brown, and Christopher Shores. *The Guinness History of Air Warfare.* Enfield, Middlesex: Guinness, 1976.

Macksey, Kenneth. *The Penguin Encyclopedia of Weapons and Military Technology.* New York: Viking Press, 1993.

Magoun, Alexander and Eric Hodgins. *A History of Aircraft.* London: Whittlesey House, 1931.

Manchester, William. *American Caesar.* Boston: Little, Brown, & Co., 1978.

Mark, Eduard. *Aerial Interdiction in Three Wars.* Washington, DC: Center for Air Force History, 1994.

Markman, Steve and Bill Holder. *One-of-a-Kind Research Aircraft.* Atglen, PA: Schiffer Publishing, 1995.

Marshall, Chris. *The World's Great Interceptor Aircraft.* New York: Gallery Books, 1989.

Mason, David. *Breakout.* New York: Ballantine Books, 1969.

Mason, Francis K. *Aces of the Air.* New York: Mayflower Books, 1981.

_____. *Battle over Britain.* London: McWhinter Twins Ltd., 1969.

_____. *War in the Air.* New York: Crescent Books, 1985.

Mason, Herbert Molloy. *The U.S.A.F. - a Turbulent History.* New York: Charter, 1976.

Mason, Herbert, Randy Bergeron, and James Renfrow. *Operation Thursday.* Washington, DC: Office of Air Force History, 1994.

Maurer, Maurer. *Air Force Combat Units of W.W.II.* Edison, NJ: Chartwell Books, 1994.

_____. *Aviation in the U.S. Army 1919-39.* Washington, DC: Office of Air Force History, 1987.

_____. *The U.S. Air Service in W.W.1.* Washington, DC: Office of Air Force History, 1978.

McAulay, Lex. *Battle of the Bismarck Sea.* New York: St. Martin's Press, 1991.

McCullough, David. *Truman.* New York: Simon & Schuster, 1992.

McFarland, Stephen Lee and Wesley Philips Newton. *To Command the Sky.* Washington, DC: Smithsonian Institution Press, 1991.

McKay, Ernest A. *A World to Conquer.* New York: Arco Publishing, 1981.

Micheletti, Eric. *Air War over the Gulf.* London: Windrow & Greene, 1991.

Middlebrook, Martin. *The Schweinfurt-Regensburg Mission.* London: Allen Lane, 1983.

Middleton, Drew. *Air War Vietnam.* New York: Bobbs-Merrill Co., 1978.

_____. *Crossroads of Modern Warfare.* New York: Doubleday, 1983.

Military History Magazine. *Desert Storm.* Leesburg, VA: Empire Press, 1991.

Miller, Roger G. *Seeing off the Bear.* Washington, DC: Office of Air Force History, 1995.

Mitcham, Samuel W. *Eagles of the Third Reich.* Shrewsbury, UK: Airlife, 1989.

Momyer, William W. *Air Power in Three Wars.* Washington, DC: Government Printing Office, 1983.

Mondey, David and Lewis Nalls. *U.S.A.F. at War in the Pacific.* New York: Scribners, 1980.

Mondey, David. *Aviation.* London: Octopus Books, 1980.

_____. *The Illustrated Encyclopedia of the World's Aircraft.* New York: A&W Publishers, 1978.

Morocco, John. *The Vietnam Experience.* Boston: Boston Publishing Co., 1984.

Morrison, Wilbur H. *Fortress Without a Roof.* New York: St. Martin's Press, 1982.

Morse, Stan. *Gulf Air War Debrief.* Westport, CT: Airtime Publishing, 1992.

Murray, Williamson. *Strategy for Defeat.* Secaucus, NJ: Chartwell Books, 1986.

Nalty, Bernard C. *Pearl Harbor and the War in the Pacific.* New York: Smithmark, 1991.

Neufeld, Jacob. *Ballistic Missiles in the U.S.A.F.* Washington, DC: Office of Air Force History, 1990.

_____. *Research and Development in the U.S.A.F.* Washington, DC: Center for Air Force History, 1993.

Nevin, David. *Architects of Air Power.* Alexandria, VA: Time-Life Books, 1981.

Nicholls, Jack C. and Warren E. Thompson. *Korea: the Air War 1950-53.* London: Osprey, 1991.

Office of ACAS, Intelligence. *Airborne Assault on Holland.* Washington, DC: Center for Air Force History, 1992.

_____. *Air-Ground Teamwork on the Western Front.* Washington, DC: Center for Air Force History, 1992.

_____. *Condensed Analysis of the Ninth Air Force.* Washington, DC: Office of Air Force History, 1984.

_____. *Sunday Punch in Normandy.* Washington, DC: Center for Air Force History, 1992.

_____. *The A.A.F. in N.W. Africa.* Washington DC: Center for Air Force History, 1992.

_____. *The A.A.F. in the Invasion of Southern France.* Washington, DC: Center for Air Force History, 1992.

_____. *Pacific Counterblow.* Washington, DC: Center for Air Force History, 1992.

Ogden, Bob. *Great Aircraft Collections of the World*. New York: Gallery Books, 1988.

Overy, R.J. *The Air War 1939-45*. New York: Scarborough Books, 1982.

Pace, Steve. *Edwards Air Force Base*. Osceola, WI: Motorbooks International, 1994.

_____. *X-Fighters*. Osceola, WI: Motorbooks International, 1991.

Pape, Garry R. and Ronald C Harrison. *Queen of the Midnight Skies*. Westchester, PA: Schiffer Military History, 1992.

Patterson, Dan and Paul Perkins. *The Lady*. Charlottesville, VA: Howell Press, 1993.

_____. *Mustang*. Charlottesville, VA: Howell Press, 1995.

Patterson, Dan, Paul Perkins, and Michelle Crean. *The Soldier*. Charlottesville, VA: Howell Press, 1994.

Peacock, Lindsay T. *Strategic Air Command*. London: Arms & Armour Press, 1983.

Pimlott, John. *Strategic Bombing*. New York: Gallery Books, 1990.

Pitt, Barrie. *Military History of W.W.II*. New York: Military Press, 1989.

Platt, Frank C. *Great Battles of W.W.1 in the Air*. New York: The New American Library, 1966.

Polmar, Norman. *Strategic Air Command*. Annapolis, MD: Nautical & Aviation Publishing, 1979.

Prange, Gordon E. *At Dawn We Slept*. New York: McGraw-Hill, 1981.

Price, Alfred. *The Bomber in W.W.II*. New York: Charles Scribner's Sons, 1979.

_____. *Aircraft Versus Submarine*. London: Jane's, 1980.

_____. *Luftwaffe*. New York: Ballantine Books, 1969.

_____. *Spitfire at War*. London: Ian Allan, 1985.

Redding, Robert and Bill Yenne. *Boeing: Planemaker to the World*. New York: Crescent Books, 1983.

Rhodes, Richard. *The Making of the Atomic Bomb*. New York: Simon & Schuster, 1986.

Rickenbacker, Eddie. *Fighting the Flying Circus*. New York: Avon Books, 1967.

Rickenbacker, Edward V. *Rickenbacker*. New Jersey: Prentice-Hall, 1968.

Rooney, D.D. *Stilwell*. New York: Ballantine Books, 1971.

Scutts, Jerry and Patrick Stephens. *Lion in the Sky*. Wellingborough, Northamptonshire: P. Stephens, 1987.

Seagrave, Sterling. *Soldiers of Fortune*. Alexandria, VA: Time-Life Books, 1981.

Sherry, Michael S. *The Rise of American Air Power*. New Haven, CT: Yale University Press, 1987.

Shores, Christopher. *Air Aces*. Greenwich, CT: Bison Books, 1983.

_____. *Duel for the Sky*. New York: Doubleday, 1985.

Shultz, Jr., Richard H. and Robert L. Pfaltzgraff, Jr. *The Future of Air Power in the Aftermath of the Gulf War*. Maxwell Air Force Base, AL: Air University Press, 1992.

Speer, Albert. *Inside the Third Reich*. London: Sphere Books, 1971.

Spick, Mike. *Milestones of Manned Flight*. New York: Smithmark, 1994.

Steijger, Cees. *A History of U.S.A.F.E.* Shrewsbury, UK: Airlife Publishing, 1991.

Strategic Bombing Survey Team. *U.S. Strategic Bombing Surveys (Summaries)*. Maxwell Air Force Base, AL: Air University Press, 1987.

Sweetman, Bill. *YF-22 and YF-23*. Osceola, WI: Motorbooks International, 1991.

Taylor, John W.R. and Kenneth Munson. *History of Aviation*. New York: Crown Publishers, 1972.

Taylor, John W.R. *A History of Aerial Warfare*. London: Hamlyn, 1974.

_____. *Combat Aircraft of the World*. New York: G.P. Putnam's Sons, 1969.

_____. *Jane's All the World's Aircraft*. London: Jane's, annually.

Taylor, John W.R. and Fred T. Jane. *Jane's Fighting Aircraft of W.W.1*. New York: Military Press, 1990.

Taylor, John W.R., Michael J.H. Taylor, and David Mondey. *The Guinness Book of Air Facts and Feats*. Enfield, Middlesex: Guinness, 1977.

Taylor, Michael J.H. *Jane's Encyclopedia of Aviation*. New York: Portland House, 1989.

Taylor, Michael J.H. and Anthony Robinson. *In the Cockpit*. Secaucus, NJ: Chartwell Books, 1991.

Thomas, Gordon and Max Morgan Witts. *Enola Gay*. New York: Stein and Day, 1977.

Thompson, R.W. *D-Day*. New York: Ballantine Books, 1968.

Tibbets, Paul, Clair Stebbins, and Harry Franken. *The Tibbets Story*. New York: Stein & Day, 1978.

Tilford, Jr., Earl H. *Setup*. Maxwell Air Force Base, AL: Air University Press, 1991.

_____. *U.S.A.F. Search and Rescue in S.E. Asia*. Washington, DC: Center for Air Force History, 1992.

Tuchman, Barbara W. *Stilwell and the American Experience in China*. New York: Macmillan, 1971.

Vader, John. *New Guinea*. New York: Ballantine Books, 1971.

_____. *Pacific Hawk*. New York: Ballantine Books, 1970.

van der Vat, Dan. *The Pacific Campaign*. New York: Simon & Schuster, 1991.

Ethell, Jeffrey L. and Rikyu Watanabe. *The Great Book of W.W.II Airplanes*. New York: Bonanza Books, 1984.

Wagner, Ray. *Mustang Designer*. New York: Orion, 1990.

Walker, Bryce. *Fighting Jets*. Alexandria, VA: Time-Life Books, 1983.

Walker, Lois and Shelby Wickam. *From Huffman Prairie to the Moon*. Washington, DC: Government Printing Office, 1986.

Warnock, A. Timothy. *The Battle Against the U-Boat in the American Theater*. Washington, DC: Center for Air Force History, 1993.

Weigley, Russell F. *Eisenhower's Lieutenants*. Bloomington: Indiana University Press, 1981.

Weinberg, Gerhard L. *A World at Arms*. New York: Cambridge University Press, 1994.

Wilkinson, Roy. *The World's Great Attack Aircraft*. New York: Gallery Books, 1988.

Willmott, H. P. *B-17 Flying Fortress*. London: Arms & Armour Press, 1980.

Wohl, Robert. *A Passion for Wings*. New Haven, CT: Yale University Press, 1994.

Wolfe, Martin. *Green Light*. Washington, DC: Center for Air Force History, 1993.

Wood, Tony and Bill Gunston. *Hitler's Luftwaffe*. New York: Crescent Books, 1979.

Yeager, Chuck and Leo Janos. *Yeager*. New York: Bantam Books, 1985.

Yenne, Bill. *History of the U.S. Air Force*. Stamford, CT: Longmeadow Press, 1992.

MAGAZINES & PERIODICALS

Air Force Magazine
Air Force Association

Air Power History
Air Force History Support Office and the Air Force Historical Foundation

Military History Quarterly
American Historical Publications and the Society for Military History

Military History
Cowles History Group, Leesburg, VA

Air & Space Smithsonian
Smithsonian Institution, Washington, DC

Wings of Fame
Aerospace Publishing, London

Various unpublished papers and articles prepared in the Air Force History Support Office, including:

Hallion, Richard P. *The New Air Force*.

Hallion, Richard P. *Out of the Past, Into the Future*.

Peebles, Curtis. *The United States Air Force and the Military Space Program*.

Index

Manufacturers and aircraft

454